Law and Biotechnology

Law and Biotechnology

Cases and Materials

Victoria Sutton
Robert H. Bean Professor of Law
Texas Tech University
School of Law

Carolina Academic Press
Durham, North Carolina

ISBN 10: 0-89089-191-5, ISBN 13: 978-0-89089-191-9
LCCN 2006924478

Carolina Academic Press
700 Kent Street
Durham, North Carolina 27701
Telephone (919) 489-7486
Fax (919) 493-5668
www.cap-press.com

Printed in the United States of America

Contents

Table of Cases

Foreword

As you embark on this interdisciplinary and multidisciplinary study of Law and Biotechnology, my hope is that this book will assist you in examining the immense impact that biotechnology and law has on our society. It will undoubtedly affect you in your practice of law, in some way, during the course of your career; if not directly in many areas of practice which include not only intellectual property, but international trade, criminal law, agricultural law, business law and environmental law, to name but a few areas.

The practice of law is increasingly requiring a level of science literacy that will be required of anyone who is graduating from law school, today. This is particularly true in the field of biotechnology, which is a scientific field enjoying an explosion in growth and understanding, much like the scientific field of physics in the first half of the last century. As law develops to shape the way that our society regulates behaviors, it must quickly respond to the new and exciting possibilities of biotechnology. The opportunities to provide legal expertise and guidance in this field are great; and it is with an understanding of the science, scientists and engineers as well as the regulatory mechanisms that we can best optimize these opportunities for the benefit of society and future generations.

As this book goes to press, it is with the realization that new discoveries and new applications of the law in biotechnology will be developing as the ink is drying. But the foundations that are set forth in this text, provide you with the intellectual toolkit that should serve you well as you enter what will certainly be an exciting time in our history for judges, practicing lawyers and legal scholars in the field of Law and Biotechnology.

Victoria Sutton
Lubbock, TX

March 2007

Preface

This book provides a systematic look at law, policy, science and technology of biotechnology in the context of the traditional fields of law and practice. Chapter One begins with an introduction to the categories of biotechnologies as a way of understanding the scope of applications that are possible, raising awareness of law and policy issues. In this chapter, biotechnology is defined and the historical relationship between law and biotechnology is examined beginning with the earliest biotechnologies of food processing, animal breeding and winemaking and continuing up to the biotechnology explosion beginning in the 1980s. The chapter introduces the definitions for genomics, proteonomics, bionanotechnology and bioinformatics. An introduction to the scientific method and the sciences of biotechnology is explained at this early point in the book as a foundation to understanding. The chapter concludes by an introduction to the issue of whether life can be patented through examination of the case, *Diamond v. Chakrabarty*.

Chapter Two addresses issues of distributions of power in the regulation of biotechnology and a discussion of the earliest regulatory approaches in the development of the federal regulatory framework. The scope of authority for the regulation of biotechnology is examined through the litigation concerning genetically engineered foods with the Food and Drug Administration and Environmental Protection Agency, including administrative decisionmaking and Constitutional issues. The regulation of genetically modified organisms including plants and the environmental impact is examined through the litigation with the U.S. Environmental Protection Agency and Department of Agriculture and the National Institutes of Health. The work of biopharming is examined in the context of litigation with the U.S. Department of Agriculture. Completing this chapter is an examination of federal legislation which has been introduced concerning various policy issues of biotechnology, and the efforts of states to regulation biotechnology.

Chapter Three turns to the private sector and corporate activities in biotechnology, the unique features of biotechnology patents as well as the new professions which are developing around the emergence of biotechnologies in our lives. Unique problems for biotechnology of patent ownership, enforcement and infringement are examined in *Monsanto v. Schmeiser*.

Chapter Four, addresses some of the unique law and policy issues of biotechnology in human health, medical care and medical information. The constitutional right to privacy, adoption right to know, experimental and treatment decisions, informed consent and predisposition to disease as it relates to health insurance are among the ideas discussed in this chapter.

Chapter Five addresses international laws in biotechnology which affect the United States in the context of patenting, biological diversity, trade, security, biodefense, human rights, indigenous peoples, bioprospecting and biopiracy. Discussions of the

FAO International Treaty on Plant Genetic Resources for Food and Agriculture, the WTO Agreement on Trade-related Aspects of Intellectual Property Rights, the WIPO conventions and treaties, the International Convention for the Protection of New Varieties of Plants, the United Nations Convention on the Law of the Sea, the Convention on International Trade in Endangered Species of Wild Fauna and Flora, the Antarctic Treaty and the Human Genome Project are discussed in the context of biotechnologies.

Chapter Six tackles the broad area of ethics, religion and biotechnology by first examining religion and biotechnology and then ethics and biotechnology. Work of the National Bioethics Advisory Committee is reviewed as it explored the religious views of stem cell research and cloning among religious denominations. The family perspective is also reviewed from the question of who is family? Legal vs. biological definitions of family, reproductive technologies, eugenics, stem cell research and cloning are considered in this broad field of ethics, law and biotechnologies. The chapter concludes with consideration of the ethics of contamination of indigenous crops with genetically modified crops.

Chapter Seven considers criminal law and the role biotechnology has played in a range of legal contexts. Federal criminal statutes both new and old are explored in their application to biotechnologies. The use of DNA, and mitochondrial DNA in criminal law, the changing "expectation of privacy" with the use of new biotechnologies, human behavioral genetics and criminal predisposition are among the topics examined in this chapter. This is followed with cases which raise issues of ineffective representation by counsel where knowledge of biotechnology proves essential. A newly characterized crime of biopiracy is a final thought for the future in this chapter.

Chapter Eight reviews the foundation cases in scientific evidence and builds on these to introduce DNA testing and evidence. The emerging study of historical forensics examines some recent cases of interest to historians with legal consequences and raises new ethical issues for its practice.

Chapter Nine is introduced with the landmark case, of *Moore v. Regents of University of California* addressing the issue of ownership with human tissues. Special property protection problems of biotechnology are examined including the ownership of human organs, fertilized human eggs, sperm and umbilical cord blood storage banks.

Chapter Ten considers the application of traditional tort law to the new biotechnologies in the categories of intentional and unintentional torts, specifically trespass to land, conversion, private nuisance, public nuisance and negligence. Other torts are newly emerging areas which may utilize biotechnologies including wrongful birth and wrongful life, medical malpractice and products liability and strict liability.

The book necessarily concludes with a look at the future of law and biotechnology in the last Chapter Eleven.

Four appendices have been created specifically for the use of this book to assist in clarifying terms in biotechnology and general principles in the major scientific disciplines which are used to develop biotechnologies: cell biology, molecular biology, a primer on DNA and a glossary.

About the Author

Victoria Sutton, M.P.A., Ph.D., J.D.
Robert H. Professor of Law, Texas Tech University

Victoria Sutton is the Director of the Center for Biodefense, Law and Public Policy, Director of the Law and Science Certificate Program and the Robert H. Bean Professor of Law at Texas Tech University.

She holds a Ph.D. in Environmental Sciences from The University of Texas at Dallas; a J.D. from American University, *magna cum laude;* and a Master's Degree in Public Administration (MPA), from Old Dominion University, who awarded her the Distinguished Alumni Award in 2005. She also has two Bachelor of Science degrees in Zoology and Animal Science, *cum laude*, from North Carolina State University.

Before coming to Texas Tech, she was Assistant Director in the Bush Administration from 1990 to1993, in the Office of Science and Technology Policy in the White House Science Office, where she worked on national energy and environmental policy. Prior to that, she worked in the U.S. Environmental Protection Agency as a Special Assistant in Policy, Planning and Evaluation and EPA Liaison to the Office of Science and Technology Policy of the White House. Following the Bush Administration, she was appointed as the Executive Director of the Ronald Reagan Institute of Emergency Medicine in Washington, DC.

Since coming to Texas Tech, Dr. Sutton was a Visiting Lecturer at Yale Law School in 2004 and also served in the President George W. Bush Administration as Chief Counsel of the Research and Innovative Technology Administration, U.S. Department of Transportation from 2005 to 2007.

Dr. Sutton is a member of the District of Columbia Bar, U.S. Federal Circuit Bar and the U.S. Supreme Court Bar. She has served as a consultant to a number of federal agencies in the area of biodefense, and is a frequent speaker for audiences of lawyers as well as scientists.

Her awards include receiving the Distinguished Alumni Award from Old Dominion University. She received the Texas Tech University Book Award in 2003 for *Law and Science: Cases and Materials*; and the Law School Distinguished Research Award in 2002, 2003 and 2005. She is also the author of *Law and Bioterrorism*, a first in the field, released January 2003.

Acknowledgments

First, I want to acknowledge Professor D. Allan Bromley, Sterling Professor of the Sciences, Yale University, for his tireless review of several drafts of the book and for sharing with me his incredible insight and knowledge of science, technology, science policy and life.

I would also like to thank the following contributors:

Anna McMinn for her research and explanations for Appendix 3. Primer on DNA.

Law students in my course, Law and Biotechnology, Texas Tech University School of Law, who used previous drafts of this book.

Chapter One

U.S. Department of Energy, Argonne National Laboratory, "Scientific Excellence," *Frontiers* 2001 4–5 (2001).

These biotechnology descriptions are summarized from Helen Kreuzer, Ph.D. and Adrianne Massey, Ph.D., *Recombinant DNA and Biotechnology: A Guide for Teachers*, 2d ASM Press, Washington, D.C. (2001).

James Robert Dean, Jr, "FDA at War: Securing the Food That Secured Victory," 53 Food Drug L.J. 453, 467–8 (1998).

U.S. Department of Energy's Lawrence Livermore National Laboratory, "Research Highlights," *Science and Technology Review,* 10–13 (January/February 2001).

"The Birth of Biotech: Herbert Boyer and Stanley Cohen started a revolution," Association of Alumni and Alumnae of the Massachusetts Institute of Technology, *Technology Review* 120 (July/August 2000).

Chapter Two

Executive Office of the President, Federal Coordinating Council for Science, Engineering and Technology, "Biotechnology for the 21st Century," (February 1992).

Stuart Auchincloss, "Does Genetic Engineering Need Genetic Engineers?: Should the Regulation of Genetic Engineering Include a New Professional Discipline?" 20 B.C. Envtl. Aff. L. Rev. 37 (Fall 1993).

Jesse D. Lyon, "OPEN FORUM: Coordinated Food Systems and Accountability Mechanisms for Food Safety: A Law and Economics Approach," 53 Food Drug L.J. 729 (1998) describes the history of law governing food.

Alliance for bio-Integrity website at http://www.bio-integrity.org/list.html.

Linda Beebe, "Symposium Issue II Pesticides: What Will the Future Reap? Note: In re Starlink Corn: The Link between Genetically Damaged Crops and an Inadequate Regulatory Frame Work for Biotechnology," 28 Wm. & Mary Envtl. L. & Pol'y Rev. 511 (Winter 2004).

Rebecca M. Bratspies, *Consuming (F)ears of Corn: Public Health and Biopharming,* 30 Am. J. L. and Med. 371 (2004).

Meredith A. Jagutis, "Comment: Insurer's Access to Genetic Information: The Call for Comprehensive Federal Legislation," 82 Marq. L.Rev. 429, 434–435 (Winter 1999).

11 Biotechnology Newswatch 11 (1991).

Kourtney L. Pickens, "Don't Judge Me By My Genes: A Survey of Federal Genetic Discrimination Legislation," 34 Tulsa L.J. 161, 170–172 (Fall 1998).

Natalie E. Zindorf, in "Comment: Discrimination in the 21st Century: Protecting the Privacy of Genetic Information in Employment and Insurance," 36 Tulsa L. J. 703, 714–715 (2001).

Chapter Three

Becca Alley, "The Biotechnology Process Patent Act of 1995: Providing Unresolved and Unrecognized Dilemmas in U.S. Patent Law," 12 J. Intell. Prop. L. 229 (Fall 2004).

Margaret M .Duncan, Kathleen Harris, Duncan Curley and Patrick D. Richards, McDermott, Will & Emery, "Legal Implications for Patenting Genomics and Proteomics" Proceedings of The Biotech Law & Litigation Summit, Palo Alto, California (April 30–May 1, 2001).

Beth Panitz, "Bioengineering: A Growing New Discipline," *PRISM American Society for Engineering Education* 22–24 (November 1996).

Jeri E. Reutenauer: "NOTE: Medical Malpractice Liability in the Era of Genetic Susceptibility Testing," 19 Quinnipiac L. Rev. 539 (2000).

Ernst and Young, LLP, Annual Biotechnology Industry Reports, 2000; Ernst and Young, *Beyond Borders,* 2002 and http://www.bio.org/speeches/pubs/er/statistics.asp are the sources of statistics for the biotechnology industry table in section 3.1.

Chapter Four

Renee C. Esfandiary, "NOTE: The Changing World of Genetics and Abortion: Why the Women's Movement Should Advocate for Limitations on the right to Choose in the Area of Genetic Technology," 4 Wm. & Mary J. Of Women & L. 499 (Spring 1998).

Jeri E. Reutenauer, NOTE: Medical Malpractice Liability in the Era of Genetic Susceptibility Testing," 19 Quinnipiac L. Rev. 539 (2000).

Chapter Six

Winona LaDuke, "Wild Rice and Ethics," Cultural Survival Quarterly Issue 28.3 (September 15, 2004).

Gregg Zoroya, USA Today, February 12, 2007, Science makes a new father of a fallen American soldier: Banked sperm produces a son: 'He's a blessing'.

Jennifer S. Bard, "Immaculate Gestation? How Will Ectogenesis Change Current Paradigms of Social Relationships and Values?" Chap. Eleven, Ecotogensis: Artificial Womb Technology and the Future of Human Reproduction, eds. Scott Gelfand and John R. Shook (2006) [excerpt].

Chapter Seven

Justin Gillis, "20 Years Later, Stolen Gene Haunts a Biotech Pioneer," Washington Post Staff Writer (Monday, May 17, 1999; Page A01).

Cecilee Price-Huish, "COMMENT: Born to Kill?"Agression Genes" and Their Poten-tial Impact on Sentencing and the Criminal Justice System," 50 SMU L. Rev. 603 (Jan/Feb 1997).

Chapter Eight

Philip R. Reilly, *Abraham Lincoln's DNA and Other Adventures in Genetics* 6–13 (Cold Spring Harbor Laboratory Press, 2000).

Chapter Nine

Sara Dastgheib-Vinarov, "COMMENT: A Higher Nonobviousness Standard for Gene Patents: Protecting Biomedical Research from the Big Chill," Marq. Intell. Prop. L. Rev. 143 (2000).

Michael E. Sellers, "Patenting Nonnaturally Occurring, Man-Made Life: A Practical Look at the Economic, Environmental, and Ethical Challenges Facing Animal Patents," 47 Ark. L. Rev. 269 (1994) New York Times, Blood Cord Banks.

Chapter Ten

Excerpt from Julie A. Davies and Lawrence C. Levine, *"SYMPOSIUM: Biotechnology and the Law: Biotechnology's Challenge to the Law of Torts,"* 32 McGeorge L. Rev. 221 (Fall 2000).

Jeri E. Reutenauer, "NOTE: Medical Malpractice Liability in the Era of Genetic Suscep-tiblity Testing," 19 Quinnipiac L. Rev. 539 (2000).

Chapter Eleven

Henry Greely, "SPEECH: The Revolution in Human Genetics: Implications for Human Societies," 52 S.C. L. Rev. 377 (Winter 2001).

Appendix 4. Glossary

This entire appendix is from "A Survey of the Use of Biotechnology in Industry," (Dept. of Commerce, 2003) at: http://www.technology.gov/reports/Biotechnology/CD120a_0310.pdf.

Law and Biotechnology

Chapter One

Introduction

1.1 The Relationship between Law and Biotechnology

Law and biotechnology is the application of law to the broad range of activities encompassed within the field of biotechnology, as well as the utilization of sciences and technologies within the field of biotechnology by the field of law.

Biotechnology is a set of technologies utilizing the biological sciences. The scientific disciplines—biology, cell biology, molecular biology, immunology, microbiology, chemical engineering, genetics, chemistry, biochemistry, physics, computer science, forensic science, and mathematics—encompass the range of activities which comprise the underlying scientific principles of biotechnology. The integration of these fields of science represent interdisciplinary applications of science among the traditional "hard" sciences. Other fields, such as ethics, bioethics, sociology and psychology—traditional "soft" sciences—have grown to include new specialty areas with interdisciplinary applications to biotechnology.

The relationship of law to biotechnology, as an interdisciplinary study, has scientific, social, political, and economic consequences which add to the complexity of the development of this growing body of law addressing the issues of biotechnology. Almost every traditional area of law has an application in biotechnology—constitutional law, property law, tort law, criminal law, evidence, as well as the specialty fields of international law, intellectual property law, environmental law, indigenous peoples law, patent law, and public health law. There are certainly areas of the law which are "behind" in addressing the new issues created by the rapidly growing areas of biotechnology, such as cloning and ownership issues. There are also areas of law which are waiting for biotechnology to "catch up" to the demands of the courtroom, such as the application of reliable biotechnological techniques which can be increasingly relied upon in criminal evidentiary matters. Technology has created legal constraints for privacy, for example, with new technologies directed to biodefense surveillance, which must be shaped around those constraints.

The study of law and biotechnology encompasses the theoretical and the practical issues of concern to law and biotechnology; and considerations of the current state of the law and biotechnology as well as the future development of law and biotechnology. This understanding is essential for preparation for legal practice, whether in the public sector or private sector.

The growing importance of science in law and the need for more preparation for lawyers have not gone unnoticed by the courts. Justice Breyer, U.S. Supreme Court Associate Justice, in an unusual public advocacy posture, has been actively encouraging and promoting the education of lawyers and judges in the sciences. During a conference at Harvard University's Kennedy School of Government in November 2000, Justice Breyer stated, "Traditionally, some have believed that we need not know science but only law to make decisions. This view is increasingly unrealistic. Since the implications of our decisions in the real world often can and should play a role in our legal decisions, the clearer our understanding of the relevant science, the better…." USA TODAY, Nov 24, 2000, reported, "Although it remains rare for Supreme Court Justices to speak out on public issues, Breyer has publicly urged greater scientific education for judges at least three times this year."

1.1.1 Defining Biotechnology

Biotechnology's simplest definition is the application of biology to human needs. More specifically, biotechnology is a set of technologies that use biological molecules and cells to make products, solve problems, and do research, based upon an understanding of cellular and molecular structure and processes.

These technologies include

(1) monoclonal antibody technology, which is the use of cells and enzymes to make and break down products; (2) cell culture technology, which comprises the techniques used to grow cells in laboratory containers or bioreactors; (3) genetic engineering technology, which involves changing an organism's genetic makeup with molecular techniques; (4) biosensor technology, which is the use of biological molecules and transducers for detection and quantification; (5) antisense technology, which is the use of the mechanism of blocking gene expression with oligonucleotides; (6) DNA chip technology, which is the use of DNA probes to detect mutations and monitor gene expression; (7) tissue engineering, which comprises the techniques used in the growing of semisynthetic tissues and organs; (8) bioprocessing technology, which consist of techniques using cells and enzymes to make and break down products; and (9) bioinformatics, which is the use of computational tools to organize, access, and study information about biology.

1.1.1.1 Monoclonal Antibody Technology

Monoclonal antibody (MCAb) technology uses cells of the immune system that make proteins called antibodies. The immune system is composed of a number of cell types that work together to locate and destroy substances that invade the body. One type of immune system cell, the B lymphocyte, responds to invaders by producing antibodies that bind to the foreign substance with extraordinary specificity. The technology to harness the ability of B lymphocytes to make these very specific antibodies is being developed.

The substances that an MCAb detects, quantifies, and localizes are remarkably varied and are limited only by the substance's ability to trigger the production of antibodies. Home pregnancy kits use an MCAb that binds to a hormone produced in the placenta. Many of these antibodies are currently being used to diagnose a number of infectious diseases such as strep throat and gonorrhea. Because cancer cells differ biochemically from normal cells, we can make monoclonal antibodies that detect cancers by binding selectively to tumor cells. In addition to diagnosing diseases in humans, such antibodies are being used to detect plant and animal diseases, food contaminants, and environmental pollutants.

This technology has the potential to be used with a radioisotope or toxin tag to a cancerous tumor antibody, and then these tumor-killing agents are delivered directly to the target cells, while bypassing the healthy cells. Monoclonal antibodies can also be used to treat autoimmune diseases, such as multiple sclerosis and lupus, and to prevent complications following heart bypass surgery.

1.1.1.2 Cell Culture Technology

This technology involves the growing of cells in appropriate nutrients in laboratory containers or in large bioreactors in manufacturing facilities.

Plant cell culture technology is based upon the potential of one differentiated cell to generate an entire multicellular plant. This is called the cell's totipotency, or the potential to generate an entire organism.

Animal cell culture technology, using, for example, an insect cell culture, could isolate viruses that infect insects and then might be grown and used as an insect control agent to protect the treated plant or animal. Mammalian cell culture technology is also being used in livestock breeding. Large numbers of bovine zygotes from genetically superior bulls and cows can be produced and cultured before being implanted into surrogate cows. In its medical application, animal cell culture is used to study such areas as the safety and efficacy of pharmaceutical compounds, the molecular mechanism of viral infection and replication, the toxicity of compounds and basic cell biochemistry.

Embryonic stem cell culture has been recently developed as having major potential medical benefits. Embryonic stem cells in their development eventually grow into a differentiated cell. However, early in the development they have the potential to differentiate into several different kinds of cells. This complete developmental plasticity sets them apart from other stem cells and opens the possibility of using them therapeutically. For example, if we develop the capability to control the differentiation of human embryonic stem cells, we may be able to produce replacement cells to treat diabetes, Parkinson's disease, and many other diseases.

1.1.1.3 Genetic Engineering Technology

Genetic engineering is often referred to as recombinant DNA (rDNA) technology and is carried out by joining or recombining genetic material from two different sources. DNA recombines naturally during the crossing over of chromosomes that occurs in gamete formation, during egg fertilization, and when bacteria exchange genetic material through conjugation, transformation, and transduction. The result of the recombination of DNA is increased genetic variation.

The early domestication of animals through selective breeding is an approach to altering the genetic makeup of an organism to adapt to human needs. As a result of this genetic selection, the animals were dramatically changed over time.

The recombination of DNA refers to the specific recombination of DNA through the use of restriction enzymes designed to cut and join DNA in predictable ways at the molecular level. To accomplish this process, bacteria and viruses are used to transport the

DNA segments. The use of this technology allows the transfer of genetic material across species, something which was not possible through selective breeding.

1.1.1.4 Biosensor Technology

A biosensor is a detecting device composed of a biological substance linked to a transducer. The biological substance might be a microbe, a single cell from a multicellular animal, or an enzyme or an antibody. Biosensors can detect substances at extremely low concentrations.

Biosensors generate digital electronic signals by exploiting the specificity of biological molecules. When the substance we want to measure collides with the biological detector, the transducer produces a tiny electrical current. This electrical signal is proportional to the concentration of the substance.

These biosensors are being developed to measure nutritional value, safety of food, analyses of blood gases, electrolyte concentrations, and blood-clotting capability in emergency rooms. Monitoring industrial processes and locating and measuring pollutants will also utilize biosensors. For example, by coupling a glucose biosensor to an insulin infusion pump, the correct blood concentration of glucose could be maintained at all times in those with diabetes. Currently under development are biosensor chips that combine the sensor element with an arithmetic analysis and a wireless transmitter so that a wide range of biological systems can be remotely monitored. In many cases these chips can be permanently implanted in the human body and powered for indefinite periods by the voltage normally present in the body.

1.1.1.5 Antisense Technology

Blocking or decreasing the production of certain proteins is the specific process of antisense technology. Blocking is achieved by using small nucleic acids (oligonucleotides) that prevent translation of the information encoded in DNA into a protein.

The potential applicability of this technology includes circumstances where blocking a gene would be beneficial. For example, antisense technology may be used to slow food spoilage, control viral diseases, inhibit the inflammatory response, and treat asthma, cancers, and thalassemia, a hereditary anemia.

Metabolic engineering is another use for antisense technology. Many compounds in nature that have commercial application are not proteins; for example, most compounds produced by plants to deter insect feeding could be useful as crop protectants but are not proteins. By using antisense technology to block the production of enzymes in certain pathways, the plant's metabolism is altered to favor the production of these compounds.

1.1.1.6 DNA Chip Technology

DNA chip technology is a hybrid of semiconductor technology and molecular biology technology. This technology can perform genetic analysis of tens of thousands of genes through a single "microchip." The manufacturing processes of microchips and DNA chips are similar in principle, but instead of shining light through a series of masks to etch circuits into silicon, automated DNA chip makers use a series of masks to create a sequence of DNA probes on a glass slide.

The DNA is removed from cells, tagged with fluorescent markers, and placed on the chip. Hybridized sequences attach to the probes, and unmatched bits of DNA are then washed away. Using a laser reader, computer, and high-powered microscopes, scientists can analyze thousands of sequences at a time and determine where the tagged DNA finds a match with a chip-mounted DNA probe.

This DNA chip technology is being used to detect mutations in disease-causing genes, to monitor gene expression in yeast and cancer cell lines, diagnose infectious diseases, and tell us whether a pathogen is resistant to certain drugs. DNA chips are continuing to develop for crop biotechnology, to improve screening for microbes used in bioremediation, and to hasten drug discovery. DNA chip technology is one of the scientific research priorities in the development of biodefense technologies and has been used experimentally to detect the presence of pathogens in the ambient air through existing air monitoring stations in major cities.

1.1.1.7 Tissue Engineering

Tissue engineering combines the technologies of cell biology with those of materials science to create semisynthetic tissues in the laboratory. These tissues are made up of living cells held together with biodegradable scaffolding material, usually collagen.

One of the first products was the two-layer skin, made by infiltrating a collagen gel with fibroblasts, allowing them to grow, multiply, and become the dermis, then by adding a layer of deratinocytes to serve as the epidermis. In other tissue engineering methods, the scaffolding, made of a synthetic polymer, is shaped and then placed in the body where new tissue is needed. Adjacent cells stimulated by the appropriate growth factors invade the scaffolding, which is eventually degraded and absorbed.

The simple tissues of cartilage and skin were the first to be engineered, successfully. The goal is to create more complex organs made up of a number of tissue types to serve as replacement organs.

1.1.1.8 Bioprocessing Technology

Bioprocessing technology uses living cells or components of living cells to synthesize products, to break down substances, and to release energy. These living cells are typically one-celled organisms, such as bacteria or yeasts or mammalian cells; and the cellular components most often used are enzymes, which are proteins.

Enzymes catalyze all cellular biochemical reactions, which create energy in the breaking down of molecules and the creation of chemical building blocks to assemble new molecules.

Fermentation and mammalian cell culture are two types of bioprocessing technologies that rely on cellular enzymes. The oldest bioprocessing technology is microbial fermentation. In the process of metabolizing glucose in fruits, microbes synthesize byproducts which are useful: carbon dioxide for leavening bread, ethanol for brewing wine and beer, lactic acid for making yogurt, and acetic acid (vinegar) for pickling foods. Microbial fermentation is used to synthesize antibiotics, amino acids, hormones, vitamins, industrial solvents, pesticides, food processing aids, pigments, enzymes, enzyme inhibitors, and pharmaceuticals.

Biodegradation, bioremediation, and phytoremediation are biotechnological processes that are utilized for useful processes. Biodegradation can be useful by utilizing microorganisms to dissolve oil from oil spills or toxic waste. Bioremediation is the result of such cleanups of the environment. Phytoremediation is the use of plants to remove toxic substances and contaminants from the environment through the utilization of plant-specific enzymes.

Many advances in manufacturing are also expected. In manufacturing, for example, use of enzymes can lead to chemical products produced without the high temperatures and pressure characteristics of current chemical technology and with enormous savings in energy.

1.1.1.9 Bioinformatics

Computer technology manages the extraordinary volume of information of gene sequences, protein structure, carbohydrate structure, and genetic maps for many species.

Methods for organization and utilization of this information involve computational tools, such as algorithms, graphics, artificial intelligence, statistical software, simulation, and database management technologies to map and compare genomes, structures, and functions. It is essential to remember that data do not become knowledge until the data are analyzed.

Bioinformatics for Lawyers

This is a field which is of particular interest to both lawyers and scientists. Although it is primarily technical in identifying catalogs of DNA information in computer searchers among scientists, it is also a useful data base which can be utilized in legal research.

At Argonne National Laboratory, the Computational Biology Group developed WIT3, an interactive database that stores genomics and metabolic information and provides tools for users to access the data and construct their own models of the sequences of [bases] As, Cs, Gs and Ts. The researchers originally developed a computer program called WIT, or What Is There, to store and compare genomics information on the World Wide Web. The new WIT3 is automated, speeding the process of retrieving data and constructing models. WIT3 is available to researchers on the World Wide Web. The site has about 20,000 users and receives between 3,000 and 5,000 visits a day. The success of Argonne's structural genomics program depends on the technological advances of synchrotron facilities such as the APS [Advanced Proton Source], molecular biology and crystallography methods, robotics, and computer hardware and software. But the process begins with two time-consuming, vital tasks in a more traditional laboratory.

First biologists clone a protein by snipping pieces out of its genome and placing them in "expression bacteria," which make many protein copies. Argonne researchers created a modern production line using robots to automate this time-consuming cloning task. The Robotic Molecular Biology Facility can produce 400 to 800 protein clones each week; manual methods produce only 20 to 40. Then biologists coax these purified proteins to form crystals for X-ray crystallography in the Structural Biology Center [SBC].

Argonne researchers continue to refine the structural genomics process to make it even faster. For example, the robotic lab plans to quadruple production in 2001 by increasing from 96 to 384 the number of miniature test-tube-like wells the robot can handle at a time. Also, the SBC will take advantage of the APS's brighter X-rays using new larger, faster X-ray detectors that provide information in greater detail. In the future Argonne maybe able to offer a structural genomics assembly line to many users.... and researchers can send their crystals to be placed in the beamline using robots and have the data remotely collected and processed in real time.

Scientific Excellence, FRONTIERS (U.S. Dep't of Energy, Argone Nat'l Lab.) 2001 at 4–5.

These biotechnology descriptions are summarized from HELEN KREUZER, PH.D. AND ADRIANNE MASSEY, PH.D., RECOMBINANT DNA AND BIOTECHNOLOGY: A GUIDE FOR TEACHERS, (2d ed. 2001).

1.1.2 Defining Bioengineering

Bioengineering is an interdisciplinary field that applies physical, chemical, and mathematical sciences and engineering principles of the study of biology, medicine, behavior, and health. It advances knowledge from the molecular to the organ systems level, and develops new and novel biologics, materials, processes, implants, devices, and informational approaches for the prevention, diagnosis, and treatment of disease, for patient rehabilitation, and for improving health. (NIH)

Bioengineering has made enormous contributions to the advancement of health care in the United States. It has been instrumental in establishing the U.S. as the world leader in health care technology, as evidenced by a $4.6 billion trade surplus for this sector in 1993. The field through basic and applied research and technology assessment, has given us such devices as the pacemaker, orthopedic implants, and noninvasive diagnostic imaging. Bioengineers have developed new processes for manufacturing products in the pharmaceutical and biotechnology industries. An example is human insulin, the first product to be based on recombinant DNA technology, where bioengineering was critical to the ability to commercialize the product.

Winfred M. Phillips, Ph.D., Dean, College of Engineering, University of Florida; Past-President American Institute for Medical and Biological Engineering Testimony before The Subcommittee on Public Health and Safety, Committee on Labor and Human Resources (July 24, 1997).

1.1.3 Defining Genomics

Genomics's simplest definition is the study of the genome. Structural genomics is the study of gene structure, that is DNA mapping and sequencing. Functional genomics is the study of DNA function, or gene expression.

Genomics is the study of the map of the set of genes which comprise a living organism—the genome. Genomics is the study of the sequence of genes and the identification of the proteins which these genes code for, and further study of other functions of the genes which have not yet be discovered.

1.1.4 Defining Proteomics

Sequencing the human genome was a major landmark in science, which revealed the next layer of the onion—proteomics, which is the understanding of the action of the gene which has been sequenced. The term "proteome" was coined around 1994 by an Australian academic, and is defined generally as the identification and characterization of proteins produced by genes which are part of a biological process.

Three leaders in the field of genomics and proteomics defined the new field of proteomics in the following article by Stu Borman, *Any New Proteomics Techniques Out There?* 79 CHEMICAL AND ENGINEERING NEWS 31–33, Nov. 26, 2001 at 31–33.

"The genome is static. It's the blueprint, and no one lives in the blueprint of their house," explains Ruth A. Van Bogelen, head of genomics and proteomics at Pfizer, Ann Arbor, Mich. "Proteomics tells us about the biology—how it feels to live in the house: Does the heat and air conditioning work? Is there enough water pressure? Will the house stand up in a tornado? And so on." Proteomics studies include "what cells and organisms do, how they respond, what disease looks like, how drugs reverse disease—all the parts of cells and how they work."

"Proteomics is many different things," says Leroy Hood of the Institute for Systems Biology, Seattle, who in the 1980s led a California Institute of Technology team that invented the automated gene sequencer. "It's being able to identify complex mixtures of proteins; it's being able to quantitate [sic] their behavior in interesting biological systems; it's looking at their modifications and how that changes their biological activity; it's looking at their interactions, their compartmentalization, their turnover times—all of these kinds of things."

Collins says he likes the proteomics definition given by genetics and medicine professor and Howard Hughes Medical Institute investigator Stanley Fields of the University of Washington, Seattle, in *Science* [*291*, 1221 (2001)]: "the analysis of complete complements of proteins. Proteomics includes not only the identification and quantification of proteins, but also the determination of their localization, modifications, interactions, activities, and, ultimately, their function." To this definition, Collins adds structural genomics, the rapid 3-D structure determination of large numbers of proteins (on a proteome scale).

1.1.5 Defining Nanobiotechnology

Nanotechnology is the application of nanoscience to practical problems, measured in nanometers, or 1/1,000,000,000th (one trillionth) of a meter. One million nanometers is equal to one millimeter. The National Nanotechnology Initiative, an organization of the Office of Science and Technology Policy of the federal government, defines nanotechnology only if it involves all of the following: (1) research and technology development at the atomic, molecular or macromolecular levels, in the length scale of approximately 1–100 nanometer range; (2) creating and using structures, devices and systems that have novel properties and functions because of their small and/or intermediate size; and (3) ability to control or manipulate on the atomic scale.

To conceptualize nano-size, the size of a red blood cell is 2.5 micrometers, DNA is 2.5 nanometers, viruses are between 100 and 10 nanometers, biological molecules are approximately 1 nanometer.

The Foresight Institute has developed guidelines for professionals, industries, and governments for the regulation of nanotechnologies at http://www.foresight.org/guidelines/current.html.

The nanobiotechnologies involve the use of biological processes at the molecular level to do constructing or to operate in an environment where only nano-size objects can operate. Nanobiotechnology is biological in origin and may include composites of biological and nonbiological materials, or mimetics of biological systems. These technologies possess unique and useful properties conferred on them by virtue of the nanoscale of operation.

1.2 The History of Biotechnology and Law in Eurasia and the Americas

The beginning of biotechnology, defined as the application of biology to human needs, occurred when humans began both the selective crossing of plants for crops and the domestication of animals through selective breeding more than 10,000 years ago. Sheep and goats were domesticated around 9,000 B.C., swine around 7,000 B.C. and cattle around 6,500 B.C. In 4,000 B.C. the Sumerians and Babylonians began making beer. It was around 3,200 B.C. when yogurt and cheese were developed, and thus microorganisms were utilized for human needs. R.K. ROBINSON, A COLOUR GUIDE TO CHEESE AND FERMENTED MILKS, (Chapman & Hall 1995). [See Figure 1.1].

Figure 1.1

Sheep and goats	9000 BC
Swine	7000 BC
Cattle	6500 BC
Beer-making	4000 BC
Cheese and yogurt	3200 BC
Moldy soybean curds for antibiotic	500 BC
Pesticides—chrysanthemum	100 BC
Genetics—diseases run in families observation	1000 BC
Dark ages	1200 AD
Harvey	1630 AD
Leeuwenhoek	1660 AD
Jenner—inoculation	1797 AD
Term "biology" coined	1802 AD
Mendel, Pasteur	1860 AD
Fleming—penicillin reported	1929 AD
Monoclonal antibodies technology	1972 AD
DNA engineering	1980 AD

In the Americas, the Native Americans were involved in the pharmacological development of plants, which is a part of the oral history of tribes.

The first law applied to biotechnology was probably the standards for a bioprocessing technology. This first recorded relationship between law and biotechnology was found in the Hammurabi code, which required an "eye for an eye." Contained within that code were precise instructions and regulations for the manufacture of beer in ancient

Babylonia. Around 4,000 B.C. the brewing of beer began in Sumeria, Babylonia, and Egypt.

The period around 3200 B.C. marks the beginning of the cheesemaking processes. It has been theorized that cheese may have been discovered through the slaughter of un-weaned calves with fermented milk remaining in their stomachs. Around 500 B.C., the Chinese recorded the practice of using moldy soybean curds as an antibiotic treatment for pustules and open sores. The use of crop rotation to preserve soil fertility was prac-ticed by the Greeks as early as 250 B.C. The use of pesticides was first recorded around 100 B.C., when the Chinese used chrysanthemum pollen as an insecticide.

From A.D. 100 to 300 Hindu philosophers became curious about the nature of re-production and genetic inheritance. Around A.D. 1,000, the Hindus observed that cer-tain diseases may run in families. The laws of Manu set forth the principle that "[a] man of base descents can never escape his origins." The period from A.D 1,100 to 1,500 can be considered the dark age of biotechnology and law. Spontaneous generation re-mained the dominant explanation of the origin of living organisms, such as maggots originating from horsehair.

A vinegar manufacturing operation in Orleans in the 1500s was the next develop-ment, marking an end to the dark ages of biotechnology development in Europe.

Around A.D. 1630, William Harvey concluded that sexual reproduction existed in the lower organisms and that males contribute sperm and females contribute an egg in the process. In A.D. 1,665, Robert Hooke observed the cellular structure of cork, and in that same period the idea of spontaneous generation was disproven by the work of Francesco Redi, who with a simple experiment showed that maggots arose from uncov-ered meat, while covered meat did not produce maggots. Then in A.D. 1,680 Leeuwen-hoek observed the fermentation process of yeast through his first microscope.

Prior to the use of cowpox, the Moravians, a religious sect, in North Carolina in the early 1700s recorded in their detailed diaries, the use of a small infection of smallpox to guard against a more serious case. This often resulted in deaths from an unexpectedly serious case. It was not until 1797, that Edward Jenner used a different living organism (cowpox) to protect people from diseases through innoculation. Louis Pasteur, in 1864, proved the existence of microorganisms and that they reproduced. Thereafter in 1865, Gregor Mendel demonstrated the inheritance of traits from one generation to another in the pea plant, establishing the beginning of the field of genetics. Then in 1869, Jo-hann Meische isolated DNA from the nuclei of white blood cells. It is noteworthy that the work of these scientists was beyond any regulatory mechanism of the time.

The regulation of cheese has been largely driven by the cultures in which it is pro-duced and consumed. A comparison of European regulation and U.S. regulation illus-trates this point:

> The acceptance of raw milk cheeses necessarily implies the rejection of a pasteurization requirement. This rejection has both negative aspects (the pos-sibility of contamination) and positive aspects (better taste). Consumers in Eu-rope generally value the flavor and tradition of raw milk cheeses. Since the cheeses have been produced and eaten for hundreds of years with few public health consequences, consumers do not believe these cheeses present a food safety risk, provided that certain sanitary practices are followed. EC law reflects this view. In contrast, in the U.S., unpasteurized cheeses—products not sub-jected to modern scientific standards—are considered risky. U.S. law reflects this view by prohibiting fresh raw milk cheeses. Only those products that have

been aged for at least sixty days may be imported and sold. Marsha A. Echols, *Food Safety Regulation in the European Union and the United States: Different Cultures, Different Laws*, 4 COLUM. J. EUR. L. 525, 533 (1998).

Butter and margarine became an issue in the United States when margarine was first introduced in 1873. Concern for content of the product was largely driven by politics rather than product quality or content. "New York enacted an antimargarine law in 1877 at the direct urging of the butter interests. Missouri followed suit the same year. Six states adopted labelling laws in 1878: California, Connecticut, Maryland, Massachusetts, Ohio, and Pennsylvania. Three more states passed legislation in 1879: Delaware, Illinois, and Tennessee. Others soon fell into line; by 1886, thirty-four states and territories had enacted some version of margarine labelling legislation." Geoffrey P. Miller, *Public Choice at the Dawn of the Special Interest State: The Story of Butter and Margarine*, 77 CALIF. L. REV. 83 (1989).

The strong mercantile, commerce and regulatory interests in butter and cheese led to the development of the New York Stock Exchange. The Exchange began when the Butter and Cheese Exchange of New York was created. On June 1, 1875, this exchange became the American Exchange of New York, and then on April 26, 1880, it became the Butter, Cheese and Egg Exchange of the City of New York. Finally, on June 5, 1882, the Exchange changed its name to the New York Mercantile Exchange. See N.Y. Mercantile Ex. Guide (CCH)PP 51, 61, 65, 59 (1986).

The 1800s were the culmination of the discoveries of the Enlightenment Era, and the word "biology" was coined in 1802. Appert invented the canning process in 1809, and proteins were discovered in 1830, followed in 1833 with the first isolation of enzymes. Then in 1855, *Escherichia coli*, a common bacteria, was first isolated, and continues to be an important tool in biotechnology research. The famous work of Gregor Mendel occurred in 1863, when he discovered the first principles of genetics. From 1881 to 1900, the first rabies vaccine was discovered.

The possible societal evils of the fermentation of fruit, were recognized, however, and as early as 1855, states were regulating alcohol production. The regulation of alcohol in the United States has a long history, culminating in the twenty-first Amendment to the U.S. Constitution. As Judge Hopkins wrote in a judicial opinion, "Kansas has been one of the pioneers, first, in the regulation, and second, in the prohibition of the beverage liquor traffic. Indeed as early as 1855, her Territorial Legislature passed acts regulating such traffic. Those interested in the subject will find a synopsis of all the liquor laws of Kansas from 1855 to 1933, together with citations pertaining thereto, in a note or appendix to the opinion in *Chapman v. Boynton*, 4 F.Supp. 43, 47 (D.C. Cir.), from which it appears that prohibition of the beverage liquor traffic had a progressive development in Kansas from regulation of the saloon and tavern down to and including 'bone dry.'" *United States v. Robason*, 38 F. Supp. 991, 992 (1941).

In the United States, concern for food safety and regulation began in 1862, the beginning years of the U.S. Civil War. The following excerpt from James Robert Dean, Jr., *FDA at War: Securing the Food That Secured Victory*, 53 FOOD DRUG L.J. 453, 456–7 (1998), provides a brief overview of the history of that regulatory agency which was to oversee food safety and the resulting development of regulation:

> The agency now known as FDA began in 1862, when the Chemical Division of the U.S. Department of Agriculture (USDA) was established. The Agriculture Department was charged with undertaking research aimed at furthering American agriculture. As other divisions of the growing department became more

focused on particular lines of research, such as livestock or crop research, the Chemical Division remained a general scientific laboratory. Only because of the growing interest in food adulteration of Harvey W. Wiley, the head of the division, did FDA's predecessor begin to emphasize food and drug matters. After a lengthy legislative fight, the 1906 Pure Food and Drugs Act vested the recently renamed Bureau of Chemistry with regulatory authority. This authority entailed a significant shift in FDA's focus. The pre-1906 Bureau of Chemistry furthered the interests of farmers. The 1906 Act created a new federal consumer protection agency. FDA appropriations jumped from $ 17,100 in 1900 to $ 888,560 in 1910, reflecting these additional responsibilities. The number of FDA personnel also increased from 20 in 1897 to 110 in 1906 and then to 425 by 1908. In the following decades, FDA developed a regulatory model based on frequent seizures and criminal prosecutions of adulterated products.

FDA remained a division of the Agriculture Department until 1940 when it was moved into the Federal Security Agency (FSA). This move ended a long period of institutional conflict between the former Chemical Division and the other divisions of the Agriculture Department. Combined with the new mandate of the 1938 Act, the move marked a new era in FDA's history. Separation from the Agriculture Department that was becoming increasingly concerned with promoting the welfare of farmers, as opposed to the consumer protection mission of FDA, allowed the newly empowered agency to expand fully into its new responsibilities. FSA had fewer institutional biases than the Agriculture Department, making FSA a more suitable home for FDA. President Roosevelt, in his message to Congress explaining the new arrangement, stated that he found it desirable to group together those agencies of the government whose major purpose was to promote social and economic security, educational opportunity, and the health of the citizens of the Nation. FDA, while located in a new home more attuned to its mission, was still a small agency, however, and was allocated only $ 2.5 million from an FSA total budget of $ 1 billion. Despite its strong congressional mandate and history of excellent work, the FDA of 1940 needed to establish its new identity and power quickly.

The 1938 Act changed the philosophy behind food and drug regulation. Under the 1906 Act, the agency generally had banned "adulterated" and "misbranded" foods and drugs. The definition of these terms, however, largely remained for the courts to determine. Every violation had to be proven in court to meet the terms of the Act. The 1906 Act could be described as a legal, as opposed to administrative, regime.

The 1938 Act reflected a different approach, one more in tune with the emerging New Deal regulatory model. FDA received authority to promulgate standards of identity for common foods, an important exercise of administrative discretion. Where a standard of identity existed, foods sold under the common name established by the standard would be in violation of the FDCA if they did not meet the FDA-established requirements. Furthermore, foods packed in conditions where they might become adulterated were subject to seizure, without a full adjudication of whether the particular item in question was, in fact, adulterated. Another important expansion of FDA's powers was its new authority to review new drugs before they could be marketed legally. While the agency's name remained the same, the 1938 Act provided for the replacement of a traditional police force with an independent regulatory body empowered to create and enforce the law. This marked a significant change for both the regulators and the regulated. FDA was charged with developing a body of law, a task that required both expert knowledge and political deftness.

The regulation of these activities was limited primarily to the recipes and processes as a quality control and public health matter.

World War II produced a need for antimalarial drugs as well as penicillin. The following account describes the role of regulation in the development of these pharmaceuticals:

> Malaria was prevalent in the entire Pacific theater and areas in North Africa and Sicily, where millions of American troops soon were to be stationed. While quinine had been used successfully for centuries to treat malaria, supplies of the drug were reduced drastically following the Japanese capture of the East Indies. Although cinchona was native to South America, production was concentrated in the East Indies where the tree grew particularly well. In 1941, ninety-five percent of American quinine came from territory soon to be under Japanese control.
>
> To complicate the situation, quinine did not actually cure or prevent malaria; it only relieved the debilitating symptoms. Prolonged use of quinine also produced unpleasant side effects, such as ringing in the ears, blurry vision, and nausea. FDA had recognized some of these problems before the war while investigating how quinine should be marketed under the FDCA. In 1939, FDA had issued a statement requiring that all anti-malarial preparations comply with the requirements of the FDCA, which limited certain labeling claims.... The germicidal properties of penicillin had been reported by Alexander Fleming in 1929, but it had not been used as an antibiotic before World War II. British scientists at Oxford began investigating penicillin for medicinal use in the late 1930s.... Penicillin comes from a mold, *Penicillium notatum*. While relatively easy to grow in a laboratory, it proved exceedingly difficult to extract the chemical substance from the organism on a commercial scale. Early attempts involved arrays of large Petri dishes, each harboring an active culture of the penicillin-producing mold. Eventually it proved possible to grow the molds in a solution rather than on the surface of a culture medium, making larger-scale production possible. After considerable effort, the penicillin program proved to be a huge success. By the end of the war all military needs were met and substantial supplies were available for public consumption.... The pattern that emerged during World War II has continued after the war. FDA became a reviewer of scientific research, but not a major patron of science or a research organization itself. Other nonregulatory agencies, such as the National Institutes of Health and the National Science Foundation, became the primary federal sponsors of scientific research. Soon after the war ended, OSRD canceled FDA's outstanding research projects on synthetic penicillin. The cancellation noted that the major portion of the work in this program has been performed in commercial and academic laboratories, and recent developments require a readjustment of all projects, especially those involving non-governmental groups. Progress in methods of producing penicillin by fermentation and the end of active hostilities have removed the justification for continued governmental sponsorship of this research on its present basis. James Robert Dean, Jr, *FDA at War: Securing the Food That Secured Victory*, 53 FOOD DRUG L.J. 453, 497–500 (1998).

Penicillin and the development of other drugs came after the passage of the Food, Drug and Cosmetic Act in 1938, providing a regulatory vehicle for the control of the development and dispensing of drugs. Foods were also regulated under this Act, and many foods such as salt, flour and sugar were classified under the GRAS provision of the Act—generally recognized as safe food products, which meant *de facto* approval for human consumption.

The scientific approach to regulation prevailed at FDA, but it was not without criticism. As one author described the situation:

> FDA's "scientific" approach badly served the goal of food and drug regulation. The most famous example is Harvey W. Wiley's crusade against all food additives. The man known for creating the modern system of food and drug regulation also was "seriously deficient" in his grasp of scientific matters. Dupree notes that "although the bureau made steady progress in enforcing pure-food-and-drug standards, it became a correspondingly serious problem to the responsible political chiefs to be sure in the face of pressure that Wiley's facts were straight." This controversy, which developed in food and drug law soon after the turn of the century, was the crux of the late New Deal debate over the future of administrative law. Regulating in the name of expertise can succeed only when the underlying scientific justification generally is accepted as valid. As FDA moved into its broader power granted by the 1938 Act, it frequently approached the edge of scientific knowledge and had correspondingly less legitimating force behind its regulatory plans.... The quantum leap in food technology during and after the war eventually led to the food and color additives amendments, which further transformed the agency from Wiley's group of "G-men" into a scientific bureaucracy. Dean, *supra.*

The development of biotechnology has been compared to the rapid advances made in the field of physics in the early part of the 20th century through the 1980s. Almost everything we know about the universe as well as subatomic particles was discovered during this period. But, hundreds of years passed between the discoveries of Ptolemy and Newton before the revolution in physics began. The phenomena of revolutions of science have been described by Thomas S. Kuhn in THE STRUCTURE OF SCIENTIFIC REVOLUTIONS 92, 111 (1962).

> [S]cientific revolutions are taken to be those non-cumulative developmental episodes in which an older paradigm is replaced in whole or in part by an incompatible new one.... Led by a new paradigm, scientists adopt new instruments and look in new places. Even more important, during revolutions scientists see new and different things when looking with familiar instruments in places they have looked before. Nevertheless, paradigm changes do cause scientists to see the world of their research-engagement differently.

In physics, perhaps the two most important discoveries were those of relativity and of quantum mechanics in 1905 and 1925, respectively. In biology the two most important were the structure of the DNA molecule as the blueprint of life and the completion of the mapping of the human genome in 1956 and 2001, respectively.

Similarly, the revolution in biotechnology has created a revolution in the legal field, as well, causing lawyers, legislators, and judges to "see different things when looking with familiar *laws and political institutions* in places they have looked before,"(to apply Kuhn's description of the scientists of a revolution). So, too, biotechnology allows us to ask questions not only in science but in law, which we have never asked before.

The Hungarian engineer, Karl Ereky, is credited with coining the term "biotechnology" in 1919. Ereky used this term to refer to the use of living organisms in the utilization of raw materials to make useful commodities.

The following accounts of the beginnings of modern biotechnology demonstrate the wide range of biological research taking place which produced the synergy that created the development of the biotechnology industry.

The first successful biomolecular project at Livermore took place in the late 1970s with the production of made-to-order monoclonal antibodies. (Antibodies are nature's defender molecules, and monoclonal means that they are produced by a single clone.) [It is possible to] select for and form single clones or copies of immunologically active cells. Such cells make only one antibody, and when isolated, they can be produced infinitely with complete purity and remarkable specificity. Two of Livermore's products are the monoclonal antibodies that recognize the subtle distinction between normal and mutant red blood cells in the glycophorin-A assay. Other Livermore monoclonal antibodies can indicate whether a blood stain is human or whether a child has sickle cell anemia. Still others are useful for making the individual proteins involved in the complex process of repairing DNA.

Perhaps the most important antibodies to come out of this work were those of bromodeoxyuridine in DNA, a substance that can substitute for a normal building block of DNA. A small amount injected into a subject or in a culture will be synthesized into the DNA of any cells that are dividing. When this monoclonal antibody is coupled to a fluorescent marker, all the cells in division become fluorescent and can be seen under a microscope or detected and measured in a a glow cytometer. A Livermore team used this technique ... to develop methods that revolutionized the study of cell growth and that today are standard procedure worldwide. Cancer patients are routinely evaluated by these methods to see how fast their cancer cells are dividing....

In 1974, Livermore scientists for the first time performed an experiment that successfully measured and sorted Chinese hamster chromosomes using flow cytometry. Not until 1979 did scientist learn how to do the same with human chromosomes, which are much smaller and more varied....

In 1984, Mort Mendelsohn organized a meeting of molecular geneticists from around the world to brainstorm the potential for DNA-oriented methods to detect human heritable mutation in A-bomb survivors. It became clear to those at the meeting that despite the enormous scale of this effort, analysis of the entire human genome was feasible.

In 1986, the Department of Energy was the first federal agency to launch a major initiative to completely decipher the human genetic code. A year later, Livermore researchers began to study all of chromosome 19, which they had earlier learned was the home of several genes important for DNA repair.

In 1990, the Department of Energy joined forces with the National Institutes of Health to kick off the Human Genome Project, the largest biological research project ever.

Early groundbreaking Livermore work in flow cytometry, a technique for separating specific cells from other cells has come to have numerous medical research applications. Some biosensors to detect the specific agents used in biological weapons are based on flow cytometry.

Research Highlights, SCIENCE AND TECHNOLOGY REVIEW (U.S. Dep't of Energy's Lawrence Livermore Nat'l Lab), Jan./Feb. 2001 at 10–13.

From the University of California, San Francisco:

> In the fall of 1972, there was no such thing as genetic engineering.... In the early 1970s, Herbert Boyer's lab at the University of California, San Francisco, isolated an enzyme that cut DNA at specific locations. At the same time, Stanley Cohen's Stanford lab was working out methods for introducing small circular pieces of DNA called "plasmids" into bacteria, which act as living Xerox machines, copying genes each time the microbes divide. At a November 1972 conference in Hawaii, both researchers presented their work—and realized that if they combined their techniques they would have a remarkable tool.... within months their labs had jointly proved the possibility of gene "cloning": splicing a gene of interest—say, one that encodes a human hormone—into a microorganism or other cell. The technique is at the heart of DNA sequencing, genetic engineering and indeed, biotechnology.
>
> Stanford seized on the potential of the work, and did something that was quite unusual at the time: They patented the technique. But that might not have happened it if weren't for a 1974 *New York Times* story on Boyer and Cohen's accomplishment by TR board member Victor K. McElheny, then the Times' technology writer. Clipped by Stanford's news director, the story landed on the desk of the school's director of technology transfer, Niels Reimers. Reimers quickly called Cohen; patents must be filed within a year of the first public disclosure of an invention, and Boyer and Cohen had published their results in 1973. By the time all of the researchers and institutions involved agreed on a strategy, Reimers had only a week to file.
>
> In 1980, Boyer and Cohen received the first of three patents. All told, the patents generated over $250 million in royalties before expiring in 1997.
>
> In 1976, Boyer with venture capitalist Robert Swanson, founded the now-giant Genentech.

The Birth of Biotech: Herbert Boyer and Stanley Cohen started a revolution, TECHNOLOGY REVIEW (Ass'n of Alumni and Alumnae of the Mass. Inst. of Tech.), July/Aug. 2000 at 120.

1.3 Introduction to the Scientific Method and Biotechnology

The scientific method is the basis of logical empirical study in the sciences, and following the scientific method ensures that the scientific work is reliable, repeatable, and is acceptable to peer researchers in the same field of study in terms of methodology. The biological sciences, physics, chemistry and other sciences are utilized in research in basic knowledge in the field of biotechnology. Biotechnology is the application of this research knowledge to practical problems and problem-solving, which requires reliable basic science research and conclusions based in the scientific method.

In formulating research in the sciences, a researcher will begin with a hypothesis, which is part of the scientific method. To understand the purpose of a hypothesis, it is helpful in the beginning to formulate the question as an "if-then" statement. For example, if I expose this microbe to light, then it will produce a particular biochemical. Carrying out the experiment, then will test the truth of that statement. The hypothesis will then be proved or disproved. A reformulation of another hypothesis may be required, and another experiment tried, in order to reach a true conclusion.

This hypothesis, then gives rise to the experimental design, which is the plan of an experiment. In the case of the previous example, the design would call for exposing some microbes to light and other microbes remain in the dark as the control, or the part of the experiment that ensures that it is only the variable of light that makes the production of the biochemical, and not some other unknown factor. The type of procedure and statistical analysis that you would use to interpret the results of the experiment would also be part of the design. In psychology, the design of the experiment would include selection of subjects who receive treatment and a control group who do not receive treatment, procedures, and statistical analyses to be performed.[1] When the experimental design has been well studied, the data collection can begin. The data collection is the process of measurement of an experiment by quantitative and qualitative means, yielding nominal, ordinal or metric data. The collection of the data must ultimately lead to the analysis of the data. In the case of quantitative data, the analysis of the collected data may be examined using statistical methods. In the case of qualitative data, the data may be analyzed and presented in a descriptive or interpretive form. Data is often presented in terms of level of confidence upon which the data may be considered reliable. A level of one chance in 20 (.05) or one chance in 100 (.01)[2] is stated as a 95% or 99% level of confidence, respectively. When the data analysis has been completed and enough data has been collected which can yield an acceptable level of confidence in attributing the results to the experiment, then a discussion of the results and ultimately a conclusion can be made. A scientific conclusion describes the quantitative and qualitative results of the analysis and concludes whether the hypothesis was correct or incorrect.

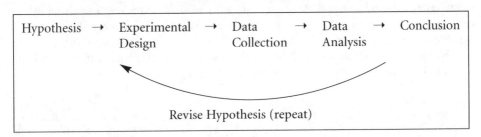

Basic biotechnology research involves research in the relevant basic sciences—physics, chemistry, biochemistry, biology and other interdisciplinary areas—to discover principles of science which have application in biotechnology processes. Research that is presented in the courtroom must survive the scrutiny of admissibility and reliability based upon the proper application of the scientific method. Conclusions of sci-

---

1. National Science Foundation, *User-Friendly Handbook for Project Evaluation*, Glossary (1993).
2. *Id.*

ence must be based upon plausible and reliable scientific evidence gathered using an acceptable scientific process. The use of scientific evidence is discussed in Chapter Eight.

Biotechnology involves the application of these principles and the solving of problems for human needs. Biotechnology requires the skill and experience of the expert and the application of scientific principles which are generally accepted in the relevant fields.

1.4 Biotechnology — What New Questions Have Been Raised?

The first genetics case decided by the U.S. Supreme Court involved the patentability of a living organism. In *Diamond v. Chakrabarty* the U.S. Supreme Court was faced with the question of wether a living organism created by human ingenuity could be patented.

Diamond v. Chakrabarty
447 U.S. 303 (1980)

Chief Justice Burger, delivered the opinion of the Court, in which Stewart, Blackmun, Rehnquist and Stevens, JJ, joined. Brennan, J. filed a dissenting opinion, in which White, Marshall and Powell, JJ joined.

Chief Justice Burger delivered the opinion of the Court.

We granted certiorari to determine whether a live, human-made micro-organism is patentable subject matter under 35 U. S. C. §§ 101.

I

In 1972, respondent Chakrabarty, a microbiologist, filed a patent application, assigned to the General Electric Co. The application asserted 36 claims related to Chakrabarty's invention of "a bacterium from the genus *Pseudomonas* containing therein at least two stable energy-generating plasmids, each of said plasmids providing a separate hydrocarbon degradative pathway."[1] This human-made, genetically engineered bacterium is capable of breaking down multiple components of crude oil. Because of this property, which is possessed by no naturally occurring bacteria, Chakrabarty's invention is believed to have significant value for the treatment of oil spills.[2]

---

1. Plasmids are hereditary units physically separate from the chromosomes of the cell. In prior research, Chakrabarty and an associate discovered that plasmids control the oil degradation abilities of certain bacteria. In particular, the two researchers discovered plasmids capable of degrading camphor and octane, two components of crude oil. In the work represented by the patent application at issue here, Chakrabarty discovered a process by which four different plasmids, capable of degrading four different oil components, could be transferred to and maintained stably in a single *Pseudomonas* bacterum, which itself has no capacity for degrading oil.

2. At present, biological control of oil spills requires the use of a mixture of naturally occurring bacteria, each capable of degrading one component of the oil complex. In this way, oil is decomposed into simpler substances which can serve as food for aquatic life. However, for various reasons, only a portion of any such mixed culture survives to attack the oil spill. By breaking down multiple components of oil, Chakrabarty's micro-organism promises more efficient and rapid oil-spill control.

Chakrabarty's patent claims were of three types: first, process claims for the method of producing the bacteria; second, claims for an inoculum comprised of a carrier material floating on water, such as straw, and the new bacteria; and third, claims to the bacteria themselves. The patent examiner allowed the claims falling into the first two categories, but rejected claims for the bacteria. His decision rested on two grounds: (1) that micro-organisms are "products of nature," and (2) that as living things they are not patentable subject matter under 35 U. S. C. §§ 101.

Chakrabarty appealed the rejection of these claims to the Patent Office Board of Appeals, and the Board affirmed the examiner on the second ground.[3] Relying on the legislative history of the 1930 Plant Patent Act, in which Congress extended patent protection to certain asexually reproduced plants, the Board concluded that §§ 101 was not intended to cover living things such as these laboratory created micro-organisms....

II

The Constitution grants Congress broad power to legislate to "promote the Progress of Science and useful Arts, by securing for limited Times to Authors and Inventors the exclusive Right to their respective Writings and Discoveries." Art. I, §§ 8, cl. 8. The patent laws promote this progress by offering inventors exclusive rights for a limited period as an incentive for their inventiveness and research efforts. The authority of Congress is exercised in the hope that "[the] productive effort thereby fostered will have a positive effect on society through the introduction of new products and processes of manufacture into the economy, and the emanations by way of increased employment and better lives for our citizens."

The question before us in this case is a narrow one of statutory interpretation requiring us to construe 35 U. S. C. §§ 101, which provides:

"Whoever invents or discovers any new and useful process, machine, manufacture, or composition of matter, or any new and useful improvement thereof, may obtain a patent therefor, subject to the conditions and requirements of this title."

Specifically, we must determine whether respondent's micro-organism constitutes a "manufacture" or "composition of matter" within the meaning of the statute.

III

In cases of statutory construction we begin, of course, with the language of the statute. And "unless otherwise defined, words will be interpreted as taking their ordinary, contemporary, common meaning." We have also cautioned that courts "should not read into the patent laws limitations and conditions which the legislature has not expressed."

Guided by these canons of construction, this Court has read the term "manufacture" in §§ 101 in accordance with its dictionary definition to mean "the production of articles for use from raw or prepared materials by giving to these materials new forms, qualities, properties, or combinations, whether by hand-labor or by machinery." Similarly, "composition of matter" has been construed consistent with its common usage to include "all compositions of two or more substances and ... all composite articles, whether they be the results of chemical union, or of mechanical mixture, or whether they be gases, fluids, powders or solids." In choosing such expansive terms as "manufacture" and "composition of matter," modified by the comprehensive "any," Congress plainly contemplated that the patent laws would be given wide scope.

---

3. The Board concluded that the new bacteria were not "products of nature," because *Pseudomonas* bacteria containing two or more different energy-generating plasmids are not naturally occurring.

The relevant legislative history also supports a broad construction. The Patent Act of 1793, authored by Thomas Jefferson, defined statutory subject matter as "any new and useful art, machine, manufacture, or composition of matter, or any new or useful improvement [thereof]." Act of Feb. 21, 1793. The Act embodied Jefferson's philosophy that "ingenuity should receive a liberal encouragement." 5 Writings of Thomas Jefferson 75–76 (Washington ed. 1871). Subsequent patent statutes in 1836, 1870, and 1874 employed this same broad language. In 1952, when the patent laws were recodified, Congress replaced the word "art" with "process," but otherwise left Jefferson's language intact. The Committee Reports accompanying the 1952 Act inform us that Congress intended statutory subject matter to "include anything under the sun that is made by man." S. Rep. No. 1979, 82d Cong., 2d Sess., 5 (1952); H. R. Rep. No. 1923, 82d Cong., 2d Sess., 6 (1952).

This is not to suggest that §§ 101 has no limits or that it embraces every discovery. The laws of nature, physical phenomena, and abstract ideas have been held not patentable. Thus, a new mineral discovered in the earth or a new plant found in the wild is not patentable subject matter. Likewise, Einstein could not patent his celebrated law that E=mc2; nor could Newton have patented the law of gravity. Such discoveries are "manifestations of . . . nature, free to all men and reserved exclusively to none."

Judged in this light, respondent's micro-organism plainly qualifies as patentable subject matter. His claim is not to a hitherto unknown natural phenomenon, but to a nonnaturally occurring manufacture or composition of matter—a product of human ingenuity "having a distinctive name, character [and] use." The point is underscored dramatically by comparison of the invention here with that in *Funk*. There, the patentee had discovered that there existed in nature certain species of root-nodule bacteria which did not exert a mutually inhibitive effect on each other. He used that discovery to produce a mixed culture capable of inoculating the seeds of leguminous plants. Concluding that the patentee had discovered "only some of the handiwork of nature," the Court ruled the product nonpatentable:

"Each of the species of root-nodule bacteria contained in the package infects the same group of leguminous plants which it always infected. No species acquires a different use. The combination of species produces no new bacteria, no change in the six species of bacteria, and no enlargement of the range of their utility. Each species has the same effect it always had. The bacteria perform in their natural way. Their use in combination does not improve in any way their natural functioning. They serve the ends nature originally provided and act quite independently of any effort of the patentee."

Here, by contrast, the patentee has produced a new bacterium with markedly different characteristics from any found in nature and one having the potential for significant utility. His discovery is not nature's handiwork, but his own; accordingly it is patentable subject matter under §§ 101.

IV

Two contrary arguments are advanced, neither of which we find persuasive.

(A)

. . . Prior to 1930, two factors were thought to remove plants from patent protection. The first was the belief that plants, even those artificially bred, were products of nature for purposes of the patent law. This position appears to have derived from the decision of the Patent Office in *Ex parte Latimer*, 1889, in which a patent claim for fiber found in the needle of the *Pinus australis* was rejected. The Commissioner reasoned that a contrary result would permit "patents [to] be obtained upon the trees of the forest and the plants of the earth, which of course would be unreasonable and impossible." The *Latimer* case, it seems, came to "[set] forth the general stand taken in these matters" that plants were natural products not subject to patent protection.[4] The second obstacle to patent protection for plants was the fact that plants were thought not amenable to the "written description" requirement of the patent law. Because new plants may differ from old only in color or perfume, differentiation by written description was often impossible.

In enacting the Plant Patent Act, Congress addressed both of these concerns. It explained at length its belief that the work of the plant breeder "in aid of nature" was patentable invention. And it relaxed the written description requirement in favor of "a description ... as complete as is reasonably possible." ... No Committee or Member of Congress, however, expressed the broader view, now urged by the petitioner, that the terms "manufacture" or "composition of matter" exclude living things.

Moreover, there is language in the House and Senate Committee Reports suggesting that to the extent Congress considered the matter it found the Secretary's dichotomy unpersuasive. The Reports observe:

"There is a clear and logical distinction *between the discovery of a new variety of plant and of certain inanimate things*, such, for example, as a new and useful natural mineral. The mineral is created wholly by nature unassisted by man.... On the other hand, a plant discovery resulting from cultivation is unique, isolated, and is not repeated by nature, nor can it be reproduced by nature unaided by man...."

Congress thus recognized that the relevant distinction was not between living and inanimate things, but between products of nature, whether living or not, and human-made inventions. Here, respondent's micro-organism is the result of human ingenuity and research. Hence, the passage of the Plant Patent Act affords the Government no support.

Nor does the passage of the 1970 Plant Variety Protection Act support the Government's position. As the Government acknowledges, sexually reproduced plants were not included under the 1930 Act because new varieties could not be reproduced true-to-type through seedlings.

In particular, we find nothing in the exclusion of bacteria from plant variety protection to support the petitioner's position. The legislative history gives no reason for this exclusion. As the Court of Customs and Patent Appeals suggested, it may simply reflect congressional agreement with the result reached by that court in deciding *In re Arzberger* (1940), which held that bacteria were not plants for the purposes of the 1930 Act. Or it may reflect the fact that prior to 1970 the Patent Office had issued patents for bacteria under §§ 101.[9] In any event, absent some clear indication that Congress "focused on [the] issues ... directly related to the one presently before the Court," there is no basis for reading into its actions an intent to modify the plain meaning of the words found in §§ 101.

---

4. Writing three years after the passage of the 1930 Act, R. Cook, Editor of the Journal of Heredity, commented: "It is a little hard for plant men to understand why [Art. I, §§ 8] of the Constitution should not have been earlier construed to include the promotion of the art of plant breeding. The reason for this is probably to be found in the principle that natural products are not patentable." Florists Exchange and Horticultural Tade World, July 15, 1933, p. 9.

9. In 1873, the Patent Office granted Louis Pasteur a patent on "yeast, free from organic germs of disease, as an article of manufacture." And in 1967 and 1968, immediately prior to the passage of the Plant Variety Protection Act, that Office granted two patents which, as the petitioner concedes, state claims for living micro-organisms. See Reply Brief for Petitioner 3, and n. 2.

(B)

The petitioner's second argument is that micro-organisms cannot qualify as patentable subject matter until Congress expressly authorizes such protection. His position rests on the fact that genetic technology was unforeseen when Congress enacted §§ 101. From this it is argued that resolution of the patentability of inventions such as respondent's should be left to Congress. The legislative process, the petitioner argues, is best equipped to weigh the competing economic, social, and scientific considerations involved, and to determine whether living organisms produced by genetic engineering should receive patent protection. In support of this position, the petitioner relies on our recent holding in *Parker* v. *Flook*, 437 U.S. 584 (1978), and the statement that the judiciary "must proceed cautiously when … asked to extend patent rights into areas wholly unforeseen by Congress."

It is, of course, correct that Congress, not the courts, must define the limits of patentability; but it is equally true that once Congress has spoken it is "the province and duty of the judicial department to say what the law is." *Marbury* v. *Madison*, 1 Cranch 137, 177 (1803). Congress has performed its constitutional role in defining patentable subject matter in §§ 101; we perform ours in construing the language Congress has employed. In so doing, our obligation is to take statutes as we find them, guided, if ambiguity appears, by the legislative history and statutory purpose. Here, we perceive no ambiguity. The subject-matter provisions of the patent law have been cast in broad terms to fulfill the constitutional and statutory goal of promoting "the Progress of Science and the useful Arts" with all that means for the social and economic benefits envisioned by Jefferson. Broad general language is not necessarily ambiguous when congressional objectives require broad terms….

Congress employed broad general language in drafting §§ 101 precisely because such inventions are often unforeseeable.

To buttress his argument, the petitioner, with the support of *amicus*, points to grave risks that may be generated by research endeavors such as respondent's. The briefs present a gruesome parade of horribles. Scientists, among them Nobel laureates, are quoted suggesting that genetic research may pose a serious threat to the human race, or, at the very least, that the dangers are far too substantial to permit such research to proceed apace at this time. We are told that genetic research and related technological developments may spread pollution and disease, that it may result in a loss of genetic diversity, and that its practice may tend to depreciate the value of human life. These arguments are forcefully, even passionately, presented; they remind us that, at times, human ingenuity seems unable to control fully the forces it creates — that, with Hamlet, it is sometimes better "to bear those ills we have than fly to others that we know not of."

It is argued that this Court should weigh these potential hazards in considering whether respondent's invention is patentable subject matter under §§ 101. We disagree. The grant or denial of patents on micro-organisms is not likely to put an end to genetic research or to its attendant risks. The large amount of research that has already occurred when no researcher had sure knowledge that patent protection would be available suggests that legislative or judicial fiat as to patentability will not deter the scientific mind from probing into the unknown any more than Canute could command the tides. Whether respondent's claims are patentable may determine whether research efforts are accelerated by the hope of reward or slowed by want of incentives, but that is all.

What is more important is that we are without competence to entertain these arguments — either to brush them aside as fantasies generated by fear of the unknown, or to act on them. The choice we are urged to make is a matter of high policy for resolution within the legislative process after the kind of investigation, examination, and study that legislative bodies can provide and courts cannot. That process involves the balancing of competing values and interests, which in our democratic system is the business of elected representatives. Whatever their validity, the contentions now pressed on us should be addressed to the political branches of the Government, the Congress and the Executive, and not to the courts.[11]

We have emphasized in the recent past that "[our] individual appraisal of the wisdom or unwisdom of a particular [legislative] course ... is to be put aside in the process of interpreting a statute." *TVA* v. *Hill*, 437 U.S., at 194. Our task, rather, is the narrow one of determining what Congress meant by the words it used in the statute; once that is done our powers are exhausted. Congress is free to amend §§ 101 so as to exclude from patent protection organisms produced by genetic engineering.... Or it may choose to craft a statute specifically designed for such living things. But, until Congress takes such action, this Court must construe the language of §§ 101 as it is. The language of that section fairly embraces respondent's invention.

Accordingly, the judgment of the Court of Customs and Patent Appeals is

Affirmed.

Dissent by Justice Brennan, with whom Justice White, Justice Marshall, and Justice Powell join, dissenting.

I agree with the Court that the question before us is a narrow one. Neither the future of scientific research, nor even the ability of respondent Chakrabarty to reap some monopoly profits from his pioneering work, is at stake. Patents on the processes by which he has produced and employed the new living organism are not contested. The only question we need decide is whether Congress, exercising its authority under Art. I, §§ 8, of the Constitution, intended that he be able to secure a monopoly on the living organism itself, no matter how produced or how used. Because I believe the Court has misread the applicable legislation, I dissent.

The Court protests that its holding today is dictated by the broad language of §§ 101, which cannot "be confined to the 'particular [applications] ... contemplated by the legislators.'" ... [T]he Court's decision does not follow the unavoidable implications of the statute. Rather, it extends the patent system to cover living material even though Congress plainly has legislated in the belief that §§ 101 does not encompass living organisms. It is the role of Congress, not this Court, to broaden or narrow the reach of the patent laws. This is especially true where, as here, the composition sought to be patented uniquely implicates matters of public concern.

---

11. We are not to be understood as suggesting that the political branches have been laggard in the consideration of the problems related to genetic research and technology. They have already taken action. In 1976, for example, the National Institutes of Health released guidelines for NIH-sponsored genetic research which established conditions under which such research could be performed. 41 Fed. Reg. 27902. In 1978 those guidelines were revised and relaxed. 43 Fed. Reg. 60080, 60108, 60134. And Committees of the Congress have held extensive hearings on these matters. See, *e. g.,* Hearings on Genetic Engineering before the Subcommittee on Health of the Senate Committee on Labor and Public Welfare, 94th Cong., 1st Sess. (1975); Hearings before the Subcommittee on Science, Technology, and Space of the Senate Committee on Commerce, Science, and Transportation, 95th Cong., 1st Sess. (1977); Hearings on H. R. 4759 et al. before the Subcommittee on Health and the Environment of the House Committee on Interstate and Foreign Commerce, 95th Cong., 1st Sess. (1977).

Notes

1. A number of Amici curiae briefs were filed in the *Chakrabarty* case, in support of the patentability of life. However, one brief was filed in opposition by the Peoples Business Commission led by co-Director, Jeremy Rifkin. In part, they write:

> The interest of the amicus herein is PBC's belief that the present cases are of critical importance to the potential development and direction of the burgeoning genetic engineering industry. Most financial and scientific observers concur that during the coming two decades, genetic engineering technologies will have a profit potential and social impact akin to the development of transistors and computer during the past twenty years. PBC contends that a ruling in favor of life form patents in *Bergy* or *Chakrabarty* would serve as a precedent in a host of related areas of genetic manipulation, most particularly in the field of recombinant DNA or "gene splicing". Such a ruling would significantly contribute to the profit potential of the genetic industry, thus generating a greater momentum in research and development of genetic engineering technologies.... It is PBC's contention that such a proliferation of genetically-based technologies is not in the public interest for a host of reasons. PBC believes that the ecological, evolutionary, ethical, philosophical, political and economic questions that surround the patenting of living organisms have been given insufficient consideration by the Congress, the country as a whole and the lower court in issuing its ruling in favor of such patents.

Specifically, the PBC goes on to describe the ecological and evolutionary disaster that might result from patenting life:

> The General Electric Company *Pseudomonas* may well be a case in point. GE hopes to one day unleash its microorganism on an oil slick, thus preventing a tanker spill from polluting the shoreline. Environmentalists, however, are voicing concern about where the "oil eater" will go once the petroleum is consumed.... [W]hat if natural conditions turn out to be more complicated than the laboratory controlled environment? ... Once out of the laboratory, there is no recalling a life form.

The claimed threat to the environment of the "oil eaters" has not proven to be real, and in fact, most of the difficulty has been in keeping a large enough supply of the bacteria alive.

2. Another *amicus curiae* brief was filed in support of the respondent, Chakrabarty, by Genetech, Inc. which cites the exciting contributions of biotechnology rather than the dire predictions of disaster suggested by the Jeremy Rifkin *amicus* in note one, *supra*:

> The new biology holds enormous promise in application for the public good. Much tangible benefit is already in hand. Despite the contrary view of Amicus The People's Business Commission, it is the job of the Patent System to generate greater momentum in such research ... [G]rant of microorganism patent protection is required to avoid opportunities for cynical evasion of patent laws as they attach to processes....

In 2001, another case was before the U.S. Supreme Court on *writ of certiorari*, challenging the interpretation of § 101 in *Chakrabarty*. The following opinion is that of the Federal Circuit U.S. Court of Appeals in January 2000:

Pioneer Hi-Bred International, Inc. v. J.E.M. Ag Supply
200 F.3d 1374 (Fed. Cir. 2000)

Chief Judge Mayer, Newman and Lourie, Circuit Judges.

Circuit Judge Newman

… The patents in suit, owned by Pioneer Hi-Bred International, Inc., are directed to plants and seed for new varieties of hybrid and inbred corn. The United States District Court for the Northern District of Iowa, denying the defendants' motion for summary judgment, ruled that seeds and plants grown from seed, that is, sexually reproduced plants, are patentable subject matter within the scope of 35 U.S.C. §101. On interlocutory appeal of the denial of summary judgment under 28 U.S.C. §1292(b), we affirm the district court's ruling.

DISCUSSION

The district court held that the Supreme Court in *Diamond v. Chakrabarty*, in stating that "Congress intended statutory subject matter to 'include anything under the sun that is made by man,'" (quoting S. Rep. No. 1979 at 5 (1952)), confirmed that there is no basis in law for excluding living things, in this case seeds and seed-grown plants and parts thereof, from the subject matter included in 101:

> 35 U.S.C. '101 Whoever invents or discovers any new and useful process, machine, manufacture, or composition of matter, or any new and useful improvement thereof, may obtain a patent therefor, subject to the conditions and requirements of this title.

In *Chakrabarty* the Court dealt directly with this provision, responding to the arguments concerning patentability of Dr. Chakrabarty's new bacterium that was engineered to consume oil spills. The Court explained that the patent system is directed to the inventive works of mankind, and is not otherwise limited: "In choosing such expansive terms as 'manufacture' and 'composition of matter,' modified by the comprehensive 'any,' Congress plainly contemplated that the patent laws would be given wide scope."

The defendants do not dispute that the subject matter of the patents in suit is within the scope of the *Chakrabarty* decision; their argument is that this decision does not apply to plants because plants were intended to be excluded from the patent system, as evidenced by the enactment of other statutes to provide protection to plants. Thus the defendants argue that seeds and seed-grown plants are excluded from Title 35 and may be protected only under the Plant Variety Protection Act, 7 U.S.C. '2321 et seq.

The district court observed that the Patent and Trademark Office has been granting patents on new and unobvious varieties of seed-grown plants for at least fifteen years. In In re Hibberd, 227 U.S.P.Q. (BNA) 443, 444 (Bd. Pat. App. & Interf. 1985) the Board confirmed this PTO position, rejecting the argument that "the plant-specific Acts (PPA [Plant Protection Act] and PVPA [Plant Variety Protection Act]) are the exclusive forms of protection for plant life covered by those acts." Although the defendants criticize Hibberd, the district court reached the same conclusion as did the Board. Indeed, the "increasing adaptation [of the patent laws] to the uses of society" was remarked by the Court a century earlier, in Kendall v. Windsor, 62 U.S. (21 How.) 322, 328, 16 L. Ed. 165 (1859).

The district court discerned no historical basis for excluding seed-grown plants from the scope of '101, referring to the Supreme Court's explanation of why plants were not previously deemed to be patent able: first, plants are "products of nature," and second, plants could not be described with sufficient precision to satisfy the written description requirement of the patent statute. Now, however, mankind is learning how to modify plants in ways unknown to nature. In addition, precision of description is no longer an insurmountable obstacle, due both to rules authorizing the deposit of new species in publicly available depositories, and advances in botanical understanding and analysis. The Court, cognizant of advances in science, has ratified the traversal of these past impediments to the compass of 101. Although there remain the traditional categories that have never been viewed as patent able subject matter, viz., laws of nature, natural phenomena, and abstract ideas, the policy underlying the patent system fosters its application to all areas of technology-based commerce.

On appeal, the defendants argue that the history of plant protection legislation shows that plants were never intended to be included in the patent statute. The defendants state that the existence of the P.A. and the PAPA precludes application to plants of 35 U.S.C. 101, citing the rule of construction that a general statute must give way to a specific one. ("specific terms prevail over the general in the same or another statute which otherwise might be controlling"). The defendants argue that the *Chakrabarty* decision can not overtake this rule of statutory construction, and thus that the Court's interpretation of '101 does not apply to plants because there are statutes specific to plant protection.

The district court viewed *Chakrabarty* as resolving the uncertainty that previously existed as to the patentability of living things, and concluded that there is no impediment to reading all of the statutes concerning plant protection in harmony. ("when two statutes are capable of co-existence, it is the duty of the courts … to regard each as effective"). Thus the district court concluded that a person who develops a new plant variety may have recourse either to patenting under Title 35 or to registration under the PAPA....

The defendants point out that at the time of enactment of the PAPA Congress believed that seed-grown plants were not included in the patent statute, and argue that 101 can not now be interpreted as available to seed-grown plants, when Congress believed otherwise. A similar argument was presented by Justice Brennan in his dissent from the *Chakrabarty* decision. Dissenting opinions are often helpful in showing positions that were not adopted by the court. However, they are not the law.

. . . .

The defendants also object that Pioneer has obtained patents under Title 35 as well as certificates under the PAPA, and state that these statutes are in conflict. The district court observed, correctly, that the asserted conflict is simply the difference in the rights and obligations imposed by the two statutes. It is not unusual for more than one statute to apply to a legal or property interest. For example, an ornamental design may qualify for protection under both copyright and design patent law. The fact that laws are of different scope does not invalidate the laws....

We conclude that patent able subject matter under 35 U.S.C. 101 includes seeds and seed-grown plants.

AFFIRMED

Notes

1. The Federal government's brief in the *Pioneer Hi-Bred* case addresses the challenges attempting to overturn *Chakrabarty*:

SUMMARY OF ARGUMENT

1. In *Diamond v. Chakrabarty*, 447 U.S. 303 (1980), this Court held that patent able subject matter under 35 U.S.C. 101 "includes] anything under the sun that is made by man." 447 U.S. at 309. The *Chakrabarty* Court rejected the argument that the P.A. and the PAPA demonstrate a congressional understanding that living things are not protect able under Section 101....

Petitioners urge the Court to overrule *Chakrabarty's* construction of Section 101 and to revisit *Chakrabarty's* reasoning concerning the relationship between Section 101 and the PAPA. Those aspects of *Chakrabarty*, however, are quintessentially deserving of repose. *Chakrabarty* involved statutory rather than constitutional construction, and Congress could have overridden this Court's interpretation of Section 101 if it disagreed. In the two decades since *Chakrabarty*, plant breeders and genetic engineers have invested time and resources in reliance upon the availability of patent protection, and such protection has proved workable in practice. Finally, petitioners' arguments for overruling *Chakrabarty* are not materially different from the arguments the Court rejected 21 years ago.

2. Congress has acquiesced, both implicitly and explicitly, in the patenting of sexually reproduced plants. Congress has not overruled *Chakrabarty*, even though legislators have acknowledged the PTO's practice of granting utility patents for sexually reproduced plants. In 1999, moreover, Congress added a new provision to Title 35 (35 U.S.C. 119(f) (Supp. V 1999)), which assumes the patentability of plants under Section 101.

The revisit to the *Chakrabarty* decision confirms the concerns that the legislature might speak to the patenting issue of life in a different way. Decades later, Congress has not only declined to pass legislation to overturn *Chakrabarty*, they have facilitated the ability for inventors to patent a broader scope of life.

2. The *amicus curiae* brief for the People's Business Commission, led by Jeremy Rifkin, concludes with a warning, which reflects the same viewpoint that has arisen around the recent cloning technology. Dr. Leon Kass provides eloquent testimony to the enormity of what is at stake.

> We have paid some high prices for the technological conquest of nature, but none perhaps so high as the intellectual and spiritual costs of seeing nature as mere material for our manipulation, exploitation and transformation. With the powers for biological engineering now gathering, there will be splendid new opportunities for a similar degradation of our view of man. Indeed, we are already witnessing the erosion of our idea of man as something splendid or divine, as a creature with freedom and dignity. And clearly, if we come to see ourselves as meat, then meat we shall become. The new technologies for human engineering may well be "the transition to a wholly new path of evolution." They may, therefore, mark the end of human life as we and all other humans know it. It is possible that the non-human life that may take our place will in some sense be superior—though I personally think it most unlikely, and certainly not demonstrable. In either case, we are ourselves human beings;

therefore, it is proper for us to have a proprietary interest in our survival, and in our survival as human beings. This is a difficult enough task without having to confront the prospect of a utopian, constant remaking or our biological nature with all-powerful means but with no end in view.

Dr. Leon Kass, a University of Chicago bioethicist serves as the Chairman of the U.S. President's Council on Bioethics (2002).

The concerns expressed with this quote which ended the People's Business Commission brief, makes the point that the greatest concern is the threat to our own existence or freedom. Are the risks outweighed by the benefits and who decides?

3. Since genes exist in humans just as the bacteria applied to leguminous plants in *Funk* existed and continued to operate on nature as it always has done—how can genes be patented?

Some differences in performance and utilization of genes are possible in their isolated and purified form which are not possible as they exist in nature. *See* Rebecca S. Eisenberg, *Re-examining the Role of Patents in Appropriating the Value of DNA Sequences*, 49 EMORY L. J. 783 (2000).

Chapter Two.

Federalism: Distributions of Power to Regulate Biotechnology

2.1 Federal Government

The United States federal government has traditionally funded emerging technologies which are too new and undeveloped to be supported by private sector research, but which are promising enough to merit federal funding in anticipation of their contribution to the national economy, public well-being and international trade.

Eleven agencies and departments in the federal government have been formally identified as having critical roles in the development of biotechnology: Department of Agriculture (USDA); Department of Commerce (DOC); Department of Defense (DOD); Department of Energy (DOE); Department of Health and Human Services (DHHS); Department of the Interior (DOI); Department of Veterans Affairs (DVA); Agency for International Development (AID); Environmental Protection Agency (EPA); National Aeronautics and Space Administration (NASA); and the National Science Foundation (NSF). The understanding of the roles of these agencies and the federal government in biotechnology policy and law is addressed in this section.

The federal government is also expected to regulate and control unwanted effects of technologies, and to rely upon ethical and legal constraints to protect the public. Biotechnology has been challenged with existing laws as it affects the environment, as well as human health. This chapter includes those legal challenges and the direction from the judiciary as these new technologies continue to develop.

2.1.1 Executive Branch

In 1992, the leadership of the federal government in biotechnology was first realized when President Bush made Biotechnology one of his five Presidential Initiatives in scientific research. This involved the coordination of twelve federal agencies in order to coordinate both research strategies and budget resources to accelerate the developments in biotechnology in a synergistic manner. This Presidential Initiative was coordinated by the White House Science Office, or the Office of Science and Technology Policy as it is more formally known. This involved a year-long effort to coordinate the budget items with the research programs across all twelve agencies prior to submission of the budget to Congress. The ultimate success of the coordinated budget was then dependent upon Congressional approval by each of the congressional committees, having budget authority for each of the twelve agencies or departments.

In 1992, the President proposed a budget of $4.03 billion, representing an 18% increase over the preceding two years of federal investment—$3.76 billion in FY 1992, and $3.38 billion in FY 1991. The majority of the funding (80%) was for basic science and health; reflecting the early federal support for the National Institutes of Health research; a smaller fraction (12%) of the total supported environmental, agricultural and manufacturing/bioprocessing research; about the same fraction was dedicated to infrastructure in biotechnology, such as personnel training (about 12%); and a very small percentage (less than 1%) was for the support of research in marine biotechnology. In the letter of transmittal to the Congress the President's Science Adviser, D. Allan Bromley, wrote the following:

> This Presidential Initiative [Biotechnology] recognizes the critical role of biotechnology in our nation's future technological strength, economic growth, and the health and quality of life of its people. This country has been the world leader in biological research for the past thirty years which has provided the foundation for the current U.S. pre-eminence in biotechnology research. This leadership, however, is clearly being challenged as the field changes and expands rapidly.

> The strategic framework ... is a coordinated, interagency effort intended to develop and implement a national Biotechnology Research Program to assure the nation of a vigorous base of science and engineering for future development of this critical technology. If aggressively exploited, this effort will maintain the momentum of U.S. leadership in health-directed biotechnology research and will expand research in critical areas where applications of biotechnology research promise significant breakthroughs including agriculture, energy and environment. Executive Office of the President, Federal Coordinating Council for Science, Engineering and Technology, "Biotechnology for the 21st Century," (February 1992).

There was a serious concern that if the United States did not support the emerging biotechnologies, it would lose its world lead in this field. Remaining the world leader in biotechnology research and applications was a matter of securing the future of the national economy as well as one of national security.

During the Bush Administration (1989–1993), Vice President Quayle chaired the Council on Competitiveness, whose mission was to remove unnecessary or outdated regulatory barriers and to maximize national productivity and quality of life. The Vice President appointed a biotechnology working group with the directive to ensure that regulatory barriers did not prevent the successful development of biotechnologies.

2.1.1.1 Regulation of Biotechnology

2.1.1.1.1 Early Developments in Modern Biotechnology Regulation

The rapid development of biotechnology in the 1970s spurred questions about the need to regulate the science, the technology, and even the scientists themselves. The following excerpt from Stuart Auchincloss, *Does Genetic Engineering Need Genetic Engineers?: Should the Regulation of Genetic Engineering Include a New Professional Disci-*

pline? 20 B.C. ENVTL. AFF. L. REV. 37 (Fall 1993), provides an overview of biotechnology regulation by the federal government, beginning with the 1973 Gordon Research Conference on Nucleic Acids.

... III. THE CURRENT REGULATION OF BIOTECHNOLOGY

A. *The Historical Roots*

When scientists in the early 1970s realized the power of biotechnology, they agreed on collective self-restraint in conducting experiments which might be hazardous ... When the scientists' concern became public, the safety of their work became a political issue. This Section describes those early actions and the political debate that took place as a result, showing that with the exception of the participation of a few non-governmental organizations, the scientists themselves have created all the federal regulation of biotechnology primarily on the basis of technical considerations, with only grudging acknowledgment of the existence of social issues.

1. The 1973 Gordon Research Conference

In 1973, Maxine Singer, a biochemist with NIH, was one of the two co-chairs of the Gordon Research Conference on Nucleic Acids, a meeting of professional molecular biologists.... On the last day of the conference, after the announcement of the powerful new technology of using restriction enzymes to combine the DNA of unrelated organisms, there was an unscheduled debate on the question of the potential hazards from dangerous synthetic mutant germs made possible by this process.... A large majority of those scientists who participated in this discussion favored expressing their concern to the National Academy of Sciences.... Just a little over half of these scientists also favored making their concerns known more widely in the scientific community....

Acting on this vote, Maxine Singer and her co-chair wrote to the president of the National Academy of Science and to the president of the National Institute of Medicine, 181 SCIENCE 1114, 1114 (1973). The letter announced the scientists' concern that certain hybrid molecules may be hazardous to laboratory workers and the public.... The letter requested the National Academy of Sciences to establish a committee to consider the problem and recommend specific actions or guidelines.... As a result of the letter, the National Academy of Sciences established a committee of scientists to consider the matter in the Fall of 1973.

A year later, on July 26, 1974 *Science* published an open letter from the National Academy of Sciences Committee to all scientists throughout the world suggesting a voluntary moratorium on certain genetic engineering experiments because the experiments were too risky for currently available laboratory containment technology, Paul Berg *et al.*, *Potential Biohazards of Recombinant DNA Molecules,* 185 SCIENCE 303, 303 (1974). Although the concerned scientists intended only to encourage voluntary self-restraint among molecular biologists, the scientists' letter began to alert journalists and the general public to the potential dangers of genetic engineering.... Six months after the publication of the letter, an international conference of molecular biologists convened at Asilomar, California on February 24–27, 1975 to consider what the scientists themselves should do next ...

2. The 1975 Asilomar Conference

Maxine Singer and four other concerned scientists organized the pivotal Asilomar Conference of molecular biologists in February 1975 to discuss the future of biotechnology.... The organizers proclaimed the following two principles to guide genetic engineering experiments: containment as an essential consideration in the design of experiments, and the containment's effectiveness equaling the experiment's estimated risk, Paul Berg *et al., Asilomar Conference on Recombinant DNA Molecules,* 188 SCIENCE 991, 992 (1975). Even bearing these principles in mind, the conferees agreed that there were certain experiments which ought not to be conducted with the then available containment facilities....

Beginning at Asilomar, eminent molecular biologists disagreed among themselves about the risk of the genetic engineering experiments, *see generally,* Michael Rogers, *The Pandora's Box Congress,* 189 ROLLING STONE 36 (1975) ... While most molecular biologists believed that raising the issues and warning each other was enough, a few molecular biologists felt that the experiments should be halted altogether ...

B. The Beginning of Federal Regulation

1. The NIH Guidelines

On October 7, 1974, four months before the Asilomar conference, the NIH's director already had formed the Recombinant DNA Molecule Program Advisory Committee (RAC) to consider three aspects of the new genetic engineering technology: potential hazards, the spread of genetically modified organisms in the environment, and guidelines for scientists working with such organisms ... After the Asilomar conference, however, RAC focused almost exclusively on its third task, preparing guidelines for researchers, *see* 41 Fed. Reg. 27903 (1976); Collin Norman, *Genetic Manipulation: Guidelines Issued,* 262 NATURE 2, July 1, 1976.

On June 23, 1976, the Director of the NIH formally issued the guidelines which effectively halted experiments using DNA from warm blooded animals and viruses, 41 Fed. Reg. 27,902–43 (1979); *Norman, supra* note 82, at 2. NIH, the main source of federal funds for biotechnology research, required an institutional biosafety committee to review proposed experiments before the applicant could receive his or her grant to perform certain experiments. 41 Fed. Reg. 27,920–21 (1976); WATSON & TOOZE, *supra* note 5, at 63. The regulations also specified the degree of containment necessary for certain particularly dangerous genetic engineering experiments.

Despite their strict limitations on biotechnology experiments, the guidelines appear to apply only to entities receiving research grants from NIH, *see generally* 41 Fed. Reg. 27,920 (1976). In addition, the only sanction the guidelines imposed was cutting off funding for institutions that did not follow the guidelines....

As scientists around the world have carried out safely many laboratory experiments with genetic engineering, RAC steadily relaxed the guidelines until now most experiments require no more than local peer review, *see,* NIH Section of the Coordinated Framework, 55 Fed. Reg. 23,349 (1990). Thus, early in the regulation of biotechnology, the NIH guidelines established the pattern of making compliance voluntary for laboratories operating without government funds, most notably industrial and commercial laboratories....

2. Congressional Study and Inaction

Two months after the Asilomar conference, on April 22, 1975, Senator Edward Kennedy, as Chairman of the Subcommittee on Health, held a hearing on the relationship of a free society to its scientific community.... The hearing used genetic engineering as a case study to consider the public's role in both the direction of scientific research and the application of the research's results ...

The April 22 hearing was followed by another hearing on September 22, 1976 on the same subject.... In his opening remarks, Senator Kennedy drew particular attention to the problem of industry's "voluntary" compliance with the NIH guidelines.... Senator Kennedy singled out General Electric for its unwillingness to participate in the hearing as an example of industry's unwillingness to follow the NIH guidelines (Opening Statement of Senator Edward M. Kennedy at a Hearing of the Senate Health Subcommittee on Recombinant DNA Research and the NIH Guidelines, Wednesday, Sept. 22, 1976 ...)

Following these hearings, efforts to adopt a biotechnology control act continued in both the United States Senate and the House of Representatives until March 1978 when legislative action ceased.... Academic scientists opposed biotechnology regulation by taking the extreme position that the proposed government regulation was similar to the subjugation of Russian biological science to communist ideology during the middle of the Twentieth Century.

Congressional interest in a biotechnology bill disappeared in the Fall of 1978 for many reasons including a lack of support from the executive branch, NIH's relaxation of its guidelines thereby implying that the threat of biotechnology was less than feared, and the complexities of congressional politics. At the same time, Secretary of Health, Education and Welfare (HEW), Joseph Califano stated that his agency, which controlled NIH, did not intend to invoke existing statutory authority to regulate DNA activities, preferring to continue with voluntary control of industry based on NIH's guidelines.... Over the next five years RAC steadily relaxed the NIH guidelines by determining that ever more classes of experiments posed no special hazard....

C. The Coordinated Framework

In the Spring of 1984 the Council on Natural Resources and the Environment formed a Working Group on Biotechnology, 49 Fed. Reg. 50,856 (1984). The Working Group prepared and published the Coordinated Framework as a proposal for the regulation of biotechnology by existing agencies, under existing statutes, 49 Fed. Reg. 50,856 (1985) (proposed Dec. 31, 1984).

On October 31, 1985, the [Reagan] Domestic Policy Council formed the Biotechnical Science Coordinating Committee (BSCC), 50 Fed. Reg. 47,174 (1985); *see also* 51 Fed. Reg. 23302 (1986), to establish for all regulatory agencies common definitions of "intergeneric organism" and "pathogen," and to limit federal regulation to these entities. (The Coordinated Framework's definitions are intended to determine what organisms should be appropriate for certain types of review, 51 Fed. Reg. 23302 (1986)).

The BSCC ruled that an intergeneric organism is a microorganism that is "deliberately formed to contain an intergeneric combination of genetic material." ... Basing a regulatory definition on the location of microbes in the taxonomic system, however, is questionable because of the lack of scientific agreement on the taxonomic classifications and the categories' relation to each other, see, "Principles for Federal Oversight of Biotechnology: Planned Introduction into the Environment of Organisms with Modified Hereditary Traits," 55 Fed. Reg. 31118, (1990) [hereinafter referred to as the "Proposed Refinement"] " ... Taxonomy ... is imprecise for microorganisms." Id. at 31119.

Likewise, a pathogen is a "virus or microorganism ... [broadly defined] that has the ability to cause disease in other living organisms," 51 Fed. Reg. 23,302 (1986). This is followed by a long gloss stating, in effect, that an organism is a regulated pathogen when the organism is dangerous, see, 51 Fed. Reg. 23,306–07 (1986). Up until July 31, 1990 the Coordinated Framework used these two definitions to describe reviewable genetically modified organisms, see 51 Fed. Reg. 23,307 (1986) (Coordinated Framework).

After an eighteen month comment period, the Working Group published the final Coordinated Framework on June 26, 1986, 51 Fed. Reg. 23,301 (1986). The Coordinated Framework expressed the Executive Branch's opinion that the existing statutes provide a basic network of agency control over biotechnology's research and products sufficient for the regulation of the plants, animals, and microorganisms created by the new genetic engineering techniques, 51 Fed. Reg. 23,302–03 (1986) The White House Office of Science and Technology Policy (OSTP) reaffirmed this opinion when the agency issued its "Principles for Federal Oversight of Biotechnology." 55 Fed. Reg. 31,118 (1990). The Coordinated Framework provides a chart which summarizes agency jurisdiction and authority over the approval of biotechnology products, Chart 1, 51 Fed. Reg. 23,304 (1986).

2.1.1.1.2 Federal Regulations — What Is Regulated?

Genetically modified organisms are controlled through the regulations developed by the Office of Science and Technology Policy in 1990. In addition to these regulations, recipients of funding from the National Institutes of Health are also subject to NIH regulations for researchers and the release of genetically modified organisms.

---

51 Fed. Reg. 23,304 (1986):

CHART I.
COORDINATED FRAMEWORK —
APPROVAL OF COMMERCIAL BIOTECHNOLOGY

PRODUCTS

Subject	Responsible agency(ies)
Foods/Food Additives	FDA, *
	FSIS. n1
Human Drugs, Medical Devices and Biologics	FDA
Animal Drugs	FDA.
Animal Biologics	APHIS
Other Contained Uses	EPA
Plants and Animals	APHIS, *
	FSIS n1
	FDA. n2

Pesticide Microorganisms Released in the Environment All.	EPA, * APHIS n3
Other Uses (Microorganisms): Intergeneric Combination	EPA, * APHIS n3
Intrageneric Combination: Pathogenic Source Organism: 1. Agricultural Use 2. Non-Agricultural use	APHIS. EPA, * n4 APHIS n3
No Pathogenic Source Organisms	EPA Report
Nonengineered Pathogens: 1. Agricultural Use 2. Non-Agricultural Use	APHIS EPA, n4 APHIS n3
Nonengineered Nonpathogens	EPA Report

* Lead agency.

n1 FSIS, Food Safety and Inspection Service, under the Assistant Secretary of Agriculture for Marketing and Inspection Services is responsible for food use.

n2 FDA is involved when in relation to a food use.

n3 APHIS, Animal and Plant Health Inspection Service, is involved when the microorganism is plant pest, animal pathogen or regulated article requiring a permit.

n4 EPA requirements will only apply to environmental release under a "significant new use rule" that EPA intends to propose.

Jurisdiction over the varied biotechnology products is determined by their use, as has been the case for traditional products. The detailed description of the products and their review are found in the individual agency policy statements contained in this Federal Register Notice. The following is a brief summary of jurisdiction as described in Chart I.

Foods, food additives, human drugs, biologics and devices, and animal drugs are reviewed or licensed by the FDA. Food products prepared from domestic livestock and poultry are under the jurisdiction of the USDA's Food Safety Inspection Service (FSIS).

Animal biologics are reviewed by the Animal and Plant Health Inspection Service (APHIS). APHIS, also reviews plants, seeds, animal biologics, plant pests, animal pathogens and "regulated articles," i.e., certain genetically engineered organisms containing genetic material from a plant pest. An APHIS permit is required prior to the shipment (movement) or release into the environmental of regulated articles, or the shipment of a plant pest or animal pathogen.

"Other contained uses" refers to the closed system uses of those microorganisms, subject to the TSCA, that are intergeneric combinations, i.e., deliberately formed microorganisms which contain genetic material from dissimilar source organisms. These are subject to EPA's PMN requirement. EPA is considering promulgating a rule to exempt certain classes of microorganisms from this requirement.

Microbial pesticides will be reviewed by EPA, with APHIS involvement in cases where the pesticide is also a plant pest, animal pathogen, or regulated article requiring a permit. (FDA may become involved in implementing pesticide tolerances for foods.)

"Other uses (microorganisms)" include uses involving release into the environment. For these, jurisdiction depends on the characteristics of the organism as well as its use.

"Intergeneric combination" * microorganisms will be reported to EPA under PMN requirements, with APHIS involvement in cases where the microorganism is also a regulated article requiring a permit.

"Intrageneric combinations" are those microorganisms formed by genetic engineering other than intergeneric combinations. For these, when there is a pathogenic n1 source organism, and the microorganism is used for agricultural purposes, APHIS has jurisdiction. If the microorganism is used for nonagricultural purposes, then EPA has jurisdiction, with APHIS involvement in cases where the microorganism is also a regulated article requiring a permit. Intrageneric combinations with no pathogenic source organisms are under EPA jurisdiction although EPA will only require an informational report.

n1 "Intergeneric organisms (new organisms)" and "pathogen" are defined in section D. of the preamble.

"Nonengineered pathogens" that are used for an agricultural use will fall under APHIS jurisdiction. Those that are for a nonagricultural use come under EPA jurisdiction, with APHIS involvement in cases where the microorganism is also a plant pest or animal pathogen requiring a permit. Nonengineered nonpathogenic microorganisms are under EPA jurisdiction which will require only an informational report.

CHART II.
COORDINATED FRAMEWORK —
BIOTECHNOLOGY RESEARCH JURISDICTION

Subject	Responsible agency(ies)
Contained Research, No Release in Environment:	
1. Federally Funded	Funding agency n1
2. Non-Federally Funded	NIH or S&E voluntary review APHIS. n2
Foods/Food Additives, Human Drugs, Medical Devices, Biologics, Animal Drugs:	
1. Federally Funded	FDA *, NIH guidelines & review
2. Non-Federally Funded	FDA *, NIH voluntary review
Plants, Animals and Animal Biologics:	
1. Federally Funded	Funding agency, n1 * APHIS. n2
2. Non-Federally Funded	APHIS *, S&E voluntary review
Pesticide Microorganisms: Genetically Engineered: Intergeneric	EPA, * APHIS, n2 S&E

Pathogenic Intergeneric	voluntary review EPA, * APHIS, n2 S&E
Intrageneric Nonpathogen	voluntary review EPA, * S&E
Nonengineered: Nonindigenous Pathogens	voluntary review EPA, * APHIS
Indigenous Pathogens	EPA, * n3 APHIS
Nonindigenous Nonpathogen	EPA, *
Other Uses (Microorganisms) Released in the Environment: Genetically Engineered: Intergeneric Organisms: 1. Federally Funded	Funding agency, * n1 APHIS, n2 EPA n4
2. Commercially Funded	EPA, APHIS, S&E
Intrageneric Organisms: Pathogenic Source Organism: 1. Federally Funded	voluntary review Funding agency, * n1 APHIS, n2 EPA. n4
2. Commercially Funding	APHIS, n2 EPA (* if non-agricul use)
Intrageneric Combination: No Pathogenic Source Organisms	EPA Report
Nonengineered	EPA Report, * APHIS n2

* Lead Agency.

n1 Review and approval of research protocols conducted by NIH, S&E, or NSF.

n2 APHIS issues permits for the importation and domestic shipment of certain plants and animals, plant pests and animal pathogens, and for the shipment or release in the environment of regulated articles.

n3 EPA jurisdiction for research on a plot greater than 10 acres.

n4 EPA reviews federally funded environmental research only when it is for commercial purposes.

The Auchincloss article, cited above, includes a note on the development and refinement of the Framework by the Office of Science and Technology Policy in 1990:

> Regulatory authority under the Framework, however, extends only to risks from the use or misuse of biotechnology products which are regulated already in the stream of commerce. As an example of the Framework's maintenance of the *status quo*, the Department of Labor declared that its regulations under the Occupational Safety and Health Act were adequate and that the new biology did not require new regulations to protect workers. Thus the Occupational Safety and Health Act does nothing to narrow the class of unregulated organisms or to regulate releases not covered by the Framework.
>
> The Coordinated Framework does not cover animals which are not insects, plants which are not parasites, or insects which are not plant pests, Even though the FDA regulates the use of plants and animals for food and medicine, the FDA and United States Department of Agriculture regulate veterinary medicine; Virus, Serum, Toxin Act, and the Public Health Service regulates the interstate movement of etiologic agents, a considerable range of transgenic plants and animals are still free of federal regulation.
>
> The residual class of life forms which are not regulated under any federal program will be referred to in this Article as "unregulated organisms." As examples of unregulated organisms, an industrial enterprise might engineer transgenic fish for weed and mosquito control, or oysters for pearl production and release them to the environment without any intent that people would use the organisms for food. If the genetic engineering work did not have government funding, the organisms' release would be unregulated even if the release occurred in the waters of the United States. No reported case or lawsuit has suggested that such a release might be covered by § 404 of the Clean Water Act or the Rivers and Harbors Appropriations Act of 1899.
>
> Furthermore, the Coordinated Framework does not apply to a large amount of biotechnology work because research does not have a product ... Most genetically modified organisms that scientists release to the environment are experiments, not commercial products, therefore the Framework does not apply to the resulting organisms unless experimenters receive government funding, or come under the experimental use permit section of the laws. For experiments involving unregulated organisms and carried on without government funding, reporting and peer review are only voluntary.... While some such research on future commercial products might fall under the experiment provisions of, for example, Toxic Substance Control Act (TSCA) ... one can imagine uses which might escape even these definitions.

D. The Proposed Refinement of the Coordinated Framework

In hopes of clarifying the Framework, the President's Office of Science and Technology Policy (OSTP), the parent body of the BSCC, referred the problem of what organisms the Coordinated Framework covered to the White House Council on Competitiveness. In late July 1990, on the basis of the Council on Competitiveness's recommendation, OSTP proposed a refinement of the Coordinated Framework for regulation of biotechnology.... As the refinement itself declares, the "Coordinated Framework was expected to evolve in accordance with the experience of the industry, and, thus, modifications to the framework were anticipated." ... This modification, however, goes to the heart of the Coordinated Framework—the definition of organism and the need for government supervision of releases to the environment of genetically modified organisms.

The Coordinated Framework limited its application to two classes of organisms—organisms formed by the combination of genetic material from sources in different genera and microorganisms containing genetic material from pathogenic species—with each class having several exceptions. The proposed 1990 refinement declares that the Coordinated Framework now applies to all "organisms with deliberately modified hereditary traits." Because regulation under the refinement requires deliberate modification, regulation is limited to the products of genetic engineering and does not include the products of selective breeding and intentional mutation.... [*See id.* Because the Framework is based on risk rather than on strict classifications, only those organism introductions for which safety data already exist, or for which there are existing, adequate safety regulations will be excluded from oversight.

For years scientists and representatives of industry have maintained that the regulation of biotechnology products should be no different from the regulation of hybrids because the risks from genetically modified organisms are comparable to the risks from organisms modified by conventional breeding techniques and possibly less risky because the genetic changes are so specific.... Now, the refined Coordinated Framework reflects this view, and all such organisms will be brought within its purview [*see* 55 Fed. Reg. 31120 (1990)]. The refined Framework discloses the principle that planned introductions "should not be subject to oversight ... unless information concerning the risk posed by the introduction indicates that oversight is necessary." ... The refinement thus has something for everyone—a broader definition of genetically modified organisms and a vaguely worded prohibition on their regulation.

The refinement's definitions feature a no-oversight-until-risk-is-known approach, implying that the burden is on the regulator to demonstrate the risk and bear the cost of showing the risk's existence.... The problem is that regulation turns on the existence of "information concerning the risk posed," information which in most cases today does not exist yet....

———————

Jeremy Rifkin, an activist opposed to genetic engineering, and biotechnology in general, began initiating a number of complaints against the federal government for actions taken which might lead to the release of the genetically-engineered plants into the environment. His actions and the publicity he received raised the public awareness of biotechnology and perpetuated many of his "scientific" ideas which were not science-based principles.

2.1.2 Patents for Biotechnology

The United States Patent and Trademark Office (USPTO) has responsibility for implementing the Patent Act, determining which patent applications should be granted, and keeping a register of those patents. The USPTO is part of the U.S. Department of Commerce, and includes a Patent and Trademark Appeals Board, with appeal to the Federal Circuit, U.S. Court of Appeals.

2.1.3 Food and Drug Administration and the Environmental Protection Agency: Genetically Engineered Foods

2.1.3.1 History of Law and Food Regulation

The following excerpt from Jesse D. Lyon, *OPEN FORUM: Coordinated Food Systems and Accountability Mechanisms for Food Safety: A Law and Economics Approach*, 53 FOOD DRUG L.J. 729 (1998) describes the history of law governing food.

––––––––––––

Laws governing the production and marketing of food were recorded from the time of Moses. Moses' book of *Leviticus* proclaimed that "thou shalt not sow thy field with mingled seed." In addition, in the book of *Deuteronomy*, Moses' law required "a perfect and just weight, a perfect and just measure." The consequence of disobeying the laws of Moses was God's wrath, often exacted by the offender's enemies: "Thou shalt plant a vineyard, and shalt not gather the grapes thereof. Thine ox shall be slain before thine eyes, and thou shalt not eat thereof." Such rules are consistent with "primitive law's concept of thing responsibility, whereby vengeance was wrought upon the thing itself which caused the damage, as if it were possessed of demons." Imposing this kind of "strict" liability on the products appeased those harmed and prevented tensions from escalating without imposing a subjective finding of fault on the food producer.

As early as the second century B.C., the Han Dynasty in China prohibited "the making of spurious products, and the defrauding of purchasers." This is consistent with the Confucian value of societal harmony, which could be achieved only by universal compliance with the rules of moral behavior. Even at these early stages, Chinese law saw the unsafe or unfair provision of food as an offense against society. An official named the "Supervisor of Markets" and his agents attempted to provide a central mechanism to ensure that societal harmony was not disrupted by debauchery in food-making or marketing.

"Because of the enormous importance of food to the Roman Empire, a substantial portion of the Roman civil law was designed to assure a sufficient supply at reasonable prices." Where food was sold publicly, the government sometimes intervened. The Theodosian Code (A.D. 438) required bread made for pubic sale to be arranged on the steps of a building according to grades. Such rules aimed to protect against fraud, but more often "relied upon the concept of *caveat emptor*." In the end, this reliance was imperfect. Pliny the Elder's writings particularly evidence the common consumer's inability to detect adulterations during this era, making findings of fault based on objective standards problematic.

Comparative law and economics suggests that food safety rules and institutions originated as general concepts of *moral accountability* in ancient times, when the food supply chain was not fragmented and individual enterprises were not anonymous. Because exchange frequently was confined within relationships defined not by community, contract, or government, but by a pre-existing familial or parochial bond, food production and marketing norms were most efficiently left to an individual's piety. The provision of food during ancient times was regulated primarily out of prevailing notions of moral obligation....

....

2. *Food Safety Mechanisms in the Medieval Period (1000 to 1500 A.D.)*

The food supply chain in the medieval period was composed of farmer-sellers and mer-chant-manufacturers. "The transformation of agriculture in the eleventh and twelfth centuries created both the opportunity and the need for the rapid expansion of the merchant class. There were large agricultural surpluses to be traded."

Food manufacturing became more prevalent during the medieval period. "In the first historical stage of food manufacturing, foods were essentially handmade by farmers or artisans." "By the Middle Ages over [two hundred] varieties of processed meats were being made commercially by European craftsmen." Because winter feeding of livestock was difficult, most non-breeding animals were slaughtered prior to the onslaught of bad weather, and their meat was salted for safe sale and consumption throughout the win-ter. "Spices were ground, flour was milled or baked into bread, milk and cheese became articles of commerce. Each offered more opportunity for hidden sophistication," that is food manufacturers could modify or adulterate products to their advantage in increas-ingly subtle ways that consumers could not detect. Food manufacturers usually were the ultimate seller of their own products.

During this period, farm products and manufactured food products were bought and sold at local markets. "Expanded trade in the countryside was initially a result of the 'agricultural revolution'... ; indeed, the growth of agriculture was itself a precondition for the growth of the cities." "Methods were known to medieval cultivators which would have increased ... yields ... but these methods were simply unprofitable...."

Market information during the medieval period was confined to local markets. "Diffi-culties of communication" and "sparseness of settlement" contributed to the "local character of the economy." The local character of the economy, however, also meant that a merchant's reputation was well known, and much relied on by consumers....

....

The integrity of the food supply during the medieval period was protected by commu-nity extralegal sanctions, reputational constraints, and self-adjudication. Extralegal sanctions discouraged food producers and sellers from adulteration and fraud. In 1315 in France, angry citizens "staged a mass punishment of bakers who had been found guilty of mixing their flour with animal droppings. Sixteen bakers were lashed to wheels in public squares and made to hold bits of rotten bread in outstretched hands, while they were beaten and reviled by the multitude." Additionally, "history records the inci-dent of a butcher being paraded through the streets, his face close to a horse's tail, for selling 'measly' meat ... [and] of a dishonest brewer who was drawn around town in the garbage cart."

Manorial law regulated agricultural production, but soon "merchants constituted a self-governing community." Carrying forward the moral accountability of ancient times, "[a] social and economic morality was developed which purported to guide the souls of merchants...." That morality came to be enforced by "market and fair courts" in Italy and "courts of the staple" in England and Ireland where food sellers were subject to a system of customary merchant law.

Mercantile law was transaction-based and arranged to protect the commercial reputa-tion of the merchant class and their need for speedy, informal, and equitable dispute resolution. Its principle of reciprocal rights mandated a fair exchange so that there was a procedural and substantive "equality of burdens or benefits as between the parties to the transaction." The principle of good faith also emerged as a fundamental precept of the mercantile law system. Food adulteration and fraudulent food sales violated both these principles. Because violators risked expulsion from the merchant community, the system ensured fair transactions in food and farm products among parties whose livelihood depended on their perpetually reversing roles as buyers and sellers and on their market access to the merchant community. In England, trade guilds eventually developed among businesspersons in "every important food category." They performed an even narrower regulatory function, at times even exercising "power to search all premises and to seize all unwholesome products."

. . . .

Comparative law and economics thus suggests that while *moral accountability* remained, *community accountability* was added to protect the integrity of the food supply during the medieval period, when the food supply chain was only minimally fragmented and the relative anonymity of individual players was still quite low. Community accountability comports with "the old 'golden rule' of the Middle Ages—do unto others as you would wish them to do to you." The behavior of food producers and sellers was constrained most efficiently by their reputation in the local community.

. . . . That local ordinances were the most notable and effective medieval legislative attempts to regulate the food supply shows that the food system remained predominantly local, and that its players were constrained most efficiently by accountability to their market community.

C. *The Evolution of Traditional Food Safety Mechanisms*

The evolution of traditional rules and institutions governing the integrity of the food supply corresponded to increased fragmentation and anonymity as food systems matured. *Moral accountability* and *community accountability* remained, but were no longer sufficient. Food system rules and institutions during the development of commerce relied on notions of contractual accountability. As the food supply became widely recognized in the legislative period as a public good, *strict* societal accountability was added to govern its integrity.

1. *Food System Rules and Institutions in Development of Commerce (1500–1800 A.D.)*

The sixteenth through eighteenth centuries were marked by the development of commerce and the "era of colonial expansion." Some agricultural historians characterize the first half of this period as a rural economic depression. During this time, food production increasingly separated producers from sellers. During the development of commerce, "urbanization and improved transportation increased the effective demand for even highly perishable foods and beverages." "Colonial America [initially] was an agrarian economy. People consumed the food ... they produced at home. Even those who lived in small towns kept livestock and maintained their own gardens. [But as] urban centers grew, local food markets were established to serve them." European populations also became increasingly urbanized, in part because of cheaper food supplies brought on by free trade.

. . . .

The sixteenth century marked the development of notions of natural law, with its focus on law common to all mankind, essential for human coexistence, and found by reason, not by divine help or the influence of special interests. Any activities of lobbying groups to protect food supply integrity (a noted factor later driving the development of product safety and liability standards) would not result in legislative preference being given to producer or consumer interests. Locke's theories of economic liberalism followed in the seventeenth century; under this view, freedom of contract was revered.

Early English common law recognized a civil cause of action for damages for the sale of adulterated food. Civil remedies became prevalent in the sixteenth century when food system rules for the development of commerce became marked by notions of product liability and privity. The concept of product liability "originated in English common law, in which the brewer, butcher, cook, or other person was held responsible for tainted or adulterated drink or food ... Liability of [such food manufacturers] was limited to the person to whom he or she directly sold a product." Under doctrines of privity of contract, "a contract can generate rights and obligations only for the parties to it."

Thus, products liability often depended on a breach of some (often fictional) contractual duty, although liability generally was limited to cases where the manufacturer effectively was held negligent....

Broad, public laws were of little use given the lack of analytical tools to detect subtle adulterations. Nonetheless, regulators strove for effective enforcement. In the mid-1600s, the English Parliament enacted statutes to regulate butter quality. "In order to trace violations [of those statutes], every butter packer was required to brand the container with his full surname and the first initial of his Christian name." The integrity of imported food was more easily protected, for port authorities had incentives to prevent "frauds in the revenue of excise."

....

Centralized government administration had not yet sufficiently evolved to enforce legislated mechanisms to protect the food supply. Rather, societal conviction in the freedom of contract meant that contracts were the favored means for defining relationships and corresponding legal rights and obligations, and food product liability remedies evolved as a corollary to these contractual relationships.

2. *Food Safety Mechanisms in the Legislative Period (1800 A.D. to Present)*

In the legislative period, the food supply chain became characterized by task specialization and technological efficiencies. "In the agrarian economies of Europe and America, increases in food supplies were obtained in part by bringing marginal lands into cultivation. Production increased, but productivity diminished. Farmers worked harder to extract a smaller crop from stubborn fields of poor productivity. Some people responded to these problems by introducing new methods of farm management.... In the process, farming tended to become more intensive. In the early [nineteenth] century there was nearly [five] times as much investment in land improvements as in the middle ages."

"The nineteenth century [also] saw the widespread adoption of machine technologies; craftsmen were replaced by factories using motive power to produce more uniform foods ... [Subsequent development] brought automation to food manufacturing, but with application to basically physiochemical processes." Most methods of food processing, including "canning, freezing, and chemical preservation (except salting) have all been invented since 1800." Mechanical refrigeration and freezing also were products of nineteenth century ingenuity. "The factory system ... encouraged increasing specialization within the food industries" and resulted in the "disintegration of food manufacturing functions. As handicrafts [were] replaced by mass production with its great markets and transportation facilities, the close relationship between the producer and consumer of a product [was] altered."

During the legislative period, exchange of food products along the supply chain began to take place in multiple, atomistic markets. As a consequence, market information was often incomplete and complicated, resulting in high information search costs. Consumers were wealthier and more highly educated, but now faced "bewildering problems in evaluating products ... [given] differences of technology, function, price, and promotion on the basis of ... information that [was] occasionally misleading, often irrelevant, and always imperfect. Manufacturing processes, frequently valuable secrets, are ordinarily either inaccessible to or beyond the ... general public. The consumer no longer has means or skill enough to investigate for himself the soundness of a product, even when it is not contained in a sealed package."

Cost became the primary emphasis of exchange during the legislative period. "Factory production usually lowered costs by the application of mass production techniques on ever larger scales." Quality was correspondingly de-emphasized.

The earliest statement of English law concerning the criminal status of food adulteration appeared in the mid-1600s. It was not until the legislative period, however, that food markets became intensely regulated, and food system rules were enforced by sanctions beyond the community level. The public clamored against food adulteration. Food regulation in the modern era was made possible by the introduction of the microscope into food analysis in the 1850's, providing unprecedented detection of germs in adulterated food.

The nineteenth century saw the first enactment of general nationwide statutes prohibiting food adulteration, directing penalties for violations, and establishing administrative responsibility for enforcement. "France passed a general food law rather early—1851. In 1855, it was amended to include beverages." The English Parliament enacted its first general food laws in 1860, and the German Empire followed suit in 1879. The United States enacted the comprehensive Pure Food and Drugs Act in 1906. President Woodrow Wilson in 1913 acknowledged that "the first duty of law is to keep sound the society it serves. Sanitary laws [and] pure food laws ... are intimate parts of the very business of justice and legal efficiency."

In 1959, the New York state court deciding *Linn v. Radio Center Delicatessen*, held that it was "against natural justice and good morals to permit an individual or corporation to manufacture food containing dangerous foreign substances and escape the consequences of his acts...." *Linn* evidenced that the unsafe provision of basic human needs in the legislative period was viewed as an offense against society, requiring criminal punishment where civil remedies were insufficient to protect the public.

Accordingly, food safety regulation is highly representative of the aspects of law protecting the public good. "Under customary law [such as the medieval period's merchant law systems], offenses are treated as torts (private wrongs or injuries) rather than crimes (offenses against the state or the 'society')." Nineteenth-century lawmakers, however, decided that the provision of foods that threaten the integrity of our food supply should be treated as a crime against society. This development occurred after there was a centralized system capable of enforcing national food laws. Once general standards for food production and handling were in place, the government agencies enforcing them could not exclude select individuals from the protection that those rules afforded. All citizens benefitted from food manufacturers' incentive to provide safe food for consumption, while developing general standards essentially are sunk costs. Thus, the marginal costs of food regulation are negligible with increases in food production and consumption.

2.1.3.2 *The Controversy over Genetically Engineered Foods*

RACHEL CARSON, the famous environmentalist/author of the 1960s, authoring the book, SILENT SPRING, which started a nationwide awareness of the destructive use of pesticides, identified the use of a bacteria, *Bacillus thuringiensis* (Bt), as a promising alternative to pesticides. Again, Carson was prophetic.

By 1980, scientists had isolated the proteins in Bt bacteria that were poisonous to insects. Specifically, the genes for producing the crystalline proteins Cry1A group and Cry9C have been isolated for splicing into the DNA of crop plants. This new characteristic of the crop plant, which includes the crystalline protein, protects the plant from insects. Once ingested by the insect, the crystalline protein binds to specific sites in the insect stomach, causing death.

1988 witnessed the first field test of an engineered Bt tomato, and 1990 was the first successful Bt field test, which was with a cotton plant. By 1995, the first commercial use of a Bt potato was underway and by 1998, 25% of U.S. corn was genetically engineered.

This new characteristic in our food indicated that either the Food and Drug Administration, which regulates food safety, or the Environmental Protection Agency, which regulates the use of pesticides, were the agencies most likely to begin regulatory oversight for these products. The U.S. Environmental Protection Agency initially took responsibility for regulating the engineering of food because of the pesticide component. The Food and Drug Administration classified these foods as generally accepted as safe (GRAS), needing no regulation. Developers of these genetically engineered foods were required only to consult with the FDA before marketing, to demonstrate the safety of the new food. No labeling requirements were imposed on genetically engineered foods.

The test data to determine safety of these genetically engineered foods focuses on any allergenicity properties which might have been created. Food allergies are reactions to protein molecules. When new proteins are created by engineered plants the potential for a food allergy exists. The approach to determining whether these proteins might be allergenic is simply to compare the structure of the new protein to proteins that are known to cause food allergies, such as those in peanuts. Once it is demonstrated that the new protein has no properties or structure similar to known allergenic proteins, the food is assumed to be safe. The second part of the test for safety, is simply to determine whether the plant is toxic to humans, which can be determined by toxicity tests.

Specifically, a U.S. EPA Science Advisory Board Panel in November 2000 wrote that "To have a high likelihood of allergenicity the protein could be expected to have an amino acid sequence similar to known allergens." The Panel specified that it also would have three or more of the presumed risk factors, relative resistance to acid treatment, relative resistance to protease digestion, general molecular weight range of 10 to 70 kilodalton, probably would be a glycoprotein with the ability to induce an immunologic response in Brown Norway rats, and have the ability to be found intact in the bloodstream.

Although the protein is present in the engineered crop, processing the food destroys fragile proteins which are sensitive to heat. The DNA, however, remains and provides a way of identifying the presence of engineered food, although the protein has been destroyed by processing. The destruction of the protein also precludes the allergic reaction possibility. There have been no confirmed allergic reactions to these proteins which have been approved by the FDA. However, approximately 34 complaints (as of 2000) have been filed with the FDA regarding reported incidences of allergenic reactions.

Using the legal tools to address biotechnology issues, a number of cases have been brought for resolution to the courts. The theories used to challenge federal governmental actions have been based upon existing environmental statutes, consumer information, or food labeling statutes. The following case raises issues concerning the labeling of genetically engineered foods, utilizing claims under the Food, Drug and Cosmetic Act, the National Environmental Policy Act, as well as the Administrative Procedure Act. In 1995, the court heard a challenge to the use of Bovine Somatotropin (rBST) in cows for increased production of milk, without disclosing its use on the consumer label.

Stauber v. Shalala and Kessler

895 F. Supp. 1178 (W.D. Wisc. 1995)

Opinion by Barbara B. Crabb, District Judge:

This is a civil action for declaratory and injunctive relief brought pursuant to the Food, Drug and Cosmetic Act, the National Environmental Policy Act, and the Administrative Procedure Act. Plaintiffs are American consumers of commercially sold dairy products. Defendants are Donna Shalala, Secretary of the Department of Health and Human Services, and Dr. David Kessler, Commissioner of the Food and Drug Administration. Plaintiffs challenge defendants' approval of intervenor-defendant Monsanto Company's new drug application for Posilac(r)), a milk production-enhancing, synthetic bovine growth hormone drug. Specifically, plaintiffs contend that: 1) the approval was arbitrary and capricious because the FDA failed to consider health and safety issues related to the use of Posilac; 2) defendants failed to require mandatory labeling of products from cows treated with Posilac; and 3) defendants failed to conduct an adequate environmental assessment or issue an environmental impact statement assessing the environmental effects of Posilac's approval. Plaintiffs request both a declaration that defendants failed to perform their statutory duties in approving Posilac and a permanent injunction suspending the approval of Posilac until defendants comply with their statutory obligations.

The case is before the court on the parties' cross-motions for summary judgment. After a close review of the parties' submissions, I find that plaintiffs have offered no admissible, relevant evidence putting any material facts into dispute. Plaintiffs have not shown that defendants acted arbitrarily and capriciously in approving Posilac or in declining to require product labeling and they have not shown that defendants' environmental assessment was inadequate. Therefore, plaintiffs' claims must be dismissed.

From the proposed findings of fact of the parties, I find that the following material facts are undisputed.

UNDISPUTED FACTS

Bovine somatotrophin (bST), a bovine growth hormone, is a naturally occurring protein hormone produced in the pituitary gland of all cattle. In the 1930s, scientists discovered that injecting dairy cows with bovine growth hormone from other cattle could increase the cows' milk production but the discovery was not pursued on a wide scale because extraction of the hormone from cattle was not cost effective. In the 1980s, however, scientists developed a synthetic recombinant bovine growth hormone. Scientists can now isolate the gene responsible for natural bovine growth hormone, transfer that genetic material into bacterial cells called a "recombinant fermentation organism" and "program" the bacterial cells to produce a synthetic version of the hormone.

In the early 1980s, the FDA approved intervenor-defendant Monsanto Company's investigative new animal drug application for Posilac, a synthetic recombinant bovine somatotrophin. In 1987, Monsanto submitted a new animal drug application for Posilac to the FDA. Over the next several years, Monsanto supported the application with studies and reports documenting the safety and effectiveness of the drug. After reviewing those materials, the FDA approved Monsanto's application for the subcutaneous (injectable) use of Posilac on November 5, 1993. Posilac is the first genetically engineered animal drug to be approved for use in dairy cows and the first milk production enhancement drug to be approved for sale by the FDA.

The FDA approved Posilac despite criticism that the drug would have a significant negative effect on the health of dairy cows and despite concern about potential negative health effects on human consumers of dairy products derived from cows treated with rbST. Scientists, economists, farmers, and environmental and animal welfare organizations have questioned the safety and quality of rbST-derived products. In addition, the FDA received thousands of letters from consumers asking it either to deny approval of rbST or to require labeling of rbST-derived products. The General Accounting Office advised the FDA to withhold approval of Posilac until further research of rbST's potential negative impact on human health could be conducted. After the FDA approved Posilac for marketing, Congress delayed sale of the drug for 90 days while an interagency task force supervised by the Office of the President reviewed the data upon which the FDA based its decision. In January 1994, the task force concluded that the FDA's position was adequately supported. The FDA made available to the public a summary of the safety and effectiveness data submitted by Monsanto on which the agency relied in approving Posilac for mass marketing.

A. Cow Safety

Use of Posilac may affect cows adversely in several ways. Posilac increases the risks of reduced pregnancy rates, ovarian cysts and uterine disorders, decreased lengths of gestation periods and lower birth weight of calves. Posilac increases the risk of retained placentas and twinning rates in cows. It may cause increased bovine body temperatures, indigestion, bloating, diarrhea, enlarged hocks, enlarged lesions and injection site swellings. Additionally, use of Posilac increases the risk of clinical and subclinical mastitis, a bacterial infection of the udder. In absolute terms, rbST increases the risk of mastitis by about 0.1 case per cow per year. This risk is less than the risk of mastitis posed by seasonal change.

Before approving Posilac, the FDA reviewed the data submitted by Monsanto as part of its new drug application and considered Posilac's effects on animal health, including: 1) the acute and chronic toxicity of the drug; 2) its effects on reproduction; 3) calf birth traits, growth and health; 4) increased incidence of mastitis; 5) musculoskeletal effects; 6) digestive disorders including indigestion, bloating and diarrhea; 7) injection site reactions; 8) nutrient intake, body weight and body condition; 9) general cow health; and 10) miscellaneous health variables, including circulating anti-somatotrophin binding, blood variables, body temperature and urinalysis results. The agency determined that the risks to cows associated with the use of Posilac could be managed properly under a "manageable risk" criteria and that the risks to animal health were not significant enough to warrant denial of the drug application. (The FDA has never applied a zero risk standard when assessing the safety of new animal drugs.) Monsanto conducted a 14-day drug tolerance study that involved injecting a herd with dosages of rbST up to thirty times the normal dosage. Analysis of both cow and fetal blood and tissue revealed only one health side effect: slight swelling at the injection site.

B. Human Consumer Safety

Before approving Posilac, the FDA considered Posilac's possible negative effects on human health, including the possible effects of 1) increased levels of rbST in milk; 2) increased levels of insulin growth factor in milk; and 3) increased amounts of antibiotic drug residues in milk.

1. RbST

BST and its synthetic counterpart rbST are protein hormones that are orally inactive in humans. Upon ingestion, protein hormones (unlike steroid hormones) are broken down by enzymes in the intestines and digested. BST and rbST are orally inactive in cows as well. Like insulin, which must be injected to take effect, bST and rbST must be injected to stimulate milk production in cows. Even if injected into humans, however, rbST would not stimulate growth because human somatotrophin has a significantly different amino acid sequence from that of rbST and human receptors will not bond with rbST. Furthermore, heat destroys rbST, so that pasteurizing milk and cooking meat would tend to destroy at least 90% of the rbST in milk or beef. The FDA found that even at exaggerated doses the ingestion of rbST poses no significant risk to human safety.

2. Mastitis and antibiotics

Antibiotics are used to treat bovine mastitis. Trace residues of the antibiotics can appear in the milk of dairy cows. The level of antibiotic residue in milk is regulated, however. Forty-nine states have adopted the Grade A Pasteurized Milk Ordinance, established by the FDA and the Public Health Service in cooperation with state and local regulatory agencies and members of the milk industry. The ordinance defines standards for milk purity, establishes standards for production of pasteurized milk and milk products, details the method of inspections of farms and processing plants and provides that only producers, haulers, processors and distributors who meet the requirements of the ordinance shall be given permits. Under the milk ordinance, milk that is inspected and found to contain drug residues in excess of the standard must be discarded and the responsible producer is subject to regulatory sanctions.

Although states test milk routinely for drug residues in accordance with the milk ordinance, they generally test only for the presence of four of the antibiotics most commonly used to treat bovine infection, the beta-lactams, which are penicillin-like antibiotics. It has been estimated, however, that over fifty different drugs are used to treat bovine infections, some not approved for use on dairy cows, and the presence of residues from these other drugs would go undetected by most current testing procedures. The General Accounting Office has concluded that there is currently no means of assessing the degree to which current milk supplies are contaminated by these other drugs. One concern surrounding Posilac is that its use will increase the frequency of bovine infection, particularly mastitis, which will in turn lead to an increased need for antibiotics to treat dairy cow infections. Because the current regulatory scheme does not detect the presence of all drug residues in dairy products, there is a risk that greater amounts of antibiotic drug residue will be ingested by human dairy consumers.

To date there have been no long term studies of the impact on human health of increased antibiotics in milk. However, the FDA determined that the increased risk of bovine mastitis caused by Posilac did not present a risk to human health because 1) the increased risk of mastitis from the use of Posilac is not great, and in fact is much lower than the increased risk caused by the many other factors that contribute to mastitis; 2) milk is tested for beta-lactam drugs, and any milk found to contain illegal residues is discarded; and 3) the beta-lactams are the most commonly used antibiotics to treat mastitis. The FDA and its Veterinary Medicine and Food Advisory Committees determined that state and local regulation of milk production and distribution ensures that milk is free from the most widely used antibiotics and that introduction of Posilac to the market would not cause a statistically significant increase in the amount of antibiotic residues found in milk.

3. Somatic cell count

Mastitis brings with it an increase in the amount of somatic cells (i.e., white blood cells) present in dairy milk. Studies by Monsanto showed a significant increase in the somatic cell count in milk from rbST-treated cows in some herds, although the increase was not found in all herds studied. When the various studies conducted by Monsanto on somatic cell count were pooled, the results demonstrated no significant increase in somatic cell counts attributable to rbST treatment. The FDA did not consider somatic cell count from the standpoint of human safety. However, the agency did conclude from Monsanto's studies that rbST did not increase somatic cell count any more than factors such as lactation stage and cow parity. (Cow "parity" is a term that refers to whether and how many times a cow has given birth.)

4. Insulin-like growth factor

Insulin-like growth factor (IGF-1) is protein hormone whose production is regulated at least in part by somatotrophin. It has the same biochemical composition in humans and cows and is present in all milk, human saliva and human digestive juices. RbST increases the amount of IGF-1 in milk. IGF-1 is denatured in the process of making baby formula, but it is not destroyed by pasteurization.

At the time Monsanto filed its new drug application for Posilac, not much was known about the hormone. Defendants have done no long term studies on the effects of increased levels of IGF-1 on human health. However, Monsanto did conduct a two week study of rats administered IGF-1 either by gavage (forced feeding) or systemically by implanted pump. The study indicated no negative health impact on the esophagus, stomach and intestines of the rats from increased levels of IGF-1 administered orally.

The FDA considered IGF-1 when it evaluated the safety and effectiveness of Posilac and concluded that any increase in IGF-1 levels posed no significant health risks to consumers. This conclusion was based on the FDA's determinations that: 1) IGF-1 levels in milk from rbST-treated cows were not significantly higher than milk from untreated cows; 2) IGF-1 was not orally active; 3) even if IGF-1 from milk was absorbed intact, levels of IGF-1 in the human bloodstream are so much higher (100 to 1000 times) than the levels found in cows' milk that the addition of small amounts of IGF-1 from cows' milk would be physiologically insignificant; and 4) the manufacturing process for infant formula denatures almost all of the IGF-1 in cows' milk. The agency concluded that IGF-1 was unlikely to affect either the gastrointestinal track of adults or infants in general.

C. Labeling

The FDA determined that the risks of Posilac to dairy cows could be addressed adequately by labeling the drug itself. The Posilac label contains a "precautions and side-effects" section that lists the potential adverse effects on cows, including reduced pregnancy rates, cystic ovaries, disorders of the uterus, decreases in length of gestation, increased twinning rates, decreased calf birth weight, an increased risk of clinical and subclinical mastitis, digestive disorders and infection site reactions. In bold letters, the warning section informs the dairy farmer that "use of Posilac should be preceded by implementation of a comprehensive and ongoing herd reproductive health program," and "mastitis management practices should be thoroughly evaluated prior to initiating use of Posilac."

The FDA considered whether special labeling should be required for milk and milk products derived from rbST-treated cows in addition to the drug's packaging label. In May 1993, the FDA's Veterinary Medicine and Food Advisory Committees held a meeting to address the issue. The committees received testimony from doctors, scientists, dietitians, dairy farmers, veterinarians, members of medical and scientific organizations and universities, dairy organizations and farm and agricultural groups. On the basis of testimony from the hearings and the data submitted by Monsanto, the FDA concluded that there is no significant difference between milk from cows treated with Posilac and milk from untreated cows. The agency concluded also that rbST had no significant effect on the organoleptic properties of milk or on the lactose, fat, protein, ash, phosphorous and vitamin content of milk. On February 3, 1994, the FDA issued interim guidance on voluntary labeling of milk from untreated cows, concluding that such milk cannot be labeled as "BST free" because BST occurs naturally in milk, but that farmers may label their milk "from cows not treated with rbST," if the statement is placed in proper context. 59 Fed. Reg. 6279–80 (February 10, 1994).

D. Environmental Issues

The FDA approved Monsanto's new drug application for Posilac without preparing an environmental impact statement, concluding that no statement was necessary because approval of Posilac would not have a significant impact on the environment within the meaning of the National Environmental Policy Act. The FDA based this conclusion on an environmental assessment prepared by Monsanto that addressed Posilac's potential impact on the environment.

The FDA assumes responsibility for the scope and content of the environmental assessment prepared by Monsanto. Agency officials have reviewed the information contained in that document. The environmental assessment refers to studies that evaluated the impact Posilac was likely to have on the dairy industry and concluded that its introduction to the market would not do fundamental damage to current structural trends. The environmental assessment addressed the possibility of shifts in land use patterns as a result of the use of Posilac, concluding that the drug would be unlikely to have any significant effect on land use. The assessment also addressed two alternatives to the current approval of Posilac: 1) additional controls on production; and 2) use of the drug, including labeling. Both alternatives were addressed only with regard to the environmental concerns surrounding the biotechnological aspects of the drug's preparation.

Neither the environmental assessment nor the finding of no significant impact addressed consumer health risks posed by increased IGF-1 levels and antibiotic residue levels in milk derived from rbST-treated cows, the impact of Posilac on the health of dairy cows or the potential risks to consumers caused by increases in IGF-1 and antibiotic residues. However, the agency's policy is not to reexamine issues under the

National Environmental Policy Act already considered as part of its evaluation of a new animal drug application. The assessment failed to address the impact of Posilac on family dairy farms. Finally, the environmental assessment did not address possible alternatives of 1) approving the drug at lower doses; 2) approving Posilac only as a prescription drug; or 3) approving the drug for use only when accompanied by detailed instructions or educational seminars regarding methods to minimize health risks....

OPINION

... 1. Standing under the Food, Drug, and Cosmetic Act

Defendants raised their standing argument once before in this litigation in a motion to dismiss. In an opinion and order entered September 1, 1994, I concluded that standing could be premised on plaintiffs' allegations that they were unable to consume dairy products known to be free of milk from rbST-treated cows. Defendants do not challenge plaintiffs' alleged inability to consume milk products known to be free of milk from rbST-treated cows. Rather, they attack the minor premise of plaintiffs' allegation, that consuming dairy products derived from rbST treated cows is harmful. This argument misconstrues plaintiffs' rights under the Food, Drug, and Cosmetic Act.

The federal Food, Drug, and Cosmetic Act, 21 U.S.C. §§§§ 301–394, is intended to protect American consumers from the risks of consuming unsafe or ineffective food and drugs and thus requires new drug applicants to demonstrate the safety and effectiveness of new drugs before they may be marketed. One aspect of plaintiffs' challenge to the FDA's approval of rbST is that the agency did not hold Monsanto to its burden under the act of demonstrating the safety of Posilac. If this allegation is true, plaintiffs' injury is their exposure to a potentially dangerous drug whose safety has not been demonstrated in accordance with the act.

2. Standing under the National Environmental Policy Act

To have standing under the National Environmental Policy Act, plaintiffs must show that an agency's alleged noncompliance with the act has adversely affected them and that they are within the zone of interests protected by the act. Under the act, individuals are aggrieved by an agency's failure to prepare an environmental impact statement if they can show that the failure creates a reasonable risk that "'environmental impacts will be overlooked'" and that they have a "sufficient geographical nexus to the site of the challenged project that [they] may be expected to suffer whatever environmental consequences the project may have."

Defendants contend that plaintiffs have failed to allege an injury cognizable under the National Environmental Policy Act and have made no showing of a sufficient nexus between the agency's decision not to prepare an environmental impact statement and the alleged harm. Defendants do not challenge plaintiffs' allegations that they are consumers of milk. Rather, defendants' challenge assumes that plaintiffs must prove that rbST is actually harmful. This assumption is flawed, however, because it collapses the standing inquiry into the merits of plaintiffs' claims.

Plaintiffs have introduced evidence tending to show that rbST creates an increased risk of mastitis that will increase dairy farmers' reliance on antibiotics in the treatment of their dairy cows. Plaintiffs offer additional evidence that over 50 drugs are used to treat infections in cows, only 4 of which are seriously regulated. (I note that in analyzing standing, I am able to consider evidence that is outside the administrative record and for that reason may not be considered when assessing plaintiffs' claims of violations of the Food, Drug, and Cosmetic. See infra, section C.) For standing purposes, I conclude that this evidence demonstrates a reasonable risk that 1) farmers will rely increasingly on illegal or otherwise unregulated drugs to treat the higher incidence of mastitis, which in turn will 2) increase the levels of drug residues that might show up in consumers' milk. Plaintiffs argue that there is a risk that increased exposure to drug residues may affect human bioimmune systems and the bacteria living in our digestive systems. Whether plaintiffs are likely to succeed on this claim does not determine whether they have standing under the National Environmental Policy Act. The evidence they have proffered demonstrates a reasonable risk of serious environmental harm caused by the proposed agency action that would clearly affect them as dairy product consumers, were it ever to come to fruition. Therefore, I conclude that the consumer plaintiffs satisfy the requirements for Article III standing under the National Environmental Policy Act....

D. The FDA's Approval of Posilac

The FDA is the federal agency responsible for assuring that new animal drugs are safe and effective for their intended use. Before approving a new animal drug application, the FDA requires a new drug sponsor to demonstrate that the food products from the subject animals will be safe for human consumption, that the drug is safe and effective for the animals in question and that the manufacture and use of the drug will not harm the environment. Approval proceeds in two steps. First, the drug sponsor seeks approval of its investigative new animal drug application, which outlines how the sponsor will conduct the necessary research. This research covers human food safety, animal safety and drug efficacy and includes clinical and field trials, laboratory studies, on-site inspections and other investigative methods. Second, upon completion of the studies, the sponsor submits a new animal drug application that employs investigational studies to establish the safety and efficacy of the drug.

Throughout the application process, the burden is on the applicant or drug sponsor to show that the new animal drug is both effective and safe under the proposed conditions of use. Effectiveness must be demonstrated on the basis of "substantial evidence" that the drug "will have the effect it purports or is represented to have under the conditions of use prescribed, recommended, or suggested in the proposed labeling thereof." The Food, Drug, and Cosmetic Act does not indicate the standard an applicant must meet to demonstrate a new drug's safety or the evidence upon which the FDA must base its safety determination. However, the act requires the FDA to consider four specific factors when assessing safety: 1) the likelihood that the drug or a substance formed in food because of the drug will be consumed; 2) the cumulative effect that the drug will be likely to have on man or other animals; 3) safety factors that experts consider appropriate for extrapolating from animal experimentation data; and 4) whether it is likely that the conditions of use proposed or suggested in the labeling will be followed. The FDA is required to take into account the drug's effect on the health of the target animal. A new drug application must contain "full reports of adequate tests by all methods reasonably applicable to show whether or not the drug is safe for use under the conditions prescribed, recommended, or suggested in the proposed labeling." Such testing includes preclinical acute, subacute and chronic toxicity testing, clinical studies and filed investigations.

Plaintiffs contend that the FDA should not have approved Posilac because of safety concerns. For the reasons set out above in section C, supra, none of plaintiffs' proffered evidence indicating that rbST poses a danger to human health may be considered because it is outside the administrative record. The focus narrows, therefore, to plaintiffs' arguments that are grounded properly on the administrative record. Despite the limited amount of evidentiary support plaintiffs have collected, they continue to maintain that Monsanto failed to meet its burden under the Food, Drug, and Cosmetic Act. To survive summary judgment, plaintiffs must raise a genuine issue on the reasonableness of the FDA's conclusion that Monsanto met its burden of showing the safety of Posilac.

In identifying what they consider to be arbitrary and capricious FDA determinations, plaintiffs begin with the assertion that the Posilac label does not adequately counteract the health risks to cows associated with the drug's use. The FDA approved Posilac, notwithstanding its admitted risks of side effects to cows, on the theory that this safety risk is "manageable" if farmers adopt herd management techniques and ongoing herd reproductive health programs as the Posilac label recommends. Plaintiffs contend that this manageable risk criterion is arbitrary and capricious because the drug's label is vague and farmers will not know how to interpret it. Defendants respond by noting that mastitis is not a new problem to dairy farmers and that the increased incidence of mastitis caused by Posilac is not significantly great (0.1 per cow per year). It was on these two findings that the agency grounded its conclusion that the risk was "manageable," and in any event not so great as to warrant denying approval of the drug. Defendants note also that under the Food, Drug, and Cosmetic Act, neither the sponsors of new animal drugs nor the FDA is held to a "zero risk" standard.

Although plaintiffs raise valid concerns about the manageable risk approach, I cannot conclude that the agency's decision was arbitrary and capricious. First, nothing in the record indicates that the agency overlooked some aspect of cow health when reviewing the Posilac application. To the contrary, the record demonstrates that the agency evaluated the target animal's safety as it was required to do, considering each and every one of the known side effects associated with Posilac. Second, I cannot say it was irrational for the agency to conclude that the increased risk of mastitis caused by Posilac is not sufficiently great to warrant denying approval of the drug. This conclusion was based on the agency's determination that the risk of mastitis caused by Posilac is much less than the risk caused by other variables such as seasonal change. Finally, although mastitis is a serious health concern, it is one familiar to dairy farmers, who know how to detect and treat it. I add, however, that in the future it would be helpful to reviewing courts for the FDA to set out the factors it looks at in determining whether a particular risk is a manageable one.

Plaintiffs argue that defendants' decision to approve Posilac was arbitrary and capricious because defendants did not adequately consider the risk of higher levels of antibiotic drug residues in milk that could have an adverse impact on human health because of the greater resistance of certain bacteria, particularly human digestive bacteria. The FDA determined that the risk of exposure to increased amounts of antibiotics was slim because, among other things, the risk of increased mastitis is slight and the level of antibiotic drug residues in milk is highly regulated. Plaintiffs characterize this decision as arbitrary and capricious because many of the drugs used to treat bovine infections are not tested routinely under the current regulatory scheme. Defendants counter that the four antibiotics most commonly screened are also the ones most commonly used to treat bovine infection. The controversy boils down to whether it was proper for the FDA to rely on the current regulatory mechanism to assure that drug residues will be kept out of the milk supply.

Although plaintiffs have raised valid concerns about the adequacy of the current regulatory scheme to assure the purity of the nation's milk supply, they have not shown the agency's reliance on that scheme to be arbitrary and capricious. First and most important, the agency determined that the increased risk of mastitis was not overly great and on that basis concluded that the rise in the use of antibiotics would not be overly great either. Given these conclusions, it was rational for the agency to rest a determination of safety on the current milk purity regulatory scheme especially because milk is tested for the drugs most commonly used to treat mastitis, the beta-lactams. Although I understand plaintiffs' concerns, I conclude that the agency considered the relevant factors and that the record contains support for its determination.

Third, plaintiffs are dissatisfied with the FDA's exploration of the potential risks associated with an increased level of IGF-1 in milk from cows treated with Posilac. The FDA concluded that an increased level of IGF-1 in milk presented no significant human health concerns. This conclusion was based on Monsanto's two-week rat study indicating no adverse effects from oral ingestion of IGF-1 and on other evidence indicating that IGF-1 levels rise only slightly when the producing cow is treated with rbST, that IGF-1 exists in the human blood stream at levels much higher than those appearing in milk and that IGF-1 is denatured when milk is boiled. Plaintiffs are correct that no long term studies have been done, but they have presented no admissible evidence that would show either that longer studies were required or that the two-week rat study was not scientifically adequate to permit the FDA to conclude that IGF-1 poses no significant risk to human health. Without any admissible evidence indicating that the two-week study did not support the conclusions that the agency drew from it, I cannot conclude that the agency's decision lacked a rational basis in the record.

E. The FDA's Decision Not to Require Labeling of Products Derived from rbST-treated Cows

Under the Food, Drug, and Cosmetic Act, food is deemed misbranded if its labeling is "false or misleading in any particular." provid [ing] further that:

> If an article is alleged to be misbranded because the labeling or advertising is misleading, then in determining whether the labeling or advertising is misleading there shall be taken into account (among other things) not only representations made or suggested by statement, word, design, device, or any combination thereof, but also the extent to which the labeling or advertising fails to reveal facts material in the light of such representations or material with respect to consequences which may result from the use of the article to which the labeling or advertising relates under the conditions of use prescribed in the labeling or advertising thereof or under such conditions of use as are customary or usual.

> Plaintiffs contend that food products derived from rbST-treated cows must be labeled as such if the products are to comply with these two provisions. They argue that milk derived from rbST-treated cows differs organoleptically from ordinary milk in several respects and that these differences are "material facts" requiring labeling. In addition, they argue that there is widespread consumer desire for mandatory labeling of rbST-derived milk and that such a degree of demand is also a "material fact" requiring labeling.

> An organoleptic difference is one capable of being detected by a human sense organ. See Webster's Collegiate Dictionary 953 (1991). In a different context from the one presented here, the FDA has stated:

Information disclosing differences in performance characteristics (e.g., physical properties, flavor characteristics, functional properties and shelf life) is a material fact under section 201(n) of the act because it bears on the consequence of the use of the article. Accordingly, this information must be communicated to the consumer on the product label, or labeling would be misleading, and the product would be misbranded under section 403(a) of the act.

58 Fed. Reg. 2431, 2437 (January 6, 1993) (notice of final FDA rule regarding standards for products named with nutrient content claims, i.e., "fat free," and "low calorie"). However, plaintiffs have been able to point to no evidence in the administrative record indicating that milk derived from rbST-treated cows has performance characteristics or organoleptic properties different from milk from untreated cows. The increased incidence of mastitis in cows would not provide a basis for labeling because plaintiffs have provided no evidence that milk that finds its way to the consumer actually will contain higher levels of drug residues. Plaintiffs assert that the increased somatic cell counts and IGF-1 levels in rbST-derived milk are material facts warranting a label. However, they offer no evidence that increased somatic cell counts and increased IGF-1 levels in rbST-derived milk are organoleptic differences or that they alter the performance characteristics of milk. Indeed, plaintiffs have been unable to put into dispute the agency's conclusion that "administration of sometribove [rbST] has no significant effect on the overall composition of milk."

Regarding widespread consumer demand, plaintiffs are incorrect in their assertion that by itself consumer opinion could suffice to require labeling. The FDA does consider consumer opinion relevant when determining whether a label is required to disclose a material fact, but a factual predicate to the requirement of labeling is a determination that a product differs materially from the type of product it purports to be. If there is a difference, and consumers would likely want to know about the difference, then labeling is appropriate. If, however, the product does not differ in any significant way from what it purports to be, then it would be misbranding to label the product as different, even if consumers misperceived the product as different. In the absence of evidence of a material difference between rbST-derived milk and ordinary milk, the use of consumer demand as the rationale for labeling would violate the Food, Drug, and Cosmetic Act. Because plaintiffs have not presented any evidence demonstrating organoleptic differences between regular and rbST-derived milk or of any harmful effects of rbST on consumers, they have failed to carry their burden of demonstrating the arbitrary and capricious nature of the agency's determination....

F. The National Environmental Policy Act

The National Environmental Policy Act, 42 U.S.C. §§ 4321–4370, requires federal agencies to prepare an environmental impact statement if the agency plans to undertake a "major" action "significantly affecting the quality of the human environment." ...

Plaintiffs contend that the FDA failed to comply with the National Environmental Policy Act when it determined that an environmental impact statement was unnecessary. In particular, plaintiffs contend that the decision not to prepare an environmental impact statement was arbitrary and capricious in light of the failure to address Posilac's socioeconomic effects on the dairy farmer and Posilac's likely effects on human and bovine health in either the environmental assessment or the finding of no significant impact. In addition, plaintiffs challenge the failure to discuss feasible alternatives in the environmental assessment and the finding of no significant impact.

Regarding socioeconomic effects, the regulations promulgated under the National Environmental Policy Act provide that "economic or social effects are not intended by themselves to require preparation of the environmental impact statement." 40 C.F.R. §§ 1508.14. Plaintiffs are wrong when they assert that Posilac's socioeconomic effects on the dairy farmer require the preparation of an environmental impact statement.... It is true that an environmental impact statement must discuss economic or social effects of the proposed action to the extent those effects interrelate to its natural or physical environmental effects, but the regulations do not contemplate an independent consideration of socioeconomic effects when there is no determination that the proposed agency activity will significantly effect the environment....

Because defendants were not required to include a discussion of socioeconomic effects in their environmental assessment, it was not arbitrary and capricious to omit consideration of those nonenvironmental effects from the environmental assessment.

The next question is whether, to comply with the National Environmental Policy Act, the FDA was required to take an independent and second look at the effects Posilac might have on the health of cows and consumers or whether the agency could rely on the safety evaluations it made pursuant to its statutory duties under the Food, Drug, and Cosmetic Act. Plaintiffs do not seem to argue that the analysis of the human and bovine health issues required under the two statutes differ in some way or that the analysis required under the Food, Drug, and Cosmetic Act is somehow less rigorous than that required under National Environmental Policy Act. Rather, plaintiffs' argument appears to be simply that the agency must review the issues twice to satisfy the requirements of both statutes....

Plaintiffs contend that at a minimum, the agency should have been required to incorporate by reference its health and safety findings into the environmental assessment and the finding of no significant impact. This argument is not without merit. Such incorporation of the health and safety data by reference in the environmental assessment and finding of no significant impact would provide an interested party (or reviewing court) with a complete picture of all analysis bearing on the agency's obligations under the National Environmental Policy Act.

Plaintiffs' argument fails, however, for two interrelated reasons. First, at bottom, their argument is a purely informational one, which fails because they allege no harm stemming from the asserted procedural defect. Cf. Foundation for Economic Trends v. Lyng, ... (D.C. Cir. 1991) (informational injury alone is not enough to satisfy standing requirements under NEPA). Second, environmental assessments and findings of no significant impact are informal agency actions subject to judicial review under the arbitrary and capricious standard....

The final issue plaintiffs raise is the omission of any discussion of feasible alternatives from the environmental assessment and the finding of no significant impact. Plaintiffs argue that the agency should have considered the possibilities of a delay on approving the Posilac application until further studies on health and safety could be conducted, a lower recommended dosage to the cows, or approval of Posilac only as a prescription drug. (Plaintiffs proposed as fact that the environmental assessment did not address the alternative of approving the drug for marketing only when accompanied by detailed instructions or educational seminars regarding methods to minimize health risks, but they have not pursued this argument in their briefs.) The first alternative, a delay in approving the drug, was suggested to the agency. During the review process the Foundation on Economic Trends, a non-profit consumer organization and a former plaintiff in this action, suggested that approval of the drug be postponed until further safety research could occur. However, plaintiffs have failed to offer evidence that the other two alternatives (a lower recommended dosage or prescription drug status) were ever presented to the agency for consideration. If an alternative is not presented to the agency for consideration, the agency cannot be attacked in federal court for not considering it....

Even if I assume that plaintiffs made a presentation of their alternative of delayed approval pending further research into health and safety that was adequate to require the agency to consider the proposal, see *Vermont Yankee Nuclear Power Corp. v. Natural Resources Defense Council*, ... (1978) (proponents of alternatives must make a preliminary showing that proposed alternative merits review before agency required to consider alternative during agency proceedings), plaintiffs would still not meet their burden of showing that an environmental impact statement should have been prepared. When an agency determines that a proposed action poses a significant risk of harm to the environment, the agency must consider alternatives to the proposed action.... However, if the agency determines that a proposed action will not significantly effect the environment, it is required to consider alternatives only when the proposal involves "unresolved conflicts concerning alternative uses of available resources." ... In this situation, I cannot perceive any unresolved conflict concerning uses of available resources. Plaintiffs' proposed alternative involves only a delay in approving the drug until further tests have been conducted. This situation does not involve an "available resource" as the term is used in §§ 4332(E)(2).

ORDER

IT IS ORDERED that the motions for summary judgment of defendants Donna Shalala, Secretary of Health and Human Services, and David Kessler, Commissioner of the Food and Drug Administration, and intervenor defendant Monsanto Company's motions for summary judgment are GRANTED. Plaintiffs' motion for summary judgment is DENIED. The clerk of court is directed to enter judgment for defendants and the intervenor defendant and close this case.

———————

Five years later, the effort to utilize the National Environmental Policy Act and the Food, Drug and Cosmetic Act were again used to raise labeling and environmental concerns, after thirty-six foods, derived from GMOs were released into the market.

———————

Alliance for Bio-Integrity v. Shalala
116 F. Supp. 2d 166 (D.D.C. 2000)

MEMORANDUM OPINION:

Technological advances have dramatically increased our ability to manipulate our environment, including the foods we consume. One of these advances, recombinant deoxyribonucleic acid (rDNA) technology, has enabled scientists to alter the genetic composition of organisms by mixing genes on the cellular and molecular level in order to create new breeds of plants for human and animal consumption. These new breeds may be designed to repel pests, retain their freshness for a longer period of time, or contain more intense flavor and/or nutritional value. Much controversy has attended such developments in biotechnology, and in particular the production, sale, and trade of genetically modified organisms and foods. The above-captioned lawsuit represents one artic-ulation of this controversy.

Among Plaintiffs, some fear that these new breeds of genetically modified food could contain unexpected toxins or allergens, and others believe that their religion forbids consumption of foods produced through rDNA technology. Plaintiffs, a coalition of groups and individuals including scientists and religious leaders concerned about genet-ically altered foods, have brought this action to protest the Food and Drug Administra-tion's ("FDA") policy on such foods in general, and in particular on various genetically modified foods that already have entered the marketplace. The parties have filed cross-motions for summary judgment on plaintiffs' multiple claims. Upon careful considera-tion of the parties' briefs and the entire record, the Court shall grant Defendants' mo-tion as to all counts of Plaintiffs' Complaint.

I. BACKGROUND

On May 29, 1992, the FDA published a "Statement of Policy: Foods Derived From New Plant Varieties" (Statement of Policy, 57 Fed. Reg. 22,984). In the Statement of Policy, FDA announced that the agency would presume that foods produced through the rDNA process were "generally recognized as safe" (GRAS) under the Federal Food, Drug and Cosmetic Act ("FDCA"), 21 U.S.C. §§ 321(s), and therefore not subject to regulation as food additives. While FDA recommended that food producers consult with it before marketing rDNA-produced foods, the agency did not mandate such con-sultation. In addition, FDA reserved the right to regulate any particular rDNA-devel-oped food that FDA believed was unsafe on a case-by-case basis, just as FDA would reg-ulate unsafe foods produced through conventional means.

The Statement of Policy also indicated that rDNA modification was not a "material fact" under the FDCA, and that therefore labeling of rDNA-produced foods was not necessarily required. FDA did not engage in a formal notice-and-comment process on the Statement of Policy, nor did it prepare an Environmental Impact Statement or Envi-ronmental Assessment. At least thirty-six foods, genetically altered through rDNA tech-nology, have been marketed since the Statement of Policy was issued.

Plaintiffs filed a Complaint in this Court challenging the FDA's policy on six different grounds: (1) the Statement was not properly subjected to notice-and-comment proce-dures; (2) the FDA did not comply with the National Environmental Protection Act (NEPA) by compiling an Environmental Assessment or Environmental Impact State-ment; (3) the FDA's presumption that rDNA-developed foods are GRAS and therefore do not require food additive petitions under 21 U.S.C. §§ 321(s) is arbitrary and capri-cious; (4) the FDA's decision not to require labeling for rDNA-developed foods is arbi-trary and capricious ...

II. DISCUSSION

A. Subject Matter Jurisdiction

.... Although the Court may not review FDA's policy-laden individual enforcement decisions, the Court has jurisdiction to review whether or not FDA's Statement of Policy comports with Congressional directives.

B. Notice and Comment

Plaintiffs argue that the Statement of Policy should be set aside because it was not subjected to notice and comment proceedings, as required under the Administrative

Procedure Act ("APA"), 5 U.S.C. §§ 553. While conceding that the Statement of Policy did not undergo a formal notice and comment process, Defendants maintain that the Statement of Policy is a policy statement or an interpretive rule not subject to notice and comment requirements. Plaintiffs contend instead that the Statement of Policy is a substantive rule, and that therefore it was improperly exempted from a formal notice and comment process....

A substantive rule, which must undergo a formal notice-and-comment process, is a rule that "implement[s]" a statute and has "the force and effect of law." Policy statements, on the other hand, are "statements issued by an agency to advise the public prospectively of the manner in which the agency proposes to exercise a discretionary power." Although the distinction between these categories is not entirely clear, the Court of Appeals articulated a two-part test for determining when an agency action is a policy statement. Policy statements (1) must not impose any new rights or obligations, and (2) must "genuinely leave the agency and its decision-makers free to exercise discretion." In weighing these criteria, "the ultimate issue is the agency's intent to be bound." An agency's own characterization of its statement deserves some weight, but it is not dispositive. Rather, courts will look to the actual language of the statement.

By its very name, the Statement of Policy announces itself as a policy statement. More importantly, the plain language of the Statement suggests that it does not have a binding effect. For example, the Statement does not declare that transferred genetic material will be considered GRAS; rather, it announces that "such material is *presumed* to be GRAS." This presumption of safety is rebuttable, because FDA will "require food additive petitions in cases where safety questions exist sufficient to warrant formal premarket review by FDA to ensure public health protection." Rebuttable presumptions leave an agency free to exercise its discretion and may therefore properly be announced in policy statements.

In response to the argument that the Policy Statement vests broad discretion with the agency, Plaintiffs contend that the FDA's application of the Statement has given it a "practical effect" that has effectively bound the agency's discretion, as evidenced by the thirty-six genetically engineered foods that are currently on the market and not regulated by the FDA. Although courts will look to the "agency's actual applications" to determine the nature of an agency statement, such an inquiry occurs "where the language and context of a statement are inconclusive." Here, the plain language of the Statement clearly indicates that it is a policy statement that merely creates a presumption and does not ultimately bind the agency's discretion.

Even if, as Plaintiffs argue, FDA has previously used notice-and-comment procedures to determine GRAS status, in the instant case FDA has not determined GRAS status but has rather announced a GRAS presumption.... Because the Statement is a policy statement merely announcing a GRAS presumption, the omission of formal notice-and-comment procedures does not violate the Administrative Procedure Act.

C. NEPA

Plaintiffs have also alleged that FDA violated the National Environmental Protection Act (NEPA), 42 U.S.C. §§ 4321 *et seq.*, by not performing an Environmental Assessment (EA) or an Environmental Impact Statement (EIS) in conjunction with the Statement of Policy. NEPA requires "all agencies of the Federal Government ... [to] include in every recommendation or report on proposals for legislation and other major Federal actions significantly affecting the quality of the human environment, a detailed statement ... on the environmental impact of the proposed action." 42 U.S.C. §§ 4332(2)(c)(I).

"Major federal action," as defined in the Code of Federal Regulations, includes actions such as "adoption of official policy ... adoption of formal plans ... adoption of programs ... [and] approval of specific projects." 40 C.F.R. §§ 1508.18(b)(1–4). For major federal actions, agencies must either prepare an EIS examining the environmental impact of the proposed action, prepare an EA determining whether or not to prepare an EIS, or claim that the action falls within a Categorical Exclusion, "a category of actions which do not individually or cumulatively have a significant effect on the human environment." 40 C.F.R. §§ 1508.4 (1999). If the agency is not engaging in a major federal action, NEPA requirements do not apply.

In the Statement of Policy, FDA announces that "the activities [FDA] may undertake with respect to foods from new plant varieties ... will [not] constitute agency action under NEPA." FDA's determination that the Statement is not a major federal action is essentially an interpretation of the meaning of "major federal action" in 42 U.S.C. §§ 4332(2)(c) and 40 C.F.R. §§ 1508.18. Agencies enjoy wide discretion in interpreting regulations, and the agency's interpretation will be upheld unless it is arbitrary and capricious.

The FDA's determination that the Statement was not a major federal action comports with the holdings of this Circuit, and is therefore neither arbitrary nor capricious. While declaring a rebuttable presumption that foods produced through rDNA technology are GRAS, the FDA has neither made a final determination that any particular food will be allowed into the environment, nor taken any particular regulatory actions that could affect the environment. In order to trigger the NEPA requirement of an EIS, the agency must be prepared to undertake an " 'irreversible and irretrievable commitment of resources' to an action that will affect the environment." Because the FDA's presumption does not bind its decisionmaking authority, it has neither taken nor prepared to take the irreversible action that is necessary to require preparation of an EIS ... Evidencing this non-binding effect is the FDA's 1993 decision to open the labeling issue for further discussion, requesting additional public comment on the possible implementation of a general labeling requirement. 58 Fed. Reg. 25,837 (1993).

Moreover, agency decisions that maintain the substantive status quo do not constitute major federal actions under NEPA. Defendants maintain correctly that their actions have not altered the status quo because "rDNA modified foods ... were regulated no differently before the publication of the Policy Statement than they are now." Because the announcement of a rebuttable presumption of GRAS does not affect the substantive regulatory status quo, it is not a major federal action.

The Statement of Policy is not only reversible and consistent with the status quo ante; it is also not properly an "agency action." The core of Plaintiff's NEPA claim is that FDA has failed to regulate rDNA-modified foods, and that this failure to act engenders environmental consequences. But NEPA applies only to agency actions, "even if inaction has environmental consequences." *Defenders of Wildlife v. Andrus*, 201 U.S. App. D.C. 252, 627 F.2d 1238, 1243 (D.C. Cir. 1980). The *Defenders of Wildlife* court reasoned that Congress did not intend for agencies to perform environmental studies when the agencies were not acting. *See* 627 F.2d at 1244. In certain cases, agencies may take action by authorizing private action, but in such cases the government still must undertake some overt act, such as issuing a permit or affirming a substance as GRAS.

In the instant case, FDA has not taken an overt action, but instead has merely announced a presumption that certain foods do not require special regulation. This presumption against regulation does not constitute an overt action, and is therefore not subject to NEPA requirements.

In sum, because FDA's Statement of Policy is reversible, maintains the substantive status quo, and takes no overt action, the Statement of Policy does not constitute a major federal action under NEPA. FDA was not required to compile an Environmental Assessment or an Environmental Impact Statement in conjunction with the Statement of Policy, and therefore its failure to do so does not violate NEPA....

D. GRAS Presumption

In their challenge to the FDA's Statement of Policy, Plaintiffs further claim that the Statement of Policy's presumption that rDNA-engineered foods are GRAS violates the GRAS requirements of the Federal Food, Drug, and Cosmetic Act ("FDCA"), 21 U.S.C. §§ 321(s), and is therefore arbitrary and capricious. The FDCA provides that any substance which may "become a component or otherwise affect[] the characteristics of any food" shall be deemed a food additive. A producer of a food additive must submit a food additive petition to FDA for approval unless FDA determines that the additive is "generally recognized [by qualified experts] ... as having been adequately shown through scientific procedures ... to be safe under the conditions of its intended use."[6]

In the Statement of Policy, FDA indicated that, under §§ 321(s), it is the intended or expected introduction of a substance into food that makes the substance potentially subject to food additive regulation. Thus, in the case of foods derived from new plant varieties, it is the transferred genetic material and the intended expression product or products that could be subject to food additive regulation, if such material or expression products are not GRAS. Accordingly, FDA reasoned that the only substances added to rDNA engineered foods are nucleic acid proteins, generally recognized as not only safe but also necessary for survival. ("Nucleic acids are present in the cells of every living organism, including every plant and animal used for food by humans or animals, and do not raise a safety concern as a component of food"). Therefore, FDA concluded that rDNA engineered foods should be presumed to be GRAS unless evidence arises to the contrary. The Statement of Policy does acknowledge, however, that certain genetically modified substances might trigger application of the food additives petitioning process. In that vein, FDA recognized that "the intended expression product in a food could be a protein, carbohydrate, fat or oil, or other substance that differs significantly in structure, function, or composition from substances found currently in food. Such substances may not be GRAS and may require regulation as a food additive."

This Court's evaluation of the FDA's interpretation of §§ 321(s) is framed by *Chevron, U.S.A. v. Natural Resources Defense Council*, 467 U.S. 837 (1984). Since "'statutory interpretation begins with the language of the statute itself,'" as a general matter the Court first must determine whether Congress has spoken directly to the issue at hand, a line of analysis that has become known as *Chevron* step one.... The Court answers this inquiry in the affirmative, then "that is the end of the matter; for the court, as well as the agency, must give effect to the unambiguously expressed intent of Congress."

---

6. The term 'food additive' means any substance the intended use of which results or may result, directly or indirectly, in its becoming a component or otherwise affecting the characteristics of any food (including any substance intended for use in producing, manufacturing, packing, processing, preparing, treating, packaging, transporting, or holding food; and including any source of radiation intended for any such use), if such substance is not generally recognized, among experts qualified by scientific training and experience to evaluate its safety, as having been adequately shown through scientific procedures (or, in the case as a substance used in food prior to January 1, 1958, through either scientific procedures or experience based on common use in food) to be safe under the conditions of its intended use....

But *Chevron* review also concerns itself with the extent and application of agency discretion in interpreting the statute at issue. In other words, "a reviewing court's inquiry under *Chevron* is rooted in statutory analysis and is focused on discerning the boundaries of Congress' delegation of authority to the agency." To resolve the issue, "the question for the reviewing court is whether the agency's construction of the statute is faithful to its plain meaning, or, if the statute has no plain meaning, whether the agency's interpretation 'is based on a permissible construction of the statute.'" If this interpretation is "reasonable and consistent with the statutory scheme and legislative history."…, then the Court must defer to the agency. This inquiry into the agency's interpretation constitutes *Chevron* step two.

When Congress passed the Food Additives Amendment in 1958, it obviously could not account for the late twentieth-century technologies that would permit the genetic modification of food. The "object and policy" of the food additive amendments, is to "require the processor who wants to add a new and unproven additive to accept the responsibility … of first proving it to be safe for ingestion by human beings." S. Rep. No. 85-2422, at 2 (1958). The plain language of §§ 321(s) fosters a broad reading of "food additive" and includes "any substance intended for use in producing, manufacturing, packing, processing, preparing, treating, packaging, transporting, or holding food; and … any source of radiation intended for any such use." §§ 321(s).

Nonetheless, the statute exempts from regulation as additives substances that are "generally recognized … to be safe under the conditions of its intended use.…" §§ 321(s). Plaintiffs have not disputed FDA's claim that nucleic acid proteins are generally recognized to be safe. Plaintiffs have argued, however, that significant disagreement exists among scientific experts as to whether or not nucleic acid proteins are generally recognized to be safe when they are used to alter organisms genetically. Having examined the record in this case, the Court cannot say that FDA's decision to accord genetically modified foods a presumption of GRAS status is arbitrary and capricious.… this court must proceed with particular caution, avoiding all temptation to direct the agency in a choice between rational alternatives."*Environmental Defense Fund, Inc. v. Costle*, 188 U.S. App. D.C. 95, 578 F.2d 337, 339 (D.C.Cir.1978).

To be generally recognized as safe, a substance must meet two criteria: (1) it must have technical evidence of safety, usually in published scientific studies, and (2) this technical evidence must be generally known and accepted in the scientific community. *See* 21 C.F.R. §§ 170.30(a–b); 62 Fed. Reg. 18940. Although unanimity among scientists is not required, "a severe conflict among experts … precludes a finding of general recognition." 62 Fed. Reg. at 18939. Plaintiffs have produced several documents showing significant disagreements among scientific experts.[7] …

… Moreover, pointing to a 44,000 page record, the FDA notes that Plaintiffs have chosen to highlight a selected few comments of FDA employees, which were ultimately addressed in the agency's final Policy Statement. As a result, Plaintiffs have failed to convince the Court that the GRAS presumption is inconsistent with the statutory requirements.

---

7. Plaintiff scientist affidavit describing dangers of rDNA technology, Scientist affidavit describing rDNA technology as "inherently risky", Scientist affidavit describing risks of rDNA technology; FDA scientist comments on the Statement of Policy, noting difference between genetic engineering and cross-breeding; FDA scientist criticizing scientific basis of Statement of Policy; FDA scientists arguing that pre-market review of genetically engineered foods is necessary; FDA scientist arguing that Food Additives Amendment should be applied to rDNA engineered foods; FDA toxicology group head warning that genetically modified plants could have high levels of toxins.

E. Labeling

Plaintiffs have also challenged the Statement of Policy's failure to require labeling for genetically engineered foods, for which FDA relied on the presumption that most genetically modified food ingredients would be GRAS. Plaintiffs claim that FDA should have considered the widespread consumer interest in having genetically engineered foods labeled, as well as the special concerns of religious groups and persons with allergies in having these foods labeled.

The FDCA, 21 U.S.C. §§ 321(n), grants the FDA limited authority to require labeling. In general, foods shall be deemed misbranded if their labeling "fails to reveal facts ... material with respect to consequences which may result from the use of the article to which the labeling ... relates under the conditions of use prescribed in the labeling ... or under such conditions of use as are customary or usual." Plaintiffs challenge the FDA's interpretation of the term "material." Thus, the question is again one of statutory interpretation. As is apparent from the statutory language, Congress has not squarely addressed whether materiality pertains only to safety concerns or whether it also includes consumer interest....

Because Congress has not spoken directly to the issue, this Court must determine whether the agency's interpretation of the statute is reasonable. Agency interpretations receive substantial deference, particularly when the agency is interpreting a statute that it is charged with administering. Even if the agency's interpretation is not "the best or most natural by grammatical or other standards," if the interpretation is reasonable, then it is entitled to deference.

The FDA takes the position that no "material change," under §§ 321(n), has occurred in the rDNA derived foods at issue here. Absent unique risks to consumer health[8] or uniform changes to food derived through rDNA technology, the FDA does not read §§ 321(n) to authorize an agency imposed food labeling requirement. More specifically irksome to the Plaintiffs, the FDA does not read §§ 321(n) to authorize labeling requirements solely because of consumer demand. The FDA's exclusion of consumer interest from the factors which determine whether a change is "material" constitutes a reasonable interpretation of the statute. Moreover, it is doubtful whether the FDA would even have the power under the FDCA to require labeling in a situation where the sole justification for such a requirement is consumer demand. *See Stauber v. Shalala*, 895 F. Supp. 1178, 1193 (W.D.Wis. 1995) ("In the absence of evidence of a material difference between [milk from cows treated with a synthetic hormone] and ordinary milk, the use of consumer demand as the rationale for labeling would violate the Food, Drug, and Cosmetic Act.").

Plaintiffs fail to understand the limitation on the FDA's power to consider consumer demand when making labeling decisions because they fail to recognize that the determination that a product differs materially from the type of product it purports to be is a factual predicate to the requirement of labeling. Only once materiality has been established may the FDA consider consumer opinion to determine whether a label is required

---

8. In other contexts, the FDA has identified that the presence of an increased risk to consumer safety constitutes a "material change." Likewise, should a material consequence exist for a particular rDNA-derived food, the FDA has and will require special labeling. However, the Policy Statement at issue here provides only a very general rule regarding the entire class of rDNA derived foods. Thus, without a determination that, *as a class*, rDNA derived food pose inherent risks or safety consequences to consumers, or differ in some material way from their traditional counterparts, the FDA is without authority to mandate labeling.

to disclose a material fact. Thus, "if there is a [material] difference, and consumers would likely want to know about the difference, then labeling is appropriate. If, however, the product does not differ in any significant way from what it purports to be, then it would be misbranding to label the product as different, even if consumers misperceived the product as different." The FDA has already determined that, in general, rDNA modification does not "materially" alter foods, and as discussed in Section II.E, *supra*, this determination is entitled to deference. Given these facts, the FDA lacks a basis upon which it can legally mandate labeling, regardless of the level of consumer demand.

Plaintiffs also contend that the *process*[10] of genetic modification is a "material fact" under §§ 321(n) which mandates special labeling, implying that there are new risks posed to the consumer. However, the FDA has determined that foods produced through rDNA techniques do not "present any different or greater safety concern than foods developed by traditional plant breeding," and concluded that labeling was not warranted. That determination, unless irrational, is entitled to deference. Accordingly, there is little basis upon which this Court could find that the FDA's interpretation of §§ 321(n) is arbitrary and capricious.

CONCLUSION

For the foregoing reasons, the Court determines that Defendant's 1992 Policy Statement did not violate the Administrative Procedures Act, the National Environmental Policy Act, or the procedures mandated by the FDCA and FDA regulations. Furthermore, Defendant was not arbitrary and capricious in its finding that genetically modified foods need not be labeled because they do not differ "materially" from non-modified foods under 21 U.S.C. §§ 321(n).... Hence, the Court denies Plaintiffs' motion for summary judgment and grants Defendant's motion for same. An appropriate order accompanies this memorandum opinion.

ORDERED that Judgment is hereby entered for Defendant and the case is DISMISSED.

SO ORDERED.

———————

Notes

1. A list of documents collected during discovery can be found on the Alliance for Bio-Integrity website at http://www.bio-integrity.org/list.html. The organization posted its explanation of the outcome of the preceding case:

> The judge did not rule that GE foods actually have been shown to be safe. Nor did she determine that there ever was a general recognition of safety among the FDA scientists or within the scientific community. Moreover, she did not even say that the FDA could justifiably continue to presume that GE foods are safe. Her decision was limited to the particular exercise of discretion made by the FDA in May of 1992. She ruled that at that specific point in time, the FDA was entitled to have presumed there was a general recognition of safety among sci-

———————

10. Disclosure of the conditions or methods of manufacture has long been deemed unnecessary under the law. The Supreme Court reasoned in 1924, "When considered independently of the product, the method of manufacture is not material. The act requires no disclosure concerning it." *U.S. v. Ninety-Five Barrels (More or Less) Alleged Apple Cider Vinegar*, 265 U.S. 438 (1924).

entific experts; but she indicated we had presented evidence showing that there currently is not a general recognition of safety. Further, she emphasized that the FDA's presumption is supposed to be rebuttable by evidence it receives to the contrary. Nonetheless, the FDA continues to pretend that there is an overwhelming consensus among experts that GE foods have been demonstrated to be safe.

Because of the major flaws in the judge's opinion, we filed an appeal in November 2000. Then in January 2001, the FDA proposed new regulations on GE foods. Although these regulations still did not require any safety testing or labeling of GE foods, had they been implemented, they would have replaced the less formal policy decision of May 1992 against which our lawsuit was brought. This appeared to render it a waste of time for us to further pursue our suit, because if the proposed regulations had been enacted, our suit would have become moot and we would have needed to proceed against the new regulations by filing a new lawsuit. Therefore, the Alliance for Bio-Integrity and the other plaintiffs in our lawsuit dropped our appeal, intending to bring a new lawsuit when the regulations took effect.

However, after we dropped our appeal, and after a two year delay in enacting the proposed regulations, the FDA announced it was withdrawing them. So the FDA continues to rely on its policy statement of 1992, and we cannot revive our appeal of the court's decision. Further, because the 1992 policy has already been upheld in a federal court, it is unlikely that anyone else would be able to sustain a new lawsuit against it. This means that GE foods will continue to be unknowingly consumed by most Americans on a daily basis even though they are on the market in stark violation of the food safety laws.

On balance, our lawsuit accomplished a lot by exposing the FDA's fraud and revealing the unsoundness of its policy and the irresponsibility of its behavior. Even though we failed to overturn the FDA's policy, the court's ruling refutes the standard claims of the biotech industry about the rigor of FDA oversight and the proven safety of its own products. It gives the FDA nothing to be proud of nor does it give the biotech industry anything to brag about. But it does give all consumers something to be very concerned about.

2.1.3.3 The Regulation of Genetically Engineered Foods

The use of Starlink corn began a controversy about the use of engineered foods in the Fall 2000, when a member of the Friends of the Earth, part of the coalition of groups opposed to genetically engineered foods, went to a Safeway grocery store in Silver Spring, Maryland and collected corn products for analysis. One of the twenty-three products showed the presence of the DNA strand for the production of the Bt protein, Cry9C. While the Cry1A group of Bt proteins had been approved by the U.S. EPA and FDA, Cry9C, in Starlink corn, had been approved only for animal feed use. The presence of Cry9C, as well as Cry1A proteins in Starlink, gave it added protection against insect pests, but also resulted in a plant with higher levels of toxicity than in previously approved plants.

The finding of the Cry9C DNA in Kraft's Taco Bell taco shells was released to the news media on September 18, 2000 and an investigation ensued. Aventis, the producer of the Starlink variety bought over a million test kits for detecting the presence of Star-link corn, and farmers throughout the nation were contacted and cautioned about the mixing of their corn production.

Attorney Generals in the sixteen major corn-growing states including Iowa, which made up 39% of the Starlink production in 2000, began to look to Aventis for compensation to the farmers for their lost profits. Concerns about liability to farmers for the use of their corn after it is sold is a significant issue which farmers have raised. Further, seed manufacturers require grower agreements which may create further liability for farmers if their crop is used illegally, even after the seed has left their control. In March 2001, EPA issued guidance ending the split registration—approved feed uses for animals, but not for human consumption—stating that StarLink would "no longer be considered a regulator option for products of biotechnology."

Starlink is regulated under both the authority of EPA and the FDA. FIFRA is the statutory authority, which is implemented by EPA through the use of labels which denote genetically altered material as "plant-incorporated protectants." "Plant-incorporated protectants" are regulated based upon the definition of a pesticide under FIFRA, which encompasses both chemical or biological methods of insect or pest control. FDA regulates foods based on the presence of these pesticides in the food. Under the Food, Drug and Cosmetic Act, the FDA regulates these GMOs where they result in "pesticide residues in feed and food," because of the inserted genes' continued presence in the food.

The damage caused by the StarLink controversy was litigated in part on a theory of tort liability, which is discussed *infra* in Chapter Ten, Biotechnology and Tort Law.

The following excerpt describes the regulation of genetically engineered food through the statutory authorities of EPA and FDA.

In practice, the Coordinated Framework places the burden on USDA to ascertain "whether GMOs are 'safe to grow,'" on EPA to "ensure[] that GMOs are 'safe for the environment,'" and on FDA to "determine[s] whether they are 'safe to eat.'"

A. *USDA*

USDA has authority over genetically modified crops under the Plant Protection Act ("PPA"). PPA provides USDA with rather narrow authority to investigate GMOs. Under this Act, USDA can regulate the "movement of organisms that may endanger plant life, and to prevent the introduction, dissemination or establishment of such organisms."

USDA deals with genetically modified crops in two different ways. If a genetically modified crop "uses genetic material from a known plant pest," the agency issues a permit. A USDA permit, however, is not required for crops not using "genetic material from a known plant pest." In this second case, the party using the crops is required to give USDA "advance notice of intent to conduct field trials." USDA then has the authority to refuse to grant authorization, but if it fails to act, authorization is presumed.

USDA also has the authority to identify genetically modified crops as "non-regulated." The developer of the crop can petition USDA for this status. Before granting the petition, the agency must decide that the crop is not a plant pest risk and conduct an Environmental Assessment. There are no USDA restrictions on crops that are "non-regulated." Therefore, USDA's regulation of genetically modified crops extends only to those that use known plant pests. USDA is only obliged to issue permits for, and therefore is only obliged to do a comprehensive examination of, genetically modified crops that use known plant pests.

B. *EPA*

EPA regulates genetically modified organisms primarily under FIFRA. FIFRA regulates pesticide labeling and registration. It authorizes EPA to evaluate genetically modified organisms with "pesticidal properties." FIFRA requires any party intending to market pesticides commercially to register with EPA. This process is supposed to ensure that the product will not cause "unreasonable adverse effects on the environment." As Professor Rebecca Bratspies points out, "absolute safety is not the goal. 'Unreasonable' (and therefore forbidden) risk falls somewhere in the realm of harm that is not certain and risk that is not de minimus." It is significant to note that FIFRA grants EPA power "to exempt whole classes of pesticides" if it concludes that the pesticide is "of a character which is unnecessary to be subject to this [Act]."

EPA also regulates genetically modified plants that contain pesticide chemicals under the federal Food Drug and Cosmetic Act ("FDCA"). Under FDCA, EPA must either set tolerance levels for pesticide residues in foods or create exemptions from the tolerance levels. EPA, relying on the aforementioned "substantial equivalence doctrine," has created "broad categorical exemptions" for several genetically modified organisms. EPA exempted many genetically modified foods after "concluding that [they] did not endanger public health" and "that there was a reasonable certainty that 'aggregate dietary exposure to these modifications' would not cause harm." Overall, EPA has broad discretion regarding the regulation of genetically modified organisms.

C. *FDA*

FDCA also gives FDA authority to regulate genetically modified organisms. Under FDCA, FDA regulates genetically modified foods through provisions that allow it to prohibit "adulterated foods." An "adulterated food" is a food that "bears or contains any poisonous or deleterious substance which may render it injurious to health." FDA's policy towards genetically modified foods, in line with the "substantial equivalence doctrine," is that they are not inherently dangerous; it regulates genetically modified foods in the same manner as regular foods.

Although FDA otherwise would have jurisdiction over genetically modified plants, such as StarLink, that contain pesticidal properties, the agency specifically relinquished this authority in 1992. FDA handed over all regulatory authority concerning genetically modified plants with pesticidal characteristics to EPA. FDA and EPA concluded that "such plants are in fact pesticides and thus subject to EPA's exclusive jurisdiction." The policy statement on the matter admitted that "there may be cases in which the jurisdictional responsibility for a substance is not clear." Confusingly, EPA does not classify plants genetically modified to be resistant to chemical herbicides as pesticides. Therefore, these types of GMOs fall only under FDA's jurisdiction.

Even more confusingly, FDA biotechnology regulation grants a great deal of discretion to manufacturers. FDA regulates genetically modified foods under its authority to regulate food additives. A "food additive," however, is only regulated if the substance "is not generally recognized, among experts qualified by

scientific training and experience to evaluate its safety, as having been adequately shown through scientific procedures … to be safe under the conditions
of its intended use.…" Therefore, many ingredients are not reviewed because
they are labeled "generally recognized as safe" ("GRAS"). FDA, in determining
if a product is GRAS, determines if "there is a consensus of expert opinion regarding the safety of the use of the substance." The manufacturer has significant influence on this determination.

Linda Beebe, *Symposium Issue II Pesticides: What Will the Future Reap? Note: In re
Starlink Corn: The Link between Genetically Damaged Crops and an Inadequate Regu-
latory Frame Work for Biotechnology*, 28 WM. & MARY ENVTL. L. & POL'Y REV. 511
(Winter 2004).

2.1.3.4 Constitutional First Amendment Limitations in State Labeling Regulations

State regulation requiring the use of labeling to provide information to consumers is
another approach which was tested to satisfy the public concerns about biotechnology.
However, the realistic aspect of the fear raises concerns about the stated legislative purpose in the following case and raises First Amendment "right not to speak" protections.

International Dairy Foods Association v. Amestoy, Attorney General of the State of Vermont
92 F.3d 67 (2d Cir. 1996)

Judges Altimari, McLaughlin and Leval

Altimari, *Circuit Judge:*

Plaintiffs-appellants International Dairy Foods Association, Milk Industry Foundation (MIF), International Ice Cream Association, National Cheese Institute, Grocery
Manufacturers of America, Inc. and National Food Processors Association (collectively
"appellants" or "dairy manufacturers") appeal from a decision of the district court
(Murtha, C.J.), denying their motion for a preliminary injunction. The dairy manufacturers challenged the constitutionality of Vt. Stat. Ann. tit. 6, §§ 2754(c) which requires
dairy manufacturers to identify products which were, or might have been, derived from
dairy cows treated with a synthetic growth hormone used to increase milk production.
The dairy manufacturers alleged that the statute violated the United States Constitution's First Amendment and Commerce Clause.

Because we find that the district court abused its discretion in failing to grant preliminary injunctive relief to the dairy manufacturers on First Amendment grounds, we reverse and remand.

Background

In 1993, the federal Food and Drug Administration ("FDA") approved the use of recombinant Bovine Somatotropin ("rBST") (also known as recombinant Bovine Growth
Hormone ("rGBH")), a synthetic growth hormone that increases milk production by
cows. It is undisputed that the dairy products derived from herds treated with rBST are
indistinguishable from products derived from untreated herds; consequently, the FDA

declined to require the labeling of products derived from cows receiving the supplemental hormone.

In April 1994, defendant-appellee the State of Vermont ("Vermont") enacted a statute requiring that "if rBST has been used in the production of milk or a milk product for retail sale in this state, the retail milk or milk product shall be labeled as such." The State of Vermont's Commissioner of Agriculture ("Commissioner") subsequently promulgated regulations giving those dairy manufacturers who use rBST four labeling options, among them the posting of a sign to the following effect in any store selling dairy products:

rBST INFORMATION

THE PRODUCTS IN THIS CASE THAT CONTAIN OR MAY CONTAIN MILK FROM rBST-TREATED COWS EITHER (1) STATE ON THE PACKAGE THAT rBST HAS BEEN OR MAY HAVE BEEN USED, OR (2) ARE IDENTIFIED BY A BLUE SHELF LABEL LIKE THIS

[BLUE RECTANGLE]
OR (3) A BLUE STICKER ON THE PACKAGE LIKE THIS. [BLUE DOT]

The United States Food and Drug Administration has determined that there is no significant difference between milk from treated and untreated cows. It is the law of Vermont that products made from the milk of rBST-treated cows be labeled to help consumers make informed shopping decisions. (6 V.S.A. Section 2754)

Failure to comply with the statute and companion regulations subjects manufacturers to civil, as well as criminal penalties.

Appellants filed suit in April 1994, asserting that the statute was unconstitutional. In June 1995, the dairy manufacturers moved for preliminary injunctive relief, seeking to enjoin enforcement of the statute. The dairy manufacturers alleged that the Vermont statute (1) infringed their protected rights under the First Amendment to the Constitution and (2) violated the Constitution's Commerce Clause, U.S. Const., Art. 1, §§ 8. Following an extensive hearing, the United States District Court for the District of Vermont (Murtha, *C.J.*), denied appellants' motion. The dairy manufacturers now appeal.

Because we find that the dairy manufacturers are entitled to an injunction on First Amendment grounds, we do not reach their claims made pursuant to the Commerce Clause.

Discussion

Generally, preliminary injunctive relief is appropriate when the movant shows "(a) irreparable harm and (b) either (1) likelihood of success on the merits or (2) sufficiently serious questions going to the merits to make them a fair ground for litigation and a balance of hardships tipping decidedly toward the party requesting the preliminary relief." ... ("Before a preliminary injunction will be granted in this Circuit, it must pass one of two tests. Both require a showing of irreparable harm."), However, because the injunction at issue stays "government action taken in the public interest pursuant to a statutory ... scheme," this Court has determined that the movant must satisfy the more rigorous "likelihood of success prong."

We review the district court's denial of a preliminary injunction for an abuse of discretion, and will reverse the district court only if it relied on clearly erroneous findings of fact, misapprehended the law, or erred in formulating the injunction.

1. Irreparable Harm

Focusing principally on the economic impact of the labeling regulation, the district court found that appellants had not demonstrated irreparable harm to any right protected by the First Amendment. We disagree.

Irreparable harm is "injury for which a monetary award cannot be adequate compensation." ... It is established that "the loss of First Amendment freedoms, for even minimal periods of time, unquestionably constitutes irreparable injury." ... Because the statute at issue requires appellants to make an involuntary statement whenever they offer their products for sale, we find that the statute causes the dairy manufacturers irreparable harm.

[T]he district court rejected this claim, stating that:

"the assertion of First Amendment rights does not automatically require a finding of irreparable injury, thus entitling a plaintiff to a preliminary injunction if he shows a likelihood of success on the merits."

Ordinarily, it is the purposeful suppression of speech which constitutes irreparable harm. Compliance with the Vermont Labeling Law does not prohibit the plaintiffs from disseminating a message. Instead, it requires the plaintiffs to truthfully disclose the method used in producing their product. Under these circumstances, the Court does not find that the plaintiffs' assertion of a First Amendment violation leads ineluctably to the conclusion that they will suffer irreparable harm.

We conclude, however, that the manufacturers have carried their burden of establishing irreparable harm. The wrong done by the labeling law to the dairy manufacturers' constitutional right *not* to speak is a serious one that was not given proper weight by the district court. "We begin with the proposition that the right of freedom of thought protected by the First Amendment against state action includes both the right to speak freely and the right to refrain from speaking at all."; "involuntary affirmation could be commanded only on even more immediate and urgent grounds than silence"; recognizing, along with freedom to express one's views publicly, "'concomitant freedom *not* to speak publicly'" ...

The right not to speak inheres in political and commercial speech alike ... If, however, as Vermont maintains, its labeling law compels appellants to engage in purely commercial speech, the statute must meet a less rigorous test. *See Central Hudson Gas & Elec. Corp. v. Public Serv. Comm'r*, ... ("The Constitution ... accords a lesser protection to commercial speech than to other constitutionally guaranteed expression."). The dairy manufacturers insist that the speech is not purely commercial because it compels them "to convey a message regarding the significance of rBST use that is 'expressly contrary to' their views." ... Agreeing with Vermont, the district court found that the speech was commercial in nature.

We need not resolve this controversy at this point; even assuming that the compelled disclosure is purely commercial speech, appellants have amply demonstrated that the First Amendment is sufficiently implicated to cause irreparable harm. *See* (First Amendment implicated by mandatory assessment on almond handlers to fund almond marketing program); *United States v. Frame* ... (3d Cir. 1989) (federal Beef Promotion & Research Act implicated beef producer's right to refrain from speaking because it required that producer help fund commercial message to which producer did not necessarily subscribe), ... *Cf. National Comm'n on Egg Nutrition*, ... (modifying remedial order provision that required egg producers "to argue the other side of the controversy, thus interfering unnecessarily with the effective presentation of the pro-egg position."). The dairy manufacturers have clearly done more than simply "assert" their First Amendment rights: The statute in question indisputably requires them to speak when they would rather not.... Because compelled speech "contravenes core First Amendment values," appellants have "satisfied the initial requirement for securing injunctive relief."

In *Central Hudson*, the Supreme Court articulated a four-part analysis for determining whether a government restriction on commercial speech is permissible.... We need not address the controversy concerning the nature of the speech in question—commercial or political—because we find that Vermont fails to meet the less stringent constitutional requirements applicable to compelled commercial speech.

Under *Central Hudson*, we must determine: (1) whether the expression concerns lawful activity and is not misleading; (2) whether the government's interest is substantial; (3) whether the labeling law directly serves the asserted interest; and (4) whether the labeling law is no more extensive than necessary.... Furthermore, the State of Vermont bears the burden of justifying its labeling law.... As the Supreme Court has made clear, "this burden is not satisfied by mere speculation or conjecture; rather, a governmental body seeking to sustain a restriction on commercial speech must demonstrate that the harms it recites are real and that its restriction will in fact alleviate them to a material degree." ...

> In our view, Vermont has failed to establish the second prong of the *Central Hudson* test, namely that its interest is substantial. In making this determination, we rely only upon those interests set forth by Vermont before the district court.... As the district court made clear, Vermont "does not claim that health or safety concerns prompted the passage of the Vermont Labeling Law," but instead defends the statute on the basis of "strong consumer interest and the public's 'right to know'...." 898 F. Supp. at 249. These interests are insufficient to justify compromising protected constitutional rights.[1]

Vermont's failure to defend its constitutional intrusion on the ground that it negatively impacts public health is easily understood. After exhaustive studies, the FDA has "concluded that rBST has no appreciable effect on the composition of milk produced by treated cows, and that there are no human safety or health concerns associated with food products derived from cows treated with rBST." ... Because bovine somatotropin ("BST") appears naturally in cows, and because there are no BST receptors in a cow's mammary glands, only trace amounts of BST can be detected in milk, whether or not the cows received the supplement. Moreover, it is undisputed that neither consumers nor scientists can distinguish rBST-derived milk from milk produced by an untreated cow. Indeed, the already extensive record in this case contains no scientific evidence from which an objective observer could conclude that rBST has any impact at all on dairy products. It is thus plain that Vermont could not justify the statute on the basis of "real" harms....

---

1. Although the dissent suggests several interests that if adopted by the state of Vermont may have been substantial, the district court opinion makes clear that Vermont adopted no such rationales for its statute. Rather, Vermont's sole expressed interest was, indeed, "consumer curiosity." The district court plainly stated that, "Vermont takes no position on whether rBST is beneficial or detrimental. However," the district court explained, "Vermont has determined that its consumers want to know whether rBST has been used in the production of their milk and milk products." 898 F. Supp. at 252 (emphasis added). It is clear from the opinion below that the state itself has not adopted the concerns of the consumers; it has only adopted that the consumers are concerned. Unfortunately, mere consumer concern is not, in itself, a substantial interest.

We do not doubt that Vermont's asserted interest, the demand of its citizenry for such information, is genuine; reluctantly, however, we conclude that it is inadequate. We are aware of no case in which consumer interest alone was sufficient to justify requiring a product's manufacturers to publish the functional equivalent of a warning about a production method that has no discernable impact on a final product....

Although the Court is sympathetic to the Vermont consumers who wish to know which products may derive from rBST-treated herds, their desire is insufficient to permit the State of Vermont to compel the dairy manufacturers to speak against their will. Were consumer interest alone sufficient, there is no end to the information that states could require manufacturers to disclose about their production methods. For instance, with respect to cattle, consumers might reasonably evince an interest in knowing which grains herds were fed, with which medicines they were treated, or the age at which they were slaughtered. Absent, however, some indication that this information bears on a reasonable concern for human health or safety or some other sufficiently substantial governmental concern, the manufacturers cannot be compelled to disclose it. Instead, those consumers interested in such information should exercise the power of their purses by buying products from manufacturers who voluntarily reveal it.

Accordingly, we hold that consumer curiosity alone is not a strong enough state interest to sustain the compulsion of even an accurate, factual statement, ... (compelled disclosure of "fact" is no more acceptable than compelled disclosure of opinion), in a commercial context. *See, e.g., United States v. Sullivan* ... (1948) (upholding federal law requiring warning labels on "*harmful* foods, drugs and cosmetics") *see also Zauderer* ... (disclosure requirements are permissible "as long as [they] are reasonably related to the State's interest in preventing deception of consumers.") ... Because Vermont has demonstrated no cognizable harms, its statute is likely to be held unconstitutional.

Conclusion

Because appellants have demonstrated both irreparable harm and a likelihood of success on the merits, the judgment of the district court is reversed, and the case is remanded for entry of an appropriate injunction.

DISSENT by Leval, Circuit Judge:

I respectfully dissent. Vermont's regulation requiring disclosure of use of rBST in milk production was based on substantial state interests, including worries about rBST's impact on human and cow health, fears for the survival of small dairy farms, and concerns about the manipulation of nature through biotechnology. The objective of the plaintiff milk producers is to conceal their use of rBST from consumers. The policy of the First Amendment, in its application to commercial speech, is to favor the flow of accurate, relevant information. The majority's invocation of the First Amendment to invalidate a state law requiring disclosure of information consumers reasonably desire stands the Amendment on its ear. In my view, the district court correctly found that plaintiffs were unlikely to succeed in proving Vermont's law unconstitutional.

Background

Because many of the most important facts of this case are omitted from the majority's opinion, I briefly review the facts.

Recent advances in genetic technologies led to the development of a synthetically isolated metabolic protein hormone known as recombinant bovine somatotropin (rBST), which, when injected into cows, increases their milk production. Monsanto Company, an amicus in this action on the side of the plaintiff milk producers, has developed the only commercially approved form of rBST and markets it under the brand name "Posilac." This is, of course, at the frontiers of bio-science. A 1994 federal government study of rBST describes it as "one of the first major commercial biotechnology products to be used in the U.S. food and agricultural sector and the first to attract significant attention." Executive Branch of the Federal Government, Use of Bovine Somatotropin (BST) in the United States: Its Potential Effects (January 1994) [hereafter "Federal Study"] …

The United States Food and Drug Administration ("FDA") and others have studied rBST extensively. Based on its study, the FDA authorized commercial use of rBST on November 5, 1993, concluding that "milk and meat from [rBST-treated] cows is safe" for human consumption.

The impending use of rBST caused substantial controversy throughout the country. The Federal Study reports, based on numerous surveys, that consumers favor the labeling of milk produced by use of rBST. In Vermont, a state highly attuned to issues affecting the dairy industry, use of rBST was the subject of frequent press commentary and debate, and provoked considerable opposition. In response to public pressure, the state of Vermont enacted a law requiring that "if rBST has been used in the production of milk or a milk product for retail sale in this state, the retail milk or milk product shall be labeled as such." 6 V.S.A. §§2754(c). The statute authorized Vermont's Commissioner of Agriculture to adopt implementing rules. Id. at §§2754(d). The Department of Agriculture, Food and Markets (hereafter "the Agriculture Department") proceeded to adopt the regulations described in the majority opinion, which essentially require manufacturers to identify dairy products produced with rBST with a blue dot, and retailers to display a sign telling consumers that the blue-dotted products "contain milk from rBST-treated cows" and that the FDA "has determined that there is no significant difference between milk from treated and untreated cows." The sign concludes that the law of Vermont requires that the information be given "to help consumers make informed shopping decisions."

The interests which Vermont sought to advance by its statute and regulations were explained in the Agriculture Department's Economic Impact Statement accompanying its regulations. The Statement reported that consumer interest in disclosure of use of rBST was based on "concerns about FDA determinations about the product as regards health and safety or about recombinant gene technology"; concerns "about the effect of the product on bovine health"; and "concerns about the effect of the product on the existing surplus of milk and in the dairy farm industry's economic status and well-being." This finding was based on "consumer comments to Vermont legislative committees" and to the Department, as well as published reports and letters to the editors published in the press.

The state offered survey evidence which demonstrated similar public concern. Comments by Vermont citizens who had heard or read about rBST were overwhelmingly negative. The most prevalent responses to rBST use included: "Not natural," "More research needs to be done/Long-term effects not clear," "Against additives added to my milk," "Worried about adverse health effects," "Unhealthy for the cow," "Don't need more chemicals," "It's a hormone/Against hormones added to my milk," "Hurts the small dairy farmer," "Producing enough milk already."

On the basis of this evidence the district court found that a majority of Vermonters "do not want to purchase milk products derived from rBST-treated cows," … and that the reasons included:

(1) They consider the use of a genetically-engineered hormone in the production unnatural; (2) they believe that use of the hormone will result in increased milk produc-

tion and lower milk prices, thereby hurting small dairy farmers; (3) they believe that the use of rBST is harmful to cows and potentially harmful to humans; and, (4) they feel that there is a lack of knowledge regarding the long-term effects of rBST.

The court thus understandably concluded that "Vermont has a substantial interest in informing consumers of the use of rBST in the production of milk and dairy products sold in the state."

Discussion

A. The Majority Opinion

In the face of this evidence and these explicit findings by the district court, the majority oddly concludes that Vermont's sole interest in requiring disclosure of rBST use is to gratify "consumer curiosity," and that this alone "is not a strong enough state interest to sustain the compulsion of even an accurate factual statement." Maj. Op. at 12. The majority seeks to justify its conclusion in three ways.

First, it simply disregards the evidence of Vermont's true interests and the district court's findings recognizing those interests. Nowhere does the majority opinion discuss or even mention the evidence or findings regarding the people of Vermont's concerns about human health, cow health, biotechnology, and the survival of small dairy farms.

Second, the majority distorts the meaning of the district court opinion. It relies substantially on Judge Murtha's statement that Vermont "does not claim that health or safety concerns prompted the passage of the Vermont Labeling Law," but "bases its justification ... on strong consumer interest and the public's 'right to know'."... The majority takes this passage out of context. The district court's opinion went on, as quoted above, to explain the concerns that underlie the interest of Vermont's citizenry. Unquestionably the district court found, and the evidence showed, that the interests of the citizenry that led to the passage of the law include health and safety concerns, among others. In the light of the district judge's further explicit findings, it is clear that his statement could not mean what the majority concludes.[2] More likely, what Judge Murtha meant was that Vermont does not claim to know whether rBST is harmful. And when he asserted that Vermont's rule was passed to vindicate "strong consumer interest and the public's right to know," this could not mean that the public's interest was based on nothing but "curiosity," because the judge expressly found that the consumer interest was based on health, economic, and ethical concerns.

Third, the majority suggests that, because the FDA has not found health risks in this new procedure, health worries could not be considered "real" or "cognizable." ...

I find this proposition alarming and dangerous; at the very least, it is extraordinarily unrealistic. Genetic and biotechnological manipulation of basic food products is new and controversial. Although I have no reason to doubt that the FDA's studies of

---

2. Indeed had the judge really intended such a finding, it would be unsupportable in view of the evidence that the concerns of the citizenry were communicated to the legislature. When the citizens of a state express concerns to the legislature and the state's lawmaking bodies then pass disclosure requirements in response to those expressed concerns, it seems clear (without need for a statutory declaration of purpose) that the state is acting to vindicate the concerns expressed by its citizens, and not merely to gratify their "curiosity." Vermont need not, furthermore, take the position that rBST is harmful to require its disclosure because of potential health risks. The mere fact that it does not know whether rBST poses hazards is sufficient reason to justify disclosure by reason of the unknown potential for harm.

rBST have been thorough, they could not cover long-term effects of rBST on humans.... Furthermore, there are many possible reasons why a government agency might fail to find real health risks, including inadequate time and budget for testing, insufficient advancement of scientific techniques, insufficiently large sampling populations, pressures from industry, and simple human error. To suggest that a government agency's failure to find a health risk in a short-term study of a new genetic technology should bar a state from requiring simple disclosure of the use of that technology where its citizens are concerned about such health risks would be unreasonable and dangerous. Although the FDA's conclusions may be reassuring, they do not guarantee the safety of rBST.

Forty years ago, when I (and nearly everyone) smoked, no one told us that we might be endangering our health. Tobacco is but one of many consumer products once considered safe, which were subsequently found to cause health hazards. The limitations of scientific information about new consumer products were well illustrated in a 1990 study produced at the request of Congress by the General Accounting Office. Looking at various prescription drugs available on the market, the study examined the risks associated with the drugs that became known only after they were approved by the FDA, and concluded:

Even after approval, many additional risks may surface when the general population is exposed to a drug. These risks, which range from relatively minor (such as nausea and headache) to serious (such as hospitalization and death) arise from the fact that preapproval drug testing is inherently limited.

....

In studying the frequency and seriousness of risks identified after approval, GAO found that of the 198 drugs approved by FDA between 1976 and 1985 for which data were available, 102 (or 51.5 percent) had serious postapproval risks, as evidenced by labeling changes or withdrawal from the market. All but six of these drugs ... are deemed by FDA to have benefits that outweigh their risks. The serious postapproval risks are adverse reactions that could lead to hospitalization ... severe or permanent disability, or death.

GAO Report, "FDA Drug Review: Postapproval Risks, 1976–85," April 1990, at 2–3. As startling as its results may seem, this study merely confirms a common sense proposition: namely, that a government agency's conclusion regarding a product's safety, reached after limited study, is not a guarantee and does not invalidate public concern for unknown side effects.

In short, the majority has no valid basis for its conclusion that Vermont's regulation advances no interest other than the gratification of consumer curiosity, and involves neither health concerns nor other substantial interests.

B. Substantial State Interests

Freedom of speech is not an absolute right, particularly in the commercial context. In Central Hudson Gas v. Public Service Comm'n of New York ... the Supreme Court announced standards for governmental regulation of commercial speech. At the outset, commercial speech enjoys no First Amendment protection at all unless it is not misleading (and relates to lawful activity). If the speech passes that test, it is nonetheless subject to regulation if the government has a substantial interest in regulating the speech, the regulation directly advances that interest, and it is no more intrusive than necessary to accomplish its goal.... The Supreme Court later clarified that government's power to regulate commercial speech includes the power to compel such speech. Zauderer v. Office of Disciplinary Counsel (upholding state law requiring attorneys who advertised contingent fee services to disclose specific details about how contingent fee would be calculated and to state that certain costs might be borne by the client even in the event of loss).

Except for its conclusion that Vermont had no substantial interest to support its labeling law, the majority finds no fault with the district court's application of these governing standards. Nor do I. Accordingly, the sole issue is whether Vermont had a substantial interest in compelling the disclosure of use of rBST in milk production.

In my view, Vermont's multifaceted interest, outlined above, is altogether substantial. Consumer worries about possible adverse health effects from consumption of rBST, especially over a long term, is unquestionably a substantial interest. As to health risks to cows, the concern is supported by the warning label on Posilac, which states that cows injected with the product are at an increased risk for: various reproductive disorders, "clinical mastitis [udder infections] (visibly abnormal milk)," "digestive disorders such as indigestion, bloat, and diarrhea," "enlarged hocks and lesions," and "swellings" that may be permanent. As to the economic impact of increased milk production, caused by injection of rBST, upon small dairy farmers, the evidence included a U.S. Department of Agriculture economist's written claim that, "if rBST is heavily adopted and milk prices are reduced, at least some of the smaller farmers that do not use rBST might be forced out of the dairy business, because they would not be producing economically sufficient volumes of milk." Public philosophical objection to biotechnological mutation is familiar and widespread.

Any one of these concerns may well suffice to make Vermont's interest substantial; all four, taken together, undoubtedly constitute a substantial governmental justification for Vermont's labeling law.

Indeed, the majority does not contend otherwise. Nowhere does the majority assert that these interests are not substantial. As noted above, the majority justifies its conclusion of absence of a substantial interest by its assertion that Vermont advanced no interest other than consumer curiosity, a conclusion that is contradicted by both the record and the district court's findings.

The Supreme Court has upheld governmental impositions on commercial speech in numerous instances where the governmental interest was no more substantial than those advanced here by Vermont. See Florida Bar v. Went For It, Inc.... (upholding 30-day waiting period for lawyers' solicitation of business from accident victims because of state's interests in promoting privacy ...) ...

C. Plaintiffs' Contentions

Plaintiffs rely on invalid arguments and authorities that are easily distinguishable. In Ibanez v. Florida Dep't of Business & Professional Regulation, 512 U.S. 136, 129 L. Ed. 2d 118, 114 S. Ct. 2084 (1994), the Supreme Court struck down a disciplinary sanction based on a law requiring one who advertised as a "Certified Financial Planner" to disclose in the advertising that her certification came from an unofficial private organization, rather than from the state. The Court found the state's purported interest—the likelihood of consumer confusion—to be "purely hypothetical." ... Plaintiffs contend that Vermont's health concerns are similarly "hypothetical" because there is no demonstrated health risk in rBST. This misreads the Supreme Court's meaning. The point in Ibanez was that there was no demonstration that Florida's citizenry was confused or cared whether a financial planner's certification was from a private organization or the state. Here, it was clearly shown that Vermont's citizens want rBST disclosure.[4] ...

The milk producers argue that because the sign which Vermont's law requires retailers to post goes beyond disclosure of rBST use and makes statements about it, they, like the fund raisers in Riley, are entitled to the full protection of the First Amendment, rather than the more limited protection afforded to commercial speech. They contend that the disclosure required of them is "inextricably intertwined" with fully protected speech.... Because the blue dot they affix to their milk containers is linked to the sign retailers post in the stores, they also contend they are forced to subscribe to a message on that sign with which they do not agree.

This argument is merely a contrivance. In the first place, apart from disclosing use of rBST, Vermont's law imposes no speech requirements on the plaintiff milk producers. It is the retailers who are obligated to post signs containing text that relates to the rBST process....

Second, the text posted by retailers under Vermont's law is innocuous. Apart from enabling the consumer to tell which products derive from rBST-treated cows, the only additional required text states:

> The United States Food and Drug Administration has determined that there is no significant difference between milk from treated and untreated cows. It is the law of Vermont that products made from the milk of rBSt-treated cows be labeled to help consumers make informed shopping decisions.

The producers cannot contend they disagree with the first sentence, whose only function is to reassure consumers that the FDA found no health hazard in rBST products.[5] They focus rather on the second sentence, asserting that they disagree with the proposition that "informed shopping decisions" are advanced by disclosure of rBST treatment because they contend it is irrelevant to any legitimate consumer concern. Their argument has no force. The "informed shopping decisions" statement is clearly identified as made by the state of Vermont, not by the milk producers. Furthermore, the statement is virtually meaningless and harmless, especially following the sentence stating that the FDA found no significant difference between milk from treated and untreated cows. The producers cannot even contend that they are obligated by Vermont's regulation to enter into debate....

It is quite clear that the producers' real objection is to the mandatory revelation of the use of rBST, which many Vermonters disfavor, and not to the bland sentence announcing that products are labeled "to help consumers make informed shopping decisions."

----

4. The evidence included a cartoon, published in the Burlington Free Press: in frame 1, a man declares his confidence in the safety of rBST milk; in frame 2, he drinks the milk; in frame 3, he turns into a werewolf. Plaintiffs cite this cartoon as a demonstration that the concerns of Vermonters are fantastical. They overlook the fact that the cartoon is a joke. But like most jokes it has a basis in reality. The cartoon does not mean that Vermonters think rBST will turn them into werewolves. What it reflects is that, notwithstanding the FDA's assurances, consumers are worried about the effects of rBST.

5. Indeed, a statistical sampling shows that this labeling makes milk from rBST-treated cows more acceptable to Vermont consumers. Before reading this sign, 86% of respondents preferred milk from untreated cows; after reading the sign, preference for milk from untreated cows fell to 73%.

D. Disclosure v. Concealment

Notwithstanding their self-righteous references to free expression, the true objective of the milk producers is concealment. They do not wish consumers to know that their milk products were produced by use of rBST because there are consumers who, for various reasons, prefer to avoid rBST. Vermont, on the other hand, has established a labeling requirement whose sole objective (and whose sole effect) is to inform Vermont consumers whether milk products offered for sale were produced with rBST.[6] The dispute under the First Amendment is over whether the milk producers' interest in concealing their use of rBST from consumers will prevail over a state law designed to give consumers the information they desire. The question is simply whether the First Amendment prohibits government from requiring disclosure of truthful relevant information to consumers.

In my view, the interest of the milk producers has little entitlement to protection under the First Amendment. The caselaw that has developed under the doctrine of commercial speech has repeatedly emphasized that the primary function of the First Amendment in its application to commercial speech is to advance truthful disclosure—the very interest that the milk producers seek to undermine.

The milk producers' invocation of the First Amendment for the purpose of concealing their use of rBST in milk production is entitled to scant recognition. They invoke the Amendment's protection to accomplish exactly what the Amendment opposes. And the majority's ruling deprives Vermont of the right to protect its consumers by requiring truthful disclosure on a subject of legitimate public concern....

I am comforted by two considerations: First, the precedential effect of the majority's ruling is quite limited. By its own terms, it applies only to cases where a state disclosure requirement is supported by no interest other than the gratification of consumer curiosity. In any case in which a state advanced something more, the majority's ruling would have no bearing....

Second, Vermont will have a further opportunity to defend its law. The majority's conclusion perhaps results from Vermont's failure to put forth sufficiently clear evidence of the interests it sought to advance....

Notes

1. Vermont's Legislature responded and passed legislation making the labeling of milk that was "BST-free" voluntary:

6 V.S.A. § 2 760. Substantial state interest

(a) Role of state government. The Vermont general assembly finds, as does the U.S. Food and Drug Administration, that the states under our federal system of

---

6. I disagree with the majority's contention, Maj. Op. at 12, that voluntary labeling by producers who do not use rBST can be relied on to effectuate Vermont's purpose. There is evidence that, notwithstanding the FDA's determination to permit such voluntary labeling, certain states, no doubt influenced by the rBST lobby, will "not allow any labeling concerning rBST." Affidavit of Ben Cohen, at 3–4. This effectively prevents multistate distributors from including such labeling on their packaging. Producers complying with Vermont's law do not face the same problem. The blue dot has meaning only in conjunction with the signs posted in Vermont retail establishments. Thus producers can inexpensively affix the blue dot without violating the laws of states that forbid all rBST labeling.

government have traditionally undertaken the role of overseeing milk production. The Vermont general assembly also finds that the intent of the U.S. Food and Drug Administration is to rely primarily on state governments to validate rbST labeling claims regarding milk and dairy products and to ensure that such claims are truthful and not misleading.

(b) State policy. It is the policy of this state:

(1) that Vermont citizens should have an opportunity to choose to consume milk or dairy products which have not had rbST used in their production ("rbST-free"), based on truthful and nonmisleading product labeling;

(2) that Vermont dairy product manufacturers who want to sell rbST-free products in Vermont or out of state should be able to do so, based on a state-sanctioned process for certifying rbST-free labeling claims;

(3) that the economic health and vitality of the Vermont dairy industry is critical to the health of the overall Vermont economy, which depends in part on the high reputation of Vermont farmers and their dairy products, and the associated good-will toward other Vermont enterprises, and that this economic asset should not be jeopardized by consumer doubts about the integrity of Vermont milk or dairy products caused by false, misleading or unverifiable rbST-free labeling claims; and

(4) to support the right of Vermont dairy farmers to choose to use rbST, and of rbST manufacturers and suppliers to sell their product to Vermont dairy farmers.

(c) Substantial state interest. Therefore, the Vermont general assembly:

(1) finds a substantial state interest in ensuring the availability of milk and dairy product labeling information that is accurate and nonmisleading, and in which Vermont and out-of-state consumers can place their confidence; and

(2) seeks to serve this interest through this subchapter by:

(A) authorizing a program of voluntary labeling of milk and dairy products which have not had rbST used in their production; and

(B) providing for the verification of claims that rbST has not been used in the production of milk or dairy products offered for sale in Vermont; but

(C) without unduly intruding into the businesses of Vermont dairy farmers who choose to use rbST, or of rbST manufacturers or suppliers who choose to sell their product to Vermont dairy farmers. (Added 1997, No. 154 (Adj. Sess.), §1, eff. April 29, 1998.

2. On November 16, 1999, the Genetically Engineered Food Right To Know Act was introduced in the House of Representatives. The bill proposed amending FDCA, the Federal Meat Inspection Act, and the Poultry Products Inspection Act, to require food that contains a genetically engineered material, or that is produced with a genetically engineered material, be labeled accordingly. *See* H.R. 3377, 106th Cong. (1999). Is this advisable?

3. A scientist in Germany has created a genetically engineered rice plant, called "yellow rice," which includes the DNA code for producing Vitamin A. This rice is intended to supplement the diet of millions of people who primarily eat rice, and have Vitamin A deficiencies. Many groups are opposing the widespread use of this rice. What are the policy and legal issues which might be considered in making a determination as to whether this rice should be used?

2.1.4 U.S. Environmental Protection Agency and Department of Agriculture: Genetically Engineered Plants

Genetically engineered plants have raised concerns primarily for their use as food, but the other concerns involve the risk to ecological systems.

On May 20, 1999, an article appeared in NATURE suggesting that there could be a potential environmental problem with genetically engineered crops. John Losey, Cornell University, reported in this article that Bt corn was deadly for Monarch butterfly larvae. This created a new focus for groups fearing the effects of engineered plants placed in the ecosystem.

March 15, 2001, the U.S. Environmental Protection Agency's Independent Panel on Biotechnology released their report on the reassessment of the Bt corn, cotton, and potato plants. The U.S. EPA registrations for corn and cotton Bt products (plant incorporated protectants) expired September 2001. This time-sensitive conditional permit was designed to allow the U.S. EPA to evaluate the effects on human health and the environment.

The report concluded that an environmental impact statement under NEPA should include a consideration of risk, and a determination as to whether the methods used are sufficient to mitigate gene flow between feral and Bt crops. Standards for isolation distance were modified and greater borders were recommended for the protection of feral crops from the Bt crops. The Panel also considered whether a Section 7 consultation with the Department of Interior under the Endangered Species Act was necessary. The Panel concluded that the formal consultation was unnecessary but an informal consultation would be recommended. In summary, the Panel found no significant risk to human health or the environment and made recommendations for improvements in the current management scheme.

The following cases challenge a federal action based upon the environmental impact statement considered pursuant to the National Environmental Policy Act (NEPA).

Foundation on Economic Trends v. Thomas
637 F.Supp. 25 (D.D.C., 1986)

District Judge Thomas F. Hogan.

Plaintiffs, various individuals and non-profit environmental organizations, seek injunctive relief against the Environmental Protection Agency's ("EPA") issuance of an experimental use permit ("EUP") to Advanced Genetic Sciences, Inc. ("AGS"), which authorized AGS to conduct a field test of bacteria strains altered by recombinant DNA technology. Plaintiffs contend that the EPA's issuance of the permit violated the requirements of the Federal Insecticide, Fungicide and Rodenticide Act, 7 U.S.C. §§§§ 136–136y ("FIFRA"), the National Environmental Policy Act, 42 U.S.C. §§§§ 4321, et seq. ("NEPA"), and the Administrative Procedure Act, 5 U.S.C. §§ 706(2)(A) ("APA"). Industrial Biotechnology Association ("IBA"), of which AGS is a member, was permitted to intervene as a defendant. The case is before the Court on plaintiffs' motion for preliminary injunction, the motions for summary judgment filed by defendants and IBA, and plaintiffs' motion for relief under Rule 56(f) of the Federal Rules of Civil Procedure. The Court heard oral argument of counsel on the pending motions on February 28, 1986. Upon consideration of the memoranda in support of and opposition to the motions, the arguments and representations of counsel in open court, and the entire record of this case, the Court concludes that the motion for preliminary injunction should be denied and that the Rule 56(f) motion should be denied. The Court withholds decision on the motions for summary judgment filed by defendants and intervenor.

FINDINGS OF FACT

EPA regulates the sale and distribution of pesticides in the United States under FIFRA through the statute's registration scheme, which prohibits the registration, and hence the use and marketing of pesticides which cause "unreasonable adverse effects on the environment." Any person seeking to test an unregistered pesticide may apply to the EPA for an EUP, which will control the conditions under which the testing may take place. EPA may only issue a permit if it finds that the proposed experiment is needed to produce data necessary for registration, and that the experiment will not cause unreasonable adverse effects on the environment. Tests involving genetically engineered microbial pesticides must be presented to the EPA, to determine whether an EUP is necessary. The agency set out this requirement in a policy statement in the Federal Register, on October 12, 1984, as an interim measure to ensure agency supervision of the release of genetically engineered organisms into the environment. Pursuant to their interim policy, EPA began its review of AGS' proposed recombinant DNA experiments involving genetically altered strains of *Pseudonomas Syringae (P. syringae)* and *Pseudonomas Flourescens (P. fluorescens)* late in 1984. The naturally-occurring strains of these bacteria are involved in the formation of ice crystals on plant surfaces, known as "ice nucleation." Ice-nucleating active (INA+) bacteria promote frost formation and non-ice nucleating active (INA-) bacteria inhibit frost formation. Both forms of bacteria coexist in nature, although INA+ predominate. Through recombinant DNA technology, AGS has deleted genetic material from the INA-bacteria to produce INA-bacteria, in an effort to control frost damage on plants.

In August, 1984, following a request by several of the plaintiffs herein, the Hazard Evaluation Division ("HED") of the EPA Office of Pesticide Programs initiated its interim policy with review of several proposed recombinant DNA experiments which had been recommended for approval by the Recombinant DNA Advisory Committee of the National Institutes of Health. When informed of EPA's notification and EUP requirements, AGS submitted its INA-proposal to EPA, with supporting data, and formal EPA review began on October 31, 1984. HED concluded that the test was not likely to pose significant risks to humans or the environment, but determined that AGS would have to provide more information before testing could be conducted under an EUP. HED's specific areas of environmental concern were the dissemination of the mutant bacteria from the test site, the survivability and colonization abilities of the bacteria, and the possible effects from its release on precipitation patterns....

HED's preliminary conclusions were reviewed by independent scientists on a subpanel of the FIFRA Scientific Advisory Panel ("SAP") in January, 1985. The SAP subpanel generally agreed with HED's conclusions. In February, 1985 HED informed

AGS that an EUP would be required for its proposed field test, and that additional data would have to be submitted on the bacteria's competitiveness, ability to colonize, host specificity and pathogenicity. AGS submitted a modified proposal in June, 1985, and included data responsive to the HED's requests. In addition, AGS requested a waiver of some of the EPA's additional standard data requirements. EPA published notice of this application in the *Federal Register* on August 21, 1985, and requested public comments. HED's initial scientific position that the proposal presented no foreseeable risk issued on August 27, 1985, was reviewed by the U.S. Department of Agriculture, the Food & Drug Administration and NIH. Public comments from plaintiff the Foundation on Economic Trends ("FOET") questioned the agency's conclusions about the bacteria's novelty, competitiveness, pathogenicity, and atmospheric role. FOET also urged more laboratory study of the bacteria's effects....

HED responded to FOET's concerns about the bacteria's role in precipitation by contacting the scientists FOET had referenced in their comments, and by contacting other meteorological scientists. The SAP subpanel finally concluded that the experiment was unlikely to pose significant risks and recommended approval of the application. On November 5, 1985 HED summarized their final position, and responded specifically to public comments, concluding that, in light of the evaluated data and the limited scale of the proposed tests, the lack of the mutant's competitive advantage over the natural INA bacteria, AGS' experiment "does not pose a significant risk of adverse environmental impact." HED addressed FOET's concerns about precipitation effect, "novelty" of the mutant, the need for further testing, the toxicology of the bacteria, and EPA's waiver of certain additional data requirements.

The agency issued EUPs to AGS on November 14, 1985, effective December 1, 1985 through November 30, 1986. Plaintiffs filed this suit the same day, alleging that the agency action violated FIFRA, and was arbitrary, capricious and an abuse of discretion. Plaintiffs filed an amended preliminary injunction request on January 26, 1986.

Under the EUP, AGS can conduct a field test of INA-bacteria on a 0.2 acre site, in Monterey County, California, not less than 15 days after it notifies the agency of its intent to begin testing. An interim local ordinance passed in Monterey County prohibits the release of any genetically altered bacteria prior to March 28, 1986, preventing the test from occurring before that time. Additionally, the EPA has begun an investigation of AGS and its research facility following media reports that possible unauthorized open-air tests of the mutant bacteria have occurred. EPA represented to the Court that it will complete its investigation no later than March 24, 1986, and the parties have stipulated that no testing shall occur under the EUP before then.

CONCLUSIONS OF LAW

[P]laintiffs must establish that there was a procedural defect in the agency EUP process, or that the agency's substantive decision to issue the EUP was arbitrary, capricious or an abuse of discretion, based on the record before the agency.

The data submission and agency review requirements for EUPs are set out at 40 C.F.R. §§ 172.4–172.5. The EPA imposed additional data and review procedures for microbial pesticide EUP applications.... These procedures are to ensure that the permit is needed to accumulate information necessary for pesticide registration under FIFRA, and that the proposed testing will not have unreasonable adverse effects on the environment.

Plaintiffs contend that the EPA improperly waived certain data submission requirements for AGS in their EUP application. Data requirements for this type of test are set out at 40 C.F.R. §§ 158, *et seq.*, and may be waived on a case-by-case basis. HED recommended granting the waivers, and upon consideration of the available information, the limited size and scope of the experiment and AGS' proposed safeguards, the EPA concluded that the waivers were appropriate. No further procedure is required in a waiver determination.

Plaintiffs also challenge the substantive result of this EUP procedure, contending that EPA did not adequately consider the potential pathogenicity and toxicity of the bacteria, the likelihood of its dissemination and off-site reproduction, and the impact of release of INA—on atmospheric precipitation patterns. Plaintiffs also claim that the EPA did not give sufficient consideration to alternatives to the proposed test. In reviewing the adequacy of the EPA's consideration of these factors, the Court notes that the stringent procedural and substantive requirements of NEPA's EIS standards do not literally apply to actions of the EPA in this case. The rationale for this exception is that EPA's actions already occur within a substantive regulatory framework that emphasizes the quality of man's environment, and a procedural framework that provides "full opportunity for thorough consideration of the environmental issues and for ample judicial review." This framework is functionally equivalent to NEPA, and to require formal compliance with the statute, when its purpose and policies have been fulfilled, would be "a legalism carried to the extreme." Based upon its review of the record for purposes of the injunction, the procedures in the present case do not appear to the Court to have fallen short of this goal of "functional equivalence" with NEPA. The EPA appears to have considered at each level of review each of the substantive elements plaintiffs raise in their challenge. The administrative record is, at worst, equivocal on these substantive claims, and in light of the deferential "arbitrary and capricious" standard of review applied to this decision, the Court does not find that plaintiffs have made a "strong showing" that they will succeed on the merits of their claims. Further, plaintiffs have not shown that they will be irreparably injured if an injunction does not issue at this stage, since the parties stipulated in open Court that no testing would be conducted under the EUP prior to completion of the EPA's investigation of AGS on March 24. The county ordinance restricting such testing is also in effect until March 28, preventing the release of INA-bacteria by AGS. Accordingly, the motion for preliminary injunction must be denied....

Plaintiffs have moved under Fed.R.Civ.P. 56(f) for a continuance of the Court's decision on summary judgment to enable them to conduct discovery related to the media reports of AGS' alleged testing violations. Specifically, plaintiffs contend that discovery may provide evidence of the pathogenicity of the mutant bacteria, which they claim is relevant to their challenge to the agency's EUP review. The Court is of the opinion that discovery involving these issues is not warranted, since it would not aid in plaintiffs' challenge to the adequacy of the record before the agency at the time the decision was made or to the adequacy of the agency's procedure. Plaintiffs admit that the evidence they seek to discover was not before EPA during the EUP review. Affidavit of Jeremy Rifkin. When the permit was issued, the EPA had no reason to doubt the accuracy of AGS' data. Plaintiffs have access to the entire record that was before the agency when it decided to issue the EUPs, and additional data not before the agency cannot serve as a basis to challenge the decision. A continuance to permit discovery of such data is therefore not appropriate in light of the present posture of the case ...

———————

Foundation on Economic Trends v. Lyng

680 F. Supp. 10 (D.C. Cir., 1988)

Opinion by: Thomas F. Hogan, United States District Judge.

MEMORANDUM OPINION

Plaintiffs[1] brought this action on April 23, 1986, seeking to suspend and revoke the license defendants[2] issued permitting marketing of the pseudorabies vaccine "Omni-vac." The case is before the Court on the parties' cross-motions for summary judgment. After consideration and review of the motions, oppositions, replies, supporting memoranda, and the entire administrative record, the Court shall grant defendants' motion and deny plaintiffs' motion.

I. BACKGROUND

The United States Department of Agriculture Animal & Plant Health Inspection Service ("USDA-APHIS") controls the production and marketing of veterinary medicines including vaccines through a licensing process under the Virus-Serum-Toxin Act ("VSTA"), 21 U.S.C. §§ 151–158 (1982), and applicable regulations, 9 C.F.R. pt. 102 (1987). USDA-APHIS may grant a license only after reviewing a product and evaluating its safety, efficacy, purity, and potency. 9 C.F.R. § 102.3(b) (2) (ii) (1987). Vaccines and other veterinary biological products that are prepared using biotechnological or "genetic engineering" procedures must comply with these licensing regulations. *E.g.*, Final Policy Statement for Research and Regulation of Biotechnology Processes and Products, 51 Fed. Reg. 23,336 (June 26, 1986).

In addition, USDA-APHIS is subject to the requirements of the National Environmental Policy Act ("NEPA"), and the agency must prepare an environmental impact statement for any major federal action having a significant impact on the human environment. No environmental impact statement is required if the agency finds that the action will have no significant impact. To determine the impact of an action, the agency must prepare an environmental assessment, which summarizes the available environmental evidence and presents the agency's analysis of relevant data. USDA-APHIS guidelines implementing NEPA require preparation of an environmental assessment "for each proposed new action." The parties do not dispute that the licensing of Omni-vac was a "proposed new action" requiring an environmental assessment.

The license application at issue was submitted to USDA-APHIS in December, 1984, by Biologics Corporation, a subsidiary of TechAmerica Group Inc. Novagene, Inc., had developed the vaccine in 1982, under the guidance of Dr. Saul Kit. The vaccine was designed to combat pseudorabies, a contagious disease affecting swine and other livestock. In its natural state, the pseudorabies virus may retreat to the nerve cells of a recovered animal and lie dormant, unaffected by the body's immune system. The dormant virus

---

1. Plaintiffs are the Foundation on Economic Trends ("FET"), a private nonprofit organization active on issues of biotechnology and genetic engineering; Jeremy Rifkin, president of FET and an activist in the area of biotechnology and genetic engineering; and Dr. Michael W. Fox, Scientific Director of the Humane Society of the United States. All plaintiffs reside in the District of Columbia.

2. Defendants are Richard Lyng, Secretary, United States Department of Agriculture ("USDA"); Bert W. Hawkins, Administrator of the Animal & Plant Health Inspection Service ("APHIS"), USDA; and J.K. Atwell, Deputy Administrator, Veterinary Services, USDA-APHIS. All are sued in their official capacities.

may be reactivated in this outwardly healthy animal and may then spread to other animals as the carrier "sheds" the virus.

Existing pseudorabies vaccines have been prepared from killed or modified live strains of the virus. The modified live virus vaccine is assertedly the most effective, but generally retains the ability to be harbored in the host's nerve cells and then spread to other animals. While these animals are not infected with a disease-producing virus, they will test positive for infection, complicating diagnosis and health programs.

Omnivac was developed by weakening an existing modified live strain of the virus (Bucharest strain). Researchers deleted the gene that produces the enzyme thymidine kinase ("TK"), which is essential for the survival and replication of the virus. As a result, the TK-vaccine virus cannot survive and multiply in nerve cells, unlike the existing wild strain and weakened vaccine virus strain.

The Administrative Record documents the progress of TechAmerica's application through USDA-APHIS's review process. Dr. George Shibley, Senior Staff Microbiologist at the Veterinary Services Division of USDA-APHIS, monitored the license procedure for Omnivac. After a little more than one year of review, testing, and reporting, USDA-APHIS issued a United States Veterinary Biological Product License to TechAmerica on January 16, 1986. USDA-APHIS did not issue or prepare an environmental assessment or environmental impact statement before it granted the license. The Foundation on Economic Trends petitioned USDA-APHIS in early April, 1986, to revoke or suspend the Omnivac license, based in part on USDA-APHIS's failure to comply with NEPA. The agency suspended the license and prepared a lengthy environmental assessment to document the environmental concerns that were "fully identified and reviewed by Department officials prior to licensing the vaccine."

USDA-APHIS concluded that the licensing of Omnivac would not have a significant impact on the environment, based on the following facts:(1) deletion of the genetic element necessary for reproduction prevents the TK-virus from establishing latency; (2) conventional methodology had been used to render the Bucharest virus strain noninfectious prior to the gene deletion; (3) studies on susceptible host animals demonstrated no transmission of the TK-virus; (4) deletion of the TK gene and the consequent inability of the virus to replicate will result in reduced dissemination of the virulent virus through shedding; (5) TK deletion is a stable characteristic, and any reversion and reacquisition of the TK gene would produce latency but not virulency; (6) there is no likelihood of oncogenicity, as the TK-virus contains no new genetic information from the non-oncogenetic wild pseudorabies virus; (7) the TK-virus demonstrated reduced virulence in other animals; (8) like the existing virus strains, the TK-virus is avirulent to humans; and (9) demonstrated inability of the TK-virus to revert to the wild virus strain, as distinct from the weakened strain from which it is crafted. *Id.* The scientific data requested and submitted from which USDA-APHIS drew these conclusions are presented in the environmental assessment and are discussed more fully below.

The belated Omnivac environmental assessment was released on April 22, 1986, and notice of its availability was published in the Federal Register. 51 Fed. Reg. 15,657 (Apr. 25, 1986). The suspension was lifted immediately and Omnivac production resumed. Plaintiffs filed this action on April 23, 1986, seeking declaratory and injunctive relief. Plaintiffs did not apply for temporary or preliminary injunctive relief. Cross-motions for summary judgment were submitted after the Administrative Record was filed. Plaintiffs contend that USDA-APHIS violated the VSTA and applicable regulations in issuing the license, and that the agency failed to comply with NEPA. Defendants challenge plaintiffs' standing, and assert that USDA-APHIS complied with the law in issuing the license.

II. DISCUSSION ...

B. *Plaintiffs' Claim Under NEPA*

Plaintiff FET has standing to seek review of USDA's compliance with NEPA, based on its claim that the agency's noncompliance affected FET's ability to provide information to the public. *E.g., Scientists' Institute for Public Information, Inc. v. AEC,* 156 U.S. App. D.C. 395, 481 F.2d 1079, 1086–87 n.29 (D.C. Cir. 1973); *see also Foundation on Economic Trends v. Lyng,* 260 U.S. App. D.C. 159, 817 F.2d 882 (D.C. Cir. 1987) (reviewing gravamen of plaintiffs' challenge to USDA's compliance with NEPA; implicitly assuming existence of standing). FET alleges that USDA-APHIS's environmental assessment ("EA") on Omnivac was inadequate.... The Court must ordinarily ask four questions in deciding whether an agency's finding of "no significant impact" in an environmental assessment is arbitrary and capricious:

(1) whether the agency took a "hard look" at the problem; (2) whether the agency identified the relevant areas of environmental concern; (3) as to the problems studied and identified, whether the agency made a convincing case that the impact was insignificant; and (4) if there was an impact of true significance, whether the agency convincingly established what changes in the project sufficiently reduced it to a minimum.

Cabinet Mountains Wilderness v. Peterson, 222 U.S. App. D.C. 228, 685 F.2d 678, 682 (D.C. Cir. 1982). Within this framework, review of USDA-APHIS's decision not to prepare an EIS "must be undertaken with a view merely to determine if the agency has taken the 'hard look' at the environmental consequences of the action that NEPA requires." *Foundation on Economic Trends v. Weinberger,* 610 F. Supp. 829, 838–39 (D.D.C. 1985). To survive review, the agency's environmental assessment "must indicate, in some fashion, that the agency has taken a searching, realistic look at the potential hazards and, with reasoned thought and analysis, candidly and methodically addressed those concerns." *Id.* at 841.

The EA prepared on Omnivac found that use of recombinant TK-pseudorabies vaccine would not have significant impact on the environment. The EA discusses the characteristics of existing strains of wild and modified pseudorabies, describing among other factors the transmission, range, pathogenesis, latency, and survival of the pseudorabies vaccine. The EA then presents the agency's review of the same characteristics of the TK-pseudorabies vaccine, and summarizes the data supporting the scientific conclusions. USDA-APHIS concluded that the TK-virus is stable, avirulent, unlikely to be transmitted, and unable to establish latency, and accordingly, would have no significant impact on the environment.

FET initially asserts that USDA-APHIS failed to consult with other agencies, internal advisory committees, and the public, in violation of applicable regulations. None of the regulations, internal memoranda, or policy statements requires the review plaintiffs seek. Applicable APHIS regulations implementing NEPA require public involvement where program changes will have significant adverse effects on the environment, when APHIS intends to prepare an EIS, and when a draft or final EIS or a finding of no significant impact is available. APHIS Guidelines Concerning Implementation of NEPA Procedures, 44 Fed. Reg. 50,381, 50,383 (Aug. 28, 1979). Applicable USDA regulations leave to the agency's discretion when to seek additional public involvement. 7 C.F.R. § 1b.1(a) (1987) (incorporating Council on Environmental Quality ("CEQ") regulations); 40 C.F.R. § 1506.6 (1987) (CEQ regulation concerning public involvement). The guidelines upon which FET relies to establish interagency and advisory committee review requirements apply, if at all, to the licensing process, and are not mandated by NEPA and its implementing regulations.... To the extent regulations and protocol required preliminary consultation, USDA-APHIS provided it.

FET challenges the substance of USDA's conclusions in the EA, delineating what it considers to be deficient testing and inadequate review of data submitted in support of the application. FET's principal concern is with the "safety data" USDA received and compiled. FET raises legitimate complaints about the failure of the original researcher, Dr. Saul Kit, to comply with established reporting and notification requirements in the conduct of an open air test of the vaccine. Even if USDA knew of Dr. Kit's transgressions, the Court cannot conclude that it was "arbitrary and capricious" to consider the data collected....

FET finally argues that the tests and data reflected in the EA do not resolve issues it asserts are central to the nature and effect of Omnivac. USDA presents evidence contradicting these claims, rebutting both the assertion that specific issues were not resolved and the claim that the issues are "central" to the nature and effect of the vaccine.[6] FN6 After careful review of the record, the Court notes that some of the testing "deficiencies" FET recounts reflect the nascency of the field of genetic engineering rather than truncated examination of the product by the agency.

The Court is not in the same position as the agency in its review of the scientific data submitted, and cannot replace the agency's judgment with its own. Upon examination of the environmental assessment and the supporting Administrative Record, the Court concludes that the finding of no significant impact was not arbitrary and capricious. Accordingly, summary judgment shall be granted in defendants' favor under the NEPA claim.

An appropriate order accompanies this opinion.

ORDER OF DISMISSAL

Notes

1. Vermont enacted legislation in 2003 to require the identification and labeling of genetically engineered seeds that are brought into the state, the Farmer Protection Act.

> (4) For all seed containing genetically engineered material, the manufacturer or processor shall cause the label or labeling to specify the identity and relevant traits or characteristics of such seed, plus any requirements for their safe handling, storage, transport, and use, the contact point for further information and, as appropriate, the name and address of the manufacturer, distributor, or supplier of such seed....

> (b) The secretary may develop rules for labeling procedures consistent with the provisions of this section, which take into account: origin, presence of

---

6. FET's principal concern is the lack of conclusive data on the potential teratogenicity of Omnivac when ingested by pregnant sows. The vaccine was not specifically approved for administration to pregnant sows, however, until teratogenicity data was received and reviewed, after the initial license was granted.

weed seed, mixtures, hermetically sealed containers, coated seed, "crop seeds," genetically engineered material, genetically engineered plant parts, hybrids, germination medium, and preplanted containers. (Added 1989, No. 85, §2; amended 2003, No. 42, §2, eff. May 27, 2003; 2003, No. 97 (Adj. Sess.), §3, eff. Oct. 1, 2004; 2003, No. 149 (Adj. Sess.), §13, eff. Oct. 2, 2004.)

2. Vermont enacted S.182 in the 2002–2003 Session adding this provision: §611. SERVICE FOR CERTIFICATION OF SEED: STANDARDS AND REGULATIONS: Sec. 1. 6 V.S.A. §611 (c) This chapter requires the identification of seeds modified by the presence of living modified organisms resulting from modern biotechnology and intended for intentional introduction into the environment. The purpose of such identification is to help to avoid through the use of such seeds any adverse effects on the conservation and sustainable use of biological diversity in this state.

2.1.5 U.S. Environmental Protection Agency, National Institutes of Health: Genetically Modified Organisms

Foundation on Economic Trends v. Heckler
756 F.2d 143 (D.C. Cir. 1985)

Circuit Judge J. Skelly Wright:

Almost 14 years ago, soon after passage of the National Environmental Policy Act (NEPA), this court faced the challenge of ensuring that the Act's " important legislative purposes, heralded in the halls of Congress, [were] not lost or misdirected in the vast hallways of the federal bureaucracy." *Calvert Cliffs' Coordinating Committee v. USAEC,....* This case poses a no less formidable challenge: to ensure that the bold words and vigorous spirit of NEPA are not similarly lost or misdirected in the brisk frontiers of science.

For this appeal presents an important question at the dawn of the genetic engineering age: what is the appropriate level of environmental review required of the National Institutes of Health (NIH) before it approves the deliberate release of genetically engineered, recombinant-DNA-containing organisms into the open environment? More precisely, in the context of this case, the question is whether to affirm an injunction temporarily enjoining NIH from approving deliberate release experiments without a greater level of environmental concern than the agency has shown thus far.

In September 1983 three environmental groups and two individuals filed suit against the federal officials responsible for genetic engineering decisions. Arguing that NIH had not complied with the requirements of NEPA, plaintiffs sought to enjoin a proposed NIH-approved experiment by University of California scientists that would represent the first deliberate release of genetically engineered organisms into the open environment. They also sought to enjoin NIH's approval of any other deliberate release experiments. Plaintiffs later added Regents of the University of California as a defendant. On May 18, 1984 the District Court granted the requested relief and enjoined both the University of California experiment and NIH approval of all other deliberate release experiments.

We emphatically agree with the District Court's conclusion that NIH has not yet displayed the rigorous attention to environmental concerns demanded by law. We there-

fore affirm the District Court's injunction prohibiting the University of California deliberate release experiment until an appropriate environmental assessment is completed.
We also share the District Court's view that NIH should give greater consideration to
the broad environmental issues attendant on deliberate release of organisms containing
recombinant DNA, and to its own responsibility for approving these deliberate release
experiments. We find, however, that the part of the injunction enjoining NIH from approving all other deliberate release experiments is, at this juncture, overly broad, and
we therefore vacate the part of the injunction that prohibits NIH approval of those experiments. We wish to emphasize, however, that if NIH fails to give appropriate environmental consideration to any other experiment, as it has failed to do with the University of California experiment, injunctive relief would be clearly proper.

I. BACKGROUND

This case arises against a backdrop of the National Environmental Policy Act, the emergence of genetic engineering, and federal attempts to regulate genetic engineering....

A. *National Environmental Policy Act*

On January 1, 1970 the National Environmental Policy Act became law. Recognizing
"the profound impact of man's activity on the interrelation of all components of the
natural environment," Congress sought to "fulfill the responsibilities of each generation
as trustee of the environment for succeeding generations." The major "action-forcing"
provision of NEPA is the requirement that "all agencies of the Federal government" prepare a detailed environmental analysis for "major Federal actions significantly affecting
the quality of the human environment." Congress mandated that this detailed statement, long known as an Environmental Impact Statement (EIS), include such considerations as "the environmental impact of the proposed action," "any adverse environmental effects which cannot be avoided should the proposal be implemented," and
"alternatives to the proposed action."

Realizing that NEPA would be toothless if agencies could merely issue a conclusory
statement that the action did not significantly affect the environment (and that therefore no EIS was required), the Council on Environmental Quality (CEQ), an entity created by NEPA, issued regulations establishing that, unless the major federal action falls
within an agency-established "categorical exclusion," the agency should support each
finding of "no significant impact" with a "concise public document" called an "environmental assessment" (EA). The environmental assessment must "briefly provide sufficient evidence and analysis for determining whether to prepare an environmental impact statement or a finding of no significant impact." CEQ regulations apply to all
federal agencies.

Two fundamental principles underlie NEPA's requirements: federal agencies have the
responsibility to consider the environmental effects of major actions significantly affecting environment, and the public has the right to review that consideration.... NEPA's
dual mission is thus to generate federal attention to environmental concerns and to reveal that federal consideration for public scrutiny.

In passing NEPA Congress emphasized its particular concern with the role of new
technologies and their effect on the environment. The statute explicitly enumerates
"new and expanding technological advances" as one of the activities with the potential to threaten the environment. The legislative history reveals an underlying concern with "[a] growing technological power ... far outstripping man's capacity to un-

derstand and ability to control its impact on the environment." S.Rep. No. 91-296. One of NEPA's main functions was to bolster this capacity to understand and control the effects of new technology. *See Scientists' Institute for Public Information v. AEC,*....

NEPA thus stands as landmark legislation, requiring federal agencies to consider the environmental effects of major federal actions, empowering the public to scrutinize this consideration, and revealing a special concern about the environmental effects of new technology.

B. *Genetic Engineering*

Genetic engineering is an important development at the very cusp of scientific advances. More than a decade ago scientists discovered a method for transplanting deoxyribonucleic acid (DNA), the principal substance of genes. Although exchanges and mutations of DNA occur in nature, genetic engineering provides the ability to control these fundamental processes of life and evolution. DNA segments can be recovered and cloned from one organism and inserted into another. The result is known as "recombinant DNA."

Recombinant DNA technology has been limited primarily to small organisms, usually bacteria. This production of new bacteria through altering genetic material has been confined to the laboratory; organisms with recombinant DNA have never been released into the general environment.

Broad claims are made about both the potential benefits and the potential hazards of genetically engineered organisms. Use of recombinant DNA may lead to welcome advances in such areas as food production and disease control. At the same time, however, the environmental consequences of dispersion of genetically engineered organisms are far from clear. According to a recent report by a House of Representatives subcommittee, "The potential environmental risks associated with the deliberate release of genetically engineered organisms or the translocation of any new organism into an ecosystem are best described as 'low probability, high consequence risk '; that is, while there is only a small possibility that damage could occur, the damage that could occur is great." *The Environmental Implications of Genetic Engineering*, Report by Subcommittee on Investigations & Oversight to House Committee on Science & Technology, 98th Cong., 2d Sess. 9 (1984) (hereinafter cited as *Genetic Engineering Report*), JA 167.

C. *Federal Oversight of Genetic Engineering*

Spurred by scientists involved in genetic research, NIH began efforts to oversee genetic engineering in the mid-1970's. Federal oversight of deliberate release experiments falls into four periods: (1) NIH's 1976 standards, which prohibited deliberate release of organisms containing recombinant DNA; (2) NIH's 1978 revision, which gave the NIH Director power to approve deliberate release experiments; (3) the NIH Director's approval of three such experiments in the early 1980's; and (4) the District Court's injunction prohibiting the University of California experiment and enjoining NIH approval of all other deliberate release experiments.

1. *NIH's 1976 standards: prohibition on deliberate release.* In 1976 the NIH Director issued "Guidelines for Research on Recombinant DNA Molecules." 41 Fed. Reg. at 27902, JA 230. The Guidelines were an historic development, representing the first major federal effort to oversee genetic research and the culmination of intense scientific attention to the possible hazards of genetic research.

In 1974 scientists working in genetic research voluntarily called for a moratorium on certain kinds of experiments until an international meeting could be convened to consider the potential hazards of recombinant DNA molecules. On October 7, 1974 NIH established the Recombinant DNA Advisory Committee (RAC) to consider genetic research issues. And in February 1975 NIH, the National Science Foundation, and the National Academy of Sciences sponsored an international conference at the Asilomar Conference Center in Pacific Grove, California to review the questions posed by the possibility of genetic engineering.

Finally, in the summer of 1976 the NIH Director announced the Guidelines that would govern NIH-supported genetic research experiments. In broad terms, the Guidelines permitted certain laboratory experiments to go forward under carefully specified conditions; certain other types of experiments were flatly prohibited. Deliberate release—"deliberate release into the environment of any organism containing a recombinant DNA molecule"—was one of five categories explicitly banned. In announcing the Guidelines the Director noted that deliberate release of organisms with recombinant DNA was not yet feasible and that, if it became feasible, the ban could be reconsidered. But he stressed that, if such reconsideration occurred, environmental concerns should be paramount: " "It is most important that the potential environmental impact of the release be considered."

Significantly, NIH prepared an EIS to accompany its Guidelines—the only EIS NIH has ever completed on the subject of genetic engineering. The EIS did not specifically refer to deliberate release experiments; such experiments were banned. The EIS did, however, note that dispersion of organisms with recombinant DNA molecules loomed as a potential environmental hazard from the permitted experiments:

Should organisms containing recombined DNA be dispersed into the environment, they might, depending on their fitness relative to naturally occuring [sic] organisms, find a suitable ecological niche for their own reproduction. A potentially dangerous organism might then multiply and spread. Subsequent cessation of experiments would not stop the diffusion of the hazardous agent.

Thus in 1976 the NIH Guidelines prohibited deliberate release; the Director emphasized the importance of full environmental consideration of any possible future release; and the EIS identified dispersion of organisms with recombinant DNA as a possible environmental hazard.

2. *The 1978 revision: permission to waive the prohibition against deliberate release.* In 1978 the NIH Director undertook an effort to revise the Guidelines "in light of NIH's experience operating under them and in light of [NIH's] increasing knowledge about the potential risks and benefits of this research technique." 43 Fed.Reg. 33042 (July 28, 1978). Proposed in July and adopted in December, the revision changed the Guidelines in several respects. Most importantly for this appeal, the 1978 revision allowed the NIH Director authority to grant exceptions to the five absolute prohibitions in the Guidelines—including the prohibition on deliberate release of organisms containing recombinant DNA into the environment....

NIH announced that the standard governing the use of this waiver authority would be the standard generally applicable to the Director's exercise of his duties: "The Director shall weigh each proposed action, through appropriate analysis and consultation, to determine that it complies with the Guidelines and presents no significant risk to health or the environment." NIH also declared that the Director would exercise his authority "with the advice of the Recombinant DNA Advisory Committee after appropriate notice and opportunity for public comment." The Director further stated that his "waiver decisions [would] include a careful consideration of the potential environmental impact, and certain decisions may be accompanied by a formal assessment or statement. This must be determined on a case-by-case basis."

On the subject of deliberate release experiments in particular, the Director suggested that clear standards might be necessary to guide his waiver discretion: "Recognizing the need expressed by ... commentators for more definitive standards [to govern deliberate release waiver decision], I will refer the matter to the Recombinant Advisory Committee (RAC) for its consideration.... The RAC will be asked to address conditions under which exceptions to various prohibited categories of experiments may be granted." 43 Fed. Reg. at 60083. Thus the Director perceived a possible need for more definitive standards and suggested that such standards might be forthcoming.

NIH did not prepare an EIS to accompany its 1978 revision. It prepared two Environmental Assessments—one for the revision as proposed, and one for the revision as adopted. The assessments said little about the Director's new waiver authority for deliberate release experiments. The first simply declared, "Waiver decisions will include a careful consideration of potential environmental impact;" the second did not mention the waiver authority.

The 1978 revision also extended the coverage of the Guidelines to all experiments at institutions receiving NIH funds for recombinant DNA research, whether or not the particular experiment had received NIH funds....

3. *Approval of deliberate release experiments.* The 1978 revision was the last significant revision of NIH's guidelines regarding deliberate release experiments. A 1982 revision was largely semantic, 47 Fed. Reg. 17186–17187 (April 21, 1982); a 1983 revision establishing slightly different procedures for deliberate release involving certain plants, is not part of this appeal. The "more definitive standards" suggested by the Director never emerged.

Although the guidelines have not changed, NIH's role has begun to change dramatically. For, with the maturation of genetic engineering technology, NIH has been faced with applications for approval of deliberate release experiments.

The NIH Director, acting on the advice of RAC, has approved three deliberate release experiments at institutions receiving NIH funds for recombinant DNA research. On August 7, 1981 the Director approved a request by Dr. Ronald Davis of Stanford University to field-test corn plants containing recombinant DNA molecules. The goal was to increase the corn's dietary value by improving its ability to store protein. However, the field tests were never conducted because feasibility problems developed. *Genetic Engineering Report* ...

On April 15, 1983 the Director approved a request by Dr. John Sanford of Cornell University to field-test tomato and tobacco plants with recombinant DNA. The goal was to prove that pollen could serve as a "vector" for insertion of recombinant DNA. Again, however, due to feasibility problems, the experiment never went forward. *Genetic Engineering Report* ...

On June 1, 1983 the Director gave final approval to the experiment at issue on appeal—the request by Drs. Nickolas Panopoulos and Steven Lindow of the University of California at Berkeley to apply genetically altered bacteria to plots of potatoes, tomatoes, and beans in northern California. As discussed in greater detail below, the goal was to increase the crops' frost resistance. Because of the cancellation of the previous two experiments, the Panopoulos-Lindow experiment would be the first NIH-approved deliberate release experiment actually to be conducted....

In February 1984 a congressional subcommittee report sharply criticized NIH's method of reviewing deliberate release experiments. The report concluded that "the current regulatory framework does not guarantee that adequate consideration will be given to the potential environmental effects of a deliberate release." In particular, "the RAC's ability to adequately evaluate the environmental hazards posed by deliberate releases is limited by both its expertise and its jurisdiction." The subcommittee report recommended a moratorium on deliberate release approvals until an interagency review panel was established to consider the potential environmental effects of each deliberate release experiment. "Each [deliberate release experiment] could result in major environmental damage or adverse public health effects." ...

4. *The injunction.* In September 1983 three public interest organizations and two individuals filed suit against the three federal officials ultimately responsible for NIH deliberate release decisions; they later added Regents of the University of California as a defendant. The University of California experiment was scheduled to begin on or about May 25, 1984. On May 18 the District Court issued an injunction enjoining the University of California experiment and NIH approval of other deliberate release experiments. The District Court found that plaintiffs were likely to succeed in showing that NIH should have completed at least a more complete environmental assessment, and perhaps an EIS, before approving the University of California experiment; it also found them likely to succeed in showing that NIH should have completed an Environmental Impact Statement in connection with both its 1978 policy change and its imminent "program" of deliberate release approvals....

A. *Review of an Agency Decision Not to Prepare an EIS*

That courts must play a cardinal role in the realization of NEPA's mandate is beyond dispute. As the Supreme Court recently emphasized, the critical judicial task is "to ensure that the agency has adequately considered and disclosed the environmental impact of its actions and that its decision is not arbitrary or capricious." ... Since NEPA requires the agency to "take a 'hard look ' at the environmental consequences before taking a major action," *id. (quoting Kleppe v. Sierra Club)*, the judiciary must see that this legal duty is fulfilled. Although the "agency commencing federal action has the initial and primary responsibility for ascertaining whether an EIS is required," ... the courts must determine that this decision accords with traditional norms of reasoned decision-making and that the agency has taken the "hard look" required by NEPA....

A. *The Adequacy of the Environmental Review*

1. *The proposed experiment.* On September 17, 1982 Drs. Lindow and Panopoulos, scientists at Berkeley, submitted a request for NIH approval of an experiment that would involve deliberate release of genetically altered organisms in the open environment. NIH approval was required because the University of California receives NIH funds for recombinant DNA research. Lindow and Panopoulos proposed to apply the genetically altered bacteria to various crops, including potatoes, tomatoes, and beans. By changing the bacteria's genetic composition, Lindow and Panopoulos hoped that the bacteria would change from frost-triggering bacteria to non-frost-triggering bacteria; they further hoped that the engineered non-frost-triggering bacteria would displace the natural frost-triggering bacteria. The ultimate goal was to protect the crops from frost and thus to extend their growing season. Such non-frost-triggering bacteria occur in nature as

products of natural mutation, but Lindow and Panopoulos apparently hoped that the genetically engineered organisms would be more stable than the natural mutants. They sought to treat crops at six sites; the workers applying the recombinant-DNA-containing bacteria would wear respirators to reduce the risk of inhalation....

2. *NIH review.* NIH announced the Lindow-Panopoulos request for approval, the RAC meeting at which it would be considered, and the opportunity to comment. No comments were received. At the RAC meeting on October 25, 1982 RAC members raised questions about the number of sites, the lack of adequate information, and the possible effects on rainfall. RAC voted to recommend that the Director approve the project; the vote was seven in favor, five opposed, with two abstentions. The Director decided to postpone approval and suggested further consideration.

Lindow and Panopoulos resubmitted their proposal with some modifications, including a reduction of experiment sites from six to one. On April 11, 1983, after some discussion, RAC voted to recommend approving the proposal by a vote of 19–0, with no abstentions. The Director then approved the experiment....

3. *NEPA compliance.* NIH's consideration of the Lindow-Panopoulos experiment falls far short of the NEPA requirements. And, despite the government's apparent belief, the deficiency is not a question of which document contains the environmental analysis. Rather, the deficiency rests in NIH's complete failure to consider the possibility of various environmental effects.

Neither the government nor the University seriously disputes that an environmental assessment is necessary. The government has conceded that the approval is a "major action" and that it does not fall into a categorical exclusion to the EIS requirements, Federal Defendants' Response to Plaintiffs' Second Set of Interrogatories at 17, JA 50; *see also Foundation on Economic Trends v. Heckler*, 587 F. Supp. 753, 767 (D.D.C.1984). The University's contention here—and the government's contention below, as well as its apparent continuing belief—is that the environmental consideration given by NIH was equivalent to the necessary environmental assessment and that the injunction requires only a document labelled "Environmental Assessment." We thus fear that the University and the government completely misapprehend the District Court's holding and the requirements imposed by NEPA.

The most glaring deficiency in NIH's review of the Lindow-Panopoulos experiment is its treatment of the possibility of dispersion of recombinant-DNA-containing organisms. As noted, NIH's only EIS on genetic engineering specifically identified dispersion as one of the major environmental concerns associated with recombinant DNA research. The consequences of dispersion of genetically altered organisms are uncertain. Some observers believe that such dispersion would affect the environment and the climate in harmful ways. ("the risk presented by the deliberate release of a genetically engineered organism is that it may cause environmental changes that perturb the ecosystem it encounters and/or that the organism itself may have negative effects if it establishes itself outside of the specific environment for which it was intended").

Thus the problem of dispersion would seem to be one of the major concerns associated with the Lindow-Panopoulos experiment, the first experiment that would actually release genetically engineered organisms in the open environment. Yet in the minutes of the RAC meeting—the only document on appeal that records *any* NIH consideration of the environmental impact of dispersion—the entirety of the consideration of dispersion is the following statement: according to a RAC evaluator, "Although some movement of bacteria toward sites near treatment locations by insect or aerial transport *is possible*, the numbers of viable cells transported has been shown to be very small; and these cells are subject to biological and physical processes limiting survival." In this sentence, which was taken almost verbatim from the Lindow-Panopoulos proposal, the RAC evaluator thus conceded the possibility of aerial or insect transport, but merely commented that the number of viable cells would be small, and that they were subject to processes limiting survival. Remarkably, therefore, RAC completely failed to consider the possible environmental impact from dispersion of genetically altered bacteria, however small the number and however subject to procedures limiting survival.[6]

In light of this complete failure to address a major environmental concern, NIH's environmental assessment utterly fails to meet the standard of environmental review necessary before an agency decides not to prepare an EIS. The argument that this consideration would be adequate if contained in a document labelled "Environmental Assessment" simply misconceives the clear requirements of NEPA as articulated by the courts ... An environmental assessment that fails to address a significant environmental concern can hardly be deemed adequate for a reasoned determination that an EIS is not appropriate.... Appellants also contend that the adequacy of the environmental assessment can be divined from the NIH Director's final approval—and his accompanying statement of "no significant risk," ... This contention also reveals a fundamental misunderstanding about the adequacy of an environmental assessment. Simple, conclusory statements of "no impact" are not enough to fulfill an agency's duty under NEPA....

To reiterate, NIH must first complete a far more adequate environmental assessment of the possible environmental impact of the deliberate release experiment than it has yet undertaken. That assessment must "provide sufficient evidence and analysis for determining whether to prepare an environmental impact statement or a finding of no significant impact," 40 C.F.R. §§ 1508.9(a)(1). Ignoring possible environmental consequences will not suffice. Nor will a mere conclusory statement that the number of recombinant-DNA-containing organisms will be small and subject to processes limiting survival. Instead, NIH must attempt to evaluate seriously the risk that emigration of such organisms from the test site will create ecological disruption. Second, until NIH completes such an evaluation the question whether the experiment requires an EIS remains open. The University of California experiment clearly presents the possibility of a problem identified by NIH in its EIS as a potential environmental hazard. This fact weighs heavily in support of the view than an EIS should be completed, unless NIH can demonstrate either that the experiment does not pose the previously identified danger, or that its assessment of the previously identified danger has changed through a process of reasoned decisionmaking. Nor is it sufficient for the agency merely to state that the environmental effects are currently unknown. Indeed, one of the specific criteria for determining whether an EIS is necessary is "the degree to which the possible effects on the

---

6. The University's arguments defending the NIH review are completely unconvincing. For instance, the University emphasizes that the use of chemically induced non-frost-triggering bacteria has produced "no untoward environmental consequences." Brief for appellant Regents at 42. But the Lindow-Panopoulos proposal itself stressed that the genetically engineered bacteria would have greater "genetic stability" and "competitive fitness" than the chemically-induced bacteria. Similarly, the University points to the presence of non-frost-triggering bacteria in nature. At oral argument, however, the University reported that these natural populations, like the chemical mutants, are probably less stable and competitive than the genetically engineered bacteria.

human environment are highly uncertain or involve unique or unknown risks." 40 C.F.R. §§ 1508.27(b)(5).

Thus we approve the District Court's determination that, as a matter of law, plaintiffs are likely to prevail in showing that NIH's environmental assessment of the University of California experiment—and its discharge of its statutory duty to consider the propriety of an EIS—was wholly inadequate....

Senior Circuit Judge MacKinnon (concurring).

I am of opinion that the Foundation should have made its original application to NIH. I do not agree that the failure to exhaust can be disposed of by the cases cited holding that exhaustion is "ultimately an exercise of judicial discretion." This is not a case of just failure to exhaust in a pending proceeding before an agency, but a case of a complete failure of the Foundation to present any claim or objection whatsoever to the agency—NIH. Thus, the normal exhaustion cases where the parties have appeared before the agency are not applicable. However, since the issues in this case are of great importance, new and novel I do not dissent because we are remanding the major issues in the case to the agency where what should have been done by all parties will now be done, and we are reversing in other major respects....

Had the Foundation submitted its objections to the agency, it is thus more than likely, given the demonstrated sensitivity of NIH and its scientists to such matters, that the University and the agency would have responded to any objections and the record here, if the Foundation were not satisfied, would have been more complete and useful. I am thus not so concerned about the fairness to the agency and to the litigants as I am that the Foundation's delay deprived this court of the normal administrative record and consideration by the district court that are required to meet the issues raised by the Foundation.

The Foundation's conduct also has delayed this vital experiment for a very considerable period of time. The use of delaying tactics by those who fear and oppose scientific progress is nothing new. It would, however, be a national catastrophe if the development of this promising new science of genetic engineering were crippled by the unconscionable delays that have been brought about by litigants using the National Environmental Policy Act and other environmental legislation in other areas. The protracted litigations involving the Alaska pipeline, nuclear power plants, and the Clean Air Act present only a few examples.

These concerns extend to the court's comments concerning the possibility of a Programmatic EIS. It is my opinion that because the possibilities of genetic engineering, an industry still in its infancy, extend to so many areas, and because the development of a programmatic EIS would be vulnerable to delaying tactics, composing a programmatic EIS at this time would be neither justified, practical, nor prudent.

Two cases followed in the District of Columbia federal district court, again brought by the Foundation on Economic Trends. Both used NEPA to challenge the impact on the environment. The second case was based on a challenge of the consideration of the environmental impact of a genetically engineered plant which had a bacteria gene that is intended to prevent frost damage to the plant. The court examines the procedural requirements of NEPA, and finds there is no basis to issue a preliminary injunction to prevent the experiment from going forward, based on compliance with NEPA.

Foundation on Economic Trends v. Block
No. 84-3045 (D.D.C. 1986)

An EA or EIS need not be prepared unless a proposal or major federal action may have a significant impact on the environment. 42 U.S.C. §4322 (1)(c).

Plaintiffs allege that defendants' animal productivity research is directed solely at producing larger, more productive animals which are best suited to capital intensive breeding operations. According to plaintiffs, this research focus significantly impacts the environment by decreasing the gene pool of farm animals, pollutes air and water resources, erodes the soil, makes the traditional family farm unit economically obsolete and alters the animal husbandry industry.

Most of these effects are indirect. However, NEPA requires that impact statements consider indirect effects, including a proposal's social and economic consequences. Relying on Sierra Club, plaintiffs urge that the social and economic consequences of defendants' animal breeding research put these activities under the reach of NEPA.

However, as defendants' correctly note, Sierra Club does not require that "highly speculative or indefinite impacts" be considered. Before an EA or EIS is prepared the Sierra Club court required that the following factors be considered:

With what confidence can one say that 'the impacts are likely to occur? Can one describe them 'now with sufficient specificity to make their consideration useful? If the decisionmaker does not take them into account 'now', will the decisionmaker be able to take account of them before the agency is so firmly committed to the project that further environmental knowledge, as a practical matter, will prove irrelevant to the government's decision?

Applying these criteria, it becomes clear that it is premature to require the defendants in this case to prepare an EA or an EIS evaluating the possible direct and indirect consequences of its animal breeding research. As previously discussed, when research has just begun, and when its success is uncertain, discussion of its eventual applications and the consequences of these applications can be no more than speculation. Furthermore, defendants' experiments in animal breeding and reproduction do not set the USDA on a path of no return. The direction this research takes can be changed at any time. Thus, at this stage, an EA or EIS would be, at most, of limited value, and thus is not required by law.

Another day, on a different record, the result might be otherwise.

Finally, there is a logical rebuttal to plaintiffs' claim of significant environmental impact: Defendants' experiments are only conducted in laboratories and other controlled environments. The animals are not released into the general environment. Thus, by definition, there can be no "environmental impact". Defendants' have detailed the safeguards now being used to insure that the products of genetic engineering remain under their control. Moreover, even the products of conventional selective breeding research are isolated. (Cattle used in a current USDA breeding experiment in Montana are descended from cattle involved in this same experiment when it began in 1931 at this same location. Given the controls defendants' place on their experimental subjects and products, allegations of significant environmental impact are now nothing but sheerest speculation.

DEFENDANTS' ALLEGED FAILURE TO CONSIDER ALTERNATIVE APPROACHES TO ITS ANIMAL BREEDING RESEARCH IS NOT A VIOLATION OF THE ADMINISTRATIVE PROCEDURES ACT

Plaintiffs allege that defendants' breeding programs focus almost exclusively on producing larger, more productive, more fecund animals and ignore alternative research approaches which would achieve these objectives without the allegedly harmful effects caused by the current program. Failure to consider such alternatives is, in plaintiffs' opinion, arbitrary agency action in violation of the Administrative Procedures Act (APA).

Defendants respond in the alternative: (1) their research is not as limited in direction as plaintiffs say, (2) judicial review of USDA research decisions should be highly deferential and under such a standard the programs must be upheld as rational exercises of agency discretion; and (3) plaintiffs lack standing to raise an APA claim.

This Court need not tarry long over plaintiffs' APA claim because defendants also raise a jurisdictional defense which neatly disposes of plaintiffs' argument: the challenged research activities have been "committed to agency discretion by law".

This phrase has been interpreted to mean that judicial review is precluded when a statute is so broadly drawn that "a court would have no meaningful standard against which to judge the agency's exercise of discretion". In such cases, agencies have absolute discretion.

That is the case here. The relevant statute authorizes the USDA to research agriculture's "basic problems" in their "broadest aspect". The statute does not establish priorities, goals, means or methods. No distinction is made between animal and crop research, basic and applied technology, or producer and consumer needs.

This wide ranging statute does not supply a reviewing court with "meaningful standards" against which to measure agency action for possible abuse of discretion. Therefore, USDA research activities are not subject to APA review and plaintiffs' APA claim must fall.

CONCLUSION

The issues raised by plaintiffs' complaint go to the heart of the interrelationships among man, nature, and science. However, the relief plaintiffs seek is not available under either NEPA or the APA. Defendants' animal breeding research is not a "proposal for legislation or other major Federal action significantly affecting the environment". Thus, neither a programmatic EA or EIS is required. And, defendants' choices as to the priorities, means, and ends of its animal productivity research is a matter of absolute discretion and thus not subject to judicial review under the APA. Accordingly, defendants' Motion for Summary Judgment will be granted.

This is not the last suit which will challenge some aspect of rDNA research. With this in mind it is prudent to emphasize the exceedingly limited nature of the Court's holding. The Court has determined on the basis of the record now before it that defendants' animal productivity research in general, and its rDNA research in particular, need not be the subjects of either a programmatic EA or an EIS. Plaintiffs have failed to prove either that defendants' independent studies are a cohesive program or that its genetic engineering research is sufficiently mature so that an impact statement would be more than an unfounded hypothesis.

However, science is not a static discipline. The structure of DNA was discovered only three decades ago. Twenty years ago genetic engineering was only performed by authors of science fiction. Eventually (and sooner rather than later) genetic engineering will reach the stage when an impact statement may well be required. Perhaps this will be when whole animal rDNA research is ready to leave the laboratory for field tests. Perhaps future rDNA studies may threaten the environment even when conducted under controlled conditions. Perhaps rDNA research will become so expensive that its pursuit can be legitimately said to foreclose alternative approaches to animal productivity research. When the technology is mature an analysis of the benefits and hazards of the proposed activity can be the product of a calculated and informed estimate of the probabilities and not merely haphazard speculation.

This Opinion should not be taken as deprecating plaintiffs' concerns. These merit serious attention but Congress is the place where they should be addressed in the first instance, not the courts.

An Order in accordance with the foregoing will issue of even date herewith.

ORDER

In accordance with the Opinion issued in the above captioned case of even date herewith and for the reasons set forth therein it is, by the Court, this day of April, 1986,

ORDERED, that defendants' Motion for Summary Judgment shall be, and the same is hereby granted, and the case will stand dismissed from the dockets of this Court.

———

While the previous case was involved biotechnology activities in a laboratory, the next case involved a field test, and the court would have to consider how NEPA applied to biotechnological field tests.

———

Foundation on Economic Trends v. Bowen
722 F. Supp. 787 (D.D.C., 1989)

Opinion by George H. Revercomb, District Judge:

The plaintiffs have sued the chiefs of various federal government entities to enjoin the National Institute of Health (NIH) from supporting any research involving various aspects of genetic, AIDS, and cancer research until NIH completes an Environmental Impact Statement (EIS) on the research, pursuant to the National Environmental Policy Act (NEPA). Oral argument was heard on February 28, 1989. In this Opinion and Order, the Court grants the defendants' motion for summary judgment.

I. The Current Legal Standards

NEPA requires the federal government to create a "detailed" statement on all "major Federal actions significantly affecting the quality of the human environment." Such a statement must discuss:

(I) the environmental impact of the proposed action,

(ii) any adverse environmental effects which cannot be avoided should the proposal be implemented,

(iii) alternatives to the proposed action,

(iv) the relationship between local short-term uses of man's environment and the maintenance and enhancement of long-term productivity, and

(v) any irreversible and irretrievable commitments of resources which would be in-volved in the propose action should it be implemented.

Such statements are to be made available to the public, and are designed to inform the governmental policy-makers and the public about the environmental effects of ac-tion undertaken with governmental support.

Once an agency has completed an EIS on a major federal action, the agency must supplement the EIS if (1) the agency makes substantial changes to the action that changes the environmental impact, or (2) there are "significant new circumstances or information relevant to environmental concerns and bearing on the proposed action or its impacts."

There is no hard-and-fast rule regarding when there are significant enough new cir-cumstances to require a new EIS. It is clear to the Court, however, that an agency should not have to generate an EIS every time a researcher develops a new project—such a requirement would be oppressively burdensome and would effectively prevent a tremendous amount of research from going forward. Rather, a supplementary EIS should be required when new developments have so increased the effects and risks to the environment that the old EIS does not properly address them. It is safe to say, then, that a supplementary EIS should not be required when there are new developments in a field of research that scientists believe either have less effect than preceding research or that reveal that the field of research is likely to have less effect on the environment than originally estimated.

The NIH in 1976 published detailed Guidelines on NIH-sponsored rDNA research. The Guidelines set standards for safety and environmental protection in rDNA research, including physical containment of particular experiments, and discouraged certain ex-periments. They also established groups to review research and determine whether the Guidelines were being followed properly.

In 1977, NIH published the final draft of an EIS on the 1976 Guidelines after accept-ing public comments. 41 Fed. Reg. 38425 (1977). The statement evaluated the likely consequences of research under the Guidelines and concluded that although following the Guidelines would guard against many possible environmental harms, they would not and could not guarantee that rDNA research would be free from all risk. The EIS also stated that the Guidelines should remain flexible in order to take account of new biological developments and new evaluations of the environmental impact of certain research.

This Court upheld the adequacy of the 1977 EIS in a lawsuit to enjoin NIH-spon-sored rDNA research. *Mack v. Califano*, 447 F. Supp. 668 (D.D.C. 1978). Since *Mack*, NIH has published a number of smaller Environmental Assessments ("EA's") to supple-ment the 1977 EIS. An EA is a "concise public document" that provides "sufficient evi-dence and analysis for determining whether to prepare an environmental impact state-ment of a finding of no significant impact" and aids the agency's compliance with NEPA when a full EIS is not necessary.... Like an EIS, an EA must include a discussion of the environmental impact of the topic, as well as alternatives to the action involved....

In the years after the formulation of 1976 Guidelines, the experts at NIH determined that the initial level of concern over the dangers of rDNA research was too high, and that some relaxation of the Guidelines was warranted. This conclusion was based on the fact that there had been little or no environmental harm caused by rDNA research and that additional research showed that rDNA did not pose the level of risk that was once feared. The Guidelines thus have been relaxed somewhat nearly each year since 1976, most recently in 1987. The defendants' position is that there is no need for a new EIS on the revised Guidelines because both the new scientific evidence and the excellent environmental record of rDNA research so far prove that the environmental impact of rDNA research is likely to be less than expected in 1977.

II. The Standard of Review

The Court reviews the decision of an agency that an EIS is not necessary under the deferential "arbitrary or capricious" test, 5 U.S.C. §§ 706, which essentially means that the Court cannot "second-guess" the agency unless it has acted unreasonably. The Court must give a hard and thorough look at the evidence presented to it on the record. Nonetheless, the Court thus must uphold scientific evaluations and conclusions by an agency if the decision was a reasonable one, even if there are good—or even, in the Court's opinion, slightly more convincing—arguments made on the other side.

With regard to the question of whether an agency has been reasonable in deciding not to create a supplementary EIS for new information or a new development in major federally sponsored action, the Court should consider the likely environmental impact of the new development and the degree of care that the agency appeared to take in evaluating the new development and making its decision not to create a supplement to the EIS. Moreover, the Court should determine whether it was reasonable to conclude that the new developments have not increased the likelihood or changed the form of environment impact significantly. If the Court finds that it was unreasonable to conclude that the new developments do not significantly change the likelihood of environmental impact, it must overturn the agency decision. When there is a debate among scientists as to the environmental impact of new developments, the Court must defer to the agency's decision if its appears to supported by "substantial evidence."

III. The Plaintiff's Challenges

It is settled that NIH approval of experiments involving rDNA constitute "major federal action" under NEPA and thus is subject to the EIS requirement when appropriate. *FOET v. Heckler*, 244 U.S. App. D.C. 122, 756 F.2d 143 (D.C. Cir. 1985). The plaintiffs in this case allege that certain research and experimentation approved by NIH in the years after the 1977 EIS have triggered the requirement of an EIS supplement, but that NIH has failed to create such a supplement.

An agency may not rest on an EIS if there is significant new information to be gathered that would change the environment evaluation. Moreover, NIH is obligated to create a supplement to an EIS when new scientific developments in a biomedical field make an earlier EIS insufficient to evaluate adequately the environmental impact of the new developments. *See, e.g., FOET v. Heckler*, 244 U.S. App. D.C. 122, 756 F.2d 143 (D.C. Cir. 1985).

The plaintiffs disagree that the 1977 EIS is legally sufficient under NEPA to cover all current rDNA research conducted under the auspices of NIH since 1977. Specifically, plaintiffs argue that there are three new areas of research and experimentation that were not evaluated by the 1977 EIS: (1) the ability to clone oncogenes into bacteria using shuttle vectors; (2) the cloning of the HIV (human immunodeficiency virus); and (3) the engineering of genetic codes of AIDS (acquired immune deficiency syndrome) into animal species. On each of these three broad points, the Court concludes that it is reasonable to maintain that the new developments are not so significant in their likely impact on the environment that a new EIS is necessary.

A. Oncogenic Cloning

The first area of debate is over the purported new development of the ability to clone oncogenic—i.e., tumor-causing—viruses into bacteria by using shuttle vectors. Vectors are DNA molecules used to introduce foreign DNA into a cell. The plaintiffs fear that this ability could lead to a situation in which oncogenic viruses entered into *E. coli* could reproduce, causing danger to other organisms.

The defendants argue persuasively, however, that the ability to clone oncogenic viruses using shuttle vectors does not create any greater risk or harm than cloning using other methods. Indeed, in 1978 NIH published an Environmental Assessment (EA) on changes in oncogenic research. Noting that the new Guidelines removed the ban on research involving oncogenic viruses classified as moderated risk, the EA stated that the change would not have a significant environmental impact and that cloning oncogenic viruses posed a "conceivable" but "unlikely" biohazard. The principles of basic molecular biology provide that it is virtually impossible for a viral segment to generate a oncogenic virus…. This conclusion, and the decision to remove the ban on research involving oncogenic viruses, resulted from an in-depth analysis that included a series of workshops attended by experts from all over the world, n1 various reviews of the workshop conclusions, examination of the guidelines of other countries, hours of public hearings, and various public and scientific comment.

The new technique of using shuttle vectors is still the use of gene or DNA segments and therefore does not increase the risk beyond that was evaluated carefully by the EA in 1978. The Court concludes that there was substantial evidence and that it was reasonable to conclude that the new oncogenic cloning research does not require a supplementary EIS.

B. Cloning the HIV Virus

The second area of new research and experimentation identified by plaintiffs is the ability to genetically engineer the HIV virus into HeLa cells and other types of cells not normally susceptible to HIV. Because these HeLa cells would for the first time be a host to the HIV virus, the plaintiffs argue, this new development would increase the risk of environmental harm.

The defendants note, however, that the new capabilities do *not* extend the host range of the HIV virus. Making HeLa cell lines—which are human cell lines—susceptible to the HIV virus does not put any new species at greater risk, the defendants point out, because humans are already susceptible to HIV and AIDS. Because the practical effect of the development does not appear to pose any serious additional threat, the Court concludes that it reasonable not to require a supplement to the EIS for this research.

C. Transgenic Experimentation

Finally, the third area of research and experimentation about which the plaintiffs allege that the government has failed to provide adequate environmental impact statement concerns the engineering of the genetic code for viruses causing human disease into other animals. This transgenic research, the plaintiffs claim, has the potential for serious harm should these animals enter man's environment. Particularly, the plaintiffs point to current experimentation at NIH in which the AIDS DNA has been placed in mice.

NIH approved the mice/AIDS experimentation pursuant to the NIH Guidelines. NIH concluded that if the experimentation was controlled using the highest safety level under the Guidelines, there would be no chance that any of the mice could escape the contained environment.

The plaintiffs argue that NIH is legally required to prepare a supplementary EIS to set forth and assess the possible environmental impact of the experiment and other similar experiments. NIH is in the process, however, of working on amendments to its Guidelines regarding the use of transgenic animals. As part of the Guideline amendments, NIH is preparing an environmental assessment (EA). The Court concludes that this EA should satisfy the legal requirements of NEPA.

The Court also concludes that NIH is acting reasonably in permitting the mice/AIDS experimentation to go forward while the EA is being prepared. First, the Court notes that although the AIDS virus was discovered after the original NIH EIS was published in 1977, the mere existence of a new disease that is being researched does not mean that the analyses, safeguards, and assessments of previous environmental evaluations are worthless.

Second, even if the mice/AIDS research does raise new environmental concerns and problems that have not been addressed satisfactorily to the requirements of NEPA, the Court concludes that the proper legal solution is to await the creation of the EA by NIH, instead of enjoining the mice/AIDS research.

NIH has presented persuasive evidence that mice/AIDS experimentation poses only the smallest possible risk to the environment. Under the highest-level containment pursuant to the NIH Guidelines, the mice are stored in "glove box" — a completely sealed unit with built-in gloves for handling the mice without having to open the box. The mice area is surrounded by a Clorox-filled dunk tank designed to stop the mice. Even if a mouse somehow did escape the unit, it would then have to work its way out of the high-level contained laboratory, which contains mouse traps, and a screen door to enable scientists to examine the area before entering. The defendant states that each of the safety features is inspected once every 10 days.

NIH also has guarded against the harm to humans should the mice somehow escape the laboratory building altogether. The mice have been blinded, to prevent their escape and to put them at a selective disadvantage in the wild. Mice injected with the viral DNA while still in embryo have all died before reaching sexual maturity. Singer Declaration at para. 5. Finally, the AIDS virus has not been found in the saliva or the urine of the mice — making further remote the possibility that a mouse biting a human or an escaping mouse could spread the AIDS virus.

In sum, the Court does not subscribe completely to the argument that because the mice are not released to the general environment there is no environmental impact. *See FOET v. Block*, Civ. No. 84-3045 (D.D.C. slip op. April 29, 1986) (concluding that there was no environmental impact to an experiment in which animals were kept in the laboratory), *aff'd sub nom. FOET v. Lyng*, 260 U.S. App. D.C. 159, 817 F.2d 882 (D.C. Cir. 1987). The Court realizes that the environmental impact of an experiment or research should be judged while considering the *possibility* that the experiment could affect the environment, as well as the expected impact. In the NIH's mice/AIDS experimentation, the Court concludes that the EA currently being created appears to satisfy the requirements of NEPA, and that the proven very low possibility of any environmental impact before the EA is complete justifies not enjoining NIH from continuing to sponsor the research pending the publication of the EA.

The defendants' motion for summary judgment is granted.

Notes

1. Is the application of the National Environmental Policy Act (NEPA) an effective way to challenge biotechnology? So far, the cases brought by Jeremy Rifkin and other similar groups have not been successful in their challenges under NEPA. *See*, Elie Gendloff, *Stauber v. Shalala: Are Environmental Challenges to Biotechnology Too Difficult?* 4 Wis. Envtl. L.J. 41 (Winter 1997). See also, Paul S. Naik, *Biotechnology Through the Eyes of an Opponent: The Resistance of Activist Jeremy Rifkin*, 5 Va. J.L. & Tech. 5 (Spring 2000) (Naik observes that despite all of the litigation by Rifkin, he has had little affect on biotechnology policy.)

2. Genetically Modified Organisms have been sensationalized in terms of their potential for escaping and destroying the environment. For example, the Smithsonian Institutes in the Museum of American History, designed an exhibit to explain the history of biotechnology. Their designers made the unfortunate decision to greet the museumgoers with a large image of Frankenstein with various products of biotechnology. The scientific community was enraged with this perpetuation of misinformation, and several scientific societies wrote letters to that effect to the Smithsonian Secretary. Within about six months, the exhibit was dismantled, but by that time millions of visitors had passed by the image of Frankenstein.

2.1.6 U.S. Department of Agriculture and BioPharming

BioPharming, or the production of crops which are designed to produce pharmaceuticals, vaccines, enzymes, antibodies, hormones or industrial chemicals using food as the vehicle poses potential threats to native plants, food crops and humans through ingestion. These plants, known as GEPPV (genetically engineered pharmaceutical-producing plant varieties), are regulated by the U.S. Department of Agriculture, yet have features of products regulated by FDA because they may be drugs.

The following excerpt provides a succinct introduction to the legal and scientific issues of biopharming, from Rebecca M. Bratspies, *Consuming (F)ears of Corn: Public Health and Biopharming*, 30 Am. J. L. and Med. 371 (2004).

> One of the most controversial and exciting prospects of biotechnology is biopharming—a process in which plants are genetically modified so that they endogenously produce specialty pharmaceutical or industrial proteins. Many such crops are currently being planted in small test plots throughout the country. Once they are fully developed and approved, these biopharm crops will be grown in the same agricultural fields that are currently devoted to producing traditional agricultural crops.

> Biopharm companies envision a lucrative future in which agricultural fields, converted into biofactories, grow the raw materials for industrial or pharmaceutical production. Among the dazzling possibilities are plants that produce specialty industrial compounds like biodegradable plastics or drugs to treat a variety of human diseases, such as cancer, HIV, and Alzheimer's. The allure of these crops is clear—an environmentally sustainable and inexpensive replacement for costly drugs and petrochemicals.

At the same time, there are some jarring points of tension, if not outright contradiction, between widespread planting of biopharm crops and the ongoing expectation of a safe and secure food supply. Biopharming frequently uses corn and other food crops as production vehicles, but these crops are emphatically not food and are not intended for human consumption. Biopharm crops, therefore, pose "a wholly different order" of environmental and human health risks. Despite the unique risks, biopharm crops have been tested in fields across the country under the same laissez-faire standards used for first-generation genetically modified ("GM") crops—with minimal and poorly enforced safety precautions based on physical containment. In the last decade, biotech companies and research universities have violated even those minimal safety precautions more than a hundred times. Because many of these open-air field tests of experimental biopharm crops take place in the Corn Belt, these violations put the food supply at a high risk for contamination.

Contamination of food crops with non-food, biopharm compounds is a serious threat to human safety and could result in rapid dissemination of non-food pharmaceutical or industrial compounds through the world food supply. There is no room for trial and error. Once contamination occurs, it will be next to impossible to reverse this process and "uncontaminate" the food supply. Unfortunately, important safety issues have been sidelined in order to facilitate rapid growth of this nascent industry. First and foremost, readily available and far safer alternatives could be used instead of food crops for biopharm production. But, because market forces diverge from the public's interest on this point, those safer options have not been pursued. Without government action forcing innovation towards achieving public health ends, it is clear that these options will remain unexplored. At the very least, there should be a moratorium on field testing these crops until a host of health-related questions are answered. Among the most pressing questions are: Do biopharm residues bioaccumulate? Is there a threshold below which these compounds can be safely consumed? Are there low-level, long-term health effects? Are these compounds allergens Are biopharmed crops anti-nutrients? How persistent are these compounds in the soil? How toxic are they to wildlife? How likely is the prospect that these non-food compounds could be spread to wild relatives?

… Part of the problem is that no regulatory agency has a clear statutory mandate to regulate biopharming. As a result, there are no coherent overarching government policies capable of ensuring that this new technology is safely explored and exploited.

The crisis is on our doorstep. According to some predictions, at least 10% of U.S. agricultural lands will be devoted to biopharming by the end of the decade. Thousands of inedible and potentially harmful compounds may soon be grown in corn fields throughout the country. Without detailed and enforceable standards for responsible use of this new technology, it is inevitable that these biopharm crops will contaminate crops destined for use as human food. The health risks from consuming these adulterated foods could be considerable.

Nevertheless, industry and governmental regulators have failed to impose obvious biological controls that would greatly protect the public's safety, while still permitting exploitation of this technology. For example, biopharming ought not be done in food crops, or, at the very least, ought not be released into the open environment of an agricultural field (as opposed to being grown in a greenhouse) before basic research has demonstrated that there will be no negative health effects from consuming contaminated foods. Instead of adopting these sensible precautions, regulators have simply assumed that contamination can be avoided through use of physical containment measures. This wildly optimistic assumption is not shared by biopharm developers who admit that biopharm proteins will likely wind up in the food supply. Moreover, physical containment measures have not shown much success in existing GM crops.

The limited scope of existing biopharm regulation leaves the public unprotected and exposed to an unacceptable level of risk. Moreover, the mere threat of commingling may be enough to destroy the United States' multi-billion dollar export trade in corn and other commodities. These failures to address the problem of contamination and commingling become even more critical now that the Cartagena Protocol on Biosafety has entered into force. Article 10 of the Protocol gives states the power to refuse import of the products of biotechnology (called living modified organisms or LMOs in the Protocol) in order to avoid or minimize adverse effects on human health or the conservation and sustainable use of biological diversity. It is hard to imagine anything more likely to justify a refusal to import under the Cartagena Protocol than undetectable commingling of industrial or pharmaceutical crops containing non-food proteins with export food crops. Protecting the public's interest in this context will require government to assume a far more active role than the hands-off attitude that has been the hallmark of conventional agricultural policy ...

BIOPHARMING 101

During the 1990s, researchers around the world embarked on the most ambitious biotechnology project ever—the sequencing of the human genome. and related biomedical research spawned a generation of highly specialized drugs based on antigens (vaccines), recombinant proteins (biologies) and human antibodies (collectively "therapeutics"). Demand for therapeutics is growing rapidly, especially those designed for chronic illnesses like psoriasis, allergic asthma, and rheumatoid arthritis. Meeting the projected demand for these therapeutics will require thousands of kilograms of purified proteins.

Commercial production of these products currently relies on abiotic fermentation (primarily in E. coli or yeast) or on mammalian cell culture (primarily in Chinese hamster ovary cells ("CHO cells")). These expression systems have some serious drawbacks: they tend to be expensive, labor intensive, and they produce relatively low yields that fall short of supplying all patients in need. Generally, recombinant mammalian systems can produce about 1–4 grams of a therapeutic protein per liter of media every 2–3 weeks, while recombinant E. coli systems yield 1–4 grams per liter every 1–2 days. Recombinant monoclonal antibody culture in CHO cells yields .5–1 gram per liter per day, and mammalian cell perfusion bioreactor systems yield about .3 gram per liter each day. Biopharming represents the cutting edge of the research on increasing yields with at least 120 different research institutions currently developing a staggering array of biopharm products.

At least in theory, plants can be engineered to express high levels of the desired pharmaceutical protein. One 200-acre biopharm field could therefore produce significantly greater quantities of therapeutics than current methods. More-over, biopharm crops offer some other distinct advantages for producing phar-maceutical proteins. Large-scale biopharming of these compounds should be more economical than current production techniques that rely on mammalian cell cultures. Because biopharming can be done by ordinary farmers in ordi-nary fields, rather than by highly skilled workers in high-tech facilities, the capital investment costs are relatively low. Some estimates indicate that bio-pharming could reduce production costs for these therapeutics by an order of magnitude. Biopharming can also draw on a wealth of existing agronomic ex-perience with growing, harvesting and processing these crops in their conven-tional forms. Unlike CHO cell or E. coli production techniques, biopharming does not require a highly educated and tech-savvy workforce. Biopharmed therapeutics may also be safer than those produced via existing techniques, be-cause plant-produced therapeutics have a reduced risk of carrying human pathogens.

The range of possible biopharm products under development is truly stagger-ing. For example, researchers at the Washington State University have trans-formed barley so that it produces a[1]-antitrypsin, a human blood plasma protein used to treat cystic fibrosis and various skin diseases. Barley has also been transformed to produce Antithrombin III, a human anticoagulant. There has been a great deal of research on antibody production in biopharm plants, so-called "plantibodies," and various research teams have demon-strated the possibilities of growing biovaccines against infectious diseases like cholera, Norwalk virus, Pre-clinical trials for these biovaccines have demon-strated that plant-grown vaccines can be effective in humans. Researchers at ProdiGene and Epicyte have transformed corn to produce human mono-clonal antibodies to treat HIV, and a team at Cornell has developed individu-alized biovaccines to treat non-Hodgkin's lymphoma. ProdiGene currently biopharms avidin corn for use as a research grade chemical, and Epicyte has developed a corn-grown spermicidal plantibody that it hopes to market as a contraceptive.

Although biopharm research has been conducted on a wide variety of plant species, corn has become the crop of choice for biopharm companies looking to commercialize their products. Indeed, the number of corn field tests dwarfs experimentation in all other crops combined. Corn does offer a num-ber of advantages—particularly the utility of corn cobs as a pre-packaged, cheap, and easily transported storage system. Unfortunately, his use of corn raises some serious safety questions because of the likelihood of contaminat-ing the food supply. Corn is, after all, a promiscuously outcrossing, wind-pollinated plant. Although companies routinely claim that test site locations are confidential business information ("CBI"), rendering that information unavailable to the public, much of this testing apparently occurred in the Corn Belt.

———————

The following case was a NEPA challenge to the continued use of land for biopharm-ing by plaintiffs in Hawaii, one of the most active regions for biopharming, based upon the number of permits granted from the U.S. Department of Agriculture.

———————

Center for Food Safety v. Veneman
364 F. Supp. 2d 1202 (D. HI 2005)

Plaintiffs allege that Defendants permitted open-air field tests of experimental, genetically engineered, pharmaceutical-producing plant varieties ("GEPPVs") of crops such as corn. These plant varieties are engineered to produce biologically active drugs, hormones, vaccines and industrial chemicals. [Plaintiffs state that Defendants have issued permits allowing companies to grow crops in Hawaii to produce proteins such as cytokines, which suppress the immune system, interferon alpha, which may cause dementia and neurotoxicity, avidin, known to cause Vitamin B deficiency, and trypsin, an inhalant allergen known to cause occupational asthma in workers, amongst others.]

Plaintiffs assert that Hawaii has become a preferred site for field testing genetically engineered crops at thousands of plot locations throughout the islands. Plaintiffs' first through fifth claims involve Defendants' alleged failure to comply with NEPA in the promulgation of the field tests at issue in the instant case. Plaintiffs maintain that Defendants never prepared an Environmental Impact Statement ("EIS") or environmental assessment ("EA") as they claim was required by NEPA before approving the permits at issue. Plaintiffs allege violations of ESA, 16 U.S.C. § 1533 et seq. in their sixth through tenth claims in part for Defendants' failure to consult with the United States Fish and Wildlife Service ("FWS") prior to issuing the permits.

Plaintiffs next assert in their eleventh claim for relief that Defendants violated the Plant Protection Act ("PPA"), 7 U.S.C. § 7701 et seq., and the Administrative Procedure Act ("APA"), 5 U.S.C. 551 et seq., by arbitrarily and capriciously denying their request to promulgate regulations under the PPA to both prohibit the challenged field tests generally and also prohibit the use of food crops affected by the tests. Plaintiffs seek declaratory and injunctive relief to compensate Plaintiffs for the risks Defendants' actions pose to public health, the environment, and the economy.

The "capable of repetition, yet evading review" exception to the general principle that a court must dismiss claims that are rendered moot was first established by the Supreme Court in Southern Pacific Terminal Co. v. ICC. (1911). There are two requirements that must exist for the exception to apply: "(1) the duration of the challenged action is too short to allow full litigation before it ceases, and (2) there is a reasonable expectation that the plaintiffs will be subjected to it again.

In the instant case, the Court finds evidence supporting the existence of both required elements. First, the Court evaluates whether the underlying action is almost certain to run its course before a court can give the case full consideration. Regarding the field test plantings at issue, the period between the first planting and the last harvest ranged from less than a week to more than a year; all terminated in less than two years. Moreover, APHIS announced in a letter dated January 14, 2004, a rule limiting the duration of biopharmaceutical permits and plantings to one growing season, or a maximum of one year. No stretch of the imagination would allow this Court to conclude that one year is sufficient time for a claim to be adjudicated from the trial level through appellate review. Indeed, in the instant case, one year was not sufficient time to allow even the completion of discovery or the litigation of jurisdictional issues. This finding is consistent with Ninth Circuit precedent, which has held that challenges to two-year permits meet the durational requirement for the exception, because two years is not a sufficient period of time to allow full litigation.

The second, the Court must assess whether the challenged action will probably affect the Plaintiffs in the future. As Plaintiffs note, Defendants have themselves repeatedly asserted that the activity will recur on these cites. Indeed, Defendants own declarant, Dr. Neil Hoffman, stated the following:

> Historically, biotechnology companies have used the same field-test sites repeatedly. This is particularly true in Hawaii where much of their breeding work goes on year round. BRS staff contacted Dow and Garst, two companies that recently had GEPPV trials in Hawaii. Garst has been at the same site since 1985 and has a 30 year lease on the property they are using. Dow has been using the same site since the 1960s. Therefore, it is a certainty that the locations previously used for GEPPVs will be used in the near future for other field trials, both pursuant and subject to future permits.

Moreover, the Court finds that not only is it likely that such testing will continue in Hawaii, but it is also likely that the testing will continue under the circumstances to which Plaintiffs object. During the pendency of this lawsuit, at least 25 applications have been filed seeking permission to conduct biopharmaceutical field tests in other jurisdictions across the nation, and at least 10 have been approved by Defendants without an EIS or EA. As such, the Court finds that the record evidences a probability that the challenged action will affect Plaintiffs in the future.

The Court finds that declaratory and equitable relief is still available to Plaintiffs, regardless of the completion of the testing at issue. As shown in the Ninth Circuit's previous decisions, such equitable relief could include a court order requiring of study of the impact the crop testing ultimately had on the surrounding environment, and if necessary, to take remedial measures. The Court does not reach any ruling regarding the propriety of such a remedy, should Plaintiffs ultimately prevail on the merits of their case; the possibility is only raised hypothetically to show that equitable remedies remain available and the case is not mooted. Moreover, claims ten and eleven of Plaintiffs' complaint, which seek declaratory judgment regarding alleged programmatic violations of the Endangered Species Act, Plant Protection Act, and Administrative Procedure Act, are not affected by Defendants' mootness argument at all.

The case which follows, is the final determination by the court on the question of whether an environmental impact statement is required under NEPA for these permits for biopharm crops.

Center for Food Safety v. Johanns
451 F.Supp.2d 1165 (D.Hawai'i 2006)

J. MICHAEL SEABRIGHT, District Judge.

I. *INTRODUCTION*

From 2001 to 2003, four companies—ProdiGene, Monsanto, Hawaii Agriculture Research Center (HARC), and Garst Seed—planted corn and sugarcane that had been genetically modified to produce experimental pharmaceutical products. The companies modified the genetic structure of the corn or sugarcane so that, when harvested, the plants would contain hormones, vaccines, or proteins that could be used to treat human illnesses. For example, one company engineered corn to produce experimental vaccines for the Human Immunodeficiency Virus and the Hepatitis B virus, while another company engineered corn and sugarcane to produce cancer-fighting agents. These techniques are still experimental, and from 2001 to 2003 these four companies conducted limited field tests of these genetically engineered pharmaceutical-producing plant varieties ("GEPPVs") on Kauai, Maui, Molokai, and Oahu.

ProdiGene, Monsanto, HARC, and Garst Seed received permits to plant these crops from the United States Department of Agriculture, Animal and Plant Health Inspection Service ("APHIS"). The companies have already planted and harvested these crops, the permits have expired, and the companies are no longer planting crops pursuant to these permits.

The Plaintiffs argue that APHIS2 broke the law in issuing these permits. Because these crops produce experimental pharmaceutical products, the Plaintiffs argue, their effect on Hawaii's ecosystem (especially Hawaii's 329 endangered and threatened species) is unclear. The Plaintiffs contend that these experimental crops could cross-pollinate with existing food crops, thus contaminating the food supply. The Plaintiffs also argue that animals that feed on corn (as well as animals further up the food chain that feed on corn-eating animals) would become unwitting carriers of experimental pharmaceutical products, causing even more widespread dissemination of these experimental vaccines, hormones, and proteins. According to the Plaintiffs, APHIS was required to evaluate the environmental impact of these genetically engineered crops before issuing the permits. In failing to do so, the Plaintiffs argue, APHIS violated both the National Environmental Policy Act ("NEPA") and the Endangered Species Act ("ESA"). The Plaintiffs also argue that these four permits were part of a broader "GEPPV program": a collection of policies and protocols which, taken together, form a comprehensive program for the promotion and regulation of GEPPV development and testing. The Plaintiffs contend that APHIS was required to consider the environmental impact of the program as a whole and that APHIS's failure to do so constitutes an additional violation of NEPA and the ESA. As a remedy for failing to follow NEPA and the ESA in implementing this "GEPPV program," the Plaintiffs seek a nationwide ban on all GEPPV open-air field testing until APHIS complies with NEPA and the ESA. APHIS, on the other hand, argues that it fulfilled its statutory obligations. APHIS contends that it placed strict conditions on the permits to ensure that the genetically modified crops would not contaminate the environment, such that it complied with both the ESA and NEPA.

According to APHIS, because the Plaintiffs have failed to demonstrate any environmental harm from these open-air field tests, the Plaintiffs' claims necessarily fail. And as for the alleged "GEPPV program," APHIS argues that its internal policies and protocols do not rise to the level of "final agency action"; consequently, APHIS contends, the Plaintiffs are not entitled to judicial review of this "program."

In addition to the dispute over the four permits and the alleged "GEPPV program," there is a dispute over a petition for rulemaking submitted to APHIS by the Plaintiffs. The Plaintiffs submitted their Petition to APHIS on December 16, 2002; the Petition sought five specific actions from APHIS, and the Plaintiffs argue that APHIS arbitrarily and capriciously denied the Petition. APHIS contends that the Plaintiffs' claims are not ripe and must be dismissed.

After more than two and a half years of contentious litigation, the court heard the parties' motions for summary judgment on July 7, 2006.

Based on the following, the court GRANTS IN PART and DENIES IN PART the Plaintiffs' motion for summary judgment and GRANTS IN PART and DENIES IN PART the Defendants' motion for summary judgment.

The court concludes that APHIS violated both the ESA and NEPA in issuing the four permits, but concludes that injunctive relief is not necessary to remedy these violations. The court then concludes that APHIS's alleged "GEPPV program" was neither a "final agency action" subject to review under the Administrative Procedure Act nor "agency action" subject to the requirements of the ESA.

II. BACKGROUND

A. Legal Framework

A brief description of the legal framework applicable to the instant case may assist in placing the facts in context. The Plaintiffs allege APHIS violated the ESA, NEPA, and the Plant Protection Act ("PPA"); the court first discusses the Administrative Procedure Act ("APA"), which provides for judicial review of agency action, and then examines the ESA, NEPA, and the PPA.

1. Administrative Procedure Act

The APA allows for judicial review of "[a]gency action made reviewable by statute and final agency action for which there is no other adequate remedy in a court[.]" 5 U.S.C. § 704. The APA defines "agency action" as "includ[ing] the whole or a part of an agency rule, order, license, sanction, relief, or the equivalent or denial thereof, or failure to act[.]" 5 U.S.C. § 551(13). As discussed more fully *infra*, some statutes (such as the ESA) contain provisions allowing for greater judicial review than that provided in the APA, whereas many statutes (such as NEPA) do not contain their own review standards (such that the APA standards control). As set forth in 5 U.S.C. § 706, the "arbitrary and capricious" standard of review applies to judicial review of agency actions:

The reviewing court shall—

(1) compel agency action unlawfully withheld or unreasonably delayed; and

(2) hold unlawful and set aside agency action, findings, and conclusions found to be—

(A) arbitrary, capricious, an abuse of discretion, or otherwise not in accordance with law;

(B) contrary to constitutional right, power, privilege, or immunity;

(C) in excess of statutory jurisdiction, authority, or limitations, or short of statutory right; [or]

(D) without observance of procedure required by law

2. Endangered Species Act [1]

One of the express policies of the Endangered Species Act, 16 U.S.C. § 1531 et seq., is to ensure "that all Federal departments and agencies shall seek to conserve endangered species and threatened species[.]" 16 U.S.C. § 1531(c)(1). The ESA mandates interagency collaboration, through a series of procedural requirements outlined in the statute, to effectuate Congress's goals of protecting endangered and threatened plant and animal species. 16 U.S.C. §§ 1532, 1536. Specifically, the ESA requires the following:

[E]ach Federal agency shall request of the Secretary [of the Interior] information whether any species which is listed or proposed to be listed [as an endangered species or a threatened species] may be present in the area of such proposed action. If the Secretary advises, based on the best scientific and commercial data available, that such species may be present, such agency shall conduct a biological assessment for the purpose of identifying any endangered species or threatened species which is likely to be affected by such action. 16 U.S.C. § 1536(c)(1); 50 C.F.R. § 402.12(c) (requiring federal agencies to request information regarding listed species and critical habitat from the Department of the Interior). In other words, whenever an agency is considering taking an "action," that agency must request a list, from either the United States Fish and Wildlife Service ("FWS") or the National Marine Fisheries Service ("NMFS"), of those endangered and threatened species present in the geographic area of the proposed action.

[T]he APA allows for judicial review of "[a]gency action made reviewable by statute and final agency action for which there is no other adequate remedy in a court[.]" 5 U.S.C. §704. The ESA falls into the former category, as it contains a broad citizen suit provision allowing suits "to enjoin any person, including the United States and any other governmental instrumentality or agency, who is alleged to be in violation of any provision of this chapter or regulation issued under the authority thereof to enforce the ESA." 16 U.S.C. § 1540(g)(1)(A).

The Plaintiffs allege that APHIS failed to follow the procedures outlined in 16 U.S.C. § 1536. These procedural requirements, however, only apply to "agency action," a term defined by the ESA as "any action authorized, funded, or carried out by" a federal agency. 16 U.S.C. § 1536(a)(2). The joint regulations (promulgated by the United States Fish & Wildlife Service and the National Marine Fisheries Service) implementing the ESA similarly provide:

"Action" means all activities or programs of any kind authorized, funded, or carried out, in whole or in part, by Federal agencies in the United States or upon the high seas. Examples include, but are not limited to: (a) actions intended to conserve listed species or their habitat; (b) the promulgation of regulations; (c) the granting of licenses, contracts, leases, easements, rights-of-way, permits, or grants-in-aid; or (d) actions directly or indirectly causing modifications to the land, water, or air. 50 C.F.R. §402.02. APHIS does not dispute that issuance of the four permits is "agency action" sufficient to trigger the requirements of the ESA. The parties disagree, however, as to whether APHIS's purported "GEPPV program" is an "agency action" within the meaning of the ESA. As discussed *infra*, the court concludes that this "GEPPV program" is not an "agency action" under the ESA.

3. National Environmental Policy Act

The National Environmental Policy Act, 42 U.S.C. §4321 et seq., states that "each person should enjoy a healthful environment and that each person has a responsibility to contribute to the preservation and enhancement of the environment." 42 U.S.C. §4331(c). To that end, NEPA requires federal agencies to evaluate the impact of their actions on the natural environment. *See* 42 U.S.C. §4332. Specifically, NEPA requires all federal agencies to "include in every recommendation or report on proposals for legislation and other major Federal actions significantly affecting the quality of the human environment, a detailed statement by the responsible official on the environmental impact of the proposed action[.]" 42 U.S.C. §4332(2)(c). Through NEPA, Congress established the Council on Environmental Quality ("CEQ"), which has promulgated regulations requiring all agencies to comply with certain procedures before acting. 42 U.S.C. §4342; 40 C.F.R. Part 1500. The CEQ regulations require agencies to prepare an "environmental assessment"("EA") and/or an "environmental impact statement" ("EIS") before acting, except in limited circumstances. 40 C.F.R. §§ 1501.3, 1501.4. An EIS is "a detailed written statement as required by" NEPA, and an EA is "a concise public document"that an agency prepares when deciding whether it needs to prepare a more extensive EIS. 40 C.F.R. §§ 1508.9, 1508.11.

There are circumstances under which an agency may avoid preparing either an EA or an EIS. The CEQ regulations allow federal agencies to develop "categorical exclusion[s]" to the EA/EIS requirements for routine agency actions that are known to have no significant effect on the human environment:

Categorical exclusion means a category of actions which do not individually or cumulatively have a significant effect on the human environment and which have been found to have no such effect and for which, therefore, neither an environmental assessment nor an environmental impact statement is required. Any procedures under this section shall provide for extraordinary circumstances in which a normally excluded action may have a significant environmental effect. 40 C.F.R. § 1508.4.

APHIS promulgated its own regulations to ensure that its actions complied with NEPA and with the CEQ regulations. In 7 C.F.R. § 372.5, APHIS describes four categories of actions: "Actions normally requiring environmental impact statements"; "Actions normally requiring environmental assessments but not necessarily environmental impact statements"; "Categorically excluded actions"; and "Exceptions for categorically excluded actions." (Italics omitted.) In other words, 7 C.F.R. § 372.5 generally tracks the CEQ's requirements (as set forth in 40 C.F.R. § 1508.4): it allows federal agencies to develop categorical exclusions, but requires agencies to "provide for extraordinary circumstances in which a normally excluded action may have a significant environmental effect."

The APHIS regulations regarding categorically excluded actions provide in relevant part: This class of APHIS actions shares many of the same characteristics as the class of actions that normally requires environmental assessments but not necessarily environmental impact statements. The major difference is that the means through which adverse environmental impacts may be avoided or minimized have actually been built right into the actions themselves. The efficacy of this approach generally has been established through testing and/or monitoring [Types of categorically excluded actions] include: (3) *Licensing and permitting* (ii) Permitting, or acknowledgement of notifications for, confined field releases of genetically engineered organisms and products[.] 7 C.F.R. § 372.5(c). The relevant exception to this categorical exclusion appears in 7 C.F.R. § 372.5(d): Whenever the decisionmaker determines that a categorically excluded action may have the potential to affect "significantly" the quality of the "human environment," as those terms are defined at 40 CFR 1508.27 and 1508.14, respectively, an environmental assessment or an environmental impact statement will be prepared.

For example: (4) When a confined field release of genetically engineered organisms or products involves new species or organisms or novel modifications that raise new issues. In sum, APHIS does not need to prepare an EA or an EIS when it issues permits for actions in which "the means through which adverse environmental impacts may be avoided or minimized have actually been built right into the actions themselves" — such as "confined field release[s] of genetically engineered organisms and products" — so long as those field releases do not "involve[ ] new species or organisms or novel modifications that raise new issues." In interpreting the statutes and regulations cited *supra,* the Ninth Circuit has held that, "[w]hen an agency decides to proceed with an action in the absence of an EA or EIS, the agency must adequately explain its decision." *Alaska Ctr. For the Env't v. U.S. Forest Serv.,* 189 F.3d 851, 859 (9th Cir.1999). "NEPA's procedural requirements require agencies to take a 'hard look' at the environmental consequences of their actions. A hard look includes 'considering all foreseeable direct and indirect impacts.'" *Earth Island Inst. v. U.S. Forest Serv.,* 442 F.3d 1147, 1159 (9th Cir.2006) (quoting *Idaho Sporting Cong. v. Rittenhouse,* 305 F.3d 957, 973 (9th Cir.2002)). "'An agency cannot avoid its statutory responsibilities under NEPA merely by asserting that an activity it wishes to pursue will have an insignificant effect on the environment.'" *Alaska Ctr. for the Env't,* 189 F.3d at 859 (quoting *Jones v. Gordon,* 792 F.2d 821, 828 (9th Cir.1986)). To comply with NEPA, "'[t]he agency must supply a convincing statement of reasons why potential effects are insignificant.'" *Id.* (quoting *Steamboatersv. Fed. Energy Regulatory Comm'n*, 759 F.2d 1382, 1393 (9th Cir.1985)).

There does not appear to be any specific process an agency must follow in determining that a categorical exclusion applies and that an exception to that exclusion does not apply; the agency must simply explain its decision in a reasoned manner. Once again, however, a court may only review an agency's activity if that activity rises to the level of "final agency action." Unlike the ESA, NEPA does not contain its own definition of "agency action." Instead, NEPA uses the definition from the APA, which provides that "'agency action' includes the whole or a part of an agency rule, order, license, sanction, relief, or the equivalent or denial thereof, or failure to act[.]" 5 U.S.C. §551(13). As with the Plaintiffs' ESA claims, APHIS does not dispute that issuance of the four permits is "agency action" sufficient to trigger the requirements of NEPA, but APHIS argues that the alleged "GEPPV program" is not "agency action" within the meaning of NEPA and the APA. As discussed *infra*, the court concludes that this "GEPPV program" is not a "final agency action" under NEPA.

4. Plant Protection Act

The Plant Protection Act ("PPA"), 7 U.S.C. §7701 et seq., was enacted in 2000 to attempt to detect, control, eradicate, and suppress plant pests and noxious weeds. 7 U.S.C. §7701(1). The PPA gives the Secretary of Agriculture the authority to promulgate regulations to prevent the introduction and dissemination of plant pests. 7 U.S.C. §§7702(16), 7711(a). The PPA regulations appear in 7 C.F.R. Part 340.

The Plaintiffs do not claim that APHIS violated the PPA. Instead, as discussed more fully *infra*, the Plaintiffs contend that they asked APHIS to promulgate rules pursuant to the PPA; that APHIS ignored the Plaintiffs' request for the past three and a half years; and that APHIS's inaction violated the APA. [T] the court concludes that some of the Plaintiffs' claims are unripe inasmuch as they do not address "final agency action"; the court concludes that the remaining claims are ripe but that APHIS's actions were neither arbitrary nor capricious.

IV. *DISCUSSION*

In its Second Amended Complaint, the Plaintiffs allege the following: (1) APHIS violated NEPA and the ESA in issuing each of the four permits at issue in this case (Counts One through Four and Six through Nine, respectively); (2) APHIS violated NEPA and the ESA in implementing its "GEPPV program" (Counts Five and Ten, respectively); and (3) APHIS violated the PPA and the APA in failing to respond to the Plaintiffs' Petition (Count Eleven).

Finally, in Section E, the court considers the appropriate remedies in this case and concludes that injunctive relief is not appropriate as to those Counts on which the Plaintiffs prevail.

A. *Endangered Species Act*

Hawaii is known not only for its remarkable landscape and beaches, but also for its considerable number of endangered and threatened species. The Fish and Wildlife Service reports on its website that there are 329 endangered and threatened plant and animal species in Hawaii, including thirty-two types of birds. Hawaii has more endangered and threatened species than any other state, and Hawaii's 329 listed species represent approximately twenty-five percent of all listed species in the United States. Although strict compliance with the ESA's procedural requirements is always critically important, these requirements are particularly crucial in Hawaii given Hawaii's extensive number of threatened and endangered species.

APHIS argues that it complied with the ESA in issuing the four permits. APHIS points to 50 C.F.R. §402.14, which provides that "[e]ach Federal agency shall review its actions at the earliest possible time to determine whether any action may affect listed species or critical habitat"; APHIS argues that it determined that its proposed actions would not affect listed species or critical habitat, such that formal consultation was not required. APHIS's argument misses the mark. The problem is not with APHIS's decision not to conduct a formal consultation: APHIS may ultimately be correct that formal consultation was not required (though the court makes no findings on this point), but this is not the real issue. Instead, the problem is that APHIS skipped the initial, mandatory step of obtaining information about listed species and critical habitats from FWS and NMFS.

Regardless of whether the field tests of the genetically modified crops were "confined" (as discussed more fully *infra*), and regardless of whether APHIS's actions were in fact innocuous with respect to listed species and habitats, APHIS violated the ESA. APHIS engaged in "agency action"—granting a series of permits to field test genetically modified crops—without fulfilling its congressionally mandated duty to obtain information from FWS and NMFS regarding endangered species, threatened species, and critical habitats.

Even if APHIS is ultimately correct in its assertion that no listed species or habitats have been harmed, APHIS's actions are nevertheless tainted because APHIS failed to comply with a fundamental procedural requirement. APHIS's utter disregard for this simple investigation requirement, especially given the extraordinary number of endangered and threatened plants and animals in Hawaii, constitutes an unequivocal violation of a clear congressional mandate.

In an apparent effort to mitigate, APHIS turns to its second argument: "No harm, no foul." APHIS argues that, because the Plaintiffs have not provided any evidence to show that a single listed species or habitat was harmed in any way, the Plaintiffs' claims necessarily fail. This argument is absurd. An agency violates the ESA when it fails to follow the procedures mandated by Congress, and an agency will not escape scrutiny based on the fortunate outcome that no listed plant, animal, or habitat was harmed. APHIS's argument essentially asks the court to believe that APHIS is immune from suit, no matter how egregious the violation of the ESA, so long as APHIS does not cause any substantive harm to any listed species or habitat.

In other words, APHIS argues that the Plaintiffs may not proceed with a lawsuit against the agency unless APHIS actually facilitates an organism's extinction. This after-the-fact justification (and good fortune) cannot absolve APHIS of its failure to follow a clear congressional mandate. If a project is allowed to proceed without substantial compliance with those procedural requirements, there can be no assurance that a violation of the ESA's substantive provisions will not result. The latter, of course, is impermissible. In sum, the

Defendants' argument is utterly without merit. The court therefore grants summary judgment in favor of the Plaintiffs as to Counts Six, Seven, Eight, and Nine of the Second Amended Complaint.

B. *National Environmental Policy Act*

The court concludes that APHIS violated NEPA because APHIS failed to articulate its reasons for declining to prepare an EA or EIS. There is nothing in the administrative record to indicate that, contemporaneously with the issuance of the four permits, APHIS considered the applicability of NEPA, categorical exclusions, or the exceptions to those exclusions. In other words, APHIS failed to provide a reasoned explanation for its apparent determinations that a categorical exclusion applied and that the exceptions to the exclusion did not apply. Consequently, APHIS's actions—granting the four permits—were arbitrary and capricious.

1. APHIS cannot rely on a categorical exclusion post hoc

The court could find nothing in the administrative record to indicate that APHIS considered NEPA when deciding whether to issue the four permits. Nowhere in the administrative record does APHIS discuss the applicability of the categorical exclusion or the exceptions to that exclusion. As the Ninth Circuit has explained: It is difficult for a reviewing court to determine if the application of an exclusion is arbitrary and capricious where there is no contemporaneous documentation to show that the agency considered the environmental consequences of its action and decided to apply a categorical exclusion to the facts of a particular decision.

APHIS argues that the four permits fit within its broad categorical exclusion in 7 C.F.R. § 372.5(c) (environmental mitigation measures built into the agency action itself) and its own more specific categorical exclusion in 7 C.F.R. § 372.5(c)(3)(ii) ("confined field releases of genetically engineered organisms").

APHIS cannot, however, abdicate its responsibilities during the administrative process and expect the court to defer to the agency's post hoc explanations. Furthermore, the fact that a field test is "confined" or "controlled" for purposes of the PPA does not necessarily mean that the field test is "confined" within the meaning of the categorical exclusion within APHIS's NEPA regulations. While there may be substantial or complete overlap between 7 C.F.R. Part 340 and 7 C.F.R. § 372.5(c)(3)(ii), there must be some indication in the administrative record that APHIS considered the environmental consequences of its actions. NEPA requires no less. APHIS's effort to justify its actions falls short.

Based on the administrative record, the court concludes that APHIS's issuance of the four permits—without an EA, an EIS, or an explanation as to why neither an EA nor an EIS was required—was arbitrary and capricious. Furthermore, as explained in the following section, APHIS's issuance of the four permits without considering the exceptions to the applicable categorical exclusion was also arbitrary and capricious.

2. APHIS's failure to consider the exceptions to the categorical exclusion renders APHIS's actions arbitrary and capricious. APHIS also argued that it should be held to a lower standard because this was "informal" rather than "formal" agency action. This argument is similarly without merit. The court agrees with APHIS that no formal NEPA document was required and that, as a general rule, an agency action will survive the arbitrary and capricious standard even if the agency was disorganized in performing its review. Nevertheless, an agency action will not survive judicial review where the administrative record fails to reflect any consideration of environmental harm as required by NEPA. "[w]hen a confined field release of genetically engineered organisms or products involves new species or organisms or novel modifications that raise new issues." The Plaintiffs argue that this exception applies to the four permits at issue, such that APHIS violated NEPA by failing to prepare an EA or EIS. In the instant case, whether the exception in 7 C.F.R. § 372.5(d)(4) *does* apply is unclear, but there is substantial evidence that it *may* apply. Applications and correspondence submitted by two of the four permittees state that the proposed field tests involve "novel" proteins. Whether the remain-

ing two permit applications involve "novel modifications" that "raise new issues" is unclear. While the idea of genetically modifying food crops to produce experimental pharmaceutical products may certainly appear "novel" to a layperson, this court lacks the expertise to make this kind of determination.

Whether the proposed field tests involve "novel modifications," and whether these modifications "raise new issues," are questions best left to APHIS; the court will defer to APHIS's judgment on these issues, but APHIS must articulate a reasoned decision based on the information available to it. In the instant case, APHIS has simply failed to provide *any* explanation for its implied determination that the exceptions to the categorical exclusion do not apply. This is not the type of reasoned decisionmaking required of federal agencies, and it cannot stand. The court finds that there is substantial evidence that an exception to the categorical exclusion *may* apply and that APHIS was required to provide *some* explanation as to why, in its view, the exceptions did not apply. Consequently, the court concludes that APHIS's issuance of the four permits, without considering the exceptions to the categorical exclusions, was arbitrary and capricious. Therefore, the court grants summary judgment in favor of the Plaintiffs as to Counts One, Two, Three, and Four of the Second Amended Complaint.

C. The "GEPPV Program"

The Plaintiffs argue that APHIS did more than just issue a series of individual permits: they argue that APHIS developed and implemented an organized, national program (with coordinated policies, protocols, and regulations) and that APHIS was required by NEPA and the ESA to study the impact of this program on the environment and endangered species. The Plaintiffs contend that APHIS's failure to consider the cumulative impact of its national GEPPV program constitutes a separate violation of NEPA and the ESA (Counts Five and Ten, respectively, of the Plaintiffs' Second Amended Complaint). APHIS argues that there was no "final agency action" for purposes of the NEPA claim and no "agency action" for purposes of the ESA claim, such that the Plaintiffs' claims necessarily fail. The court agrees with APHIS. The court first examines the NEPA claim and then turns to the ESA claim.

1. NEPA

The APA provides that "[a]gency action made reviewable by statute and final agency action for which there is no other adequate remedy in a court are subject to judicial review." 5 U.S.C. § 704. And second, the action must be one by which "rights or obligations have been determined," or from which "legal consequences will flow," *Port of Boston Marine Terminal Assn. v. Rederiaktiebolaget Transatlantic*, 400 U.S. 62, 71, 91 S.Ct. 203, 209, 27 L.Ed.2d 203 (1970).

The Plaintiffs allege that APHIS has a national "GEPPV program" and that this national program has a substantial environmental impact. The court is not persuaded. [I]t is clear that APHIS has some internal policies and procedures by which it operates. An agency's decision to publicly share its internal guidelines and policies does not automatically mean that "final agency action" exists.

Obviously, federal agencies routinely develop internal procedures and protocols in attempting to fulfill their statutory duties, but ... these procedures and protocols do not rise to the level of "final agency action" for purposes of NEPA unless the agency engages in some activity with some direct impact on the environment. Thus, even if the Plaintiffs are correct that "APHIS, through its program, promotes and oversees the development and testing of GEPPVs," the Plaintiffs have not pointed to any "final agency action," apart from issuance of the four permits, that allows for judicial review.

Similarly, the court is unpersuaded that APHIS's PPA regulations evince a broader "GEPPV program" that, in turn, constitutes "final agency action." The Plaintiffs admit that they are not bringing a facial challenge to the regulations themselves; instead, they appear to argue that the regulations, when viewed in concert with APHIS's internal procedures and protocols, constitute a "final agency action" subject to judicial review. Plaintiffs have failed to demonstrate, in their briefing and in oral argument, how these regulations have transformed internal procedures into a "final agency action." The Plaintiffs' fourth argument—that APHIS's programmatic EIS ("PEIS"), currently underway, demonstrates that APHIS has always had a "GEPPV program"—is similarly without merit. The Plaintiffs would have the court believe that, any time an agency decides to conduct a PEIS, all agency activity that preceded the PEIS necessarily violated NEPA (because the agency was "acting" without a PEIS in place). If the court were to agree with the Plaintiffs, agencies would have a tremendous disincentive to prepare programmatic environmental impact statements because, according to the Plaintiffs, initiation of the PEIS process is essentially an admission that the agency had been violating NEPA prior to initiating the PEIS process. The law is clear as to when a PEIS must be prepared, and no PEIS was necessary for the agency activity relied upon by the Plaintiffs. The fact that APHIS decided to initiate a PEIS does not demonstrate that APHIS engaged in "final agency action" before beginning the PEIS. The Plaintiffs have failed to produce any evidence or point to any genuine issue of material fact demonstrating that there is a reviewable agency action. None of the four items relied upon by the Plaintiffs—either individually or cumulatively—shows that the "GEPPV program" is "final agency action" sufficient to allow for judicial review under the APA. Because there is no "final agency action" for the court to review, APHIS is entitled to summary judgment as to Count Five.

2. ESA

[T]he ESA contains a broad citizen suit provision. Consequently, the Plaintiffs' ESA claim is not limited by the "final agency action" restriction applicable to the NEPA claim. 16 U.S.C. §540(g)(1)(A). Nevertheless, federal agencies are only required to comply with the ESA's procedural requirements when an agency proposes an "agency action".

Although ESA provides a slightly broader definition of "agency action" than NEPA, the ESA, like NEPA, still contemplates something more tangible than internal agency protocols and policies. Even if the Plaintiffs are correct that APHIS has established an organized method of running a "GEPPV program," the court fails to see how these coordinated polices and regulations constitute an "agency action" separate and distinct from APHIS's action in issuing the individual permits. In sum, the Plaintiffs have failed to produce evidence of an "agency action," and with no "agency action," there can be no violation of the ESA (because an agency is only required to comply with the ESA's procedural requirements where the agency proposes to engage in "agency action"). Consequently, the court grants summary judgment in favor of APHIS as to Count Ten of the Plaintiffs' Second Amended Complaint.

D. *Plant Protection Act*

In Count Eleven of their Second Amended Complaint, the Plaintiffs contend that APHIS has essentially denied their December 16, 2002 Petition and that this effective denial was arbitrary and capricious. The Defendants argue that APHIS never denied the Petition, such that the Plaintiffs' claims are unripe. Consequently, the court concludes that [some of]he Plaintiffs' claim is unripe and grants summary judgment in favor of the Defendants.

[E. Remedies]

The court agrees with Plaintiffs' assessment of the situation: injunctive relief is inappropriate as to Counts One through Four and Six through Nine. The most the court could do is issue an injunction stating that APHIS must comply with NEPA, the ESA, and the APA; given that APHIS is already required to do all those things, and given that the permits have all expired (such that there is no ongoing or pending agency action to enjoin), the court sees no reason to issue an injunction.

V. *CONCLUSION*

Based on the foregoing, the court GRANTS summary judgment in favor of the Plaintiffs as to Counts One, Two, Three, Four, Six, Seven, Eight, and Nine of their Second Amended Complaint, and the court GRANTS summary judgment in favor of the Defendants as to Counts Five, Ten, and Eleven of the Plaintiffs' Second Amended Complaint....

IT IS SO ORDERED.

DATED: Honolulu, Hawaii, August 31, 2006.

2.2 Legislative Branch

2.2.1 Legislation and Problems with Biotechnology

In response to public concern about genetically engineered foods, and as noted in the previous case, a bill was introduced to provide for an amendment of food labeling requirements to define and require labeling for genetically engineered foods.

H.R. 3377, 106th Cong.

The Genetically Engineered Food Right to Know Act, H.R. 3377, 106th Cong. (1999), introduced November 16, 1999.

To amend the Federal Food, Drug, and Cosmetic Act, the Federal Meat Inspection Act, and the Poultry Products Inspection Act to require that food that contains a genetically engineered material, or that is produced with a genetically engineered material, be labeled accordingly.

Be it enacted by the Senate and House of Representatives of the United States of America in Congress assembled, ...

SEC. 2. FINDINGS. The Congress finds as follows: (1) The process of genetically engineering foods results in the material change of such foods. (2) The Congress has previously required that all foods bear labels that reveal material facts to consumers. (3) Federal agencies have failed to uphold Congressional intent by allowing genetically engineered foods to be marketed, sold and otherwise used without labeling that reveals material facts to the public. (4) Consumers wish to know whether the food they purchase and consume contains or is produced with a genetically engineered material for a variety of reasons, including the potential transfer of allergens into food and other health risks, concerns about potential environmental risks associated with the genetic engineering of crops, and religiously and ethically based dietary restrictions. (5) Consumers have a right to know whether the food they purchase contains or was produced with genetically engineered material. (6) Reasonably available technology permits the detection in food of genetically engineered material, generally acknowledged to be as low as 0.1 percent.

SEC. 3. LABELING REGARDING GENETICALLY ENGINEERED MATERIAL; AMENDMENTS TO FEDERAL FOOD, DRUG, AND COSMETIC ACT.

(a) In General. Section 403 of the Federal Food, Drug, and Cosmetic Act (21 U.S.C. 343) is amended by adding at the end the following paragraph:

"(t)(1) If it contains a genetically engineered material, or was produced with a genetically engineered material, unless it bears a label (or labeling, in the case of a raw agricultural commodity, other than the sale of such a commodity at retail) that provides notices in accordance with the following: (A) A notice as follows: 'GENETICALLY ENGINEERED'. (B) A notice as follows: 'UNITED STATES GOVERNMENT NOTICE: THIS PRODUCT CONTAINS A GENETICALLY ENGINEERED MATERIAL, OR WAS PRODUCED WITH A GENETICALLY ENGINEERED MATERIAL'. (c) The notice required in clause (A) immediately precedes the notice required in clause (B) and is not less than twice the size of the notice required in clause (B).... (A) The term 'genetically engineered material' means material derived from any part of a genetically engineered organism, without regard to whether the altered molecular or cellular characteristics of the organism are detectable in the material.

(B) The term 'genetically engineered organism' means—(I) an organism that has been altered at the molecular or cellular level by means that are not possible under natural conditions or processes (including but not limited to recombinant DNA and RNA techniques, cell fusion, microencapsulation, macroencapsulation, gene deletion and doubling, introducing a foreign gene, and changing the positions of genes), other than a means consisting exclusively of breeding, conjugation, fermentation, hybridization, in vitro fertilization, or tissue culture, and (ii) an organism made through sexual or asexual reproduction (or both) involving an organism described in subclause (I), if possessing any of the altered molecular or cellular characteristics of the organism so described. (3) For purposes of subparagraph (1), a food shall be considered to have been produced with a genetically engineered material if—(A) the organism from which the food is derived has been injected or otherwise treated with a genetically engineered material (except that the use of manure as a fertilizer for raw agricultural commodities may not be construed to mean that such commodities are produced with a genetically engineered material);

(B) the animal from which the food is derived has been fed genetically engineered material, or

(c) the food contains an ingredient that is a food to which clause (A) or (B) applies. (4) This paragraph does not apply to food that—(A) is served in restaurants or other establishments in which food is served for immediate human consumption, (B) is processed and prepared primarily in a retail establishment, is ready for human consumption, which is of the type described in clause (A), and is offered for sale to consumers but not for immediate human consumption in such establishment and is not offered for sale outside such establishment, or (c) is a medical food as defined in section 5(b) of the Orphan Drug Act.

The bill includes civil penalties up to $100,000 for each violation of misbranding food.

This bill failed in the House of Representatives in the 106th Congress, but in the Second Session of the 106th Congress, a similar bill was introduced in the U.S. Senate by Barbara Boxer (D-Ca). Her remarks in 146 Cong. Rec. S 680 (February 22, 2000) on S. 2080 demonstrate the public pressure to label genetically modified foods.

Mrs. BOXER: Mr. President, today I am pleased to introduce the Genetically Engineered Food Right-to-Know Act. This legislation requires that all foods containing or produced with genetically engineered material bear a neutral label stating that: "this product contains a genetically engineered material or was produced with a genetically engineered material."

The bill adds this labeling requirement to the provisions of the Federal Food, Drug, and Cosmetic Act (FFDCA), the Federal Meat Inspection Act, and the Poultry Products Inspection Act which contain the general standards for labeling foods.

Recent polls have demonstrated that Americans want to know if they are eating genetically engineered food. A January 1999 Time magazine poll revealed that 81% of respondents wanted genetically engineered food to be labeled. A January 2000 MSNBC poll showed identical results.

This pressure has already led some companies not to use genetically engineered materials in their foods. Gerber and Heinz have said they will no longer use genetically engineered material in their baby food. Whole Foods and Wild Oats Supermarkets also have said they will use no genetically engineered material in their own products.

Great Britain, France, Germany, the Netherlands, Belgium, Luxembourg, Denmark, Sweden, Finland, Ireland, Spain, Austria, Italy, Portugal, Greece, New Zealand, and Japan already require genetically engineered food to be labeled.

If the U.S. wants to sell its genetically engineered food to these countries, it will have to label the food for foreign consumers. It is only fair that American consumers be given similar information.

Why do I feel it's important for consumers to know that their food is genetically engineered?

First, we don't know whether genetically engineered food is harmful or whether it is safe. However, scientists have raised concerns about genetically engineered food. These concerns include the risks of increased exposure to allergens, decreased nutritional value, increased toxicity and increased antibiotic resistance.

In addition, scientists have raised concerns about the ecological risks associated with genetically engineered food. Some of those risks include the destruction of species, cross pollination that breeds new weeds that are resistant to herbicides, and increases in pesticide use over the long-term.

Earlier this year, for example, researchers at Cornell University reported that Monarch butterflies were either killed or developed abnormally when eating milkweed dusted with the pollen of Bt-corn, a genetically engineered food.

Second, the Food and Drug Administration does not require pre-market health and safety testing of genetically engineered foods. Therefore, it is only fair that consumers know they are eating products that have not been tested.

Third, the Environmental Protection Agency and the Department of Agriculture do not require substantive environmental review of genetically engineered materials under their jurisdiction.

My Genetically Engineered Food Right-to-Know Act not only mandates labels, but does something even more important: it authorizes $5 million in grants to conduct studies into the health and environmental risks raised by genetically engineered food.

Specifically, it directs the Secretary of HHS to make grants to individuals, organizations and institutions to study risks like increased toxicity, increased allergenicity, negative effects on soil ecology and on the environment in general.

What is the extent of genetically engineered crops today?

Last year, 98.6 million acres in the U.S. were planted with genetically engineered crops. More than one-third of the U.S. soybean crop and one-quarter of corn were genetically engineered. This represents a 23-fold increase in genetically engineered crop production from just four years ago.

And waiting to come into the marketplace are more than 60 different genetically engineered crops—from apples and strawberries to potatoes and tomatoes.

Providing consumers with information about the foods they eat is hardly new.

For example, I was proud to be the author of the law to provide for the "dolphin safe" label on tuna. The label indicated that the tuna was harvested by methods that don't harm dolphins.

I was also proud to lead the fight in the Senate to make sure that chicken frozen as solid as a bowling ball could not be labeled fresh. At the time, USDA's position was that frozen chicken could be labeled "fresh."

In 1996, I succeeded in amending the Safe Drinking Water Act to require that drinking water providers give their consumers annual reports concerning the quality of their water.

Others in Congress led the fight to tell consumers whether their products contain artificial colors or sweeteners, preservatives, additives, and whether they are from concentrate. I supported those labels as well.

Food manufacturers also label their products with information that is of little value to consumers. Certain brands of pretzels, for example, bear a label which states that the manufacturer is a "Member of the Snack Food Association: An International Trade Association."

I don't think this is information consumers are clamoring for, yet the manufacturer is willing to go through the trouble of putting it on the bag.

My legislation builds on the existing food labeling system, and would be simple to implement. It would require that all foods containing or made with genetically engineered foods be labeled with this information: "this product contains a genetically engineered material or was produced with a genetically engineered material."

For example, corn flakes made with genetically engineered corn would be a "product that contains" genetically engineered material. To take another example, milk from a cow treated with genetically engineered bovine growth hormone would be a product "produced with" genetically engineered material.

Specifically, my bill requires that food that contains or was produced with genetically engineered material be labeled at each stage of the food production process—from seed company to farmer to manufacturer to retailer. The labeling requirement in my bill, however, does not to apply to drugs or to food sold in restaurants, bakeries, and other similar establishments.

Genetically engineered material is defined under the bill as material that "has been altered at the molecular or cellular level by means that are not possible under natural conditions or processes." Food developed through traditional processes such as crossbreeding is not considered to be genetically engineered, and the legislation's labeling requirement would not apply to foods produced in that way.

Under the bill, persons need not label food if they obtain a written guaranty from the party from whom they received the food that the food does not contain and was not produced with genetically engineered material. Persons who obtain a valid guaranty are not subject to penalties under the bill if they are later found to have failed to label food that contains genetically engineered material.

For example, a farmer who plants genetically engineered corn must label that corn. Each person who then buys and then sells that corn, or food derived from it, will also be required to label it as genetically engineered.

Conversely, farmers who obtain a guaranty that the corn they are planting is not genetically engineered may issue a guaranty to purchasers that their corn is not genetically engineered. The purchaser then would not have to label that corn or product made with that corn.

If the corn or food is later found to have contained or been produced with genetically engineered material but was not labeled accordingly, the purchaser would not be subject to penalties under the bill.

This guaranty system is used today to enforce provisions of existing law concerning the distribution of adulterated or mislabeled foods. The system is much less expensive than a system which would require food to be tested at every phase of the food production process.

Failure to label food that contains or was produced with genetically engineered material carries a civil penalty of up to $1,000 amount for each violation.

Importantly, the bill provides that if a party fraudulently warrants that a product is not genetically engineered, no party further down the chain of custody may be held liable for mislabeling. This provision is particularly meant to protect small farmers from the possibility that their suppliers would by contract provide that any liability for mislabeling be borne by the farmer regardless of the suppliers' own actions.

The bill also provides another protection for farmers. Under the bill, a farmer who plants a non-genetically engineered crop, but whose crop came to contain genetically engineered material from natural causes such as wind carrying pollen from a genetically engineered plant is not subject to penalties under the bill. This is the case so long as the farmer did not intend or did not negligently permit this to occur.

And, finally, the bill directs the Secretary of HHS to make grants to study the possible health and environmental risks associated with genetically engineered foods. The bill authorizes $5 million for this purpose.

In closing, Mr. President, during the recent negotiations on the Biosafety Protocol, it was the United States' negotiating position that international shipments of seeds, grains and plants that may contain genetically engineered material be labeled accordingly.

If the United States took the position that it is appropriate to provide this information to its trading partners, shouldn't we make similar information available to American consumers?

I am hopeful that my House and Senate colleagues can act quickly to ensure the passage of my legislation to give American families the right-to-know whether their food contains or was produced with genetically engineered material.

This Act may be cited as the "Genetically Engineered Food Right-to-Know Act".

SEC. 2. FINDINGS. Congress finds the following:

(1) In 1999, 98,600,000 acres in the United States were planted with genetically engineered crops, and more than 1/ 3 of the soybean crop, and 1/4 of the corn crop, in the United States was genetically engineered.

(2) The process of genetically engineering foods results in the material change of such foods.

(3) The health and environmental effects of genetically engineered foods are not yet known.

(4) Individuals in the United States have the right to know whether food contains or has been produced with genetically engineered material.

(5) Federal law gives individuals in the United States the right to know whether food contains artificial colors and flavors, chemical preservatives, and artificial sweeteners by requiring the labeling of such food.

(6) Requirements that genetically engineered food be labeled as genetically engineered would increase consumer knowledge about, and consumer control over consumption of, genetically engineered food.

(7) Genetically engineered material can be detected in food at levels as low as 0.1 percent by reasonably available technology.

SEC. 3. LABELING REGARDING GENETICALLY ENGINEERED MATERIAL; AMENDMENTS TO FEDERAL FOOD, DRUG, AND COSMETIC ACT.

"(t)(1) If it contains a genetically engineered material, or was produced with a genetically engineered material, unless it bears a label (or labeling, in the case of a raw agricultural commodity) that provides notices in accordance with each of the following requirements:

"(A) The label or labeling bears the following notice:

GENETICALLY ENGINEERED'.

"(B) The label or labeling bears the following notice:

THIS PRODUCT CONTAINS A GENETICALLY ENGINEERED MATERIAL, OR WAS PRODUCED WITH A GENETICALLY ENGINEERED MATERIAL'.

"(c) The notice required in clause (A) immediately precedes the notice required in clause (B) and the type for the notice required in clause (A) is not less than twice the size of the type for the notice required in clause (B).

"(D) The notice required in clause (B) is the same size as would be required if the notice provided nutrition information that is required in paragraph (q)(1).

"(E) The notices required in clauses (A) and (B) are clearly legible and conspicuous.

"(2) This paragraph does not apply to food that—

"(A) is served in restaurants or other similar eating establishments, such as cafeterias and carryouts;

"(B) is a medical food as defined in section 5(b) of the Orphan Drug Act; or

"(c) was grown on a tree that was planted before the date of enactment of the Genetically Engineered Food Right-to-Know Act, in a case in which the producer of the food does not know if the food contains a genetically engineered material, or was produced with a genetically engineered material.

"(3) In this paragraph: ,

"(A) The term genetically engineered material' means material derived from any part of a genetically engineered organism, without regard to whether the altered molecular or cellular characteristics of the organism are detectable in the material.

"(B) The term genetically engineered organism' means—

"(I) an organism that has been altered at the molecular or cellular level by means that are not possible under natural conditions or processes (including recombinant DNA and RNA techniques, cell fusion, microencapsulation, macroencapsulation, gene deletion and doubling, introduction of a foreign gene, and a process that changes the positions of genes), other than a means consisting exclusively of breeding, conjugation, fermentation, hybridization, in vitro fertilization, or tissue culture; and

"(ii) an organism made through sexual or asexual reproduction, or both, involving an organism described in subclause (I), if possessing any of the altered molecular or cellular characteristics of the organism so described.

"(c) The term produced with a genetically engineered material', used with respect to a food, means a food if—

"(I) the organism from which the food is derived has been injected or otherwise treated with a genetically engineered material (except that the use of manure as a fertilizer for raw agricultural commodities may not be construed to be production with a genetically engineered material);

"(ii) the animal from which the food is derived has been fed genetically engineered material; or

"(iii) the food contains an ingredient that is a food to which subclause (I) or (ii) applies.".

On March 9, 2000, HR 3883 was introduced in the House of Representatives, which now included labeling requirements for genetically engineered food additives:

This Act may be cited as the "Genetically Engineered Food Safety Act".

SEC. 2. FINDINGS. The Congress finds as follows:

(1) Genetic engineering is an artificial gene transfer process wholly different from traditional breeding.

(2) Genetic engineering can be used to produce new versions of virtually all plant and animal foods. Thus, within a short time, the food supply could consist almost entirely of genetically engineered products.

(3) This conversion from a food supply based on traditionally bred organisms to one based on organisms produced through genetic engineering could be one the most important changes in our food supply in this century.

(4) Genetically engineered foods present new issues of safety that have not been adequately studied.

(5) The Congress has previously required that food additives be analyzed for their safety prior to their placement on the market.

(6) Adding new genes into a food should be considered adding a food additive, thus requiring an analysis of safety factors.

(7) Federal agencies have failed to uphold congressional intent of the Food Additives Amendment of 1958 by allowing genetically engineered foods to be marketed, sold and otherwise used without requiring pre-market safety testing addressing their unique characteristics.

(8) The food additive process gives the Food and Drug Administration discretion in applying the safety factors that are generally recognized as appropriate to evaluate the safety of food and food ingredients.

SEC. 3. FEDERAL DETERMINATION OF SAFETY OF GENETICALLY ENGINEERED FOOD; REGULATION AS FOOD ADDITIVE.

(a) Inclusion in Definition of Food Additive. Section 201 of the Federal Food, Drug, and Cosmetic Act (21 U.S.C. 321) is amended—

(1) in paragraph (s), by adding after and below subparagraph

(6) the following sentence:

"Such term includes the different genetic constructs, proteins of such constructs, vectors, promoters, marker systems, and other appropriate terms that are used or created as a result of the creation of a genetically engineered food (as defined in paragraph (kk)), other than a genetic construct, protein, vector, promoter, or marker system or other appropriate term for which an application under section 505 or 512 has been filed. For purposes of this Act, the term 'genetic food additive' means a genetic construct, protein, vector, promoter, or marker system or other appropriate term that is so included."; and (2) by adding at the end the following:

"(kk)(1) The term 'genetically engineered food' means food that contains or was produced with a genetically engineered material.

"(2) The term 'genetically engineered material' means material derived from any part of a genetically engineered organism, without regard to whether the altered molecular or cellular characteristics of the organism are detectable in the material.

"(3) The term 'genetically engineered organism' means—

"(A) an organism that has been altered at the molecular or cellular level by means that are not possible under natural conditions or processes (including but not limited to recombinant DNA and RNA techniques, cell fusion, microencapsulation, macroencapsulation, gene deletion and doubling, introducing a foreign gene, and changing the positions of genes), other than a means consisting exclusively of breeding, conjugation, fermentation, hybridization, in vitro fertilization, or tissue culture, and (B) an organism made through sexual or asexual reproduction (or both) involving an organism described in clause (A), if possessing any of the altered molecular or cellular characteristics of the organism so described.

(4) For purposes of subparagraph (1), a food shall be considered to have been produced with a genetically engineered material if the organism from which the food is derived has been injected or otherwise treated with a genetically engineered material (except that the use of manure as a fertilizer for raw agricultural commodities may not be construed to mean that such commodities are produced with a genetically engineered material).

(c) In the case of genetic food additives:

(I) The Secretary shall maintain and make available to the public through telecommunications a list of petitions that are pending under this subsection and a list of petitions for which regulations under subsection (c)(1)(A) have been established. Such list shall include information on the additives involved, including the source of the additives, and including any information received by the Secretary pursuant to clause (ii).

[A further provision was made to prevent the categorical exclusion of claims under NEPA:]

(c) In the case of genetic food additives, petitions under subsection (b)(1) may not be categorically excluded for purposes of the National Environmental Policy Act.".

In the 107th Congress, H.R. 4814, Genetically Engineered Foods Right to Know Act, was introduced and included a provision for labeling foods and additives which contain genetically engineered foods as defined by the act. The bill was introduced, but died in the House.

In the 108th Congress, H.R. 2916, The Genetically Engineered Food Right to Know Act, H.R. 2916 was introduced, but died in the House . The labeling requirement for any food or food containing an additive that is defined under the act as a GMO is that such label must contain this statement: "THIS PRODUCT CONTAINS A GENETICALLY ENGINEERED MATERIAL, OR WAS PRODUCED WITH A GENETICALLY ENGINEERED MATERIAL."

In the 109th Congress, there are no bills pending which address genetically engineered food regulation.

Notes

1. The definition of genetically engineered foods is fairly broad. The bill did not leave the Committee for further consideration; it "died in Committee." Why might this bill have failed to gain enough support for passage?

2. Would the statement for the label proposed in H.R. 2916 (108th, 1st Sess.) pass constitutional muster in light of *International Dairy Foods Association v. Amestoy* ?

2.2.2 Genetic Preservation

Other interests of Congress, such as endangered species have now been re-cast as genetic preservation. One example is a bill introduced by the late Representative from Hawaii (Cong. Patsy Mink):

Vol. 145, No. 9 145 Cong. Rec. 85 (Tuesday, January 19, 1999) HON. PATSY T. MINK of Hawaii in the House of Representatives:

> Mrs. MINK of Hawaii: Mr. Speaker, today I am introducing the Plant Genetic Conservation Appropriations Act of 2000 that provides $1.5 million for a genetic plant conservation project that collects and preserves genetic material from our Nation's endangered plants.

> While the Fish and Wildlife Service continues to make strides in battling the war against further extinction of endangered species, we must do more. As of 1997 when I originally introduced this legislation, there were 513 plants listed as Endangered and 101 as threatened under the Endangered Species Act. Today,

there are 567 plants listed as endangered and 135 as threatened. The need to supplement the Fish and Wildlife Services work is critical.

I believe a crucial part of the solution to save our endangered species is the genetic plant conservation project, which can help save and catalog genetic material for later propagation. As genetic technology develops, we will have saved the essential materials necessary to restore plant populations.

The Plant Genetic Conservation Appropriations Act of 2000 requests $1.5 million for activities such as rare plant monitoring and sampling, seed bank upgrade and curation, propagation of endangered plant collections, expanded greenhouse capacity, nursery construction, cryogenic storage research, and in-vitro storage expansion. In my home state of Hawaii, the endangered plant population sadly comprises 46 percent of the total U.S. plants listed as endangered. And our endangered plant list continues to grow. We cannot afford to wait any longer. By allocating the resources and allowing scientists to collect the genetic samples now, we can ensure our endangered plants will survive.

I strongly urge my colleagues to support the Plant Genetic Conservation Appropriations Act 2000. This necessary bill can lead us to preserving plants that many of our ecosystems cannot afford to lose.

The text of the bill reads as follows: H. R. 398, 106th Cong., 1st Sess.:

PLANT GENETIC CONSERVATION

For expenses necessary to carry out a plant genetic conservation program to store material from rare, endangered, and threatened plants in Hawaii and other States and areas of the United States, including expenses for construction and maintenance of a temperature-controlled facility for such purpose, $1,500,000.

2.2.3 Cloning Prohibition

Congress was also confronted in 1999 with the world-shaking news of the cloning of "Dolly" the sheep. This was a call for Congress to respond to the spectre of cloning humans with an immediate prohibition against such activities, as well as advising other countries of the world to do likewise.

The text of this bill is as follows: H.R. 2326, 106th Congress, 1st Session

HUMAN CLONING RESEARCH PROHIBITION ACT

Cloning Research Prohibition Act Human Cloning Research Prohibition Act—Prohibits the expenditure of Federal funds to conduct or support any research on the cloning of humans. Directs the Director of the National Science Foundation to enter into an agreement with the National Research Council for a review of the implementation of this Act. Mandates a report to the Congress containing the results of that review, including the conclusions of the National Research Council on: (1) the impact that the implementation of this Act has had on research; and (2) recommendations for any appropriate changes to this Act. States that nothing in this Act shall restrict other areas of scientific research not specifically prohibited by this Act, including important and promising work that involves: (1) the use of somatic cell nuclear transfer or other cloning technologies to clone molecules, DNA, cells other than human embryo cells, or tissues; or (2) the use of somatic cell nuclear transfer techniques to create animals other than humans. Expresses the sense of the Congress that other countries should establish substantially equivalent prohibitions.

H.R. 2505, 107th Cong., 1st Sess., a bill was introduced entitled the Human Cloning Prohibition Act of 2001. It was engrossed in the House, and sent to the U.S. Senate where it died.

H.R. 534, 108th Congress, 1st Sess., a bill was introduced entitled, the Human Cloning Prohibition Act of 2003. It was engrossed in the House and sent to the U.S. Senate where it died.

H.R.222, 109th Cong., 1st Sess., a bill has been introduced to prohibit the expenditure of Federal funds to conduct or support research on the cloning of humans, and to express the sentiments of Congress that other countries should establish substantially equivalent restrictions.

The Congress has not yet passed legislation to prohibit human cloning.

The issue of cloning is addressed in Chapter Six.

2.3 State Governments and Biotechnology Regulation

2.3.1 Biotechnology and State Support

States have created biotechnology centers as cooperatives for universities and the private sector in order to promote commercialization of biotechnology. The North Carolina Biotechnology Center is one example of these centers created by state legislation. The mission of the Center is "to ensure that the state gains long-term economic benefits from development of the biotechnology industry. The Center works toward five goals: biotechnology business development; strengthen the biotechnology capabilities of state's universities; educate the public about biotechnology; encourage collaborations among the state's universities, industry and government; and strengthen the state's leadership in biotechnology." North Carolina Biotechnology Center, *BT Catalyst* (September 1994).

Another Center, The Maryland Biotechnology Institute, was also created by the state for promotion of biotechnology. One of their cooperative projects involved a collaborative research program in marine biotechnology with Israel's National Steering Committee on Biotechnology. *Financial Times Business Information*, BIOTECHNOLOGY BUSINESS NEWS, April 22, 1994.

The Oregon Biotechnology Association (OBA), was formed in 1990 from the Biotechnology Industry Council and BioForum groups. The mission of the OBA is to "contribute more effectively to the growth and quality of this important new industry," and the goal of the OBA is primarily "to provide the public with accurate, balanced and

understandable information about biotechnology activities in Oregon." 10 BIOTECH-
NOLOGY NEWSWATCH 2 (July 2, 1990).

2.3.2 State Codes

The states have taken the initiative to pass various forms of legislation to deal with
biotechnology and genetics issues where the federal government has no regulatory controls.

By 1990, eleven states had passed biotechnology laws. The Industrial Biotechnology
Association's year-end survey of state governments revealed six states enacting legislation concerning DNA testing; four states with legislation for limiting or studying bovine
growth hormones in milk production; and on regulation of environmental releases in
one state. 11 BIOTECHNOLOGY NEWSWATCH 11 (1991).

In 1993, six states had biotechnology regulatory statutes that dealt with genetic engineering and specifically releases of genetically modified organisms into the environment. In an excerpt from Stuart Auchincloss, *Does Genetic Engineering Need Genetic Engineers?: Should the Regulation of Genetic Engineering Include a New Professional
Discipline?* 20 B.C. ENVTL. AFF. L. REV. 37 (Fall 1993), the following summary of legislation was made.

> Six states have their own biotechnology regulatory statutes [ILL. ANN. STAT.
> ch. 111 ½, §§ 7601–7611 (Smith-Hurd Supp. 1992); ME. REV. STAT. ANN. tit.
> 7, §§ 231–236 (West 1989, Supp. 1991); MINN. STAT. ANN. § 116C.91-96
> (West Supp. 1992); N.C. GEN. STAT. §§ 106-765–780 (Supp. 1991); OKLA.
> STAT. ANN. tit. 2, §§ 2011–2018 (West Supp. 1992); WIS. STAT. ANN.
> § 146.60 (West Supp. 1992)]. The North Carolina statute requires a permit for
> any release into the environment of any, broadly defined, genetically modified
> organism [N.C. GEN. STAT. § 106-772 (Supp. 1991)]. The Oklahoma statute is
> similar to the North Carolina statute except that releases approved under fed-
> eral law are exempt from regulation under Oklahoma law [OKLA. STAT. ANN.
> tit. 2, § 2016 (West Supp. 1992)]. The Illinois and Wisconsin statutes provide
> for state commissions to intervene in the federal review of releases in their re-
> spective states, and to protect the states' interests in the federal review process
> [ILL. ANN. STAT. ch. 111 ½, § 7602 (Smith-Hurd Supp. 1992); WIS. STAT.
> ANN. § 146.60 (West Supp. 1992)].

In 1998, it was reported that at lease 26 states had enacted legislation the regulate the use of genetic information for purposes of preventing discrimination
by insurers and employers. At least fourteen states have laws prohibiting discrimination. The following summary of these laws, from Kourtney L. Pickens,
"Don't Judge Me By My Genes: A Survey of Federal Genetic Discrimination
Legislation," 34 Tulsa L.J. 161, 170–172 (Fall 1998), demonstrates the variance
in state regulation and a national patchwork of genetics laws with which employers and insurance companies must consider:

[A] California law prohibits employers from using any genetic information including information obtained from genetic tests, family medical histories, or
genetic information obtained from other sources in making any employment
decisions. Although other states possess non-discrimination laws in employment areas, many of the laws contain loopholes such as allowing discrimina-

tion if a belief exists that a particular genetic trait would produce an occupational hazard. Similar to the Oklahoma law, Texas prohibits the use of genetic test results in employment and some insurance plans; however, genetic information derived from family histories is not addressed.

Some states have passed laws forbidding insurance companies from dropping an individual's coverage based upon the results of a genetic test. A New Mexico law enacted on May 9, 1998, prohibits such discrimination. Other states have enacted laws criminalizing genetic discrimination. "Seven states have even gone so far as to give people property rights to their genetic information." Still other states have dealt with this issue by passing laws requiring confidentiality of medical records. One survey, according to the Electronic Privacy and Information Center, reported: thirty-seven states create a duty to physicians to maintain confidential medical records; twenty-six states place this duty on other health care providers; four states impose this duty on insurers; nine states impose the duty on employers; twelve states impose criminal penalties as a result of discrimination; nineteen states allow for civil penalties; and three states can impose both criminal and civil penalties. With so many different state regulations, the scope of protection is inconsistent. Uniform federal legislation will provide security to those individuals with genetic conditions who relocate to other states with no genetic discrimination protection. Additionally, federal legislation will protect those family members who are without the genetic condition but whose state laws do not provide reciprocal protection.

One of the most comprehensive state laws is the Genetic Privacy Act enacted by New Jersey. New Jersey's law not only applies to insurance companies and employers but expands its scope by amending New Jersey's anti-discrimination laws to apply to other societal discrimination. The Genetic Privacy Act explicitly states "the improper collection retention or disclosure of genetic information can lead to significant harm to the individual, including stigmatization and discrimination in areas such as employment, education, health care and insurance." The Act requires informed consent before obtaining genetic information and requires consent for retention of genetic information. The New Jersey law also restricts the disclosure of genetic information prohibiting the disclosure of the identity of the person upon whom the genetic test was performed, including disclosure of any genetic information gained from the actual individual. Penalties for violations of this Act include: (1) a fine of $ 1,000, six-month imprisonment, or both; (2) for willful violations, a $ 5,000 fine, a one-year imprisonment term, or both; and (3) all actual damages suffered by the individual as a proximate result of the genetic disclosure.

The Genetic Privacy Act also supplements other areas of the New Jersey statutes. With relation to insurance coverage, the statute prohibits insurance companies from discriminating on the basis of "genetic information" or the refusal to submit or make available the results of genetic testing. Genetic information is defined as "information about genes, gene products or inherited characteristics that may derive from an individual or family member." Unlike Oklahoma, New Jersey does not limit its prohibition of genetic discrimination to the results of genetic tests. Furthermore, genetic test is broadly defined as "a test for determining the presence or absence of an inherited genetic characteristic in an individual, including tests of nucleic acids such as DNA, RNA and mitochondrial DNA, chromosomes or proteins in order to identify a predisposing genetic characteristic." The Genetic Privacy Act supplements this provision to provide more comprehensive coverage of genetic information. This broad definition captures individuals linked to genetic conditions through personal diagnoses and through familial associations, resulting in greater protection against genetic discrimination....

These trends in state government were discussed in Meredith A. Jagutis, Comment, *Insurer's Access to Genetic Information: The Call for Comprehensive Federal Legislation*, 82 MARQ. L.REV. 429, 434–435 (Winter 1999):

> .... Scholars have identified three periods of laws regarding genetic testing. First, laws emerged that prohibited underwriting or rating based on specifically identified genetic traits. Next, states began barring genetic testing altogether from underwriting or rating. Finally, laws barring insurance industry use of genetic information broadened beyond information collected in laboratory tests. This third phase began with the passage of a Wisconsin law shortly after the Human Genome Project began. Other states have continued to pass their own laws preventing genetic discrimination by insurers out of concern that the federal government is acting too slowly. Last year alone, legislators saw 153 bills in various states. Even states that currently have laws prohibiting insurers from discriminating based on genetic information are considering new laws. Ohio, for example, is now concerned that its law does not address family histories. Other states are trying to be proactive and establish safeguards. Apparently, the underlying goal in most states is to encourage the use of genetic tests by individuals by protecting the privacy of the results.
>
> The change in laws exhibited in the past five years illustrates the rapid developments in research. Unfortunately, hasty decision making by state legislatures creates laws that will long outlive their usefulness, as some already have. For example, a bill in Florida sought to prohibit insurers from soliciting information from any other source if that information could be obtained through genetic tests. Without knowing even what genetic tests can reveal, this law could have been potentially dangerous. Even Wisconsin, the state that passed one of the first genetic testing laws, has considered a new bill in order to keep pace with scientific progress.
>
> The driving force behind these laws is the fear of unfair discrimination. However, the term "discrimination" misconstrues the method and use of genetic information by insurers. Insurance is essentially a system based on fair "discrimination" and selection. Many of these new laws restrict an insurer's ability to evaluate risk. The spokesman from HIAA articulated this concern by stating that insurance companies do not want to require tests, but they need to be able to evaluate medical history. Not only are state laws limiting the function of insurance, they may be limiting future coverage if a genetic test reveals methods of possible treatment. The difficulty presented with prohibiting discrimination lies in the way that these laws define genetic information or genetic testing, coupled with the specific activities prohibited or restricted.

Then in 2001, it was reported that nearly half of all states had employed some genetic employment or insurer legislation. Natalie E. Zindorf, in Comment, *Discrimination in the 21st Century: Protecting the Privacy of Genetic Information in Employment and Insurance*, 36 TULSA L. J. 703, 714–715 (2001):

Currently, nearly half of the states have legislation prohibiting genetic discrimination in the workplace. Most states prohibit employers from requiring genetic testing as a condition of employment unless the employer is conducting genetic monitoring. However, existing state laws vary widely in coverage, with some of the earlier laws only protecting individuals with specific genetic characteristics or particular genetic disorders. For instance, Louisiana has not adopted legislation addressing genetic discrimination since the 1982 statute prohibiting employers and labor organizations from discriminating against individuals due to sickle cell trait, which is only one of a yet unknown number of genetic disorders.

Other states vary widely in genetic discrimination legislation. Some states have broad bans on discrimination while others specify particular types of discrimination that are prohibited. Connecticut, Iowa, Kansas, North Carolina and Oklahoma are among the states that prohibit discrimination based on genetic discrimination and provide for no exceptions or qualifying circumstances. In contrast, some states, including Delaware, Maine, Michigan, New Jersey and New York, allow employers to collect genetic information if it can be proved to be job related and consistent with business necessity.

In 2005, all fifty states have some form of legislation addressing genetic testing, usually in the Insurance Code.

———————

Stuart Auchincloss, *Does Genetic Engineering Need Genetic Engineers?: Should the Regulation of Genetic Engineering Include a New Professional Discipline?* 20 B.C. Envtl. Aff. L. Rev. 37 (Fall 1993) discussed the North Carolina Statute.

1. The North Carolina Statute

The North Carolina statute is the only law in the United States, including the Coordinated Framework, that provides for comprehensive regulation of genetic engineering. For this reason it warrants a more complete description than the other state regulatory schemes.

The North Carolina permit process is the only state biotechnology statute totally separate from the complexities and ambiguities of the federal process; not relying on federal law even for definitions [N.C. GEN. STAT. § 106-768 (Supp. 1991)]. The North Carolina statute applies to living organisms changed by "the introduction of new genetic material or the regrouping of [their] genes," except for organisms changed by traditional methods of selective breeding [*Id.* § 106-768(6)-(8)].

The statute requires a permit for any "release," defined simply as the placement of genetically modified organisms outside of a containing enclosure.... Although the statute allows the Genetic Engineering Review Board to request any information necessary in the permit application, the statute encourages the board to use applicable federal application information.... Fifteen days after the state's receipt of the application, the statute requires local notification and a public hearing in the county of the proposed release when there is "significant public interest." ... The statute also provides for written notice to interested parties who request information concerning the release....

One of the North Carolina statute's most interesting provisions concerns the handling of confidential business information ... While permitting an applicant to designate parts of its application as confidential, the statute provides that any person may petition to see the information as long as the petition contains an affidavit from the petitioner stating that the petitioner does not have any commercial interest in the confidential information.... This petition triggers a required negotiating process between the petitioner and the applicant.... If the parties cannot reach an agreement on what information the petitioner will receive from the applicant, either party may appeal to the Board.... The Board can deny or grant the petition, and give the applicant the choice either to provide the information or withdraw its application.... The statute also provides that the disclosure or use of confidential business information for the benefit of any person other than the applicant is punishable by the same daily penalties as those the statute established for any other violation of the act.... This section does not apply to publicizing any information about adverse effects from a proposed release because the applicant knows in advance that it is accountable for such effects....

The statute was the outcome of an eighteen-month study of the regulation of biotechnology in North Carolina by a committee made up of manufacturers, users, universities, state government, and the environmental community.... During the process it appeared that the interests represented were not as divergent as most had at first expected, and the final law had the support of all factions.... This observation holds promise for the success of a more serious federal process to develop a national biotechnology law....

Chapter Three

Private Sector Profits and Biotechnology

3.1 Introduction

The biotechnology industry has existed, only to a significant degree, during the past decade. In 2000, the industry reached its highest point yet with biotech companies raising $37.5 billion from public and private sources. This was equivalent to that raised from 1993 through 1999 combined. Much of this surge was the result of interest generated by the mapping of the human genome. *The BioWorld Biotechnoogy State of the Industry Report 2001*, BIOWORLD TODAY (2001). The stock value of the overall biotechnology sector rose more than 60% in 2000. *News of the Week*, CHEMICAL AND ENGINEERING NEWS 11 (January 29, 2001).

Following the simultaneous sequencing of the human genome by Celera and the federal Human Genome Project, the next logical commercial venture is to identify the proteins that are made by the DNA sequences, and to find out what they do. Currently, not many protein configurations are known, and the synthesis of new proteins would turn the industry of drug discovery on its head. Instead of the hit and miss approach of looking at current protein structures, the process used will be to examine protein structures first and design the protein to create a chemical that designed for one, very specific task.

But the task is the ability to quickly produce protein structures. Currently, pharmaceutical companies only achieve isolating about twenty proteins a year; the next step is to speed that process to about that many a week. For example, in 2000, Structural GenomiX (San Diego, CA) had the early lead in structural genomics with a $40 million venture capital infusion; Syrrx, (San Diego, CA) an academic spin-off of Structural GenomiX planned to generate 1,000 protein structures in 2003; Structure Function Genomics (Princeton, N.J.) planned to use nuclear magnetic resonance to determine protein structure; and Astex Technology (Cambridge, England) concentrated on protein-drug complexes of interest to pharmaceutical companies. IBM announced its plan to spend $100 million over five years to create a computer capable of answering the protein folding question, with the use of IBM's Deep Blue computer which defeated chess grandmaster, Garry Kasparov, dubbed "Blue Gene". The National Institutes of Health recently announced their Protein Structure Initiative with which they expect to generate 10,000 protein structures during the next ten years. Ken Garber, *The Next Wave of the Genomics Business*, TECHNOLOGY REVIEW 47–56 (July/Aug. 2000).

Growth of the Biotechnology Industry in the United States

Year	Number of Companies	Number of Employees	Worldwide Sales ($billions)
1986	850	40,000	1.1
1991	1,107	66,000	2.9
1996	1,308	108,000	9.3
1999	1,283	153,000	13.4
2003	1,473	198,300	39

Growth of the Biotechnology Industry, Globally

2001	4,282	188,000	35

3.2 Biotechnology Issues in Fraud

The growth of the biotechnology sector in publicly traded companies has created a corporate environment which demands rapid discoveries and announcement of their applications in order to continue the flow of investor money into the fledgling industries. Further pressure to acquire intellectual property has also brought the good with the bad.

The pressure to produce new drugs and new products has led to the overzealousness of some companies to stray into behaviors and actions constituting securities fraud. The following case is such an example.

3.2.1 Securities Fraud

In Re Ribozyme Pharmaceuticals, Inc. Securities Litigation
119 F. Supp.2d 1156 (D.Col. 2000)

Opinion by Chief Judge, Lewis T. Babcock

MEMORANDUM OPINION AND ORDER

Defendants move pursuant to Rule 12(b)(6) to dismiss Plaintiff's *Consolidated Class Action Complaint (Consolidated Complaint)*, and for judicial notice of several documents in support of their Rule 12(b)(6) motion. The motions are adequately briefed, and the parties presented oral argument on October 20, 2000. For the reasons set forth below, I grant in part and deny as moot in part Defendants request for judicial notice, and deny the motion to dismiss....

I.

The material facts, with disputes resolved in Plaintiff's favor, are as follows. This case involves a class action on behalf of all persons who purchased or otherwise acquired the common stock of Defendant Ribozyme Pharmaceuticals, Inc. ("Ribozyme") between the close of trading on November 15, 1999, and the close of trading on November 17, 1999. Defendant Ribozyme is a Delaware corporation with its principal executive offices in Colorado. Defendant Ralph E. Christoffersen resides in Colorado, and has been the Chief Executive Officer, President, and Director of Defendant Ribozyme since 1992.

Defendant Ribozyme is developing a new class of drugs containing ribozymes, a form of ribonucleic acid, to treat or prevent human disease. Defendant Ribozyme is developing one of those drugs, Angiozyme, in collaboration with Chiron Corporation. Angiozyme is designed to inhibit the production of a protein essential to angiogenesis, the process by which new blood vessels are formed. Because cancerous tumors rely on a supply of blood to develop and metastasize, it is hoped that Angiozyme will inhibit the growth of new blood vessels surrounding such tumors, and thereby restrict or halt the development, or spread of certain types of cancer in individuals suffering from the disease.

In its Form 10-K covering the period ending on December 31, 1998 and filed with the Securities and Exchange Commission on May 7, 1999, Defendant Ribozyme summarized the U.S. Government regulations governing the process by which new drugs receive approval by the Food and Drug Administration (FDA):

> Before testing of any agents with potential therapeutic value in healthy human test subjects or patients may begin, stringent government requirements for preclinical data must be satisfied. The data, obtained from studies in several animal species, as well as from laboratory studies, are submitted in an IND application or its equivalent in countries outside the United States where clinical studies are to be conducted. The preclinical data must provide an adequate basis for evaluating both the safety and the scientific rationale for the initiation of clinical trials.

Clinical trials are typically conducted in three sequential phases, although these phases may overlap. In Phase I, which frequently begins with initial introduction of the compound into healthy human subjects prior to introduction into patients, the product is tested for safety, adverse effects, dosage, tolerance, absorption, metabolism, excretion and clinical pharmacology. Phase II typically involves studies in a small sample of the intended patient population to assess the efficacy of the compound for a specific indication to determine dose tolerance and the optimal dose range as well as to gather additional information relating to safety and potential adverse effects. Phase III trials are undertaken to further evaluate clinical safety and efficacy in an expanded patient population at geographically dispersed study sites to determine the overall risk-benefit ratio of the compound and to provide an adequate basis for product labeling....

Data from preclinical and clinical trials are submitted to the FDA as an NDA for marketing approval and to other health authorities as a marketing authorization application. The process of completing clinical trials for a new drug is likely to take a number of years and requires the expenditure of substantial resources....

As to where in the process Angiozyme stood as of December 31, 1998, Defendant Ribozyme stated that it "had commenced Phase Ib clinical trials testing safety and tolerability in approximately 16 cancer patients with a broad spectrum of solid tumors and metastasis.... [and] expected to initiate Phase II clinical trials prior to the end of 1999."

On August 11, 1999, Defendant Ribozyme issued a press release indicating that it had successfully completed the Phase Ia and Ib trials, and that it was "preparing to enter multi-dose Phase I/II clinical trials in Q4 1999." The press release also stated that "studies at several independent centers have demonstrated significant inhibition of both growth and metastases in preclinical trials." Finally, the press release included accounts by Dr. Nassim Usman, Vice President of Research at Defendant Ribozyme "and Angiozyme program director" that Angiozyme "completely inhibited metastases in a clinically relevant colorectal cancer model," and "halted tumor growth and metastases in a Lewis Lung murine model."

On November 15, 1999, Defendant Ribozyme issued a "Media Advisory" entitled "Colorado Pharmaceutical Co. Makes Cancer Drug History" announcing a press conference scheduled for November 17, 1999 (Press Release). The Press Release stated in part

[Defendant Ribozyme] presently has several drug compounds in development, of these Angiozyme—it's cancer drug—has made significant progress. Angiozyme is now in human clinical trials at the Cleveland Clinic Foundation and has taken an important step forward ... making both clinical history and industry news. [At the November 17, 1999 press conference, Defendant] Christoffersen, Ph.D., and other senior RPI staff, will explain Angiozyme and its recent history-making leap, an achievement which may be of great significance to cancer patients everywhere.

On November 16, 1999, the price of a share of stock in Defendant Ribozyme traded on NASDAQ opened at $ 13.625 after closing on November 15, 1999 at $ 10.0625. Because the price then rose to $ 22 within one hour and twenty-five minutes, trading of Defendant Ribozyme's stock was halted. During the halt, Maurice Wolin, vice president of medical affairs for Chiron Corporation (Chiron), stated both that "we don't know if we're going to break ground here or not," and he "doesn't expect any major cancer—drug history to be made since it's too early to say whether the drug works in humans." Later on November 16, 1999, Shari Annes, vice president of corporate communications at Chiron, stated that the Press Release was "very overstated," and "there is always pressure [on small biotechnology companies] when anything good happens, no matter how small, to make it into big news."

Also during the halt in trading, Defendant Ribozyme issued a press release indicating that Angiozyme had entered Phase I/II testing as predicted by the May 7, 1999 Form 10-K and the August 11, 1999 press release. After the close of trading on NASDAQ, Defendant Christoffersen stated to reporters that the press release issued earlier in the day had disclosed all of the material information Defendant Ribozyme intended to reveal at the planned November 17, 1999 press conference. At the close of trading on November 16, 17, 1999, the price of Defendant Ribozyme's stock was $ 12.25 and $ 9.3125, respectively.

Between November 19, 1999 and January 5, 2000, four separate class action complaints were filed with this court claiming in essence that the information contained in the Press Release was misleading and/or false, and artificially raised the price of Ribozyme shares on November 16, 1999.

B.

Section 10(b) makes it unlawful for any person "to use or employ, in connection with the purchase or sale of any security ... any manipulative or deceptive device or contrivance in contravention of such rules and regulations as the Commission [SEC] may prescribe as necessary or appropriate in the public interest or for the protection of investors." 15 U.S.C. §§ 78j(b). Rule 10b-5, prescribed by the SEC under Section 78j(b), declares it unlawful for a person "to make any untrue statement of a material fact or to omit to state a material fact necessary in order to make the statements made, in light of the circumstances under which they were made, not misleading." 17 C.F.R. §§ 240.10b–5 (1997). To state a claim under Rule 10b-5, a plaintiff must allege: (1) a misleading statement or omission of a material fact; (2) made in connection with the purchase or sale of securities; (3) with intent to defraud or recklessness; (4) reliance; and (5) damages.

III.

A.

I.

Defendants first assert that Plaintiffs have failed to plead adequately that the Press Release was materially false or misleading. They contend that the *Consolidated Complaint* fails to satisfy the pleading requirements of 15 U.S.C. §§ 78u–4(b)(1). Defendants also assert that Plaintiffs have not established the materiality of any allegedly false or misleading statements insofar as the statements in the Press Release are protected by the "bespeaks caution doctrine" and/or the Reform Act's safe haven for forward-looking statements, and the "truth on the market" doctrine. I will address each argument in turn.

a.

In the *Consolidated Complaint*, Plaintiffs allege that, as of November 15, 1999, the expected commencement of the Phase II trials of Angiozyme had been announced previously in both the May 7, 1999 Form 10-K, and August 11, 1999 press release. *Consolidated Complaint* at paras. 31–32. Plaintiffs further allege that, in light of this background, they construed the Press Release's announcement of "important corporate and product news" constituting "a history-making leap" as something other than, and perhaps beyond, the previously disclosed commencement of Phase II trials. Finally, Plaintiffs allege that not only the run-up in the stock price, but also the announcements by Mr. Wolin and Ms. Annes, indicate that the interpretation of the Press Release alleged in the *Consolidated Complaint* is reasonable. Hence, Plaintiffs conclude in the *Consolidated Complaint* that the Press Release was in fact false and/or misleading because as of November 17, 1999 Angiozyme had only entered Phase II trials. Plaintiffs' allegations thus "specify each statement alleged to have been misleading, [and] the reason or reasons why the statement is misleading." 15 U.S.C. §§ 78u–4(b)(1). As Judge Brimmer stated in similar circumstances, "neither Rule 9(b) nor the Reform Act requires that Plaintiffs do more." *Queen Uno Ltd. Partnership v. Coeur D'Alene Mines Corp.*, 2 F. Supp. 2d 1345, 1354 (D. Colo. 1998). Accordingly, I will not dismiss the *Consolidated Complaint* on the basis that it fails to satisfy the pleading requirements of 15 U.S.C. §§ 78u–4(b)(1).

b.

The statements in the Press Release are also not immaterial under the "bespeaks caution doctrine" and the Reform Act's safe harbor provision for forward-looking statements, as Defendants contend. Both the "bespeaks caution doctrine" and 15 U.S.C. §§ 78u–5(c)(1)(A)(I) apply to forward looking statements.... However, under Plaintiffs' allegations at least part of the Press Release upon which they relied concerned purported historical fact. Indeed, Defendants' statement in the Press Release that "Angiozyme ... has taken an important step forward ... making both clinical history and industry news. [At the November 17, 1999 press conference, Defendant] Christoffersen, Ph.D., and other senior RPI staff, will explain Angiozyme's [] recent history-making leap" was falsifiable at the time it was made.

In arguing that the Press Release contains only forward-looking statements, Defendants focus exclusively on the statement that the alleged "history-making leap ... may be of great significance to cancer patients everywhere." (emphasis added). Defendants thus argue in effect that the latter forward-looking clause necessarily renders all other statements in the Press Release forward-looking as well. Nevertheless, it is possible that Angiozyme could have completed a "history-making leap" within the trials, but not a sufficiently large leap to warrant the definitive statement that

Angiozyme "[will] be of great significance to cancer patients everywhere." Defendants' statements that Angiozyme had made "both clinical history and industry news," and a "history-making leap," are not necessarily forward-looking given the full context of the Press Release. Under these circumstances, neither the "bespeaks caution" doctrine nor 15 U.S.C. §§ 78u–5 require dismissal of Plaintiffs' *Consolidated Complaint*.

c.

Defendants' argument that the "truth on the market" doctrine renders immaterial any allegedly false or misleading statements in the Press Release is also unpersuasive. The "truth on the market" doctrine excuses "the defendant's failure to disclose material information ... where that information has been made credibly available to the market by other sources."....

Assuming the Tenth Circuit would adopt the "truth on the market" doctrine, Plaintiffs' claims nevertheless survive dismissal. Construing the alleged facts in the light most favorable to Plaintiffs as I am required to do, the *Consolidated Complaint* alleges that because of the publicly available information regarding Angiozyme, Plaintiffs construed the Press Release's announcement of "important corporate and product news" constituting "a history-making leap" as something other than the previously disclosed commencement of Phase II trials. Consequently, Plaintiffs have alleged that, notwithstanding the cautionary language in the May 17, 1999 Form 10-K filing, they believed based on the Press Release that Defendants would reveal at the November 17, 1999 press conference information not already "on the market." I conclude the "truth on the market" doctrine does not require dismissal of the *Consolidated Complaint*. Plaintiffs have met their burden in pleading that Defendants' statements were materially false or misleading.

ii.

Defendants next argue that Plaintiffs cannot take advantage of the "fraud on the market" presumption of reliance. Specifically, Defendants claim that Plaintiffs have not plead adequately an efficient market, which is a prerequisite to triggering the presumption. I disagree.

The "fraud on the market" doctrine ... recognizes that in an open, efficient, and developed market, where millions of shares are traded daily, investors must rely on the market to perform a valuation process which incorporates all publicly available information, including misinformation.

Consequently, the reliance of individual plaintiffs on the integrity of a price in such a market, and implicitly the misinformation that contributed to that price, may be presumed.... In order to take advantage of the doctrine, however, a plaintiff must plead, and ultimately prove, that the market on which the security is traded is efficient.... Courts assessing the efficiency of markets consider: (1) whether the stock trades at a high weekly volume; (2) whether securities analysts follow and report on the stock; (3) whether the stock has market makers and arbitrageurs; (4) whether the company is eligible to file SEC Form S-3; and (5) whether there are empirical facts showing a cause and effect relationship between unexpected corporate events or financial releases and an immediate response in the stock price.... No bright-line rules exist as to how many factors must be plead before a plaintiff is entitled to the presumption of reliance....

Here, Plaintiffs assert that the trading volume of Defendant Ribozyme's stock was substantial, ... and that analysts followed and reported on Defendant Ribozyme. In addition, Plaintiffs allege in effect that the Press Release was the sole factor that caused the rise in the stock price from $ 10.0625 to $ 22 in less than one and a half hours. The timing of the Press Release and the dramatic increase in the stock price support Plaintiffs' alleged cause and effect relationship. Hence, Plaintiffs allege empirical facts showing a cause and effect relationship between unexpected corporate events and an immediate response in the stock price.

Accordingly, IT IS ORDERED that [d]efendants' motion to dismiss is DENIED.

Notes

1. This is an example of a "safe harbor" statement for a biotechnology medical company, Biosphere Medical, in discussing new products which are described as bioengineered microspheres for the minimally invasive treatment of hypervascularized tumors and vascular malformations:

> *Cautionary Statement Regarding Forward-Looking Statements: This website contains forward-looking statements within the meaning of the Private Securities Litigation Reform Act of 1995. The Company uses words such as "plans," "seeks," "projects," "believes," "may," "expects," "anticipates," "estimates," "should"' and similar expressions to identify these forward-looking statements. These statements are subject to risks and uncertainties and are based upon the Company's beliefs and assumptions. There are a number of important factors that may affect the Company's actual performance and results and the accuracy of its forward-looking statements, many of which are beyond the Company's control and are difficult to predict. These important factors include, without limitation, risks relating to: the failure of the Company and its distributors to successfully market and sell the Company's products; the failure of the Company to achieve or maintain necessary regulatory approvals, either in the United States or internationally, with respect to the manufacture and sale of its products and product candidates; the failure of the Company to successfully commercialize and achieve widespread market acceptance of the Embosphere(R) Microspheres and EmboGold Microspheres; risks relating to the Company's ability to obtain and maintain patent and other proprietary protection for its products; the absence of or delays and cancellations of, product orders; delays, difficulties or unanticipated costs in the introduction of new products; competitive pressures; the inability of the Company to raise additional funds in the near term to finance the development, marketing, and sales of its products; and general economic conditions. These risk factors are further described in the section titled "Certain Factors That May Affect Future Results of Operations" in the Company's Quarterly Report on Form 10-Q for the quarter ended June 30, 2004, as filed by the Company with the Securities and Exchange Commission. In addition, the forward-looking statements included in this website represent the Company's estimates as of the date of this release. The Company anticipates that subsequent events and developments may cause its forward-looking statements to change. The Company specifically disclaims any obligation or intention to update or revise these forward-looking statements as a result of changed events or circumstances after the date of this website update.*

[http://www.biospheremed.com/safe.cfm, visited March 31, 2007].

Does this statement allow corporations to make exaggerated claims in their press releases and still be protected?

2. Advanced Cell Technology, a company with only 27 employees had been struggling financially, when it announced that it had extracted stem cells from single cells in embryos. Stockholders, debentures and warrants holders bought more stock, and they raised $13.5 million. In addition, the headlines in the news was followed by an increase in the stock price by 500 percent in two days, going from 40 cents the day before the press release to $2 the day after the announcement. The following day, the stock dropped back down to around $0.80.

The press release read: that this new discovery was "a way out of the current political impasse in this country and elsewhere" referring to the prohibition on federal funding for stem cells not derived from a list of pre-existing stem cell lines. The news release claim was repeated through broadcasts and newspapers in lead stories and headlines. While the research, published in the highly respected journal Nature, was not exaggerated, the idea that it would solve the world's problems and the current ethical dilemma with stem cell research *was* misleading.

This action avoided violating security laws, but it raises an ethical issue of making exaggerated claims about resolving policy problems, with the end result of raising huge amounts of cash for the company. Should regulation be proposed to prevent this kind of activity?

See Robert Bazell, "Slippery slope: Inflated Science claims equal $$: News of breakthroughs raise money—even if later disputed," MSNBC News at http://www.msnbc.msn.com/id/14561404/ (August 29, 2006).

3.2.2 Contract Fraud

Rhone-Poulenc Agro S.A. v.
Monsanto Company and Dekalb Genetics Corp.
73 F. Supp.2d 540 (M.D.N.C. 1999)

N. Carlton Tilley, Jr., District Judge

For the reasons set forth below, Defendants' motions for summary judgment are DENIED as to Count IV. Decision regarding all other motions is postponed until after it is determined whether the 1994 agreement is rescinded.

I.

RPA is "a leading worldwide manufacturer and vendor of diversified agricultural products, and is engaged in chemical and biotechnological research and development with particular interests in the area of weed control and crops." (Compl. [Doc. # 68], P 6.) Monsanto manufactures and sells a diversified line of agricultural products as well, including herbicides, and is engaged in biotechnological research and development. (Id. P 7.) DeKalb, which is at least partially owned by Monsanto, n2 (id. P 3), is involved in agricultural genetics and biotechnology for seed, and is one of the largest seed suppliers in the United States, (id. P 7). RPA and Monsanto compete directly with each other in the general agricultural market and particularly in the fields of herbicides and biotechnology. (Id. P 8.)....

This case involves sophisticated biotechnology and genetic engineering. However, for the purposes of these summary judgment motions, the essence of the case can be reduced to the following explanation. Monsanto produces an herbicide called Roundup, whose active ingredient is "glyphosate." Glyphosate is apparently a very powerful, yet relatively safe, herbicide that will kill all green foliage with which it comes into contact. This case revolves around the attempt to use genetic engineering to create corn that is tolerant to glyphosate herbicides, such as Roundup. The ability to grow glyphosate-tolerant corn would increase the efficiency of farmers, because they could spray glyphosate-herbicide over the entire crop of corn, killing all of the weeds but not damaging any of the corn plants.

In 1985, DeKalb and Calgene, Inc. ("Calgene") entered into an agreement for the joint development of crops containing Calgene's C-AroA gene that would make corn crops tolerant to glyphosate (the "1985 Agreement"). The 1985 Agreement called for the formation of a "Project Review Committee," composed of scientists from each company, that would have general oversight responsibility for the progress of each party under the agreement. It also provided for various royalty payments to be made by DeKalb to Calgene for products developed under the agreement. As part of the 1985 Agreement, DeKalb received an exclusive license for two patents of certain mutated genes (the "Comai" patents) in the field of use of corn. In 1991, RPA, DeKalb, and Calgene entered into an "Assignment and Assumption Agreement," (the "1991 Agreement") whereby RPA assumed Calgene's rights and obligations under the 1985 Agreement.

At a November 1992 meeting, RPA stated that it would provide to DeKalb new genetic material containing an OTP/maize double mutant EPSPS construct ("EPSPS construct"). At some point after that meeting DeKalb received the genetic material. Moreover, the record indicates that at this meeting RPA notified DeKalb of its decision to withdraw from at least some of its responsibilities under the 1985 and 1991 Agreements. There is a factual dispute as to the extent of this withdrawal, and as to the responsibilities of each party under the 1985 and 1991 Agreements afterwards. RPA claims that it was "generally suspending work on glyphosate tolerance.", while DeKalb asserts that RPA "ceased its participation in the joint project,".

In late 1993 and early 1994, in a greenhouse, DeKalb succeeded in growing transformed corn plants containing RPA's EPSPS construct that were tolerant to Roundup herbicide at potentially commercial levels. On February 18, 1994, DeKalb sent RPA a report of its results, stating that:

We have now demonstrated tolerance in transgenic plants in the greenhouse to up to four times the field application recommended by Monsanto for tolerant corn! We will repeat these experiments in the field in the summer of 1994. It is obvious from these results that the mutant maize gene has been the key to success.

RPA responded with a three sentence letter stating: "I thank you for the report on development of glyphosate resistant corn. The results look good. I hope they will be confirmed by the field experiments." Then, on March 10, 1994, DeKalb sent RPA another letter that once again mentioned the summer field trials and the gains DeKalb had achieved in the greenhouse regarding the glyphosate tolerance of corn with the EPSPS construct. (Id. at Ex. 25.) In addition, that letter requested RPA's opinion regarding the use of the EPSPS construct for other projects, and also requested a response to the "many questions" that need to be answered regarding the "recent success" of the EPSPS construct. (Id.)

DeKalb conducted field tests occurred in the summer of 1994, and on September 6, 1994, DeKalb received results indicating that corn plants containing RPA's EPSPS construct were resistant to four-times the normal level of Roundup herbicide. The report from the field testing was not sent to RPA. Rather, on September 7, 1994, DeKalb sent RPA a letter which stated, in its entirety, that:

> As the results that we have obtained in maize with the glyphosate resistant double mutant maize gene provided by RPA to DEKALB have been very encouraging, we are interested in whether this gene would also function as a selective marker in soybeans. Is it possible for DEKALB to use this gene in soybeans as a selectable marker?
>
> I will await your answer.

These letters seem to be the extent of the communications between DeKalb and RPA regarding the EPSPS construct and its introduction into corn lines.

Also during the summer of 1994, Calgene and RPA filed a patent infringement action against Monsanto in which Calgene and RPA accused Monsanto of using the patented technology contained in the Comai patents in making, using, and selling glyphosate resistant soybeans. Calgene owned the Comai patents, and RPA had certain exclusive rights under these patents in soybeans. DeKalb also had an interest in the litigation, because under the 1985 Agreement, DeKalb was the exclusive licensee of the Comai patents in the field of use of corn.

In December 1994, two agreements were negotiated arising from these events. First, RPA, Calgene, and Monsanto agreed to a settlement of the patent litigation begun in July 1994. Monsanto paid $ 8 million in return for an exclusive license (shared with DeKalb) under the Comai patents, for use in all fields. Concurrent with this settlement process, RPA and DeKalb entered a new agreement (the "1994 Agreement") in which DeKalb agreed to share its exclusive license under the Comai patents in the field of use of corn with Monsanto. Under the 1994 Agreement, DeKalb was provided with $ 500,000, as its share of the Monsanto settlement proceeds. Moreover, the 1994 Agreement dissolved the 1985 and 1991 Agreements, and RPA granted DeKalb the "worldwide, paid-up right to use" various technologies, including the EPSPS construct, in the field of use of corn. The 1994 Agreement also gave DeKalb "the right to grant sublicenses to the aforementioned right to use."

DeKalb eventually developed a glyphosate-tolerant corn line from the EPSPS construct, named the "GA21 corn line." In January 1996, DeKalb and Monsanto entered an agreement to work together on a variety of projects, including glyphosate-tolerant corn, and DeKalb licensed the GA21 corn line to Monsanto. Subsequently, corn seeds containing the GA21 corn line were commercialized and marketed under the brand name "Roundup Ready." Sales of Roundup Ready corn seeds began in 1998....

III.

In Count IV, RPA alleges that DeKalb failed to disclose to RPA the results of field tests conducted by DeKalb in the summer of 1994 that "successfully demonstrated for the first time that the transgenic corn plants incorporating RPA's genetic material produced commercially viable glyphosate resistant corn plants." The corn seed produced in these field trials formed the basis of what became the GA21 corn line. RPA alleges that these results were "highly material information" that DeKalb had a duty to disclose to RPA, and that if DeKalb had revealed that information to RPA, RPA would not have entered into the Monsanto Settlement Agreement and the 1994 Agreement in December 1994 on the terms that it did. Therefore, RPA asserts that the 1994 Agreement should be rescinded because DeKalb's actions constitute fraud in the inducement to enter into the

1994 Agreement, and because DeKalb's contractual and fiduciary duties required DeKalb to disclose the results of the field tests,....

Two possible bases for rescission created by DeKalb's alleged misconduct exist: constructive fraud and actual fraud. The Court will discuss each theory in turn.

A.

Constructive fraud arises when a party to a confidential or fiduciary relationship breaches a duty which has been implied by law because of the special relationship between the parties....

When a fiduciary relationship exists, a presumption of fraud is raised when the superior party obtains a possible improper benefit from the relationship.... RPA may raise this presumption if it demonstrates the facts and circumstances "(1) which created the relation of trust and confidence, and (2) led up to and surrounded the consummation of the transaction in which [DeKalb] is alleged to have taken advantage of [its] position of trust to the hurt of [RPA]."....

A fiduciary relationship sufficient for a constructive fraud claim "exists in all cases where there has been a special confidence reposed in one who in equity and good conscience is bound to act in good faith and with due regard to the interests of the one reposing confidence." ...

However, as a matter of law, no fiduciary relationship exists in the instant case based upon "special circumstances" resulting in one party having "superiority and influence" over the other. In North Carolina, no fiduciary relationship exists between mutually interdependent businesses with equal bargaining positions who dealt at arms-length.... RPA is attempting to impose upon DeKalb a "duty to disclose" that relates to the EPSPS construct, which is an entirely different venture from the consortium's activities. Similarly, if Doug Fisher owed any fiduciary duty to RPA based upon his negotiations with Monsanto, the scope of that duty would not include a duty to disclose field results from different genetic materials. Also, RPA removed Mr. Fisher from the negotiations, and took over much of the responsibilities itself, while it was represented by its own attorneys. Therefore, the consortium activities and Doug Fisher's alleged attorney relationship with RPA do not provide the necessary confidential or fiduciary relationship to give rise to a duty to disclose....

B.

The elements of an actual fraud claim are: (1) a false representation or concealment of a material fact; (2) that was reasonably calculated to deceive; (3) which was made with the intent to deceive; (4) that did in fact deceive (or reasonably induce reliance); and (5) resulted in injury or damage....

(1) RPA does not allege that DeKalb made any statement that, taken alone, was false or contained a misrepresentation. Rather, RPA claims that DeKalb had a duty to disclose the results of the field tests to RPA, and DeKalb's nondisclosure of those results resulted in a fraudulent concealment or omission by DeKalb. [n6] In both North Carolina and Illinois, fraud can be practiced by silence as well as by a positive misrepresentation, if a duty to speak exists....

RPA has alleged that DeKalb was under several "legal duties" to disclose the results of the field tests to RPA: a fiduciary relationship based upon either the parties' alleged joint venture relationship, the parties' consortium, or an attorney-client relationship; DeKalb's contractual obligations toward RPA; and DeKalb's superior knowledge, obtained by virtue of the RPA-DeKalb relationship of trust and confidence....

The first question is whether DeKalb had a contractual obligation to disclose the field test results. RPA seems to present two possible sources for this obligation: the 1985 and 1991 Agreements or a separate, oral contract beginning in November 1992 when RPA agreed to send DeKalb the EPSPS construct. If the source is the 1985 and 1991 Agreements, then there is evidence that DeKalb had a duty to keep RPA "apprised of [DeKalb's] efforts." ...

DeKalb asserts that the 1985 and 1991 Agreements required them only to report results to the Project Review Committee, and once those meetings were abandoned by RPA, DeKalb had no obligation to continue reporting the results under the Agreements. Yet, the facts surrounding RPA's withdrawal remain unclear, and do not necessarily lead to the conclusion that DeKalb would be relieved of its obligation to report its testing results.

The second issue is whether a duty to disclose material facts may arise if RPA placed trust and confidence in DeKalb, thereby placing DeKalb in a position of influence and superiority over RPA.... As this Court decided that such a special relationship does not exist in this case under a constructive fraud theory, see supra Part III(A), RPA will not be able to rely on the "special relationship" theory to require a duty to disclose under its actual fraud claim either....

A third issue is that courts have acknowledged a duty to disclose, which may arise without a fiduciary relationship, if one party makes a partial or ambiguous statement that requires additional disclosure to avoid misleading the other party.... North Carolina courts acknowledge that once a party speaks, it "must make full and fair disclosure as to the matter [it] discusses." ...

RPA alleges that the September 7, 1994 letter "was a 'partial and ambiguous statement,' which misled RPA into believing that DeKalb had not had much success with its 1994 field trials." Furthermore, the September 7, 1994 letter, in combination with the February 1994 report and DeKalb's subsequent letters, "created a belief that DeKalb was being forthright and honest, and was keeping RPA abreast of its material developments." In other words, even if DeKalb did not have a duty to disclose the results of the field tests, see discussion supra, once DeKalb did speak, DeKalb had a duty to be straightforward and direct regarding the tests....

RPA has created an issue of material fact as to whether DeKalb's actions over the course of its business dealings with RPA created the reasonable belief that DeKalb would affirmatively disclose any and all significant results from testing of the EPSPS construct. Given DeKalb's past history of reporting its positive results to RPA without inquiry, it would be reasonable for a jury to conclude that the September 7, 1994 letter led RPA to believe that it was receiving, and would receive, all of the results of testing done with the EPSPS construct....

The next question to answer in order to satisfy the first element of actual fraud is whether the omission was material. "A false representation is material when it deceives a person and induces him to act."....

(2)

The second and third elements that RPA must demonstrate are that DeKalb's omission was reasonably calculated to deceive and that it was made with the intent to deceive, respectively. A showing that DeKalb acted with the intent to deceive is an essential element of RPA's fraud claim.... In the instant case, intent to deceive may be inferred from the fact that DeKalb kept RPA updated and informed on all of

DeKalb's research with the EPSPS construct until DeKalb actually discovered extremely positive results with the field tests. At that point, DeKalb sent RPA a brief letter that focused on another issue (asking for permission to use the gene with soybeans) and that did not mention the field test results specifically. Then, less than four months later, RPA — never having learned of the results from the field tests — transferred to DeKalb the right to use the EPSPS construct for arguably much less than its full value. From these facts, a reasonable jury could conclude that DeKalb actively misled RPA with the intent to deceive it about the true value of the EPSPS construct....

(3)

The fourth element of a fraud claim is that the omission did in fact deceive (or reasonably induce reliance). DeKalb asserts that it was not reasonable for RPA to rely on DeKalb's omission because RPA failed to satisfy a "duty of inquiry" prior to signing the 1994 Agreement. There is no doubt, as DeKalb contends, that the law requires an individual to exercise ordinary prudence in relying upon persons with whom they conduct their business affairs. "The question is whether it is better to encourage negligence in the foolish or fraud in the deceitful.... Just where reliance ceases to be reasonable and becomes such negligence and inattention that it will, as a matter of law, bar recovery for fraud is frequently very difficult to determine." ...

For the reasons set forth in the Memorandum Opinion filed contemporaneously with this Order, it is ORDERED that Defendants' Motion for Summary Judgment as to Count IV of RPA's Complaint is DENIED. Decisions regarding all other summary judgment motions are postponed until after it is determined whether the 1994 agreement is rescinded.

3.3 Intellectual Property Protection Issues

3.3.1 Trade Secrets as an Approach to Protecting Corporate Knowledge

Trade secrets includes formulas, patterns, programs, devices, methods, techniques, drawings, processes or other data that is sufficiently secret to derive economic value for not being generally known by others; and that efforts are made to keep it secret. This method of protecting corporate knowledge has the advantage of not being in the public domain through publication of a patent, if it was patentable material, thereby preventing anyone from ever using the information, unlike a patent which has a limited period of protection to the property owner.

In the biotechnology industry, trade secrets present the difficult problem of keeping them secret in an area where there are rapid advancements, publications of discoveries, and frequent movement of employees from one laboratory to another, taking with them, their experiences and knowledge. In the next case, Microbix Biosystems v. Biowhittaker, what the company believed was protected trade secret property failed to meet the statutory requirements for protection, in part, due to the frequent movement of laboratory technicians and scientists among biotechnology companies.

Microbix Biosystems, Inc. v. Biowhittaker, Inc.
184 F. Supp. 2d 434 (D. Md. 2000)
JUDGE Marvin J. Garbis, District Judge

1. Abbott's Expired Patents

Abbott held three patents on urokinase production that expired in 1994 and became publicly available: (a) United States Patent No. 3,930,944, January 6, 1976 ("the '944 Patent"); (2) United States Patent No. 3,930,945, January 6, 1976 ("the '945 Patent"); and United States Patent No. 3,957,582, May 18, 1976 ("the '582 Patent").

a. The '944 Patent

The '944 Patent disclosure discusses the addition of a chemical called pronase to the urokinase-production medium. The patent describes the need to increase urokinase yields from kidney cell cultures to make commercially feasible volumes....

b. The '945 Patent

The '945 Patent discloses a procedure similar to that presented in the '944 Patent for producing urokinase from embryonic kidney cells and concludes that the addition of between 0.3 and 1.2 percent glycine to the production medium significantly increases the quantity of urokinase obtained....

c. The '582 Patent

The '582 Patent discloses a detailed description of a urokinase purification method that yields a purity of between 55,000 and 64,000 CTA....

3. Scientific Publications

Abbott scientists have published papers relating to the manufacture of urokinase from kidney cells....

5. Duff's Expertise

Prior to working at Abbott, Duff was a Postdoctoral Fellow at the Baylor School of Medicine (specializing in virology and epidemiology) from 1968 to 1969, and then an Associate Professor in microbiology at the Milton S. Hershey Medical School ("Hershey") from 1969 to 1974. At Hershey, Duff specialized in virology and cell biology. In that capacity, he conducted experiments on tissue cell culture. Moreover, as a Postdoctoral Fellow and Associate Professor, Duff published various papers concerning the process of culturing cell. Duff then worked at Abbott from 1974 to 1983 as head of the viral and cell biology groups in the experimental biology division of Abbott.

II. LEGAL STANDARD

A motion for summary judgment shall be granted if the pleadings and supporting documents "show that there is no genuine issue of material fact and that the moving party is entitled to a judgment as a matter of law." Fed. R. Civ. P. 56(c)). The well-established principles pertinent to such motions can be distilled to a simple statement....

III. DISCUSSION

Abbott alleges that Microbix misappropriated and used Abbott's trade secrets in violation of the Illinois Trade Secret Act ("ITSA"). A plaintiff seeking damages under ITSA must show (1) secrecy, (2) misappropriation, and (3) use of the trade information at issue. Microbix contends that Abbott has not presented evidence adequate to establish the "secrecy"and "use" elements.

A. Secrecy of Trade Information

Abbott alleges that the information which Duff disclosed to Microbix includes trade secrets. The ITSA defines a "trade secret" as information, including but not limited to, technical or non-technical data, a formula, pattern, compilation, program, device, method, technique, drawing, process, financial data, or list of actual or potential customers or suppliers, that:

(1) is sufficiently secret to derive economic value, actual or potential, from not being generally known to other persons who can obtain economic value from its disclosure or use; and

(2) is the subject of efforts that are reasonable under the circumstances to maintain its secrecy or confidentiality.

As to the secrecy requirement of subsection 1065/2(d)(1) of ITSA, Abbott must prove that the trade information at issue (a) is sufficiently secret to derive economic value, (b) is not within the realm of general skills and knowledge of the relevant industry, and (c) cannot be readily duplicated without involving considerable time, effort or expense.

B. Use of Information

It is undisputed that Microbix's current procedures for urokinase production are distinct from those of Abbott. That is, there is no evidence, and indeed Abbott has not alleged, that Microbix's procedures contain any Abbott's trade secrets. Abbott alleges only that Microbix "exploited" the alleged trade secrets to (1) obtain funding and partners n15 and (2) conduct initial research and development. However, for purposes of this motion, Abbott must present evidence to show that each piece of trade information allegedly disclosed by Duff to Microbix is a "trade secret" and that the information was actually used in Microbix's business.

Moreover, the Court notes a possible threshold problem with Abbott's trade secret counterclaim that could render an analysis of the claim in detail a moot exercise. The undisputable fact is that Microbix never produced its planned product and, on the evidence, has no reasonable prospect of doing so in the future. Accordingly, even if Microbix had used Abbott's trade secrets in its attempts to develop a product, there is no evidence, or conceivable evidence, of any possible damages to Abbott resulting from the use. Nor is there any threatened use or disclosure warranting injunctive relief.

Finally, the Court finds unpersuasive Abbott's "one size fits all" argument that the fact that Abbott, without disclosing it, uses generally known information is itself a trade secret....

1. Procedures and Specifications for Testing and Acceptance of HNK Cells

a. Secrecy

Abbott alleges that Duff provided to Microbix an Abbott document describing protocols for the processing and screening of HNK cells for potential use in the production of urokinase, and that Abbott has not publicly disclosed the document.... Abbott appears to focus on page MBX003145 of the document, which contains the specifications for minimum urokinase yields for a lot of cells to be accepted for use in urokinase production. This page consists of a chart which states that (1) with respect to subculture three at week four, "must assay at least 475 units/ml or reject lot"; (2) with respect to subculture three at week five, "must assay at least 760 units/ml or reject lot"; and (3) with respect to both subcultures three and four at six weeks, "must assay at least 1100 units/ml or reject lot."

As noted above, Abbott alleges that it has not publicly disclosed the document. However, Abbott has not alleged (or presented any evidence to show) that the information contained in the document namely, the specifications on page MBX003145) is not generally known in the industry. Duff testified that the document contains information that he originally wrote as a graduate student and as a professor at Hershey. Specifically, Duff testified that he derived the specifications at issue from the 1975 and 1977 scientific papers published by Abbott scientists. The Court concludes that, on the evidence, no reasonable jury could find the subject information secret rather than generally known in the industry.

b. Use

Use of the information is moot in light of the ruling as to secrecy. Nevertheless, it should be noted that Abbott does not allege that either Abbott or Microbix has ever used the data from page MBX003145 as their actual specifications. To the contrary, none of the specifications from page MBX003145 appear anywhere in Microbix's procedures....

4. Use of Newborn Calf Serum in Place of Fetal Calf Serum

Abbott alleges that Duff disclosed to Microbix that, as part of Abbott's manufacturing protocols, Abbott substitutes newborn calf serum for fetal calf serum as a media supplement during the last passage of the cell growth phase, and that Abbott has not disclosed publicly this information.... It appears that a switch from fetal calf serum to newborn calf serum was an obvious cost-saving measure generally known in the industry (citing a similar switch published in a scientific journal)....

IV. CONCLUSION

Counterclaim-Defendant Microbix Biosystems, Inc.'s Motion for Summary Judgment is GRANTED.

The next case opines that there cannot be a trade secret in animals.

North Carolina Farm Partnership v. Pig Improvement Company, Inc.
593 S.E.2d 126 (2004)

In 1996, North Carolina Farm Partnership (NCF), a North Carolina partnership, and PIC, a Wisconsin corporation, entered into a contract whereby NCF agreed to lease pigs and facilities in Warren County, North Carolina for pig breeding and nursery to PIC. At the expiration of the lease term, NCF was to retain possession of the pigs and the facilities, subject to the contractual options available to both parties on or before the termination of the lease.

Following expiration of the lease on 31 March 2000, NCF filed a complaint in Wake County, North Carolina on 27 July 2000 alleging breach of the lease terms by PIC. In its answer and counterclaim, PIC in turn alleged NCF breached the lease terms by continuing, "after termination of the lease, to use the progeny of [pigs] in the breeding herd as breeding stock in [NCF's] own herd and/or [by] transferr[ing] and/or s[elling] said progeny to other herds, rather than selling said progeny to slaughter as permitted in the lease." The answer and counterclaim also sought injunctive relief because "[t]he genetics incorporated into [PIC's] breeding animals are confidential, proprietary and secret information."

The [c]ourt accepts PIC's contention, as supported by the evidence, that each pig contains unique genetics in its make-up and that the genetics and breeding processes which led to the breeding of the pigs containing such genetics are valuable intellectual property. However, this fact does not make a pig[ ] a trade secret. Because of the pig's genetic makeup, it may be a valuable pig, but it is not a trade secret.

On the contract issue, the trial court concluded NCF was not restricted in its use of the breeding herd left on the leased premises at the expiration of the lease.PIC does not cite, and our research did not reveal, any cases involving the application of trade secrets law to animals. Furthermore, PIC provided two affidavits containing general allegations but no specific scientific evidence to support those allegations. PIC's technical director in one affidavit states generally that PIC has used "molecular biological research and ... selective breeding" to develop favorable traits in pigs and that PIC's competitors could use the pure-line pigs in NCF's possession to duplicate those traits. The other affidavit, by a doctorate holder who provides no information on his specialty and other credentials, simply states that the breeding of great-grandparent female pigs in NCF's possession with pure-line boars would produce offspring with "one-half of the positive genetic qualities and characteristics" of the sow.

On the other hand, NCF provided a detailed affidavit of a North Carolina State University professor, explaining the current selection methodology for breeding swine, the feasibility of obtaining PIC pigs on the market, and the degree of difficulty competitors would face in attempting to discover and exploit favorable traits in PIC pigs. The professor, a published Professor of Animal Science and Genetics, has taught at the university since 1959 and been involved in research in the swine industry for more than thirty years. According to the professor: selective breeding is the exclusive method of genetic improvement in the swine industry and is not a secret; "[a]ny competitor could buy a[] sample of PIC product on the open market and test against these pigs"; and PIC's competitors would not be able to "work backwards to figure out what [PIC] did to develop [a] pig" or "to take the pigs in the possession of [NCF] and determine whether the PIC line was a superior line of pigs without first performing years of tests."

Affirmed.

3.3.2 Patenting as an Approach to Protecting Corporate Knowledge in Corporate Competitive Research

The generic pharmaceutical industry necessarily utilizes the patent of the drug product for which it seeks to develop a generic. However, if the generic company was forced to wait until the expiration of the patent it is using, this would result in a de facto extension of the patent term, possibly as many as four years during the development of the generic.

In 1984, the U.S. Federal Circuit opined in *Roche Products, Inc. v. Bolar Pharmaceutical*, 733 F.2d 858 (1984), 221 USPQ 937, that Bolar, a generic drug manufacturer, had infringed the Roche patent, when they conducting testing before the expiration of Roche's patent. This research was required by the FDA to gain approval for marketing Bolar's new generic. The court held that this kind of experimental testing was a patent infringement under 35 U.S.C. 271(a).

In 1984, Congress responded to *Roche Product, Inc. v. Bolar Pharmaceutical*, by passing the Drug Price Competition and Patent Term Restoration Act, 98 Stat. 1535 (1984). The Act established an expedited procedure for FDA approvals of generic equivalents of previously approved drugs (ANDA), and established guidelines for the extension of terms of patents for medical devices, food additives, color additives and pharmaceuticals if there are resulting delays by FDA for their approval.

The amended 35 U.S.C. 271(e)(1) states:

> "It shall not be an act of infringement to make, use or sell a patented invention (other than a new animal drug or veterinary biological product (as those terms are used in the Federal Food, Drug and Cosmetic Act and the Act of March 4, 1912)) solely for uses reasonably related to the development and submission of information under a Federal law which regulates the manufacture, use or sale of drugs."

Under this new provision, can a patent be used in research for purposes of obtaining another patent, without infringing? This would go beyond the sole use requirement of the statute which the court opined in the following case when Genentech relied on this provision to conduct this kind of research.

———

Scripps Clinic and Research Foundation v. Genentech, Inc.
666 F.Supp. 1379, 3 U.S.P.Q.2d 1481 (N.D. Calif, July 20, 1987)

I. Introduction

This action alleges infringement of a patent covering a protein known as Factor VIII:C which plays an essential part in blood clotting. Hemophiliacs commonly suffer from an absence or deficiency of this protein and as a result are exposed to the risk of hemorrhaging from even a minor wound. The patent at issue claims highly concentrated and purified Factor VIII:C and a process for deriving it from human blood plasma. The principal issue raised is whether defendant Genentech, Inc.'s production of Factor VIII:C using recombinant technology infringes plaintiffs' patent.

VI. Non-Infringement Under 35 U.S.C. §271(e)(1)

Genentech has renewed its motion for dismissal or summary judgment of noninfringement under 35 U.S.C. §271(e)(1), which the Court denied without prejudice as premature by order of August 1, 1986. The Court has reconsidered its prior order in light of the memoranda submitted and the arguments made in connection with these motions, and for the reasons stated denies the motion.

Section 271(e)(1) provides:

It shall not be an act of infringement to make, use, or sell a patented invention (other than a new animal drug or veterinary biological product (as those terms are used in the Federal Food, Drug, and Cosmetic Act and the Act of March 4, 1913)) solely for uses reasonably related to the development and submission of information under a Federal law which regulates the manufacture, use, or sale of drugs.

This provision, enacted under the Drug Price Competition and Patent Term Restoration Act of 1984 ("Act"), Pub.L. 98-417, 98 Stat. 1585, overruled the Federal Circuit's 1984 decision in Roche Products, Inc. v. Bolar Pharmaceutical Co., Inc., 733 F.2d 858 (Fed.Cir.), cert. denied, 469 U.S. 856, 105 S.Ct. 183, 83 L.Ed.2d 117 (1984). The defendant in Roche had obtained from a foreign manufacturer a generic drug covered by a domestic patent in order to conduct bioequivalency tests necessary for FDA approval. The Federal Circuit held this use infringing, notwithstanding that it was "limited" to "testing and investigation strictly related to FDA drug approval." The 1984 Act established a streamlined procedure for FDA approval of generic drugs to hasten their introduction into the marketplace. Section 271(e)(1), enacted as § 202 of the 1984 Act, responded to congressional concern that under Roche the arrival of generics on the market would be delayed because bioequivalency testing required by the FDA could not begin until after expiration of the patent.

Genentech argues that all its uses of Factor VIII:C, though not solely for purposes related to FDA testing, bear some reasonable relationship to such purposes and hence are noninfringing under § 271(e)(1). The construction of § 271(e)(1) that Genentech urges the Court to adopt would, in effect, eliminate the express statutory limitation "solely for" and thereby immunize any use of a patented invention so long as some aspect of that use is reasonably related to FDA testing. This broad construction defies the plain mandate of the statute and the intent of Congress.

The statute's meaning is clear: the use of a patented invention is protected so long as that use is solely for purposes reasonably related to meeting the reporting requirements of federal drug laws. Therefore, to establish entitlement to the statutory exemption, Genentech must demonstrate that it made and used plasma-derived and recombinant Factor VIII:C preparations solely for the purpose of meeting FDA reporting requirements.

This interpretation accords with the intent of Congress in enacting § 271(e)(1). The comments of the authors of the House Report emphasize the narrowness of the exemption. For example, the Report states that "a generic drug manufacturer may obtain a supply of a patented drug product during the life of the patent and conduct tests using that product if the purpose of those tests is to submit an application to FDA for approval." It further states that the only activity which will be permitted by the bill is a limited amount of testing so that generic manufacturers can establish the bioequivalency of a generic substitute. The patent holder retains the right to exclude others from the major commercial marketplace during the life of the patent. Thus, the nature of the interference with the rights of the patent holder is not substantial.

Even if the uses to which Genentech and Cutter put the Factor VIII:C were reasonably related to meeting FDA requirements, they certainly were not solely related to that purpose. Those uses also related, among other things, to preparation of Genentech's application for a European patent and to performance of the Genentech-Cutter agreement to develop a process for manufacturing Factor VIII:C on a commercial scale. Pursuant to that agreement, Genentech supplied Cutter with Factor VIII:C and received substantial sums from and agreed to share proprietary rights with Cutter. Furthermore, the agreement contemplates the marketing of recombinant Factor VIII:C outside the United States before expiration of the Scripps patent. These sales and uses of Factor

VIII:C, serving multiple purposes unrelated to meeting FDA requirements, clearly lie beyond the protection of §271(e)(1).

Genentech's motion to dismiss or for summary judgment under 35 U.S.C. §271(e)(1) is therefore denied.

3.4 Bioprospecting — Private Sector Agreements with the Government

Private sector exploration for useful biological plants and organisms requires permission for companies to enter land, probably owned by others, in order to carry out their explorations. National Parks in the United States are places where harvesting of timber and many other private sector activities take place with the permission of the federal government. The United States federal government, however, used the CRADA mechanism to enter into a private-public partnership in granting permission to enter the National Parks for "bioprospecting."

The following case represents the new conflicts which arise when permission and partnership in "bioprospecting" is granted by the federal government to private sector companies for use of the National Parks, a national public resource.

Edmonds Institute v. Babbitt, Secretary of Interior
93 F. Supp. 2d 63 (D.D.C. 2000)

PINION by: District Judge Royce C. Lamberth

This matter comes before the court on the parties cross-motions for partial summary judgment. Plaintiffs, three environmental advocacy organizations and a frequent visitor to Yellowstone National Park ("Yellowstone" or "Park"), challenge as arbitrary and capricious the Department of the Interior's ("Interior") entry into a research agreement with a private biotechnology company for the "bioprospecting" of microbial organisms from geysers and other thermal features in Yellowstone. Upon consideration of the motions, the oppositions thereto, the relevant record, and the applicable law, the court GRANTS defendants' motion for summary judgment and DENIES plaintiffs' motion for summary judgment.

I. BACKGROUND

This court has previously detailed the factual background underlying the present dispute. *Edmonds Institute v. Babbitt*, 42 F. Supp. 2d 1, 4–9 (D.D.C. 1999). Accordingly, the court now provides only an abbreviated review the salient facts and procedural history of this case.

A. The Yellowstone-Diversa CRADA

Yellowstone is the nation's oldest national park. To commemorate its 125th anniversary, defendants hosted a ceremony on August 17, 1997, which was attended by top environmental policymakers, including Vice President Al Gore, Secretary of the Interior Bruce

Babbitt, National Park Service Director Robert Stanton, and Yellowstone Superintendent Mike Finley. At the ceremony, it was announced that the federal government had entered into a novel contract with San Diego-based Diversa Corporation, by which Diversa would obtain a nonexclusive right to "bioprospect" n1 microbial organisms in Yellowstone, in exchange for an agreement to share with Yellowstone a portion of any financial returns generated by commercial applications or products developed from these research materials.

SELECTED FOOTNOTES

FN1 As this court has previously explained, bioprospecting refers to a relatively new method of natural resource utilization that targets microscopic resources, such as the genetic and biochemical information found in wild plants. *Edmonds Institute v. Babbitt*, 42 F. Supp. 2d 1, 5–6 (D.D.C. 1999). Bioprospecting is an extension of the field of biotechnology, which uses biological resources like genes and enzymes to develop beneficial pharmaceutical and industrial products and applications. *Id.*

This novel agreement, officially termed a Cooperative Research and Development Agreement ("CRADA"), was the first of its kind to involve a national park. The Statement of Work in the CRADA explains how Yellowstone and Diversa will cooperate in researching and cataloguing the Park's biological diversity, primarily in the Park's thermal features such as geysers, hot springs, fumaroles, and mud pots, as well as in Yellowstone's "alpine tundra ecosystems, subalpine forests; riparian habitats, sedge marshes, bogs, swamps, streams and lakes." CRADA, Statement of Work at 2. Following an initial survey, sites will be "prioritized and systematically sampled by [Diversa] scientists," using techniques to be "jointly selected by YNP and [Diversa] to ensure that there is no significant impact to park resources or other appropriate park uses." *Id.* Once raw samples have been extracted from the selected sites, nucleic acids will be isolated, purified and used to create a library of genetic information. *Id.* at 2–3. The resulting gene libraries will be the starting point for the discovery and cloning of biocatalytic and bioactive compounds, which will be evaluated for potential commercial applications. *Id.* These libraries of genetic information will also be available to Park scientists for their own research. The CRADA and Statement of Work explicitly state that all activity carried on under the agreement will be in accordance with applicable law, including Yellowstone's management policy. Accordingly, to conduct the research under the CRADA, Diversa applied for and was issued a Research Authorization/Collection Permit, which authorized the collection of certain biological materials from Yellowstone. Since 1994, prior to its entry into the CRADA, Diversa, under its previous name Recombinant Biocatalysis, Inc., had already been conducting the same sort of sampling from Yellowstone, pursuant to permits issued in accordance with Park regulations. The main difference, however, is that prior to the CRADA, the company was under no obligation to share any of the economic or other benefits that might result from its research on Park resources.

Thus, perhaps the most notable feature of the CRADA is the consideration that Yellowstone stands to receive in exchange for access to its biodiversity. Defendants have disclosed that Diversa will make annual payments of around $ 20,000 to the defendants, as well as provide research equipment and other support for Yellowstone's use and benefit. More importantly, however, Diversa will pay royalties to Yellowstone on any future commercial use or product derived from the company's bioprospecting activities in the Park. Although the specifics are not public, Yellowstone has indicated that it will receive royalties of between .5% and 10% depending upon the nature of the raw material and the final product. By virtue of the CRADA, Yellowstone will share in any revenues generated by future beneficial applications or products developed from Diversa's research at Yellowstone.

B. Bioprospecting in Yellowstone

Notwithstanding the novelty of the Yellowstone-Diversa CRADA itself, this agreement is not the first time that the National Park Service has permitted scientific research and collection of microbial specimens from Yellowstone's thermal features. To the contrary, the earliest research permit authorizing collection of microbial samples from Yellowstone was in 1898. Indeed, in recent years, the number of annual requests by researchers for access to Yellowstone has averaged 1,500, with some 250–300 research permits issued each year (between 40 and 50 of which are for microbial research projects). Declaration of Michael Soukoup ("Soukoup Decl."), at P 8 Exhibit 1 to Defendants' Motion to Dismiss and for Summary Judgment. National Park Service regulations govern this permit system and ensure that research activities are consistent with the Yellowstone and Interior's overall goals.

Prior to the CRADA, Diversa or other researchers were free to remove any specimen within the purview of their permit and develop it as they wished. If such development led to commercial uses, the Park Service never saw any proceeds from the derivative products. Thus, recognizing that resources yielding potentially valuable properties were being removed from Yellowstone with no remuneration to Yellowstone or the American people, see Soukup Decl. P 9, officials at Interior began to consider a resource management scheme, patterned on the successes of Costa Rica and other nations, which would use bioprospecting to provide funds and incentives for the conservation of biological diversity. To that end, the defendants opened negotiations in 1995 with the Diversa Corporation and other biotechnology companies to explore possible bioprospecting contracts. These potential agreements would be drafted as cooperative research and development agreements (CRADA) under the Federal Technology Transfer Act of 1986, which authorizes federal laboratories to enter into CRADAs with nonfederal entities to facilitate the sharing of research developed in conjunction with government scientists. By the fall of 1996, Diversa and the defendants had begun drafting a CRADA that would permit the collection of raw environmental materials from Yellowstone. The final version of the CRADA was signed by National Park Service Director Robert Stanton and Yellowstone Superintendent Mike Finley on May 4, 1998.

C. Procedural History

Plaintiff Edmonds Institute is a nonprofit public interest organization based in Edmonds, Washington. The group advocates the regulation of biotechnology and the maintenance and protection of biodiversity. Plaintiff Alliance for the Wild Rockies is a nonprofit organization committed to the preservation and protection of the native biodiversity of the Northern Rockies Region. Plaintiff International Center for Technology Assessment (CTA) is a Washington, D.C.-based nonprofit corporation focused on the environmental, economic, and ethical issues surrounding the biotechnology industry (including bioprospecting), particularly as it relates to the national parks. Finally, plaintiff Phil Knight is a resident of Bozeman, Montana who allegedly visits Yellowstone some twelve times a year to hike, photograph, and otherwise enjoy its aesthetic and recreational qualities.

Defendants, of course, are Secretary of the Interior Bruce Babbitt, sued in his official capacity, and Robert Stanton, Director of the National Park Service, also sued in his official capacity only.

In 1997, plaintiffs filed a petition requesting that the agency not enter into the Yellowstone-Diversa CRADA (or similar agreements) because the agency had failed to provide public notice of its proposed change in policy and had not undertaken the environmental impact assessment required by law. The defendants denied plaintiffs' request in January of 1998.

The court ordered defendants to suspend implementation of the CRADA pending the completion of "any and all review mandated by [NEPA], including but not limited to the preparation of an Environmental Assessment." *Edmonds Inst.*, 42 F. Supp. 2d at 20. The parties now move for summary judgment as to the remaining claims under Counts I, II and III.

II. DISCUSSION

Where a controversy presents no genuine issue as to any material fact, summary judgment is appropriate and the moving party is entitled to judgment as a matter of law. Here, the parties agree that no genuine issue of material fact exists and that the central dispute concerns whether defendants acted in accordance with the FTTA, the National Park Service Organic Act, the Yellowstone National Park Organic Act, and Park Service regulations by entering into the CRADA with Diversa.

Under the Administrative Procedure Act, courts must set aside agency action found to be "arbitrary, capricious, an abuse of discretion, or otherwise not in accordance with law." As the Supreme Court has instructed, the 'arbitrary and capricious standard' is 'highly deferential' and presumes the validity of agency action. If the court can discern a rational basis for the agency's decision, the decision must be affirmed. Similarly, the court must uphold the agency's construction of the statute unless it is unreasonable ... In light of this standard, the starting point for this court's review is the language of the FTTA, for where Congress has spoken to a particular matter, Congress' plainly expressed intent governs. The validity of this CRADA under the FTTA turns upon whether Yellowstone falls within the meaning of "laboratory" as that term is defined in the statute. By its terms, the FTTA defines "laboratory" as a facility or group of facilities owned, leased, or otherwise used by a Federal agency, a substantial purpose of which is the performance of research, development, or engineering by employees of the Federal Government.

Plaintiffs object to the application of the FTTA to the Yellowstone CRADA because they assert that the plain meaning of "laboratory" forecloses application of that term to the research facilities in Yellowstone. Specifically, plaintiffs argue that Yellowstone is not a "facility" because Yellowstone's organic statute describes the Park only as a "tract of land." 16 U.S.C. § 21.

While the court agrees that a national park does not immediately conjure the term "laboratory," the court finds that defendants have provided a reasoned basis for concluding that the broad, statutorily-assigned definition encompasses Yellowstone's extensive research facilities.... 1986 U.S.C.A.A.N. 3442, 3453 (stating that statutory definition of "laboratory" in FTTA was "a broad definition which is intended to include the *widest possible range of research institutions operated by the Federal Government*")(emphasis added). As a preliminary matter, the court notes that because the statute has specifically defined laboratory to include facilities owned or otherwise used by a federal agency, plaintiffs "plain meaning" argument with respect to the term "laboratory" is misplaced. As noted above, where Congress has assigned a particular definition to a term, courts may not simply cast such definitions aside in favor of the term's "ordinary" meaning. Thus, the specific definition of laboratory provided in the statute governs the court's review.

Yellowstone's research facilities fall within the definition of laboratory under the FTTA as a "facility owned ... or otherwise used by a Federal agency," a "substantial purpose of which is the performance of research." While the term "laboratory" is defined in the statute, "facility" is not. Thus, the court must look to the ordinary meaning of that word. "Facility" is broadly defined as "*something* (as a hospital, machinery, plumbing) that is built, constructed, installed *or established* to perform some particular function or *to serve or facilitate some particular end*". WEBSTER'S THIRD NEW INTERNATIONAL DICTIONARY 812 (1961) (emphasis added). The extensive array of research facilities at Yellowstone plainly satisfy this definition. To begin with, as defendants correctly note, the statute makes no requirement that the entire facility be used exclusively for research. To the contrary, the only statutory restriction is that a "substantial purpose" of the facility be for "the performance of research, development or engineering by employees of the Federal government." 15 U.S.C. § 3710a(2)(A). Defendants have adequately demonstrated that a substantial purpose of the facilities at Yellowstone is scientific research. *See* Affidavit of John Varley, at P3 ("Varley Aff."), September 16, 1999, Attachment to Defendant's Motion for Partial Summary Judgment. Specifically, Yellowstone employs approximately 43 individuals engaged in scientific activities. Many of these scientific researchers possess doctorates or other advanced degrees, and are members of leading scientific societies. And, to coordinate scientific research at the Park, Yellowstone has established the Yellowstone Center for Resources ("YCR"), which oversees all aspects of research by Park scientists, including research concerning the Park's abundant mammalian wildlife such as bison or wolf populations, as well as the vast array of microorganisms contained in Yellowstone's hot springs and thermal features. Moreover, the plethora of scientific and research structures and equipment at Yellowstone plainly fall within the FTTA definition. For instance, Yellowstone maintains "wet" and "dry" laboratories at Yellowstone headquarters that are approved and regulated by the Occupational Safety and Health Administration, in addition to other scientific research facilities throughout the Park. Varley Aff., at P 10-12. And, many of the research facilities at Yellowstone are equipped with standard laboratory equipment, including spectrophotometers, microscopes, stereoscopes, genetic thermal cyclers, balancers, centrifuges, refrigerators, freezers, evaporators, dryers, ovens, bunsen burners, deionizers, and other chemical, physical, and biological measuring and processing instruments, and computers....

This laboratory equipment enables YNP personnel to perform a wide range of scientific analyses and tests that include but are not limited to animal necroscopies, DNA extraction, water analysis, soil characterization, and acid rain sampling and analysis. Yellowstone's research facilities also include geographic information systems ("GIS") and a remote sensing facility, which collects, records and analyzes environmental data from satellites and aircraft. Thus, in light of these extensive scientific research facilities, the court finds that Yellowstone falls within the meaning of "laboratory" under the FTTA.

Legislation enacted subsequent to the Yellowstone-Diversa CRADA also reinforces the conclusion that application of the FTTA to this CRADA is consistent with Congressional intent regarding cooperative scientific research agreements with units of the National Park System. Notably, in 1998, Congress enacted the National Parks Omnibus Management Act ("Parks Management Act"), 16 U.S.C. §§ 5901–6011, for the purpose of "enhancing management and protection of national park resources by providing clear legal authority and direction for the conduct of scientific study in the National Park System and to use information gathered for management purposes" and "to encourage others to use the National Park System for study to the benefit of park management as well as broader scientific value." 16 U.S.C. § 5931. To achieve this end, the statute specifically authorizes the Secretary of the Interior to "solicit, receive and consider requests from Federal or non-Federal public or private agencies, organizations, individuals, or other entities for the use of any unit of the National Park System for purposes of scientific study." *Id.* at § 5935(a). Moreover, the statute further empowers the Secretary to "enter into negotiations with the research community and private industry for equitable, efficient benefits-sharing arrangements." *Id.* at § 5935(d). Under these broad terms, the CRADA at issue here plainly constitutes an "equitable, efficient benefits-sharing arrangement" with a private entity for the purposes of scientific study. *Id.* Had Congress wished to foreclose units of the National Park System from entering into cooperative scientific research agreements with private industry in the wake of the Yellowstone-Diversa CRADA, its subsequent enactment displays a contrary intent. Instead, the far-reaching terms of the Parks Management Act reinforce the conclusion that the Yellowstone-Diversa CRADA is proper.

Having concluded that defendants have provided a rational basis for their determination that the FTTA definition of laboratory encompasses Yellowstone's myriad scientific research facilities, the court must next consider whether the CRADA is consistent with the relevant Park Service statutes and regulations. Plaintiffs contend that the CRADA conflicts with defendants' statutory mandates under the relevant organic statutes, the National Park Service Organic Act ("NPS Act"), 16 U.S.C. § 1, et seq., and the Yellowstone National Park Organic Act ("YNP Act"), 16 U.S.C. § 21, et seq. Specifically, plaintiffs maintain that the CRADA constitutes a "consumptive use," and hence, is contrary to the conservation emphasis of the NPS Act and the YNP Act. Plaintiffs further argue that the CRADA violates the Park Service's own regulations, which prohibit the "sale or commercial use of natural products." As explained below, this court disagrees with plaintiffs' contentions and finds that defendants have offered a reasoned basis explaining how the CRADA is consistent with the organic statutes and regulations.

Review of plaintiffs' challenges under the Park Service authorizing statutes, like plaintiffs' FTTA claim, is governed by the APA. Thus, as Congress has delegated the administration and preservation of national park resources to Interior and the Park Service, these agencies enjoy broad discretion in implementing their statutory responsibilities under the authorizing statutes. Accordingly, their actions should be upheld as long as they are "based on a reasoned, permissible construction of the statute."

As its name indicates the National Park Service Organic Act ("NPS Act") is the general authorizing statute for the National Park Service. In relevant part, the NPS Act provides that there is created in the Department of the Interior a service to be called the National Park Service.... The service thus created shall promote and regulate the use of the Federal areas known as national parks, monuments, and reservations hereinafter specified ... by such means and measures as conform to the fundamental purpose of said parks, monuments, and reservations, which purpose is to conserve the scenery and the natural and historic objects and the wild life therein and to provide for the enjoyment of the same in such manner and by such means as will leave them unimpaired for the enjoyment of future generations. 16 U.S.C. § 1. The Yellowstone National Park Organic Act ("YNP Act") established Yellowstone as a unit of the National Park service, by providing that :

The tract of land in the States of Montana and Wyoming [within specified boundaries] is reserved and withdrawn from settlement, occupancy, or sale under the laws of the United States, and dedicated and set apart as a public park or pleasuring ground for the benefit and enjoyment of the people; and all persons who locate, or settle upon, or occupy any part of the land thus set apart as a public park, except as provided in section 22 of this title, shall be considered trespassers and removed therefrom. 16 U.S.C. §21.

The court finds that defendants reasonably determined that the Yellowstone-Diversa CRADA is consistent with the above-quoted statutory authority and is not an impermissible "consumptive use" of park resources. *Michigan United Conserv. Clubs v. Lujan*, 949 F.2d 202, 206 (6th Cir. 1992). Specifically, defendants concluded that the CRADA does not authorize consumptive use of natural resources because it does not grant Diversa the authority to sell any living material taken from the Park. Varley Aff., P 37. In fact, as Yellowstone's Research Permitting Policy makes clear, Diversa never actually owns the specimens its collects, and thus has no right to transfer ownership of them. A.R. I.1, at 3 ("All specimens collected within the park are the property of the National Park Service and, regardless of where the collections are housed, must be properly accessioned and catalogued into the National Park Service's cataloguing system."); *see also* Varley Aff., P 75 ("A sale of [Yellowstone's] resources will not occur pursuant to a CRADA.").

More fundamentally, however, the CRADA does not conflict with the conservation mandate of the organic statutes because it does not grant Diversa the right to collect any research specimens at all. Indeed, contrary to plaintiffs' assertion, neither the CRADA nor its Scope of Work authorizes Diversa to take any natural materials from Yellowstone. Rather, the CRADA outlines the rights and responsibilities of Yellowstone and Diversa with respect to information and inventions developed after the conclusion of research specimen collection and analysis. Thus, the legal force and scope of the CRADA covers the use, ownership, development and allocation of revenues from useful discoveries or potential proprietary information developed from the research activities. By contrast, to conduct its research activities at Yellowstone, Diversa-like all other researchers in the Park—must apply for and obtain a research permit, which prescribes the terms and conditions of on-site research activities. 36 C.F.R. §2.5; *see also* A.R. §II.20, P2.18 (noting that "the term 'Research Specimen' means those items [Diversa] has the authority to collect under the collection permit or permits issued by [Yellowstone]"). Thus, while in certain respects the CRADA may impose restrictions on Diversa's research activities over and above those provided by a permit alone, the research permit, not the CRADA, provides the legal basis for Diversa to collect specimens.

In mounting a frontal attack on the CRADA, plaintiffs fail to recognize this critical legal distinction. While they challenge the CRADA, they do not in any way contend that the research permit issued to Diversa is improper or is otherwise invalid. Indeed, plaintiffs' misconception of the legal force of the CRADA reveals the fundamental flaws in their challenge. If the court were to find that the CRADA was improper under the relevant statutes, Diversa could still collect specimens under a research permit, as it has since 1994. The only—albeit critical—difference would be that Yellowstone could not share in any of the potential benefits from Diversa's research. Instead, the positive gains from the research would go exclusively to Diversa. Plaintiffs' challenge is further undermined by the fact that finding the CRADA to be an impermissible "consumptive use" of Park resources would necessarily imply that every other scientific research permit issued over the past century was equally invalid. But plaintiffs have offered no argument, evidence or suggestion that Diversa's research permit or the research permit program at Yellowstone are improper.

Thus, in light of the longstanding policy and practice of allowing specimen collection at the Park, and because they are not properly before the court, the court need not reach the questions of the validity of the permit or the permit program.

Finally, the court finds that defendants properly determined that the CRADA was consistent with the governing statutes because it would produce direct, concrete benefits to the Park's conservation efforts by affording greater scientific understanding of Yellowstone's wildlife, as well as monetary support for Park programs. As early as 1994, defendants recognized that cooperation between Park officials and private researchers would be mutually beneficial. Defendants determined that the potential scientific and economic benefits resulting from collaboration with private industry would support and strengthen the Park Service's primary mission of resource conservation. Agreements like the Yellowstone-Diversa CRADA would allow the Park to share in revenues generated by beneficial developments, and thus, provide a valuable source of funding to support the Park Service's ongoing wildlife preservation, protection, and study initiatives. Equally critical to the Park's conservation efforts as adequate funding, improved scientific knowledge and understanding of Yellowstone's habitat generated by these types of joint research projects would be shared with the Park and used to support its efforts to preserve the environment.

In addition to their challenges under the organic statutes, plaintiffs also contend that the CRADA violates a Park Service regulation that bars the "sale or commercial use" of natural materials from the Park. 36 C.F.R. §2.1(c)(3)(v) ("Section 2.1"). Specifically, plaintiffs advance that Park Service officials proceeded with the CRADA despite their awareness that such action was "illegal" under Park regulations But, as both the Court of Appeals for the District of Columbia Circuit and the Supreme Court have recognized, "the [Park] Service's interpretation of its own regulations will prevail unless it is 'plainly erroneous or inconsistent' with the plain terms of the disputed regulations."

The court finds that the Park Service reasonably determined that the Yellowstone-Diversa CRADA does not involve the "sale or commercial use" of park resources within the meaning of Section 2.1. The record discloses that defendants have provided a thoughtful and rational approach to research conducted on Park resources. In concluding that the regulations did not foreclose the CRADA, the Park Service determined that there was a critical distinction between researchers profiting from the sale of the actual specimens themselves, which is prohibited by Section 2.1, and profiting from a future development based on scientific discoveries resulting from research on those resources, which is permitted. In reaching this conclusion, the Park Service considered several critical factors. First, it recognized that permit holders, such as Diversa, do not, by virtue of either the permit or the CRADA, acquire title to the specimens or the right to transfer them to third parties. A.R. II.1, Yellowstone Permitting Policy, at 3 (stating that "all specimens collected within the park are the property of the National Park Service and regardless of where the collections are housed, must be properly accessioned and catalogued in the National Park Service's cataloging system"); *id.* at 5 (noting that the "sale of collected research specimens and other transfer to third parties is prohibited"). Second, the Park Service determined that permittees like Diversa, who later develop useful products, information or applications, are making "commercial use" of scientific discoveries, not Park resources. A.R. II. 45.m, at 3 (noting that "to date no firm has asked Yellowstone for a permit to collect research specimens for the purpose of replication and subsequent commercialization"). This interpretation accords with the fact that patent rights derive from human ingenuity brought to bear on scientific specimens, not the specimens themselves. *See Diamond v. Chakrabarty*, 447 U.S. 303, 313, 65 L. Ed. 2d 144, 100 S. Ct. 2204 (1980) (stating that "the relevant distinction was not between living and inanimate things, but between products of nature, whether living or not, and human-made inventions, ... the result of human ingenuity and research"); *see also* Varley Aff. at P 39.

Plaintiffs do not persuade the court that the defendants' interpretation of the regulation is unreasonable. Plaintiffs aver that because patent law allows scientists to obtain intellectual property rights over natural organisms, the CRADA at issue in this case necessarily involves the prohibited sale of natural materials. But this view of the scope of patent law ignores relevant precedent, which instructs that a substance occurring in nature may not be patented in that form. *Diamond*, 447 U.S. at 313. Instead, to obtain a patent rights, a researcher must bring to a naturally-occurring substance a contribution that is non-obvious, novel and demonstrably useful. *See* 35 U.S.C. § 101-103. Thus, in accord with these fundamental principles, the Park Service has interpreted its regulations only to allow researchers to study, not sell, Park resources. The CRADA, in turn, accords with the regulations because any "commercial use" flowing from such research is limited to applications or products generated from the scientific study of the resources, not the resources themselves. Accordingly, the court finds that defendants reasonably construed Park regulations and concluded that the CRADA was consistent with their requirements.

V. CONCLUSION

For the reasons set forth above, the court hereby GRANTS defendants' motion for partial summary judgment and DENIES plaintiffs' motion for partial summary judgment.

A separate order shall issue this date. SO ORDERED.

ORDER AND FINAL JUDGMENT

ORDERED that FINAL JUDGMENT shall be entered for the defendants.

SO ORDERED.

3.5 Patents in Biotechnology

Biotechnology patents in the United States follow statutory guidelines, judicial interpretations, and the guidelines and standards of the U.S. Patent and Trademark Office (USPTO). The issues in international patenting of biotechnology are addressed in Chapter Five at 5.2. *supra.*

The U.S. Supreme Court established three requirements for a biotechnology patent in the case, *Diamond v. Chakrabarty*, 447 U.S. 303 (1980), discussed in Chapter One, 1.4, *supra.:* that "anything under the sun that is made by man" is patentable subject matter in accordance with 35 U.S.C. § 101. 447 U.S. 303 at 309. The three requirements are: (1) that the plant or animal invention must be a non-naturally occurring substance; (2) that the invention have a substantial amount of human intervention; and (3) the invention must have some useful industrial applicability, and is included in the *Manual of Patent Examination Procedure § 2105.*

In USPTO policy, patentable subject matter is described as "non-naturally occurring, non-human, multicellular organisms" which does not recognize human creations because of the application of the U.S. Constitution, Thirteenth Amendment, prohibiting slavery. Donald J. Quigg, *Policy Announcement by Assistant Secretary and Commissioner of Patents and Trademarks*, 69 J. PAT. & TRADEMARK OFF. SOC'Y 328 (1987).

In 1995, Congress passed legislation to provide for an exemption for the non-obvious requirement for biotechnology patents. The non-obviousness statutory requirement is that "the subject matter sought to be patented and the prior art are such that the subject matter as a whole would have been obvious at the time the invention was made to a person having ordinary skill in the art to which said subject matter pertains." 35 U.S.C. § 103(a) (2004). Because of the nature of the development of biotechnology, and the case *In re Mancy*, 499 F.2d 1289 (Ct. Cl., 1974) it appeared that the nonobvious requirement would prevent the patenting of biotechnology in the United States and thereby leave inventors of many biotechnology products without protection in other countries where it could be patented.

In re Mancy involved a known process method, but a novel starting material, which was a new strain of bacteria, Streptomyces. This process produced a novel antibiotic, daunorubicin. The USPTO denied the patent because they argued that one skilled in the art would find obvious, the process of developing the antibiotic. However, the Court of Claims held that it was the "invention as a whole," rather than each part of the invention that must be non-obvious. Further, they held that the novelty of the starting material was determinative to non-obviousness, not the end product, or in this case, the antibiotic.

In 1998, the USPTO announced that § 101 carried a morality element which would be applied in the review of patent applications that included biotechnologies. Donald J. Quigg, *Patent and Trademark Office Issues Statement on Patenting of Partial Human Life Forms*, 10 No. 6 J. Proprietary Rts. 17 (1998).

The Biotechnology Patent Act of 1995

> Biotechnology is defined much more broadly in science than it is defined in patent law and limits the processes of biotechnology in § 103(b) to:
>
> (A) A process of genetically altering or otherwise inducing a single- or multi-celled organism to—
>
>> (i) express an exogenous nucleotide sequence,
>>
>> (ii) inhibit, eliminate, augment, or alter expression of an endogenous nucleotide sequence, or
>>
>> (iii) express a specific physiological characteristic not naturally associated with said organism;
>
> (B) cell fusion procedures yielding a cell line that expresses a specific protein, such as a monoclonal antibody; and
>
> (C) a method of using a product produced by a process defined by subparagraph (A) or (B), or a combination of subparagraphs (A) and (B).93

These two processes, genetic alteration and cell line production and the problems with this narrow definition of biotechnology processes is described in the following article:

Becca Alley, *The Biotechnology Process Patent Act of 1995: Providing Unresolved and Unrecognized Dilemmas in U.S. Patent Law*, 12 J. INTELL. PROP. L. 229 (Fall 2004)

> Genetic Alteration. Genetic alteration, in general, is the manipulation of genetic material, or deoxyribonucleic acid (DNA). All living cells possess DNA, which

are complex molecules which code for the production of proteins. These proteins, in turn, drive all of the basic functions of life. Specifically, each DNA molecule is composed of two polynucleotides associated to form a double helix. On the inside of this helix is a series of nucleic acid base pairs. There are only four nucleic acid bases which always pair the same way: adenine with thymine and guanine with cytosine. The sequence of these base pairs carries the organism's genetic information, providing instructions for the production of proteins (via ribonucleic acid (RNA)). In particular, series of three bases, called codons, encode for twenty specific amino acids which join together in certain combinations to compose specific proteins. These proteins play a central role in regulating the cell's functions and in determining the physiological characteristics of the organism as a whole.

The statute describes genetic alteration as those procedures which stimulate a living thing to (1) express an exogenous nucleotide sequence, (2) change the expression of an endogenous nucleotide sequence, or (3) express a physiological trait not naturally associated with the organism. "Expression" of a nucleotide sequence refers to the process of protein synthesis from the genetic code. Expression of an exogenous nucleotide sequence thus involves an organism responding, via protein synthesis, to genetic information originating outside the organism. This new genetic information may be incorporated into an organism's pre-existing DNA through a number of recombinant DNA techniques. For example, in gene splicing, scientists use proteins called restriction enzymes to cut DNA molecules at specific locations and then insert foreign DNA, from the same or different species, at these locations. Similarly, altering the expression of an endogenous nucleotide sequence refers to a process of inducing an organism to express its original genetic material differently by starting, ceasing, or otherwise adjusting the production of certain proteins.

The third type of genetic alteration within the statutory definition involves the expression of a new physiological characteristic. This category is significantly more expansive than the previous two, apparently covering processes which do not involve the manipulation of DNA and thus are not processes of genetic alteration in the scientific sense. Specifically, a new physiological characteristic broadly refers to any change in the normal functioning of a living organism. The exact scope of this clause is somewhat vague and depends upon the definition of the word "express," which in the context of the statute may be interpreted either as a genetics term of art or in its generic sense.

As mentioned earlier, expression in the field of genetics refers to the process of synthesizing proteins from the genetic code. Applying this definition would limit the scope of clause (iii) to those physiological changes which result from altered protein synthesis due to adjustments in the genetic code. This interpretation, however, would render clause (iii) superfluous given that the previous two clauses already cover such genetic alterations. That is, at a basic level, clause (i) covers processes incorporating outside genetic information while clause (ii) covers all other genetic alterations, specifically those involving changes to the organism's original DNA. Additionally, the statute refers to "a process of genetically altering or otherwise inducing" new physiological characteristics. Since, "otherwise inducing" cannot apply to either of the previous clauses (because changes in nucleotide sequences are, by definition, processes of genetic alteration), these words too would be rendered superfluous if not applied to clause (iii).

The difficulties surrounding the term of art definition suggest that "express" should be interpreted in its generic sense to denote an outward manifestation. Under this extremely broad—but perhaps necessary—interpretation, any procedure which stimulates an organism to manifest an unnatural physiological characteristic (i.e., to change its normal functioning) is a biotechnology process under the statute. This definition could include procedures, such as injecting an organism with an inorganic chemical compound, which are beyond the bounds of genetic alteration in the scientific world.

2. The Production of Cell Lines. The second statutory category of biotechnology process involves the production of cell lines. Cell lines are populations of cells cultured in vitro (i.e., outside a living organism) that are descended from a single primary culture. These cells have common characteristics, and for this reason, researchers frequently utilize cell lines to produce specific proteins. The statute expressly mentions monoclonal antibodies, which are immune proteins secreted by a clone of cells, as an example of such a protein. Because these proteins specifically bind to particular antigens (i.e., foreign agents, such as bacterial and viral molecules, which elicit an immune response), monoclonal antibodies are particularly useful in laboratory research, clinical diagnosis, and the treatment of disease. The statute limits the production of cell lines, however, to those which result from cell fusion procedures, leaving out other production methods.

Additionally, the statute fails to incorporate numerous procedures involving isolated cells and cell products, which scientists generally categorize as biotechnology processes. That is, part (A) of the statutory definition applies only to "single and multi-celled organisms" while part (B), which applies to isolated cells, is limited to the production of cell lines through cell fusion procedures. This indicates that all other processes involving isolated cells or cell products are excluded under the statute (with the exception of those defined by part (C), described below). In other words, the statutory definition leaves out various biotechnological procedures, such as isolation of enzymes from animal and plant sources, incorporation of amino acids in food products and pharmaceuticals, and even certain developments in stem cell research.

A summary of the requirements for a biotechnology patent below, are taken from Margaret M. Duncan, Kathleen Harris, Duncan Curley and Patrick D. Richards, McDermott, Will & Emery, "Legal Implications for Patenting Genomics and Proteomics" Proceedings of The Biotech Law & Litigation Summit, Palo Alto, California (April 30–May 1, 2001).

3.5.1 Biotechnology Patents Applications Requirements

There are three patentability requirements for biotechnology patent applications: the utility requirement in 35 U.S.C. § 101; the written description requirement of 35 U.S.C. § 112; and the enablement requirement of 35 U.S.C. § 112. Those three patent requirements are described below.

3.5.1.1 *The Utility Requirement*

35 U.S.C. §101. The utility requirement was established in *Brenner v. Manson*, 383 U.S. 519, 534 (1966) wherein the U.S. Supreme Court held that an invention must have a definite, immediate, and demonstrable utility to meet the utility requirement of §101. The USPTO applied the *Brenner* standards to biotechnology patent applications and required human clinical data to demonstrate biotechnology invention utility. *See, Ex parte Balzarini*, 21 U.S.P.Q.2d 1892, 1897 (Bd. Pat. App. & Interferences 1991), until 1995. In 1995, the USPTO issued guidance for biotechnology patent utility. Utility Examination Guidelines, 60 Fed. Reg. 36,263 (1995).

The USPTO also issued a series of interim utility guidance for comment between 1995 and 1999 which addressed the rising concerns regarding the legality and morality of issuing gene patents. Revised Utility Examination Guidelines; Request for Comments, 64 Fed. Reg. 71,440 (1999); Revised Utility Examination Guidelines; Request for Comments, Correction, 65 Fed. Reg. 3,425 (2000). These guidelines required the applicant to "explicitly identify, unless already well-established, a specific, substantial, and credible utility" for the claimed invention. These guidelines were intended to provide examiners a basis for rejecting a gene patent application disclosing only theoretical utility.

Final utility guidance was issued in January 5, 2001, Utility Examination Guidelines, 66 Fed. Reg. 1,092 (2001). The final guidance requires that examiners "review the claims and the supporting written description to determine if the applicant has asserted for the claimed invention any 'specific and substantial utility' that is credible, based on the view of one of ordinary skill in the art and any record evidence." Failure to meet the utility requirements of the guidance will result in a rejection under §101 for lack of utility and under §112 ¶1 for failure to teach how to use the invention.

Still, the guidance is criticized for not establishing distinctions between the classic discovery verses invention. According to the USPTO, "an inventor's discovery of a gene can be the basis for a patent on the genetic composition isolated from it's natural state and processed through purifying steps that separate the gene form other molecules naturally associated with it." *PTO Finalizes Guidelines For Examiners on Utility Requirement*, 61 Pat. Trademark & Copyright J. (BNA) 252 (January 12, 2001).

3.5.1.2 *The Written Description Requirement. 35 U.S.C. §112*

The written description requirement is codified at 35 U.S.C. §112 ¶1, "Written Description" Requirement, 66 Fed. Reg. 1,099 (2001). The published guidance for examiners in evaluating biotechnology patents requires the following procedure: (1) compare what the applicant possesses and what the applicant claims; (2) determine whether there is sufficient written description to inform a skilled artisan that the applicant is in possession of the claimed invention as a whole; (3) for species claims, determine whether the application (i) includes a reduction to practice; (ii) is complete based on the drawings; or (iii) identifies sufficient distinguishing characteristics to show the applicant was in possession of the claimed invention; and (4) for genus claims, determine whether the application: (i) describes a representative number of species by reduction to practice, drawings, or disclosure of identifying characteristics; or (ii) disclosed functional characteristics correlated with structure or a combination of identifying characteristics that indicate the inventor was in possession of the claimed invention.

For example, these heightened written description requirements for biotechnology patents may not require the exact DNA sequence to meet the written description requirement, but it appears likely that the USPTO will only grant, and the Federal Circuit, U.S. Court of Appeals, will only enforce patent protection to the extent of the scope of the invention at the time of the invention.

The guidance indicate that, in general, as knowledge and skill in the relevant art improve, the written description requirements may begin to relax. *See,* Margaret Sampson, *The Evolution of the Enablement and Written Description Requirement Under 35 U.S.C. 112 in the Area of Biotechnology,* 15 BERKELEY TECH.L.J. 1233, 1266 (2000).

3.5.1.3 The Enabling Requirement. 35 U.S.C. § 112

The Federal Circuit, U.S. Court of Appeals, has reinforced the enabling requirement by invalidating broad biotechnology claims requiring "undue experimentation." In 1999, in *Enzo Biochem, Inc. v. Calgene, Inc.,* 188 F.3d 1362 (Fed. Cir. 1999), the Federal Circuit, U.S. Court of Appeals, returned to the *Wands* factors from *In re Wands,* 858 F.2d 731 (Fed. Cir. 1988), in determining where there was "undue experimentation.

The *Wands* factors are: (1) the quantity of experimentation required; (2) the amount of guidance provided; (3) the presence or absence of working examples; (4) the nature of the invention; (5) the state of the prior art; (6) the relative skill of those in the art; (7) the predictability of the art; and (8) the breadth of the claims.

The first case to address genetics in the U.S. Supreme Court was *Diamond v. Chakrabarty,* 447 U.S. 303 (1980), which was discussed in Chapter One, *supra.* The principles established in *Chakrabarty* made possible the great proliferation of biotechnology patents which followed.

In 1997, Amgen filed suit against Transkaryotic Therapies (TKT) and Hoechst Marion Rouseel alleging patent infringement for Dynepo, erythropoietin, a recombinant red blood cell stimulant. Dynepo is used primarily in the treatment of anemia associated with kidney dialysis, chemotherapy, and AIDS. In 2000, Amgen's sales of Dynepo were $1.96 billion; and receives royalties for the licensing of Dynepo from Johnson and Johnson. Ann Thayer, *Amgen Prevails,* CHEMICAL AND ENGINEERING NEWS 11 (Jan. 29, 2001).

In Re Thomas Deuel

51 F.3d 1552 (1995)

JUDGES: Before ARCHER, Chief Judge, NIES and LOURIE, Circuit Judges.

LOURIE, Circuit Judge.

Thomas F. Deuel, [et. al.] (collectively "Deuel") appeal from the November 30, 1993 decision of the U.S. Patent and Trademark Office Board of Patent Appeals and Interferences affirming the examiner's final rejection of claims 4–7 of application Serial No. 07/542,232, entitled "Heparin-Binding Growth Factor," as unpatentable on the ground of obviousness under 35 U.S.C. §§ 103 (1988). Ex parte Deuel, 33 USPQ2d 1445 (Bd. Pat. App. Int. 1993). Because the Board erred in concluding that Deuel's claims 5 and 7 directed to specific cDNA molecules would have been obvious in light of the applied references, and no other basis exists in the record to support the rejection with respect to claims 4 and 6 generically covering all possible DNA molecules coding for the disclosed proteins, we reverse.

BACKGROUND

The claimed invention relates to isolated and purified DNA and cDNA molecules encoding heparin-binding growth factors ("HBGFs"). HBGFs are proteins that stimulate mitogenic activity (cell division) and thus facilitate the repair or replacement of damaged or diseased tissue. DNA (deoxyribonucleic acid) is a generic term which encompasses an enormous number of complex macromolecules made up of nucleotide units. DNAs consist of four different nucleotides containing the nitrogenous bases adenine, guanine, cytosine, and thymine. A sequential grouping of three such nucleotides (a "codon") codes for one amino acid. A DNA's sequence of codons thus determines the sequence of amino acids assembled during protein synthesis. Since there are 64 possible codons, but only 20 natural amino acids, most amino acids are coded for by more than one codon. This is referred to as the "redundancy" or "degeneracy" of the genetic code.

DNA functions as a blueprint of an organism's genetic information. It is the major component of genes, which are located on chromosomes in the cell nucleus. Only a small part of chromosomal DNA encodes functional proteins.

Messenger ribonucleic acid ("mRNA") is a similar molecule that is made or transcribed from DNA as part of the process of protein synthesis. Complementary DNA ("cDNA") is a complementary copy ("clone") of mRNA, made in the laboratory by reverse transcription of mRNA. Like mRNA, cDNA contains only the protein-encoding regions of DNA. Thus, once a cDNA's nucleotide sequence is known, the amino acid sequence of the protein for which it codes may be predicted using the genetic code relationship between codons and amino acids. The reverse is not true, however, due to the degeneracy of the code. Many other DNAs may code for a particular protein. The functional relationships between DNA, mRNA, cDNA, and a protein may conveniently be expressed as follows:

genomic
DNA   mRNA   protein
               cDNA   other DNAs

Collections ("libraries") of DNA and cDNA molecules derived from various species may be constructed in the laboratory or obtained from commercial sources. Complementary DNA libraries contain a mixture of cDNA clones reverse-transcribed from the mRNAs found in a specific tissue source. Complementary DNA libraries are tissue-specific because proteins and their corresponding mRNAs are only made ("expressed") in specific tissues, depending upon the protein. Genomic DNA ("gDNA") libraries, by contrast, theoretically contain all of a species' chromosomal DNA. The molecules present in cDNA and DNA libraries may be of unknown function and chemical structure, and the proteins which they encode may be unknown. However, one may attempt to retrieve molecules of interest from cDNA or gDNA libraries by screening such libraries with a gene probe, which is a synthetic radiolabelled nucleic acid sequence designed to bond ("hybridize") with a target complementary base sequence. Such "gene cloning" techniques thus exploit the fact that the bases in DNA always hybridize in complementary pairs: adenine bonds with thymine and guanine bonds with cytosine. A gene probe for potentially isolating DNA or cDNA encoding a protein may be designed once the protein's amino acid sequence, or a portion thereof, is known.

As disclosed in Deuel's patent application, Deuel isolated and purified HBGF from bovine uterine tissue, found that it exhibited mitogenic activity, and determined the first 25 amino acids of the protein's N-terminal sequence. Deuel then isolated a cDNA molecule encoding bovine uterine HBGF by screening a bovine uterine cDNA library with an oligonucleotide probe designed using the experimentally determined N-terminal sequence of the HBGF. Deuel purified and sequenced the cDNA molecule, which was found to consist of a sequence of 1196 nucleotide base pairs. From the cDNA's nucleotide sequence, Deuel then predicted the complete amino acid sequence of bovine uterine HBGF disclosed in Deuel's application....

During prosecution, the examiner rejected claims 4–7 under 35 U.S.C. §§ 103 as unpatentable over the combined teachings of Bohlen and Maniatis. n4 The Bohlen reference discloses a group of protein growth factors designated as heparin-binding brain mitogens ("HBBMs") useful in treating burns and promoting the formation, maintenance, and repair of tissue, particularly neural tissue. Bohlen isolated three such HBBMs from human and bovine brain tissue. These proteins have respective molecular weights of 15 kD, 16 kD, and 18 kD. Bohlen determined the first 19 amino acids of the proteins' N-terminal sequences, which were found to be identical for human and bovine HBBMs. Bohlen teaches that HBBMs are brain-specific, and suggests that the proteins may be homologous between species. The reference provides no teachings concerning DNA or cDNA coding for HBBMs....

The examiner asserted that, given Bohlen's disclosure of a heparin-binding protein and its N-terminal sequence and Maniatis's gene cloning method, it would have been prima facie obvious to one of ordinary skill in the art at the time of the invention to clone a gene for HBGF. According to the examiner, Bohlen's published N-terminal sequence would have motivated a person of ordinary skill in the art to clone such a gene because cloning the gene would allow recombinant production of HBGF, a useful protein. The examiner reasoned that a person of ordinary skill in the art could have designed a gene probe based on Bohlen's disclosed N-terminal sequence, then screened a DNA library in accordance with Maniatis's gene cloning method to isolate a gene encoding an HBGF. The examiner did not distinguish between claims 4 and 6 generically directed to all DNA sequences encoding human and bovine HBGFs and claims 5 and 7 reciting particular cDNAs.

In reply, Deuel argued, inter alia, that Bohlen teaches away from the claimed cDNA molecules because Bohlen suggests that HBBMs are brain-specific and, thus, a person of ordinary skill in the art would not have tried to isolate corresponding cDNA clones from human placental and bovine uterine cDNA libraries. The examiner made the rejection final, however, asserting that the starting materials are not relevant in this case, because it was well known in the art at the time the invention was made that proteins, especially the general class of heparin binding proteins, are highly homologous between species and tissue type. It would have been entirely obvious to attempt to isolate a known protein from different tissue types and even different species.

No prior art was cited to support the proposition that it would have been obvious to screen human placental and bovine uterine cDNA libraries for the claimed cDNA clones. Presumably, the examiner was relying on Bohlen's suggestion that HBBMs may be homologous between species, although the examiner did not explain how homology between species suggests homology between tissue types....

The Board affirmed the examiner's final rejection. In its opening remarks, the Board noted that it is "constantly advised by the patent examiners, who are highly skilled in this art, that cloning procedures are routine in the art." According to the Board, "the examiners urge that when the sequence of a protein is placed into the public domain, the gene is also placed into the public domain because of the routine nature of cloning techniques." Addressing the rejection at issue, the Board determined that Bohlen's disclosure of the existence and isolation of HBBM, a functional protein, would also advise a person of ordinary skill in the art that a gene exists encoding HBBM. The Board found that a person of ordinary skill in the art would have been motivated to isolate such a gene because the protein has useful mitogenic properties, and isolating the gene for HBBM would permit large quantities of the protein to be produced for study and possible commercial use. Like the examiner, the Board asserted, without explanation, that HBBMs are the same as HBGFs and that the genes encoding these proteins are identical. The Board concluded that "the Bohlen reference would have suggested to those of ordinary skill in this art that they should make the gene, and the Maniatis reference would have taught a technique for 'making' the gene with a reasonable expectation of success." Responding to Deuel's argument that the claimed cDNA clones were isolated from human placental and bovine uterine cDNA libraries, whereas the combined teachings of Bohlen and Maniatis would only have suggested screening a brain tissue cDNA library, the Board stated that "the claims before us are directed to the product and not the method of isolation. Appellants have not shown that the claimed DNA was not present in and could not have been readily isolated from the brain tissue utilized by Bohlen." Deuel now appeals.

On appeal, Deuel challenges the Board's determination that the applied references establish a prima facie case of obviousness. In response, the PTO maintains that the claimed invention would have been prima facie obvious over the combined teachings of Bohlen and Maniatis. Thus, the appeal raises the important question whether the combination of a prior art reference teaching a method of gene cloning, together with a reference disclosing a partial amino acid sequence of a protein, may render DNA and cDNA molecules encoding the protein prima facie obvious under §§ 103....

Deuel argues that the PTO failed to follow the proper legal standard in determining that the claimed cDNA molecules would have been prima facie obvious despite the lack of structurally similar compounds in the prior art. Deuel argues that the PTO has not cited a reference teaching cDNA molecules, but instead has improperly rejected the claims based on the alleged obviousness of a method of making the molecules. We agree

Because Deuel claims new chemical entities in structural terms, a prima facie case of unpatentability requires that the teachings of the prior art suggest the claimed compounds to a person of ordinary skill in the art. Normally a prima facie case of obviousness is based upon structural similarity, i.e., an established structural relationship between a prior art compound and the claimed compound. Structural relationships may provide the requisite motivation or suggestion to modify known compounds to obtain new compounds. For example, a prior art compound may suggest its homologs because homologs often have similar properties and therefore chemists of ordinary skill would ordinarily contemplate making them to try to obtain compounds with improved properties. Similarly, a known compound may suggest its analogs or isomers, either geometric isomers (cis v. trans) or position isomers (e.g., ortho v. para).

In all of these cases, however, the prior art teaches a specific, structurally-definable compound and the question becomes whether the prior art would have suggested making the specific molecular modifications necessary to achieve the claimed invention....

Thus, one could not have conceived the subject matter of claims 5 and 7 based on the teachings in the cited prior art because, until the claimed molecules were actually isolated and purified, it would have been highly unlikely for one of ordinary skill in the art to contemplate what was ultimately obtained. What cannot be contemplated or conceived cannot be obvious....

We today reaffirm the principle, stated in Bell, that the existence of a general method of isolating cDNA or DNA molecules is essentially irrelevant to the question whether the specific molecules themselves would have been obvious, in the absence of other prior art that suggests the claimed DNAs. A prior art disclosure of a process reciting a particular compound or obvious variant thereof as a product of the process is, of course, another matter, raising issues of anticipation under 35 U.S.C. §§ 102 as well as obviousness under §§ 103. Moreover, where there is prior art that suggests a claimed compound, the existence, or lack thereof, of an enabling process for making that compound is surely a factor in any patentability determination....

Amgen, Inc. v. Hoechst
126 F. Supp. 2d 69 (D.Mass. 2001)

Opinion by: William G. Young, Chief Judge

In this jury waived declaratory judgment action, Amgen, Inc. ("Amgen") seeks a declaration that certain of the patents protecting its best selling drug EPOGEN(r)) are infringed by the conduct of the defendants, Hoechst Marion Roussel, Inc. and Transkaryotic Therapies, Inc. (collectively "TKT"). TKT denies infringement and, in turn, counterclaims that Amgen's patents are invalid on a number of grounds.

Amgen, the first to discover and manufacture a recombinant DNA product similar to natural erythropoietin ("EPO") and useful in various medical treatments, has reaped significant commercial rewards from its discoveries ... EPO was then the "biggest-selling biotechnology drug ever developed" and that Amgen's EPO sales accounted for over fifty percent of its 1997 $ 2.4 billion revenue). As one would expect, Amgen has sought to preserve its commercial success through a cluster of related patents that it has defended with skill and perseverance.

In conjunction with Hoechst Marion Roussel, Inc., now known as Aventis Pharmaceuticals, Inc., TKT, a smaller company, seeks to capitalize upon apparent advances in genetic engineering by targeting the most lucrative commercial recombinant DNA products and designing around them. It, too, as one might expect, is no stranger to litigation. The present litigation, in fact, has been brewing for some time, and when it ultimately erupted in June of 1999, the parties were ready.

As an aside, it is only just to note that this case has been presented with high integrity, an unswerving fidelity to court rules and procedures, and a consummate excellence in trial practice that makes it a model not only for the intellectual property bar, but for lawyers everywhere. Any failings in understanding are mine, and mine alone.

The course of the litigation may be briefly sketched.

Early on, the parties agreed on a list of experts upon whom the Court might call for technical assistance. The Court chose Professor Chris Kaiser of the Massachusetts Institute of Technology from this list, and has met privately with him for background tutorial assistance.[3]

---

3. While not in any way original to this Court, the use of and protocol followed by the Court with technical advisors is extensively discussed in MediaCom Corp. v. Rates Tech., Inc., 4 F. Supp. 2d 17, 29–30 (D. Mass. 1998) (tracing Judge Richard Stearns' technique of using technical advisors in Biogen, Inc. v. Amgen, Inc., 1996 U.S. Dist. LEXIS 22617, No. 95-10496-RGS [D. Mass. Dec. 10, 1996]). As this Court remarked in MediaCom, the technique employed by Judge Stearns is extraor-

Towards the close of discovery, Amgen moved for summary judgment on the issue of infringement. This motion necessitated construction of the patent claims, and the Court held a Markman hearing on March 27, March 28, and April 10, 2000. Thereafter, the Court granted summary judgment to Amgen on a particular claim in one of the five patents in issue. The motion for summary judgment was otherwise denied.

Trial commenced on May 15, 2000 and continued for twenty-three days spread over four months. At the close of Amgen's case in chief, the Court held, pursuant to Fed. R. Civ. P. 52(c), that TKT had not infringed the process claims of Amgen's U.S. Patent No. 5,618,698 (issued Apr. 8, 1997). Trial concluded on September 8, 2000, and the matter was taken under advisement....

I. THE PATENTS AT ISSUE

There are five patents at issue in this case: U.S. Patent No. 5,547,933 (issued Aug. 20, 1996) ("'933 patent"), Trial Ex. 2; U.S. Patent No. 5,618,698 (issued Apr. 8, 1997) ("'698 patent"), Trial Ex. 4; U.S. Patent No. 5,621,080 (issued Apr. 15, 1997) ("'080 patent"), Trial Ex. 3; U.S. Patent No. 5,756,349 (issued May 26, 1998) ("'349 patent"), Trial Ex. 5; and U.S Patent No. 5,955,422 (issued Sept. 21, 1999) ("'422 patent"), Trial Ex. 6.

II. "THE NAME OF THE GAME IS THE CLAIM": n6 CLAIM CONSTRUCTION

It is appropriate to pause for a moment to emphasize the particular procedural approach that this Court used in conducting the Markman hearing. District courts have differed significantly in the timing and procedure for Markman hearings—some engaging in claim construction prior to trial and others after hearing all of the evidence at trial.... I have consistently taken the procedural approach of conducting the Markman hearing at the summary judgment stage of litigation or at the point when discovery has closed and trial is approaching.... I have taken care to note that the benefits of so doing range from constitutional concerns arising from conducting such a hearing too soon to efficiency concerns arising from conducting the hearing too late.

Here, however, I want more specifically to emphasize that when the Markman hearing is conducted at the summary judgment stage, it is also important to conduct the two hearings independently of each other—the Markman hearing being held prior to and entirely independently of the summary judgment hearing. This is exactly the procedure that the Court followed in the case at hand, although other courts have chosen to address the issues raised with respect to claim construction in the context of the motion for summary judgment and hence conduct the Markman hearing in conjunction with the hearings on summary judgment....

This Court's Markman procedure turns on what this Court sees as the crucial distinction between construing patent claims in the context of considering motions for summary judgment as opposed to construing the patent claims without regard to the alleged infringement issue presented in the summary judgment motion. With this distinction in mind, this Court scrupulously kept the issues separate in order to avoid conflating the legal explication required by Markman with the fact finding that the Seventh Amendment ultimately reserves for the American jury.

Although, under current law, both approaches are permitted in the wake of Markman, just as the Federal Circuit has spoken to the question of what evidence a court should

---

dinarily helpful to any judge faced by complex technical litigation.... In this case, every contact with Professor Kaiser has been made a matter of record. While this record remains sealed, it is, of course, available to any appellate court should it so require.

consider in a Markman hearing ... perhaps it ought similarly fashion flexible procedural boundaries within which to conduct such a hearing. Failure to do so not only deprives litigants of the benefit of consistent treatment among districts (or even among
specific judges), but also risks descending a slippery slope toward the erosion of the role
of the fact finder in patent litigation.

During the course of the Markman hearing, the positions of each party remained generally consistent. On the one hand, Amgen consistently advocated what the Court referred
to as the "ordinary meaning" of a particular claim term. On the other hand, TKT often
sought to insert a limitation by arguing that without such limitation, the claim would be
invalid for lack of adequate description or enablement. Their positions, of course, were not
surprising. As the patent holder, Amgen had every incentive to persuade the Court to
adopt the broadest possible interpretation in order to sweep within its patents' span the
greatest possible amount of its competitors' activities. TKT meanwhile proffered limiting
interpretations with an eye toward distinguishing its products and process from the scope
of the patents' language. This dance is well known. Both parties cite Federal Circuit case
law that appears to support their conflicting views, thus creating the impression that the
case law itself is contradictory. A close examination of this case law, however, reveals that
TKT's approach — though accepted in some limited circumstances — is inappropriate here.

In many instances, Amgen relied primarily on the familiar notion that "first, and
most importantly, the language of the claim defines the scope of the protected invention." ..."The claim construction inquiry, therefore, begins and ends in all cases with
the actual words of the claim. The resulting claim interpretation must, in the end, accord with the words chosen by the patentee to stake out the boundary of the claimed
property." ..."The language of the claim frames and ultimately resolves all issues of
claim interpretation.".... Relatedly, absent a clear and specific statement in the patent
specification giving a claim term a special definition, the Court must adopt the plain
and ordinary meaning given by persons experienced in the field of the invention. Ad-
hering to these cardinal principles of claim construction, this Court discharges its duty
of claim construction by interpreting the claim terms pursuant to the plain and ordinary meaning ascribed to them by one skilled in the art....

Derived from these core principles is the additional canon of claim construction that
a court may not read a limitation into a claim from the written description, but may
look to the written description to define a term already in a claim limitation, for a claim
must be read in light of the specification. Thus, even when the Court looks at intrinsic
evidence to assist it in identifying the meaning of a claim term, the words of the claim
should still be given their preeminence. This canon creates a fine but important line for
the Court to walk: "It is entirely proper to use the specification to interpret what the
patentee meant by a word or a phrase in the claim. But this is not to be confused with
adding an extraneous limitation appearing in the specification, which is improper." ...
To ensure that a litigant does not improperly cross this line, a party wishing to use statements in the written description to confine a patent's scope must first point to a term in
the claim with which to incorporate those statements...."Without any [such] claim
term that is susceptible of clarification by the written description, there is no legitimate
way to narrow the property right." Under such circumstances, use of the specifications
to "define" the claim term would impermissibly cross over the line by using the specifications to add extraneous limits on the patent.[9]

---

9. The line between interpreting claim language in light of the specification and adding an extraneous limitation from the specification is relevant in other canons of construction. As will be

In contrast, TKT relies most heavily upon a number of Federal Circuit cases standing for the proposition that claims ought be construed so as to sustain their validity. During the claim construction phase of the case, counsel for TKT implored the Court to reject Amgen's proffered interpretations because such broad interpretations were not adequately disclosed in the patents' specification. In short, TKT argued that while Amgen taught the production of EPO using a precise process and specific cells, Amgen went on to claim far beyond its teachings. Thus, if the Court adopted a claim construction commensurate with the plain and ordinary meaning of the overbroad claim terms, its construction would run counter to the Federal Circuit's command that claims be construed so as to sustain their validity.

Indeed, incorporating validity concerns during claim construction may apply "where there are several common meanings for a claim term" and thus "the patent disclosure serves to point away from the improper meanings and toward the proper meaning." In this sense, the canon that claim terms ought be construed to sustain their validity is simply an interpretation tool to aid courts in determining what a reasonably disputed claim term means in light of the specifications. The Federal Circuit has warned, however, that the canon that claims ought be interpreted to sustain their validity is not without limits:

> The [Supreme] Court has consistently limited the axiom [that claims should be interpreted to preserve their validity] to cases where the construction is "practicable" and does not conflict with the explicit language of the claim. [The Federal Circuit also has] consistently employed the caveat, "if possible," to our instruction that claims should be construed to sustain their validity. We have also admonished against judicial rewriting of claims to preserve validity....

> In this case, the Court ruled during the Markman hearing that TKT's claim construction theory extends the canon that claims ought be construed in favor of their validity far beyond its intended reach. Instead, as explained below, because the terms to be construed simply are not reasonably capable of the interpretation proffered by TKT, it became apparent that TKT was actually attempting to add limitations to claim terms rather than merely attempting to define the disputed terms. At the end of the day, the canon that claims ought be construed so as to sustain their validity simply does not include under its umbrella TKT's arguments as they apply in this matter.

B. The Biological Activity of Erythropoietin

As explained in the patent specification:

> Erythropoiesis, the production of red blood cells, occurs continuously throughout the human life span to offset cell destruction. Erythropoiesis is a very precisely controlled physiological mechanism enabling sufficient numbers of red blood cells to be available in the blood for proper tissue oxygenation, but not so many that the cells

---

seen, the doctrine upon which TKT relied that claims ought be construed so as to sustain their validity should be subject to the same restriction. Thus, although the Federal Circuit has stated that "if the claim is susceptible to a broader and a narrower meaning, and the narrower one is clearly supported by the intrinsic evidence while the broader one raises questions of enablement under §§ 112, P 1, we will adopt the narrower of the two," Digital Biometrics, 149 F.3d at 1344, this is nonetheless subject to the limitation that the party seeking to incorporate a limitation by relying on the specification must first identify a claim term hook susceptible of the narrower meaning upon which to hang the limitation.

would impede circulation. The formation of red blood cells occurs in the bone marrow and is under the control of the hormone, erythropoietin.

In more basic terms, hemoglobin is the protein in red blood cells that transports oxygen. The amount of hemoglobin in the body correlates to the amount of oxygen that can be supplied to the body's tissues. Hematocrit is a measurement of the ability of the blood to supply oxygen to the body. Hematocrit level indicates the relative proportion of red blood cells to the total volume of blood. An increase or decrease in the hematocrit or hemoglobin results in an increase or decrease in the ability of the blood to supply oxygen to the body. Under normal conditions, forty-five to fifty percent of the blood is made up of red blood cells, and in such circumstances, the hematocrit would be referred to as forty-five to fifty. Anemia occurs when a person does not have a steady, sufficient supply of red blood cells to carry oxygen to all the tissues of the body. Thus, the primary cause of anemia incident to chronic renal failure is a decrease in the production of red blood cells in the patient's blood....

From these uncontested factual conclusions, it is but a short hop to infer that, prior to Amgen's pathbreaking invention, there was a long-felt need for a human EPO preparation that was therapeutically effective in treating the anemia of chronic renal failure. Despite researchers all across the globe seeking to fulfill that need (and commercial entities desperately hoping to capitalize on it), Amgen was the first to succeed. Amgen's invention opened the floodgates for EPO production and ultimately led to a therapeutically effective pharmaceutical composition containing human EPO. One cannot help but wonder if achieving such an outcome by combining certain known prior art techniques were truly obvious to those of ordinary skill in the art, why didn't one of the myriad competitors do it? Consequently, the Court finds that the secondary considerations strongly counsel the Court against a finding of obviousness....

As the contending parties sail into the culminating melee, however, Amgen is aided by two strong, though not impregnable, legal principles. First, as the owner of issued patents, Amgen is entitled to the "presumption of validity." The presumption of validity is, in patent law, not a true evidentiary presumption at all, i.e. an aid to proof that vanishes once the opponent produces evidence to rebut the presumed fact. Rather, the presumption of validity shifts the burden of proof to TKT and places on it not only the burden of going forward but also the burden of persuasion itself.... Moreover, in order to overcome the presumption of validity, TKT must convince the Court, not by a fair preponderance but by clear and convincing evidence, to adopt one or more of its defenses. As will be seen in this most complex case, at least in part, it is this heightened standard of proof to which Amgen ultimately clings as a piece of flotsam among the wreckage of its evidentiary presentation....

Of great significance here, however, once the Patent and Trademark Office issues the patent, the presumption of validity takes hold requiring the Court to presume that the specification adequately describes the claimed subject matter. As a result, the burden falls upon TKT to prove by clear and convincing evidence that the specification fails to describe Amgen's claimed inventions. Although TKT persuades the Court by a preponderance of the evidence that the specification is deficient in some regards, it fails to make its case by clear and convincing evidence. Consequently, Amgen's patents narrowly survive TKT's written description challenge....

Another issue merits consideration, however. Throughout this litigation, TKT has made every effort to point out the fact that whereas Amgen recombines exogenous EPO DNA sequences, TKT activates the endogenous EPO gene. As previously mentioned,

TKT attempted to insert an exogenous DNA limitation somewhere within nearly every asserted claim. Then and now, the Court maintained that the claim language could not reasonably be read to incorporate such a limitation. Instead, the Court opined that if the exogenous-endogenous dispute belonged anywhere in this case, it ought be faced in the context of the validity arguments. Well, here it is.

As an initial matter, TKT's contention must be clarified. Taking the Court's claim construction as issued, TKT notes (as it must) that the claimed pharmaceutical composition is not defined by the EPO gene's relationship to its host. Having lost that battle during the Markman hearing, TKT now comes about and argues, essentially, that "if the claim construction is that broad, then Amgen's disclosure better meet it." Fair enough.

TKT is correct that HMR4396 Injection is produced by activating the endogenous EPO gene and that, in contrast, all of Dr. Lin's specific examples are devoted to the insertion of exogenous EPO DNA into host cells. As earlier detailed with respect to the written description analysis of the '422 patent, TKT's evidence tends to show that Amgen's invention was limited to the expression of exogenous DNA. While the Court is willing to assume that this contention has been proven by clear and convincing evidence, a finding of invalidity for lack of enablement does not follow. Like the written description requirement, see supra Section IV.F.2.a, at 200–03, where the method is immaterial to the claim, the enablement inquiry simply does not require the specification to describe technological developments concerning the method by which a patented composition is made that may arise after the patent application is filed. Moreover, the law makes clear that the specification need teach only one mode of making and using a claimed composition. As a result, contrary to what TKT proposes here, there is no requirement that the specification enable every mode for making and using the claimed products.[56] Thus, the facts that (1) TKT makes the same pharmaceutical composition but by a different method; and (2) that such method is not taught in the Amgen patent, are wholly immaterial. As a result, because the record is replete with persuasive evidence that Dr. Lin's disclosure taught those skilled in the art at least one method of making and using the pharmaceutical composition of Claim 1 of the '422 patent, the specification is sufficient to overcome this enablement challenge.

3.5.2 Unique Problems in Patenting Biotechnology

Monsanto Canada, Inc. v. Schmeiser

File No. T-1593-98
Federal Court Trial Division
2001 ACWSJ LEXIS 2163 (March 29, 2001)

Judge MacKay

This is an action heard in Saskatoon, against the defendants, pursuant to the Patent Act, R.S.C. 1985, c. P-4 (the " Act "), for alleged infringement of the plaintiffs' Canadian Letters

---

56. The reason for such a rule is clear. What would be the value in patenting a composition at all if, by making the slightest alteration in the method of making what is nonetheless the same product, a competitor were able to evade liability? A patent system that permitted such conduct would remove the carrot dangling in front of the inventor's nose. If inventors were so easily divested of their limited monopoly rights attendant to their novel, useful, and nonobvious contributions, they would likely abandon their pursuits and thereby inhibit progress. The law does not permit such an outcome....

Patent No. 1,313,830. The infringement alleged is by the defendants using, reproducing and creating genes, cells and canola seeds and plants containing genes and cells claimed in the plaintiffs' patent, and by selling the canola seed they harvested, all without the consent or licence of the plaintiffs. The commercial product resulting from the plaintiffs' development, from its patent and licensing agreements, is known as "Roundup Ready Canola", a canola seed that is tolerant of glyphosate herbicides including the plaintiffs' "Roundup".

On consideration of the evidence adduced, and the submissions, oral and written, on behalf of the parties I conclude that the plaintiffs' action is allowed and some of the remedies they seek should be granted. These reasons set out the bases for my conclusions, in particular my finding that, on the balance of probabilities, the defendants infringed a number of the claims under the plaintiffs' Canadian patent number 1,313,830 by planting, in 1998, without leave or licence by the plaintiffs, canola fields with seed saved from the 1997 crop which seed was known, or ought to have been known by the defendants to be Roundup tolerant and when tested was found to contain the gene and cells claimed under the plaintiffs' patent. By selling the seed harvested in 1998 the defendants further infringed the plaintiffs' patent....

Introduction

The plaintiff Monsanto Canada Inc. ("Monsanto Canada") is incorporated under the laws of Canada, and has its principal place of business in Mississauga, Ontario. The plaintiff Monsanto Company ("Monsanto US") is incorporated under the laws of the state of Delaware, U.S.A., and has its principal place of business in St. Louis, Missouri, U.S.A. Reference to both corporations in these reasons is made by the terms "Monsanto" or "the plaintiffs."

On February 23, 1993, Monsanto US was issued Canadian Letters Patent No. 1,313,830 ("the '830 patent") for an invention termed "Glyphosate-Resistant Plants." ...

The defendant, Percy Schmeiser ("Mr. Schmeiser"), is an individual who resides near Bruno, Saskatchewan, and who has farmed in that region for more than 50 years. The defendant, Schmeiser Enterprises Ltd., is a corporation organized under the laws of Saskatchewan. It has existed since 1960 in relation to a number of other businesses operated by Mr. Schmeiser, and it was assigned control of his farming business in 1996. The only shareholders and directors of the corporation are Mr. Schmeiser and his wife. Reference to both defendants in these reasons is made by the terms "Schmeiser" or "the defendants."

Mr. Schmeiser has been farming near Bruno in the Rural Municipality of Bayne, Saskatchewan, for approximately 50 years. He has grown canola since the 1950's. There, in 1998, the year giving rise to the plaintiffs' claim, his corporation farmed nine fields, in which 1030 acres were devoted exclusively to growing canola. In addition to his farming, Mr. Schmeiser has an extensive history in municipal and provincial politics, and as a businessman and an adventurer.

The plaintiffs' claim alleges that in 1998 the defendants planted glyphosate-resistant seeds to grow a crop of canola, for harvest, having a gene or cell that is the subject of the plaintiffs' patent. By so doing the defendants are said to use, reproduce and create genes, cells, plants and seeds containing the genes and cells claimed in the plaintiffs' patent. The parties agree that the defendants did not at any time sign a Technology Use Agreement ("TUA"), the plaintiffs' form of license for growers of the seed containing the patented gene....

The defendants do not deny the presence of Roundup Ready canola in their fields in 1998, but they urged at trial that neither Mr. Schmeiser nor Schmeiser Enterprises Ltd.

have ever deliberately planted, or caused to be planted, any seeds licensed by the plaintiffs containing the patented gene. The defendants further asserted that substantial damage and loss has been suffered by them because of the herbicide-resistant plants. It is said for them that it is not possible to control the growth of the Roundup Ready canola with normal herbicides, it interferes with crop selection, making it difficult to plant anything other than canola, and it requires the adoption of new farming practices. I note that despite this claim no counterclaim by the defendants is before the Court. They do urge that, even if the plaintiffs' patented gene is present in the canola grown by the defendants, that gene must be used, in the sense that the crop must be sprayed with the herbicide Roundup, before any infringement of the patent can be found.

The defendants urged at trial that by the unconfined release of the gene into the environment the plaintiffs have not controlled its spread, and did not intend to do so, and they have thus lost or waived their right to exercise an exclusive patent over the gene.

The defendants further asserted at trial that Canadian Patent No. 1,313,830 is, and always has been, invalid and void because:

(a)the alleged invention is a life; form intended for human consumption and is not the proper subject matter for a patent; it is self-propagating and can spread without human intervention;

(b)the patent was obtained for an illicit purpose of creating a noxious plant that would spread by natural means to the lands of innocent parties so as to entrap them with nuisance patent infringement claims. I note that no evidence was adduced and no argument was directed at trial to the alleged illicit purpose; ...

The patent in issue, entitled "Glyphosate-Resistant Plants", concerns man-made genetically-engineered genes, and cells containing those genes which, when inserted in plants, in this case canola, make those plants resistant to glyphosate herbicides such as Monsanto's product sold under the trade-mark Roundup. Glyphosate herbicides inhibit the enzyme known as EPSPS, required to produce a particular amino acid essential for the growth and survival of a very broad range of plants. The herbicide so inhibits the enzyme EPSPS that most plants sprayed with Roundup or other glyphosates do not survive.

By laboratory developments scientists of Monsanto US created a genetic insert, known as RT73, which, when introduced into the DNA of canola cells by a transformation vector, produces a variety of canola with a high level of tolerance to glyphosate. Once the modified gene is inserted in the DNA of the plant cells, the plant, its stem, leaves, seeds, etc., contain the modified gene. The plant's progeny, growing from seed with the patented gene and cells, will largely be comprised of cells with the modified gene. Thus the offspring or seeds of Roundup Ready canola, which is mainly self-germinating, contain the modified gene so that they too are glyphosate-tolerant....

Glyphosate herbicides such as Roundup have been widely used in Canada for many years. Canola tolerant to glyphosate first became available commercially in Canada in 1996. It has been marketed under licensing arrangements through Monsanto Canada under Monsanto's trade-mark Roundup Ready Canola. In 1996 approximately 600 farmers in Canada planted Roundup Ready canola, on some 50,000 acres. By 2000, approximately 4.5 to 5 million acres of Roundup Ready canola were planted in Canada, by about 20,000 farmers, producing nearly 40% of canola grown in Canada....

Canola growing in western Canada is a great Canadian success story. Rape seed was grown on a relatively small scale for many years. Now with the development, largely by

Canadian scientists, of high yield seed, now called canola, crops for oil for human consumption and meal for animal feed, provide the greatest annual value of all grain crops in Canada.

The advantage of Roundup Ready canola is that it is tolerant to the glyphosate herbicide Roundup which can be sprayed after the desired crop has emerged, killing other plants. This procedure is said to avoid any need to delay seeding for early weed spraying, to avoid the use of other special types of herbicides, and to eliminate the need for extensive tillage of the land, thus preserving moisture in the ground.

Because the progeny of glyphosate-resistant canola will contain the modified gene and will also be glyphosate-resistant, Monsanto developed a licensing arrangement to protect its patent, and its market, by limiting the opportunity of a grower, under licence, to sell or give seed to another or to retain it for his own use.

All of the plaintiffs' licensing arrangements in Canada are made by or on behalf of Monsanto Canada. It licenses commercial seed growers to grow Roundup Ready canola for seed purposes. Farmers are required to attend a Grower Enrollment Meeting conducted by Monsanto representatives who describe the gene technology and the licensing terms for its use, A grower must be certified to use the gene technology by signing a Roundup Ready grower agreement. This entitles a farmer to purchase Roundup Ready canola seed from an authorized Monsanto agent, but to acquire seed the farmer must also sign a Technology Use Agreement provided by the retail seed agent acting for Monsanto Canada. Under the latter agreement, the farmer can use the seed for planting only one crop, to be sold for consumption to a commercial purchaser authorized by Monsanto. The farmer undertakes not to sell or give seed to any other third party and not to save seed for his own replanting or inventory. Under the TUA Monsanto has the right to inspect the fields of the contracting farmer and to take samples to verify compliance with the agreement.

Mr. Schmeiser's farming practices

As is apparently common practice for a number of canola farmers in the Bruno area, Mr. Schmeiser routinely saved a portion of the canola harvested on his property to serve as seed for the next generation of crops. Through this procedure, Mr. Schmeiser was able to avoid purchasing canola seed after 1993, until 1999, and over the years he believes he was able to develop his own strain of canola that was relatively resistant to various forms of diseases that tend to attack canola.

It is the defendants' usual practice to grow a conventional variety of canola known as Argentine canola. They also grow wheat and peas, and in addition portions of his land are subject to summer fallow from time to time. For a number of years, Mr. Schmeiser has chosen to grow canola crops back-to-back in the same fields for a period of up to four years. At trial, he asserted that the advantage to such a farming practice is that one may then utilize the benefits of the fertilizer applied the year before, thereby using less and often creating a greater crop yield in the subsequent years. It is also the general practice of Mr. Schmeiser to time the cultivation of his land so as to avoid tilling potentially diseased plant remains into the soil and thereby reducing the possibility of certain diseases developing in new crops. Through this practice over the long-term the defendants say Mr. Schmeiser has been able to grow canola crops that are relatively free of weeds and the common diseases of blackleg and sclerotinia that plague canola. He claims his crops have been better-than-average yields in the Bruno, Saskatchewan area....

In the 1996 crop year, from which Mr. Schmeiser's 1998 seed was said to be derived through the 1997 crop, there were five other growers with farms in the Rural Municipality of Bayne No. 371 who grew Roundup Ready canola. It is the evidence of Aaron Mitchell, Biotechnology Manager, Research Development Department of Monsanto, at Saskatoon, that of the farms licensed to grown Roundup Ready canola in 1996 the closest field to the defendants' field number 2, from which seed was saved in 1997, was approximately five miles.

I note that in 1996 one of the licensed farmers, Mr. Huber, a neighbour of Mr. Schmeiser, grew seed under license from Monsanto on a quarter section just north and west of, and diagonally adjacent to, Mr. Schmeiser's field No. 6. It was the evidence at trial of Mr. Schmeiser's hired man, Carlysle Moritz, that at the end of the 1996 crop year, a substantial swath of canola had blown from Mr. Huber's land onto field No. 6. There was no evidence that seed from Schmeiser's field No. 6 was saved in 1996 to be used as seed for his 1997 crop.

The evidence of Mr. Mitchell for Monsanto is that after both the 1996 and 1997 crop years, the crop was collected from licensed growers by commercial truckers who delivered all of the canola to crushing plants in trucks with tight tarpaulins. In the case of the Bruno crop area, the crushing plants were located at Nipawin or Clavet.

Testing of Mr. Schmeiser's canola

Despite inconsistencies in the recollections of witnesses for the plaintiffs on the one hand, and for the defendants on the other, the chronology of events leading to the commencement of this action can be generally described.

In the summer of 1997, the plaintiffs, through Robinson Investigations, a private agency in Saskatoon, undertook random audits of canola crops growing in Saskatchewan. The farms were identified by Monsanto from among their licensed farmers, or from leads or tips suggesting that Roundup Ready seed might be growing on property of an unlicensed farmer, or from random inspections undertaken to audit a farming area. The defendants' farm was included in this audit process after an anonymous tip was received indicating that Roundup Ready canola was being grown in Schmeiser's fields, where it was not licensed.

As we have noted Mr. Schmeiser testified that in 1997 he planted his canola crop with seed saved from 1996 which he believed came mainly from field number 1. Roundup resistant canola was first noticed in his crop in 1997, when Mr. Schmeiser and his hired hand, Carlysle Moritz, hand-sprayed Roundup around the power poles and in ditches along the road bordering fields 1, 2, 3 and 4. These fields are adjacent to one another and are located along the east side of the main paved grid road that leads south to Bruno from these fields. This spraying was part of the regular farming practices of the defendants, to kill weeds and volunteer plants around power poles and in ditches. Several days after the spraying, Mr. Schmeiser noticed that a lame portion of the plants earlier sprayed by hand had survived the spraying with the Roundup herbicide.

In an attempt to determine why the plants had survived the herbicide spraying, Mr. Schmeiser conducted a test in field 2. Using his sprayer, he sprayed, with Roundup herbicide, a section of that field in a strip along the road. He made two passes with his sprayer set to spray 40 feet, the first weaving between and around the power poles, and the second beyond but adjacent to the first pass in the field, and parallel to the power poles. This was said by him to be some three to four acres in all, or "a good three acres". After some days, approximately 60% of the plants earlier sprayed had persisted and continued to grow.

Despite this result Mr. Schmeiser continued to work field 2, and, at harvest, Carlysle Moritz, on instruction from Mr. Schmeiser, swathed and combined field 2. He included swaths from the surviving canola seed along the roadside in the first load of seed in the combine which he emptied into an old Ford truck located in the field. That truck was covered with a tarp and later it was towed to one of Mr. Schmeiser's outbuildings at Bruno. In the spring of 1998 the seed from the old Ford truck was taken by Mr. Schmeiser in another truck to the Humboldt Flour Mill ("HFM") for treatment. After that, Mr. Schmeiser's testimony is that the treated seed was mixed with some; bin-run seed and fertilizer and then used for planting his 1998 canola crop.

Derbyshire samples, 1997 crop

Before the 1997 crop was harvested, acting for Robinson Investigations, on August 18, 1997, Mr. Wayne Derbyshire, after trying unsuccessfully to speak with Mr. Schmeiser at his garage and at his residence, took pod samples of canola from the west side, along the road allowance, beside field 2 and from the south and east sides along the road allowances bordering field 5. He testified he did not trespass on Schmeiser's land, taking his samples from the crop apparently planted, as Mr. Schmeiser does and many other farmers do, in the road allowance bordering his fields. Mr. Derbyshire placed the samples of pods from three or four plants in separate bags, marking them for identification by Mr. Schmeiser's name, the date, his own file number and the number of the sample. The location of the sample gathering was described by Mr. Derbyshire in a document dated August 21, 1997, which, with the samples, was delivered to Robinson Investigations in Saskatoon on August 27, by courier. Until then the samples had been retained, sealed, in Mr. Derbyshire's car until his work in the Bruno area was completed on August 19....

At the University of Saskatchewan in the fall of 1997, four seeds of each sample were planted and two, three or four of the seeds germinated from each sample. When these reached the two or three leaf stage they were sprayed with Roundup herbicide. More than three weeks later all plants from five of these samples had survived the spraying....

Rather, in his view, the high percentage of glyphosate-tolerant plants, among those which had germinated, indicated they were grown from commercial Roundup Ready canola seed.

As a result of the 1997 test on samples of Schmeiser's canola, in March 1998, Mr. Robinson, on instruction from Monsanto, visited Mr. Schmeiser in Bruno, and advised him that it was believed that Schmeiser had grown Roundup Ready canola the previous summer. Mr. Robinson testified he told Mr. Schmeiser that he was representing Monsanto and that samples had been taken the previous summer. Mr. Schmeiser denies this was said....

Sample in June 1995

In late July, 1998, Mr. E. L. Shwydiuk, a representative of Robinson Investigations, acting for Monsanto, collected random samples of leaves from several canola plants growing in the rights of way near the boundary of each of Schmeiser's nine fields. These were subjected by Mr. Shwydiuk to a "quick test", developed and used by Monsanto for detecting the presence of a protein found within Roundup Ready canola as a result of the inserted patented gene and cell. Each sample, from all the locations, tested positive for the presence of the tell-tale protein.... As a result of tests by Monsanto all of these samples were positive for the presence of the patented gene....

As earlier noted, the defendants did not purchase canola seed from 1993 until 1999. In 1999, because this action had been initiated, on the advice of their counsel the defendants destroyed all canola seed held from previous crops and purchased an entirely new inventory of seed for the planting of their 1999 canola crop, the source of which would be unquestioned. However, volunteer plants of Roundup Ready canola were said to be found within the 1999 canola fields grown by the defendants.

The issues

The issues arising in this action concern

—the admissibility of evidence of the tests conducted on samples of Schmeiser's canola,

—the validity of the plaintiffs' patent,

—possible waiver of patent rights by the plaintiffs,

—infringement of the patent, ...

I conclude that the samples taken under Court order in August 1998 were obtained in accord with the law. Evidence of tests using those samples is relevant to the issues before the Court and is admissible.

As for the samples taken in 1997 by Mr. Derbyshire, in the road allowances of fields and 5, and the samples obtained by the plaintiffs from HFM, it is urged that these were samples of the defendants' products, of their property, taken without their knowledge or approval. The same could be said of the nine leaf samples taken on July 30, 1998 by Mr. Shwydiuk, for the Robinson firm, which he selected from the public rights of way or road allowances bordering the nine fields on which Mr. Schmeiser's canola was growing. Taking the samples in all these cases is said to be unlawful, a conversion of the defendants' property, without permission. Even if the samples were taken from the public rights of way it is urged the plants were still the property of the defendants. It is urged that property in the samples taken by Messrs. Derbyshire and Shwydiuk, and the samples provided by HFM, originally withheld from Schmeiser for HFM's own purposes, was vested in the defendant corporation, and results of tests based on those samples should be excluded....

In my opinion, the evidence of tests conducted on all of the samples taken of the 1997 and 1993 canola crops of the corporate defendant is admissible. It is clearly relevant to the issues. It was not obtained illegally. I conclude that its admission would not bring the administration of justice into disrepute....

It is also urged that the sampling procedures were not designed to support scientific grow-out tests that could be accepted as indicating the extent of Roundup tolerant canola grown by the defendants in 1998, or in 1997. Moreover, the sampling was done by Robinson's investigators with police backgrounds and experience, but no reputed scientific qualifications, and the integrity of the samples, once collected, was in some cases said to be questionable.

These concerns require that the Court carefully weigh the evidence from any of the tests but, in my opinion, there is no basis, in this case, for disregarding all of the evidence from various tests. Particularly is this so where the evidence of more than one or two tests points to the same conclusions. I consider conclusions of fact that, in my opinion, may be drawn from evidence of the various tests, when I come to consider the issue of infringement, after considering argument concerning the validity of the plaintiffs' patent and concerning the loss or waiver of the plaintiffs' rights.

Validity of the plaintiffs' patent

The defendants question the validity of the plaintiffs' patent on the ground that the subject matter of the patent is not patentable. Further, it is urged that the enactment of the Plant Breeders' Rights Act, S.C. 1990, c.30 (the "PBRA") is a clear indication of Parliament's intent "that intellectual property rights pertaining to new plant varieties are to be governed by legislation other than the Patent Act and only to the extent permitted under the former Act". The PBRA preserves the right of a farmer to save and reuse seed. Monsanto does not deny that it seeks protection under the Patent Act for its intellectual property rights, to promote its commercial interests, including its interest to preclude by licensing agreements the saving of seed for use by farmers licensed to grow Roundup Ready canola.

Finally, the defendants say that the gene Monsanto claims protection for has been inserted in many different registered varieties of canola and each canola plant is potentially different from others. At least within a particular variety those plants with the gene cannot be distinguished visually from those without, unless both are sprayed with Roundup herbicide. Moreover, the replication of the gene is not caused by human intervention but by natural means and it cannot be contained or controlled. For these reasons it is urged it is not the proper subject matter of a patent, and the patent should be declared invalid.

The defendants refer to the Patent Manual which describes Patent Office practice to regard as not patentable "subject matter for a process for producing a new genetic strain or variety of plant or animal, or the production thereof." (s. 12.03.01(a))....

This manual is to be considered solely as a guide and should not be quoted as an authority. Authority must be found in the Patent Act, the Patent Rules, and in decisions of the Courts interpreting them.

The PBRA was intended to create a new form of intellectual property right in new plant varieties, as defined, for registered plant breeders....

In my opinion the PBRA was not intended to, and by its terms it does not, preclude registration under the Patent Act of inventions that relate to plants, and that may lead to new varieties or characteristics of plants. The plaintiffs point to a similar issue raised under United States' statutes of the same general nature which was resolved in an analogous manner. The Court there concerned found no conflict in the application of the patent and plant breeders' legislation in that country. (See Pioneer Hi-Bred International Inc. v. J.E.M. Ag Supply Inc. (2000), 53 USPQ (2d) 140 (U.S.C.A., Fed.Crt.)).

The fact that the plaintiffs may have inserted the patented gene in a number of varieties of canola, each of which is different from the others, in my opinion, does not render the subject matter of the patent an improper subject for a patent. The patent is not granted in relation to any claim for a particular variety of canola, or indeed for canola plants exclusively. The subject matter is thus probably inappropriate, it seems to me, for registration under the PBRA, but not inappropriate for registration under the Patent Act .

Moreover, the fact that replication of the gene may occur in the natural course of events, without human intervention after insertion of the gene in the original plant cells, and plants, produced for seed, and that this may result in differences between individual canola plants does not in itself preclude registration, under the Patent Act, of the invention, that is, creation of the gene and the process for inserting the gene. Not all progeny from pollen of Roundup Ready plants will be Roundup tolerant if outcrossing with Roundup susceptible plants occurs, but only use of those plants containing the gene can be subject to Monsanto's claims as patent holder.

In this case the Patent Office issued a patent to Monsanto US as owner of the patent. That patent is "valid in the absence of any evidence to the contrary" (the Act, s. 45).

The grant of the patent is consistent with the implications of the decision of Mr. Justice Lamer, as he then was, for the Supreme Court of Canada in Pioneer Hi-Bred. In that case he dismissed an appeal from a decision of the Federal Court of Appeal that a new variety of soybean produced by cross-breeding (hybridization) was not patentable under the Patent Act . He found that the description of the plant was insufficient to qualify under that Act . In the course of that decision he distinguished between a product resulting from hybridization and a product resulting from a process for change in genetic material caused by human intervention within a gene. As I read his decision Lamer J. was careful to restrict his comments to the facts of the case, a product resulting from hybridization. The processes of genetic engineering, properly described, were not excluded from patent protection by implication of that decision.

In President and Fellows of Harvard College v. Canada (Commissioner of Patents), [1998] 3 F.C. 510 (F.C.T.D.), Mr. Justice Nation dismissed an appeal from a decision of the Commissioner of Patents denying an application for a patent for a transgenic mouse, which contained a gene artificially introduced into the chromosomes of the mammal at the embryonic stage. That decision was reversed by a majority decision of the Court of Appeal in President and Fellows of Harvard College v. Canada (Commissioner of Patents).

The Harvard Mouse case is not of direct use in resolution of the matter before the Court. There the issue concerned patentability under the Act of a mammal, a higher life form, the oncomouse resulting from reproduction of mice, one of whom bears the gene introduced by invention to affect its susceptibility to cancerous growth. It was the claim to the mouse containing the genetically engineered material that the Commissioner had rejected but the Court of Appeal allowed.

It is essentially matters similar to those recognized by the patent granted originally to the applicant for the patent of the mouse that are the subjects of the claims patented in this case. Here it is the gene and the process for its insertion which can be reproduced and controlled by the inventor, and the cell derived from that process, that is the subject of the invention. The decision of the Trial Judge and of the Court of Appeal in the Harvard Mouse case implicitly support the grant of the patent to Monsanto.

The patent granted in this case would not appear to be revolutionary in recognizing, by the Patent Office, that certain life forms maybe patentable.

I sum up my conclusions in regard to the defendants' arguments concerning validity of the plaintiffs' patent. I am not persuaded on any of the grounds urged that the patent in issue is invalid....

Loss or waiver of the plaintiffs' patent rights

For the defendants it is urged Monsanto has no property interest in its gene, only intellectual property rights. While I acknowledge that the seed or plant containing the plaintiffs' patented gene and cell may be owned in a legal sense by the farmer who has acquired the seed or plant, that "owner's" interest in the seed or plant is subject to the plaintiffs' patent rights, including the exclusive right to use or sell its gene or cell, and they alone may license others to use the invention.

Thus a farmer whose field contains seed or plants originating from seed spilled into them, or blown as seed, in swaths from a neighbour's land or even growing from germination by pollen carried into his field from elsewhere by insects, birds, or by the wind, may own the seed or plants on his land even if he did not set about to plant them. He does not, however, own the right to the use of the patented gene, or of the seed or plant containing the patented gene or cell.

I do not agree that the situation is comparable to the "stray bull" cases that recognize that the progeny of stray bulls impregnating cows of another belong to that other, and that the owner of the straying bull may be liable in damages that may be caused to the owner of the cows. Further, the circumstances here are not akin to those cases that the defendants urge are part of the larger law of admixture, where property of A introduced by A without B's intervention to similar property of B from which it is indistinguishable, becomes the property of B. Monsanto does have ownership in its patented gene and cell and pursuant to the Act it has the exclusive use of its invention. That is an important factor which distinguishes this case from the others on which the defendants rely.

Here the defendants urge that having introduced its invention for unconfined release into the environment without control over its dispersion, the plaintiffs, as inventor and licensee have lost any claim to enforcement of their rights to exclusive use. It is said for the defendants that Monsanto obtained regulatory approval for the "unconfined release" into the environment of the patented gene pursuant to the Seeds Regulations, C.R.C. c. 1400. Whether that is so is not significant in my view.

On the basis of the evidence of pictures adduced by Mr. Schmeiser, of stray plants and of plants in fields, in Bruno and its environs, it is urged that unconfined release and lack of control of Monsanto over the replication of the plants containing their patented gene clearly demonstrates extensive uncontrolled release of the plaintiffs' invention. Indeed it is urged this is so extensive that the spread of the invention cannot be controlled and Monsanto cannot claim the exclusive right to possess and use the invention. It is further urged that it was the plaintiffs' obligation to control its technology to ensure it did not spread and that Monsanto has not attempted to do so.

That assessment places much weight on photographs of stray plants in Bruno, said to have survived spraying with Roundup, in addition to photographs of canola in fields which is said to be of canola, some with the potential gene incorporated. With respect, the conclusion the defendants urge would ignore the evidence of the licensing arrangements developed by Monsanto in a thorough and determined manner to limit the spread of the gene. Those arrangements require agreement of growers not to sell the product derived from seed provided under a TUA except to authorized dealers, not to give it away and not to keep it for their own use even for reseeding. It ignores evidence of the plaintiffs' efforts to monitor the authorized growers, and any who might be considered to be growing the product without authorization. It ignores the determined efforts to sample and test the crops of the defendants who were believed to be growing Roundup Ready canola without authorization. It ignores also the evidence of Monsanto's efforts to remove plants from fields of other farmers who complained of undesired spread of Roundup Ready canola to their fields.

Indeed the weight of evidence in this case supports the conclusion that the plaintiffs undertook a variety of measures designed to control the unwanted spread of canola containing their patented gene and cell.

I am not persuaded that the plaintiffs have lost the right to claim exclusive use of their invention, or that they have waived any such claim. There clearly is no expressed waiver, and none can be implied from the conduct of the plaintiffs so far as that is a matter of record before the Court....

In my opinion the conduct of the plaintiffs does not support a conclusion that it has lost or waived its exclusive rights arising by statute as a result of the grant of its patent.

Infringement of the Patent

The plaintiffs claim that the defendants infringed Monsanto's '830 patent by growing, in 1998, seed that Mr. Schmeiser knew was from his 1997 crop and was from plants that were Roundup resistant. By so doing the defendants reproduced the patented gene and cells. The canola crop so grown in 1998 was harvested and sold by the defendants.

The evidence of Mr. Schmeiser is that seed for his 1998 crop was saved from seed harvested in 1997 in field number 2 by his hired man Mr. Moritz. That seed was placed by Mr. Moritz in the old Ford truck, then located in field number 2, directly from the combine after it was harvested from the area of that field previously sprayed with Roundup by Mr. Schmeiser. That "testing" by him resulted, by his estimate, supported by Mr. Moritz, of about 60% of the sprayed canola plants surviving in the "good three acres" that he sprayed. The surviving plants were Roundup resistant and their seed constituted the source of seed stored in the old Ford truck.

Knowledge of the nature of that seed by Moritz, the hired hand, is attributable to Mr. Schmeiser and to the corporate defendant. Mr. Schmeiser must be presumed to know the nature of the seed stored in the truck by Mr. Moritz who acted under Schmeiser's general instructions in harvesting the crop....

Despite questions raised about particular aspects of the sampling and the handling of samples of the defendants' 1998 canola crop, subject to consideration of any defence raised, the balance of probabilities supports a conclusion that the growing and sale of Roundup tolerant canola by the defendants infringed the exclusive rights of the plaintiffs to use the patented gene and cell. I reach that tentative conclusion having also concluded on a balance of probabilities that the samples taken from the borders of nine fields in July 1998 and three samples taken at random from within each field in August 1998 are representative of the entire crop, bearing in mind that all of the nine fields were planted with seed that was saved in 1997 in field number 2, which seed was known to be Roundup tolerant.

I turn to submissions of the defendants in reply to the claim for infringement. First, the defendants urge that there was no intention to infringe the patent. However, it is well settled that infringement is any act which interferes with the full enjoyment of the monopoly rights of the patentee ...

In the course of their defence, it was urged by defendants that the source of contamination by Roundup resistant canola of their 1996 crop, from which seed was saved for 1997, was uncertain. Indeed so was the source of contamination in the 1997 crop.

A variety of possible sources were suggested, including cross field breeding by wind or insects, seed blown from passing trucks, or dropping from farm equipment, or swaths blown from neighbours' fields. All of these sources, it is urged, could be potential contributors to cross-breeding of Schmeiser's own canola or to deposit of seeds on his land without his consent. Mr. Borstmayer, who farmed on the same grid road but further north from Bruno than Mr. Schmeiser's fields numbers 1, 2, 3 and 4, testified that in the winter of 1996–97 a bag of Roundup Ready canola seed had fallen from his truck in Bruno and broken open, and some seed was lost before he put the broken bag back on his truck to be hauled past Schmeiser's fields to his own. Further, after harvesting his 1997 crop he trucked it to the elevator on the grid road to Bruno, past Schmeiser's fields, with at least two loads in an old truck with a loose tarp. He believes that on those journeys he lost some seed.

It may be that some Roundup Ready seed was carried to Mr. Schmeiser's field without his knowledge. Some such seed might have survived the winter to germinate in the spring of 1998. However, I am persuaded by evidence of Dr. Keith Downey, an expert witness appearing for the plaintiffs, that none of the suggested sources could reasonably explain the concentration or extent of Roundup Ready canola of a commercial quality evident from the results of tests on Schmeiser's crop. His view was supported in part by evidence of Dr. Barry Hertz, a mechanical engineer, whose evidence scientifically demonstrated the limited distance that canola seed blown from trucks in the road way could be expected to spread. I am persuaded on the basis of Dr. Downey's evidence that on a balance of probabilities none of the suggested possible sources of contamination of Schmeiser's crop was the basis for the substantial level of Roundup Ready canola growing in field number 2 in 1997.

Yet the source of the Roundup resistant canola in the defendants' 1997 crop is really not significant for the resolution of the issue of infringement which relates to the 1998 crop. It is clear from Mr. Schmeiser himself that he retained seed grown in 1996 in field number 1 to be his seed for the 1997 crop. In 1997 he was aware that the crop in field number 2 showed a very high level of tolerance to Roundup herbicide and seed from that field was harvested, and retained for seed for 1998.

I find that in 1998 Mr. Schmeiser planted canola seed saved from his 1997 crop in his field number 2 which seed he knew or ought to have known was Roundup tolerant, and that seed was the primary source for seeding And for the defendants' crops in all nine fields of canola in 1998.

The principal defence raised by the defendants is that they did not use the patent because they did not spray their 1998 canola crop with Roundup after it had commenced growing. Thus they say they did not make use of the invention as the inventor intended and so, did not use the patented gene or cell.

It is accepted, as the defendants urge, that the claims of a patent are to be construed purposefully. That does not mean that the utility of a patent defines or confines its purpose or its possible uses. It is the taking of the essence of the invention without leave or licence of the owner that constitutes infringement. Here the essence of the claims at issue in this case concerns the patented gene invented by Monsanto and the patented plant cells in which the gene may be found. The claims make no specific direction for or reliance upon the use, after germination of the plant containing the patented gene, of Roundup or other glyphosate herbicide as a part of the invention. The invention does improve glyphosate resistance of the plant that includes the patented gene and the cell, but that characteristic is unaffected by use or lack of use of glyphosate herbicides upon the plant once the seed germinates and the plant begins to grow.

Here the defendants grew canola in 1998 in nine fields, from seed saved from their 1997 crop, which seed Mr. Schmeiser knew or can be taken to have known was Roundup tolerant. That seed was grown and ultimately the crop was harvested and sold. In my opinion, whether or not that crop was sprayed with Roundup during its growing period is not important. Growth of the seed, reproducing the patented gene and cell, and sale of the harvested crop constitutes taking the essence of the plaintiffs' invention, using it, without permission. In so doing the defendants infringed upon the patent interests of the plaintiffs.

For the defendants it is urged that a finding of infringement will adversely affect the longstanding right of a farmer to save his own seed for use for another crop. In particular it is urged that those who do not purchase Roundup Ready canola seed but find the plant invading their land would be precluded from saving their own seed for use another year since their crop maybe contaminated without action by the farmer on whose land plants containing the patented gene are found.

That clearly is not Mr. Schmeiser's case in relation to his 1998 crop. I have found that he seeded that crop from seed saved in 1997 which he knew or ought to have known was Roundup tolerant, and samples of plants from that seed were found to contain the plaintiffs' patented claims for genes and cells. His infringement arises not simply from occasional or limited contamination of his Roundup susceptible canola by plants that are Roundup resistant. He planted his crop for 1998 with seed that he knew or ought to have known was Roundup tolerant.

Other farmers who found volunteer Roundup tolerant plants in their fields, two of whom testified at trial, called Monsanto and the undesired plants were thereafter removed by Monsanto at its expense.

In the result, I find on a balance of probabilities, and taking into account the evidence of Ms. Dixon about the results of genetic testing of the samples of the defendants' 1998 canola crop, that by growing seed known to be Roundup tolerant and selling the harvested seed, the defendants made use of the invention without permission of the plaintiffs.

Remedies or infringement

The plaintiffs claim the following relief for the infringement by the defendants: an injunction; delivery up of any canola remaining from Schmeiser's 1998 crop; profits of $105,000.00 for Monsanto US; damages of 515,450.00 for Monsanto Canada; exemplary damages of $25,000.00 and pre judgment and post judgment interest.

A declaration of validity of the patent

… The usual bases for alleging invalidity are not raised in this case. Nevertheless, insofar as the defendants challenge validity of the patent, the Court is prepared to issue such a declaration without foreclosing any possible claim on grounds not here considered, that the patent is invalid.

An injunction

While discretion to grant an injunction restraining further use or sale of the subject matter of the patent is expressly vested in the Court under s. 57 of the Act, the defendants here submit such relief, if it be to restrain the growing of Roundup Ready canola, would be impossible to comply with in light of the uncontrollable spread of the patented gene.

In my opinion, the plaintiffs are entitled to an injunction restraining action of the sort here found to constitute infringement. With this judgment the Court orders that pending settlement of the terms of judgment concerning an appropriate injunction, the defendants are enjoined from planting seed retained from their 1997 or 1998 canola crops, or any seed saved from plants which are known or ought to be known to be Roundup tolerant, and from selling or otherwise depriving the plaintiffs of their exclusive right to use plants which the defendants know or ought to know are Roundup tolerant, or using the seeds from such plants.…

Personal liability of Mr. Schmeiser

While Mr. Schmeiser is a defendant in this action it is urged for the defendants that since the farming operations were legally those of the corporate defendant, it alone should be liable in any relief awarded and Mr. Schmeiser should not be personally liable.…

I am not persuaded that Mr. Schmeiser's conduct, though deliberate and however uncooperative it appeared to the plaintiff, was such that personal liability in regard to damages or interest is here warranted. Of course any claim to profits could only be in relation to the corporate defendant. As for the other orders here authorized, i.e. the injunction, the order for delivery up, should be directed to both defendants. Mr. Schmeiser is the directing mind and the active director of Schmeiser Enterprises. He may be made responsible for carrying out those orders. Judgment for damages or recovery of profits will be awarded against Schmeiser Enterprises only.

Conclusions

I find on a balance of probabilities that the growing by the defendants in 1998 of canola on nine fields, from seed saved in 1997 which was known or ought to have been known by them to be Roundup tolerant, and the harvesting and sale of that canola crop, infringed upon the plaintiffs' exclusive rights under Canadian patent number 1, 313, 830 in particular claims 1, 2, 5, 6, 22, 23, 27, 28 and 45 of the patent.

The plaintiffs' action for infringement is allowed and will be confirmed by Judgment to be filed after opportunity for counsel to consult, and, if appropriate, to make further submissions about the terms of Judgment to give effect to these Reasons and, in particular, to the relief which these Reasons provide are to be ordered to protect the plaintiffs' patent interests and to compensate them for the defendants' infringement of those interests.

––––––––––

Mr. Schmeiser challenged this outcome, and the Canada Supreme Court heard this case in 2004. The outcome was a positive one for Mr. Schmeiser, and as he wrote on his website: "Schmeiser views the decision as a draw as the Court determines Monsanto's patent is valid, but Schmeiser is not forced to pay Monsanto anything as he did not profit from the presence of RR canola in his fields ..." at http://www.percyschmeiser.com/ (last visited Feb. 6, 2005).

Percy Schmeiser, photo at
http://percyschmeiser.com

The Canada Supreme Court decision follows.

––––––––––

Schmeiser v. Monsanto Canada Inc.

2004 SCC 34
Supreme Court of Canada (May 21, 2004)

McLachlin C.J. and Major, Binnie, Deschamps and Fish JJ.; dissenting in part Iacobucci, Bastarache, Arbour,Lebel JJ.

The Chief Justice and Fish J. —

Introduction

1 This case concerns a large scale, commercial farming operation that grew canola containing a patented cell and gene without obtaining licence or permission. The main

issue is whether it thereby breached the *Patent Act*, R.S.C. 1985, c. P-4. We believe that it did.

In reaching this conclusion, we emphasize from the outset that we are not concerned here with the innocent discovery by farmers of "blow-by" patented plants on their land or in their cultivated fields. Nor are we concerned with the scope of the respondents' patent or the wisdom and social utility of the genetic modification of genes and cells— a practice authorized by Parliament under the *Patent Act* and its regulations. Our sole concern is with the application of established principles of patent law to the essentially undisputed facts of this case.

II. The Salient Facts

Percy Schmeiser has farmed in Saskatchewan for more than 50 years. In 1996 he assigned his farming business to a corporation in which he and his wife are the sole shareholders and directors. He and his corporation grow wheat, peas, and a large amount of canola.

In the 1990s, many farmers, including five farmers in Mr. Schmeiser's area, switched to Roundup Ready Canola, a canola variety containing genetically modified genes and cells that have been patented by Monsanto. Canola containing the patented genes and cells is resistant to a herbicide, Roundup, which kills all other plants, making it easier to control weeds. This eliminates the need for tillage and other herbicides.

It also avoids seeding delays to accommodate early weed spraying. Monsanto licenses farmers to use Roundup Ready Canola, at a cost of $15 per acre.

Schmeiser never purchased Roundup Ready Canola nor did he obtain a licence to plant it. Yet, in 1998, tests revealed that 95 to 98 percent of his 1,000 acres of canola crop was made up of Roundup Ready plants.

The origin of the plants is unclear. They may have been derived from Roundup Ready seed that blew onto or near Schmeiser's land, and was then collected from plants that survived after Schmeiser sprayed Roundup herbicide around the power poles and in the ditches along the roadway bordering four of his fields. The fact that these plants survived the spraying indicated that they contained the patented gene and cell. The trial judge found that "none of the suggested sources [proposed by Schmeiser] could reasonably explain the concentration or extent of Roundup Ready canola of a commercial quality" ultimately present in Schmeiser's crop (*Monsanto Canada Inc. v. Schmeiser* (2001), 202 F.T.R. 78, at para. 118).

The issues on this appeal are whether Schmeiser infringed Monsanto's patent, and if so, what remedies Monsanto may claim.

III. Analysis

A. *The Patent: Its Scope and Validity*

The trial judge found the patent to be valid. He found that it did not offend the *Plant Breeders' Rights Act*, S.C. 1990, c. 20, and held that the difficulty of distinguishing canola plants containing the patented gene and cell from those without it did not preclude patenting the gene. The trial judge also rejected the argument that the gene and cell are unpatentable because they can be replicated without human intervention or control.

The scope of the patent is largely uncontroversial.

Everyone agrees that Monsanto did not claim protection for the genetically modified plant itself, but rather for the genes and the modified cells that make up the plant. Unlike our colleague, Arbour J., we do not believe this fact requires reading a proviso into the claims that would provide patent protection to the genes and cells only when in an isolated laboratory form.

The appellant Schmeiser argues that the subject matter claimed in the patent is unpatentable. While acknowledging that Monsanto claims protection only over a gene and a cell, Schmeiser contends that the result of extending such protection is to restrict use of a plant and a seed. This result, the argument goes, ought to render the subject matter unpatentable, following the reasoning of the majority of this Court in *Harvard College v. Canada (Commissioner of Patents)*, [2002] 4 S.C.R. 45, 2002 SCC 76 ("*Harvard Mouse*"). In that case, plants and seeds were found to be unpatentable "higher life forms."

This case is different from *Harvard Mouse*, where the patent refused was for a mammal. The Patent Commissioner, moreover, had allowed other claims, which were not at issue before the Court in that case, notably a plasmid and a somatic cell culture. The claims at issue in this case, for a gene and a cell, are somewhat analogous, suggesting that to find a gene and a cell to be patentable is in fact consistent with both the majority and the minority holdings in *Harvard Mouse*. Further, all members of the Court in *Harvard Mouse* noted in *obiter* that a fertilized, genetically altered oncomouse egg would be patentable subject matter, regardless of its ultimate anticipated development into a mouse.

Whether or not patent protection for the gene and the cell extends to activities involving the plant is not relevant to the patent's validity. It relates only to the factual circumstances in which infringement will be found to have taken place, as we shall explain below. Monsanto's patent has already been issued, and the onus is thus on Schmeiser to show that the Commissioner erred in allowing the patent. He has failed to discharge that onus. We therefore conclude that the patent is valid.

B. Did Schmeiser "Make" or "Construct" the Patented Gene and Cell, Thus Infringing the Patent?

The *Patent Act* confers on the patent owner "the exclusive right, privilege and liberty of making, constructing and using the invention and selling it to others to be used": s. 42. Monsanto argues that when Schmeiser planted and cultivated Roundup Ready Canola seed, he necessarily infringed their patent by making the gene or cell.

We are not inclined to the view that Schmeiser "made" the cell within the meaning of s. 42 of the *Patent Act*. Neither Schmeiser nor his corporation created or constructed the gene, the expression vector, a plant transformation vector, or plant cells into which the chimeric gene has been inserted.

It is unnecessary, however, to express a decided opinion on this point, since we have in any event concluded that Schmeiser infringed s. 42 by "using" the patented cell and gene.

C. Did Schmeiser "Use" the Patented Gene or Cell, Thus Infringing the Patent?

(1) The Law on "Use"

The central question on this appeal is whether Schmeiser, by collecting, saving and planting seeds containing Monsanto's patented gene and cell, "used" that gene and cell.

The onus of proving infringement lies on the plaintiff, Monsanto.

Infringement is generally a question of fact. In most patent infringement cases, once the claim has been construed it is clear on the facts whether infringement has taken place: one need only compare the thing made or sold by the defendant with the claims as construed. Patent infringement cases that turn on "use" are more unusual. In those rare cases where a dispute arises on this issue, as in this case, judicial interpretation of the meaning of "use" in ... the Act may be required.

Determining the meaning of "use" under s. 42 is essentially a matter of statutory construction. The starting point is the plain meaning of the word, in this case "use" or "*exploiter.*" *The Concise Oxford Dictionary* defines "use" as "cause to act or serve for a purpose; bring into service; avail oneself of": *The Concise Oxford Dictionary of Current English* (9th ed.1995), at p. 1545. This denotes utilization for a purpose. The French word "*exploiter*" is even clearer. It denotes utilization with a view to production or advantage: "*tirer parti de (une chose), en vue d'une production ou dans un but lucratif, [...] [u]tiliser d'une manière advantageuse ...*": *Le Nouveau Petit Robert* (2003), at p. 1004.

Three well-established rules or practices of statutory interpretation assist us further. First, the inquiry into the meaning of "use" under the *Patent Act* must be **purposive**, grounded in an understanding of the reasons for which patent protection is accorded. Second, the inquiry must be **contextual**, giving consideration to the other words of the provision. Finally, the inquiry must be attentive to the wisdom of the **case law**. We will discuss each of these aids to interpretation briefly, and then apply them to the facts of this case.

We return first to the rule of purposive construction. Identifying whether there has been infringement by use, like construing the claim, must be approached by the route of purposive construction, "purposive construction is capable of expanding or limiting a literal [textual claim]": Similarly, it is capable of influencing what amounts to "use" in a given case.

The guiding principle is that patent law ought to provide the inventor with "protection for that which he has actually in good faith invented". Applied to "use," the question becomes: did the defendant's activity deprive the inventor in whole or in part, directly or indirectly, of full enjoyment of the monopoly conferred by law?

A purposive approach is complemented by a contextual examination of s. 42 of the *Patent Act*, which shows that the patentee's monopoly generally protects its business interests. Professor D. Vaver, in *Intellectual Property Law: Copyright, Patents, Trade-marks* (1997), suggests that the common thread among "(making, constructing and using the invention and selling it to others to be used) ... is that the activity is usually for commercial purposes—to make a profit or to further the actor's business interests ..." (p.151). This is particularly consistent with the French version of s. 42, which uses the word "*exploiter.*"

As a practical matter, inventors are normally deprived of the fruits of their invention and the full enjoyment of their monopoly when another person, without licence or permission, uses the invention to further a business interest. Where the defendant's impugned activities furthered its own commercial interests, we should therefore be particularly alert to the possibility that the defendant has committed an infringing use.

With respect for the contrary view of Arbour J., this does not require inventors to describe in their specifications a commercial advantage or utility for their inventions. Even in the absence of commercial exploitation, the patent holder is entitled to protection. However, a defendant's commercial activities involving the patented object will be particularly likely to constitute an infringing use. This is so because if there is a commercial benefit to be derived from the invention, a contextual analysis of s. 42 indicates that it belongs to the patent holder. The contextual analysis of the section thus complements—and confirms—the conclusion drawn from its purposive analysis. It is the reverse side of the same coin.

We turn now to the case law, the third aid to interpretation. Here we derive guidance from what courts in the past have considered to be use. As we shall see, precedent confirms the approach proposed above and it is of assistance as well in resolving some of the more specific questions raised by this case.

First, case law provides guidance as to whether patent protection extends to situations where the patented invention is contained within something else used by the defendant. This is relevant to the appellants'submission that growing *plants* did not amount to "using" their patented *genes* and *cells*.

Infringement through use is thus possible even where the patented invention is part of, or composes, a broader unpatented structure or process. This is, as Professor Vaver states, an expansive rule. It is, however, firmly rooted in the principle that the main purpose of patent protection is to prevent others from depriving the inventor, even in part and even indirectly, of the monopoly that the law intends to be theirs: only the inventor is entitled, by virtue of the patent and as a matter of law, to the *full* enjoyment of the monopoly conferred.

This confirms the centrality of the question that flows from a purposive interpretation of the *Patent Act*: did the defendant by his acts or conduct, deprive the inventor, in whole or in part, directly or indirectly, of the advantage of the patented invention?

In determining whether the defendant "used" the patented invention, one compares the object of the patent with what the defendant did and asks whether the defendant's actions involved that object.

In fact, the patented invention need not be deployed precisely for its intended purpose in order for its object to be involved in the defendant's activity....

The general rule is that the defendant's intention is irrelevant to a finding of infringement. The issue is "what the defendant does, not ... what he intends". And the governing principle is whether the defendant, by his actions, activities or conduct, appropriated the patented invention, thus depriving the inventor, in whole or part, directly or indirectly, of the full enjoyment of the monopoly the patent grants.

However, intention becomes relevant where the defence invoked is possession without use. Where the alleged use consists of exploitation of the invention's "stand-by" utility, as discussed above, it is relevant whether the defendant intended to exploit the invention should the need arise.

The onus of proving infringement would become impractical and unduly burdensome in cases of possession were the patent holder required to demonstrate the defendant's intention to infringe. As Professor Vaver explains, "mere possession may not be use, but a business that possesses a patented product for trade may be presumed either to have used it or to intend to use it, unless it shows the contrary"(*supra*, at p. 151 (emphasis added)).

Thus, a defendant in possession of a patented invention in commercial circumstances may rebut the presumption of use by bringing credible evidence that the invention was neither used, nor intended to beused, even by exploiting its stand-by utility.

The court does not inquire into whether the patented invention in fact assisted the defendant or increased its profits.

The defendant's benefit or profit from the activity may be relevant at the stage of remedy, but not in determining infringement.

These propositions may be seen to emerge from the foregoing discussion of "use" under the *Patent Act*:

1 "Use" or "*exploiter.*" in their ordinary dictionary meaning, denote utilization with a view to production or advantage.

2 The basic principle in determining whether the defendant has "used" a patented invention is whether the inventor has been deprived, in whole or in part, directly or indirectly, of the full enjoyment of the monopoly conferred by the patent.

3 If there is a commercial benefit to be derived from the invention, it belongs to the patent holder.

4 It is no bar to a finding of infringement that the patented object or process is a part of or composes a broader unpatented structure or process, provided the patented invention is significant or important to the defendant's activities that involve the unpatented structure.

5 Possession of a patented object or an object incorporating a patented feature may constitute "use" of the object's stand-by or insurance utility and thus constitute infringement.

6 Possession, at least in commercial circumstances, raises a rebuttable presumption of "use."

7 While intention is generally irrelevant to determining whether there has been "use" and hence infringement, the absence of intention to employ or gain any advantage from the invention may be relevant to rebutting the presumption of use raised by possession.

(2) Application of the Law

In summary, it is clear on the findings of the trial judge that the appellants saved, planted, harvested and sold the crop from plants containing the gene and plant cell patented by Monsanto. The issue is whether this conduct amounted to "use" of Monsanto's invention—the glyphosate-resistant gene and cell.

The preliminary question is whether this conduct falls within the meaning of "use" or "*exploiter.*"

We earlier concluded that these words, taken together, connote utilization with a view to production or advantage. Saving and planting seed, then harvesting and selling the resultant plants containing the patented cells and genes appears, on a common sense view, to constitute "utilization" of the patented material for production and advantage, within the meaning of s. 42.

We turn next to whether the other considerations relevant to "use" support this preliminary conclusion.

In this regard, the first and fundamental question is whether Monsanto was deprived in whole or in part, directly or indirectly, of the full enjoyment of the monopoly that the patent confers. And the answer is "yes."

Monsanto's patent gives it a monopoly over the patented gene and cell. The patent's object is production of a plant which is resistant to Roundup herbicide. Monsanto's monopoly enabled it to charge a licensing fee of $15 per acre to farmers wishing to grow canola plants with the patented genes and cells. The appellants cultivated 1030 acres of plants with these patented properties without paying Monsanto for the right to do so. By cultivating a plant containing the patented gene and composed of the patented cells without licence, the appellants thus deprived Monsanto of the full enjoyment of its monopoly.

The complementary question is whether the appellants employed or possessed the patented invention in the context of their commercial or business interests. The initial answer must again be "yes."

One of the appellants' businesses was growing canola. It used seeds containing the patented qualities in that business. Subject to the appellants' argument discussed below that they did not use the patented invention itself (whether because they used only the plant or because they did not spray with Roundup), the appellants' involvement with the disputed canola is clearly commercial in nature.

The answers to the two questions of principle that lie at the heart of "use" under the *Patent Act* both thus suggest that the trial judge and the Court of Appeal were correct in finding that the appellants "used"the protected invention and hence infringed Monsanto's patent. It is helpful as well, however, to consider the insights gained from the case law discussed above and their impact on arguments raised against this conclusion.

First, it is suggested that because Monsanto's claims are for genes and cells rather than for plants, it follows that infringement by use will only occur where a defendant uses the genes or cells in their isolated, laboratory form. This argument appears not to have been advanced in any detail at trial or on appeal, but is the position taken by our colleague, Arbour J.

It is uncontested that Monsanto's patented claim is only for the gene and cell that it developed. This, however, is the beginning and not the end of the inquiry. The more difficult question—and the nub of this case—is whether, by cultivating plants containing the cell and gene, the appellants used the patented components of those plants. The position taken by Arbour J. assumes that this inquiry is redundant and that the only way a patent may be infringed is to use the patented invention in isolation.

This position flies in the face of century-old patent law, which holds that where a defendant's commercial or business activity involves a thing of which a patented part is a significant or important component, infringement is established. It is no defence to say that the thing actually used was not patented, but only one of its components.

Professor Vaver, *supra*, observes that this is an "expansive doctrine." This is so because otherwise the inventor would be deprived of the full enjoyment of the monopoly that the law of patent confers on him or her. It is rare that patented components or processes are used in isolation; without this principle, an infringer could use the invention to his advantage, and take shelter in the excuse that he or she was not using the invention in isolation.

Provided the patented invention is a significant aspect of the defendant's activity, the defendant will be held to have "used" the invention and violated the patent. If Mr. Schmeiser's activities with Roundup Ready Canola plants amounted to use interfering with Monsanto's full enjoyment of their monopoly on the gene and cell, those activities infringed the patent. Infringement does not require use of the gene or cell in isolation.

Second, Mr. Schmeiser argued at trial that he should not be held to have "used" Monsanto's invention because he never took commercial advantage of the special utility that invention offered—resistance to Roundup herbicide. He testified that he never used Roundup herbicide as an aid to cultivation.

(That he used it in 1996 in his initial gathering of the Roundup Ready seed is clear.)

The trial judge dismissed this argument. He pointed out, at para. 122, that it "is the taking of the essence of the invention ... that constitutes infringement," and that by growing and selling the Roundup Ready crop Mr. Schmeiser took that invention. Consequently, in the judge's view, "whether or not that crop was sprayed with Roundup ... [was] not important" (para. 123).

Perhaps the appellants' failure to spray with Roundup herbicide is a way of attempting to rebut the presumption of use that flows from possession. However, the appellants have failed to rebut the presumption.

Their argument fails to account for the stand-by or insurance utility of the properties of the patented genes and cells. Whether or not a farmer sprays with Roundup herbicide, cultivating canola containing the patented genes and cells provides stand-by utility. The farmer benefits from that advantage from the outset: if there is reason to spray in the future, the farmer may proceed to do so.

Although not directly at issue in this case, cultivating Roundup Ready Canola also presents future revenue opportunities to "brown-bag" the product to other farmers unwilling to pay the licence fee, thus depriving Monsanto of the full enjoyment of their monopoly.

Further, the appellants did not provide sufficient evidence to rebut the presumption of use. It may well be that defendant farmers could rebut the presumption by showing that they never intended to cultivate plants containing the patented genes and cells. They might perhaps prove that the continued presence of the patented gene on their land was accidental and unwelcome, for example, by showing that they acted quickly to arrange for its removal, and that its concentration was consistent with that to be expected from unsolicited "blow-by" canola. Knowledge of infringement is never a necessary component of infringement.

However, a defendant's conduct on becoming aware of the presence of the patented invention may assist in rebutting the presumption of use arising from possession.

However, the appellants in this case actively cultivated canola containing the patented invention as part of their business operations. Mr. Schmeiser complained that the original plants came onto his land without his intervention. However, he did not at all explain why he sprayed Roundup to isolate the Roundup Ready plants he found on his land; why he then harvested the plants and segregated the seeds, saved them, and kept them for seed; why he next planted them; and why, through this husbandry, he ended up with 1030 acres of Roundup Ready Canola which would otherwise have cost him $15,000. In these circumstances, the presumption of use flowing from possession stands unrebutted. Third, as in their submissions on validity, the appellants seek to rely on the decision of the majority of this Court in *Harvard Mouse*. They contend that the patent should be given a narrow scope for infringement purposes, since the plants reproduce through the laws of nature rather than through human intervention. Thus, they argue, propagation of Roundup Ready Canola without a licence cannot be a "use"by them because plants are living things that grow by themselves.

This is also the perspective adopted by Arbour J. In support of the proposition that infringement of gene claims occurs only in a laboratory setting, she cites *Kirin Amgen Inc. v. Hoechst Marion Roussel Ltd.*, [2002] E.W.J. No. 3792 (QL), [2002] EWCA Civ. 1096 (C.A.). That case dealt with a protein useful in the diagnosis and treatment of blood disorders. The English court construed the claims to exclude the naturally occurring form of the DNA sequence in a human cell. However, this was done to accord with the provisions of a regulatory scheme that has no parallel in Canada: Article 5 of the European Parliament's Directive 98/44/EC, which regulates patentability of biotechnological inventions. It states that the discovery of elements of the human body, including genes, is not patentable, although such elements are patentable when isolated or otherwise produced through technical means. The legislature has not enacted a comparable statutory scheme in Canada to narrow the scope of patent construction. Thus, *Kirin Amgen* is not applicable to the case before this Court.

The appellants' argument also ignores the role human beings play in agricultural propagation. Farming is a commercial enterprise in which farmers sow and cultivate the plants which prove most efficient and profitable. Plant science has been with us since long before Mendel. Human beings since time immemorial have striven to produce more efficient plants. Huge investments of energy and money have been poured into the quest for better seeds and better plants. One way in which that investment is protected is through the *Patent Act* giving investors a monopoly when they create a novel and useful invention in the realm of plant science, such as genetically modified genes and cells.

Finally, many inventions make use of natural processes in order to work. For example, many valid patents have referred to various yeasts, which would have no practical utility at all without "natural forces." See *Re: Application of Abitibi Co.* (1982), 62 C.P.R. (2d) 81 (Pat. App. Bd.), in which the inventive step consisted of acclimatizing a known species of yeast from domestic sewage to a new environment, where it would then through its natural operation act to purify waste from pulp plants. The issue is not the perhaps adventitious arrival of Roundup Ready on Mr. Schmeiser's land in 1998. What is at stake in this case is *sowing* and *cultivation*, which necessarily involves deliberate and careful activity on the part of the farmer. The appellants suggest that when a farmer such as Mr. Schmeiser actively cultivates a crop with particular properties through activities such as testing, isolating, treating, and planting the desired seed and tending the crops until harvest, the result is a crop which has merely "grown itself." Such a suggestion denies the realities of modern agriculture.

Inventions in the field of agriculture may give rise to concerns not raised in other fields — moral concerns about whether it is right to manipulate genes in order to obtain better weed control or higher yields.

It is open to Parliament to consider these concerns and amend the *Patent Act* should it find them persuasive. Our task, however, is to interpret and apply the *Patent Act* as it stands, in accordance with settled principles. Under the present Act, an invention in the domain of agriculture is as deserving of protection as an invention in the domain of mechanical science. Where Parliament has not seen fit to distinguish between inventions concerning plants and other inventions, neither should the courts.

Invoking the concepts of implied licence and waiver, the appellants argue that this Court should grant an exemption from infringement to "innocent bystanders." The simple answer to this contention is that on the facts found by the trial judge, Mr. Schmeiser was not an innocent bystander; rather, he actively cultivated Roundup Ready Canola. Had he been a mere "innocent bystander," he could have refuted the presumption of use arising from his possession of the patented gene and cell. More broadly, to the extent this submission rests on policy arguments about the particular dangers of biotechnology inventions, these, as discussed, find no support in the *Patent Act* as it stands today. Again, if Parliament wishes to respond legislatively to biotechnology inventions concerning plants, it is free to do so. Thus far it has not chosen to do so.

The appellants argue, finally, that Monsanto's activities tread on the ancient common law property rights of farmers to keep that which comes onto their land. Just as a farmer owns the progeny of a "stray bull" which wanders onto his land, so Mr. Schmeiser argues he owns the progeny of the Roundup Ready Canola that came onto his field. However, the issue is not property rights, but patent protection. Ownership is no defence to a breach of the *Patent Act*.

We conclude that the trial judge and Court of Appeal were correct in concluding that the appellants "used" Monsanto's patented gene and cell and hence infringed the *Patent Act*.

D. Remedy

The trial judge granted injunctive relief and awarded Monsanto an accounting of the profits made by the respondents through growing Roundup Ready Canola, which he ultimately quantified at $19,832.

The record is not clear on precisely how this sum was arrived at; that it was awarded by the trial judge on account of profits is, however, undisputed.

The Court of Appeal upheld that order on the same basis and the issue is whether it erred in this regard.

The *Patent Act* permits two alternative types of remedy: damages and an accounting of profits.

Damages represent the inventor's loss, which may include the patent holder's lost profits from sales or lost royalty payments. An accounting of profits, by contrast, is measured by the profits made by the infringer, rather than the amount lost by the inventor. Here, damages are not available, in view of Monsanto's election to seek an accounting of profits.

It is settled law that the inventor is only entitled to that portion of the infringer's profit which is causally attributable to the invention.

The preferred means of calculating an accounting of profits is what has been termed the valuebased or "differential profit" approach, where profits are allocated according to the value contributed to the defendant's wares by the patent.... A comparison is to be made between the defendant's profit attributable to the invention and his profit had he used the best non-infringing option....

The difficulty with the trial judge's award is that it does not identify any causal connection between the profits the appellants were found to have earned through growing Roundup Ready Canola and the invention. On the facts found, the appellants made no profits as a result of the invention.

Their profits were precisely what they would have been had they planted and harvested ordinary canola. They sold the Roundup Ready Canola they grew in 1998 for feed, and thus obtained no premium for the fact that it was Roundup Ready Canola. Nor did they gain any agricultural advantage from the herbicide resistant nature of the canola, since no finding was made that they sprayed with Roundup herbicide to reduce weeds. The appellants' profits arose solely from qualities of their crop that cannot be attributed to the invention.

On this evidence, the appellants earned no profit from the invention and Monsanto is entitled to nothing on their claim of account.

IV. Conclusion

We would allow the appeal in part, setting aside the award for account of profit. In all other respects we would confirm the order of the trial judge. In view of this mixed result, we would order that each party bear its own costs throughout.

The reasons of Iacobucci, Bastarache, Arbour and LeBel JJ. were delivered by

ARBOUR J. (DISSENTING IN PART)—

I. Introduction

This case was decided in the courts below without the benefit of this Court's decision in *Harvard College v. Canada (Commissioner of Patents)*, [2002] 4 S.C.R. 45, 2002 SCC 76. The heart of the issue is whether the Federal Court of Appeal's decision can stand in light of our decision in that case.

More specifically, the trial judge interpreted the scope of the Monsanto patent without the benefit of the holding in *Harvard College, supra*, that higher life forms, including plants, are not patentable. Both lower court decisions "allo[w] Monsanto to do indirectly what Canadian patent law has not allowed them to do directly: namely, to acquire patent protection over whole plants".

Such a result is hard to reconcile with the majority decision in *Harvard College, supra*. It would also invalidate the Patent Office's long-standing policy of not granting exclusive rights, expressed in a patent grant, over higher life forms, that was upheld in *Harvard College, supra*: Patent Office, *Manual of Patent Office Practice* (1998 "Patent Office Manual"), at para. 16.05.

The two central issues here, the scope of Monsanto's patent and whether agricultural production of Roundup Ready Canola constitutes an infringing use, are determined by a purposive construction of the patent claims and the proper application of the majority decision in *Harvard College, supra*. Monsanto is on the horns of a dilemma; a narrow construction of its claims renders the claims valid but not infringed, the broader construction renders the claims invalid.

In light of *Harvard College, supra*, I conclude that the patent claims here cannot be interpreted to extend patent protection over whole plants and that there was no infringing use. I need not review, and take no issue with the factual overview of the case provided in my colleagues' reasons.

II. Analysis

A. *The Decision in Harvard College*

The issue in *Harvard College, supra*, was whether a mouse that was genetically modified to make it susceptible to cancer was the valid subject matter for a patent claim. The majority found that higher life forms were not "compositions of matter." Plants were clearly included in the category of higher life forms: e.g., *Harvard College, supra*, at para. 199. Accordingly, plants do not fit within the definition of an "invention":

Patent Act, R.S.C. 1985, c. P-4, s. 2.

The majority approved the line drawn by the Patent Office between unpatentable higher life forms, patentable lower life forms, and patentable processes for engineering transgenic higher life forms in the laboratory: *Harvard College, supra*, at para. 199. That line is described in the *Patent Office Manual, supra*, at para. 16.05:

Higher life forms are not patentable subject matter. However, a process for producing a higher life form may be patentable provided the process requires significant technical intervention by man and is not essentially a natural biological process which occurs according to the laws of nature ...

The line was clearly enunciated in *Re Application of Abitibi Co.* (1982), 62 C.P.R. (2d) 81 (Pat. App. Bd.), at p. 89; patents apply to:

... all micro-organisms, yeasts, moulds, fungi, bacteria, actinomycetes, unicellular algae, cell lines, viruses or protozoa; in fact to all life forms which are produced *en masse* as chemical compounds are prepared, and are formed in such large numbers that any measurable quantity will possess uniform properties and characteristics.

Thus, in *Harvard College, supra*, claims for a genetically modified plasmid and the process claims to genetically modify a mouse so that it became susceptible to cancer were found to be valid. Claims for the mouse itself were found to be invalid by the Patent Commissioner and that finding was upheld by this Court. No other claims were at issue in *Harvard College*; transgenic mammalian eggs (single cells) were not claimed, although the majority suggested in *obiter* that such a claim may be the valid subject matter of a patent claim.

B. The Patent Claims

Monsanto's Canadian Patent No. 1,313,830 is entitled "Glyphosate-Resistant Plants" (see Appendix).

The use is evident on the face of the claims, namely glyphosate resistance that a person skilled in the art would understand to mean the conferring of resistance to a glyphosate herbicide, such as "Roundup".

The Patent contained a series of hierarchical claims. The method claims are separate. The claims in the patent may be split into five general categories:

(1) the chimeric gene, claims 1–7, that does not exist in nature and is constructed through human intervention of three components;

(2) the cloning or expression vector, claims 8–14 (a vector is a DNA molecule into which another DNA segment has been integrated);

(3) the plant transformation vector, claims 15–21, 52;

(4) the glyphosate-resistant plant cell containing the chimeric gene, claims 22–28 and claims 43–51; and

(5) the method for constructing (1)–(4) and, in the laboratory, regenerating a plant from the plant cell containing the chimeric gene, claims 29–42.

All of the differentiated cells in the regenerated plant contain the chimeric gene, which will be passed to offspring of the plants through natural reproduction. However, as recognized by my colleagues, there is no claim for the regenerated plant or its progeny.

C. Purposive Construction of the Claims

The first and pivotal step in an infringement action is the purposive construction of the patent claims: *Whirlpool Corp. v. Camco Inc.*, [2000] 2 S.C.R. 1067, 2000 SCC 67, at para. 43. The claims construction will set the scope of the patent claims, which, in turn, resolves the two issues in this case: validity and infringing use. However, Monsanto's patent claims cannot be construed with an eye to either infringement or the appellants' defence to infringement, invalidity: *Whirlpool, supra*.

Purposive construction delineates the scope of the invention. It identifies what the inventor considered to be the essential elements of the invention: *Whirlpool, supra*, at para. 45.

My colleagues emphasize the commercial value of the exclusive rights to the patentee as the primary consideration in distilling the "essential elements" of the patent claims. However, commercial interests are not the only considerations. There are three further themes to purposive construction of patent claims. I will address each of these in turn.

(1) Fairness and Predictability

Fairness to the public is a recurring theme in jurisprudence on claims construction because of the severe economic consequences of patent infringement. The scope of the patent protection should be both "fair" and "reasonably predictable". "Predictability is achieved by tying the patentee to its claims; fairness is achieved by interpreting those claims in an informed and purposive way".

(2) What Is Not Claimed Is Disclaimed

The classic rule is "what is not claimed is considered disclaimed.". The inventor may not get exclusive rights to an invention that was not part of the public disclosure of the invention. The public must be able to predict the activities that will infringe on the exclusive rights granted to the patentee. So long as the claims are interpreted fairly and knowledgeably, if the patentee has limited the claims, then the public is entitled to rely on that limitation. An inventor cannot enlarge the scope of the grant of exclusive rights beyond that which has been specified.

However, the full specification may be looked at to discern the scope of the claims. The claims are invalid if they are broader than the disclosures.

(3) The Person Skilled in the Art

Patent claims must be interpreted from the point of view of the hypothetical worker skilled in the art, who has been described by Binnie J. as a: hypothetical person possessing the ordinary skill and knowledge of the particular art to which the invention relates, and a mind willing to understand a specification that is addressed to him. This hypothetical person has sometimes been equated with the "reasonable man" used as a standard in negligence cases. He is assumed to be a man who is going to try to achieve success and not one who is looking for difficulties or seeking failure.

A reasonable person skilled in the art, however, must also be taken to know the state of the law as it relates to the subject matter of his or her invention.... This interpretation is fair and predictable because the public must equally be entitled to rely on this Court's jurisprudence in determining the scope of patent claims. [T]he English Court of Appeal considered the testimony of opposing experts (persons skilled in the art) and narrowed a patent claim over a naturally occurring DNA sequence (EPO gene) so that it excluded that DNA sequence in its natural and therefore unpatentable form. In doing so, the court stated at para. 60:

The patentee could not monopolise the gene per se as that existed in nature. The patentee therefore monopolised the DNA sequence encoding for DNA when isolated and in that respect was suitable for use to express EPO in a host cell. As of 1984 such a monopoly would have seemed to give fair protection. To seek to monopolise use of the sequence when not isolated by inserting a construct into a human cell would provide a monopoly not properly supported by the description in the specification. *We also believe that third parties could reasonably expect that if they did not use a DNA sequence for insertion into a host cell, there would be no infringement.* [Emphasis added.]

In conclusion, a person skilled in the art, upon filing of Monsanto's patent, could not reasonably have expected that the exclusive rights for gene, cell, vector, and method claims extended exclusive rights over unpatentable plants and their offspring.

(4) Conclusion on the Scope of Monsanto's Claims

Accordingly, a purposive construction that limits this claim to its "essential elements," considering both the plain language of the claim and the specifications, leads me to the conclusion that the gene patent claims and the plant cell claims should not be construed to grant exclusive rights over the plant and all of its offspring.

It is clear from the specification that Monsanto's patent claims do not extend to plants, seeds, and crops. It is also clear that the gene claim does not extend patent protection to the plant. The plant cell claim ends at the point where the isolated plant cell containing the chimeric gene is placed into the growth medium for regeneration. Once the cell begins to multiply and differentiate into plant tissues, resulting in the growth of a plant, a claim should be made for the whole plant. However, the whole plant cannot be patented. Similarly, the method claim ends at the point of the regeneration of the transgenic founder plant but does not extend to methods for propagating that plant. It certainly does not extend to the offspring of the regenerated plant.

In effect, the patent claims grant Monsanto a monopoly over the chimeric gene and the cell into which it is inserted and the method for doing so. Therefore, no other biotechnology company can use the chimeric gene to create a glyphosate-resistant plant cell that can then be regenerated into a glyphosateresistant plant.

D. Validity

(1) The Law on Validity Claims that would otherwise be valid may be limited by statutory provisions or by jurisprudence.

Subject matters that are specifically precluded by statute from patent protection are natural phenomena, laws of nature, and scientific principles: s. 27(8). Other subject matter has been excluded by judicial interpretation of s. 2 definitions of "invention" and "process" and s. 27(8). For example, the following have been excluded: computer programs if the discovery involved is a method of calculation; methods of medical treatment; higher life forms; business systems and methods and professional skills and methods; printed matter producing only an artistic intellectual or literary result; mere human conduct or mental steps, or instructions; and architectural plans. These examples demonstrate that it is not unusual for courts and the Patent Office to interpret provisions of the *Patent Act* so as to exclude subject matter from patentability.

If a claim encompasses subject matter that is precluded from patentability, it is invalid.

(2) Validity of Monsanto's Claims

Applying the purposive construction of Monsanto's product claims, that they do not extend patent protection to plants, all of Monsanto's product claims are valid.

Monsanto's process claims are likewise valid. The method claims for making transgenic glyphosateresistant plant cells should be valid because an invention may be a "process": *Tennessee Eastman, supra.*A process claim may be valid even where the subject matter it manufactures is not patentable, for example,because it is obvious: *F. Hoffmann-Laroche & Co. v. Commissioner of Patents*, [1955] S.C.R. 414; or it constitutes unpatentable subject matter: *Harvard College, supra.*

The second part of the method—the regeneration of the plant cell into a plant—may, however, seem more problematic. However, since this process involves substantial human intervention and does not follow the "laws of nature" as would natural asexual or sexual reproduction, I conclude that this part of the process would likewise be patentable. The Patent Commissioner in *Harvard College, supra*, found that the process of creating a transgenic cell culture that had the intermediate step of "allowing said embryo to develop into an adult animal" was patentable as a process claim. This conclusion is consistent with the policy of the Patent Office.

E. Summary and Conclusion on Construction and Validity of the Claims

In short, properly construed, Monsanto's claims both for products and processes are valid. Neither extends patent protection to the plant itself, a higher life form incapable of patent protection. In order to avoid the claim extending to the whole plant, the plant cell claim cannot extend past the point where the genetically modified cell begins to multiply and differentiate into plant tissues, at which point the claim would be for every cell in the plant, i.e., for the plant itself.

Therefore, Monsanto's valid claims are solely for genetically modified chimeric genes and cells in the laboratory prior to regeneration—and for the attendant process for making the genetically modified plant.

F. Infringement

Infringement is not defined in the *Patent Act*. To determine what constitutes infringement, recourse must be had to the common law, the statutory provisions that define the grant of rights to the inventor and the recourse to remedies, and, most importantly, the scope of the exclusive rights claimed in the patent.

The issue at this stage is whether the appellants used the invention so as to interfere with the exclusive rights of the patentee, keeping in mind that the scope of Monsanto's patent does not extend to plants. The public is entitled to rely on the reasonable expectation that unpatentable subject matter falls outside the scope of patent protection and its use does not constitute an infringement.

I will assume, as found by the courts below, that the appellants planted seeds containing Monsanto's patented gene and cell. I agree with my colleagues that the appellants did not make or construct the gene or cell contained in the canola crop and did not use Monsanto's patented process.

(1) Statutory Interpretation of "Use" in Section 42 of the *Patent Act*

The relevant statutory provision is s. 42 of the *Patent Act* where, every patent granted under this Act shall contain the title or name of the invention, with a reference to the specification, and shall, subject to this Act, grant to the patentee and the patentee's legal representatives for the term of the patent, from the granting of the patent, the exclusive right, privilege and liberty of making, constructing and using the invention and selling it to others to be used, subject to adjudication in respect thereof before any court of competent jurisdiction.

I will use the same three principles of statutory interpretation as did my colleagues to construe the meaning of "use" in s. 42 of the *Patent Act*. These are a purposive interpretation of the word "use," a contextual analysis given the surrounding words in the provision, and the case law.

A purposive construction of "use" suggests that "use" is limited by the subject matter of the invention, and that any acts for a purpose whether foreseen or not by the inventor may constitute an infringing use. The problem with defining "use" in the manner of my colleagues as commercial use is that the inventor is not obliged to describe the utility of the invention, the inventor must merely describe the invention so as to produce it. Utility need not include commercial utility, contrary to my colleagues' opinion.

The test for determining "use" is not whether the alleged user has deprived the patentee of the commercial benefits flowing from his invention, but whether the alleged user has deprived the patentee of his monopoly over the use of the invention as construed in the claims.

Applied here, the question is whether the appellants used Monsanto's genetically modified cells and genes as they existed in the laboratory prior to differentiation and propagation—or the process of genetic alteration. The question is not whether the appellants deprived Monsanto of some or all the commercial benefits of their invention.

(2) The Law on Use

With respect, in my view, the case law does not support my colleagues' interpretation of use. Much of the jurisprudence on "use" and various analogies are unhelpful because of the unique properties of biological materials, especially higher life forms that can self-replicate and spread. The fact that self-replicating materials are difficult to place within the confines of the *Patent Act* was acknowledged by the Federal Court of Appeal, at para. 57: "it seems to me arguable that the patented Monsanto gene falls into a novel category. It is a patented invention found within a living plant that may, without human intervention, produce progeny containing the same invention."

It is well established that the use or sale of unpatented subject matter may still infringe a patent where the unpatented subject matter is made employing a patented *process*. This proposition does not assist the respondent, however. The appellants have not infringed the *process* claim because they have not used the claimed method to produce their canola crop.

The real question is whether a patented *product* (the gene or cell) extends patent protection to the unpatentable object into which it is incorporated. The respondents and the inter-vener, BIOTECanada, further contend that "[i]t is trite law that an un-patentable composition of matter can be an infringement by virtue of it incorporating *patented material*" (joint factum of BIOTECanada and the Canadian Seed Trade Association, at para. 39 (emphasis added)) but, like my colleagues, provided no authority on this point. In any event, there is no genuinely useful analogy between growing a plant in which every cell and every cell of all its progeny are remotely traceable to the genetically modified cell and contain the chimeric gene and putting a zipper in a garment, or tires on a car or constructing with Lego blocks. The analogies are particularly weak when it is considered that the plant can subsequently grow, reproduce, and spread with no further human intervention.

One option that was urged on us by the appellants was to incorporate a knowledge element into the definition of "use." Such a solution would be broadly applicable to other types of patents and lend uncertainty to a settled issue in Canadian patent law that intention is irrelevant to infringement.

Most people are not aware of the contents of patents but are effectively deemed to have knowledge.

What matters is what the person does. If the person's acts interfere with the exclusive rights granted by the patent, then there is infringement.

A truly innocent infringer may be able to rebut the presumption of use. However, that would likely prove difficult once the innocent infringer became aware that the genetically modified crop was present—or was likely to be present—on his or her land and continued to practice traditional farming methods, such as saving seed. The complexities and nuances of innocent bystander protection in the context of agricultural biotechnology should be expressly considered by Parliament because it can only be inadequately accommodated by the law on use.

(3) Conclusion on Infringement

In the result, the lower courts erred not only in construing the claims to extend to plants and seed, but in construing "use" to include the use of subject matter disclaimed by the patentee, namely the plant.

The appellants as users were entitled to rely on the reasonable expectation that plants, as unpatentable subject matter, fall outside the scope of patent protection. Accordingly, the cultivation of plants containing the patented gene and cell does not constitute an infringement. The plants containing the patented gene can have no stand-by value or utility as my colleagues allege. To conclude otherwise would, in effect, confer patent protection on the plant.

Uses that would constitute an infringement include using the chimeric gene in its isolated form to create an expression or cloning vector or a transformation vector and using the transformation vector to create a transgenic plant cell. The use claimed for the plant cell extends to the isolated plant cell in a laboratory culture used to regenerate a "founder plant" but not to its offspring.

There is no claim for a "glyphosate-resistant" plant and all its offspring. Therefore saving, planting, or selling seed from glyphosate-resistant plants does not constitute an infringing use.

Obviously, as was done here, Monsanto can still license the sale of seeds that it produces from its patented invention and can impose contractual obligations on the licencee. Licensing allows the patent owner to impose conditions on the use of the plant, such as a prohibition on saving seeds, with the concomitant ability to sue the farmer for breach of contract if the farmer violates any of the terms of the licence.

G. The Conclusion Is Consistent with Canada's International Obligations under the Agreement on Trade-Related Aspects of Intellectual Property Rights

In *Harvard College, supra,* both the majority and the minority called for Parliament's intervention on the issue of patenting higher life forms. As things stand, my conclusion on the scope of Monsanto's patent claims that is determinative of both validity and infringing use is not contrary to art. 27(1) of TRIPS whereby Canada has agreed to make patents available for any invention without discrimination as to the field of technology.

The Canadian Biotechnology Advisory Committee (CBAC), *Patenting of Higher Life Forms and Related Issues* (June 2002) suggests that the contrary may, in fact, be the case. The use of biologically replicating organisms as a "vehicle" for genetic patents may overcompensate the patentee both in relation to what was invented, and to other areas of invention. CBAC, *supra,* at p. 12, explains the point as follows:

Because higher life forms can reproduce by themselves, the grant of a patent over a plant, seed or non-human animal covers not only the particular plant, seed or animal sold, but also all its progeny containing the patented invention for all generations until the expiry of the patent term (20 years from the priority date). In addition, much of the value of the higher life form, particularly with respect to animals, derives from the natural characteristics of the original organism and has nothing to do with the invention. In light of these unique characteristics of biological inventions, granting the patent holder exclusive rights that extend not only to the particular organism embodying the invention but also to all subsequent progeny of that organism represents a significant increase in the scope of rights offered to patent holders. It also represents a greater transfer of economic interests from the agricultural community to the biotechnology industry than exists in other fields of science.

My conclusion does not violate, and indeed is supported by art. 27(3)(b) of *TRIPS,* that states:

Article 27 ...

3. Members may also exclude from patentability: ...

(b) plants and animals other than micro-organisms, and essentially biological processes for the production of plants or animals other than non-biological and microbiological processes. However, Members shall provide for the protection of plant varieties either by patents or by an effective *sui generis* system of by any combination thereof....

Allowing gene and cell claims to extend patent protection to plants would render this provision of *TRIPS* meaningless. To find that possession of plants, as the embodiment of a gene or cell claim, constitute a "use" of that claim would have the same effect as patenting the plant. Therefore, my conclusion on both the scope of the claims and the scope of use is consistent with Canada's international obligations under TRIPS.

Canada has a *sui generis* system of protection for plants. The *Plant Breeders' Rights Act*, S.C. 1990, c. 20, represents a nuanced statutory regime that takes into consideration the rights of both the developers of new plant varieties and users. There is nothing in the *Plant Breeders' Rights Act* that would exclude genetically modified new plant varieties, such as Roundup Ready Canola, from its purview. While the "rights available under the *Plant Breeders' Rights Act* fall well short of those conferred by patent, both in comprehensiveness and in duration" (*Harvard College, supra,* at para. 63), they may be all that Monsanto is entitled to.

In light of my conclusion on the issue of infringement, it is unnecessary for me to consider the other issues on appeal.

III. Disposition

I would allow the appeal with costs to the appellants throughout.

Appeal allowed in part, IACOBUCCI, BASTARACHE, ARBOUR and LEBEL JJ. *dissenting in part.*

3.6 New Professions and Legal Issues

The biotechnology revolution has brought rapid growth in the area of biotechnology and biotechnology professions. New fields have given rise to the terms, genetic engineering and bioengineering.

3.6.1 Bioengineers

Experts in the field of engineering education disagree with respect to the definition of this field. Traditional activities of engineers include designing non-biological devices to aid in a biological process or product, and this is often given as the defining limit of bioengineering. These activities would include neuroengineering, cell and tissue engineering, orthopaedic bioengineering, injury biomechanics, biofluid mechanics,[tissue culture, sensor development] and biomedical imaging.

However, other biological activities have been classified under the name of bioengineering, which extend to recombinant DNA activities used to design an organism or plant. In the simplest terms, bioengineering requires a knowledge of biology.

Bioengineering specialties in the broadest sense include: Agricultural engineering, animal systems engineering, aquacultural engineering, bioprocess engineering, biotechnical systems engineering or genetic engineering, ecological systems engineering, environmental engineering, food engineering, horticultural engineering, human engineering, medical engineering, microbial systems engineering, rehabilitation engineering. Beth Panitz, *Bioengineering: A Growing New Discipline*, PRISM AMERICAN SOCIETY FOR ENGINEERING EDUCATION 22–24, Nov. 1996 at 22–24.

3.6.2 Genetic Counselors

The genetic counseling profession as a recognized certified profession ABGC was incorporated on February 17, 1993 in the State of New York as the accrediting and credentialing body for the genetic counseling profession. In 1996, ABGC developed and administered a certification examination for genetic counselors for the first time. To be eligible to take the certification examination, the candidate must have completed an ABGC accredited Master's degree program in genetic counseling, and log 50 counseling cases in a clinical setting. There are approximately 2,000 certified genetic counselors in the United States in 2007. [See www.abgc.net]

In *Molloy v. Meier*, 679 N.W.2d 711(Minn.,2004), the court held that the mother sustained injury by the doctor's failure to diagnose her child's genetic disorder when she conceived another child, establishing that the state's four-year statute of limitations did not begin to run until conception. The mother claimed that had the child been diagnosed with the genetic disorder, Fragile X syndrome, that she would have found that any future children had a nearly 50% likelihood of inheriting the disease, and based on that information she would have made the choice not to conceive another child.

This case established third party liability for the physician who the court determined owed a duty of care to the biological parents of the child, where it is reasonably foreseeable that if the diagnosis were negligently performed, the parents would be injured by choosing to have another child.

The growing area of genetics malpractice—considerations of the standard of care for the recommendation of genetic testing—is an area in which physicians are not well-trained. Physicians are in need of genetic counselors who are informed about the genetic tests that are available, about screening techniques as well as the risks involved, if any. The following excerpt from Jeri E. Reutenauer: NOTE, *Medical Malpractice Liability in the Era of Genetic Susceptibility Testing*, 19 QUINNIPIAC L. REV. 539 (2000), describes the function of genetic counseling in the context of the standard of care:

C. Genetic Counseling

With the limited forms of genetic testing traditionally available, physicians and other healthcare providers generally have been regarded as the appropriate sources for providing genetic information. Legal precedent has established a duty for healthcare professionals to provide genetic information in a variety of situations. Courts have recognized causes of action for both wrongful birth and wrongful life. Several courts have held that a physician may have a duty to warn a patient of newly discovered risks from previously rendered services, and some have even permitted claims based on duty to warn third parties.

However, the tremendous magnitude and diversity of the genetic information that is becoming available as a result of the Human Genome Project raises questions about a physician's responsibility to provide all of the current genetic services to his or her patients. At the present time, physicians have a professional responsibility to ensure that genetic counseling is offered for the appropriate cases and that accurate information is provided within the currently accepted standards of practice.

With an increasing demand for genetic testing, the field of genetic counseling has also grown and flourished. An ad hoc committee of the American Society of Human Genetics has defined genetic counseling as "a communication process which deals with the human problems associated with the occurrence, or the risk of occurrence, of a genetic disorder in a family." Both education and counseling are vital components of the genetic testing process. Genetic counseling is a multi-step process. The genetic counselor or other healthcare provider attempts to help the family or individual to

(1) comprehend the medical facts, including the diagnosis, probable course of the disorder, and the available management; (2) appreciate the way heredity contributes to the disorder, and the risk of recurrence in specified relatives; (3) understand the alternatives for dealing with the risk of recurrence; (4) choose the course of action which seems … appropriate in view of … risk, … family goals, and … ethical and religious standards, and to act in accordance with that decision; and (5) to make the best possible adjustment to the disorder in an affected family member and/or to the risk of recurrence of that disorder.

The process of genetic counseling can be quite complex. In addition, most genetic tests yield results that are ambiguous and not readily understandable. As a result, many individuals may find themselves in need of further information and support in order to cope with the knowledge gained from genetic testing. Concurrently, many physicians and other healthcare providers are finding that they have not had adequate education and training in the areas of genetics and genetic counseling. Despite these shortcomings, physicians and other healthcare professionals, who may not be fully aware of the genetic risks and the availability of testing, may be held liable for failing to communicate the potential genetic risks to their patients. Confronted with all of the rapidly evolving genetic information, people will seek explanations and answers.

Physicians have a professional responsibility to ensure that genetic counseling is provided in the appropriate cases. Due to the explosion of genetic information resulting from the Human Genome Project, meeting this responsibility is becoming a daunting task for physicians and other healthcare providers.

Even though physicians are not expected to act as genetic counselors, it is anticipated that they will have sufficient knowledge of the capabilities of genetic testing in order to present some genetic information to their patients and to make referrals to genetic counselors when necessary. In fact, a clear legal duty exists for obstetricians to refer patients to specialists in the field of genetic counseling in cases where the patient is at sufficient risk. Therefore, it is essential for healthcare professionals to remain familiar enough with the latest information and newest technologies to know when it is appropriate to refer their patients to genetic counselors or other genetic specialists.

———

Notes

1. The conflict in defining bioengineering raises concerns that some in the field will be governed by a licensing body with a code of ethics, while others in the field will be without a licensing body and governed by the code of ethics established by the agencies from which they derive funding, such as the National Science Foundation.

In a 1927 case, the term "engineering" was determined by the Tennessee court to have exclusive use only among those licensed by the state. In that case, a company of licensed plumbers used the name "Standard Engineering Company." The state passed a statute in 1921 providing for the licensing of architects and engineers, and creating a licensing board. The court held that, "While it is doubtless true that the defendants have not undertaken to practice architecture or engineering strictly speaking, and they might pursue their business, as they have in the past without endangering the public safety or welfare, nevertheless they have seen proper to advertise themselves as engineers. This is prohibited by law unless they are in fact engineers." *State Board of Examiners for Architects and Engineers v. Standard Engineering Company*, 7 S.W.2d 47 (Tenn. 1927).

Where might the use of the term bioengineering, when used by those not licensed in the field, become an issue? In obtaining expert witnesses, identifying themselves as bioengineers, is it important that they be licensed in the field of engineering?

2. Stuart Achincloss has proposed a new licensed profession of bioengineers or genetic engineers, but based on a federal regulatory scheme:

Every release to the environment of organisms with deliberately modified hereditary traits must be supervised by a licensed professional who has personal responsibility that the release is conducted in accordance with good scientific practices.

The seven major elements of this proposal are considered in the following sections.

1. Every Release

... [T]his system requires professional supervision of every release, while the refinement limits governmental supervision to releases of demonstrable risk. In addition, this proposal is not for governmental oversight, but rather oversight by individuals with ethical obligations, who are trained to look outside the normal bounds of their specialized fields.

This requirement applies to every release because although most releases will not have any dangerous implications for society or the environment, some releases will be dangerous. There is no way to tell which releases are dangerous without the consideration of someone trained to spot the few releases needing special review.

2. To the Environment

By this clause the statute is applicable only to releases to the environment. There is no requirement that a licensed professional supervise every bakery, brewery, or pharmaceutical factory using genetically modified organisms. This clause, however, in no way relieves responsible individuals from liability for accidental releases of genetically modified organisms which escape from the premises of such facilities.

The reason for regulating is that once genetically modified organisms are in the environment, they may be impossible to eradicate. Despite the present concern with the extinction of species, it is very difficult to exterminate a specific species without doing serious collateral damage to the environment in which the species lives.

3. Organism with Deliberately Modified Hereditary Traits

... Any organism is a deliberately modified organism when human intervention has altered any of the organism's hereditary traits.... [H]owever, the proposed law would not include any exceptions to the professional supervision of releases to the environment because the problem is not only from the organism's inherent danger but also from its interaction with a specific ecological context.

4. Supervised

This law proposes supervision similar to the supervision an architect exercises in designing a large building. Although an architect is not an expert in all the special disciplines required for the design and construction of safe structures, architects must know enough about buildings in general to coordinate their specialists' work to achieve the product the owner desires while satisfying the architect's professional duty to the general public's safety.

Similarly, in biotechnology, this professional supervision would allow the coordination under one person's responsibility of the varied sciences which bear on releases to the environment. These varied sciences include the released organism's biology and molecular biology, as well as the release site's ecology. In addition, a professional scientist's expertise would include the knowledge of what other sciences are needed. This coordination of scientific specialties is necessary to manage the tremendous diversity and problems deliberately modified organism releases raise.

Because even a small release of a genetically modified organism can cause as much trouble as the gypsy moths have caused, professional supervision would be required even for small releases. This requirement applies to both academic and industrial research. Such supervision will not likely be a problem for industry because it already is accustomed to environmental regulation and reporting. This mandatory supervision will be more of a change for academic researchers who are not used to any accountability beyond the peer review of the local biohazards safety committee, or RAC. But to be fair, and to enhance public confidence, the rules must be the same for both kinds of research.

5. Licensed Professional

Certainly the release to the environment of genetically modified organisms requires competent professional judgment. Lawyers, for example, require a license to practice their profession, and all such practitioners must accept personal liability for their failure to live up to their profession's standards of competence. Because the release of genetically modified organisms to the environment may have an even larger adverse impact than the actions of other professionals, assigning similar responsibility to an individual in charge of a release is a natural step.

The proposal is that a licensed professional scientist supervise and be personally responsible that the release is carried out in an ethical manner in accordance with the law. This does not mean that the professional scientist routinely would be personally liable for the unforeseeable consequences of a release. The professional scientist would be responsible only for conducting the release in a careful manner.

The new law could create a national license requirement. Professional designation would require knowledge of molecular biology and ecology, as well as the laws of genetic engineering. The key requirement is that the person supervising any release should have a sufficiently broad, general knowledge of the relevant sciences and law to prevent mistakes arising from a failure to perceive risks outside an individual's specialty.

The cooperation of licensed professionals who have explicit obligations larger than their own interests is an important pillar in the structure of environmental law. The key to this regulatory system is personal professional accountability. Although there is no precedent for the legislative creation of licensed specialty practitioners, there are ample technically qualified candidates and adequate commercial incentives so that the creation of such a licensing law would not cause genetic engineering to cease.

6. Personal Responsibility

Personal responsibility means that professional scientists are personally liable if their review and planning of the release falls below the standard of care exercised by other professional genetic engineers in the community. This does not mean, however, that the professional engineer is responsible for damage done by a runaway deliberately modified organism if that damage was professionally unforeseeable.

Personal responsibility is important so that the general public knows there is an individual responsible for what happens, and ready to accept the consequences if anything goes wrong. This responsibility helps allay the fear that specialists who lack concern for the wider implications of their work are releasing deliberately modified organisms.

7. Good Scientific Practices

Because the possibilities from harm from releasing deliberately modified organisms to the environment are very broad, the science itself has to be equally broad. The genetic engineer will receive training to think about the organism's movement by its own power, run-off, wind, or transport on some host or vector. The genetic engineer also will consider the possibility of the deliberately modified inheritable trait transferring genetically to other organisms in the vicinity, thereby allowing modified traits to escape despite physical control over the modified organism. The genetic engineer will also receive training to look for novel interactions — ecological trouble in the target environment from an organism which has not caused a problem in a different environment.

VII. CONCLUSION

Genetic engineering is only the latest manifestation of technical progress with Promethean potential for harm or good. It is not the last. Beyond the debate over the details of regulation, it is time for legislative control to evolve from seeking to prevent harm from each new technology to preventing harm from new technology in general. One useful tool in the construction of such a meta-system would be the early imposition of professional standards on new technologies as they arise, rather than waiting for guilds of practitioners to seek such status for their own benefit.

Is this a workable proposal? A federal licensing scheme would preempt a state licensing scheme in bioengineering, which in matters of public safety and protection have typically been within those powers reserved to the states.

Chapter Four

Human Health, Medical Care, Medical Information Disclosure in Biotechnology

4.1 Disclosure of Medical Information and Privacy

4.1.1 Right to Privacy

The concept of the "right of privacy" was one which was not articulated until about 100 years ago in an article by Warren and Brandeis, according to Goldman, Schwartz and Tang in *Roundtable: Medical Privacy*, 17 Issues in Science and Technology 78 (Summer 2000). The right of privacy was referred to as the right to be left alone and as one of the most comprehensive rights known to man. With this interest, the authors discussed how the ability to have privacy "was critical to the development of self, to autonomy and to the pursuit of liberty and democracy."

There is a constitutionally protected right of privacy with respect to medical information, however, it is not absolute. The standard for disclosure of medical information is that it must be a compelling state interest and the societal interest in disclosure must be weighed against the privacy interest.

This constitutionally protected right is held against the government. The private sector community is held to the standards of tort liability.

The federal government is restricted in disclosure by the Freedom of Information Act which includes nine exceptions to the disclosure of information: (1) national security information; (2) internal personnel rules and files; (3) exemption by separate statute; (4) commercial and financial information and trade secrets; (5) inter/intra agency memoranda; (6) personnel/medical and other files disclosure of which would require a compelling state interest; (7) law enforcement and investigative files; (8) data on financial institutions; and (9) certain geological and geophysical data on oil and gas wells. 5 U.S.C. §552(b)(1)-(9).

The federal government is also restricted by a reverse Freedom of Information Act-type statute, the Federal Privacy Act, 5 U.S.C. §552a. This statute prohibits the release of private information, provides penalties for such releases, and permits the examination of these materials by the person on which the records are kept. The U.S. Supreme Court has never reviewed the Privacy Act.

The Health Insurance Portability and Accountability Act of 1996(HIPAA), Pub. L. No. 104-191, 110 Stat. 1936 (1996) (codified as amended at 26 U.S.C. 9801–9806), prohibits any group health insurance plan to base eligibility for the plan on "health status-related factors in relation to the individual or a dependent of the individual [and] ... genetic information ..." Under HIPAA, genetic information cannot be used as evidence of a pre-existing condition without further manifestation of the disease. Victoria Sutton, Law and Science: Cases and Materials 238 (Carolina Academic Press 2001). In support of this policy, former Vice-President Gore was quoted as saying, "Genetic progress should not become a new excuse for discrimination." Rueters, *Genes and Discrimination: Gore Urges Laws Banning Bias in Hiring and Insurance*, Newsday, Jan. 21, 1998, at A20.

4.1.2 Limited Right to Privacy

4.1.2.1 Limited Right to Privacy in the Military

The right of privacy is limited for individuals in the military, where there is a compelling governmental interest, typically one of national security. In *Mayfield v. Dalton* (1997), the court finds the use of DNA information by the military to be a compelling governmental interest.

Mayfield v. Dalton

109 F.3d 1423 (9th Cir. 1997)

Opinion by Schroeder, Circuit Judge:

The plaintiffs-appellants in this case, John C. Mayfield and Joseph Vlacovsky, filed this action when they were on active duty in the Marine Corps. They challenged the constitutionality of a Department of Defense program to collect and store blood and tissue samples from all members of the armed forces for future DNA analysis (the "repository"). Mayfield and Vlacovsky argued that the compulsory taking of specimens without proper safeguards to maintain the privacy of the donor was a violation of the Fourth Amendment prohibition against unreasonable searches and seizures. *Mayfield v. Dalton*, 901 F. Supp. 300, 303 (D. Hawaii 1995). In addition, they feared that information obtained from the repository samples, regarding the donors' propensities for hereditary diseases and genetic disorders, might be used to discriminate against applicants for jobs, insurance or benefit programs.

Refusing to comply with the program, Mayfield and Vlacovsky turned to the district court. They sought to represent a class of " 'all military personnel serving on active duty in the United States Navy and/or the United States Marine Corps who have been or may be compelled to provide blood and/or other tissue samples for DNA identification or testing procedures under currently applicable Navy and/or Marine Corps policies, practices and/or regulations.' " *Id.* at 305. The district court granted summary judgment in favor of the government and denied class certification.

On the merits, the district court first held that the DNA repository did not violate any constitutional rights because the taking of specimens without the service members' consent did not constitute an unreasonable seizure in violation of the Fourth Amendment. The court also stressed that the repository was instituted for the purpose of assisting in the identification of soldiers' remains, a purpose that plaintiffs-appellants did not challenge, and that other potential, more nefarious, uses were too speculative to be justiciable. The district court also held that Mayfield and Vlacovsky could not adequately represent all members of the class and therefore denied them class certification.

The district court's decision came down on September 8, 1995. In the intervening period between its decision and oral argument before this court, Mayfield and Vlacovsky have been honorably separated from active duty without ever having given any blood or tissue samples. The government suggests their claims may thus be moot. Mayfield and Vlacovsky counter that separation from active duty means that they are still contractually obligated to remain in the Marine Corps Reserves, and may thus be required to return to active duty in an emergency situation. Therefore, they argue, their case is not moot.

We agree with the government that Mayfield and Vlacovsky's challenge is moot because they are no longer subject to the DNA collection program, and face only a remote possibility that they may ever be subject to the repository policies they seek to challenge ...

Not only are Mayfield and Vlacovsky unable to challenge the regulations that might have affected them in the past, they are also unable to challenge regulations that might apply to them in the future. Such a challenge to future application is not yet ripe. "Ripeness doctrine is invoked to determine whether a dispute has yet matured to a point that warrants decision." ... [T]here is no sufficiently imminent threat of injury to Mayfield and Vlacovsky at this time.

Moreover, in the intervening time between the district court judgment and oral argument before this court, the military changed the repository in ways that appear to respond to some of plaintiffs-appellants' main concerns. As of April 1996, for example, the maximum length of time that the specimens will now be retained has been shortened from the originally challenged duration of 75 years to 50 years. In addition, upon the request of the donor, the military will now destroy individual specimen samples following the conclusion of the service member's military obligation. *See* April 2, 1996 Memorandum from the Assistant Secretary of Defense for Health Affairs. The changes made, which materially alter many aspects of the policy that Mayfield and Vlacovsky challenged in the district court, fortify our conclusion that the likelihood that these plaintiffs-appellants will ever be subject to the policy they challenged in the district court is too remote to make their suit justiciable.

The full text of the April 1996 Memorandum provides:

> Although very few concerns have been expressed regarding the repository, misgivings have been heard from a few that the specimen samples might be used to deny employment or insurance from people or otherwise discriminate based on genetic conditions. No such use is, or has ever been, authorized or contemplated by [the Department of Defense] ("DoD"). The refinements now being adopted are designed to reaffirm DoD's longstanding commitment to, and strengthen procedures for, privacy protections concerning the specimens and any DNA analysis that may be performed on any individual's specimen sample. The following refinements shall be implemented:

1. *Routine destruction schedule.* The period of retention of specimen samples in the repository, established as 75 years ... shall be reduced to 50 years.

2. *Individual specimen sample destruction.* Individual specimen samples will be destroyed upon the request of the donor following the conclusion of the donor's complete military service obligation or other applicable relationship to DoD. Upon receipt of such requests, the samples shall be destroyed within 180 days, and notification of the destruction sent to the donor.

3. *Permissible uses.* Authority to permit the use of any specimen sample in the repository for any purpose other than remains identification is further clarified. Reference (b) limited use of specimen samples to remains identification (exclusive of internal, quality assurance purposes), but did not prohibit the possibility of use under other circumstances in "extraordinary cases" when "no reasonable alternative means of obtaining a specimen for DNA profile analysis is available" and when the request is approved by the [Assistant Secretary of Defense Health Affairs]. To date, no nonconsensual exception request has been approved. This policy refinement limits "extraordinary cases" to cases in which a use other than remains identification is compelled by other applicable law. Consequently, permissible uses of specimen samples are limited to the following purposes:

a. identification of human remains;

b. internal quality assurance activities to validate processes for collection, maintenance and analysis of samples;

c. a purpose for which the donor of the sample (or surviving next-of-kin) provides consent; or

d. as compelled by other applicable law in a case in which *all* of the following conditions are present:

(1) the responsible DoD official has received a proper judicial order or judicial authorization;

(2) the specimen sample is needed for the investigation or prosecution of a crime punishable by one year or more of confinement;

(3) no reasonable alternative means for obtaining a specimen for DNA profile analysis is available; and

(4) the use is approved by the [Assistant Secretary of Defense, Health Affairs] after consultation with the DoD General Counsel.

4.1.2.2 *Adoption Right to Know*

In the Matter of Sandra L.G. v. Bouchey

576 N.Y.S.2d 767 (Fam.Court 1991)

Opinion by George G. Bernhard, Judge:

This is a proceeding to compel the clerk of this court to furnish an adopted person inspection of her adoption file. Petitioner cites as her reason for this request the possibility of some genetic factor in her background which might either predispose her to a medical problem (a) with respect to potential marriage and child bearing; or (b) with respect to later life generally. A letter from her physician alludes to unspecified "multiple medical problems" and concludes that "Some of these problems might be better diagnosed if some knowledge of her family's medical history was made known". The court attaches little or no significance to that letter.

However, although she cites no immediate compelling medical or genetic problem or marriage inquiry, her request does bring to the fore the exponential increase in the scientific knowledge of genetics and the diagnosis and treatment of problems which people can inherit from their ancestors. Moreover, it is increasingly common for persons to make genetic inquiry of themselves and potential marriage partners to avoid problems to their issue.

According to recent studies, nearly 11% of childhood deaths have been genetic in etiology and approximately 7% of pediatric admissions are for single gene and chromosomal disorders. (Epstein, New Developments in Biotechnology, ch 10, Genetic Disorders and Birth Defects [US Cong 1990].) Screening procedures are available for a few disorders which occur with relatively high frequency. Examples are Tay-Sachs disease in the Ashkenazi Jewish population, Sickle Cell Anemia in the black population and, to a limited extent, B-thalasemia in the Italian and Greek populations. Screening for cystic fibrosis is being considered.

In addition, recessive conditions are commonly observed in conditions of consanguinity of parents so that the risk of abnormal offspring of first cousins appears to be approximately twice that in the general population.

For these reasons, both the Attorney-General and Counsel to the Office of Court Administration were requested to furnish a defense so that this court can make a general ruling as opposed to treating the many requests of this nature in an inconsistent ad hoc manner.

The Legislature has taken steps to give adopted children the benefit of the advances in scientific knowledge while, at the same time, maintaining the confidence of the natural parents. (Public Health Law §§ 4138-a, 4138-b, 4138-c; Social Services Law §§ 373-a.) The issue is whether the Legislature has gone far enough so as to obviate further disclosure by this court to the adopted child.

This is an issue which must be examined with great care, particularly since natural parents from time immemorial have been assured that their identities would be thoroughly protected as an inducement toward surrendering their children to adoptive parents. Elaborate safeguards are employed to insulate natural parents from adoptive parents in the effectuation of this trust. Accordingly, it is of great concern to the courts that any exercise of discretion beyond that mandated by the Legislature will be governed by clear, consistent and effective principles. They must be clear and consistent so that attorneys and others involved in the adoption process can well explain the rules governing confidentiality to the parents and subsequently to the children over the course of a lifetime, if necessary. They must be effective so that any disclosure will pose only a demonstrable physical benefit to the person seeking access as opposed to gratuitous obtaining of emotionally charged information.

The relevant provisions are set forth in sections 4138-a, 4138-b and 4138-c of the Public Health Law. The issue is whether the information provided therein provides adequate protection against genetic hazards to the adopted child within the framework of today's medical standards, which might include submission of samples of one's own tissues for genetic examination.

With respect to discovery, the New York State Health Department is charged with the responsibility of maintaining a register with respect to adoptions which an adoptive child or a natural parent may apply as a member.

The following "non-identifying" information is required to be sent to the Health Department by the court of adoption for the purpose of prompt release to the adoptee upon request and registration:

For the purpose of this section, the term 'non-identifying information' shall only include the following information, if known, concerning the parents of an adoptee:

(a) Age of the parents in years, at birth of such adoptee.

(b) Heritage of the parents, which shall include nationality, ethnic background and race.

(c) Education, which shall be the number of years of school completed by the parents at the time of birth of such adoptee.

(d) General physical appearance of the parents at the time of the birth of such adoptee, which shall include height, weight, color of hair, eyes, skin and other information of similar nature.

(e) Religion of parents.

(f) Occupation of parents.

(g) Health history of parents.

(h) Talents, hobbies and special interests of parents.

(i) Facts and circumstances relating to the nature and cause of the adoption.

(j) Name of the authorized agency involved in such adoption." (Public Health Law §§ 4138-b [3] [a]–[j].)

Provisions are also made with respect to registrants in adoptions prior to 1984 to match natural parents with children upon joint request. (Public Health Law §§ 4138–d.) Moreover, in adoptions after 1984, provision is made to match and identify siblings who so request.

It is also true that prospective spouses of similar ethnic origins are increasingly submitting to genetic testing for problems that are frequent in their group.

It appears that the Legislature has taken definite steps to address petitioner's concerns. The non-identifying information appears to track the present state of the genetic medical arts. The day might not be far when tissue samples of natural parents might be preserved for these purposes, but that day is not at hand.

This court finds that the provisions of sections 4138-a, 4138b, 4138-c of the Public Health Law are reasonably sufficient for the purposes of satisfying general, albeit fundamental, concerns of an adopted person. This brings us to the question of whether this court should take it upon itself to provide the "non-identifying" information without need of the registration procedures of the Health Department. This court declines to do so upon the ground that the State Legislature has entrusted this disclosure to the Health Department, not the courts.

The petition is otherwise denied.

4.1.3 Use of Genetic Information

Another use of genetic information involving screening for abortions has also raised awareness for the use of genetic tests. In National Opinion Research Center, University of Chicago, General Social Surveys, 1972–1987: Cumulative Codebook (1987), noted in Fletcher & Wertz, *supra* note 13, at 787 n.56, the following public opinion was cited:

Public opinion studies show material support for genetic screening and abortion of seriously genetically defective fetuses. Between seventy-five and seventy-seven percent of persons in the United States support a woman's choice to have an abortion when a fetus has a significant genetic defect. Opposition to abortion, however, increases as the seriousness of the genetic defect decreases. In addition, eighty-nine percent of the American public approves of genetic screening for serious genetic defects. Generally, geneticists and the scientific community as a whole support a woman's right to choose abortion for fetuses with severe genetic defects. National surveys of geneticists establish common approaches to the protection of privacy and patient autonomy. In general, geneticists support the notion that the potential life of a fetus, without function in minimal nervous system, should not have a protected right of life. or serious genetic defects. [See Office of Technology Assessment, U.S. Congress, New Developments in Biotechnology: Public Perceptions of Biotechnology 74–75 (1987).] The substantial public support for genetic screening and abortions for fetuses with serious genetic defects is paralleled in the scientific community.

In 1983, President Bush created the President's Commission for the Study of Ethical Problems in Medicine and Biomedical and Behavioral Research. The Commission developed eight principles of genetic screening:

1. The disorder should be of high burden to the affected individual. 2. The inheritance and pathogenesis of the disorder should be understood. 3. The disorder should be preventable and practical therapy available, including genetic counseling and reproductive alternatives. 4. Patient's right to informed consent, voluntary participation, and confidentiality should be protected. 5. The benefit to cost ratio to the patient (public) should be greater than one. 6. The laboratory screening method should minimize false positive and exclude all false negative results. 7. A diagnostic test should be available. 8. Both screening and diagnostic tests should be available to all who require it.

In Renee C. Esfandiary, Note: *The Changing World of Genetics and Abortion: Why the Women's Movement Should Advocate for Limitations on the Right to Choose in the Area of Genetic Technology*, 4 WM. & MARY J. OF WOMEN & L. 499 (Spring 1998), she makes the following observation about the political complexity facing the Commission:

The Commission reflects Rawls' theory of justice by emphasizing the highly detrimental effect of the disease, while balancing the cost-benefit ratio to society. The successor to the President's Commission was the Biomedical Ethics Advisory Committee (BEAC). It was to discuss the issues of genetic alteration and the definition of human nature, but abortion politics deadlocked the Congressional Biomedical Ethics Board to which the BEAC reports.

These federal deadlocks have resulted in the states taking the lead role in legislating genetic testing and going about protecting privacy. This right to privacy in the protection of genetic information has been largely protected by states through the insurance code. The following is an example of one state's statutory genetic privacy protections.

Tex Insurance Code Art. 21.73. *Use of Genetic Testing Information by Insurers Definitions*

Sec. 1. In this article:

(1) "DNA" means deoxyribonucleic acid. (2) "Genetic information" means information derived from the results of a genetic test.

(3) "Genetic test" means a laboratory test of an individual's DNA, RNA, proteins, or chromosomes to identify by analysis of the DNA, RNA, proteins, or chromosomes the genetic mutations or alterations in the DNA, RNA, proteins, or chromosomes that are associated with a predisposition for a clinically recognized disease or disorder....

(b) An individual or the legal representative of an individual may authorize the disclosure of genetic information relating to that individual through an authorization that:

(1) is written in plain language;

(2) is dated;

(3) contains a specific description of the information to be disclosed;

(4) identifies or describes each person authorized to disclose the genetic information to a group health benefit plan issuer;

(5) identifies or describes the individuals or entities to whom the disclosure or subsequent redisclosure of the genetic information may be made;

(6) describes the specific purpose of the disclosure;

(7) is signed by the individual or the legal representative and, if the disclosure is for claiming proceeds of any affected life insurance policy, the claimant; and

(8) advises the individual or legal representative that the individual's authorized representative is entitled to receive a copy of the authorization form....

Right to know test results

Sec. 5. An individual who submits to a genetic test has the right to know the results of that test. On the written request of the individual, the group health benefit plan issuer or other entity that performed the test shall disclose the test results to the individual or to a physician designated by the individual. The right to information under this section is in addition to any right or requirement established under Section 3 of this article.

Retention of sample

Sec. 6. A sample of genetic material taken for a genetic test from an individual shall be destroyed promptly after the purpose for which the sample was obtained is accomplished unless:

(1) the sample is retained under a court order;

(2) the individual tested authorizes retention of the sample for purposes of medical treatment or scientific research;

(3) for a sample obtained for research that is cleared by an institutional review board, the sample is retained under the requirements that the institutional review board imposes on a specific research project or as authorized by the research participant with institutional review board approval under federal law; ...

Woman's Right to Choice in Genetic Testing

In Esfandiary, *supra*, she cautions that the progress of the women's movement should be protected in the area of genetic testing:

Although the protection of reproductive choices by the judicial branch is a tremendous accomplishment for the women's movement, this progress must be protected. To prevent a backlash, women's organizations should fight for limited legislative restraints on a woman's right to choose in the area of genetic technology. Women would be protecting their role as parental and family decision-makers while still defending their fundamental right to choose.

WOMAN'S RIGHT TO CHOICE IN GENETIC TESTING

At least one organization in the United States has determined that a woman's right to reproductive choices should always be protected. In 1975, the Committee on Inborn Errors in Metabolism, as part of the National Academy of Sciences, concluded that the privacy right should be the governing factor in all decisions, not secondary to other interests.

———————

Jeri E. Reutenauer, Note: *Medical Malpractice Liability in the Era of Genetic Susceptibility Testing*, 19 QUINNIPIAC L. REV. 539 (2000).

I. Introduction

Genetic technology, one of the great revolutions in modern medicine, is progressing rapidly as a result of both private-sector discoveries in molecular biology and the $ 3 billion federal Human Genome Project. Advances in genetic testing will permit people to learn about their personal risks of developing specific diseases, of bearing children affected with a certain genetic disorder, and of predisposition to illnesses resulting from exposure to environmental stimuli.

Intertwined with the medical ramifications of such genetic breakthroughs are a multitude of complex ethical, legal, and social concerns. As the volume of genetic information continues to increase, controversies regarding a healthcare professional's duty to convey genetic information to his or her patients are certain to develop. Although legal guidelines for healthcare professionals regarding this duty are not definitive, the potential for genetic malpractice liability does exist....

B. Genetic Testing and Its Development

In the 1940s, scientists discovered that genes consist of DNA, and in the 1950s, they further elucidated the mechanisms of inheritance. Watson and Crick were the first to describe the structure of DNA as the double helix in 1953. They were awarded the Nobel Prize in 1962 for this accomplishment. In the 1960s, genetic testing was first utilized in newborn screening for the disease phenylketonuria, a disorder of the metabolism that leads to mental retardation if the dietary intake of phenylalanine is not reduced dramatically.

Today, genetic tests include DNA-based tests, as well as chemical tests for gene products, such as enzymes and other proteins, and microscopic examination of stained or fluorescent chromosomes. As the technology has evolved, the capability to perform genetic testing not only has continued to develop in the area of newborn screening, but also has expanded in its application for other medical purposes. Such advances in genetic testing have also had a dramatic impact on the lives of many individuals. For example, prenatal diagnosis exists for a multitude of genetic diseases, providing families with the opportunity for early intervention and the potential to avoid giving birth to a child with a devastating disease. Genetic testing also can be used to detect individuals who are carriers of an abnormal gene.

Although several thousand conditions are caused by single-gene defects, many diseases occur as a result of multiple gene (polygenic) defects. With a polygenic disorder, an individual has susceptibility to, or is predisposed to, a certain disease. Accumulated evidence suggests that genetic factors underlie susceptibility to a wide range of human health problems. Virtually every polygenic disorder, however, involves some degree of interaction with the environment in order to develop. Separating the genetic component from environmental contributions that give rise to complex diseases will be one of the greatest challenges for medical researchers in the twenty-first century.

In recent years, genetic testing has begun to include testing for adult-onset disorders, such as Huntington's disease, as well as genetic susceptibility testing for both breast and colon cancer. One of the complications encountered in testing for a polygenic disorder, such as increased susceptibility to breast cancer, is determining an individual's risk of developing the disease once she tests positive for susceptibility to the disease. Genetic susceptibility testing is directed at healthy (presymptomatic) individuals who are identified as having a high-risk for the disorder due to a strong family history. Such tests provide individuals with only a probability for developing the disorder. One serious limitation of such testing, therefore, is the difficulty of interpreting a positive result because some people who carry a disease-associated mutation will never develop the disease. Scientists believe that such mutations may work in combination with other unknown mutations, or with environmental factors, to actually cause the disease.

The possibility of laboratory errors poses another problem. Such errors may result from sample misidentification, contamination of the chemicals used in testing, or other sources. In the medical community, there are many who believe that the uncertainties surrounding test interpretation, the current lack of available medical options for these diseases, the potential for provoking anxiety and the risk of discrimination and social stigmatization may outweigh the benefits of having such testing....

4.2 Informed Consent, High Risk Treatments and Research

As genetic testing and sampling becomes more widespread and standard practice, the question of research on those samples arises. However, the question of privacy and informed consent is at the center of controversial debate concerning research. Using tissues that are identifiable with a particular individual is considered research on human subjects under the federal Common Rule, and therefore informed consent is required for any research on collected human tissue samples.

Federally Funded Research v. Private Research

The conduct of research on human subjects is governed by the Common Rule[1] which applies when (1) the research is funded by a federal agency; (2) the institute performing

---

1. 45 C.F.R. §46 (2001). Applies to seventeen federal agencies funding research; while 21 C.F.R. §50 (2001) applies to the Food and Drug Administration funded research.

the research has given assurances that all human subject research will comply with the Common Rule; or (3) the research utilizes an Investigational New Drug, Device, or Biologic regulated by the Food and Drug Administration. If the research meets any of these criteria, a protocol must be submitted to an Institutional Review Board (IRB) which determines whether the benefits outweigh the risks of the research.

A "human subject" is defined as "a living individual about whom an investigator (whether professional or student) conducting research obtains (1) Data through intervention or interaction with the individual or (2) Identifiable private information."[2]

"Identifiable private information" includes "information which has been proovided for specific purposes by an individual and which the individual can reasonably expect will not be made public."[3]

In July 1996, President Clinton appointed a National Bioethics Advisory Commission to work on recommendations on the use of human biological materials. Their final report was issued August 1999, and concluded that samples that were anonymous did not constitute human research, and therefore did not require informed consent.

Failure to provide informed consent may result in a malpractice action. Such standards are guided by statutory guidelines on the failure to provide informed consent, enacted by the Texas legislature in 1989:

SUBCHAPTER F. INFORMED CONSENT

Sec. 6.01. In this subchapter, "panel" means the Texas Medical Disclosure Panel.

Theory of Recovery

Sec. 6.02. In a suit against a physician or health care provider involving a health care liability claim that is based on the failure of the physician or health care provider to disclose or adequately to disclose the risks and hazards involved in the medical care or surgical procedure rendered by the physician or health care provider, the only theory on which recovery may be obtained is that of negligence in failing to disclose the risks or hazards that could have influenced a reasonable person in making a decision to give or withhold consent.

Texas Medical Disclosure Panel

Sec. 6.03. (a) The Texas Medical Disclosure Panel is created to determine which risks and hazards related to medical care and surgical procedures must be disclosed by health care providers or physicians to their patients or persons authorized to consent for their patients and to establish the general form and substance of such disclosure.

(b) The panel established herein is administratively attached to the Texas Department of Health. The Texas Department of Health, at the request of the panel, shall provide administrative assistance to the panel; and the Texas Department of Health and the panel shall coordinate administrative responsibilities in order to avoid unnecessary duplication of facilities and services. The Texas Department of Health, at the request of the panel, shall submit the panel's budget request to the legislature. The panel shall be subject, except where inconsistent, to the rules and procedures of the Texas Department of

---

2. 45 C.F.R. §46.102(f)(1)-(2) (2001).
3. 45 C.F.R. §46.101(b)(4) (2001).

Health; however, the duties and responsibilities of the panel as set forth in the Medical Liability and Insurance Improvement Act of Texas, as amended (Article 4590i, Vernon's Texas Civil Statutes), shall be exercised solely by the panel and the board or Texas Department of Health shall have no authority or responsibility with respect to same.

(c) The panel is composed of nine members, with three members licensed to practice law in this state and six members licensed to practice medicine in this state. Members of the panel shall be selected by the Commissioner of Health....

Manner of Disclosure

Sec. 6.06. Consent to medical care that appears on the panel's list requiring disclosure shall be considered effective under this subchapter if it is given in writing, signed by the patient or a person authorized to give the consent and by a competent witness, and if the written consent specifically states the risks and hazards that are involved in the medical care or surgical procedure in the form and to the degree required by the panel under Section 6.04 of this subchapter.

Informed consent has been addressed specifically as it applies to the elderly in the Texas legislation, as well:

Tex. Hum. Res. Code §§ 102.003 (2000)

Rights of the Elderly:

(l) An elderly individual may choose and retain a personal physician and is entitled to be fully informed in advance about treatment or care that may affect the individual's well-being.

(m) An elderly individual may participate in an individual plan of care that describes the individual's medical, nursing, and psychological needs and how the needs will be met.

(n) An elderly individual may refuse medical treatment after the elderly individual:

> (1) is advised by the person providing services of the possible consequences of refusing treatment; and

> (2) acknowledges that the individual clearly understands the consequences of refusing treatment....

(t) An elderly individual may:

> (1) make a living will by executing a directive under the Natural Death Act (Chapter 672, Health and Safety Code);

> (2) execute a durable power of attorney for health care under Chapter 135, Civil Practice and Remedies Code; or

> (3) designate a guardian in advance of need to make decisions regarding the individual's health care should the individual become incapacitated.

In the 77th Texas Legislature, S.B. 355 was enacted and proved by the Governor, June 16, 2001, R.S. ch. 919. 2001 TEX. GEN. LAWS 919; 2001 Tex. SB 355, AN ACT relating to a nursing home resident's right to informed consent regarding the prescription of certain drugs. It amends the foregoing chapter on the content of the information provided to the subject.

(a) The department by rule shall adopt a statement of the rights of a resident. The statement must be consistent with Chapter 102, Human Resources Code, but shall reflect the unique circumstances of a resident at an institution. At a minimum, the statement of the rights of a resident must address the resident's constitutional, civil, and legal rights and the resident's right:

(8) to retain the services of a physician the resident chooses, at the resident's own expense or through a health care plan, and to have a physician explain to the resident, in language that the resident understands, the resident's complete medical condition, the recommended treatment, and the expected results of the treatment INCLUDING REASONABLY EXPECTED EFFECTS, SIDE EFFECTS, AND RISKS ASSOCIATED WITH PSYCHOACTIVE MEDICATIONS;

(9) to participate in developing a plan of care, to refuse treatment, and to refuse to participate in experimental research;

(2) "PSYCHOACTIVE MEDICATION" MEANS A MEDICATION THAT IS PRESCRIBED FOR THE TREATMENT OF SYMPTOMS OF PSYCHOSIS OR OTHER SEVERE MENTAL OR EMOTIONAL DISORDERS AND THAT IS USED TO EXERCISE AN EFFECT ON THE CENTRAL NERVOUS SYSTEM TO INFLUENCE AND MODIFY BEHAVIOR, COGNITION, OR AFFECTIVE STATE WHEN TREATING THE SYMPTOMS OF MENTAL ILLNESS. THE TERM INCLUDES THE FOLLOWING CATEGORIES WHEN USED AS DESCRIBED BY THIS SUBDIVISION:

(2) THE PERSON PRESCRIBING THE MEDICATION OR THAT PERSON'S DESIGNEE PROVIDED THE FOLLOWING INFORMATION, IN A STANDARD FORMAT APPROVED BY THE DEPARTMENT, TO THE RESIDENT AND, IF APPLICABLE, TO THE PERSON AUTHORIZED BY LAW TO CONSENT ON BEHALF OF THE RESIDENT:

(A) THE SPECIFIC CONDITION TO BE TREATED;

(B) THE BENEFICIAL EFFECTS ON THAT CONDITION EXPECTED FROM THE MEDICATION;

(C) THE PROBABLE CLINICALLY SIGNIFICANT SIDE EFFECTS AND RISKS ASSOCIATED WITH THE MEDICATION; AND (D) THE PROPOSED COURSE OF THE MEDICATION;

(3) THE RESIDENT AND, IF APPROPRIATE, THE PERSON AUTHORIZED BY LAW TO CONSENT ON BEHALF OF THE RESIDENT ARE INFORMED IN WRITING THAT CONSENT MAY BE REVOKED; AND

(4) THE CONSENT IS EVIDENCED IN THE RESIDENT'S CLINICAL RECORD BY A SIGNED FORM PRESCRIBED BY THE FACILITY OR BY A STATEMENT OF THE PERSON PRESCRIBING THE MEDICATION OR THAT PERSON'S DESIGNEE THAT DOCUMENTS THAT CONSENT WAS GIVEN BY THE APPROPRIATE PERSON AND THE CIRCUMSTANCES UNDER WHICH THE CONSENT WAS OBTAINED.

[Words in capitals denote changes to the statute.]

The use of informed consent has broadened to require that informed consent be as broad as possible, in anticipation of the use of samples collected for use in medical research.

The use of identifiable private information will almost always involve informed consent. Therefore, tissue samples and identifiable private information associated with those samples will require informed consent as human subjects research under federal regulations. If tissues collected in the past have no identifiable private information associated with them, presumably no informed consent is required.

The NBAC August 1999 Report discusses the use of past and future samples and the informed consent requirements. For past samples, the report provides that if the exisitng consent documents do not reveal the the sources "anticipated and agreed to participate in the type of research proposed," those document cannot constitute consent.[4] For samples collected in the future, the NBAC Report recommends that "consent forms be developed to provide potential subjects with a sufficient number of options to help them understand clearly the nature of the decision they are about to make."[5] The report provides a range of these options from a complete refusal of all types of research to "permitting the coded use of their biological materials for any kind of future study."[6] Even if informed consent is required the Common Rule provides exceptions that informed consent can be waived where four criteria are met: (1) the research poses minimal risk of disclosing private information; (2) the subject's rights and welfare will not be affected by the waiver; (3) the research is impracticable without the waiver; and (4) additional information should be provided to the subject after completion if appropriate.[7]

Further restrictions include the requirements for informed consent where specific research on human groups is proposed. Where ethnic or racial groups are concerned, the subjects must be informed that the implications of the research may extend beyond those who participate in the research to all members of the relevant group. Subjects must also be informed that unforeseen future research, to which they may be consenting, might also have such consequences for their racial or ethnic group.

After January 1, 2001, information or biological materials form or about people may not be used for research unless the people involved have either given their informed consent to the research use or have given a general permission for research with the information or materials. All such sample or data collection and the associated informed consent require IRB approval.

This rule is criticized, however, because it assumes that anonymity is sufficiently satisfying for human subjects, and that if they don't know what research is being done on their tissues, then there is no harm. There is also concern that the samples will not truly be anonymous and that private identifiable information will be linkable to the samples in some way, as a general matter. *See* Henry T. Greely, *Breaking the Stalemate: A Prospective Regulatory Framework for Unforeseen Research Uses of Human Tissue Samples and Health Information*, 34 WAKE FOREST LAW REVIEW 737, 761 (Fall 1999).

---

4. National Bioethics Advisory Commission, Research Involving Human Biological Materials: Issues and Policy Guidance (Aug. 1999), *at* http://bioethics.gov/hbm.pdf (last visited Sept. 10, 2001).

5. NBAC Report, pp. 65–66.

6. NBAC Report, pp. 66.

7. 46 C.F.R. §46.116(d) (2001).

Notes

1. The assumptions of these rules for informed consent IN research operate on the principle that, "what the subject doesn't know won't hurt her." Is that an assumption that we should hold?

2. Given the requirements for informed consent, how might you determine whether an Alzheimer's patient met the criteria for research? Further, what informed consent would be sufficient with an Alzheimer's patient, for research with little or no expectation of a benefit for the patient — purely research based work?

4.3 Insurance and Predisposition to Disease

In the following case, the court reverses a lower court finding for the insurer who refused to cover the appellant for surgery recommended because of a genetic predisposition. The court found that the genetic predisposition was an illness, therefore covered by the insurer.

Katskee v. Blue Cross/Blue Shield of Nebraska
515 N.W.2d 645 (Neb.1994)

Not every condition which itself constitutes a predisposition to another illness is necessarily an illness within the meaning of an insurance policy. There exists a fine distinction between such conditions ... Writing for the court, Chief Justice Cardozo explained that when a condition is such that in its probable and natural progression it may be expected to be a source of mischief, it may reasonably be described as a disease or an illness. On the other hand, he stated that if the condition is abnormal when tested by a standard of perfection, but so remote in its potential mischief that common speech would not label it a disease or infirmity, such a condition is at most a predisposing tendency.

The issue raised in Fuglsang was whether the disease from which the plaintiff suffered constituted a preexisting condition which was excluded from coverage by the terms of the policy. Blue Cross/Blue Shield relies on the following rule from Fuglsang as a definition of "disease":

A disease, condition, or illness exists within the meaning of a health insurance policy excluding preexisting conditions only at such time as the disease, condition, or illness is manifest or active or when there is a distinct symptom or condition from which one learned in medicine can with reasonable accuracy diagnose the disease.

This statement concerns when an illness exists, not whether the condition itself is an illness. If the condition is not a disease or illness, it would be unnecessary to apply the above rule to determine whether the condition was a preexisting illness. In the present case, Blue Cross/Blue Shield maintains that the condition is not even an illness.

Even assuming arguendo that the rule announced in Fuglsang is a definition of "disease," "illness," and "condition," the inherent problems with the argument put forth by

Blue Cross/Blue Shield undermine its reliance on that rule. Blue Cross/Blue Shield emphasizes the fact that appellant was never diagnosed with cancer and therefore, according to Blue Cross/Blue Shield, appellant did not have an illness because cancer was not active or manifest. Appellant concedes that she did not have cancer prior to her surgery. The issue is whether the condition she did have was an illness. Blue Cross/Blue Shield further argues that "no disease or illness is 'manifest or active' and there is no 'distinct symptom or condition' from which Dr. Lynch or Dr. Roffman could diagnose a disease." We stated above that lack of a physical test to detect the presence of an illness does not necessarily indicate that the person does not have an illness.

When the condition at issue—breast-ovarian carcinoma syndrome—is inserted into the formula provided by the Fuglsang rule, the condition would constitute an "illness" as Blue Cross/Blue Shield defines the term. The formula is whether the breast-ovarian carcinoma syndrome was manifest or active, or whether there was a distinct symptom or condition from which one learned in medicine could with reasonable accuracy diagnose the disease. The record establishes that the syndrome was manifest, at least in part, from the genetic deviation, and evident from the family medical history. The condition was such that one learned in medicine, Dr. Lynch, could with a reasonable degree of accuracy diagnose it. Blue Cross/Blue Shield does not dispute the nature of the syndrome, the method of diagnosis, or the accuracy of the diagnosis.

In the present case, the medical evidence regarding the nature of breast-ovarian carcinoma syndrome persuades us that appellant suffered from a bodily disorder or disease and, thus, suffered from an illness as defined by the insurance policy. Blue Cross/Blue Shield, therefore, is not entitled to judgment as a matter of law. Moreover, we find that appellant's condition did constitute an illness within the meaning of the policy. We reverse the decision of the district court and remand the cause for further proceedings.

Reversed and Remanded.

Notes

1. If a woman finds that she has the BRCA1 gene for breast cancer, she is still only 50–85% likely to have breast cancer and 20–30% likely to develop ovarian cancer. Could this be detrimental to the woman who discovers she has the gene (where she becomes certain she will have cancer) as well as the woman who discovers she does not have the gene (where she may stop self-examinations)? Because of these potentially harmful effect, should genetic testing be regulated? If so, how should it be regulated?

2. As more specific DNA evidence is made available, will insurance companies be precluded from all use of DNA evidence?

Chapter Five

International Law and Biotechnology

5.1 International Environment and Biotechnology Issues

International law and biotechnology are regulated and guided by international conventions and customary law in areas of environmental protection, biological diversity preservation, sustainable development, intellectual property, trade and indigenous peoples protection of intellectual property, and the introduction of genetically modified organisms (LMOs).

International biodefense issues have led CDC to regulate international laboratories for security standards where U.S. federal funding is being expended in collaborations with U.S. scientists. This has created an extension of U.S. control over foreign laboratories, in an unprecedented manner.

Research in ethically controversial areas of biotechnology which cannot be funded by the federal government in the United States is currently being pursued in other countries, for example stem cell research. Other countries have sought a range of legislative solutions to address the ethical issues of stem cell research.

5.2 Introduction to Biodiversity and the Convention on Biological Diversity (CBD)

In the 1970s, the realization that biodiversity must be addressed internationally led to a dialogue which concluded that all members of the biological community were important to sustaining the environment, and the preservation of just a few species was inadequate to protect the world's ecosystems. For example, the clubbing of baby seals for the fur trade stirred the ire of the public, and efforts to stop the practice were coordinated. While the endearing marine mammals could excite the public, a more comprehensive effort was required to prevent the loss of biodiversity.

Biodiversity is the complex web of life that exists and sustains the members of its scope. To protect biodiversity, equal concern for both ant and anteater, rhinoceros bee-

231

tle and the rhinoceros maintains that they are all of the members of the community. An emphasis on biodiversity, rather than simply conservation, has changed the focus of environmental protection. The threat to biodiversity occurs when one of the members of the ecosystem is eliminated, causing a degradation to the ecosystem in unanticipated ways, or a series of events lead to the degradation of the environment. In order to monitor threats to an ecosystem, the population and health of a species important to an ecosystem, i.e., sentinel species, can be monitored. Frogs have been identified as sentinel species and recent worldwide decline of their numbers has been watched by the environmental community with great concern for the sustainability of the world's ecosystems.

E.O. Wilson, a highly regarded scientist, has estimated that the absolute number of species falls between 5 million and 30 million. Only about 1½ million species have been identified and described. This describes *species diversity*. Overall species richness decreases with latitude—the further from the equator, the less the diversity. The higher altitudes also have less species diversity. Isolation and inbreeding also results in a loss of biodiversity sometimes.

Genetic diversity is the sum of genetic information contained in the genes of individual species. Number of genes ranges from 1,000 in bacteria to 400,000 in many flowering plants, and less than a million in humans—less than originally believed until the mapping of the human genome was completed in 2000.

Ecosystem diversity refers to the richness of habitats, biotic communities and ecological processes.

Sustainable development v. conservation. An illustration of the contrast between these concepts is the conflict on the ivory trade. The argument from Africa was that the control of the elephant trade in ivory would result in the long-term protection of the elephant, because killing elephants for ivory could be best controlled by monitoring and allowing some harvesting, rather than attempting a complete ban, which would result in large scale poaching. On the other hand, the conservation ethic requires that wildlife not be killed for something like ivory as a commodity. In this case, conservation ethic may have led to complete destruction of the elephant whereas sustainable development practices would lead to cultivation of the elephant for ivory harvesting.

5.2.1 The Convention on Biological Diversity

5.2.1.1 *History and Background of the Convention on Biological Diversity (CBD)*

In 1982, on the tenth year anniversary of the Stockholm Declaration, the United Nations General Assembly passed the World Charter on Nature, which had no binding force. From 1984 to 1989, the United Nations revised a set of draft articles which would be the foundation of the proposed treaty on biodiversity. The articles were ultimately rejected by the General Assembly, but the action brought attention to the issue and led to the establishment of a working group in the United Nations Environment Program in 1987. Early in the working group discussions, a plan to encompass all wildlife treaties under one treaty was considered, but it was deemed probably too politically difficult to succeed. It was also evident that the southern nations would accept terms that focused on biodiversity, rather than a treaty with a conservation focus, only. Formal negotiations for a Convention on Biological Diversity began in 1991 with the formation of the Intergovernmental Negotiating Committee (INC), with a goal of preparing the final document in time for the UNCED Earth Summit in Rio de Janeiro, Brazil in June 1992. The great pressure to finish the convention led to some conflicting and unclear language, but it succeeded in meeting the time deadline and was presented at the Earth Summit, finished the last day, and signed two weeks later at UNCED. It entered into force just eighteen months later on December 29, 1993.

The actions taken at United States at the Earth Summit reveal why the United States was perceived as presenting a hardline refusal to sign the Convention. Administrator Reilly was the delegate for the Summit, and in the course of his visit he sent a memorandum to President George H.W. Bush, which immediately leaked to the press at the meeting, and resulted in bad publicity for the US. The financial part of the agreement was controversial, and the financial mechanism required that the northern nations provide new, and additional funding to assist in biodiversity conservation. As a result of this leaked memorandum and refusal to amend the financial part of the agreement, the U.S. did not sign the agreement.

However, early in his term, President William Clinton signed the Convention, but the U.S. Senate did not ratify the treaty. In spite of President Clinton's urging that no new legislation would need to be passed if the Convention was ratified, the U.S. Senate still refused to ratify it. As a result, the United States is not a signatory to the Convention on Biological Diversity.

5.2.1.2 *Structure of the Convention on Biological Diversity*

The Convention on Biological Diversity addresses six important issues in its concept of protecting biological diversity on an international basis in the Preamble and later in Article Six. First, the establishment of the common concern of mankind establishes the agreement between the parties to proceed with other specific issues. The preamble of the CBD begins the first disassembly of the concept of a "common heritage" which suggests that all resources are free and available to any country, from any country; the southern nations objected to this language. Developed countries of the north, believed that "common heritage" might lead to a requirement for technology transfer to the southern developing countries. This was resolved by describing biological diversity as a "common concern of mankind."

Second, the aspect of common but differentiated responsibilities is established. The language reads, "Acknowledging further that special provision is required to meet the needs of developing countries, including the provision of new and additional financial resources and appropriate access to relevant technologies." Third, the precautionary principle is set forth as a guiding principle for actions taken by the parties, "Noting also that where this is a threat of significant reduction or loss of biological diversity, lack of full scientific certainty should not be used as a reason for postponing measures to avoid or minimize such a threat." Fourth, the concept of intergenerational equity is agreed upon, with the language, "Determined to conserve and sustainably use biological diversity for the benefit of present and future generations." And fifth, the right to develop is expressed as "recognizing that economic and social development and poverty eradication are the first and overriding priorities of developing countries." Finally, the sixth issue is the affirmation of the sovereignty of nations to act within their borders for their interests is addressed, "States have … the sovereign right to exploit their own resources pursuant to their own environmental policies.…"

Article one, sets out the objectives which are: conservation of biological diversity, sustainable use, equitable sharing of benefits arising from utilization of genetic resources, appropriate access, appropriate transfer, appropriate funding. This addressed concerns of both the northern and southern nations.

The definitions help to interpret the Convention:

genetic resources—genetic material of actual or potential value

genetic material—any material of plant, animal, microbial or other origin containing functional units of heredity

sustainable use—the use of components of biological diversity in ways and at a rate that does not lead to the long-term decline of biological diversity, thereby maintaining its potential to meet the needs and aspirations of present and future generations

ecosystem—a dynamic complex of plant, animal and micro-organism communities and their non-living environment interacting as a functional unit

Article six, General Measures of Conservation and Sustainable Use requires that nations develop national plans and strategies for biodiversity.

Article seven, Identification and Monitoring, requires the identify of components of biological diversity and processes and develop a system to monitor, maintain and organize the information.

Article eight, In-situ Conservation, establishes the desireability of a system for protected areas, not necessarily on the scale of a national parks system, but based upon the unique areas of each country. Article nine, Ex-situ conservation, is intended to complement in-situ measures, and established the preference for ex-situ conservation to be in the country of origin, although, not necessarily in the country of origin.

Article ten, Sustainable difficult Use of Components of Biological Diversity, integrates national decisionmaking between the private sector and governmental authorities, with an objective of avoiding adverse environmental impacts. It reads, "(c) Protect and encourage customary use of biological resources in accordance with traditional cultural practices that are compatible with conservation or sustainable use requirements."

Article 14, Impact Assessment and Minimizing Adverse Impacts, in (1)(A) specifically provides that a NEPA-like process be adopted by each party, and in (2) that parties will study issues of redress, liability, restoration and compensation for damage to biological diversity except where such liability is a purely a domestic matter.

Articles 15, 16, 17, 18 and 19 address biological trade and the biosafety protocol.

Articles 22 and 23 address the relationship with other conventions and the role of the Conference of Parties (COP).

Article 25, Subsidiary Body on Scientific, Technical and Technological Advice, provides for

(1) A subsidiary body for the provision of scientific, technical and technological advice ... with timely advice relating to the implementation of this Convention. This Body shall be open to participation by all Parties and shall be multidisciplinary. It shall comprise government representative competent in the relevant field of expertise. It shall report regularly to the Conference of the Parties on all aspects of its work; and (2) Under the authority of and in accordance

with guidelines laid down by the Conference of the Parties, and upon its request, this body shall:

(A) Provide scientific and technical assessments of the status of biological diversity;

(B) Prepare scientific and technical assessments of the effects of types of measures taken in accordance with the provisions of this Convention;

(C) Identify innovative, efficient and state-of-the-art technologies and know-how relating to the conservation and sustainable use of biological diversity and advise on the ways and means of promoting development and/or transferring such technologies;

(D) Provide advice on scientific programmes and international cooperation in research and development related to conservation and sustainable use of biological diversity; and

(E) Respond to scientific, technical, technological and methodological questions that the Conference of the Parties and its subsidiary bodies may put to the body....

Article 26, provides for the development of reports on measures and their effectiveness which have been taken for the implementation of the provisions of the CBD.

Article 27, addresses the settlement of disputes, which is to be done through negotiation, and if that fails, through the mediation of a third party. If these first two methods fail the Parties agree to accept one or both of the following means of dispute settlement as compulsory:

(A) arbitration in accordance with the procedure laid down in Part 1 of Annex II

(B) Submission of the dispute to the International Court of Justice.

5.2.1.2.1 Article 8(j)

Article 8 (j) provides that:

Each contracting Party shall, as far as possible and as appropriate: Subject to national legislation, respect, preserve and maintain knowledge, innovations and practices of indigenous and local communities embodying traditional lifestyles relevant for the conservation and sustainable use of biological diversity and promote their wider application with the approval and involvement of the holders of such knowledge, innovations and practices and encourage the equitable sharing of the benefits arising from the utilization of such knowledge, innovations and practices.

The Convention of the parties addressed specifically the mandate of Article 8(j) and its related provisions:

In 1997, in Decision III/14, the COP held a five-day workshop on Traditional Knowledge and Biological Diversity, Madrid, Spain, November 1997. The COP realized that to implement Article 8(j), the traditional knowledge, innovations, and practices of indigenous and local communities should be examined in the context of other international agreements, in particular, the World Trade Organization's Agreement on Trade-related Aspects of Intellectual Property. (Decision III/17). Thereafter, an ad hoc open-ended inter-sessional working group on Article 8(j) was established with a mandate to

(1) provide advice on the application of legal and other appropriate forms of protection for traditional knowledge; (2) to provide advice to the COP related to the implementation of Article 8(j) and related provisions; (3) to develop a program of work; and (4) to provide advice to the COP on measures to strengthen cooperation and suggest mechanisms to increase cooperation among indigenous local communities at the international level.

The principal decision on the implementation of Article 8(j) was in Decision V/16, adopted at the fifth COP meeting in Nairobi, Kenya, May, 2000. Here, the parties agreed to the following provisions:

> (1) the extension of the mandate of the Ad Hoc Working Group on Article 8(j); (2) promotion of the full and effective participation of indigenous and local communities, and particularly that of women, in implementing the Convention; (3) protection of the traditional knowledge, innovations and practices of indigenous and local communities related to the conservation of biodiversity and the sustainable use of natural resources; and (4) adoption of a programme of work for the Working Group.

5.2.1.2.2 Article 15. Access to Genetic Resources

The Convention on Biological Diversity, Article 15. "Access to Genetic Resources" reads as follows:

> 1. Recognizing the sovereign rights of States over their natural resources, the authority to determine access to genetic resources rests with the national governments and is subject to national legislation.
>
> 2. Each Contracting Party shall endeavour to create conditions to facilitate access to genetic resources for environmentally sound uses by other Contracting Parties and not to impose restrictions that run counter to the objectives of this Convention.
>
> 3. For the purpose of this Convention, the genetic resources being provided by a Contracting Party, as referred to in this Article and
>
> Articles 16 and 19, are only those that are provided by Contracting Parties that are countries of origin of such resources or by the Parties that have acquired the genetic resources in accordance with this Convention.
>
> 4. Access, where granted, shall be on mutually agreed terms and subject to the provisions of this Article.
>
> 5. Access to genetic resources shall be subject to prior informed consent of the Contracting Party providing such resources, unless otherwise determined by that Party.
>
> 6. Each Contracting Party shall endeavour to develop and carry out scientific research based on genetic resources provided by other Contracting Parties with the full participation of, and where possible in, such Contracting Parties.
>
> 7. Each Contracting Party shall take legislative, administrative or policy measures, as appropriate, and in accordance with Articles 16 and 19 and, where necessary, through the financial mechanism established by Articles 20 and 21 with the aim of sharing in a fair and equitable way the results of research and development and the benefits arising from the commercial and other utiliza-

tion of genetic resources with the Contracting Party providing such resources. Such sharing shall be upon mutually agreed terms.

Access and benefit sharing is the guiding framework for bioprospecting by pharmaceutical companies and other institutions in their search to isolate chemical compounds from genetic resources to develop and commercialize new drugs. The difficulty in implementing this section of the CBD has been the international framework for recognition of traditional knowledge and genetic resources as intellectual property which could the provide protection for indigenous communities and developing nations. The following sections outline and examine these aspects of genetic resources and commercialization.

5.3 Bioprospecting and International Biopiracy

Access and benefit-sharing is the international term of reference for utilizing the biological resources for the good of all humankind in an equitable way.

The first company to make bioprospecting equitable for all parties was Merck Pharmaceutical Company, pioneering a novel effort in 1991 to include in bioprospecting in Costa Rica, and making an agreement with the Costa Rican Institute for Biodiversity. The contract provided that 10% of any budget for a research contract and 50% of any financial benefits would be donated to the National Parks Fund, and provided for an advance payment for bioprospecting. The objective of the agreement was to develop new drugs form chemicals found in wild plants, insects and micro-organisms. Merck will own rights of any patented material, but will establish an institute in Costa Rica and provide equipment and training to the institute.

The agreement was renewed in 1994.

In India, the Neem tree controversy raised objections to western biopiracy of traditional knowledge when W. R. Grace isolated the molecular compound in the Neem tree to patent. The company was issued a patent in June 1992 for its invention. In March 1994, W.R. Grace registered Neemix as a pesticide with EPA in accordance with FIFRA.

A coalition of 200 organizations from thirty five different nations challenged the patent and filed a petition with the U.S. Patent and Trademark Office seeking to invalidate the patent. The challenge was ultimately dismissed. However, the European Patent Office revoked the W.R. Grace patent [Decision Revoking European Patent No. 0436257 (Eur. Patent Off. Feb 13, 2001)].

The anti-malarial drug, quinine, was patented based on observations that chewing the bark of south American Cinchona trees was a practice of peoples of Peru in the Eighteenth century which prevented them from getting malaria.

The San people of Africa, agreed to sell their interests in the hoodia cactus, *Hoodia gordoniis*, which was known among the San people as an appetite suppressant.

International protocols based on the Convention for Biological Diversity and the Inter-American Draft Declaration on the Rights of Indigenous Peoples, provide for bioprospecting that is equitable for both the pharmaceutical companies and the indigenous peoples. There is no international crime for biopiracy, but the CBD describes the unethical practice of appropriating the property of others.

5.3.1 International Approaches to Bioprosecting

Two treaties directly address access and benefit-sharing: the Convention on Biological Diversity and the FAO International Treaty on Plant Genetic Resources for Food and Agriculture. Other treaties with intellectual property issues relate to access and benefit-sharing such as WIPO treaties and the WTO TRIPs agreement. There are several international legal instruments which govern this process summarized below from CBD UNEP/CBD/WG-ABS/3/2 10 November 2004:

5.3.1.1 Convention on Biological Diversity

The Convention on Biological Diversity through Articles 8(j), 10 and 23, address the protection of traditional practices. The use of indigenous knowledge in the process of bioprosecting is being addressed by the Conference of the Parties. Guidelines have been developed for use by private sector companies seeking to explore the natural resources and traditional knowledge of a country.

Article 10. Sustainable Use Of Components of Biological Diversity

(c) Protect and encourage customary use of biological resources in accordance with traditional cultural practices that are compatible with conservation or sustainable use requirements.

5.3.1.2 FAO International Treaty on Plant Genetic Resources for Food and Agriculture

Adopted by the Food and Agriculture Organization of the United Nations (FAO) in November 2001 and entered into force November 29, 2004, sixty one countries and the European Union ratified the treaty. The objective is, "the conservation and sustainable use of plant genetic resources for food and agriculture and the fair and equitable sharing of benefits derived from their use, in harmony with the Convention on Biological Diversity for sustainable agriculture and food security."

The mechanism for implementation is a Material Transfer Agreement (MTA) adopted by the country's governing body, which will set out the conditions for access to genetic resources and benefit-sharing. The treaty provides for benefit sharing through payment of monetary benefits, information exchange, access to, and transfer of technology and capacity building.

5.3.1.3 WTO Agreement on Trade-Related Aspects of Intellectual Property Rights

The TRIPS agreement became effective on January 1, 1995 from the Uruguay round of multilateral trade negotiations. The main objective is to ensure that intellectual property rights do not become an impediment to legitimate trade. Article 7 of the agreement sets out as one of its objectives that the protection and enforcement of intellectual property rights should contribute to the promotion of technological innovation and the transfer and dissemination of technology, to the mutual advantage of producers and users of technological knowledge, in a manner conducive to social and economic welfare, and to a balance of rights and obligations.

The agreement establishes the minimum standards of protection to be provided by members in each of the main areas of intellectual property covered by the TRIPs Agreement. It also addresses remedies for the enforcement of intellectual property rights and makes disputes between WTO members subject to the WTO dispute-settlement procedures. The Agreement also provides for the applicability of basic GATT principles such as favored nation status.

Patentability under TRIPs requires in article 27(1) that patents shall be available for inventions that are "new, involve an inventive step and are capable of industrial application." Article 27, para. 3(b) provides that members may exclude from patentability, plants, animals and other micro-organisms and biological processes for the production of plants and animals. However, if any nation chooses to exclude plants they must provide an effective sui generis system of protection.

The Doha Declaration, Paragraph 19, requires that the TRIPS Council should examine the relationship between the TRIPS Agreement and the Convention on Biological Diversity, and the protection of traditional knowledge and folklore.

TRIPS does not require patent applicants to disclose the origin of genetic resources and associated traditional knowledge in patent applications where the subject matter of the application is based on genetic resources or related traditional knowledge; nor does it require prior informed consent from the sources of that knowledge.

WIPO has begun to address these issues through the Patent Law Treaty (PLT); the draft Substantive Patent Law Treaty (SPLT); the reform of the Patent Cooperation Treaty (PCT) and the Intergovernmental Committee on Intellectual Property and Genetic Resources, Traditional Knowledge and Folklore (IGC). WIPO will continue to consider amendments to the Patent Law Treaty and the Substantive Patent Law Treaty to address the deficiencies in addressing genetic resources and traditional knowledge intellectual property rights.

5.3.1.4 *International Convention for the Protection of New Varieties of Plants*

The Convention was signed in Paris in 1961 and entered into force in 1968. The purpose is "to ensure that the members of the union acknowledge the achievement of breeders of new varieties of plants, by granting to them an intellectual property right, on the basis of a set of clearly defined principles," forming a *sui generis* type of protection. The 1991 Act of the UPOV Convention entered into force in 1998, its objective being to encourage the development of new plant varieties, and avoiding barriers from intellectual property rights in traditional knowledge that might prevent carrying out this objective. The Convention provides a *sui generis* type of protection by its purpose "to ensure that the Members of the Union acknowledge the achievement of breeders of new varieties of plants, by granting to them an intellectual property right, on the basis of a set of clearly defined principles." To be eligible for protection under the Convention, varieties have to be "(i)distinct from existing, commonly known varieties; (ii) sufficiently uniform; (iii) stable; and (iv) new in the sense that they must not have been commercialized prior to certain dates established by reference to the date of the application for protection.

The protection is in the form of a "breeder's right," for the development of new species. However, the protection of the breeder's right is limited by two exceptions: (1) the first exception known as the "breeder's exemption" optimizes variety improvement by ensuring the germplasm sources remain available to other breeders; and (2) the second exception is known as the "farmer's exemption" continues the practice of allowing farmers to keep their seed for the purpose of resowing.

5.3.1.5 Convention on International Trade in Endangered Species of Wild Fauna and Flora

This treaty entered into force in 1975 with the purpose of regulating international trade in flora and fauna to ensure that trade does not threaten the survival of these species. The same system of permits might be used to regulate the identification of origin and ownership of biological materials exported and imported between member countries.

5.3.1.6 The Antarctic Treaty

This treaty was signed on Dec 1, 1959 and entered into force on June 23, 1961 for the purpose of regulating relations among states in the Antarctic. The purpose is to ensure "in the interests of all mankind that Antarctica shall continue forever to be used exclusively for peaceful purposes and shall not become the scene or object of international discord." The Scientific Committee on Antarctic Research (SCAR), the Committee for Environmental Protection (CEP) and the Antarctic Treaty Consultative Meeting (ATCM) are addressing the concern of unregulated bioprosecting in the region.

5.3.1.7 Universal Declaration of Human Rights

Adopted by the General Assemble of the United Nations on Dec 10, 1948, with the objective "as a common standard of achievement for all peoples and all nations to promote respect for these rights and freedoms and by progressive measures, national and international, to secure their universal and effective recognition and observance." Art 29 (1) states that "everyone has duties to the community in which alone the free and full development of his personality is possible."

5.3.1.8 International Covenant on Economic, Social and Cultural Rights

The Covenant was adopted Dec 16, 1966 and entered into force on March 23, 1976.

Article 1, para. 2, states:

"All peoples may, for their own ends, freely dispose of their natural wealth and resources without prejudice to any obligations arising out of international economic cooperation, bused upon the principle of mutual benefit, and international law. In no case may a people be deprived of its own means of subsistence."

5.3.2 Regional Agreements

Regional approaches can be utilized because of similar needs and conditions for access and benefit-sharing. Competition between countries and tribal nations in a region would be minimized, "forum shopping" by companies would be eliminated, and bioprosecting companies would have more predictability in the process. The following are some examples of existing regional agreements:

1. Andean Pact decision 391 on the Common Regime on Access to Genetic Resources

2. Draft Central American Agreement on Access to Genetic Resources and Bio-chemicals and related Traditional Knowledge

3. Draft ASEAN Framework Agreement on Access to Biological and Genetic Resources

4. African Model Law for the Protection of the Rights of Local Communities, Farmers and Breeders and for the Regulation of Access to Biological Resources.

5. Draft Pacific Model Law

5.4 International Codes of Conduct for Bioprospecting

There are two codes of conduct, the Micro-organisms Sustainable Use and Access Regulation International Code of Conduct, *at* http://www.belspo.be/bccm/mosaicc, and the "Bonn Guidelines on Access to Genetic Resources and Fair and Equitable Sharing of the Benefits Arising out of their Utilization" (Montreal: Secretariat of the Convention on Biological Diversity (2002)), which were written to address specifically Articles 8(j), 10(c), 15, 16 and 19 of the Convention on Biological Diversity.

5.4.1 The Micro-Organisms Sustainable Use and Access Regulation International Code of Conduct (MOSAICC)

The Belgian Co-ordinated Collections of Micro-organisms (BCCM) initiated the co-ordinated action to develop the MOSAICC guidelines with the support of the Directorate General XII for Science, Research and Development of the European Commission. In November 2000, the MOSAICC document was developed. It states the following about its purpose and principles:

> MOSAICC is a voluntary Code of Conduct. It is developed to facilitate access to microbial genetic resources (MGRs) and to help partners to make appropriate agreements when transferring MGRs, in the framework of the Convention on Biological Diversity (CBD)2 and other applicable rules of international3 and national laws. MOSAICC is a tool to support the implementation of the CBD at the microbial level; it can also serve as a model when dealing with genetic resources other than MGRs. Access to MGRs is a prerequisite for the advancement of microbiology and world-wide sustainable development. Furthermore, monitoring the transfer of MGRs is necessary to identify the individuals or groups that are entitled to be scientifically or financially rewarded for their contribution to the conservation and sustainable use of the MGRs. Therefore, MOSAICC combines the need for easy transfer of MGRs and the need to monitor the transfer of MGRs. It proposes a system that works through two operating principles:

1. The in situ origin of the MGRs is identified via initial Prior Informed Consent (PIC) procedure providing authorisation for sampling. The in situ origin of the MGRs is always mentioned when transfer occurs.

2. The transfer of MGRs is monitored and occurs under Material Transfer Agreement (MTA) which terms are defined by both recipient and provider. MTA is a generic term that covers either a very short shipment document, a simple standard delivery notice, a standard invoice containing minimal standard requirements or a more detailed specific contract including tailor-made mutually agreed terms. According to the use and intended distribution of the MGRs, mutually agreed terms can be short or very detailed.

[See figure 5.1 MOSAICC Process]

MOSAICC recommends that compensation for access to genetic resources should be "partly dedicated to technical and scientific co-operation programmes" and include "initial, up-front payments ... made before or after accessing the MGRs, but this always independently of the possible, successful commercial use of the MGRs. MOSAICC recommends to calculate the importance of the initial payments in terms of the actual involvement of the provider in the delivery of the MGRs." Further, the guidance suggests, "milestones payments ... related to the progress made in the development of a product or process that could be commercialised," as we; as "royalty payments ... fully dependent on the successful commercial use of the MGRs concerned." *at* http://www.belspo.be/bccm/mosaicc.

The following form letter is recommended by MOSAICC for the beginning of a prior informed consent process:

———————

(*Date*)

(*Name and address of the PIC-provider*)

Dear (...........),

According to article 15 of the Convention on Biological Diversity (CBD) stating that «the authority to determine access to genetic resources rests with the national governments and is subject to national legislation» and that «Each Contracting Party shall endeavour to create conditions to facilitate access to genetic resources for environmentally sound uses by other Contracting Parties and not to impose restrictions that run counter to the objectives of this Convention», as well that «access to genetic resources shall be subject to prior informed consent of the Contracting Party providing such resources»; and, as ratified by (*Name of the Country where one wants to access MGRs*), I would like to acquire access to (*Name of the field survey area*), as well as to its genetic resources, with your prior informed consent (PIC), during the period and under the conditions specified in annex.

To this end, I have annexed a model form of PIC-certificate to be used if you agree to provide me with such a PIC according to the principles and rules laid down in the CBD.

(*closing salutation*)

(*Name, address and signature of the PIC-applicant*)

———————

The second part of the MOSAICC guidance requires a material transfer agreement, and the following form letter is provided in the guidance:

———————

Figure 5.1

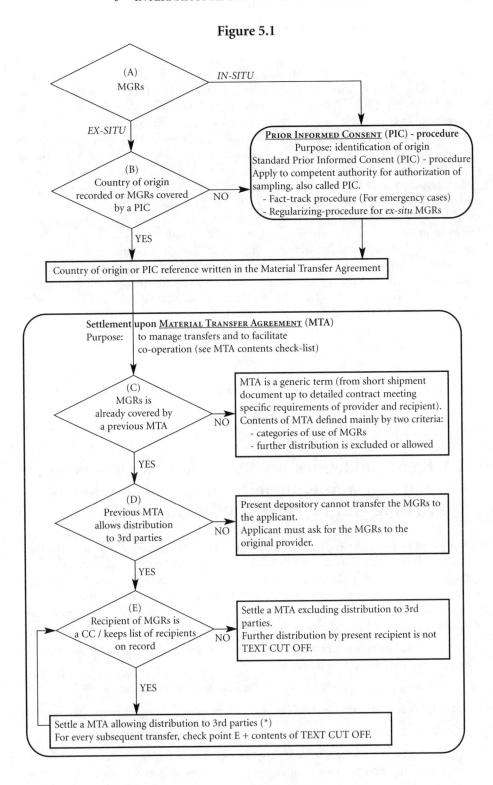

(*Name and address of the CBD PIC-provider*) (*Date*)

Dear (*Name of the PIC-applicant*),

In reply to your PIC-application of (*date of written demand*), having as a reference (*reference*), and as annexed; as well as, according to article 15 of the Convention on Biological Diversity (CBD) stating that «*the authority to determine access to genetic resources rests with the national governments and is subject to national legislation*» and that «*Each Contracting Party shall endeavour to create conditions to facilitate access to genetic resources for environmentally sound uses by other Contracting Parties and not to impose restrictions that run counter to the objectives of this Convention*», as well that «*access to genetic resources shall be subject to prior informed consent of the Contracting Party providing such resources*»; and, as ratified by (*Name of the Country providing the MGRs*), on (*Date of ratification*);as well as, in conformity with the national laws and rules referred to in annex; We, the undersigned, being (within the framework of the CBD)*, on behalf of (*Name of the country providing the MGRs*), the competent authority for surveying *in-situ* access to the genetic resources of (*Name of the geographical area of competence*), have the pleasure to provide you, exclusively for the annexed PIC-application, with the required PIC. This PIC for access to *in-situ* MGRs from (*Name of the field survey area*) grants access to this area from (*date*) to (*date*). This PIC is not transferable from one organisation to another without written agreement of the undersigned authority.

(*closing salutation*)

(*Place and date of issue, official administrative seals and signature of the CBD PIC-provider.*)

———————

5.4.2 Bonn Guidelines on Access to Genetic Resources and Fair and Equitable Sharing of the Benefits Arising Out of Their Utilization

The Bonn Guidelines were developed by the leadership of the Secretariat of the Convention on Biological Diversity in 2002. The scope of the Bonn Guidelines extends to "[a]ll genetic resources and associated traditional knowledge, innovations and practices covered by the Convention on Biological Diversity and benefits arising from the commercial and other utilization of such resources should be covered by the guidelines, with the exclusion of human genetic resources."

The Bonn Guidelines establish a set of principles for prior informed consent before beginning any bioprospecting activities:

1. The basic principles of a prior informed consent system should include:

(a) Legal certainty and clarity;

(b) Access to genetic resources should be facilitated at minimum cost;

(c) Restrictions on access to genetic resources should be transparent,based on legal grounds, and not run counter to the objectives of the Convention;

(d) Consent of the relevant competent national authority(ies) in the provider country. The consent of relevant stakeholders, such as indigenous and local communities, as appropriate to the circumstances and subject to domestic law, should also be obtained.

2. Elements of a prior informed consent system may include:

(a) Competent authority(ies) granting or providing for evidence of prior informed consent;

(b) Timing and deadlines;

(c) Specification of use;

(d) Procedures for obtaining prior informed consent;

(e) Mechanism for consultation of relevant stakeholders;

(f) Process.

The Guidelines provide a process for obtaining prior informed consent:

An application for access could require the following information to be provided, in order for the competent authority to determine whether or not access to a genetic resource should be granted. This list is indicative and should be adapted to national circumstances:

(a) Legal entity and affiliation of the applicant and/or collector and contact person when the applicant is an institution;

(b) Type and quantity of genetic resources to which access is sought;

(c) Starting date and duration of the activity;

(d) Geographical prospecting area;

(e) Evaluation of how the access activity may impact on conservation and sustainable use of biodiversity, to determine the relative costs and benefits of granting access;

(f) Accurate information regarding intended use (e.g.: taxonomy, collection, research, commercialization);

(g) Identification of where the research and development will take place;

(h) Information on how the research and development is to be carried out;

(i) Identification of local bodies for collaboration in research and development;

(j) Possible third party involvement;

(k) Purpose of the collection, research and expected results;

(l) Kinds/types of benefits that could come from obtaining access to the resource, including benefits from derivatives and products arising from the commercial and other utilization of the genetic resource;

(m) Indication of benefit-sharing arrangements;

(n) Budget;

(o) Treatment of confidential information.

37. Permission to access genetic resources does not necessarily imply permission to use associated knowledge and vice versa.

38. Applications for access to genetic resources through prior informed consent and decisions by the competent authority(ies) to grant access to genetic resources or not shall be documented in written form.

39. The competent authority could grant access by issuing a permit or licence or following other appropriate procedures. A national registration system could be used to record the issuance of all permits or licences,on the basis of duly completed application forms.

40. The procedures for obtaining an access permit/licence should be transparent and accessible by any interested party.

5.5 International Intellectual Property and Biotechnology

5.5.1 Patent Protection in the United States

In the United States a patent issued by the U.S. Patent Office will grant the right, for twenty years from the date of application, to exclude everyone from making, using or selling the patented invention without permission of the holder of the patent. The United States grants patents based on the principle of "first to invent" not "first to file" as do many other countries.

Infringement on U.S. held patents in other countries can be prosecuted in U.S. courts for injunctive relief and damages through several enforcement mechanisms. "Exclusion orders" are issued by the International Trade Commission under Sec. 337 of the Tariff Act of 1930, and are enforced by the U.S. Customs Service, where there are foreign made infringing articles.

5.5.2 Patent Protection in Other Countries

There are two major types of patenting systems in the governments of the world, which are registration and examination. Some countries grant patents upon "registration" without making an initial inquiry about patentability of the invention, such as France. The validity of such a patent grant is not questioned until there is an infringement or a need to defend the patent, and only then is it determined whether it is a patentable invention. Under the system of "examination" there is a careful examination and inquiry into the prior art and statutory criteria on patentability, as in the United States and Germany. A "deferred examination" may also be part of the process, giving notice to the public to oppose the patent. The validity of patents granted under an examination system are much more likely to survive a patentability examination in court if it must be defended or if there is an infringement claim.

In comparison to the United States, one major difference in patent protection in other countries is the difference in timing that is presented by the "first to invent" principle, which could come much earlier than "first to file", and present conflicting patents, both valid in both countries.

For patent protection in other countries, patent applications must be filed in those countries and are governed by the domestic law of each country. A decision that a patent is invalid in one country is not binding on any other country, nor is the recognition of a patent in one country binding on another.

5.5.3 International Patenting

For international patenting, it is important to know that patents are protected territorially, not internationally. Patents are granted according to national law. There is no international patent protection, which requires patents to be filed in each country. There is some limited protection provided by the Paris Convention through the World Intellectual Property Organization (WIPO) at Geneva. A "right of priority" is granted through this organization to a patent holder if they file in foreign jurisdictions within twelve months of the filing of the original patent in the first country. However, even this protection may not overcome the differences in the "first to file" jurisdictions for United States patentees seeking international protection.

There is also another international mechanism which is intended to make the patent application process more uniform and to provide protection for at least a limited international scope. Approximately forty countries have joined in The Patent Cooperation Treaty (PCT) which allows one patent filing to be done once under the PCT which will include a number of selected countries. The offices, designated as International Searching Authorities (ISA) where this filing can be done under the PCT, include the national patent offices of the United States, Russia, Sweden, Japan, and the European Patent Office at Munich and The Hague. The PCT offices provide that the patent applicant may see a preliminary examination and seek a non-binding opinion on the questions of novelty, non-obviousness and utility. This initial filing, together with the international search report is filed with each national patent office where the patentee is seeking protection. The individual countries establish their own substantive requirements for patentability and remedies for infringement, although in many countries without extensive patent systems, the report of the PCT may carry great weight.

5.6 International Trade and Biotechnology

5.6.1 Exporting Biotechnologies

Unlike many products in international trade, the import and export of many biotechnologies are regulated by the U.S. Department of Commerce. A determination of whether the biotechnology being exported is on a list, maintained through the U.S. Department of Commerce, Bureau of Export Administration, which administers non-defense and dual-use products in commerce. These Export Administration Regulations (EAR) may require a permit for the export of biotechnologies or biological material, or their export may be prohibited, if for example, the biological material could be used as a biological weapon and is being sent to a country listed as one which should not receive those types of technologies.

5.6.2 The Cartegena Biosafety Protocol

More than 130 countries adopted the Biosafety Protocol on January 29, 2000, in Montreal, Canada and it is named for the extraordinary Conference of the Parties to the

Convention on Biological Diversity (CBD) in Cartagena in 1999. The objective of the Cartegena Biosafety Protocol to the Convention on Biological Diversity is to contribute to the safe international transfer, handling, and use of living modified organisms (LMOs), and to avoid adverse effects on the conservation and sustainable use of biodiversity without burdening the world food trade.

The Biosafety Protocol, Art. 15 specifies procedures for the handling, transport, packing and identification of living modified organisms (LMOs). Shipments must be identified by traits and characteristics of the organism, include instructions for safe handling and shipment, and a point of contact for further information or in the event of an emergency. In addition, the shipment must include a declaration that the transboundary movement is being conducted in compliance with the requirements of the Biosafety Protocol.

Labeling within the meaning of the Protocol has come to mean that the requirements of the Protocol must be included on the label. The Protocol requires the parties to provide public information about safe-handling of LMOs, through the Biosafety Clearing House.

5.7 International Security

The Biological Weapons Convention of 1972

In the 1960s many countries ended their offensive military programs in biological weapons, including the United Kingdom, the United States (1969) and France (1972). In 1972, the Biological and Toxin Weapons Convention was signed and entered into force in 1975. The Biological Weapons Convention prohibits the development, production, stockpiling and acquisition of biological agents or toxins that "have no justification for prophylactic, protective or other peaceful purposes." (Art. 1). Signatories to the Convention committed to the destruction or conversion to peaceful purposes all agents, weapons, equipment, and means of delivery within nine months of the treaty's entry into force (Art. 3).

The existence of biological weapons programs are still a very real threat, and several countries including Iran and South Korea are considered to be potentially working with biological agents for use as weapons.

5.8 International Human Rights and Biotechnology

5.8.1 United Nations Treaty on Indigenous Peoples and Human Rights

Key articles of the Draft Declaration for biotechnology issues are as follows:

Article 7. [Indigenous people will have the right to prevent and seek redress for] any action which has the aim or effect of dispossessing them of their lands, territories or resources.

Article 24. [Rights of indigenous people include] the right to the protection of vital medicinal plants, animals and minerals.

Article 29. Indigenous peoples are entitled to the recognition of the full ownership, control and protection of their cultural and intellectual property.

They have the right to special measures to control, develop and protect their sciences, technologies and cultural manifestations, including human and other genetic resources, seeds, medicines, knowledge of the properties of fauna and flora, oral traditions, literatures designs and visual and performing arts.

Article 30. Indigenous peoples have the right ... to require that States obtain their free and informed consent prior to the approval of any project affecting their lands, territories and other resources, particularly in connection with the development ... of ... resources.

The term "indigenous people" is one of the most controversial in the area, in terms of defining who that is. The term "indigenous peoples" in international contexts is defined by meeting all of a list of criteria. Required criteria are (1) self-identification as a distinct ethnic group; (2) historical experience of, or contingent vulnerability to, severe disruption, dislocation, or exploitation; (3) long connection with the region; (4) wish to retain a distinct identity. Other relevant criteria are (1) nondominance in the national (or regional) society; (2) close cultural affinity with a particular area of land or territories; (3) historic continuity (especially by descent) with prior occupants of land in the region; (4) socio-economic and cultural differences from the ambient population: (5) distinct objective characteristics: language, race, material or spiritual culture; and (6) regarded as indigenous by the ambient population or treated as such in legal and administrative arrangements. [Kingsbury.]

Earlier definitions by the World Bank and IMO limited the scope of the definition of indigenous peoples to those who maintained traditional lifestyles, such as hunter-gatherer. Indigenous tribes in North America objected to this.

The World Bank has developed its own definition of indigenous peoples as: (a) a close attachment to ancestral territories and to the natural resources in these areas; (b) self-identification and identification by others as members of a distinct cultural group; (c) an indigenous language; (d) presence of customary social and political institutions; and (e) primarily subsistence-oriented production.

5.9 Human DNA

Human DNA is not within the scope of the Convention on Biological Diversity, and at the second Conference of the Parties it was declared that human genetic diversity was not subject to the Biodiversity Convention.

The United States as well as at least 17 other countries were engaged in the human genome mapping project. The mapping of the human genome was completed in 2000 by two private companies. The Human Genome Project is funded by the U.S. federal government, and has been fraught with criticism, corruption and other problems since the beginning. It was originally headed by Dr. Watson, of the Crick and Watson team who first modeled the double-helix of DNA. When the federal government moved too slowly, one of the staff, Craig Ventner went out on his own to start a private endeavor in a race to map the human genome.

Originally it was thought there were more than 100,000 genes in the human genome, but it was discovered that there were only about 30,000. The genes of flowers also were thought to be much greater in number, probably around 400,000; but it has been discovered that the number is closer to 30,000.

The following excerpt provides some insight into the questions being addressed and the potential for application of the knowledge of the human genome to human diseases, environmental remediation and industrial processes. [U.S. Department of Energy, Argonne National Laboratory, "Scientific Excellence," *Frontiers 2001* 4–5 (2001).]:

> The genome is a set of genetic instruction in the cells of all living things. Those instructions are written in the sequence of bases—adenine(A), guanine(G), cytosine(C) and thymine(T)—that form the two strands of DNA's double helix. Sequences of these bases create specific amino acids, which link in different combinations to make different proteins. These proteins are responsible for all of the genetic traits any living organism carries.... There are more than 40 known genomes including the human genome. Now researchers need to understand the structure and function of each protein, because this knowledge will ultimately help doctors treat, cure or prevent disease.

> To determine a protein's structure, the brilliant APS X-rays are shined on tiny crystals of the protein at liquid nitrogen temperatures. The pattern of X-rays produced by the sample is captured in a kind of digital camera, called a CCD detector, and the data are mathematically converted to a three-dimensional image.

> For example, the crystal structure of immune cells called CD4T cells was determined in a few hours. Data collection took less than one hour. The structure provides clues to how the immune system identifies enemy threats and is helping researchers to understand the human response system. Results of this research were published in *Science*.

> Researchers also determined the structure of a large detoxifying enzyme, cyanase, which helps certain bacteria to regulate carbon dioxide levels and neutralize toxic chemicals. It may be important for technologies that use biological species to clean the environment. The data quality was so high that researchers automatically produced the protein structure in a few days. It was published in Structure magazine. Other structures studied at the SBC may provide insights into diabetes, muscular dystrophy and high blood pressure....

> Some Argonne biologists and computer scientists are focusing on finding potential targets for antibiotics. Biologists identify genes and metabolic pathways that are unique to disease-causing organisms so that they may be used to fight the disease without harming the human.

The Human Genome Diversity Project, part of the Human Genome Project was controversial and was denied the support of the United Nation's body UNESCO's International Bioethics Committee. The project was nicknames the "Vampire Project" because of its process of taking blood samples for DNA testing from entire communities. It was not long after the failure to gain support from the UN body that the project came to an end in the 1990s.

A project sponsored by the National Geographic Society, the Genographic Project, was designed to take 100,000 samples from indigenous peoples, but in May 2006, a petition with names representing 850 indigenous nations, individuals and supporters demanded an end to the project. The United Nations Permanent Forum on Indigenous Issues (UNPFI) announced its recommendation that "the World Health Organization and the Human Rights Commissions investigate the objectives of the Genographic Project" and request "that the Genographic Project be immediately suspended ..." [Press Release, "United Nations Recommends Halt to Genographic Project," Indigenous Peoples Council on Biocolonialism (May 26, 2006) at www.ipcb.org.]

Chapter Six

Bioethics, Religion and Biotechnology

6.1 Law, Biotechnology and Religion: Humans' Relationship with Biotechnology and Religion

Religion has been raised in the context of science which offends the religious beliefs of individuals. But should governmental actions go beyond simply offending—where science begins to interfere with one's ability to practice one's religion, the question of the protection of the free exercise of religion is raised.

6.1.1 Free Exercise Clause Challenge to Biotechnology

The following case raises issues of religion in a challenge to the failure to label bio-engineered foods, as a violation of the Free Exercise Clause of the U.S. Constitution:

Alliance for Bio-Integrity v. Shalala

116 F. Supp. 2d 166 (D.D.C., 2000)

MEMORANDUM OPINION

Technological advances have dramatically increased our ability to manipulate our environment, including the foods we consume. One of these advances, recombinant deoxyribonucleic acid (rDNA) technology, has enabled scientists to alter the genetic composition of organisms by mixing genes on the cellular and molecular level in order to create new breeds of plants for human and animal consumption. These new breeds may be designed to repel pests, retain their freshness for a longer period of time, or contain more intense flavor and/or nutritional value. Much controversy has attended such developments in biotechnology, and in particular the production, sale, and trade of genetically modified organisms and foods. The above-captioned lawsuit represents one articulation of this controversy.

Among Plaintiffs, some fear that these new breeds of genetically modified food could contain unexpected toxins or allergens, and others believe that their religion forbids

253

consumption of foods produced through rDNA technology. Plaintiffs, a coalition of groups and individuals including scientists and religious leaders concerned about genetically altered foods, have brought this action to protest the Food and Drug Administration's ("FDA") policy on such foods in general, and in particular on various genetically modified foods that already have entered the marketplace. The parties have filed cross-motions for summary judgment on plaintiffs' multiple claims. Upon careful consideration of the parties' briefs and the entire record, the Court shall grant Defendants' motion as to all counts of Plaintiffs' Complaint.

I. BACKGROUND

On May 29, 1992, the FDA published a "Statement of Policy: Foods Derived From New Plant Varieties". In the Statement of Policy, FDA announced that the agency would presume that foods produced through the rDNA process were "generally recognized as safe" (GRAS) under the Federal Food, Drug and Cosmetic Act ("FDCA"), 21 U.S.C. §§ 321(s), and therefore not subject to regulation as food additives. While FDA recommended that food producers consult with it before marketing rDNA-produced foods, the agency did not mandate such consultation. In addition, FDA reserved the right to regulate any particular rDNA-developed food that FDA believed was unsafe on a case-by-case basis, just as FDA would regulate unsafe foods produced through conventional means.

F. Free Exercise

Plaintiffs have argued that the Statement of Policy unconstitutionally violates their right to free exercise of religion by allowing unlabeled genetically engineered foods on the market. Under the Supreme Court's decision in *Employment Division v. Smith*, 494 U.S. 872, 108 L. Ed. 2d 876, 110 S. Ct. 1595 (1990), however, neutral laws of general applicability do not violate the Free Exercise Clause, even if the laws incidentally burden religion. Because it is not disputed that the Statement of Policy is neutral and generally applicable, Plaintiff's Free Exercise Claim must fail. *See* Pls.' Mot. at 64 (conceding that the Statement of Policy is neutral and generally applicable).[11]

G. Religious Freedom Restoration Act

Plaintiffs also claim that the Statement of Policy burdens their religion in violation of the Religious Freedom Restoration Act (RFRA), 42 U.S.C. §§ 2000bb–2000bb-4. Congress enacted RFRA in reaction to the *Employment Division v. Smith* decision in order to "restore the compelling interest test" for Free Exercise issues. RFRA's definition of the compelling interest test provides that "Government shall not substantially burden a person's exercise of religion even if the burden results from a rule of general applicability … [unless the rule is] (1) in furtherance of a compelling governmental interest; and (2) is the least restrictive means of furthering that compelling governmental interest." §§ 2000bb-1(a–b). This test is not to be "construed more stringently or more leniently than it was prior to *Smith*." H.R. Rep. No. 103-88, at 7 (1993).

Although the Supreme Court has overruled the portions of RFRA applicable to the state governments on the grounds that Congress exceeded its authority under the Fourteenth Amendment, its holding does not affect RFRA's applicability to the federal government. [Previously], this Circuit held that Congress had the authority to enact RFRA as to federal law. While this Circuit has not squarely addressed the constitutionality of RFRA as

---

11. Plaintiffs' claim that the Statement of Policy nevertheless violates the Free Exercise Clause because it lacks a rational basis is without merit.

applied to the federal government since *Boerne,* several decisions in this and other circuits support the continuing validity of *Catholic University's* holding that RFRA applies to the federal government.

Defendants concede that RFRA applies to the FDA. Assuming arguendo that Plaintiffs' meet the RFRA requirement that their beliefs are sincerely held and can demonstrate an "honest conviction" desiring to avoid genetically engineered foods, Plaintiffs still must establish that Defendants have substantially burdened Plaintiffs' religion. A substantial burden does not arise merely because "the government refuses to conduct its own affairs in ways that comport with the religious beliefs of particular citizens." The Free Exercise Clause (as interpreted before *Smith* and incorporated into RFRA) does not require the government to take action to further the practice of individuals' religion. *See id.* Indeed, were the government to take such action, it might bring itself precariously close to violating the First Amendment's Establishment Clause.

Arguing that the government does have some obligation to facilitate the practice of religion, Plaintiffs point to several cases involving prisoners, in which the government was required to provide nutritional information and alternative diets for inmates whose religious beliefs required dietary restrictions. See *Barnett* (D.C. Cir. 1969) (rejecting the government's contention that Muslim inmates could practice their religion by simply not eating foods they found objectionable and held that the government was required to disclose the pork content of meals and make at least one pork-free meal a day available). However, the prisoner cases cited by the Plaintiffs are inapposite to the issue before this Court. In this case, the Plaintiffs' liberty is not restricted and they are free to choose their food and may obtain their food from the source of their choosing.

Still, Plaintiffs argue that in the absence of labeling they are unable to know whether the foods they consume are genetically engineered or not. While the Court recognizes the potential inconvenience the lack of labeling presents for Plaintiffs, Defendant's decision to mandate labeling of genetically modified foods does not "substantially" burden Plaintiffs' religious beliefs. Furthermore, given that the FDA functions under statutory power granted by Congress and cannot exceed that power, Plaintiffs' argument on this point is probably better directed at Congress, than at the Defendant or this Court. The Policy Statement does not place "substantial pressure" on any of the Plaintiffs, nor does it force them to abandon their religious beliefs or practices. Accordingly, Plaintiffs are not entitled to relief under RFRA.

CONCLUSION

For the foregoing reasons, the Court determines that Defendant's 1992 Policy Statement did not violate the Administrative Procedures Act, the National Environmental Policy Act, or the procedures mandated by the FDCA and FDA regulations. Furthermore, Defendant was not arbitrary and capricious in its finding that genetically modified foods need not be labeled because they do not differ "materially" from non-modified foods under 21 U.S.C. §§ 321(n). Finally, the Court finds that Defendant's Policy Statement does not violate the First Amendment Free Exercise Clause or RFRA, 42 U.S.C. §§ 2000bb–1(b). Hence, the Court denies Plaintiffs' motion for summary judgment and grants Defendant's motion for same. An appropriate order accompanies this memorandum opinion.

September 29, 2000

COLLEEN KOLLAR-KOTELLY

United States District Judge

Notes

1. The Court disposed of the Free Exercise Clause in the U.S. Constitution with very little analysis. As a practical matter, why does this law of general applicability not prevent the plaintiffs from freely exercising their religion?

2. The Court also found that under the Religious Freedom and Restoration Act the law of general applicability did not substantially burden the free exercise of the plaintiff's religious beliefs. In fact, the court cautions that to act otherwise, the federal government might violate the Establishment Clause. What test did the court use?

———————

6.1.2 Religious Views on Biotechnology

Religious views and long-standing traditions as they concern biotechnology are important, in part, because they inform and influence citizens. Citizen viewpoints, then shape our legislative responses to regulate and control new technologies without a direct role for religion.

6.1.2.1 Stem Cell Research and Religion

As part of the work of the National Bioethics Advisory Commission, a meeting was convened on the religious viewpoints concerning stem cell research. One of the participants, Rabbi Moshe Dovid Tendler, Ph.D., from Yeshiva University made this statement:

> There is something unreal about this National Bioethics Advisory Commission meeting at which the focus is on religious views on the humanhood of stem cells or of pre-embryos. The death-dealing silence of the leaders of organized religion as to the humanhood of men, women, and children subjected to murder, rape, exile, torture, and hunger, raised the question of "who cares?" ... Ambiguity and indecision in the face of crimes against humanity is an admission that organized religion has failed in its mission to humanize animal-man.... The prophet Elija cried out in exasperation (Kings I 18:21), "How long will you vacillate between God and idolatry?" If you would but take a stand I could then hope to influence you with the truth and beauty of our faith. Ambiguity and indecision are fatal to any social order based on morals and ethics.

In NBAC, ETHICAL ISSUES IN HUMAN CELL RESEARCH, VOLUME III RELIGIOUS PERSPECTIVES, (June 2000), the following viewpoints of different religions were presented:

United Church of Christ. That stem cell research go forward is consistent with the viewpoint of the church. "In fact, we go further and encourage reconsideration of the ban on federal funding for embryo research." They caution however, that "one of the conditions that we attach to the possibility of this research is that a clear and attainable benefit for science and medicine be indicated in advance. And it is reasonable to think that now, with pluripotent stem cell technology, such benefit is becoming clearer."

Holy Trinity Greek Orthodox Church. "In my view, the establishment of embryonic stem cell lines was done at the cost of human lives. Even though not yet a human person, an embryo should not be used for or sacrificed in experimentation, no matter how noble the goal may seem. For me, then, the derivation of embryonic stem cell lines is immoral because it sacrificed the human embryos, which were committed to becoming human persons." This does not square with the dignity and sanctity of life. "In summary, the Orthodox Church promotes and encourages therapeutic advances in medicine and the research necessary to realize them, but not at the expense of human life." [at B-3, B-4].

Judaism. "Stem cells for research purposes also can be procured from donated sperm and eggs mixed together and cultured in a petri dish. Genetic materials outside the uterus have no legal status in Jewish law, for they are not evan a part of a human being until implanted in a woman's womb, and even then, during the first 40 days of gestation, their status is 'as if they were simply water.' Abortion is still prohibited during that time, except for therapeutic purposes, for in the uterus such gametes have the potential of growing into a human being. Outside the womb, however, at least at this time, they have no such potential. As a result, frozen embryos may be discarded or used for reasonable purposes and so may the stem cells that are procured from them."

Roman Catholic Church. "There is no simple, single voice form the Catholic community on such questions [stem cell research]. There is, however, a shared 'community of discourse,' so that one can easily identify common convictions expressed in common language ..." Within the Catholic tradition, a case can be made both against and for such research—each dependent upon different interpretations of the moral status of the human embryo and the aborted human fetus.... [One view is that] human embryos must be protected on par with human persons—at least to the extent that they should not be either created or destroyed merely for research purposes. Moreover, the use of aborted fetuses as a source for stem cells.... should be prohibited because it is complicit with and offers a possible incentive for elective abortion.... [Another point of view is that a] growing number of Catholic moral theologians ... do not consider the human embryo in its earliest stages (prior to the development of the primitive streak or to implantation) to constitute an individualized human entity with the settled inherent potential to become a human person. The moral status of the embryo is, therefore, not that of a person, and its use for certain kinds of research can be justified." [at D-3, D-4]. "I do not oppose stem cell research per se if the cells are obtained from sources such as adult humans, miscarriages, or placental blood." [at F-3].

Roman Catholic Bishops of the United States " ... have made known their opposition to stem cell research, opposition that is based on the need to destroy human embryos in order to conduct this type of research. Because the Bishops work form an assumption that the human embryo should be treated as a human person, destruction of the embryo to conduct research is morally problematic." [at I-3].

Islam. There are traditionalists, conservatives and liberals points of view in Islam. "A majority of the Sunni and some Shi ite scholars make a distinction between two stages in pregnancy divided by the end of the fourth month (120 days) when the ensoulment takes place. On the other hand, a majority of the Shi ite and some Sunni jurists have exercised caution in making such a distinction because they regard the embryo in the pre-ensoulment stages as alive and its eradication as a sin.... [there is no] universally accepted definition of the term "embryo." ... [I]t is possible to propose the following as acceptable to all schools of thought in Islam: ... (2) The fetus is accorded the status of a legal person only at the later stages of its development, when perceptible form and voluntary movement are demonstrated. Hence, in earlier stages, such as when it lodges itself in the uterus and begins its journey to personhood, the embryo cannot be considered as possessing moral status.... Hence, in Islam, research ons tem cells made possible by biotechnical intervention in the early stages of life is regarded as a n act of faith in the ultimate will of God as the Giver of all life, as long as such an intervention is undertaken with the purpose of improving human health."

6.1.2.2 Cloning and Religion

Religion and reproductive biotechnology has been considered by theologians and other religious thinkers as four recent overlapping periods. The first phase began in the mid-1960s until the early 1970s when the choices and control of reproduction became possible. For example, the use of birth control pills, technologically-assisted reproduction such as *in vitro* fertilization, and the discussions and advocacy of cloning superior genotypes.

The Protestant and Roman Catholic viewpoints were diametrically opposed. The Protestant viewpoint found that cloning could be ethically justified by societal benefit. Joseph Fletcher, a spokesperson for the Protestant view, found cloning to be preferable to the "genetic roulette" of sexual reproduction." Five problems exist with this: (1) cloning requires reproductive management to serve the ends of science; (2) experimentation on the unborn; (3) parenthood would become something other than the human sexual expression; (4) the sin of hubris or pride is expressed; and (5) humans become a "man-God" by creating other humans.

A second era of religious thought concerning human cloning began about 1978 — the year of the birth of Louise Brown in Britain, the first baby produced by *in vitro* fertilization — through the 1980s. Protestant groups issued resolutions and position statements which cautiously supported genetic interventions for therapeutic purposes. In 1979, President Carter, created the President's Commission for the Study of Ethical Problems in Medicine and Biomedical and Behavioral Research to examine the scientific, ethical, and social issues of gene splicing. The Commission addressed genetic engineering as it relates to disease, but nothing about *in vitro* fertilization or cloning.

A third era of religious thought began in 1993 — the year that George Washington University reported the separation of cells in human blastomeres to create multiple, genetically identical embryos. The Roman Catholic Church was vigorously opposed to this practice, calling it "intrinsically perverse." Individuality, dignity and wholeness concepts were invoked in condemning this research. Conservative Protestants held that this research contravened basic notions of sanctity of life and parenthood. Other Protestants felt that its potential for medical benefits was worth exploring, but with caution.

A fourth era of thinking began in 1997 with the successful cloning of Dolly the sheep. The possibility of cloning a human became more realistic. Protestants have expressed qualified support for creating children with cloning. Some Jewish and Islamic thinkers encourage continuation of research on animals, and in laboratories toward human cloning where there is only a worthy purpose. Roman Catholics continue to reiterate previous warnings. NBAC, *Cloning Human Beings*, RELIGIOUS PERSPECTIVES, (June 9, 1997) at ch. 3.

Religious themes relating to human cloning include the biblical account of the creation of humans; responsible human dominion over nature; the quest for knowledge, human destiny, human dignity, procreation and families, and concerns about the future of the family.

The National Bioethics Advisory Committee considered viewpoints from major religions and concluded that they are pluralistic in their premises, arguments and conclusions.

> Nevertheless, several major themes are prominent in Jewish, Roman Catholic, Protestant, and Islamic positions, including responsible human dominion over nature, human dignity and destiny, procreation, and family life. Some religious thinkers argue that cloning a human to create a child would be intrinsically immoral and thus could never be morally justified; they usually propose a ban on such human cloning. Some other religious thinkers content that human cloning to create a child could be morally justified under some circumstances but hold that it should be strictly regulated in order to prevent abuses.

NBAC, *Cloning Human Beings*, Religious Perspectives, (June 9, 1997) at ch. 3.

———————

As can be expected, with new technologies that raise serious religious and ethical concerns, there will be widely varying viewpoints. One provocative website proposes cloning technology as the answer to the second coming, an event referred to in the New Testament as the return of Jesus Christ to the earth.

The Second Coming Project

The Second Coming Project is a not-for-profit organization devoted to bringing about the Second Coming of Our Lord, Jesus Christ, as prophesied in the Bible, in time for the 2,000th anniversary of his birth. Our intention is to clone Jesus, utilizing techniques pioneered at the Roslin Institute in Scotland, by taking an incorrupt cell from one of the many Holy Relics of Jesus' blood and body that are preserved in churches throughout the world, extracting its DNA, and inserting into an unfertilized human egg (oocyte), through the now-proven biological process called nuclear transfer. The fertilized egg, now the zygote of Jesus Christ, will be implanted into the womb of a young virginal woman (who has volunteered of her own accord), who will then bring the baby Jesus to term in a second Virgin Birth.

If all goes according to plan, the birth will take place on December 25, 2001, thus making Anno Domini 2001 into Anno Domini Novi 1, and all calendrical calculations will begin anew.

How Can This Be Possible?

a. Modern cloning technology enables us to clone any large mammal—including humans—using just a single cell from an adult specimen.

b. Throughout the Christian world are churches that contain Holy Relics of Jesus' body: his blood, his hair, his foreskin. Unless every single one of these relics is a fake, this means that cells from Jesus' body still survive to this day.

c. We are already making preparations to obtain a portion of one of these relics, extract the DNA from one of its cells, and use it to clone Jesus.

No longer can we rely on hope and prayer, waiting around futilely for Jesus to return. We have the technology to bring him back right now: there is no reason, moral, legal or Biblical, not to take advantage of it.

IN ORDER TO SAVE THE WORLD FROM SIN, WE MUST CLONE JESUS TO INITIATE THE SECOND COMING OF THE CHRIST.

The Second Coming Project is soliciting contributions and donations to help us is our quest. Time is short! We must have a fertilized Jesus zygote no later than April of 2001 if Baby Jesus is to come to term on the predicted date. Please send all contributions to:

The Second Coming Project
P.O. Box 295
Berkeley, CA 94701

Biblical Predictions of Cloning

"While they were eating, Jesus took bread, gave thanks and broke it, and gave it to his disciples, saying, 'Take and eat; this is my body.' Then he took the cup, gave thanks and offered it to them, saying, 'Drink from it, all of you. This is my blood of the covenant, which is poured out for many for the forgiveness of sins.'" (Matthew 26:26–28)

Many have long wondered at the strange behavior of Jesus here at the Last Supper. Was he imitating some pagan ritual? Was he encouraging cannibalism? We think: No! He was giving a clue to later generations. Honor, protect and preserve my body and blood, he was saying, for someday, far in the future, with it you will be able to save the world. How? Through unspecified magical or supernatural means? Obviously not. Through knowledge given to us by God: the knowledge of CLONING, which we can use to BRING JESUS BACK, because the faithful have preserved parts of his body and blood for all these centuries!

Jesus was very explicit about the necessity of cloning in the book of Matthew: "It is better for you to lose one part of your body than for your whole body to go into hell." (Matthew 5:30)

"He will cut him to pieces." (Matthew 24:50)

"If someone from the dead goes to them, they will repent." (Luke 16:30)

Paul knew too: here he tells us that Christ's blood is the key: "In him we have redemption through his blood." (Ephesians 1:7)

The apostle John foresaw cloning. here is what he said: "We know that, when He appears, we shall be like Him, because we shall see Him just as He is." (1Jn.3:2)

Even the Old Testament prophets knew what must occur: "The grave below is all astir to meet you at your coming; it rouses the spirits of the departed to greet you— all those who were leaders in the world; it makes them rise." (Isaiah 14:9–11)

Do not disobey the Bible. Send your contribution to The Second Coming Project today!

6.2 Ethics and Biotechnology

6.2.1 Public Sector Considers Ethics and Biotechnology

The National Bioethics Advisory Commission, created in 1997 by President Clinton, examined the biotechnologies that raised new ethical issues. The Commission was chaired by Harold T. Shapiro, President, Princeton University. The charter for the National Bioethics Advisory Commission expired October 3, 2001. In concluding its work, the Chair transmitted a letter to President Bush, outlining remaining issues to be discussed, as follows:

Outstanding Ethical and Public Policy Issues

Assisted Reproductive Technologies

The methods and frequency of use of assisted reproductive technologies are increasing. Oversight of these technologies in the United States is limited, and there is little distinction between the development and experimental use of a new assisted reproductive technology and its use as a proven clinical treatment. Key issues for consideration are the need and type of required oversight when assisted reproductive technologies are used in research or practice, identifying and assessing risks of these technologies, whether the motivations behind their use are relevant to determining acceptability, and whether there should be eligibility criteria for use of such technologies.

Horizontal Gene Transfer

Horizontal gene transfer is the insertion of new genetic material or material from another species into human beings. When horizontal gene transfer is initiated by humans (as opposed to being unplanned such as through viral infection) it raises issues about whether it should be permitted and if so, with what protections. In other words, we must be able to anticipate horizontal gene transfer applications and evaluate safety and efficacy. At a more fundamental level, horizontal gene transfer may alter an individual's humanness, especially when this involves making inheritable genetic changes.

Body as Property

Research and commercial uses of human tissues are increasing while relatively little federal or state law addresses the transfer of human tissue. The interplay of property law and personal control over one's body raises a number of questions. Should the body, in whole or in part, be treated as the property of the person who inhabits or inhabited the body? If so, questions include whether it can be disposed of by will or other testamentary measures after death, and what effect treating the body as property has on efforts to ensure the autonomy and dignity of individuals and to regulate the human tissue market.

Research Involving Children

There is increasing recognition of the value of including children as participants in research, and inclusion is encouraged by recent regulatory and legal changes. However, children can be particularly vulnerable in research. Only a few federal agencies have regulations addressing research involving children. Questions have been raised as to whether current regulations are adequate to protect children, under what circumstances healthy children should be involved in research, and the role of the child's age in determining participation in research.

Population-Based Research

There has been increasing recognition of the need to respect and protect communities or groups of people in research. Federal regulations are focused on protecting individuals, so researchers have little guidance on how to identify risks to communities and provide appropriate protections. Community issues arise even when a population is not necessarily being studied. Consideration should be given as to when and how to involve communities in planning and conducting research and in reporting research findings.

Cloning Human Beings

In 1997, NBAC recommended a prohibition on somatic cell nuclear transfer to create a child and noted that more debate on the ethical, social, and legal aspects of cloning would be necessary if safety concerns were ever resolved in the future. Today, serious safety issues remain. However, consideration should be given to the ethical, social, and legal issues associated with human cloning in the event that the risks to the fetus and mother were someday to be considered acceptable. *at* http://bioethics.georgetown.edu/nbac/stemcell3.pdf (last visited 10-7-01).

6.2.2 The Private Sector Considers Ethics and Biotechnology

Geron, a biotechnology company leading the efforts in stem cell research, discusses the company's establishment of an advisory board on ethics:

> Okarma, the vice president of Geron, testified, "The company formed an ethics advisory board to advise us on ethical issues associated with this research. The board, composed of medical ethicists of diverse religious traditions, carefully deliberated the issues and unanimously agreed that research on human pluripotent stem cells can be conducted ethically if performed within certain guidelines: treating the cells with appropriate respect due to early developmental tissue, obtaining full and informed consent from donors of the tissue, no reproductive cloning of human beings, accord for accepted norms of animal research, concern for global justice and the use of best efforts to develop and utilize technology for all peoples, and lastly, participation by an independent ethics advisory board in addition to an institutional review board to assess the appropriateness of each research protocol. Geron has and will continue to follow these guidelines."

> This statement is an instructive example of the empty Ethical Correctness that pervades biotechnology. It emphasizes procedural issues ("respect" for embryos, "informed consent," and humane "animal research"), forbids what the company doesn't plan to do ("reproductive cloning"), and ignores the significance of what the company does plan to do (manufacturing and redesigning organs) while repeatedly invoking buzzwords such as "ethics," "justice," and "religious traditions." *at* http://slate.msn.com/BraveNewWorld/98-12-09/note1.asp (last visited 10-7-01).

6.3 Family Relations: Legal v. Biological

As discussed by the National Bioethics Advisory Commission, among the religious themes of discussion is the impact on families and family relations with growing technological capabilities in the use of genetic testing. The following case illustrates one issue which can arise with the existence and utilization of reliable DNA testing in paternity and child custody cases.

Stitham v. Henderson
768 A.2d 598 (ME, 2001)

Panel: Wathen, C.J., Clifford, Rudman, Dana, Saufley, Alexander, and Calkins, J.J.

J.J. Calkins, Judge:

John C. Henderson appeals from the summary judgment of the Superior Court (Aroostook County, Pierson, J.) in favor of David B. Stitham, declaring that Henderson is not the biological father of the minor child K.M.H. and declaring that Stitham is the child's biological father. Henderson further appeals from the order denying his motion to dismiss in which he requested a dismissal of Stitham's complaint on the basis of res judicata. Henderson also appeals the order dismissing his counterclaim in which he sought to establish his equitable parental rights. We affirm the judgment and orders of the Superior Court.

I. BACKGROUND

Henderson and Norma were married in 1986. Norma gave birth to K.M.H. in 1993. Henderson was present at the birth and is named on the birth certificate as the father of K.M.H. He believed that he was the child's father, and he established and maintained a father-daughter relationship with her. His parents and the child had a grandparent-grandchild relationship. Henderson and Norma divorced in 1996, and they agreed to the terms of the divorce in a written document that was incorporated into the divorce judgment. The divorce judgment, entered in the District Court (Houlton, Griffiths, J.), awarded shared parental rights of the child to Henderson and Norma; granted primary physical residence of the child to Norma; awarded Henderson contact with the child at all reasonable and proper times; ordered Henderson to maintain health insurance for the child; and ordered Henderson to pay child support to Norma. Henderson has continued to pay Norma child support....

A few months after the divorce, Norma and Stitham married, and they, along with the child, submitted to DNA testing to determine if Stitham is the child's biological father. The test results show Stitham's probability of paternity to be 99.96%. Thereafter, Norma filed a post-divorce motion in District Court in which she sought to obtain a declaration that Henderson was not the child's biological parent. Henderson objected, and the District Court denied Norma's motion on the ground of res judicata.

In 1998, Stitham filed the instant action in Superior Court against Henderson. The complaint states that the action is brought pursuant to the Uniform Act on Paternity, 19-A M.R.S.A. §§§§ 1551–1570 (1998 & Supp. 2000), and requests that Stitham be declared the child's biological father. Henderson moved to dismiss the complaint on the ground of res judicata, and the court denied the motion. The court ordered Henderson to submit to DNA testing, and the test results exclude Henderson as the biological father of K.M.H....

After the DNA test results were obtained, Henderson brought a motion to allow a counterclaim to establish his equitable parental rights. Stitham objected to the motion on the ground that the counterclaim was untimely. Stitham moved for summary judgment on his complaint to which Henderson objected. The court granted Stitham's summary judgment motion and Henderson's motion to file the counterclaim, but it dismissed the counterclaim without prejudice as not being ripe for adjudication. The judgment declares that Henderson is not the child's biological father and that Stitham is the biological father....

The interests of a biological mother and a biological father are not identical in actions in which paternity may be determined. The biological mother may not want the paternity of the biological father determined because she does not want him to establish a relationship with the child, or she, does not want him to be allocated rights in the upbringing of the child. The determination of paternity can include, or at least lead to, visitation with the child, decision-making regarding the education and medical care of the child, and various legal and moral duties. The finances of the mother, her husband, and the biological father may be such that the mother's best hope for ongoing financial support for a child is from the husband rather than the biological father. The mother may choose not to complicate divorce proceedings by injecting a disputed paternity claim into the action. Henderson, as the party claiming res judicata, has offered nothing to indicate that the actual situation of Norma and Stitham, at the time of the District

Court divorce judgment, was such that Norma was in fact representing Stitham's interest. Although Norma and Stitham are married now, and it may be safe to assume that their interests currently are aligned, no such assumption can be made that their interests were identical at the time Norma and Henderson were divorced.

We have held that a court-approved settlement of a paternity action between the biological parents is not binding on nonparties and does not bar either the child or the Department of Human Services from litigating paternity. Webster, 398 A.2d at 794. The divorce between Henderson and Norma was by agreement, and the issue of paternity was not raised before the court. This fact alone demonstrates the divergence of interests between Stitham and Norma. Norma did not represent Stitham's interest during the divorce proceeding. Norma and Stitham were not in privity, and for this reason the doctrine of res judicata does not act as a bar to Stitham's action to determine his paternity....

Henderson next claims that summary judgment was inappropriate because the DNA test results are not dispositive and there remains a genuine issue as to the paternity of the child. Henderson has not presented his own expert or otherwise challenged the validity of the DNA tests. Those test results exclude Henderson as the biological father and state that the probability that Stitham is the biological father is 99.96%. The test result provision in the Uniform Act on Paternity, declares that if the tests demonstrate that the "alleged father" is not the father, "the question of paternity must be resolved accordingly." Given that the test results are not disputed, there is no genuine dispute that Henderson is not the biological father. Thus, a summary judgment declaring that Henderson is not the child's biological father was proper....

CONCUR:

Saufley, J. with whom Alexander and Dana join concurring:

I concur in the Court's analysis and the result in this matter. I write separately to address the Court's reference to the de facto parenthood of Henderson and the area of law that is emerging from the intersection of traditional social policies and modern biological testing abilities.

With the recent advances in biotechnology and human genetics, family law is undergoing further evolution. Because testing is now sufficiently accurate, the presumption of paternity, a hurdle once very difficult to overcome, can now be swept aside by a simple test. As a result, there now exists the real possibility, as this case demonstrates, that one man may become the legally acknowledged biological father of a child, while another, through marriage to the mother, has been the legally acknowledged and factually involved father....

Maine statutes are silent on the issue. Maine law does, however, create an avenue for biological fathers to assert a claim of paternity, even when the child has a father who was previously understood to be the father because he was married to the mother at the time of the child's birth. Thus, although the law recognizes the legal rights and responsibilities of the newly established biological father, it does not directly address the consequences of that legal recognition for the person who had previously thought himself to be the father....

Although DNA testing may provide a bright line for determining the biological relationship between a man and a child, it does not and cannot define the human relationship between father and child. When a man has been newly determined to be the biological father of a child, the courts have a responsibility to assure that the child does not, without cause, lose the relationship with the person who has previously been acknowledged to be the father both in the law, through marriage, and in fact, through the development of the parental relationship over time....

6.4 Reproductive Technologies

The following cases involve the application of the moral distinction made in state legislation between therapeutic and experimental work in the area of reproductive technologies.

Margaret S. v. Edwards
794 F.2d 994 (5th Cir. 1986)

OPINION by PATRICK E. HIGGINBOTHAM, Circuit Judge:

We are asked to decide the constitutionality of two statutory provisions through which Louisiana has sought to regulate the practice of abortion. One provision requires that the attending physician inform his patient, within twenty-four hours after she undergoes an abortion, that she may exercise one of several options for the disposition of the fetal remains. The other forbids "experimentation" on the fetal remains of an abortion. We are persuaded that the first provision must be declared unconstitutional under City of Akron v. Akron Center for Reproductive Health, Inc. (1983), and that the second is unconstitutionally vague....

IV

La. Rev. Stat. Ann. §§ 40:1299.35.13 provides: "No person shall experiment on an unborn child or a child born as the result of an abortion, whether the unborn child or child is alive or dead, unless the experimentation is therapeutic to the unborn child or child." imposes criminal penalties for violating this or any other section of the abortion statute. The district court offered several alternative rationales for invalidating this provision. Although we agree that this statutory provision is unconstitutional, we neither approve nor disapprove any of the rationales put forth by the district court. Our holding is based solely on our conclusion that the use of the terms "experiment" and "experimentation" makes the statute impermissibly vague....

A state's legislative enactment is void for vagueness under the due process clause of the fourteenth amendment if it "is inherently standardless, enforceable only on the exercise of an unlimited, and hence arbitrary, discretion vested in the state." This test requires that the law be vague "not in the sense that it requires a person to conform his conduct to an imprecise but comprehensible normative standard, but rather in the sense that no standard of conduct is specified at all." The vagueness doctrine has been applied with considerable stringency to a law that required physicians to use professional diligence in caring for the life and health of a viable aborted fetus.

The plaintiffs' expert witness offered unrebutted testimony, which we find quite plausible, that physicians do not and cannot distinguish clearly between medical experiments and medical tests. As the expert witness pointed out, every medical test that is now "standard" began as an "experiment" that became standard through a gradual process of observing the results, confirming the benefits, and often modifying the technique. Thus, as the witness concluded, "we have at one end things that are obviously standard tests and [at] the other end things that are complete experimentation. But in the center there is a very broad area where diagnostic procedures of testing types overlap with experimentation procedures...." Indeed, as the challenged statute itself seems to acknowledge, even medical *treatment* can be reasonably described as both a test and an experiment. This must be true whenever the results of the treatment are observed, recorded, and introduced into the data base that one or more physicians use in seeking better therapeutic methods. The whole distinction between experimentation and testing, or between research and practice, is therefore almost meaningless in the medical context. When one adds to this the fact that some innovative tests or treatments are done on fetal tissue in order to monitor the health of the mother, one can see that physicians who treat pregnant women are being threatened with an inherently standardless prohibition. We therefore think that this statute "simply has *no* core" that unquestionably applies to certain activities, and we hold that it is unconstitutionally vague....

CONCURRENCE:

JERRE S. WILLIAMS, Circuit Judge, specially concurring.

B. *State Interest in Prohibiting Experimentation*

A state may exercise its police powers to ensure public health, safety and welfare. The regulation of medical experimentation is a proper exercise of this authority. A state's authority in this context is admittedly broad. The exercise of these police powers, however, must be rationally related to important state interests. Section 40:1299.35.13 fails to bear such a rational relationship to an important state interest.

Although Louisiana seeks to prohibit experimentation on tissue obtained from induced abortions it imposes no comparable restrictions on experimentation on human tissue. Indeed, Louisiana law specifically provides for the use of human corpses for the purposes of research. The evidence presented at trial failed to establish that tissue derived from an induced abortion presents a greater threat to public health or other public concerns than the tissue of human corpses. Further, no rational justification is shown for prohibiting experimentation on fetal tissue from a lawful induced abortion as opposed to a spontaneous abortion. There was no showing that [the law] in prohibiting experimentation on fetal tissue only in the instance of lawful induced abortions has any rational relationship to any legitimate state interest. The record is lacking in showing valid state policy in any of these distinctions. I can only conclude that under the guise of police regulation the state has actually undertaken to discourage constitutionally privileged induced abortions. I would affirm the judgment of the district court on this ground.

Biotechnologies change so quickly that the line between experimentation and therapy is difficult or impossible to determine. The next case addresses this issue.

Lifchez v. Hartigan

735 F. Supp. 1361 (N.D. Ill., 1990)

Opinion by: Ann Claire Williams, United States District Judge.

MEMORANDUM OPINION AND ORDER

Dr. Lifchez represents a class of plaintiff physicians who specialize in reproductive endocrinology and fertility counselling. Physicians with these medical specialties treat infertile couples who wish to conceive a child. Dr. Lifchez is suing the Illinois Attorney General and the Cook County State's Attorney, seeking a declaratory judgment that a provision of the Illinois Abortion Law is unconstitutional. He also seeks a permanent injunction against the defendants from enforcing the statute. The provision at issue concerns fetal experimentation. Both sides move for summary judgment, alleging that there are no disputed facts and that each side is entitled to judgment as a matter of law. The court finds that §§ 6(7) of the Illinois Abortion Law violates the Constitution in two ways: (1) it offends Fourteenth Amendment principles of due process by being so vague that persons such as Dr. Lifchez cannot know whether or not their medical practice may run afoul of the statute's criminal sanctions, and (2) the statute impinges upon a woman's right of privacy and reproductive freedom as established in *Roe v. Wade*, (1973) ... and their progeny. The court therefore declares §§ 6(7) of the Illinois Abortion Law to be unconstitutional and permanently enjoins the defendants from enforcing it.

Section 6(7) of the Illinois Abortion Law provides as follows:

> (7) No person shall sell or experiment upon a fetus produced by the fertilization of a human ovum by a human sperm unless such experimentation is therapeutic to the fetus thereby produced. Intentional violation of this section is a Class A misdemeanor. Nothing in this subsection (7) is intended to prohibit the performance of in vitro fertilization.Ill.Rev.Stat., Ch. 38 para. 81–26, §§ 6(7) (1989).

Dr. Lifchez claims that the Illinois legislature's failure to define the terms "experimentation" and "therapeutic" renders the statute vague, thus violating his due process rights under the Fourteenth Amendment. The court agrees.

A. *Experiment or Routine Test?*

The Illinois legislature's failure to define "experimentation" and "therapeutic" in §§ 6(7) means that persons of common intelligence will be forced to guess at whether or not their conduct is unlawful. As Dr. Lifchez points out in his briefs, there is no single accepted definition of "experimentation" in the scientific and medical communities. Dr. Lifchez identifies four referents for the term. One meaning of experiment is pure research, where there is no direct benefit to the subject being experimented on, and the only goal of the research is to increase the researcher's knowledge. This definition describes the defendants' "Orwellian nightmare" of laying out fetuses in a laboratory and exposing them to various harmful agents "just for the scientific thrill" of it. A second meaning of experiment includes any procedure that has not yet been sufficiently tested so that the outcome is predictable, or a procedure that departs from present-day practice. This is the kind of definition adhered to by insurance companies, which often deny coverage for procedures whose effectiveness is not generally recognized. Dr. Lifchez also cites to the definition of experiment by the American Fertility Society, which includes as "experimental" even standard techniques when those techniques are performed by a practitioner or clinic for the first time. Finally, any medical therapy where the practitioner applies what he learns from one patient to another, could be described as an "experiment." See, e.g., *Margaret S. v. Edwards*, 794 F.2d 994, 999 (5th Cir. 1986) (medical treatment can be described as both a test and an experiment "whenever the results of the treatment are observed, recorded, and introduced into the data base that one or more physicians use in seeking better therapeutic methods.") This definition of experiment is in line with that apparently contemplated by the federal regulations on protection of human research subjects: "'Research' means a systematic investigation designed to develop or contribute to generalizable knowledge."

The legislative history of §§ 6(7) is unenlightening as far as nailing down a particular-ized meaning of "experiment" to counter the vagueness that Dr. Lifchez claims is inher-ent in the statutory language. The bill's sponsor, Representative O'Connell, responded as follows to the governor's veto of the bill (due to what the governor saw as unconstitu-tional vagueness in the word "experimentation"): "I would submit that the word exper-iment is quite clear and does not have a vague connotation to it. In fact, the American Heritage dictionary is quite clear in defining experiments as a test made to demonstrate a known truth; to examine the validity of a hypothesis or to determine the efficacy of something previously untried." ... It is hard to imagine two more opposed definitions of "experiment" than, on the one hand, "a test made to demonstrate a known truth," and, on the other hand, a test "to determine the efficacy of something previously un-tried." That the bill's sponsor could offer such wildly different definitions of "experi-ment" as if they both meant the same thing offers little help to persons of common in-telligence who want to know what the state forbids.

It is difficult to know where along this broad spectrum of possible meanings for "exper-iment" to fit the medical procedures performed by Dr. Lifchez and his colleagues. These procedures can be roughly divided into three kinds: diagnostic, *in vitro* fertilization and related technologies, and procedures performed exclusively for the benefit of the preg-nant woman. The statute's vagueness affects all three kinds of procedures, but in differ-ent ways.

It is difficult to know where along this broad spectrum of possible meanings for "experi-ment" to fit the medical procedures performed by Dr. Lifchez and his colleagues. These procedures can be roughly divided into three kinds: diagnostic, *in vitro* fertilization and related technologies, and procedures performed exclusively for the benefit of the pregnant woman. The statute's vagueness affects all three kinds of procedures, but in different ways.

Diagnostic Procedures

One of the more common procedures performed by reproductive endocrinologists is amniocentesis. Amniocentesis involves withdrawing a portion of the amniotic fluid in order to test it for genetic anomalies. It is performed on women considered to be at risk for bearing children with serious defects. The purpose of the procedure is to provide in-formation about the developing fetus; this information is often used by women in de-ciding whether or not to have an abortion. Although now routinely performed, amnio-centesis could be considered experimental under at least two of Dr. Lifchez' definitions: it could be classified as pure research, since there is no benefit to the fetus, the subject being "experimented" on; it could also be experimental (as defined by the American Fertility Society) if the particular practitioner or clinic were doing it for the first time.

Amniocentesis illustrates well the problem of deciding at what point a procedure gradu-ates from "experimental" to routine. Does this occur the fifth time a procedure is per-formed? the fiftieth? the five hundredth? the five thousandth? Shortly before the Illinois Abortion Law was first passed in 1975, amniocentesis was considered an experimental procedure by most definitions of the term....

Although the non-experimental status of amniocentesis in 1985 may be established through this reference to legislative intent, the above dialogue underscores the problem of refusing to define the key terms in §§ 6(7) in the context of the rapidly growing field of re-productive endocrinology. Dr. Lifchez can hardly be expected to know which of his med-ical activities would be illegal now if he were to look back on the quick evolution of am-niocentesis from (very likely) illegal experiment in 1975 to explicitly endorsed "process" in 1985. Statutory language that embraces both of these possibilities simply "has no core" of meaning and forces people of common intelligence to guess at what the law forbids.

For this reason, it is unconstitutionally vague.

The court is keenly aware that, because of the meteoric growth in reproductive endocrinology, any classification of a particular procedure as either "experimental" or "routine" could easily be out-of-date within six months ...

The very same procedure that is explicitly endorsed today would have been illegal ten years earlier—the illegality resulting from a legislative insistence on using a protean term such as "experiment." A statute is unconstitutionally vague if the mere passage of time can transform conduct from being unlawful to lawful....

Other procedures give rise to this and similar objections. In genetic screening of *in vitro* embryos, one cell of an eight-cell embryo is removed for testing, while the rest are frozen. If the genetic screening on the single cell is negative, the remaining seven cells can be gestated to produce a child. This experimental procedure is undisputedly non-therapeutic to the embryo, and although it could fall within the statute's *in vitro* exception, that exception speaks to fertilization, not genetic testing. A failed implantation following *in vitro* fertilization genetic screening could subject Dr. Lifchez to criminal liability....

Procedures for the Pregnant Woman

A third class of procedures that Dr. Lifchez performs for his patients are those that are exclusively for the benefit of the pregnant woman. In order to discover correal carcinoma, for example, Dr. Lifchez would need to take a sample of fetal tissue for testing. Correal carcinoma originates with the fetus and is capable of killing pregnant women. Any experimental therapy designed to detect or treat this condition is necessarily a non-therapeutic experiment upon the fetus....

Reproductive Privacy

Section 6(7) of the Illinois Abortion Law is also unconstitutional because it impermissibly restricts a woman's fundamental right of privacy, in particular, her right to make reproductive choices free of governmental interference with those choices. Various aspects of this reproductive privacy right have been articulated in a number of landmark Supreme Court cases, including *Griswold v. Connecticut.*...

Since there is no compelling state interest sufficient to prevent a woman from terminating her pregnancy during the first trimester, *Roe v. Wade*, 410 U.S. at 163; *Akron v. Akron Center for Reproductive Health*, 462 U.S. 416, 450, 76 L. Ed. 2d 687, 103 S. Ct. 2481 (1983), there can be no such interest sufficient to intrude upon these other protected activities during the first trimester. By encroaching upon this protected zone of privacy, §§ 6(7) is unconstitutional.

CONCLUSION

The court grants Dr. Lifchez' motion for summary judgment and denies the defendants' motion for summary judgment. Section 6(7) of the Illinois Abortion Law is unconstitutional and the defendants are permanently enjoined from enforcing it.

Notes

1. There are concerns that the rights of women should not be undervalued in the consideration of issues in biotechnology. Consider the following observation:

Although the protection of reproductive choices by the judicial branch is a tremendous accomplishment for the women's movement, this progress must be protected. To prevent a backlash, women's organizations should fight for limited legislative restraints on a woman's right to choose in the area of genetic technology. Women would be protecting their role as parental and family decision-makers while still defending their fundamental right to choose.

WOMAN'S RIGHT TO CHOICE IN GENETIC TESTING

At least one organization in the United States has determined that a woman's right to reproductive choices should always be protected. In 1975, the Committee on Inborn Errors in Metabolism, as part of the National Research Council, concluded that the privacy right should be the governing factor in all decisions, not secondary to other interests. From Renee C. Esfandiary, Note: *The Changing World of Genetics and Abortion: Why the Women's Movement Should Advocate for Limitations on the Right to Choose in the Area of Genetic Technology*, 4 Wm. & Mary J. of Women & L. 499 (Spring 1998).

2. Should cloning of farm animals be allowed with no restrictions on experimentation? In March 2000, PPL Therapeutics made international headlines when it announced that it had finally succeeded in cloning pigs. At the same time, Akira Onishi, an animal breeder at Japan's National Institute of Animal Industry in Tsukuba, Japan reported the cloning of Xena, a pig. The cloning of pigs creates a capability to provide an unlimited source of organs for transplantation—xenotransplantation. However, another annoucement that pig retroviruses can infect human cells has raised caution. 289 Science 1118 (August 18, 2000).

3. Would the risk of wealthy individuals pursuing human cloning as an approach to a supply of body parts be a possibility? If so, should there be criminal statutes to prevent such individual conduct?

6.4.1 Post Mortem Sperm Collection

The following article discusses the use of post-mortem sperm collection to produce a child with a surrogate mother, at the initiation of the parents of the deceased son. What legal issues might arise with regard to family law, inheritance and parental responsibility?

USA Today, February 12, 2007

Science makes a new father of a fallen American soldier: Banked sperm produces a son: 'He's a blessing'

Gregg Zoroya

AUSTIN—Seven-month-old Benton Drew Smith is the spitting image of his father, with the same blue eyes, fair hair and infectious grin.

Bouncing on his mother's lap in olive-green overalls and slippers festooned with lizards, he also holds a special place in history: He is one of the first children to have been conceived from sperm left behind by a soldier who was killed in battle. Benton's dad, Army 2nd Lt. Brian Smith, was shot by a sniper in Iraq on July 2, 2004.

"I've had some lousy luck in my life," says Smith's widow, Kathleen "K.C." Carroll-Smith, 41. "But he has worked out," she says, gazing into her son's eyes as he grins back. "He's a blessing. He is wonderful."

Benton was born July 14, 2006, a little more than two years after his father, 30, was cut down by a single shot while checking the treads of his Abrams tank in Habaniyah, Iraq, west of Baghdad. The bullet sliced Smith's liver, causing internal bleeding. His wife says she was told that her husband collapsed, muttered that he could no longer feel his legs, lost consciousness and died.

Death did not erase him, Carroll-Smith says. "I have a piece of Brian with me every day now."

How many children have been artificially conceived after their father's death in war is unclear; the Department of Veterans Affairs says it knows of two similar cases during the past three years. The commercial technology for storing sperm did not become available until 1971, so the conflicts in Iraq and Afghanistan are the first in which a significant number of combat troops have been able to take advantage of the technology.

Participation remains small, relative to the number of troops in combat. About 100 troops make such deposits each year, according to officials at the nation's three largest sperm-bank companies—Fairfax Cryobank in Fairfax, Va., California Cryobank in Los Angeles and Xytex in Augusta, Ga.

"This clearly is an area where medical technology has moved faster than most of our social thinking," says Dale Smith, professor and chairman of medical history at the Uniformed Services University of the Health Sciences in Washington, D.C. He describes the practice as "an effort to take out a social insurance policy on … mortality."

For the family of Brian Smith, the decision by his widow to become pregnant by in vitro fertilization on Oct. 29, 2005, was not without emotional turmoil.

Smith's parents, Linda and William Smith of McKinney, Texas, concede that they struggled at first to accept their daughter-in-law's decision. "There was hesitancy there in the beginning," says Linda Smith, 59. "It just didn't seem right or fair or something that Brian wouldn't be there to raise his child."

During Carroll-Smith's pregnancy, Linda Smith nonetheless remained supportive, both women say. When Carroll-Smith asked her mother-in-law for assistance late in the pregnancy, Linda Smith rushed to help prepare for the baby.

Smith's parents have since fallen in love with the baby. During the Christmas season, they took Benton to a Wal-Mart in McKinney to have his picture taken in the same sailor suit his father wore for a portrait when he was a child. The images mirror each other, Linda Smith says.

"Once you meet that little fellow," she says of her only grandchild, "you will think that there have been gobs of angels all over the place. He's absolutely the most adorable child."

Less certain is how the Pentagon and the Department of Veterans Affairs will view Benton. A child who is a legal dependent of a combat casualty is entitled under federal law to a range of educational, financial and health benefits.

No formal policy exists, however, in cases in which conception occurred after the parent died, says Lisette Mondello, a VA spokeswoman. In the two similar cases, the VA granted benefits, Mondello says.

Carroll-Smith has not yet requested that the VA declare her son a dependent of his father.

Carroll-Smith, who left her last job as a secretary in the intensive care unit at Seton Medical Center in January, says she urged her husband to deposit his sperm in a Fairfax Cryobank facility here about a month before he went to Iraq.

The decision had nothing to do with fear that he would die in combat, she says. Rather, it was for reasons that William Jaeger, Fairfax Cryobank director, says are typical of most military families that make the decision: a desire for wives to continue to try to conceive while their husbands are deployed, or a fear that a husband will lose fertility because of combat wounds or exposure to toxic chemicals.

Today, however, some families are also concerned about a husband not surviving combat.

6.4.2 Ectogenesis

[Excerpt from Jennifer S. Bard, "Immaculate Gestation? How Will Ectogenesis Change Current Paradigms of Social Relationships and Values?" Chap. Eleven, Ecotogensis: Artificial Womb Technology and the Future of Human Reproduction, eds. Scott Gelfand and John R. Shook (2006)]:

One of the much-discussed futuristic technologies is the development of an ectogenesis mechanism, reminiscent of that in Huxley's Brave New World to gestate a human fetus outside the human body in an artificial womb. The impact of ectogenesis on social relationships and values would be greater than the extraordinary reproductive technologies developed within the last twenty years....

The invention of a method to gestate a baby outside the human womb whas enormous implication sfor the way the courts, ethicists and society at large currently view the right of a fetus to be born. It also influences how society thinks about the relationship between the fetus and its parents.... If technology advances to appoint that every fetus was viable at every stage of development how can society permit abortion? ... Can the concept of viability survive in a world where every fertilized egg can be gestated without the direct involvement of a human being? It seems a short leap from the ability to continue a pregnancy in an artificial womb to the requirement that every unwanted pregnancy must be completed in an artificial womb.... Without pregnancy, would a mother's rights to make decisions about her unborn child still prevail over a father's rights? ... Recent cases about frozen embryo ownership support the idea that a mother or a father may choose for their embryo not to be born. In Davis v. Davis, 84 S.W.2d 588 (1992) the Supreme Court of Tennessee wrote that the man and woman who were the genetic parents of six frozen embryos: "must be seen as entirely equivalent gamete providers." The court concluded "none of the concerns about a woman's bodily integrity that have previously precluded men from controlling abortion decisions is applicable here."

What if the state set some minimum standards of health for a fetus to be allowed access to ectogenesis? Could parents insist, as they can now, that the most hlpelessly impaired child be gestated to birth on the grounds that every life is precious? ... How different is that form the current situation in which some health insurance companies will not pay for genetic screening unless the parents are willing to consider terminating the pregnancy?

6.5 Eugenics

The term "eugenics" was coined in 1883 by Francis Galton, Charles Darwin's cousin. It was not until the first half of the twentieth century, however, that eugenics became a societal policy.

The American Eugenics Society was founded in 1921 during the Second International Conference on Eugenics, held in New York, with its home being in New Haven, Connecticut. Alexander Graham Bell served as its "honorary President." Other leaders, Sir Winston Churchill and George Bernard Shaw were also supporters of the movement. The definition and theme of the Society, taken from that Conference was, "eugenics is the self direction of human evolution." [See "THE SECOND INTERNATIONAL CONGRESS OF EUGENICS: A Conference on the Results of Research in Race Improvement," *Journal of Heredity* 12(5): 219–223 (1921)], (Also see, American Eugenics Society archival records, kept by the American Philosophical Society for the period 1916–1973 at: http://www.amphilsoc.org/library/exhibits/treasures/aes.htm). During the peak of the eugenics movement in the 1920s and 1930s, the American Eugenics Society is most remembered for its eugenic "Fitter Family" contests, where families were divided into small, medium and large categories and competed in moral, physical and mental superiority categories. The AES is also best known for one of its more notorious exhibits, the "flashing light exhibit." This exhibit was titled, "Some people are born to be a burden on the rest," which included a flashing light to demonstrate how infrequently a "high grade" individual was born in the United States with its slow blinking, and another light, blinking rapidly, to show how often a "defective" was born.

(Source: http://www.amphilsoc.org/library/exhibits/treasures/aes.htm)

Federal and state policies in eugenics were also prevalent during the 1920s to the 1970s. The federal government is known for its public health policies of forced sterilizations of African Americans and Native Americans (*see* GAO Report, B-164031(5), November 4, 1975). One of the most well-known state policies was that of the Commonwealth of Virginia, W. A. Plecker of Virginia. Plecker was the state statistician, and the most tireless crusader for white purity with an agenda to classify all people who were not white as African-American, and to fully implement what was known as the "one drop rule" which had existed in Virginia prior to Plecker's appointment. The state regulation was as follows:

> *Va. Code. Ann. §20-54 (1950) (Vol. 4, p. 489) "Intermarriage prohibited; meaning of term 'white person.'—It shall hereafter be unlawful for any white person in this State to marry any save a white person, or a person with no other admixture of blood than white and American Indian. For the purpose of this chapter, the term 'white person' shall apply only to such person as has no trace whatever of any blood other than Caucasian but person who have one-sixteenth or less of the blood of the American Indian and have no other non-Caucasian blood shall be deemed to be white person…."*

In 1924, he became obsessive in this mission to change every vital statistic record in the state from any ethnic designation to "Black", and to re-classify as "Black" any who was classified as "White" who had even "one drop" of non-white blood.

The World War II atrocities of Nazi Germany ended the trajectory of the eugenics movement, highlighting the bizarre extremism of the objectives of eugenics.

Eugenics has been depicted in science fiction in both print and film, beginning with the film *A Brave New World* in 1932, written by Aldus Huxley to the 1997 film *Gattaca*, depicting a society where genetic engineering of the optimum human being was the ideal, and individuals had pre-determined careers and life expectancies.

The rapid advancements in biotechnology, genetic engineering, stem cell research and cloning have all contributed to the return to attention to eugenics and its moral and ethical aspects.

6.6 Stem Cell Research

The embryonic stem cells (ES), unlike the adult stem cells or other cell types, retain the special ability to develop into nearly any cell type. Embryonic germ cells (EG), which originate from the primordial reproductive cells of the developing fetus, have properties similar to ES cells. It is the potentially unique versatility of the ES and EG cells derived, respectively, from the early stage embryo and cadaveric fetal tissue that presents such unusual scientific and therapeutic promise. The possibility of using such cells to generate more specialized cells or tissue, which could allow the generation of new cells to be used to treat injuries or diseases, such as Alzheimer's, Parkinson's, heart, and kidney disease is the promise and hope of this new technology.

6.6.1 The Controversy with Stem Cell Research

The source of much of the controversy over stem cell research is the source of the stem cells. The derivation of stem cells from cadaveric fetal tissue—harvested from dead fetuses—is generally the most accepted. Stem cells derived from embryos are of two types: one is referred to as the research embryo, an embryo created through in vitro fertilization with gametes provided solely for research purposes; the second type of embryo is that which was created for infertility treatment, but is now intended to be discarded because it is unsuitable or no longer needed for such treatment. Finally, human somatic cell nuclei transferred to an oocyte might create an embryo that could be used as a source of ES cells.

The National Bioethics Advisory Commission concluded in their report, *Ethical Issues in Human Stem Cell Research, Executive Summary* (September 1999), that "federal funding for the use and derivation of ES and EG cells should be limited to two sources of such material: cadaveric fetal tissue and embryos remaining after infertility treatments."

The National Bioethics Advisory Committee was appointed by President Clinton to investigate the use of embryo stem cells as part of their mission. The NBAC includes 67 Nobel Laureates and other scientists in many disciplines, including biology, physics and economics. On August 23, 2000, the National Institutes of Health, announced that federal funds would be released for embryo stem cell biotechnological.

However, contradictory language appears in the appropriations bill for 2000:

(a) None of the funds made available in this Act may be used for—(1) the creation of a human embryo or embryos for research purposes; or (2) research in which a human embryo or embryos are destroyed, discarded, or knowingly subjected to risk of injury or death greater than that allowed for research on fetuses in utero under 45 CFR 46.208(a)(2) and section 498(b) of the Public Health Service Act (42 U.S.C. 289g(b)).

(b) For purposes of this section, the term "human embryo or embryos" includes any organism, not protected as a human subject under 45 CFR 46 as of the date of the enactment of this Act, that is derived by fertilization, parthenogenesis, cloning, or any other means from one or more human gametes or human diploid cells.

(Pub.L. No. 106-113, §510, 113 Stat. 1501, 1501A-275 (1999)).

Although the appropriations language casts doubt upon the legality of funding embryo research, the NIH has interpreted the language to permit the use of embryo stem cells in research in specific circumstances. The NIH has determined that embryonic stem cells may be used when:

(1) the cells come from excess embryos derived through in vitro fertilization at feretility clinics, (2) the donors give informed consent, (3) the donors donate the embryos, (4) no embryos are created specifically for research purposes, (5) only private firms harvest the stem cells, (6) the stem cells are not to be used to clone a human being, and (7) they cannot be combined with animal cells to create a hybrid.

See Nelle S. Paegel, *Use of Stem Cells in Biotechnological Research*, 22 WHITTIER LAW REVIEW 1183 (2001).

On August 9, 2001, President Bush made an announcement that federal funds could be used for research on stem cell lines, with limitations on the source of the cell lines. He allowed however, "more than 60 genetically diverse stem cell lines" that were derived from excess embryos before August 9, 2001. Most scientists were surprised by this number, but NIH has identified 64 such lines which meet the President's guidelines, here and abroad. However, only about 25 of these stem cell lines are suitable for stem cell research.

About one month after the announcement by President Bush, the National Academy of Sciences released a report stating that many more cell lines are needed for research than those currently meeting the President's guidelines, and they further endorsed the controversial practice of "therapeutic cloning" (The production of tissue that is genetically matched to that of the patient's tissue.). Other problems include the origin of the current cell lines—they were all developed from mouse cells, creating a problem for use in humans due to mouse viruses and other impurities.

The nonprofit, private company, WiCell has committed to making available cell lines to the research community, since they hold the patent on human embryonic stem cells. They have agreed to provide two vials of cells and technical assistance in cultivating them for $5,000. The memorandum of understanding, signed between the U.S. Public Health Service and WiCell, provides that WiCell will forego the typical "reach-through" rights which is the right to claim patent rights to any new discoveries such as a useful new molecule, that researchers make using the cell lines purchased from WiCell. Interestingly, WiCell has licensed the development of six types of human tissue from WiCell lines to Geron Corporation, a California company, who might object to commercial uses of WiCell. In a related issue, WiCell has challenged Geron's recent move to expand its commercial stem cell work, filing suit in federal district court. *See HHS Inks Cell Deal: NAS Calls for More Lines*, 293 Science 1966 (Sept. 14, 2001).

6.6.2 What Are These Embryonic Stem Cells?

James Thomson derived the first human embryonic stem cell line in November 1998. Just a few days later, John Gearhart of Johns Hopkins University announced that he had developed a stem cell line from the germ cells of aborted fetuses.

Stem cell research includes the use of pluripotent stem cells, which are those cells which do not have the capability to form a complete human being; whereas a totipotent stem cell is capable of forming a complete human being if placed into a uterine environment. *See*, National Institutes of Health, *Stem Cells: A Primer* (2000)). Pluripotent stem cells further differentiate into stem cells having a specific function, becoming multipotent.

The National Institutes of Health issued guidelines for stem cell research, 65 Fed. Reg. 51976 (August 25, 2000) which addresses the use of stem cells. The guideline provide that no federal funds will be used for embryo experimentation, and that research will be limited to the use of pluripotent stem cells, which are broadly defined as those not capable of producing a human being. Specifically, the Department of Health and Human Services General Counsel's opinion defined these pluripotent stem cells as those "that lack the capacity to become organisms if transferred to the uterus, and are not even the precursors to human organisms." Some members of Congress objected to the broadly worded guidance, interpreting the guidance to be limited only to the specific act of destruction of the human embryo and not to research which would precede or follow such destruction. Secretary Shalala verified that this was the meaning of the guidance, and its publication proceeded over this Congressional objection.

6.6.3 Sources of Embryonic Stem Cells

The sources of embryonic stem cells include those cryo-embryonic stem cells which are disposed according to agreement through family law proceedings. Only some states have addressed these issues in legislation or case law. Virginia, Tennessee, New York, Massachusetts, and New Jersey have case law in this area. *See* Paegel, *supra*.

Conflicts over the use of embryonic and fetal tissue from abortions led to the complete ban by the federal government on the use of stem cells other than those from several discrete lines of origin.

6.6.4 State Regulation of Stem Cell Research

California was the first state to establish state funding for stem cell research, after the federal government announced that it would not fund federal research on any but specific lines of stem cells. California voters in 2004, approved a $3 billion dollar finance package to support stem cell research in California. New Jersey and Massachusetts have also passed legislation to support stem cell research in their states, and other states are expected to follow.

Notes

1. The argument is made by Senator Sam Brownback, a Republican from Kansas, that embryonic stem cell research using sources of cells which would normally be disposed is like Nazi experimentation, quoted as saying, "They used that same sort of argument, that they're going to be killed anyway." Sobel, *Miracle Cells? Maybe More Research Dollars, More Ethical Quandaries*, U.S. NEWS AND WORLD REP. Sept. 4, 2000 at 22. Do you think this is a good argument?

2. Should private companies own human stem cell lines?

3. If WiCell succeeds in its limitation of Geron's commercial use of its stem cell lines, will this create a demand for patent law reform?

6.7 Cloning

As part of the work of the National Bioethics Advisory Commission, when they were asked to examine the cloning of human beings, they submitted a report on June 1997. This request came from President Clinton after the Scotland scientists cloned "Dolly" the sheep. The NBAC unanimously concluded that "given the current state of the science, any attempt to create a human being through somatic cell nuclear transfer would be terribly premature and unacceptably dangerous. Besides being morally unacceptable on safety grounds, the creation of human clones would involve risks to the children— and more broadly to society—that are serious enough to merit further reflection and deliberation before this line of research goes forward.... [C]urrent research with other mammals makes clear that any such attempt would produce many horrible outcomes not only for the children but probably also for their mothers."

Further, the NBAC recommended that "Besides being morally unacceptable on safety grounds, the creation of human clones would involve risks to the children—and more broadly to society—that are serious enough to merit further reflection and deliberation before this line of research goes forward."

Letter from Harold T. Shapiro, Chair, National Bioethics Advisory Commission (March 16, 2001).

The National Bioethics Advisory Commission made the recommendation in 1997, that the federal government prohibit somatic cell nuclear transfer to create a child [i.e., cloning] and that more debate on the ethical, social, and legal aspects of cloning would be necessary in the future if safety concerns were ever resolved. However, the Commission cautioned that these matters should be discussed in the event the risks to the fetus and the mother become acceptable. *At* http://bioethics.georgetown.edu/nbac/ (last visited Oct. 7, 2001).

Since the report by the NBAC legislation was introduced in the 105th and 106th Congresses to prohibit human cloning; however, none was enacted. Several scientists have announced their intentions to proceed with human cloning. "While it is difficult to evaluate the credibility of announced plans for such cloning, they must be taken seriously, especially when they involve researchers who have previously performed other advanced forms of reproductive experiments," cautioned the NBAC in their final letter to The President, March 16, 2001.

Congress was also confronted in 1999 with the world-shaking news of the cloning of "Dolly" the sheep. This was a call for Congress to respond to the spectre of cloning humans with an immediate prohibition against such activities, as well as advising other countries of the world to do likewise.

The text of this bill is as follows:

106th Congress,1st Session, U. S. House of Representatives,

HR 2326

HUMAN CLONING RESEARCH PROHIBITION ACT

Human Cloning Research Prohibition Act—Prohibits the expenditure of Federal funds to conduct or support any research on the cloning of humans. Directs the Director of the National Science Foundation to enter into an agreement with the National Research Council for a review of the implementation of this Act. Mandates a report to the Congress containing the results of that review, including the conclusions of the National Research Council on: (1) the impact that the implementation of this Act has had on research; and (2) recommendations for any appropriate changes to this Act. States that nothing in this Act shall restrict other areas of scientific research not specifically prohibited by this Act, including important and promising work that involves: (1) the use of somatic cell nuclear transfer or other cloning technologies to clone molecules, DNA, cells other than human embryo cells, or tissues; or (2) the use of somatic cell nuclear transfer techniques to create animals other than humans. Expresses the sense of the Congress that other countries should establish substantially equivalent prohibitions.

Since the first bill was introduced, a human cloning prohibition bill has been introduced in successive congressional session, without success. The following bills have been introduced:

H.R. 2505, 107th Cong., 1st Sess., a bill was introduced entitled the Human Cloning Prohibition Act of 2001. It was engrossed in the House, and sent to the U.S. Senate where it died.

H.R. 534, 108th Congress, 1st Sess., a bill was introduced entitled, the Human Cloning Prohibition Act of 2003. It was engrossed in the House and sent to the U.S. Senate where it died.

H.R.222, 109th Cong., 1st Sess., a bill has been introduced to prohibit the expenditure of Federal funds to conduct or support research on the cloning of humans, and to express the sense of the Congress that other countries should establish substantially equivalent restrictions.

6.8 The Ethics of Contamination of Indigenous Crops with Genetically Modified Crops

The use of genetically modified crops involves risk of cross-pollination with other species where pollen will reach them through the wind or be carried by insects. The threat to wild rice in Minnesota from the development of GMO rice at nearby University of Minnesota is described from an indigenous perspective in the following article.

Winona LaDuke, *Wild Rice and Ethics*, 28.3 CULTURAL SURVIVAL QUARTERLY (Sept. 15, 2004).

September 15, 2004

For the past five years, the Anishinaabeg community of Minnesota has asked the University of Minnesota to stop its genetic work on wild rice. "We object to the exploitation of our wild rice for pecuniary gain," wrote then Minnesota Chippewa Tribal President Norman Deschampe to the University of Minnesota in an 1998 letter. "The genetic variants of wild rice found naturally occurring on the waters in territories ceded by the Minnesota Chippewa Tribe to the state of Minnesota are a unique treasure that has been carefully protected by the people of our tribe for centuries. Rights to the rice have been the subject of treaty and it is a resource that enjoys federal trust protection.... We are of the opinion that the wild rice rights assured by treaty accrue not only to individual grains of rice, but to the very essence of the resource. We were not promised just any wild rice; that promise could be kept by delivering sacks of grain to our members each year. We were promised the rice that grew in the waters of our people, and all the value that rice holds ... a sacred and significant place in our culture."

Virtually every tribal government and Native organization in the region has repeatedly called on the University to stop genetic work on wild rice. Finally, after attorneys for the Ojibwe filed a set of Freedom of Information Act requests, Dean Charles Muscoplat at the University of Minnesota began a "dialogue." The research in contention, however, continues unabated.

100 Years of Disagreement

"Academic Freedom" sometimes collides with ethics. In the new millennium, America expects both, and that is somewhat of a challenge.

About 100 years ago the University of Minnesota dispatched its first anthropologists to the reservations in the north. Albert Jenks came, along with his colleague from the Smithsonian Institute, Ales Hrdlicka, a physical anthropologist who specialized in comparing indigenous peoples' heads to monkey heads. The two came to White Earth Reservation and other reservations with scapulars in hand, and measured the heads of the Anishinaabeg. It turns out that Jenks not only measured Anishinaabeg heads, but returned later to study wild rice. In *The Wild Rice Gatherers of the Upper Lakes*, published by the Smithsonian Institution in 1900, Jenks noted with disdain the Ojibwe harvesting practices: "Wild rice, which had led to their advance thus far, held them back from further progress, unless, indeed, they left it behind them, for with them it was incapable of extensive cultivation."

In short, Jenks surmised that Ojibwe production systems were inadequate. This assumption would become the prevailing thought at the University of Minnesota throughout the 20th century. In the 1950s, University of Minnesota researchers decided that it was time to correct the laziness and created a new domesticated crop for the state: paddy-grown wild rice.

Ervin Oelke, another researcher at the University of Minnesota, began domesticating wild rice, using germplasm from 24 natural stands from throughout the state for most of his studies. The Ojibwe would contend that those natural stands belonged to them. Absent any tribal consent, Oelke and his researchers continued with their domestication. The impact of their work was fully realized with market analysis: the wholesale wild rice price dropped $4.44 per pound in 1967 to $2.68 per pound in 1976.Wild Rice and Science

The International Wild Rice Association met in the basement of the Eldorado Casino in Reno, Nevada, in February 2003. Invited to discuss some of the concerns tribal nations have with the wild rice industry, I listened to University of Minnesota Extension Agent Raymond Porter present on the issues of agronomy and research. He also sought to dispel some of the criticism levied at the university by tribal representatives. Suggesting that the criticisms have been based, in part, on "misunderstanding and faulty conclusions," Raymond suggested that most of the issues raised by the tribes have been addressed by research and a number have been cleared up. Porter's essential argument was that the more the Native community understands about modern science and plant genomics, the more it will be happy with the research.

Porter's turf is the heart of Minnesota's cultivated wild rice research: an agricultural extension and experiment station in Grand Rapids, Minnesota. In 1963, the Bureau of Indian Affairs (keeping with Jenk's improved productivity strategy) provided funds to the station to begin work on wild rice. Subsequent funding increased beginning in 1964 and kept rising, with $100,000 a year allocated to wild rice research. By the 1990s, that amount increased even more. The U.S. Department of Agriculture awarded Porter a $237,171 grant for wild rice breeding and germplasm improvement, and other grants have continued to support the research.

Over years of research, the Minnesota Agricultural Extension office has created several strains of wild rice: 1968 Johnson, 1970 Ml, 1972 M2, 1974 M3, 1978 Netum, 1983 Voyager, 1986 Meter, 1992 Franklin, and 2000 Petrowske Purple, all borne from the hands of University of Minnesota researchers. Are the varieties developed by the University of Minnesota researchers possibly contaminating the wild rice stands of the Anishinaabeg? Put it this way: there are around 6,000 bodies of water with significant wild rice beds in Minnesota, or around 60,000 acres of rice. And there are around 20,000 acres of cultivated wild rice paddies within close proximity of the many lakes of northern Minnesota.

Pollen Drift and the Ducks

Anishinaabeg have long contended that paddy rice stands are contaminating the natural lake stands. Ronald Phillips, regents professor and McKnight Presidential Chair in Genomics at the University of Minnesota, claims there is little chance of cross pollination as long as approximately 660 feet separate the two kinds of wild rice. But research by the university extension office appears to be in keeping with criticism leveled at the university by the Ojibwe. In the summer of 2002, wild rice researchers studied possible pollen drift from paddy rice stands into wild stands. After a lot of different mathematical formulas, the bottom line is that there is a possibility that between one and five percent of the pollen from the test plots drifted up to two miles, and maybe further. Then there is the problem of the *zhishiibig*—the ducks. There have been no systematic studies simulating duck and waterfowl movement in the wild rice area. Ducks and wild rice are a part of traditional Anishinaabeg stories, and likely will be in the future. Ducks and waterfowl do not differentiate between paddy rice plots and natural stands of wild rice; they move freely between both areas, carrying the rice from one into the other.

Wild Rice's Green Revolution

In the 1960s, paddy wild rice became a crop in Minnesota. Its production grew greatly in the 1970s, and Minnesota declared it the State Grain. Shortly thereafter, most people decided that to be in the wild rice industry, they needed to move to California, where they wouldn't have to contend with hail, wind, a fickle water supply, or inclement weather. By 1983, California was producing 8.5 million pounds, to Minnesota's 5 million pounds. In 2002 California produced 18 million pounds of paddy rice, while Minnesota's supply remained constant.

One would think that this quick shift to California would spell the end of the University of Minnesota's interest in the domesticated wild rice industry. But during the last five years the university has spent at least $1 million on its wild rice research programs—not including the budgets for their large wild rice breeding and genetics projects. This money, which comes mostly from the USDA, has been spent to benefit 20 paddy rice farmers, while Minnesota's 50,000 Indian people have been pushed aside once again.

Moving Forward

The Manoomin Ogitchidaag Coalition is composed of representatives from most of the Anishinaabeg bands in the region. In September 2003, the coalition made clear its demands to the University of Minnesota in a letter to Muscoplat's office: "a moratorium on genomic research and genetic research of wild rice at the University of Minnesota, to be effective December 31, 2004; protection of Anishinaabeg Intellectual Property Rights to Wild rice, including a ban on selling these rights; a cultural consultation program to be set in place by the University to examine the ethics of research on cross cultural issues; and mutually agreed upon beneficial research to be done on behalf of Anishinaabeg people, equal to that done on behalf of the cultivated wild rice industry." The university has yet to address these concerns.

One hundred years have passed since the head-measuring doctors came to the Anishinaabeg community. Academic freedom standards at that time may have been a bit lax, but the Anishinaabeg are concerned that the standards have not changed. Universities need to start recognizing that there is academic responsibility that goes along with their academic freedom. University of Minnesota researchers have stated that they will not genetically modify wild rice, which is a first step in guiding its research in the right direction. But there is much work to be done. The Anishinaabeg community is hopeful that the University of Minnesota will bring ethics into its relationships with indigenous people and others in the new millennium, so that we may stop the destructive patterns of research, and work toward a positive future for all of our children.

Winona LaDuke is founding director of the White Earth Land Recovery Project in Minnesota and program director of the Honor the Earth Fund.

Chapter Seven

Criminal Law
and Biotechnology

7.1 Existing Federal Crimes Applicable to New Problems in Biotechnology

7.1.1 Mail Fraud

The use of mail fraud and wire fraud to prosecute criminal actions involving biotechnology issues are applicable for a broad range of issues, absent specific legislation to address specific biotechnology problems. The mail, wire, radio and television fraud statute reads as follows:

TITLE 18. CRIMES AND CRIMINAL PROCEDURE

PART I. CRIMES

CHAPTER 63. MAIL FRAUD

18 USCS §§ 1343 (2001) §§ 1343. Fraud by wire, radio, or television

Whoever, having devised or intending to devise any scheme or artifice to defraud, or for obtaining money or property by means of false or fraudulent pretenses, representations, or promises, transmits or causes to be transmitted by means of wire, radio, or television communication in interstate or foreign commerce, any writings, signs, signals, pictures, or sounds for the purpose of executing such scheme or artifice, shall be fined under this title or imprisoned not more than five years, or both. If the violation affects a financial institution, such person shall be fined not more than $ 1,000,000 or imprisoned not more than 30 years, or both.

United States v. Greene
99-10020, 2000 U.S. App. LEXIS 33925 (9th Cir. 2000)

The government produced the following evidence at trial: (1) Greene represented that the test was FDA approved; (2) the test was not FDA approved; (3) Greene represented that the blood samples were scientifically tested in a laboratory; (4) Greene did not have a laboratory and there was no record of him sending the samples to a laboratory; (5) Greene told his employee that he could determine whether a person was HIV positive by visually looking at the color of the blood on the receptacle; (6) it is not scientifically possible to determine HIV status from the color of blood on a band-aid like strip; and (7) Greene took orders for his test on the internet and accepted checks for payment through the mail. Based on this evidence a reasonable trier of fact could conclude that Greene had the intent to defraud and used the mail and wires to carry out his scheme.

AFFIRMED.

7.1.2 The Great Train Robbery in Biotechnology

The following article reveals the competitiveness of the industry. Justin Gillis, *20 Years Later, Stolen Gene Haunts a Biotech Pioneer* WASHINGTON POST, May 17, 1999 at A01.

> SAN FRANCISCO —— The men with foreign accents trod carefully through desolate hallways. They weren't supposed to be there, but the University of California at San Francisco had something they wanted, and they knew just where to find it.
>
> It was an hour before midnight on New Year's Eve and nobody was around to see the deed unfold. The men took the elevator to a ninth-floor laboratory. They retrieved vials and beakers, hauled the material downstairs, put it in their car and raced south toward the offices of a tiny new company not far from the azure waters of San Francisco Bay.
>
> A police officer pulled them over as they got to the doors of that company, Genentech Inc. They waved their employee badges and got past him. By the time the clock struck midnight on that evening two decades ago, Genentech's laboratory was freshly stocked with genetic material from the university.
>
> A few months later Genentech announced it had pulled off one of the most dazzling feats of modern science—inserting human genes into harmless germs and getting them to produce a precious and much-needed substance, human growth hormone. Genentech was the first biotechnology company, founder of an industry, and this feat more than any other demonstrated the potential of the new science. Yet if testimony unfolding in federal court here is true, that early milestone was tainted from the outset and the biotechnology industry was born amid thievery and scientific fraud.
>
> The university is suing Genentech for patent infringement in a case that has taken nine years to come to trial. In a coup, the university's lawyers persuaded one of the scientists involved in the "midnight raid"—Peter Seeburg, one of the world's most eminent molecular biologists—to testify on their behalf.
>
> Not only did he and a colleague swipe material from the university, Seeburg testified, but Genentech later used that material to achieve its big breakthrough while pretending in scientific presentations and patent applications to have done the work on its own.
>
> "It was dishonest," Seeburg said recently on the witness stand. "I regret it, but that's the way we did it 20 years ago. I really am sorry."

No one is bothering to contest that material was lifted from the university in a New Year's Eve raid. Genentech does deny making use of that material, however, claiming its scientists, Seeburg among them, independently isolated the gene for human growth hormone.

Seeburg's account, backed by the testimony of colleagues and a pile of circumstantial evidence, is that Genentech tried to do that and failed, then resorted to using a purloined gene from the university's stocks.

Given the importance of this early achievement in spurring the growth of an industry now poised, 20 years later, to transform the worlds of medicine and agriculture, Seeburg has outlined what amounts to a scientific version of original sin.

Seeburg's account is flatly denied by another eminent scientist, David V. Goeddel, chief executive of Tularik Inc. Goeddel worked with Seeburg at Genentech, served as chief scientist on the growth-hormone project, and still is closely allied with his former employer. His account, too, is backed by the testimony of former colleagues.

Thanks mostly to his pioneering work at Genentech, Goeddel was elected to the National Academy of Sciences, an honor roll of the nation's brightest researchers, becoming the first biotechnologist so honored. When he was inducted in 1995, the academy said his early experiments, including those with growth hormone, "revolutionized protein therapeutics and ushered in the age of biotechnology and molecular medicine."

According to Seeburg, he and Goeddel made a secret pact two decades ago never to tell anyone outside Genentech about using the stolen genes in their research, a pact Seeburg now has broken in the courtroom.

According to Goeddel, Seeburg is fantasizing. "I think after I figured out it wasn't just a quick practical joke," Goeddel said on the witness stand, "I couldn't believe that he could come up with such a story."

Courtroom Showdown

The events of two decades ago are coming to light in a case in federal court here. The university, which owns a patent for its work on growth hormone, is suing Genentech, claiming that company's product infringes on the university's discovery.

That discovery—the precise order of genetic building blocks for human growth hormone—was made by none other than Peter Seeburg himself, while he was a university researcher. By leaving the university in late 1978 to join Genentech, he gave up rights to his materials. But by his own account, he went back and retrieved them in the midnight raid and handed them over to Genentech.

Genentech fought for years to keep the case, filed in 1990, from coming to trial. But U.S. District Judge Charles A. Legge pushed forward. A jury of nine Californians has been hearing arguments and testimony since April 13. The case could wrap up as early as this week.

The stakes are enormous. The university has claimed damages of $400 million, and if the jury finds that Genentech willfully infringed the university's patent, the judge could triple that amount to as much as $1.2 billion. That would be nearly seven times Genentech's 1998 earnings of $182 million. If everything were to go against Genentech, the case could conceivably cripple the company.

On top of that, testimony coming out in the case has cast serious doubt on important sections of a key paper in Nature, the world's leading scientific journal, and on eight Genentech patents. Applications for those patents were submitted under oath to the U.S. patent office by, among other scientists, David Goeddel.

The outcome of the case is far from certain. It turns on the complex details of patent law. Even if the jury finds Seeburg credible—and Genentech's attorneys argue that he has motives to lie, money among them—it could well decide that his testimony is of no legal relevance.

Conversely, the university's lawyers have suggested that Goeddel's continuing ties to Genentech give him a motive to lie, too. Genentech's founder is chairman of Goeddel's new company, among other links. And Goeddel's reputation as a scientist is on the line.

In the courtroom, Goeddel has labored to explain why his meticulous laboratory notebooks grow vague at a crucial point in the growth-hormone research. That happens to be the very point at which Seeburg says theft was committed.

Genentech has admitted in court that work Goeddel described at length in Nature and in his patent applications was never performed. Goeddel claimed on the witness stand that it was performed, but acknowledged he could not back that up with written evidence.

However the case turns out, it's clear that some strange goings-on happened by the waters of San Francisco Bay at the dawn of a modern scientific revolution.

Commercial Possibilities

The world of biology entered a state of turmoil in the mid-1970s. Scientists were closing in on new techniques for manipulating deoxyribonucleic acid, or DNA, the substance the regulates all life. They were learning to slice and dice DNA at will and to stick genes from one organism into others.

This "recombinant DNA" technology offered breathtaking possibilities, including potentially unlimited supplies of substances important to human health.

Nowhere was the ferment greater than in the first-rate universities scattered around San Francisco Bay. The heart of the action was the University of California at San Francisco, a huge teaching hospital and research institution where a biologist named Herbert Boyer had pioneered genetic techniques. A venture capitalist, Robert Swanson, saw the commercial potential of the new technology and convinced Boyer to join him in 1976 in founding a new company in South San Francisco. They named it Genentech.

At the time, there wasn't much precedent for doing biology of that sort in commercial settings, and many of the most talented scientists stayed at university laboratories. These included a group of young hotshots who had been lured to San Francisco from as far away as Germany and Australia to work on the new biology.

One of those men was Peter Seeburg, a German who worked in a lab at UCSF. In early 1978, he and several colleagues pulled off a huge coup. They isolated the gene for human growth hormone, the substance that turns children into adults and that, at lower levels, remains vital to the body's functioning throughout life. They also published the complete genetic sequence—in effect, a sketchy recipe—for this substance.

Up until then, human growth hormone could be made for use as a drug only by extracting it from the pituitary glands of dead people. There wasn't enough to treat all the children suffering from dwarfism, much less to try it for other ailments. And the product was prone to contamination by germs.

Seeburg's coup offered another possibility: The chance that the gene for human growth hormone could be inserted into harmless bacteria, tricking them into making huge supplies of the stuff. People at Genentech were working on doing this for small proteins like insulin, needed by diabetics, but nobody had yet tackled a protein as large and complex as human growth hormone.

The importance of Seeburg's work was not lost on the people at Genentech. They began recruiting him heavily. He hesitated, but finally left the university and joined the company in late 1978. Under an agreement he had signed when he joined UCSF, all rights to his prior research remained with the university. Indeed, UCSF had already applied for a patent on the growth-hormone work.

By Seeburg's account, a series of frustrations attended his first months at Genentech. All attempts to duplicate the UCSF work—in effect, to re-isolate and re-sequence the growth hormone gene—ended in failure, he said. The technology at the time was finicky at best, and according to court testimony and documents, Genentech's scientists couldn't get it to work.

On top of this, Seeburg by his own account had developed a serious addiction to cocaine and liquor. Goeddel was brought into the project, some witnesses testified, in part because Seeburg was dysfunctional much of the time. "I wasn't in top form," Seeburg testified.

Midnight Raid on New Year's Eve

Genentech was then a young, thinly capitalized company, and a Swedish firm with an interest in growth hormone was paying for much of its research. Deadlines loomed—unless it made progress, the university's lawyers have argued, Genentech faced the threat of losing funds.

It was in this environment, Seeburg testified, that he decided to go back to UCSF with a colleague, Axel Ullrich, on New Year's Eve and retrieve samples of his growth-hormone gene and other materials. Thus occurred the midnight raid.

Seeburg apparently intended to hold his materials in reserve, hoping not to have to use them. But through the early months of 1979, according to testimony and laboratory notebooks, Goeddel, Seeburg and their Genentech colleagues kept running into roadblocks in their efforts to isolate the gene for growth hormone.

At the end of their rope, Seeburg testified, he and Goeddel secretly agreed to use the gene from the university's stocks and never tell anyone. According to Seeburg, they pretended to isolate a new version of the gene at Genentech, gave it a new name and put together a chart showing the order of genetic units— the sequence—of the gene. In reality, Seeburg testified, they were using the university's material and copying work he already had done a year earlier at the UCSF lab.

It is here that Goeddel's account differs markedly from Seeburg's. Far from using purloined material, he said, he and his colleagues managed to isolate their own version of the gene from human pituitary tissue, and then they unraveled the genetic sequence.

Genentech pointed in the courtroom to some references in laboratory notebooks as supporting Goeddel's claim about isolating the gene, but these were cryptic and their meaning much disputed. The second step, determining the exact sequence of the gene, has become a particular bone of contention, since no record of it can be found in any Genentech laboratory notebook. This is striking, given that this step was reported in detail in Nature and in many Genentech patents over the years. Genentech has admitted in court that the sequencing work was never done, though Goeddel has continued to dispute the point.

However they got the gene, Goeddel, Seeburg and their colleagues subsequently managed to insert it into a sort of genetic container, stuck it into the bacterium Escherichia coli, and induced that germ to produce large quantities of human growth hormone.

These were by no means trivial steps. They had never been done before for such a complex gene. The researchers' triumph complete, they reported their success to the world on Oct. 18, 1979, in the pages of Nature.

That paper proved the new biology could achieve its most ambitious goals in a commercial setting. More than any single piece of research, it can be said to have launched the biotechnology revolution now sweeping the world.

Bitter Battle Over a Breakthrough

As this work was unfolding, university officials got word of the midnight raid. They began to suspect Genentech was making unauthorized use of their property. Acrimonious negotiations ensued. Eventually, Genentech paid the university $2 million to make the theft accusations go away.

But that deal explicitly excluded any patent royalties the university might be due if Genentech turned growth hormone into a commercial product. In 1985 the Food and Drug Administration approved Protropin, Genentech's formulation of growth hormone, for sale in the United States. As time passed, the drug turned into a blockbuster and it became clearer that the university had missed out on significant royalties.

The university sued in 1990 and the case turned into a blood feud. Proud of their role in creating a new industry, Genentech's scientists did not take well to the suggestion they did it by thievery and fraud.

At Genentech's request, the case was moved from San Francisco to Indianapolis. The university eventually got it moved back to San Francisco. The combatants appealed various rulings to higher courts on at least four occasions. Legal bills in the case are conservatively estimated to exceed $20 million. A law firm working for the university has dedicated an entire floor of a downtown San Francisco office building to maintaining records in the case.

Perhaps the biggest coup for Gerald P. Dodson, the aggressive litigator heading up the university's legal team, was to convince Seeburg to testify on the school's behalf. Seeburg, now an accomplished researcher in Germany, explained that he had made mistakes in his youth and could not continue lying about them.

Genentech's attorneys have given no quarter. They pointed out that Seeburg stands to benefit if the university wins patent royalties from Genentech—as an inventor on the UCSF patent, he would be entitled to somewhat less than 10 percent of the total, potentially a large sum. Seeburg also was forced to acknowledge that he had shaded the truth about growth hormone in various sworn statements over the years, but insisted he is telling the truth now.

In principle, the university does not need to prove a direct theft of materials to prove a patent violation. It may be enough to show that university researchers came up with a fundamental idea—namely, the genetic sequence for growth hormone—and that Genentech swiped it.

Genentech doesn't deny that Seeburg made important breakthroughs while at UCSF, but claims it did so much additional, creative work to turn growth hormone into a commercial product that there was no patent violation.

If the university were to prove a violation, however, the theft of materials could then become a crucial exhibit. The judge and jury would have to decide whether the violation was willful, meriting triple damages.

In that event, a surreptitious raid on the university's laboratories late on a New Year's Eve might have some bearing on their judgment.

The Dawn of the Biotech Era

Genentech Inc. was founded in 1976 to take advantage of new genetic techniques developed in university laboratories. It was the first biotechnology company and its success spurred the creation of an industry. One of the company's earliest achievements was the development of Protropin, or human growth hormone. Now Genentech is in court defending itself from charges that it stole that invention from the University of California at San Francisco.

1976: Herbert Boyer, a UCSF researcher and pioneer in genetic techniques, founds Genentech with Robert Swanson, a venture capitalist.

Early 1978: Peter Seeburg, another researcher, and colleagues isolate the gene for human growth hormone and determine the sequence of its biochemical units. UCSF files for a patent. Genentech recruits him later that year.

Dec. 31, 1978: Seeburg and a colleague go back to UCSF in a "midnight raid" and remove genetic material.

1979: Genentech announces it has isolated the gene for growth hormone, inserted the gene into bacteria and made the germs produce the human protein.

1980: Genentech sells stock to the public, raising $35 million.

1982: A bioengineered version of human insulin, created by Genentech and sold by Eli Lilly and Co., goes on sale.

1985: Genentech receives U.S. Food and Drug Administration approval to sell Protropin, the first genetically engineered drug to be manufactured and marketed by a biotech company.

1990: UCSF files a patent infringement suit against Genentech.

1999: Genentech pays $50 million to settle federal charges it inappropriately marketed Protropin. Patent-infringement suit goes to trial.

SOURCE: Genentech company reports; court documents

7.2 The Use of DNA in Criminal Law

The use of DNA evidence in criminal cases began in 1987 with the development of the Jeffrey's scientific finding of DNA distinctions. In 1988, Timothy Spencer was tried for a gruesome murder in Virginia and convicted, in part, based upon the use of DNA evidence which connected him to the criminal acts to the victim. In 1993, Spencer became to the first person to be given the death penalty based upon DNA evidence. In the review of the challenge to the use of DNA evidence against Spencer, the Court delivered the following opinion:

Spencer v. Murray
5 F.3d 758 (E.D. Va. 1993)

On appeal, Spencer raises essentially five issues: (1) the DNA evidence in this case is unreliable; (2) defense counsel was denied an opportunity to adequately defend against the DNA evidence because the trial court denied a discovery request for Lifecodes' worknotes and memoranda, the trial court refused to provide funds for an expert defense witness, and the prosecution did not reveal evidence of problems with Lifecodes' testing methods; (3) the trial court should not have admitted the DNA evidence; (4) the prosecution improperly struck Miss Chrita Shelton from the jury for racially-motivated reasons as prohibited by Batson v. Kentucky; and (5) the future dangerousness aggravating factor in Virginia's capital sentencing scheme is unconstitutionally vague....

III Admissibility of the DNA Evidence

Spencer's first claim that we consider is whether Spencer was denied due process of law because the trial court improperly admitted the results of the DNA testing. It has been settled in this circuit for years that a claim about the admissibility of evidence under state law rarely is a claim upon which federal habeas corpus relief can be granted. In 1960 we decided:

Normally, the admissibility of evidence, the sufficiency of evidence, and instructions to the jury in state trials are matters of state law and procedure not involving federal constitutional issues. It is only in circumstances impugning fundamental fairness or infringing specific constitutional protections that a federal question is presented. The role of a federal habeas corpus petition is not to serve as an additional appeal.

The Supreme Court recently issued a similar holding in Estelle v. McGuire, 116 L. Ed. 2d 385, 60 U.S.L.W. 4015, 112 S. Ct. 475 (U.S. 1991). In McGuire, the Supreme Court was confronted with a ruling under California law that allowed prosecutors to introduce evidence of prior injuries to a child to prove "battered child syndrome" in the context of a murder trial. The Court of Appeals held that the defendant's due process rights were violated in part because the court concluded that the evidence was improperly admitted under state law. The Supreme Court stated that "such an inquiry" into the application of state evidence law is no part of a federal court's habeas review of a state conviction. We have stated many times that federal habeas corpus relief does not lie for errors of state law. Today we reemphasize that it is not the province of a federal habeas court to reexamine state court determinations on state law questions. In conducting habeas review, a federal court is limited to deciding whether a conviction violated the Constitution, laws, or treaties of the United States.

In light of the Supreme Court's directive and our own precedent on this subject, we are of opinion that the admission of the DNA test results into evidence did not create "circumstances impugning fundamental fairness or infringing specific constitutional protections." The errors Spencer argues might have occurred with his DNA test, see infra, note 5, are not even remotely suggested by the record in this case. The admissibility of the DNA evidence was contested at trial despite the fact that the defense could find no expert witnesses to assist it. On direct review the Virginia Supreme Court applied the Virginia admissibility test of O'Dell v. Commonwealth, 234 Va. 672, 364 S.E.2d 491 (Va.), cert. denied, 488 U.S. 977 (1988), and specifically found DNA evidence in general and in this case in particular to be admissible. After reviewing the trial record, the Court noted:

> The record is replete with uncontradicted expert testimony that no "dissent whatsoever [exists] in the scientific community" concerning the reliability of the DNA printing technique. Unrebutted expert testimony further established that the testing procedure performed in this case was conducted in a reliable manner.

Further, the New York trial court case of People v. Castro, 144 Misc. 2d 956, 545 N.Y.S.2d 985 (N.Y. Sup. Ct. Bronx County 1989), on which Spencer relies for its argument that DNA tests performed by Lifecodes are inherently suspect does not support that proposition and also is decided under New York law. The errors in Castro—contaminated DNA probes, bacterially contaminated samples, and procedures used in that particular test—do not appear in the record of Spencer's case.

After a review of the record with respect to the admissibility of the DNA evidence, which includes 150 pages on the motion to prohibit the introduction of the evidence, consisting largely of expert testimony, and 230 pages at trial, again consisting largely of expert testimony, the state Supreme Court affirmed the trial court's holding that the evidence was admissible under the test in O'Dell, that the test was reliable. After a review of the same record, we think the decisions of the state courts are not only free from constitutional error under the due process clause, no error at all has come to our attention. Three expert witnesses from Lifecodes, including the people who performed the tests, testified, as did three independent experts not connected with Lifecodes. The gist of all of their testimony was that the tests were reliable and properly performed, and that the DNA evidence showed Spencer to have been the man whose seminal fluid was found in Miss Davis's bed. With the district court, we see nothing improper or fraudulent about the DNA test results or any evidence of improper procedures in this case.

We are of opinion the DNA evidence was constitutionally admitted, and so hold.

———

Chapter Eight, Scientific Evidence and Biotechnology, *infra*, addresses the area of DNA in a variety of cases in addition to its use in criminal law.

7.3 New Federal Statutes for New Problems in Biotechnology

TITLE 18. CRIMES AND CRIMINAL PROCEDURE

PART I. CRIMES

CHAPTER 113B. TERRORISM

18 USCS §§ 2332a (2001)

§§ 2332a. Use of certain weapons of mass destruction

(a) Offense against a national of the United States or within the United States. A person who, without lawful authority, uses, threatens, or attempts or conspires to use, a weapon of mass destruction (other than a chemical weapon as that term is defined in section 229F), including any biological agent, toxin, or vector (as those terms are defined in section 178)—

(1) against a national of the United States while such national is outside of the United States;

(2) against any person within the United States, and the results of such use affect interstate or foreign commerce or, in the case of a threat, attempt, or conspiracy, would have affected interstate or foreign commerce; or

(3) against any property that is owned, leased or used by the United States or by any department or agency of the United States, whether the property is within or outside of the United States, shall be imprisoned for any term of years or for life, and if death results, shall be punished by death or imprisoned for any term of years or for life.

(b) Offense by national of the United State outside of the United States. Any national of the United States who, without lawful authority, uses, or threatens, attempts, or conspires to use, a weapon of mass destruction (other than a chemical weapon (as that term is defined in section 229F)) outside of the United States shall be imprisoned for any term of years or for life, and if death results, shall be punished by death, or by imprisonment for any term of years or for life.

(c) Definitions. For purposes of this section—

(1) the term "national of the United States" has the meaning given in section 101(a)(22) of the Immigration and Nationality Act (8 U.S.C. 1101(a)(22)); and

(2) the term "weapon of mass destruction" means—

(A) any destructive device as defined in section 921 of this title;

(B) any weapon that is designed or intended to cause death or serious bodily injury through the release, dissemination, or impact of toxic or poisonous chemicals, or their precursors;

(C) any weapon involving a disease organism; or

(D) any weapon that is designed to release radiation or radioactivity at a level dangerous to human life.

Biological Weapons Anti-Terrorism Act of 1989.

CRIMES AND CRIMINAL PROCEDURE

PART I. CRIMES

CHAPTER 10. BIOLOGICAL WEAPONS

18 USCS §§ 175 (2001)

§§ 175. Prohibitions with respect to biological weapons

(a) In general. Whoever knowingly develops, produces, stockpiles, transfers, acquires, retains, or possesses any biological agent, toxin, or delivery system for use as a weapon, or knowingly assists a foreign state or any organization to do so, or attempts, threatens, or conpsires to do the same, shall be fined under this title or imprisoned for life or any term of years, or both. There is extraterritorial Federal jurisdiction over an offense under this section committed by or against a national of the United States.

(b) Definition. For purposes of this section, the term "for use as a weapon" does not include the development, production, transfer, acquisition, retention, or possession of any biological agent, toxin, or delivery system for prophylactic, protective, or other peaceful purposes.

United States v. Wise
221 F.3d 140 (5th Cir. 2000)

Defendants-appellants Johnie Wise ("Wise") and Jack Abbott Grebe, Jr. ("Grebe") appeal the judgment of criminal conviction entered on 5 February 1999, in the United States District Court for the Southern District of Texas, Brownsville Division. Appellants argue that a number of errors occurred with regard to the trial, as a result of which this Court should find the evidence insufficient to sustain their conviction or, alternatively, reverse and remand for a new trial. We AFFIRM the judgment and the district court in all respects.

Wise discussed the idea of using pathogenic agents for diseases. Wise briefly described to Cain his proposal to convert an everyday Bic (R) lighter into a dart gun device from which a cactus thorn coated with some type of slow-acting poison or biological agent could be shot at unsuspecting persons. Agent Church told Cain that it was not against the law to voice one's thoughts in such a manner. But he also told Cain to listen carefully to what Wise and Grebe say when they next call him and to ask specific questions, if Cain was comfortable doing so, regarding the proposed dart gun device.

Grebe raised the notion of taking the next step, namely sending the follow-up letter to the Declaration of War. Moreover, both Wise and Grebe discussed who should be the first targeted victim, and they chose a Texas state judge whom Roberts purportedly disliked because she had not allowed ROT members to defend themselves pro se in her Texas state court. They planned to stalk her, learn her movements, and attack at the right moment. Wise suggested the use of rabies or botulism toxins for the delivery device and discussed ways to make botulism. Wise told the others that he already had purchased the parts to convert the Bic (R) lighters into delivery devices. After that meeting, Cain immediately called Agent Sharkey, who in turn advised Cain that the situation had become more serious now that a particular person was targeted.

According to the plan, Wise was to procure the biological agent and to build the delivery device. Wise discussed the possibility of using such agents as botulism, rabies, and anthrax. According to Cain, Wise and Grebe urged Cain to send the Declaration of War e-mail because they thought he was taking too long to do so.

The second letter reads:

Dear Mr. Rossotti,

Your IRS employees and their families have been targeted for destruction by revenge. These people are extremely mad and will not accept the inequities any longer. Nontraceable, personal delivery systems have been developed to inject bacteria and/or viruses for the purpose of killing, maiming, and causing great suffering. Warn all concerned so that they may protect themselves and be made aware of this threat to themselves and their families. Good luck!

3. Interstate Commerce Element

The third issue raised is whether the district court abused its discretion in refusing to charge the jury that the offense must have "substantially affected" interstate commerce. The district court gave the following jury instruction, in relevant part:

Title 18, United States Code, Section 2332a makes it a crime for anyone to threaten to use a weapon of mass destruction against any person within the United States and results of such use would have affected interstate or foreign commerce.

For you to find the Defendant guilty of this crime, you must be convinced that the government has proved each of the following beyond a reasonable doubt:

First: That the defendant intentionally and knowingly threatened to use a weapon or weapons of mass destruction;

Second: That the weapon or weapons of mass destruction were threatened to be used against persons within the United States as specifically alleged in Counts 2–8;

Third: That the results of such use would have affected interstate or foreign commerce.

(18 R., Attach. at 29–30.) In essence, Appellants argue that the district court erred in refusing to instruct the jury that a violation of 18 U.S.C. §§ 2332a(a) requires a finding by them of a substantial effect on interstate commerce.

Section 2332a(a) provides in relevant part:

> A person who, without lawful authority, uses, threatens, or attempts or conspires to use, a weapon of mass destruction…,including any biological agent, toxin, or vector (as those terms are defined in section 178) … against any person within the United States, and the results of such use affect interstate or foreign commerce or, in the case of a threat, attempt, or conspiracy, would have affected interstate or foreign commerce … shall be imprisoned for any term of years or for life…. 18 U.S.C. §§ 2332a(a)(2).

Appellants were convicted on two counts of threatening to use a weapon of mass destruction, namely a biological agent and a weapon involving a disease organism, against persons within the United States. The statute on its face makes clear that, in the case of a threat, it applies where the results would have affected interstate or foreign commerce. The jury instruction in this case tracked the language of the statute by making as an essential element the government's proof beyond a reasonable doubt that the results of use of the weapon of mass destruction would have affected interstate or foreign commerce. The statute does not require, in the case of a threat, an actual or substantial effect on commerce; it requires only a showing that the use would have affected commerce. The jury instruction given by the court below, therefore, was proper.

In any event, the e-mails, which had been sent from Texas, were received by government agencies outside of Texas. For example, the FBI received the e-mails in California; the United States Customs received the e-mails at its website in Virginia; the ATF, the Secret Service, and the Office of Correspondence for the President all received the e-mails in Washington, D.C. The threat itself crossed state boundaries; therefore, it cannot be argued that an effect on interstate commerce is lacking in this case.

Appellants call into question the sufficiency of the evidence as to the effect on interstate commerce. Specifically, Appellants allege that the government failed to present any testimony or documentary evidence that the use of the weapon specified in the threat would have affected interstate commerce. As previously discussed, the e-mails, which had been sent by Appellants from Texas, were received by government agencies outside of Texas. The threat itself, therefore, crossed state boundaries. Since the IRS and the DEA are located outside of, and received the threat letters outside of, Texas, logic dictates that had Appellants actually carried out their threat, their action would have had consequences outside of Texas, where the IRS and the DEA are located. Viewing the evidence in the light most favorable to the jury's verdict, a rational trier of fact could have found that the interstate commerce element was satisfied in this case beyond a reasonable doubt....

III. CONCLUSION

The indictment sufficiently alleged the elements of an offense under 18 U.S.C. §§ 2332a in charging that Appellants intentionally and knowingly threatened to use a weapon of mass destruction, in violation of 18 U.S.C. §§§§ 2332a(a)(2) and (c)(2)(C), and 18 U.S.C. §§ 2. The evidence fully supports the jury's verdict as to counts five and six of the indictment. The district court did not abuse its discretion in refusing to charge the jury that the offense "substantially affected" interstate commerce. The evidence supports the jury's finding that Appellants caused a threat to use a weapon of mass destruction to be communicated. Although the prosecutor made improper remarks during his closing argument, such remarks did not substantially affect the verdict. The district court did not abuse its discretion in denying Appellants' motion for judgment of acquittal based on the defense of entrapment. The district court properly declined to instruct the jury on the issue of spoliation. And finally, the district court did not abuse its discretion in allowing Agent Decker's expert opinion testimony. For these reasons, we deny the relief sought by Appellants and AFFIRM the district court's ruling and judgment in all respects.

AFFIRMED

The previous case was a successful conviction under 18 USCS §§ 2332a (2001), finding the interstate commerce provision to be satisfied. However, with a very similar set of facts in the following case, the court held that the defendant's acts did not meet the requirements of a "substantial effect on interstate commerce". Where Congress does not make a specific finding that bioterrorism substantially affects interstate commerce, it requires a case-by-case determination as to whether the specific act actually had a substantial effect on interstate commerce. Absent an amendment by Congress, these disparities in application of the bioterrorism criminal act will continue.

In the next case, *United States v. Slaughter,* the convict is found to be entitled to acquittal on the charge of violation of 18 USCS 2332a(a)(2) for mailing letters, containing a white powder, threatening that it contains anthrax, to a prosecutor and to a television station.

United States v. Slaughter
116 F. Supp. 2d 688 (2000)

S. Catherine Dodson is a deputy state prosecutor in Norfolk, Virginia. In 1997, she was a supervisor in charge of the violent crime team, and in that capacity, she successfully prosecuted George Slaughter. Slaughter was sentenced to a lengthy state prison term.

On September 7, 1999, a letter for Dodson from Slaughter arrived at Dodson's office via the United States mail. The envelope was addressed to Catherine Dodson, had the return address of G. R. Slaughter at Red Onion State Prison, in Pound, Virginia, and was postmarked Bristol, TN/VA.

The letter itself was addressed to S. Catherine Dodson and signed by G. R. Slaughter. The letter stated that in the coming months, Slaughter would contact Dodson with instructions, and that if she failed to follow the instructions, members of her family would be killed. The letter also expressed, among other things, that Dodson would be killed if she went to the police and that Slaughter had found out the names and addresses of her family members. Dodson notified her boss, who in turn notified the police and the state department of corrections about the letter.

On October 18, 1999, Dodson received another letter at her office with Slaughter's return address via the United States mail. Dodson had been instructed to wait until an agent of the department of corrections arrived before opening the letter. The unopened letter was put in a transparency cover. The next day, department of corrections special agent James Leslie arrived and opened the letter. The envelope was addressed to S. Catherine Dodson, the return address was George Slaughter at Red Onion State Prison, and the postmark was Bristol TN/VA. Inside the envelope was a white powder. Agent Leslie smelled the white powder, then transferred it to a plastic envelope container.

The letter indicated that Slaughter wanted Dodson dead, even if it cost him his life. The letter claimed that the white powder was anthrax, stating, "guess what I got over the fence? I got enough anthrax to kill you with, and it can be done by mail. That powder you just dumped out of this letter is enough to kill at least 50,000 people. You'll think you have the flu tomorrow and the next day you'll be dead." At the end of the letter, the writer threatened that if he were ever released, he would dig up Dodson's grave and violate her corpse. The letter was signed George R. Slaughter.

Agent Leslie testified that he was "a little nervous" after the letter was read. None of the people present contacted the police or emergency medical help, and Leslie did not contact a doctor. The next day, Leslie took the powdery substance to a lab, and it was determined that the substance was not anthrax and was nontoxic.

Also in October, a third letter was sent through the United States mail to the Kentucky Educational Television station in Lexington, Kentucky. The envelope was addressed to 600 Cooper Drive, Lexington, Kentucky. The return address had Slaughter's name and address at Red Onion State Prison. The letter inside read:

Hello!

I just wanted you to know that you just opened a letter which contains enough anthrax to kill over 50,000 people. You have a nice day[]!

A mail room employee opened the letter because the envelope was not addressed to a specific person. A substance that looked like chalk dust spilled onto the counter. The employee brought the letter to his supervisor's attention. The mail room supervisor notified the postal inspector, who then notified the Federal Bureau of Investigation. The five people who had been near the letter were quarantined and no one was allowed to leave or enter the building. A variety [**6] of local fire trucks, police cars, and disaster and emergency response teams responded. After about five hours, the quarantine ended.

At trial, Leanne McCoy, the mailroom supervisor for Red Onion State Prison, testified that prisoners can send mail by handing it to a floor officer, who in turn takes it to an office until the afternoon mailbags come in. Alternatively, prisoners can put it into an outside mailbox on the way to the "chow hall." The outgoing mail is then put into mail bags and sent to the mail room. McCoy testified that the envelopes that carried the letters to Dodson bore the Red Onion State Prison disclaimer on the back. It is the prison's policy that the disclaimer is stamped onto all outgoing mail. McCoy also testified that all three envelopes were postmarked by the Bristol, Tennessee and Virginia, post office which handles the Red Onion State Prison mail.

The government also offered the testimony of Lieutenant Colonel John Rowe, M.D., an officer in the Army Medical Corps and an expert regarding anthrax. Col. Rowe described the manner in which anthrax infected humans, the effects of infection including mortality rates, and the ways anthrax can be manufactured. He also testified that in one case, the release of a gram of anthrax resulted in at least seventy-nine cases of inhalational anthrax, and that if the amount it took to fill a five-pound bag of sugar was disseminated efficiently, it would be enough to kill a million people. When asked about the effect of an amount that would fill up a regular envelope used for mail, Col. Rowe stated, "it could certainly kill somebody if they opened it up and aerosolized any of that powder. Because the amount that would be aerosolized verses the amount that would be inhaled, it would be easy to inhale [a lethal dose.]"

Finally, Col. Rowe also testified that if anthrax was used as a weapon, his agency would respond "in several different modalities." He stated that, "we would probably do the lab analysis on it for one thing, and then we would also send our physicians and other microbiologists out to respond to that." The scientists would be deployed from Fort Detrick in Maryland. In addition, a specialized team from the FBI would respond, including "some people" from an Army unit in Aberdeen, Maryland.

The government also presented the testimony of FBI special agent Tom Snapp, who interviewed Slaughter in prison after the letters had been received. He testified that Slaughter had admitted writing threatening letters to Dodson in order "to scare her." ...

III. Sufficiency of the Evidence as to Interstate Commerce.

In counts one and three, Slaughter was charged with violating That statute, in relevant part, states that a person who "without lawful authority, ... threatens ... to use, a weapon of mass destruction ... against any person within the United States, and the results of such ... threat ... would have affected interstate or foreign commerce ..." shall be guilty of a crime against the United States.

Slaughter argues that the evidence that the government presented at trial was insufficient for a jury to find an effect on interstate or foreign commerce. In ruling on the motion, I must "allow the government the benefit of all reasonable inferences from the facts proven to those sought to be established."

Where Congress has written a statute to include an effect on interstate or foreign commerce as an element of the offense, it is necessary to perform a case-by-case analysis to determine whether the jurisdictional element is satisfied. Because the statute here includes such a jurisdictional element, the government need only show a minimal effect on interstate commerce.

However, in light of our federal system, "the government still must show that an effect on interstate commerce is reasonably probable." The Supreme Court has recently noted that the "regulation and punishment of intrastate violence that is not directed at the instrumentalities, channels, or goods involved in interstate commerce has always been the province of the States." United States v. Morrison, 529 U.S. 598, 146 L. Ed. 2d 658, 120 S. Ct. 1740, 1754 (2000).

In order for Congress to have regulatory power, where a statute targets noneconomic, violent criminal conduct, the conduct must have more than an aggregate effect on interstate commerce. The government must provide proof that each act prosecuted would have at least a minimal effect on interstate commerce. Thus, in this case, in order to sustain the jury's verdict, the government must have provided sufficient evidence for a jury to conclude that had Slaughter's threat been carried out, interstate commerce would have been affected.

The testimony at trial from Col. Rowe established that if the amount of anthrax in an envelope-sized container was released, it would be enough to "kill somebody." Col. Rowe also testified about the effects of a larger amount of anthrax. In addition, he stated that several military doctors and scientists would travel from Maryland to Virginia had the threatened use of anthrax been carried out.

In count one, the letter sent to Dodson, there was no evidence that the threatened use of anthrax would have affected a "tangible component of interstate commerce." Dodson is a state prosecutor, and the threatened use of a weapon of mass destruction was against her and some of her colleagues, not against a store, bank, leased vehicle, or other obvious component of interstate commerce. Slaughter's threat to Dodson would not have affected interstate commerce directly.

Similarly, there was no evidence that the use of anthrax threatened against the Kentucky Educational Television station would have affected a component of interstate commerce. No evidence was presented that the television station bought or sold interstate goods, broadcast to an interstate area, or had any other effect on interstate commerce. Thus, there was no evidence that the threatened use of anthrax had a direct effect on interstate commerce.[6]

The government may satisfy a statutory jurisdictional component indirectly if it presents evidence of "a reasonable probability that the defendant's actions would have the effect of depleting the assets of an entity engaged in interstate commerce." There is no evidence that the threatened uses of anthrax here would have affected interstate commerce under such a "depletion of assets" theory. The government did not introduce ev-

---

6. The fact that the letters were mailed, and that one of them traveled from Virginia to another state, is of no moment, since the statute requires that the results of the threat would have affected interstate commerce, and not that the threat merely be communicated through interstate commerce.

idence that either Dodson or the television station lost any money due to the threats, nor that they engaged in interstate commerce.

The only evidence offered to show that the threatened use of anthrax would have affected interstate commerce was that an unspecified number of military doctors and scientists would have responded. The entire evidence in this regard, from Col. Rowe's testimony, is as follows:

Q And in the event that actually anthrax were to be, say, discovered and be used as a weapon, would your agency respond?

A Yes. We would probably respond in several different modalities. We would probably do the lab analysis on it for one thing, and then we would also send our physicians and other microbiologists out to respond to that.

Q Where would these different representatives from your agency come from location wise? What state?

A From Maryland, from Fort Detrick.

Q And does the FBI, to your knowledge, also have a response team for weapons of mass destruction?

A Domestic Emergency Support Team from the FBI would respond, and that would include some people from the Army's unit up in Aberdeen, Maryland.

The Fourth Circuit has held that an effect upon interstate commerce can be established by proof of probabilities. That is, the government does not have to prove that identifiable transactions in interstate commerce would be affected, but that there is a probability or likelihood of such an effect.

In this case, however, there was no evidence as to what probable effect the military personnel would have had on interstate commerce. The government did not introduce evidence that the military personnel would have had to bring or use supplies that had traveled in interstate commerce, or that they would have traveled in commercial carriers, lodged in hotels, or eaten at restaurants that engage in interstate commerce.

Federal criminal jurisdiction would be largely unrestrained if it were established under the facts of this case. If travel by a federal government employee to investigate possible criminal conduct alone established federal jurisdiction, then federal agencies would themselves control whether such jurisdiction existed.

It is possible that the use of a weapon of mass destruction, unlike other crimes, would be of such magnitude that every instance would require the response of specially trained government agents being dispatched across state lines to address the problem. In that case, the effect on interstate commerce caused by the agents' emergency travel would be a more direct result of the criminal activity than a federal agent that crossed state lines merely to investigate a crime. However, there was no evidence to indicate that the dispatch of the military units described by Col. Rowe would be a necessary result of the use of anthrax, or to demonstrate why these military units would travel to the scene of an anthrax infection.

Under this limited set of facts, there is insufficient evidence that the threatened use of anthrax would have affected interstate commerce to support a conviction under counts one and three. Accordingly, I will set aside the verdict as to those counts and enter a judgment of acquittal.

———————

Notes

1. In *Slaughter*, the prosecution argued only that the interstate commerce element was met because out-of-state scientists and law enforcers would respond to any anthrax threat. The court, in *dicta*, found that the federal criminal jurisdiction would be largely unrestrained if only these facts were sufficient to establish jurisdiction. However, in *Wise*, the court had no difficulty in finding the interstate commerce element met because the letters were sent to the DEA through the mail from another state.

2. On April 2, 2001 the U.S. Supreme Court unanimously denied *Writ of Certiorari* in *Wise*.

7.4 Biotechnology and the Changing Concept of "Expectation of Privacy"

The law on the expectation of privacy begins with the Fourth Amendment which reads, "the right of the people to be secure in their persons, houses, papers and effects against unreasonable searches and seizures."

In one of the first cases to address the warrantless gathering of information without a physical trespass, the court in *Olmstead v. United States* (1928), held that overheard conversations did not meet the criteria of trespass. Therefore, the court held, the existence of a search is dependent upon whether there is a physical trespass under local property law. For example, a microphone against the wall is not search; whereas a microphone fed through the wall is a search because it is a physical trespass. The Supreme Court moved to a test based upon privacy interests, largely because of changes in technology.

In *Katz v. United States*, a listening device against a telephone booth was utilized to enable the FBI to detect illegally transmitted wagering information across state lines, without a search warrant. Here, the technology detected vibrations in the glass of the phone booth, which set the standard for against the wall, rather than through the wall tests. In that case, Justice Harlan articulated the "reasonable expectation of privacy" test and replaced the property concept of search to some degree with a two prong test: (1) expectation of privacy; and (2) that the expectation of privacy be reasonable.

Then in *Dow Chemical*, the court held about the changing technology that "the effect of modern life, with its technological and other advances, serves to eliminate or reduce a person's justified expectation of privacy...." Using the *Katz* analysis: (1) There WAS a subjective expectation of privacy; however (2) It was NOT reasonable, because anyone could have taken those pictures. Also, in *Dow*, the court determined whether an act is observable by the general public, it is unreasonable to expect privacy in that act.

Then in *California v. Greenwood* (1988), the court found no reasonable expectation of privacy where garbage bags left on the curb before pickup, were readily accessible "to scavengers, snoops and other members of the public."

The continuing criticism of the *Katz* two-prong test has been that it is a circular argument—the Supreme Court protects only those expectations that are reasonable, while the only expectations that are reasonable are those which the Supreme Court is willing to protect.

CIRCUITS HOLDINGS ON THERMAL IMAGING DEVICES

The Fifth,[7] Eighth,[8] Ninth[9] and the Eleventh[10] Circuits have held that thermal image detection was not a "search" within the meaning of the Fourth Amendment. No Circuit Court has held a conflicting opinion with these Circuits, except for a short period when the Tenth Circuit in *United States v. Cusumano*, 67 F.3d 1497 (10th Cir. 1995), found thermal imaging a search, but the opinion was vacated. A rehearing en banc resulted in that issue not being decided.[11]

The U.S. Supreme Court decided *Kyllo*, June 14, 2001 and found that thermal image searches without a warrant violated the Fourth Amendment protection against warrantless search and seizure. The Kyllo court set a new standard that the technology must be in the public use to fall outside of the reasonable expectation of privacy standard of *Katz*.

Given the new standard articulated in *Kyllo*, and new biotechnologies and bioinformatics capabilities, how will the court analyze new biotechnologies?

In *Illinois v. Wealer*, the use of DNA data banks was relatively new, where eleven states had such legislation to provide for DNA data banks. Only two other challenges to the collection of DNA samples from incarcerated persons had arisen at the time of *Illinois*.

Illinois v. Wealer
264 Ill. App. 3d 6 (1994)

Judges: Doyle, McLaren, Peccarelli

Opinion by Justice Doyle

Defendant, Clarence Wealer, entered a negotiated plea of guilty to the charge of aggravated criminal sexual abuse in the circuit court of Lake county and was sentenced to 8½ years imprisonment. Following sentencing, the state moved for an order to obtain blood and saliva samples from defendant ... Defendant objected, contending that.... the taking of blood and saliva samples in contravention of his right to be free from unreasonable searches and seizures under the Fourth Amendment to the United States Constitution ...

With recent advanced in biotechnology, public officials have recognized with increasing frequency the value and potential of DNA testing in the context of criminal law enforcement. As a result, the Illinois legislature in 1989 amended the Uniform Code of Corrections to mandate that persons convicted of certain sex offenses submit blood and saliva specimens to the Illinois Department of State Police for analysis and categorization into genetic marker groupings....

As a threshold matter, we note that neither party disputes that the collection and testing of a blood sample from an individual pursuant to the statue at issue implicated the Fourth Amendment ...

---

7. *United States v. Ishmael*, 48 F.3d 850 (5th Cir. 1995).
8. *United States v. Pinson*, 24 F.3d 1056 (8th Cir. 1994).
9. *United States v. Kyllo*, 190 F.3d 1041 (9th Cir. 1999).
10. *United States v. Ford*, 34 F.3d 992 (11th Cir. 1994).
11. See 83 F.3d 1247 (10th Cir. 1996).

We are of the view that the statutorily mandated taking of blood samples implicated the Fourth Amendment in two respects: first, drawing the blood sample intrudes on an individual's bodily integrity; and second, conducting additional analysis on the sample further implicates Fourth Amendment interests. According, it is necessary to consider further whether the DNA sampling procedure satisfies the constitutional requirement of reasonableness....

The permissibility of a particular practice 'is judged by balancing its intrusion on the individual's Fourth Amendment interests against its promotion of legitimate governmental interests....

... [T]hree approaches have been espoused as the appropriate constitutional basis on which to uphold the validity of DNA testing statues similar to the one at issue in the present case: (1) "special needs" analysis (majority view); (2) diminished privacy rights of prisoners and probationers; and (3) "traditional principles" of Fourth Amendment law.

A majority of the Supreme Court of Washington, with two justices concurring in the result only, upheld a statue allowing nonconsensual blood extraction from convicted sex offenders for the purpose of DBNA identification analysis.... [T]he majority concluded that "special needs" analysis was superior because it affirmed general privacy rights by requiring government to demonstrate a need "beyond normal law enforcement' before it could draw blood from convicted persons without probable cause or individualized suspicion.... Although the court expressly recognized that the explicit statutory purpose of DNA testing was for future identification and prosecution of criminal offenders, it was apparently persuaded by the district court's opinion ... As a "special" law enforcement need.

[The majority of the United States Circuit Court of Appeals for the Fourth Circuit] declining to apply the special needs exception ... viewing the cases which involve the Fourth Amendment rights of prison inmates as a class of cases separate form those requiring a special need, the court reasoned that the diminished privacy rights of prisoners and probationers combined with the minimally intrusive nature of taking a blood sample were outweighed by the State's interest in determining identification characteristics for the purpose of improved law enforcement.

The third approach ... relies primarily on the perceived willingness of the United States Supreme Court, under certain circumstances, to relax or eliminate any requirement of probable cause or individualized suspicion where the nature of the intrusion occasioned by a particular search or seizure is minimal and the government's interest significant ...

It is beyond dispute that the State has a legitimate interest in deterring and prosecuting recidivist acts committed by sex offenders.

[B]ecause we consider the sampling mandated under section 5-4-3 as functionally equivalent to fingerprinting, which also necessarily intrudes a convicted sex offender's diminished privacy interest, we hold that the suspicionless blood and saliva sampling of persons convicted of the sex offenses enumerated in section 5-4-3, regardless of the sentence imposed, does not violate the Fourth Amendment prohibition against unreasonable searches and seizures.

In *People v. King*, the trial court had sentenced the defendant to life in prison, based upon the use of DNA previously collected for a DNA bank. The appellant claimed that failure to obtain a search warrant prior to collecting the DNA was violative of the Fourth Amendment of the U.S. Constitution.

People v. King

82 Cal. App. 4th 1363 (August 14, 2000)

JUDGES: Opinion by Stein, J., with Strankman, P. J., and Swager, J., concurring.

Opinion by Judge Stein:

On May 28, 1997, a jury returned a verdict finding appellant James Edward King guilty of murder with special circumstances, first degree burglary, sodomy and attempted rape. The jury did not, however, find that appellant's crimes warranted the death penalty. The trial court accordingly sentenced appellant to life in prison without the possibility of parole consecutive to a determinate term of 30 years.

In appealing his conviction and sentence, appellant does not deny that he in fact committed the crimes. He contends, rather, that the jury's findings were based on inadmissible evidence; specifically evidence of deoxyribonucleic acid (DNA) profiling matching appellant's DNA profile with that of DNA recovered from the crime site, and evidence of statements taken from appellant after his arrest for the crimes.

BACKGROUND

Appellant had been convicted of forcible rape in 1984, for which he served a term in state prison.[2] In January 1991, before appellant's release, and as required by former Penal Code section 290.2, appellant provided blood samples for analysis by a DNA laboratory operated by California's Department of Justice (the DNA Lab). The samples provided by appellant were analyzed, a profile was developed, and the profile was placed in the DNA Lab's data bank.

On September 28, 1992, approximately nine months after appellant's release from prison, the body of 76-year-old Leticia Smith was found in the living room of her home. The cause of death was strangulation, apparently by means of a ligature fashioned from a pair of pantyhose. The victim had suffered blunt trauma injuries to her head and face, and it appeared that she had been sexually assaulted. Fluids from the victim's genital and anal area were collected and analyzed. The anal smears contained sperm.

The DNA Lab was not fully funded at that time, and no attempt was made to match the DNA recovered from the crime scene with profiles, such as that developed from the samples provided by appellant, maintained in the DNA Lab's data bank. In early 1995, however, samples of blood and sperm recovered from the crime scene were forwarded to the DNA Lab for analysis.

---

2. The 1984 offense was not appellant's first brush with the criminal justice system. In 1971, while a juvenile, he exposed himself, an offense that resulted in his commitment to a boys' school. The following year, while on a good conduct leave from the school, appellant raped a teacher in her classroom and stole $ 6 from her. The year after that, after receiving a one-hour pass from football practice, appellant went to a neighboring Veterans Administration hospital, where he attempted to rape a woman. Less than two years later he committed an offense that resulted in a conviction of rape, attempted rape and armed robbery. In October 1979, 19 months after his release from prison, appellant kidnapped a 16-year-old girl, raped her and forced her to orally copulate him. In 1984, he was convicted of forcible rape.

Appellant was arrested on March 6, 1995. He was interrogated on the same day, and again on March 7, 1995. During the second day of interrogation, appellant essentially admitted that he had been in the home of the victim on the day of her murder, had struggled with her, and knew that he had injured her. He stated that he had no memory of any sexual assault.

DISCUSSION

I. *Appellant's Fourth Amendment Challenge to Former Penal Code Section 290.2*

Former Penal Code Section 290.2

Penal Code former section 290.2, as in effect in 1991, required persons convicted of specified sex offenses, including rape, or of murder or felony assault and battery, and who were "discharged or paroled from" a "state prison, county jail, or any institution," to "provide two specimens of blood and a saliva sample." It provided that the blood should be withdrawn in a medically approved manner. It required the Department of Justice to perform a DNA analysis on the specimens, and provided that "DNA analysis and other genetic typing analysis" could be used only for law enforcement purposes. It authorized the Department of Justice to maintain a computerized data bank system for the purposes of filing DNA and other genetic typing information, and prohibited the inclusion of such information in the state summary criminal history information. The data could be collected only from the individuals convicted of the specified crimes or from crime scenes. Evidence taken from a crime scene was to be "stricken from the data bank when it is determined that the person is no longer a suspect in the case." DNA or other genetic typing information could be disseminated only to law enforcement agencies and district attorney offices, or to defense counsel for defense purposes in compliance with discovery.

Penal Code former section 290.2 was amended in 1993 to permit the use of samples by local public DNA laboratories, and to permit dissemination of genetic typing information to Department of Corrections parole officers and parole authority hearing officers. In 1996, Penal Code former section 290.2 again was amended to change the time for providing samples from the time of release to the time of commitment to a specified institution. [N]ew legislation has expanded the class of persons required to provide samples for DNA testing, and requires such persons to provide replacement specimens if the original samples prove to be unusable. We, however, are not concerned with whether the state legitimately can require all such persons to provide samples, or whether persons who are not incarcerated may be required to provide samples or replace samples taken while they were in a penal institution. We determine only whether one such as appellant, imprisoned for having committed a crime involving a sexual assault, might be required to provide samples of blood and saliva for DNA analysis ... It is noteworthy that although all 50 states have enacted laws comparable to California's DNA profiling laws, and although a number of other jurisdictions have considered the question of whether such laws violate Fourth Amendment principles, and have used any of several theories to resolve that question, appellant has been unable to cite one that has resolved it against DNA profiling.

Although prisons are not beyond the reach of the Constitution, "it is also clear that imprisonment carries with it the circumspection or loss of many significant rights." The nature of confinement necessarily results in a significant reduction in the expectation of privacy. It is settled, for example, that prisoners have no privacy interests in their cells. Even pretrial detainees can have no reasonable expectation of privacy with respect to their rooms or cells. The privacy interests of inmates in their own bodies bow to the interests of prison officials in ensuring that weapons or contraband are not brought into prison institutions, and inmates therefore may be required to expose their body cavities for visual inspection as part of a strip search conducted after every contact visit with a person from outside the institution. Persons convicted of sex offenses are required to provide blood samples for purposes of testing for acquired immune deficiency syndrome (AIDS). Probationers enjoy only conditional liberty properly dependent on observance of special probation restrictions, and their homes are subject to warrantless searches on less than probable cause.

The reduction in a convicted person's reasonable expectation of privacy specifically extends to that person's identity. Indeed, not only persons convicted of crimes, but also those merely suspected of crimes, routinely are required to undergo fingerprinting for identification purposes. As to convicted persons, there is no question but that the state's interest extends to maintaining a permanent record of identity to be used as an aid in solving past and future crimes, and this interest overcomes any privacy rights the individual might retain. "This becomes readily apparent when we consider the universal approbation of 'booking' procedures that are followed for every suspect arrested for a felony, whether or not the proof of a particular suspect's crime will involve the use of fingerprint identification. Thus a tax evader is fingerprinted just the same as a burglar. While we do not accept even this small level of intrusion for free persons without Fourth Amendment constraint, the same protections do not hold true for those lawfully confined to the custody of the state." *People v. Wealer* (1994) 264 Ill.App.3d 6 [201 Ill.Dec. 697, 636 N.E.2d 1129, 1136–1137].) The fingerprints, photographs and physical descriptions of convicted persons are preserved as a matter of routine. And once an individual has been convicted of a crime or crimes, and has been incarcerated in a penal institution, his or her identity clearly becomes a matter of interest to prison officials. It further is true that sex offenders such as appellant are required to register annually with the police for the remainder of their lives. "The Fourth Amendment does not protect all subjective expectations of privacy, but only those that society recognizes as 'legitimate.' What expectations are legitimate varies, of course, with context [citation], depending, for example upon whether the individual asserting the privacy interest is at home, at work, in a car, or in a public park." By their commissions of a crime and subsequent convictions, persons such as appellant have forfeited any legitimate expectation of privacy in their identities. In short, any argument that Fourth Amendment privacy interests do not prohibit gathering information concerning identity from the person of one who has been convicted of a serious crime, or of retaining that information for crime enforcement purposes, is an argument that long ago was resolved in favor of the government.[6]

On the other hand, the government has an undeniable interest in crime prevention. It has interests in solving crimes that have been committed, in bringing the perpetrators to justice and in preventing, or at least discouraging, them from committing additional crimes. The government also has an interest in ensuring that innocent persons are not needlessly investigated—to say nothing of convicted—of crimes they did

---

6. Appellant voices concerns that once DNA profiling is permitted for one purpose, it creates the possibility of misuse and makes it that much easier to permit DNA profiling for other purposes. It is enough that Penal Code former section 290.2 limited the use of DNA evidence, prohibiting its use for anything other than law enforcement purposes. Whether it constitutionally might be used for some other purpose is a question that is not before us.

not commit. n7 DNA testing unquestionably furthers these interests. The ability to match DNA profiles derived from crime scene evidence to DNA profiles in an existing data bank can enable law enforcement personnel to solve crimes expeditiously and prevent needless interference with the privacy interests of innocent persons. It has been suggested that DNA profiling may act as a deterrent to future criminal activity. It also is an unfortunate truth that many offenders commit more than one crime, and recidivism is common. Speedy identification and apprehension of an offender, therefore, will prevent crime even if DNA testing has no deterrent effect on criminal activity.

Notes

1. In 1999, the National Commission on the Future of DNA Evidence made a recommendation to the Attorney General concerning gathering DNA samples from not only convicted offenders, but from arrestees.

> The Department of Justice should not advocate a policy supporting arrestee sampling unless (1) the convicted offender database backlog is substantially eliminated, (2) significant resources are allocated for the analysis of non-suspect cases, and (3) sufficient funds are made available for the collection and analysis of arrestee samples. At http://www.ojp.usdoj.gov/nij/dna (last visited Oct.14, 2001).

The concern here, appears to be more one of administrative burden, rather than Fourth Amendment concerns.

2. In 1995, the United Kingdom became the first nation to create a national DNA data bank. While in the United States, individual states have passed legislation that allows the collection of DNA for convicted offenders. Since it varies from state to state as to which crimes allow the collection of DNA, the United States had to sort through those when it started the U.S. national data bank called CODIS in October 1998. This accounts for the massive backlog of yet-unprofiled DNA samples (about 750,000). See, *A New Breed of High-Tech Detectives*, 289 SCIENCE 854 (Aug. 29, 2000).

3. McKenney of George Mason University, who is working on a mitochondrial database with the Department of Justice support, is quoted as saying, "Once we understand the value of DNA profiling, and we put in sufficient assurances that it won't be abused or misused, then we will pass laws that say everybody will be profiled on birth," he says. "It will be just like a Social Security number." *A New Breed of High-Tech Detectives, supra*. Will this be permissible under a Fourth Amendment analysis? Or will it be the functional equivalent of social security numbers under a special needs analysis?

7.5 Human Behavioral Genetics and Criminal Predisposition

The following excerpt from Cecilee Price-Huish, Comment: *Born to Kill? Aggression Genes and Their Potential Impact on Sentencing and the Criminal Justice System*, 50 SMU

L. REV. 603 (Jan/Feb 1997) provides an overview of the history of human behavioral genetics and criminal predisposition:

History and Development

... XYY Defense

In 1968, scientists discovered what they then believed was a genetic explanation for criminal behavior when they found an extra Y chromosome trait shared by three percent of the male inmates at one hospital housing the criminally insane. Although this information has been used by a small number of criminal defendants in attempts to displace culpability, courts have generally rejected this genetic defense. Currently, the theory that XYY men are predisposed to aggression or violence is not recognized either as a valid defense or as a mitigating factor by either the medical or legal communities. In one of the most celebrated cases in which the XYY defense was attempted, the court refused to allow the evidence to reach the jury because "presently available medical evidence [was] unable to establish a reasonably certain causal connection between the XYY defect and [the] criminal conduct." It seems that any possible nitric oxide or MAOA defense is currently in the XYY stage because the findings are not yet substantive enough to prove a causal connection between the genetic abnormalities and violent behavior. In order for these new theories of genetic predisposition to criminality to gain more acceptance than the XYY defense, there must be more research with duplicative findings that will substantiate the initial findings of causation....

In February 1995, a Symposium on the Genetics of Criminal and Antisocial Behavior ("Symposium") was held at the Ciba Foundation, an international scientific and educational charity, based in London. The purpose of the Symposium was to examine "some of the newer evidence on [genetic factors and differences in antisocial behavior] and, ... [to] consider some of the crucial ethical, legal and criminal implications that stem from those findings." The Symposium was not open to the public, but the findings and conclusions of the participants were published in Genetics of Criminal and Antisocial Behaviour.

The Symposium generated considerable controversy and debate, much of which centered around the fear that genetic explanations of differences among ethnic groups and between the sexes will be "used to account for and justify the inferior social status of women and minority ethnic groups." Unlike past attempts to offer genetic hypotheses for behavioral differences, new genetic research seemingly offers explanations that are no longer simply theoretical. This is because genetic technology has made enormous strides in the last ten years, making the isolation and study of individual gene sequences possible. Private and public genetic research have further been bolstered by the founding of the Human Genome Project, a multinational effort to map and explain the functions of all 100,000 human genes.

A conference similar to the Ciba Symposium, which was partially funded by the National Institutes of Health (NIH), was scheduled in 1992, but was canceled due to accusations of racism and eugenic regression. The NIH eventually renewed its funding, and the conference, Research in Genetics and Criminal Behavior: Scientific Issues, Social and Political Implications, was finally held in September 1995 amid denunciations of racial prejudice. As would be expected, views on the genetics of criminal behavior span the spectrum. Diana Fishbein, a criminologist with the U.S. Department of Justice believes that "'there are areas where we can begin to incorporate biological approaches' to fighting crime and ... that medical treatment [for some] violent offenders should be mandatory." Still, others argue that identifying social problems with biology simply allows a society to deflect responsibility away from the state and its social welfare appendages.

During one Symposium presentation, Sir Michael Rutter, a child psychiatrist at the Institute of Psychiatry in London, argued that genetics and environmental factors are not mutually exclusive in causing violent propensities. Rutter explained that the genetic research designs presented and discussed at the Symposium were crucial for the testing of hypotheses about environmental risk mechanisms as well as for the study of genetic factors. The real importance of research into the existence of aggression genes, according to Rutter, lies in learning more about their potential causal processes when coupled with environmental elements, not solely in the predictive strength of such genes. This holistic approach seems to be shared by legal scholars who are attempting to reconcile this new evolving science with traditional theories of culpability and punishment. Examination into the relationship between genetic and environmental causal factors of violent behavior, as espoused by Rutter, is hypothetical at this point since most of the new genetic research is conducted in a "causal vacuum" and does not explore the effects that psychosocial stressors have on those carrying aggression-causing genes....

There are two relatively recent discoveries which indicate that a genetic predisposition to aggressive behavior may be identifiable. From the same article, the following findings are summarized:

Scientists at Johns Hopkins University have found that male mice lacking the gene that produces nitric oxide are highly prone to aggressive, violent behavior against other mice. Nitric oxide is a neuron-produced gas that is used by the brain as a neurotransmitter allowing neurons to communicate. The genetically abnormal male mice sexually pursued female mice for hours even though the female mice were not in heat. Normal male mice, on the other hand, will give up the chase when a female is not in heat. Additionally, normal mice will usually stop an attack when an opponent surrenders, but abnormal mice were found to fight other mice to the death, even after the opposing mice surrendered by lying on their backs. Based on this study, it is speculated that nitric oxide is the neurotransmitter that curbs sexual and aggressive behavior. "These animals were very, very aggressive—dramatically so," said Dr. Randy J. Nelson, professor of psychology at Johns Hopkins University and co-sponsor of the study. "They don't seem to recognize social cues which would normally turn off reckless, impulsive or violent behavior."

Speculative treatment models for nitric oxide deficiency are already being discussed. According to Dr. Solomon H. Snyder, a neurobiologist at Johns Hopkins University and co-sponsor of the study, examining the DNA in families with a history of aggression may lead to discovery of a defect in the "knocked out" gene that enables the brain to produce nitric oxide. Furthermore, additional research could lead to the development of new nitric oxide-boosting drugs to treat people genetically predisposed to aggressive, violent behavior. While human studies have yet to be conducted, the mouse study provides important insight into understanding human aggression due to the neurological similarity between mice and people.

... The Absence of Monoamine Oxidase A and Aggressive Behavior

Using genetic "knockout" technology, a multinational research team has developed a family of mice that lack monoamine oxidase A (MAOA), an enzyme that severely affects the amount of serotonin and norepinephrine in the brains of affected mice. Normal amounts of MAOA in the brain serve to inactivate production of serotonin, a neurotransmitter that influences moods and perception, and norepinephrine, a neurotransmitter that helps control body movement. In the genetically altered mice, however, MAOA catalytic activity ceased altogether, causing the production of unusually high levels of serotonin and norepinephrine, which in turn led to impulsive aggressive behavior.

Abnormally aggressive behavior was displayed by MAOA-deficient adult male mice, even though housed in normal rearing conditions from the time they were pups. Researchers found that these male mice repeatedly attacked one another, primarily by biting each other on the genitals and the rump. The adult males also displayed abnormal sexual aggression by grasping females repeatedly. Dr. Isabelle Seif, a molecular biologist who directed a team of MAOA researchers, believes that since the MAOA-deficient mice displayed abnormal aggression under normal rearing conditions, absent psychosocial stressors, drugs could be developed to help control enhanced aggression in human males that lack MAOA. The absence of psychosocial stressors among the disturbed mice suggests a very strong genetic link to the abnormal behavior.

... Aggression-Causing Genetic Abnormalities in Humans

1. Monoamine Oxidase A Deficiency in Humans—Dutch Family Study

A recent study of a large Dutch extended family, which spanned four generations, found fourteen males exhibiting borderline mental retardation (IQ of about eighty-five) and impulsive aggressive behavior manifested in acts of verbal and physical aggression, which included arson, aggravated assault, sexual assault, attempted rape, and exhibitionism. In all of the affected men, MAOA activity was completely absent. The Dutch family was selected for the study because a sharp, unexplainable behavioral contrast between affected and unaffected males had been noted by family members for years.

Researchers found that stagnant MAOA activity among affected males resulted in the excretion of abnormally high amounts of the neurotransmitters serotonin, norepinephrine, dopamine, and epinephrine, all of which are normally broken down in the body using MAOA. According to Xandra Breakefield, a neurogeneticist and collaborator of the Dutch family study, when these neurotransmitters accumulate in abnormal amounts due to a defect on the MAOA gene, affected individuals will have trouble handling stressful situations, causing them to respond excessively and at times, violently. While MAOA deficiency suggests a causal link for increased impulsive, aggressive behavior among male members of the Dutch family, scientists acknowledge that research is in the infancy stages and that additional MAOA-deficient families must be studied in order to test the validity of the causal association.

Because MAOA deficiency is among several tentative genetic abnormalities linked with unusually aggressive behavior, Han G. Brunner, a clinical geneticist and author of the Dutch family study, warns against viewing the data in a vacuum. While Brunner strongly supports the theory that behavior is influenced by genetic factors, he states that,

The notion of an 'aggression gene' does not make sense, because it belies the fact that behaviour should and does arise at the highest level of cortical organization, where individual genes are only distantly reflected in the anatomical structure, as well as in the various neurophysiological and biochemical functions of the brain.

Brunner also believes that genetic studies can be best used to improve our understanding of how, not why, impulsive aggressive behavior occurs.

The ramifications that the nitric oxide-deficient mouse study, the MAOA-deficient mouse study, and the Dutch family study will have on the criminal justice system are far from clear. As scientists continue to identify behavior-modifying genetic abnormalities that cause increased aggression and violence, this groundbreaking research will surely have an impact on sentencing violent criminals....

One of the first cases to address the genetic predisposition of humans and the public policy approaches to addresses those problems was the U.S. Supreme Court case that follows:

Buck v. Bell
274 U.S. 200 (1927)

Judges: Taft, Holmes, Van Devanter, McReynolds, Brandeis, Sutherland, Butler, Sanford, Stone

Opinion by Justice Holmes.

This is a writ of error to review a judgment of the Supreme Court of Appeals of the State of Virginia, affirming a judgment of the Circuit Court of Amherst County, by which the defendant in error, the superintendent of the State Colony for Epileptics and Feeble Minded, was ordered to perform the operation of salpingectomy upon Carrie Buck, the plaintiff in error, for the purpose of making her sterile. The case comes here upon the contention that the statute authorizing the judgment is void under the Fourteenth Amendment as denying to the plaintiff in error due process of law and the equal protection of the laws.

Carrie Buck is a feeble minded white woman who was committed to the State Colony above mentioned in due form. She is the daughter of a feeble minded mother in the same institution, and the mother of an illegitimate feeble minded child. She was eighteen years old at the time of the trial of her case in the Circuit Court, in the latter part of 1924. An Act of Virginia, approved March 20, 1924, recites that the health of the patient and the welfare of society may be promoted in certain cases by the sterilization of mental defectives, under careful safeguard, etc.; that the sterilization may be effected in males by vasectomy and in females by salpingectomy, without serious pain or substantial danger to life; that the Commonwealth is supporting in various institutions many defective persons who if now discharged would become a menace but if incapable of procreating might be discharged with safety and become self-supporting with benefit to themselves and to society; and that experience has shown that heredity plays an important part in the transmission of insanity, imbecility, &c. The statute then enacts that whenever the superintendent of certain institutions including the above named State Colony shall be of opinion that it is for the best interests of the patients and of society that an inmate under his care should be sexually sterilized, he may have the operation performed upon any patient afflicted with hereditary forms of insanity, imbecility, etc., on complying with the very careful provisions by which the act protects the patients from possible abuse.

The superintendent first presents a petition to the special board of directors of his hospital or colony, stating the facts and the grounds for his opinion, verified by affidavit. Notice of the petition and of the time and place of the hearing in the institution is to be served upon the inmate, and also upon his guardian, and if there is no guardian the superintendent is to apply to the Circuit Court of the County to appoint one. If the inmate is a minor notice also is to be given to his parents if any with a copy of the petition. The board is to see to it that the inmate may attend the hearings if desired by him or his guardian. The evidence is all to be reduced to writing, and after the board has made its order for or against the operation, the superintendent, or the inmate, or his guardian, may appeal to the Circuit Court of the County. The Circuit Court may consider the record of the board and the evidence before it and such other admissible evidence as may be offered, and may affirm, revise, or reverse the order of the board and enter such order as it deems just. Finally any party may apply to the Supreme Court of Appeals, which, if it grants the appeal, is to hear the case upon the record of the trial in the Circuit Court and may enter such order as it thinks the Circuit Court should have entered. There can be no doubt that so far as procedure is concerned the rights of the patient are most carefully considered, and as every step in this case was taken in scrupulous compliance with the statute and after months of observation, there is no doubt that in that respect the plaintiff in error has had due process of law.

The attack is not upon the procedure but upon the substantive law. It seems to be contended that in no circumstances could such an order be justified. It certainly is contended that the order cannot be justified upon the existing grounds. The judgment finds the facts that have been recited and that Carrie Buck "is the probable potential parent of socially inadequate offspring, likewise afflicted, that she may be sexually sterilized without detriment to her general health and that her welfare and that of society will be promoted by her sterilization," and thereupon makes the order. In view of the general declarations of the legislature and the specific findings of the Court, obviously we cannot say as matter of law that the grounds do not exist, and if they exist they justify the result. We have seen more than once that the public welfare may call upon the best citizens for their lives. It would be strange if it could not call upon those who already sap the strength of the State for these lesser sacrifices, often not felt to be such by those concerned, in order to prevent our being swamped with incompetence. It is better for all the world, if instead of waiting to execute degenerate offspring for crime, or to let them starve for their imbecility, society can prevent those who are manifestly unfit from continuing their kind. The principle that sustains compulsory vaccination is broad enough to cover cutting the Fallopian tubes. *Jacobson* v. *Massachusetts*, 197 U.S. 11. Three generations of imbeciles are enough.

But, it is said, however it might be if this reasoning were applied generally, it fails when it is confined to the small number who are in the institutions named and is not applied to the multitudes outside. It is the usual last resort of constitutional arguments to point out shortcomings of this sort. But the answer is that the law does all that is needed when it does all that it can, indicates a policy, applies it to all within the lines, and seeks to bring within the lines all similarly situated so far and so fast as its means allow. Of course so far as the operations enable those who otherwise must be kept confined to be returned to the world, and thus open the asylum to others, the equality aimed at will be more nearly reached.

Judgment affirmed.

New York v. Weinstein

591 N.Y.S.2d 715 (1992)

Opinion by Richard D. Carruthers, J.

Herbert Weinstein stands indicted for the crime of murder in the second degree. The indictment alleges that Weinstein murdered his wife, Barbara, on January 7, 1991. Weinstein allegedly strangled his wife in their 12th floor apartment in Manhattan, and then threw her body from a window to make her death appear to be a suicide.

Weinstein's attorney has filed notice that the defense at trial will be that Weinstein lacked criminal responsibility for killing his wife due to mental disease or defect. *(See,* CPL 250.10; Penal Law §§ 40.15.) Evidence to support this defense includes scans of Weinstein's brain obtained through positron emission tomography (PET) and the results of skin conductance response (SCR) tests of his autonomic nervous system. The PET scans were obtained after Weinstein's indictment. The purpose of the scans was to enable neurologists and psychiatrists to study images that depict how Weinstein's brain functions metabolically in its various regions. In accordance with the applicable protocol, a radioactive substance called flourine-18 deoxyglucose was injected into Weinstein's body several minutes before each scan was made. In each instance, when this substance reached Weinstein's brain, it was metabolized, to a point, in the same way that glucose is metabolized. The human brain uses glucose as its energy source. The radioactivity that then was emitted from Weinstein's brain during the metabolic process was captured by a highly sophisticated monitoring device. The device, in each scan, converted this radioactivity into images that showed how well or ill each region of Weinstein's brain was performing metabolically. Weinstein's PET scans confirmed that a cyst exists within the arachnoid membrane, one of the brain's protective coverings. This arachnoid cyst is an abnormality that was first detected by images of brain structure obtained by an MRI machine. The PET scans also showed metabolic imbalances exist in areas of the brain near the cyst and opposite it.

The SCR test of Weinstein's autonomic system were performed, also after indictment, at the neurological laboratory of the University of Iowa. The physicians at this laboratory are the first to use SCR tests of the autonomic nervous system as a means of indicating the existence of lesions in the frontal lobes of the brain. During the tests, a machine similar to a polygraph is used to measure a person's galvanic skin responses while that person is shown a series of photographs depicting scenes ranging in emotional content from the serene to the shocking. Unlike more familiar polygraph tests, SCR tests are not used as a purported means of determining whether a person is telling the truth. Weinstein's SCR results were consistent with those of tested individuals who were confirmed as having lesions in the frontal lobes of their brains.

PET scans and SCR test results, according to Weinstein's attorney, are factors that a psychiatrist will rely upon at trial to explain his diagnosis that, due to mental disease or defect, Weinstein was not criminally responsible for the death of his wife. The psychiatrist will explain that his diagnosis is also based upon physical and neuropsychological tests, his interviews of Weinstein, as well as other information available to him. The District Attorney has moved for an order precluding Weinstein's attorney from offering at trial any testimony or other evidence concerning the PET scans and SCR test results, arguing that PET and SCR technology have not been shown to be sufficiently reliable as diagnostic devices for brain abnormalities so as to warrant the admission of such evidence at the trial of a criminal case. Pursuant to this court's order, a pretrial hearing was held upon this motion. Many physicians, including neurologists, psychiatrists, and experts in nuclear medicine, testified at this hearing. The court resolves below the issues raised by the District Attorney's motion.

The evidence adduced at the hearing showed that Weinstein's brain is abnormal due to the presence of the arachnoid cyst, the attendant displacement of the left frontal lobe, and firm indications of metabolic imbalance near the cyst and the regions of the brain opposite it. The defendant's experts testified at length about these matters. Doctor Jonathan Brodie, the People's expert, also acknowledged in his testimony that Weinstein's brain is abnormal, "[b]ecause there is evidence of a cyst in the brain from the

MRI results. Once you have a sack in the skull, it's going to compress the brain and make it look abnormal." Doctor Brodie testified, too, that Weinstein's brain exhibited "an abnormality in his regional glucose metabolism."

Thus, a diagnostician's consideration of Weinstein's PET test results, insofar as they depict the existence of both the cyst and the metabolic imbalances in Weinstein's brain, is, a fortiori, reasonable. The District Attorney argues that the complex mathematical formulae used to quantify the results of PET tests have not gained general acceptance in relevant technological and medical fields. Doctor Alvai's testimony supports this argument. However, the evidence shows that the formulae are used with regularity by PET experts and that the results are relied upon by them. Consequently, in forming a diagnosis, a psychiatrist in an insanity defense case could reasonably consider the quantitative results derived by application of the formulae to raw data.

Having discussed what is admissible evidence, brief reference should be made to certain theories relating to human behavior that may not be mentioned in testimony at the trial. Evidence concerning these theories is not admissible because they have not been generally accepted as valid in the fields of psychiatry, psychology, and neurology. The first of these theories is that arachnoid cysts directly cause violence. Doctor Martell testified categorically that this theory was not generally accepted, noting that he had seen no scientific research to support it. Doctor Relkin, the defendant's witness, appeared to agree. Another theory that has not been generally accepted is that reduced levels of glucose metabolism in the frontal lobes of the brain directly cause violence. In his brief, the defendant disavows any intention to rely on this theory at trial. As he states, "[w]ith respect to hypometabolism causing violence, it is critical for the Court to recognize that it is a completely false issue." This position is fully justified by the record. The only evidence offered in support of the theory was a preliminary research report: Volkow and Tancredi, *Neural Substrates of Violent Behaviour, a Preliminary Study with Positron Emission Tomography* (151 Brit J Psychiatry 668 [1987]). The report concerned four patients, each of whom had a history of purposeless violent behavior. PET scans showed hypometabolism in the frontal lobes. However, each of the four patients also had long-standing personality disorders apparently resulting from such problems as alcoholism and drug abuse. It cannot be definitively stated that the behavioral problems of these four patients was due to hypometabolism and not to their personality disorders, a fact that the authors of the report fully recognized. (Volkow and Tancredi, *op. cit.*, at 670–671.) Doctor Brodie, the People's witness, trained the report's principal author, Doctor Nora Volkow, in PET scanning. He testified that her report was published because the four cases were "potentially of interest," and that the findings were "potentially to be further investigated." Thus, a conclusion based upon Volkow and Tancredi's report that hypometabolism in the frontal lobes causes violence would be entirely premature and not at the level of general acceptance in the relevant scientific disciplines....

To recapitulate: in an insanity defense case, the existence of a mental disease or syndrome or the validity of a theory of human behavior must be generally accepted in the field of psychiatry or psychology before experts may discuss such matters in their testimony at trial. If general acceptance has been attained, a psychiatric expert then "must be permitted" to state a diagnosis and to give a reasonable explanation for a finding that the defendant does or does not suffer from the mental disease, or that that person is or is not affected by the syndrome, or that a theory of human behavior does or does not explain the defendant's conduct.

Notes

1. There is a theory among some sociologists that a lower IQ score in African-Americans accounts for their higher incidence of criminal behavior, because they lack comprehension of their actions. This theory was proposed in a controversial trade book by RICHARD J. HERRNSTEIN & CHARLES MURRAY, THE BELL CURVE: INTELLIGENCE & CLASS STRUCTURE IN AMERICAN LIFE 9–10 (The Free Press 1994). Is this admissible as scientific evidence?

2. As we gain more knowledge about brain abnormalities through MRI data, should the test for insanity be modified to include this?

7.6 Criminal Law Attorneys and Obligation to Understand Science

The Model Rules of Professional Conduct state that an attorney has "a duty to use legal procedure for the fullest benefits of the client's cause," and further that the attorney must use any lawful approach for his client's cause "without regard to professional opinion as to the likelihood that the construction will ultimately prevail." Model Rules of Prof'l Conduct, Rule 3.1, Comment 1.

The American Bar Association approved a certification program for attorneys, for training in the science of DUI (driving under the influence) cases, and to learn techniques for challenging the soundness of evidence. Lawrence Taylor, principal of a Southern California DUI defense firm suggested that "attorneys who set foot in the courtroom before learning the science of DUI defense are committing malpractice," Margaret Graham Tebo, *New Test for DUI Defense*, 91 ABA J. 34 at 36, February 2005.

7.6.1 The Genetics Defense

Zealous advocacy has resulted in the use of the post-partum psychosis, premenstrual stress syndrome, post traumatic stress syndrome, and the "Twinkie" defense. In general, the "genetics defense" — the defendant is not responsible for his or her conduct because of a genetic predisposition — is the basis of the defense.

In *United States v. Dina Abdelhaq*, 246 F.3d 990 (11th Cir. 2001), the defendant, the mother of a second child found dead, attributed to Sudden Infant Death Syndrome (SIDS), was charged with murder. Her defense included that she had a "genetic predisposition" for conceiving children with SIDS, made without expert testimony. "The defendant argues that the previous death indicated a genetic predisposition that might explain the extraordinary coincidence of losing two children to SIDS, but she presented little evidence to support that conjecture (and there apparently is little evidence that could have been presented. *See* STEDMAN'S MEDICAL DICTIONARY 1768 (27th ed. 2000)), it was vigorously contested, and the jury was entitled to disbelieve it."

In *West v. Bell*, 242 F.3d. 338 (6th Cir. 2001), a Tennessee prisoner was sentenced to death for the 1986 rape and murder of two East Tennessee women. After a stay of execution had been entered, the warden moved to dismiss the stay, because counsel representing West did not have his permission. Counsel argued that West was not competent, and the court agreed that "under most circumstances, as a society we assume a fully competent individual would wish to pursue every avenue of relief available to avoid execution. The fact West does not, when viewed in light of [evidence that West may be vacillating in his decision and perceives some of his treatment during incarceration as retaliatory] raises some concerns about his mental facility [sic]." When the court ruled to remove the stay, the dissent raised concern that West's evaluation indicated that "West may have a genetic predisposition to mental illness; that the development of schizoid, paranoid, and borderline pathology have all been noted in West; and that West's decision not to seek federal habeas corpus relief "does not follow logically with his scheduled marriage seven days after the date of his anticipated execution."

7.6.2 Ineffective Assistance of Counsel

Mobley v. Head
2001 U.S. App. LEXIS 21492 (11th Cir. 2001)

OPINION by BIRCH, Circuit Judge:

Stephen A. Mobley appeals the district court's denial of his petition for a writ of habeas corpus. Two issues were certified to us on appeal from the district court's denial of habeas corpus relief: (1) whether Mobley was denied effective assistance of counsel through his attorney's use of a "genetic deficiency" defense, and (2) whether Mobley was denied due process and effective assistance of counsel because the Georgia Supreme Court's opinion in *Sabel v. State*, 248 Ga. 10, 282 S.E.2d 61 (Ga. 1981), requiring the defense to turn over all expert opinions, including those that the defense does not intend to use at trial, had a chilling effect on his counsel that prevented him from retaining experts to develop mitigating psychiatric testimony. Because we find that the Georgia Supreme Court reasonably applied the relevant law to determine that Mobley had received effective assistance of counsel at his trial and his due process claim is procedurally barred, we AFFIRM.

I. BACKGROUND

In early 1991, Mobley stole a Walther .380 pistol from a car belonging to an acquaintance. On 17 February 1991, John Collins was working as the night manager at a Domino's Pizza franchise in Hall County, Georgia, when Mobley entered the store and robbed him at gunpoint. After emptying the cash register, Mobley moved Collins from the front of the store to the back office, took additional money from the office and then shot Collins in the back of the head before fleeing out a side door.

Mobley subsequently committed six additional armed robberies of various restaurants and drycleaners over a period of three weeks. He was apprehended after a high-speed chase as he fled the scene of an attempted armed robbery. Once in custody, Mobley confessed to the robberies and the murder of Collins. A Walther .380 found on the side of the road along the chase route matched the ballistics of the murder weapon.

Mobley was indicted for malice murder, felony murder, armed robbery, aggravated assault and possession of a firearm during the commission of a crime. Daniel Summer and Andrew Maddox were assigned by the court to defend Mobley. His first trial ended in a mistrial. Following an interim appeal on several issues, Mobley was tried a second time. Summer was also lead counsel for Mobley's second trial, but Charles Taylor replaced Maddox as Summer's co-counsel.

In bifurcated proceedings, the jury returned a verdict of guilty on charges of malice murder, felony murder, armed robbery, aggravated assault and possession of a firearm during commission of a crime. At the sentencing phase of his trial, evidence was introduced that, while in pre-trial detention, Mobley sexually assaulted another inmate on two occasions. Evidence at the sentencing phase also included testimony that Mobley tattooed the word "domino" on his shoulder, hung a Domino's pizza box lid on his cell wall and threatened a guard by saying he looked more and more like a Domino's delivery boy every day.

In their mitigation presentation, Summer and Taylor called Mobley's father, Charles Mobley, to testify. After relaying a brief history of the schools and institutions to which he sent Mobley as a child, Charles Mobley asked for mercy for his son. Counsel also called Doctor J. Stephen Ziegler, the psychologist who treated Mobley at the last facility where he was treated before reaching his eighteenth birthday. Ziegler testified that, at age 16, Mobley had a conduct disorder which is the equivalent of an adult antisocial personality disorder, and that persons with this disorder can become less violent and antisocial with age. Counsel also called Mobley's aunt, Joyce Ann Childers, who was the family historian. Childers testified about a family history over several generations of violent behavior, alcoholism, abuse and other antisocial behavior among male and female members of the Mobley family tree. Counsel also introduced evidence that, since his arrest, Mobley had attempted several times to plead guilty to all charges against him in exchange for a life sentence.

At the conclusion of the sentencing phase of the trial, the jury recommended a sentence of death....

Based on his interview with Mobley and a review of Mobley's records, Doctor Gomez concluded that Mobley's antisocial personality disorder was the result of his childhood environment, including abuse, neglect and inconsistent punishment. Doctor Semone also interviewed Mobley and other family members including Mobley's maternal grandmother. He also concluded that Mobley's "dysfunctional and disorganized and punitive" family structure was the most significant factor in Mobley's violent behavior pattern. Mobley's grandmother, Mary Walraven, testified that her daughter was verbally and emotionally abusive to Mobley. The Superior Court upheld the conviction but vacated Mobley's sentence on the grounds that Mobley was denied effective assistance of counsel for two main reasons: (1) his counsel presented a genetic defect theory to explain Mobley's violent and anti-social behavior without the assistance of an expert; and (2) his counsel failed to present other mitigating psychiatric evidence....

The Georgia Supreme Court reversed and reinstated Mobley's death sentence. Reviewing the lower court's findings and the evidence produced at the habeas hearing, the court found that Mobley's counsel had conducted an extensive investigation, interviewed several witnesses, and obtained all available records from every school and treatment facility Mobley attended. The court noted that, when interviewed by counsel in preparation for trial, Mobley denied that he had ever been abused or neglected, as did his parents and sister. Based on the evidence developed by counsel, the court concluded that the sentencing phase strategy was reasonable, and, accordingly, denied Mobley's ineffective assistance claim.

B. Ineffective Assistance Claims

Mobley also raises two ineffective assistance of counsel claims. First, he argues that the trial court's entry of the Sabel order denied him effective assistance of counsel because the chilling effect of the order prevented his attorney from consulting with experts who might have assisted in preparing mitigating evidence. Mobley also argues that his trial counsel was ineffective at the sentencing phase because he attempted to put forward a "genetic deficiency" theory to explain Mobley's behavior, but did so without the benefit of an expert in genetics.

In order to establish ineffective assistance of counsel, Mobley must demonstrate that his counsel's performance "fell below an objective standard of reasonableness" and that he suffered prejudice as a result. Thus, in order to obtain habeas relief, Mobley must show that the Georgia Supreme Court's application of the ineffective-assistance test was an unreasonable one.

1. The Sabel Order

The Georgia Supreme Court correctly found that Mobley failed to demonstrate prejudice as a result of the entry of the Sabel order. n2 The experts that Mobley presented at the habeas hearing based their testimony on their understanding that Mobley's father was an alcoholic, that his parents abused him and that his mother was cruel and controlling. This testimony was contradicted by testimony from Mobley's sister that neither parent was abusive toward him. Furthermore, when counsel originally investigated Mobley's background for possible mitigating evidence, Mobley denied that he was ever abused by his parents. Summer testified at the habeas hearing that one of the reasons he chose not to hire a mental health expert was the lack of mitigating evidence and his fear of a damaging report. In light of all of these factors, we do not find that the Georgia Supreme Court's evaluation of the claim was unreasonable or contrary to established law. Mobley's ineffective assistance claim based on the Sabel order fails.

For similar reasons, Mobley also cannot demonstrate that the Georgia Supreme Court erred in its application of the ineffective-assistance standard to evaluate his claim regarding trial counsels' presentation of mitigating evidence. Mobley essentially argues that his trial counsel chose the wrong strategy and should not have attempted to put forward a genetic deficiency theory without the benefit of an expert in genetics. As discussed above, the Georgia Supreme Court found that :

> Mobley's counsel sought to find what they called "traditional mitigation evidence." They interviewed Mobley's mother, father, and sister, all of whom reported that there was no physical or sexual abuse in Mobley's childhood. Mobley's parents also denied any birth trauma or alcohol abuse. Mobley himself denied that he had ever been physically abused, sexually abused or neglected.

Mobley's counsel also obtained records from every school and institution Mobley attended and reviewed them. They spoke with some of the individuals who had treated Mobley. Id. Counsel also sought court funding for genetic testing of Mobley and for an expert geneticist to assist him in preparing mitigation testimony, but it was denied by the court.

Mobley now argues that his trial counsel pursued the wrong strategy. That strategy was informed, however, by the information provided by Mobley himself. "When a defendant has given counsel reason to believe that pursuing certain investigations would be fruitless … counsel's failure to pursue those investigations may not later be challenged as unreasonable." Trial counsel sought evidence that Mobley had been abused or neglected in the hopes of putting forward such information as an explanation for Mobley's apparent sociopathic tendencies. Mobley denied that he was abused or neglected. He cannot now complain that trial counsel failed to present such evidence to the jury.

Nor can Mobley successfully challenge trial counsels' ultimate decision to proceed with a genetic defense. Faced with almost no mitigating evidence, counsel attempted to put forward a genetic explanation based on evidence of a family history of violent temperaments and abusive behavior. Counsel did not use a genetic expert because he was denied funding for one. Our inquiry is limited to whether counsel's strategic decisions were reasonable ones at the time they were made. Given that trial counsel had almost no other mitigating evidence to work with, we cannot say that it was unreasonable to pursue the genetic deficiency theory that counsel presented to the jury. This ineffective assistance claim fails.

III. CONCLUSION

Because the Georgia Supreme Court's decision did not involve an unreasonable application of, or a decision contrary to, federal law, we AFFIRM the denial of the writ of habeas corpus by the federal district court.

Ohio v. Lane

C-970776, 1998 Ohio App. LEXIS 6417 (Ohio 1st App. D. Dec. 31, 1998)

On appeal, Lane argues trial counsel was ineffective in not presenting an expert in molecular biology to contest the credibility of Cellmark's findings. Any deficiency in defense counsel's performance must be reviewed in light of the fact that Lane was indigent and would have only been able to secure funding for an expert if the trial court found, in the exercise of its sound discretion, a reasonable probability that the requested expert would aid in Lane's defense, and that denial of the requested expert assistance would result in an unfair trial. State v. Mason (1998), 82 Ohio St. 3d 144, 694 N.E.2d 932, syllabus. In this case, the trial court did provide Lane with the funds for Laurence Mueller, Ph.D., an expert in population genetics who testified via a videotaped deposition.

In support of his claim of ineffective assistance of counsel, Lane submitted to the trial court his own affidavit, his mother's affidavit, and the affidavit of Simon Ford, Ph.D., a molecular biologist and independent biotechnology consultant. Lane and his mother both averred that they informed defense counsel of their desire and need for an expert in molecular biology to assist the defense.

In Ford's affidavit, he detailed information he gleaned from reviewing the Cellmark report dated April 29, 1993, various laboratory bench notes and copies of the case autorads, and concluded that, in his opinion, "had the defense presented a molecular biologist as an expert witness to testify to his findings attacking the credibility of the DNA evidence, then the trier of fact would have been in a much better position to assess the significance of Cellmark's findings in this case." However, Ford's affidavit did not take into account what occurred at trial. On cross-examination, defense counsel elicited from Dr. Foreman testimony similar to that contained in Ford's affidavit. Although this court held in Lane's direct appeal that Dr. Foreman was never qualified as an expert in molecular biology, which presumably invalidated the portion of her cross-examination testimony that attacked the reliability of the DNA results, we cannot ignore the fact that despite the appellate characterization of it, the trial court heard this testimony and considered it in finding Lane guilty beyond a reasonable doubt. Therefore, the outcome of the trial would not have been different had the defense presented an expert in molecular biology. Lane has failed to demonstrate prejudice as required under Strickland, supra, and, therefore, we need not determine whether his counsel violated an essential duty in this respect.

Accordingly, the record refutes Lane's claim for relief, and the trial court did not err in denying his petition for postconviction relief without a hearing.

The assignment of error is overruled, and the judgment of the trial court is affirmed.

7.7 Biopiracy

In India, the Neem tree controversy raised objections to western biopiracy of traditional knowledge when W. R. Grace isolated the molecular compound in the Neem tree to patent. The company was issued a patent in June 1992 for its invention. In March 1994, W.R. Grace registered Neemix as a pesticide with EPA in accordance with FIFRA.

A coalition of 200 organizations from 35 different nations challenged the patent and filed a petition with the U.S. Patent and Trademark Office seeking to invalidate the patent. The challenge was ultimately dismissed.

This is not a completely new act of appropriation of property. A patent was granted for a turmeric wound healing, and India claims this is traditional knowledge that has been known in India for hundreds of years. The anti-malarial drug, quinine, was patented based on observations that chewing the bark of south American Cinchona trees was a practice of peoples of Peru in the Eighteenth century which prevented them from getting malaria.

International protocols based on the Convention for Biological Diversity and the Inter-American Draft Declaration on the Rights of Indigenous Peoples, provide for bioprospecting that is equitable for both the pharmaceutical companies and the indigenous peoples. There is no international crime for biopiracy, but describes the unethical practice of appropriating property of others.

Potentially the use of CITES, the Convention on International Trade in Endangered Species, would provide some protection for listed species, and there are criminal sanctions for violation of CITES.

Chapter Eight

Scientific Evidence and Biotechnology

8.1 Introduction

In biotechnology, DNA testing, has been used in evidence since the early 1980s with increasing acceptance by the courts and by the public. In the late 1980s however, questions began to arise about the use of DNA evidence and whether mistakes had been made, particularly in death penalty cases.

DNA evidence is used to establish paternity, to determine culpability by linking a suspect to a crime, or to identify human remains. Prior to the use of DNA, blood identification techniques such as ABO blood typing, human leukocyte antigen ("HLA") typing, and the typing or red cell enzymes and serum proteins through gel electrophoresis were utilized. These techniques were very limited and could identify only that the blood came from one of four groups in the human population.

DNA testing was much more accurate and could be performed on old and degraded samples of smaller size and of various tissues. The specificity of the test was far superior to the HLA testing techniques, because DNA evidence could demonstrate that the identified DNA had a likelihood of a coincidental match was one in 2.4 million, making identification not 100% certain, but within a statistically significant range where one could be 99% confident of the match.

DNA evidence is based upon its admissibility as scientific evidence. The following three cases are the foundation of federal scientific evidence law.

8.2 The Legal Foundation of Scientific Evidence

Frye test. "That the Frye test was displaced by the Rules of Evidence does not mean, however, that the Rules themselves place no limits on the admissibility of purportedly scientific evidence. Nor is the trial judge disabled from screening such evidence. To the contrary, under the rules the trial judge must ensure that any and all scientific testimony or evidence admitted is not only relevant, but reliable." 509 U.S. at 589.

Frye v. United States

293 F. 1013 (1923)

Opinion by: Associate Justice Van Orsdel.

Appellant, defendant below, was convicted of the crime of murder in the second degree, and from the judgment prosecutes this appeal.

A single assignment of error is presented for our consideration. In the course of the trial counsel for defendant offered an expert witness to testify to the result of a deception test made upon defendant. The test is described as the systolic blood pressure deception test. It is asserted that blood pressure is influenced by change in the emotions of the witness, and that the systolic blood pressure rises are brought about by nervous impulses sent to the sympathetic branch of the autonomic nervous system. Scientific experiments, it is claimed, have demonstrated that fear, rage, and pain always produce a rise of systolic blood pressure, and that conscious deception or falsehood, concealment of facts, or guilt of crime, accompanied by fear of detection when the person is under examination, raises the systolic blood pressure in a curve, which corresponds exactly to the struggle going on in the subject's mind, between fear and attempted control of that fear, as the examination touches the vital points in respect of which he is attempting to deceive the examiner.

In other words, the theory seems to be that truth is spontaneous, and comes without conscious effort, while the utterance of a falsehood requires a conscious effort, which is reflected in the blood pressure. The rise thus produced is easily detected and distinguished from the rise produced by mere fear of the examination itself. In the former instance, the pressure rises higher than in the latter, and is more pronounced as the examination proceeds, while in the latter case, if the subject is telling the truth, the pressure registers highest at the beginning of the examination, and gradually diminishes as the examination proceeds.

Prior to the trial defendant was subjected to this deception test, and counsel offered the scientist who conducted the test as an expert to testify to the results obtained. The offer was objected to by counsel for the government, and the court sustained the objection. Counsel for defendant then offered to have the proffered witness conduct a test in the presence of the jury. This also was denied.

Counsel for defendant, in their able presentation of the novel question involved, correctly state in their brief that no cases directly in point have been found. The broad ground, however, upon which they plant their case, is succinctly stated in their brief as follows:

"The rule is that the opinions of experts or skilled witnesses are admissible in evidence in those cases in which the matter of inquiry is such that inexperienced persons are unlikely to prove capable of forming a correct judgment upon it, for the reason that the subject-matter so far partakes of a science, art, or trade as to require a previous habit or experience or study in it, in order to acquire a knowledge of it. When the question involved does not lie within the range of common experience or common knowledge, but requires special experience or special knowledge, then the opinions of witnesses skilled in that particular science, art, or trade to which the question relates are admissible in evidence."

Numerous cases are cited in support of this rule. Just when a scientific principle or discovery crosses the line between the experimental and demonstrable stages is difficult to define. Somewhere in this twilight zone the evidential force of the principle must be recognized, and while courts will go a long way in admitting expert testimony deduced from a well-recognized scientific principle or discovery, the thing from which the deduction is made must be sufficiently established to have gained general acceptance in the particular field in which it belongs.

We think the systolic blood pressure deception test has not yet gained such standing and scientific recognition among physiological and psychological authorities as would justify the courts in admitting expert testimony deduced from the discovery, development, and experiments thus far made.

The judgment is affirmed.

The Federal Rules of Evidence were created by the U.S. Congress many years after *Frye* and those rules applicable to scientific evidence were first tested in *Daubert*, more than 50 years after the common law rule for scientific evidence admissible was established. The Federal Rules of Evidence which are relevant to the admissibility and reliability of scientific evidence are as follows:

FRE Rule 702. Testimony by Experts. If scientific, technical, or other specialized knowledge will assist the trier of fact to understand the evidence or to determine a fact in issue, a witness qualified as an expert by knowledge, skill, experience, training, or education, may testify thereto in the form of an opinion or otherwise....

FRE Rule 703. Bases of Opinion Testimony by Experts. The facts or data in the particular case upon which an expert bases an opinion or inference may be those perceived by or made known to the expert at or before the hearing. If of a type reasonably relied upon by experts in the particular field in forming opinions or inferences upon the subject, the facts or data need not be admissible in evidence....

FRE Rule 704. Opinion on Ultimate Issue. (a) Except as provided in subdivision (b), testimony in the form of an opinion or inference otherwise admissible is not objectionable because it embraces an ultimate issue to be decided by the trier of fact. (b) No expert witness testifying with respect to the mental state or condition of a defendant in a criminal case may state an opinion or inference as to whether the defendant did or did not have the mental state or condition constituting an element of the crime charged or of a defense thereto. Such ultimate issues are matters for the trier of fact, alone.

FRE Rule 401. Definition of "Relevant Evidence" "Relevant Evidence" means evidence having any tendency to make the existence of any fact that is of consequence to the determination of the action more probable or less probable than it would be without the evidence.

FRE Rule 402. Relevant Evidence Generally Admissible; Irrelevant Evidence Inadmissible. All relevant evidence is admissible, except as otherwise provided by the Constitution of the United States, by Act of Congress, by these rules, or by other rules prescribed by the Supreme Court pursuant to statutory authority. Evidence which is not relevant is not admissible.

FRE Rule 403. Exclusion of Relevant Evidence on Grounds of Prejudice, Confusion, or Waste of Time. Although relevant, evidence may be excluded if its probative value is substantially outweighed by the danger of unfair prejudice, confusion of the issues, or misleading the jury, or by considerations of undue delay, waste of time or needless presentation of cumulative evidence.

Daubert v. Merrell Dow Pharmaceuticals, Inc.

509 U.S. 579 (1993)

JUSTICE BLACKMUN delivered the opinion of the Court.

In this case we are called upon to determine the standard for admitting expert scientific testimony in a federal trial.

I

Petitioners Jason Daubert and Eric Schuller are minor children born with serious birth defects. They and their parents sued respondent in California state court, alleging that the birth defects had been caused by the mothers' ingestion of Bendectin, a prescription antinausea drug marketed by respondent. Respondent removed the suits to federal court on diversity grounds.

After extensive discovery, respondent moved for summary judgment, contending that Bendectin does not cause birth defects in humans and that petitioners would be unable to come forward with any admissible evidence that it does. In support of its motion, respondent submitted an affidavit of Steven H. Lamm, physician and epidemiologist, who is a well-credentialed expert on the risks from exposure to various chemical substances. Doctor Lamm stated that he had reviewed all the literature on Bendectin and human birth defects—more than 30 published studies involving over 130,000 patients. No study had found Bendectin to be a human teratogen (*i.e.*, a substance capable of causing malformations in fetuses). On the basis of this review, Doctor Lamm concluded that maternal use of Bendectin during the first trimester of pregnancy has not been shown to be a risk factor for human birth defects. These experts had concluded that Bendectin can cause birth defects. Their conclusions were based upon "in vitro" (test tube) and "in vivo" (live) animal studies that found a link between Bendectin and malformations; pharmacological studies of the chemical structure of Bendectin that purported to show similarities between the structure of the drug and that of other substances known to cause birth defects; and the "reanalysis" of previously published epidemiological (human statistical) studies.

The District Court granted respondent's motion for summary judgment. The court stated that scientific evidence is admissible only if the principle upon which it is based is "'sufficiently established to have general acceptance in the field to which it belongs.'" 727 F. Supp. 570, 572 (SD Cal. 1989), quoting *United States* v. *Kilgus*, 571 F.2d 508, 510 (CA9 1978). The court concluded that petitioners' evidence did not meet this standard. Given the vast body of epidemiological data concerning Bendectin, the court held, expert opinion which is not based on epidemiological evidence is not admissible to establish causation. 727 F. Supp. at 575. Thus, the animal-cell studies, live-animal studies, and chemical-structure analyses on which petitioners had relied could not raise by themselves a reasonably disputable jury issue regarding causation. *Ibid.* Petitioners' epidemiological analyses, based as they were on recalculations of data in previously published studies that had found no causal link between the drug and birth defects, were ruled to be inadmissible because they had not been published or subjected to peer review. Ibid.

The United States Court of Appeals for the Ninth Circuit affirmed. 951 F.2d 1128 (1991). Citing *Frye* v. *United States*, 54 App. D.C. 46, 47, 293 F. 1013, 1014 (1923), the court stated that expert opinion based on a scientific technique is inadmissible unless the technique is "generally accepted" as reliable in the relevant scientific community. 951 F.2d at 1129–1130. The court declared that expert opinion based on a methodology that diverges "significantly from the procedures accepted by recognized authorities in the field … cannot be shown to be 'generally accepted as a reliable technique.'" *Id.*, at 1130, quoting *United States* v. *Solomon*, 753 F.2d 1522, 1526 (CA9 1985).

The court emphasized that other Courts of Appeals considering the risks of Bendectin had refused to admit reanalyses of epidemiological studies that had been neither published nor subjected to peer review. 951 F.2d at 1130–1131. Those courts had found unpublished reanalyses "particularly problematic in light of the massive weight of the original published studies supporting [respondent's] position, all of which had undergone full scrutiny from the scientific community." *Id.*, at 1130. Contending that reanalysis is generally accepted by the scientific community only when it is subjected to verification and scrutiny by others in the field, the Court of Appeals rejected petitioners' reanalyses as "unpublished, not subjected to the normal peer review process and generated solely for use in litigation." *Id.*, at 1131. The court concluded that petitioners' evidence provided an insufficient foundation to allow admission of expert testimony that Bendectin caused their injuries and, accordingly, that petitioners could not satisfy their burden of proving causation at trial.

We granted certiorari, 506 U.S. 914 (1992), in light of sharp divisions among the courts regarding the proper standard for the admission of expert testimony. Compare, *e.g.*, *United States* v. *Shorter*, 257 U.S. App. D.C. 358, 363–364, 809 F.2d 54, 59–60 (applying the "general acceptance" standard), cert. denied, 484 U.S. 817, 98 L. Ed. 2d 35, 108 S. Ct. 71 (1987), with *DeLuca* v. *Merrell Dow Pharmaceuticals, Inc.*, 911 F.2d 941, 955 (CA3 1990) (rejecting the "general acceptance" standard).

II A

In the 70 years since its formulation in the *Frye* case, the "general acceptance" test has been the dominant standard for determining the admissibility of novel scientific evidence at trial. See E. Green & C. Nesson, Problems, Cases, and Materials on Evidence 649 (1983). Although under increasing attack of late, the rule continues to be followed by a majority of courts, including the Ninth Circuit …

The *Frye* test has its origin in a short and citation-free 1923 decision concerning the admissibility of evidence derived from a systolic blood pressure deception test, a crude precursor to the polygraph machine. In what has become a famous (perhaps infamous) passage, the then Court of Appeals for the District of Columbia described the device and its operation and declared: …

> "Just when a scientific principle or discovery crosses the line between the experimental and demonstrable stages is difficult to define. Somewhere in this twilight zone the evidential force of the principle must be recognized, and while courts will go a long way in admitting expert testimony deduced from a well-recognized scientific principle or discovery, *the thing from which the deduction is made must be sufficiently established to have gained general acceptance in the particular field in which it belongs.*" 54 App. D.C. at 47, 293 F. at 1014 (emphasis added).

Because the deception test had "not yet gained such standing and scientific recognition among physiological and psychological authorities as would justify the courts in admitting expert testimony deduced from the discovery, development, and experiments thus far made," evidence of its results was ruled inadmissible. *Ibid.*

The merits of the *Frye* test have been much debated, and scholarship on its proper scope and application is legion. Petitioners' primary attack, however, is not on the content but on the continuing authority of the rule. They contend that the *Frye* test was superseded by the adoption of the Federal Rules of Evidence. F5 We agree.

SELECTED FOOTNOTES

F5. We interpret the legislatively enacted Federal Rules of Evidence as we would any statute. *Beech Aircraft Corp.* v. *Rainey*, 488 U.S. 153, 163, 102 L. Ed. 2d 445, 109 S. Ct. 439 (1988). Rule 402 provides the baseline:

"All relevant evidence is admissible, except as otherwise provided by the Constitution of the United States, by Act of Congress, by these rules, or by other rules prescribed by the Supreme Court pursuant to statutory authority. Evidence which is not relevant is not admissible."

"Relevant evidence" is defined as that which has "any tendency to make the existence of any fact that is of consequence to the determination of the action more probable or less probable than it would be without the evidence." Rule 401. The Rules' basic standard of relevance thus is a liberal one.

Frye, of course, predated the Rules by half a century. In *United States* v. *Abel*, 469 U.S. 45, 83 L. Ed. 2d 450, 105 S. Ct. 465 (1984), we considered the pertinence of background common law in interpreting the Rules of Evidence. We noted that the Rules occupy the field, *id.*, at 49, but, quoting Professor Cleary, the Reporter, explained that the common law nevertheless could serve as an aid to their application:

> "'In principle, under the Federal Rules no common law of evidence remains. "All relevant evidence is admissible, except as otherwise provided...." In reality, of course, the body of common law knowledge continues to exist, though in the somewhat altered form of a source of guidance in the exercise of delegated powers.'" *Id.*, at 51–52.

We found the common-law precept at issue in the *Abel* case entirely consistent with Rule 402's general requirement of admissibility, and considered it unlikely that the drafters had intended to change the rule. *Id.*, at 50–51. In *Bourjaily* v. *United States*, 483 U.S. 171, 97 L. Ed. 2d 144, 107 S. Ct. 2775 (1987), on the other hand, the Court was unable to find a particular common-law doctrine in the Rules, and so held it superseded.

Here there is a specific Rule that speaks to the contested issue. Rule 702, governing expert testimony, provides:

> "If scientific, technical, or other specialized knowledge will assist the trier of fact to understand the evidence or to determine a fact in issue, a witness qualified as an expert by knowledge, skill, experience, training, or education, may testify thereto in the form of an opinion or otherwise."

Nothing in the text of this Rule establishes "general acceptance" as an absolute prerequisite to admissibility. Nor does respondent present any clear indication that Rule 702 or the Rules as a whole were intended to incorporate a "general acceptance" standard. The drafting history makes no mention of *Frye*, and a rigid "general acceptance" requirement would be at odds with the "liberal thrust" of the Federal Rules and their "general approach of relaxing the traditional barriers to 'opinion' testimony." Given the Rules' permissive backdrop and their inclusion of a specific rule on expert testimony that does not mention "general acceptance," the assertion that the Rules somehow assimilated *Frye* is unconvincing. *Frye* made "general acceptance" the exclusive test for admitting expert scientific testimony. That austere standard, absent from, and incompatible with, the Federal Rules of Evidence, should not be applied in federal trials.

B

That the *Frye* test was displaced by the Rules of Evidence does not mean, however, that the Rules themselves place no limits on the admissibility of purportedly scientific evidence.... Nor is the trial judge disabled from screening such evidence. To the contrary, under the Rules the trial judge must ensure that any and all scientific testimony or evidence admitted is not only relevant, but reliable.

The primary locus of this obligation is Rule 702, which clearly contemplates some degree of regulation of the subjects and theories about which an expert may testify. "*If scientific, technical, or other specialized knowledge will assist the trier of fact* to understand the evidence or to determine a fact in issue" an expert "may testify *thereto*." (Emphasis added.) The subject of an expert's testimony must be "scientific ... knowledge." n8 The adjective "scientific" implies a grounding in the methods and procedures of science. Similarly, the word "knowledge" connotes more than subjective belief or unsupported speculation. The term "applies to any body of known facts or to any body of ideas inferred from such facts or accepted as truths on good grounds." Webster's Third New International Dictionary 1252 (1986). Of course, it would be unreasonable to conclude that the subject of scientific testimony must be "known" to a certainty; arguably, there are no certainties in science. See, *e.g.*, Brief for Nicolaas Bloembergen et al. as *Amici Curiae* 9 ("Indeed, scientists do not assert that they know what is immutably 'true' — they are committed to searching for new, temporary, theories to explain, as best they can, phenomena"); Brief for American Association for the Advancement of Science et al. as *Amici Curiae* 7–8 ("Science is not an encyclopedic body of knowledge about the universe. Instead, it represents a *process* for proposing and refining theoretical explanations about the world that are subject to further testing and refinement" (emphasis in original)). But, in order to qualify as "scientific knowledge," an inference or assertion must be derived by the scientific method. Proposed testimony must be supported by appropriate validation—*i.e.*, "good grounds," based on what is known. In short, the requirement that an expert's testimony pertain to "scientific knowledge" establishes a standard of evidentiary reliability.

Rule 702 further requires that the evidence or testimony "assist the trier of fact to understand the evidence or to determine a fact in issue." This condition goes primarily to relevance. "Expert testimony which does not relate to any issue in the case is not relevant and, ergo, non-helpful." 3 Weinstein & Berger P702[02], p. 702–18. See also *United States* v. *Downing*, 753 F.2d 1224, 1242 (CA3 1985) ("An additional consideration under Rule 702—and another aspect of relevancy—is whether expert testimony proffered in the case is sufficiently tied to the facts of the case that it will aid the jury in resolving a factual dispute"). The consideration has been aptly described by Judge Becker as one of "fit." *Ibid.* "Fit" is not always obvious, and scientific validity for one purpose is not necessarily scientific validity for other, unrelated purposes. See Starrs, *Frye v. United States* Restructured and Revitalized: A Proposal to Amend Federal Evidence Rule 702, 26 Jurimetrics J. 249, 258 (1986). The study of the phases of the moon, for example, may provide valid scientific "knowledge" about whether a certain night was dark, and if darkness is a fact in issue, the knowledge will assist the trier of fact. However (absent creditable grounds supporting such a link), evidence that the moon was full on a certain night will not assist the trier of fact in determining whether an individual was unusually likely to have behaved irrationally on that night. Rule 702's "helpfulness" standard requires a valid scientific connection to the pertinent inquiry as a precondition to admissibility.

That these requirements are embodied in Rule 702 is not surprising. Unlike an ordinary witness, see Rule 701, an expert is permitted wide latitude to offer opinions, including those that are not based on firsthand knowledge or observation. See Rules 702 and 703. Presumably, this relaxation of the usual requirement of firsthand knowledge—a rule which represents "a 'most pervasive manifestation' of the common law insistence upon 'the most reliable sources of information,'" Advisory Committee's Notes on Fed. Rule Evid. 602, 28 U.S.C. App., p. 755 (citation omitted)—is premised on an assumption that the expert's opinion will have a reliable basis in the knowledge and experience of his discipline.

C

Faced with a proffer of expert scientific testimony, then, the trial judge must determine at the outset, pursuant to Rule 104(a),..whether the expert is proposing to testify to (1) scientific knowledge that (2) will assist the trier of fact to understand or determine a fact in issue. n11 This entails a preliminary assessment of whether the reasoning or methodology underlying the testimony is scientifically valid and of whether that reasoning or methodology properly can be applied to the facts in issue. We are confident that federal judges possess the capacity to undertake this review. Many factors will bear on the inquiry, and we do not presume to set out a definitive checklist or test. But some general observations are appropriate.

Ordinarily, a key question to be answered in determining whether a theory or technique is scientific knowledge that will assist the trier of fact will be whether it can be (and has been) tested. "Scientific methodology today is based on generating hypotheses and testing them to see if they can be falsified; indeed, this methodology is what distinguishes science from other fields of human inquiry." Green 645. See also C. Hempel, Philosophy of Natural Science 49 (1966) ("The statements constituting a scientific explanation must be capable of empirical test"); K. Popper, Conjectures and Refutations: The Growth of Scientific Knowledge 37 (5th ed. 1989) ("The criterion of the scientific status of a theory is its falsifiability, or refutability, or testability") (emphasis deleted).

Another pertinent consideration is whether the theory or technique has been subjected to peer review and publication. Publication (which is but one element of peer review) is not a *sine qua non* of admissibility; it does not necessarily correlate with reliability, see S. Jasanoff, The Fifth Branch: Science Advisors as Policymakers 61–76 (1990), and in some instances well-grounded but innovative theories will not have been published, see Horrobin, The Philosophical Basis of Peer Review and the Suppression of Innovation, 263 JAMA 1438 (1990). Some propositions, moreover, are too particular, too new, or of too limited interest to be published. But submission to the scrutiny of the scientific community is a component of "good science," in part because it increases the likelihood that substantive flaws in methodology will be detected. See J. Ziman, Reliable Knowledge: An Exploration of the Grounds for Belief in Science 130–133 (1978); Relman & Angell, How Good Is Peer Review?, 321 New Eng. J. Med. 827 (1989). The fact of publication (or lack thereof) in a peer reviewed journal thus will be a relevant, though not dispositive, consideration in assessing the scientific validity of a particular technique or methodology on which an opinion is premised.

Additionally, in the case of a particular scientific technique, the court ordinarily should consider the known or potential rate of error, see, *e.g., United States* v. *Smith*, 869 F.2d

348, 353–354 (CA7 1989) (surveying studies of the error rate of spectrographic voice identification technique), and the existence and maintenance of standards controlling the technique's operation, see *United States* v. *Williams*, 583 F.2d 1194, 1198 (CA2 1978) (noting professional organization's standard governing spectrographic analysis), cert. denied, 439 U.S. 1117, 59 L. Ed. 2d 77, 99 S. Ct. 1025 (1979).

Finally, "general acceptance" can yet have a bearing on the inquiry. A "reliability assessment does not require, although it does permit, explicit identification of a relevant scientific community and an express determination of a particular degree of acceptance within that community." *United States* v. *Downing*, 753 F.2d at 1238. See also 3 Weinstein & Berger P702[03], pp. 702–41 to 702–42. Widespread acceptance can be an important factor in ruling particular evidence admissible, and "a known technique which has been able to attract only minimal support within the community," *Downing*, 753 F.2d at 1238, may properly be viewed with skepticism.

The inquiry envisioned by Rule 702 is, we emphasize, a flexible one.... Its overarching subject is the scientific validity—and thus the evidentiary relevance and reliability—of the principles that underlie a proposed submission. The focus, of course, must be solely on principles and methodology, not on the conclusions that they generate.

Throughout, a judge assessing a proffer of expert scientific testimony under Rule 702 should also be mindful of other applicable rules. Rule 703 provides that expert opinions based on otherwise inadmissible hearsay are to be admitted only if the facts or data are "of a type reasonably relied upon by experts in the particular field in forming opinions or inferences upon the subject." Rule 706 allows the court at its discretion to procure the assistance of an expert of its own choosing. Finally, Rule 403 permits the exclusion of relevant evidence "if its probative value is substantially outweighed by the danger of unfair prejudice, confusion of the issues, or misleading the jury...." Judge Weinstein has explained: "Expert evidence can be both powerful and quite misleading because of the difficulty in evaluating it. Because of this risk, the judge in weighing possible prejudice against probative force under Rule 403 of the present rules exercises more control over experts than over lay witnesses." Weinstein, 138 F.R.D. at 632.

III

We conclude by briefly addressing what appear to be two underlying concerns of the parties and *amici* in this case. Respondent expresses apprehension that abandonment of "general acceptance" as the exclusive requirement for admission will result in a "free-for-all" in which befuddled juries are confounded by absurd and irrational pseudoscientific assertions. In this regard respondent seems to us to be overly pessimistic about the capabilities of the jury and of the adversary system generally. Vigorous cross-examination, presentation of contrary evidence, and careful instruction on the burden of proof are the traditional and appropriate means of attacking shaky but admissible evidence. See *Rock* v. *Arkansas*, 483 U.S. 44, 61, 97 L. Ed. 2d 37, 107 S. Ct. 2704 (1987). Additionally, in the event the trial court concludes that the scintilla of evidence presented supporting a position is insufficient to allow a reasonable juror to conclude that the position more likely than not is true, the court remains free to direct a judgment, Fed. Rule Civ. Proc. 50(a), and likewise to grant summary judgment, Fed. Rule Civ. Proc. 56. Cf., *e.g., Turpin* v. *Merrell Dow Pharmaceuticals, Inc.*, 959 F.2d 1349 (CA6) (holding that scientific evidence that provided foundation for expert testimony, viewed in the light most favorable to plaintiffs, was not sufficient to allow a jury to find it more probable than not that defendant caused plaintiff's injury), cert. denied, 506 U.S. 826, 121 L. Ed. 2d 47, 113 S. Ct. 84 (1992); *Brock* v. *Merrell Dow Pharmaceuticals, Inc.*, 874

F.2d 307 (CA5 1989) (reversing judgment entered on jury verdict for plaintiffs because evidence regarding causation was insufficient), modified, 884 F.2d 166 (CA5 1989), cert. denied, 494 U.S. 1046 (1990); Green 680–681. These conventional devices, rather than wholesale exclusion under an uncompromising "general acceptance" test, are the appropriate safeguards where the basis of scientific testimony meets the standards of Rule 702.

Petitioners and, to a greater extent, their *amici* exhibit a different concern. They suggest that recognition of a screening role for the judge that allows for the exclusion of "invalid" evidence will sanction a stifling and repressive scientific orthodoxy and will be inimical to the search for truth. See, *e.g.*, Brief for Ronald Bayer et al. as *Amici Curiae*. It is true that open debate is an essential part of both legal and scientific analyses. Yet there are important differences between the quest for truth in the courtroom and the quest for truth in the laboratory. Scientific conclusions are subject to perpetual revision. Law, on the other hand, must resolve disputes finally and quickly. The scientific project is advanced by broad and wide-ranging consideration of a multitude of hypotheses, for those that are incorrect will eventually be shown to be so, and that in itself is an advance. Conjectures that are probably wrong are of little use, however, in the project of reaching a quick, final, and binding legal judgment—often of great consequence—about a particular set of events in the past. We recognize that, in practice, a gatekeeping role for the judge, no matter how flexible, inevitably on occasion will prevent the jury from learning of authentic insights and innovations. That, nevertheless, is the balance that is struck by Rules of Evidence designed not for the exhaustive search for cosmic understanding but for the particularized resolution of legal disputes....

IV

To summarize: "General acceptance" is not a necessary precondition to the admissibility of scientific evidence under the Federal Rules of Evidence, but the Rules of Evidence—especially Rule 702—do assign to the trial judge the task of ensuring that an expert's testimony both rests on a reliable foundation and is relevant to the task at hand. Pertinent evidence based on scientifically valid principles will satisfy those demands.

The inquiries of the District Court and the Court of Appeals focused almost exclusively on "general acceptance," as gauged by publication and the decisions of other courts. Accordingly, the judgment of the Court of Appeals is vacated, and the case is remanded for further proceedings consistent with this opinion.

It is so ordered.

Concur by REHNQUIST (In Part) ; and dissent by Rehnquist (in Part)

Dissent by CHIEF JUSTICE REHNQUIST, with whom JUSTICE STEVENS joins, concurring in part and dissenting in part.

The petition for certiorari in this case presents two questions: first, whether the rule of *Frye v. United States*, 54 App. D.C. 46, 293 F. 1013 (1923), remains good law after the enactment of the Federal Rules of Evidence; and second, if *Frye* remains valid, whether it requires expert scientific testimony to have been subjected to a peer review process in order to be admissible. The Court concludes, correctly in my view, that the *Frye* rule did not survive the enactment of the Federal Rules of Evidence, and I therefore join Parts I and II-A of its opinion. The second question presented in the petition for certiorari necessarily is mooted by this holding, but the Court nonetheless proceeds to construe Rules 702 and 703 very much in the abstract, and then offers some "general observations." *Ante,* at 593.

"General observations" by this Court customarily carry great weight with lower federal courts, but the ones offered here suffer from the flaw common to most such observations—they are not applied to deciding whether particular testimony was or was not admissible, and therefore they tend to be not only general, but vague and abstract. This is particularly unfortunate in a case such as this, where the ultimate legal question depends on an appreciation of one or more bodies of knowledge not judicially noticeable, and subject to different interpretations in the briefs of the parties and their *amici*. Twenty-two *amicus* briefs have been filed in the case, and indeed the Court's opinion contains no fewer than 37 citations to *amicus* briefs and other secondary sources.

The various briefs filed in this case are markedly different from typical briefs, in that large parts of them do not deal with decided cases or statutory language—the sort of material we customarily interpret. Instead, they deal with definitions of scientific knowledge, scientific method, scientific validity, and peer review—in short, matters far afield from the expertise of judges. This is not to say that such materials are not useful or even necessary in deciding how Rule 702 should be applied; but it is to say that the unusual subject matter should cause us to proceed with great caution in deciding more than we have to, because our reach can so easily exceed our grasp.

But even if it were desirable to make "general observations" not necessary to decide the questions presented, I cannot subscribe to some of the observations made by the Court. In Part II-B, the Court concludes that reliability and relevancy are the touchstones of the admissibility of expert testimony. *Ante*, at 590–592. Federal Rule of Evidence 402 provides, as the Court points out, that "evidence which is not relevant is not admissible." But there is no similar reference in the Rule to "reliability." The Court constructs its argument by parsing the language "if scientific, technical, or other specialized knowledge will assist the trier of fact to understand the evidence or to determine a fact in issue, ... an expert ... may testify thereto...." Fed. Rule Evid. 702. It stresses that the subject of the expert's testimony must be "scientific ... knowledge," and points out that "scientific" "implies a grounding in the methods and procedures of science" and that the word "knowledge" "connotes more than subjective belief or unsupported speculation." *Ante*, at 590. From this it concludes that "scientific knowledge" must be "derived by the scientific method." *Ibid.* Proposed testimony, we are told, must be supported by "appropriate validation." *Ibid.* Indeed, in footnote 9, the Court decides that "in a case involving scientific evidence, evidentiary reliability will be based upon *scientific validity*." *Ante*, at 591, n. 9 (emphasis in original).

Questions arise simply from reading this part of the Court's opinion, and countless more questions will surely arise when hundreds of district judges try to apply its teaching to particular offers of expert testimony. Does all of this *dicta* apply to an expert seeking to testify on the basis of "technical or other specialized knowledge"—the other types of expert knowledge to which Rule 702 applies—or are the "general observations" limited only to "scientific knowledge"? What is the difference between scientific knowledge and technical knowledge; does Rule 702 actually contemplate that the phrase "scientific, technical, or other specialized knowledge" be broken down into numerous subspecies of expertise, or did its authors simply pick general descriptive language covering the sort of expert testimony which courts have customarily received? The Court speaks of its confidence that federal judges can make a "preliminary assessment of whether the reasoning or methodology underlying the testimony is scientifically valid and of whether that reasoning or methodology properly can be applied to the facts in issue." *Ante*, at 592–593. The Court then states that a "key question" to be answered in deciding whether something is "scientific knowledge" "will be whether it can be (and has been) tested." *Ante*, at

593. Following this sentence are three quotations from treatises, which not only speak of empirical testing, but one of which states that the "'criterion of the scientific status of a theory is its falsifiability, or refutability, or testability.'" *Ibid.*

I defer to no one in my confidence in federal judges; but I am at a loss to know what is meant when it is said that the scientific status of a theory depends on its "falsifiability," and I suspect some of them will be, too.

I do not doubt that Rule 702 confides to the judge some gatekeeping responsibility in deciding questions of the admissibility of proffered expert testimony. But I do not think it imposes on them either the obligation or the authority to become amateur scientists in order to perform that role. I think the Court would be far better advised in this case to decide only the questions presented, and to leave the further development of this important area of the law to future cases.

General Electric Company v. Joiner
522 U.S. 136 (1997)

CHIEF JUSTICE Rehnquist delivered the opinion of the Court.

We granted certiorari in this case to determine what standard an appellate court should apply in reviewing a trial court's decision to admit or exclude expert testimony under *Daubert* v. *Merrell Dow Pharmaceuticals, Inc.*, 509 U.S. 579, 125 L. Ed. 2d 469, 113 S. Ct. 2786 (1993). We hold that abuse of discretion is the appropriate standard. We apply this standard and conclude that the District Court in this case did not abuse its discretion when it excluded certain proffered expert testimony.

Respondent Robert Joiner began work as an electrician in the Water & Light Department of Thomasville, Georgia (City) in 1973. This job required him to work with and around the City's electrical transformers, which used a mineral-based dielectric fluid as a coolant. Joiner often had to stick his hands and arms into the fluid to make repairs. The fluid would sometimes splash onto him, occasionally getting into his eyes and mouth. In 1983 the City discovered that the fluid in some of the transformers was contaminated with polychlorinated biphenyls (PCBs). PCBs are widely considered to be hazardous to human health. Congress, with limited exceptions, banned the production and sale of PCBs in 1978.

Joiner was diagnosed with small cell lung cancer in 1991. He sued petitioners in Georgia state court the following year. Petitioner Monsanto manufactured PCBs from 1935 to 1977; petitioners General Electric and Westinghouse Electric manufactured transformers and dielectric fluid. In his complaint Joiner linked his development of cancer to his exposure to PCBs and their derivatives, polychlorinated dibenzofurans (furans) and polychlorinated dibenzodioxins (dioxins). Joiner had been a smoker for approximately eight years, his parents had both been smokers, and there was a history of lung cancer in his family. He was thus perhaps already at a heightened risk of developing lung cancer eventually. The suit alleged that his exposure to PCBs "promoted" his cancer; had it not been for his exposure to these substances, his cancer would not have developed for many years, if at all.

Petitioners removed the case to federal court. Once there, they moved for summary judgment. They contended that (1) there was no evidence that Joiner suffered significant exposure to PCBs, furans, or dioxins, and (2) there was no admissible scientific evidence that PCBs promoted Joiner's cancer. Joiner responded that there were numerous disputed factual issues that required resolution by a jury. He relied largely on the testimony of expert witnesses. In depositions, his experts had testified that PCBs alone can promote cancer and that furans and dioxins can also promote cancer. They opined that since Joiner had been exposed to PCBs, furans, and dioxins, such exposure was likely responsible for Joiner's cancer.

The District Court ruled that there was a genuine issue of material fact as to whether Joiner had been exposed to PCBs. But it nevertheless granted summary judgment for petitioners because (1) there was no genuine issue as to whether Joiner had been exposed to furans and dioxins, and (2) the testimony of Joiner's experts had failed to show that there was a link between exposure to PCBs and small cell lung cancer. The court believed that the testimony of respondent's experts to the contrary did not rise above "subjective belief or unsupported speculation." 864 F. Supp. 1310, 1326 (ND Ga. 1994). Their testimony was therefore inadmissible.

The Court of Appeals for the Eleventh Circuit reversed. 78 F.3d 524 (1996). It held that "because the Federal Rules of Evidence governing expert testimony display a preference for admissibility, we apply a particularly stringent standard of review to the trial judge's exclusion of expert testimony." . Applying that standard, the Court of Appeals held that the District Court had erred in excluding the testimony of Joiner's expert witnesses. The District Court had made two fundamental errors. First, it excluded the experts' testimony because it "drew different conclusions from the research than did each of the experts." The Court of Appeals opined that a district court should limit its role to determining the "legal reliability of proffered expert testimony, leaving the jury to decide the correctness of competing expert opinions." Second, the District Court had held that there was no genuine issue of material fact as to whether Joiner had been exposed to furans and dioxins. This was also incorrect, said the Court of Appeals, because testimony in the record supported the proposition that there had been such exposure.

We granted petitioners' petition for a writ of certiorari, 520 U.S. (1997), and we now reverse....

III

We believe that a proper application of the correct standard of review here indicates that the District Court did not abuse its discretion. Joiner's theory of liability was that his exposure to PCBs and their derivatives "promoted" his development of small cell lung cancer. In support of that theory he proffered the deposition testimony of expert witnesses. Dr. Arnold Schecter testified that he believed it "more likely than not that Mr. Joiner's lung cancer was causally linked to cigarette smoking and PCB exposure." Dr. Daniel Teitelbaum testified that Joiner's "lung cancer was caused by or contributed to in a significant degree by the materials with which he worked."

Petitioners contended that the statements of Joiner's experts regarding causation were nothing more than speculation. Petitioners criticized the testimony of the experts in that it was "not supported by epidemiological studies ... [and was] based exclusively on isolated studies of laboratory animals." Joiner responded by claiming that his experts had identified "relevant animal studies which support their opinions." He also directed the court's attention to four epidemiological studies ... on which his experts had relied.

The District Court agreed with petitioners that the animal studies on which respondent's experts relied did not support his contention that exposure to PCBs had contributed to his cancer. The studies involved infant mice that had developed cancer after being exposed to PCBs. The infant mice in the studies had had massive doses of PCBs injected directly into their peritoneums or stomachs. Joiner was an adult human being whose alleged exposure to PCBs was far less than the exposure in the animal studies. The PCBs were injected into the mice in a highly concentrated form. The fluid with which Joiner had come into contact generally had a much smaller PCB concentration of between 0–500 parts per million. The cancer that these mice developed was alveolo-genic adenomas; Joiner had developed small-cell carcinomas. No study demonstrated that adult mice developed cancer after being exposed to PCBs. One of the experts ad-mitted that no study had demonstrated that PCBs lead to cancer in any other species.

Respondent failed to reply to this criticism. Rather than explaining how and why the ex-perts could have extrapolated their opinions from these seemingly far-removed animal studies, respondent chose "to proceed as if the only issue [was] whether animal studies can ever be a proper foundation for an expert's opinion." *Joiner*, 864 F. Supp. at 1324. Of course, whether animal studies can ever be a proper foundation for an expert's opin-ion was not the issue. The issue was whether *these* experts' opinions were sufficiently supported by the animal studies on which they purported to rely. The studies were so dissimilar to the facts presented in this litigation that it was not an abuse of discretion for the District Court to have rejected the experts' reliance on them.

The District Court also concluded that the four epidemiological studies on which re-spondent relied were not a sufficient basis for the experts' opinions. The first such study involved workers at an Italian capacitor plant who had been exposed to PCBs. Bertazzi, Riboldi, Pesatori, Radice, & Zocchetti, Cancer Mortality of Capacitor Manufacturing Workers, 11 American Journal of Industrial Medicine 165 (1987). The authors noted that lung cancer deaths among ex-employees at the plant were higher than might have been expected, but concluded that "there were apparently no grounds for associating lung cancer deaths (although increased above expectations) and exposure in the plant." Given that Bertazzi et al. were unwilling to say that PCB exposure had caused cancer among the workers they examined, their study did not support the experts' conclusion that Joiner's exposure to PCBs caused his cancer.

The second study followed employees who had worked at Monsanto's PCB production plant. J. Zack & D. Munsch, Mortality of PCB Workers at the Monsanto Plant in Sauget, Illinois (Dec. 14, 1979)(unpublished report), 3 Rec., Doc. No. 11. The authors of this study found that the incidence of lung cancer deaths among these workers was some-what higher than would ordinarily be expected. The increase, however, was not statisti-cally significant and the authors of the study did not suggest a link between the increase in lung cancer deaths and the exposure to PCBs.

The third and fourth studies were likewise of no help. The third involved workers at a Nor-wegian cable manufacturing company who had been exposed to mineral oil. Ronneberg, Andersen, Skyberg, Mortality and Incidence of Cancer Among Oil-Exposed Workers in a Norwegian Cable Manufacturing Company, 45 British Journal of Industrial Medicine 595 (1988). A statistically significant increase in lung cancer deaths had been observed in these workers. The study, however, (1) made no mention of PCBs and (2) was expressly limited to the type of mineral oil involved in that study, and thus did not support these experts' opinions. The fourth and final study involved a PCB-exposed group in Japan that had seen a statistically significant increase in lung cancer deaths. Kuratsune, Nakamura, Ikeda, & Hirohata, Analysis of Deaths Seen Among Patients with Yusho—A Preliminary Report, 16 Chemosphere, Nos. 8/9, 2085 (1987). The subjects of this study, however, had been ex-posed to numerous potential carcinogens, including toxic rice oil that they had ingested.

Respondent points to *Daubert's* language that the "focus, of course, must be solely on principles and methodology, not on the conclusions that they generate." 509 U.S. at

595. He claims that because the District Court's disagreement was with the conclusion that the experts drew from the studies, the District Court committed legal error and was properly reversed by the Court of Appeals. But conclusions and methodology are not entirely distinct from one another. Trained experts commonly extrapolate from existing data. But nothing in either *Daubert* or the Federal Rules of Evidence requires a district court to admit opinion evidence which is connected to existing data only by the *ipse dixit* of the expert. A court may conclude that there is simply too great an analytical gap between the data and the opinion proffered. See *Turpin v. Merrell Dow Pharmaceuticals, Inc.*, 959 F.2d 1349, 1360 (CA 6), cert. denied, 506 U.S. 826, 121 L. Ed. 2d 47, 113 S. Ct. 84 (1992). That is what the District Court did here, and we hold that it did not abuse its discretion in so doing.

We hold, therefore, that abuse of discretion is the proper standard by which to review a district court's decision to admit or exclude scientific evidence. We further hold that, because it was within the District Court's discretion to conclude that the studies upon which the experts relied were not sufficient, whether individually or in combination, to support their conclusions that Joiner's exposure to PCBs contributed to his cancer, the District Court did not abuse its discretion in excluding their testimony. These conclusions, however, do not dispose of this entire case.

Respondent's original contention was that his exposure to PCBs, furans, and dioxins contributed to his cancer. The District Court ruled that there was a genuine issue of material fact as to whether Joiner had been exposed to PCBs, but concluded that there was no genuine issue as to whether he had been exposed to furans and dioxins. The District Court accordingly never explicitly considered if there was admissible evidence on the question whether Joiner's alleged exposure to furans and dioxins contributed to his cancer. The Court of Appeals reversed the District Court's conclusion that there had been no exposure to furans and dioxins. Petitioners did not challenge this determination in their petition to this Court. Whether Joiner was exposed to furans and dioxins, and whether if there was such exposure, the opinions of Joiner's experts would then be admissible, remain open questions. We accordingly reverse the judgment of the Court of Appeals and remand this case for proceedings consistent with this opinion.

It is so ordered.

Concurrence by Justice Breyer

The Court's opinion, which I join, emphasizes *Daubert*'s statement that a trial judge, acting as "gatekeeper," must "'ensure that any and all scientific testimony or evidence admitted is not only relevant, but reliable.'" *Ante*, at 5 (quoting *Daubert v. Merrell Dow Pharmaceuticals, Inc.*, 509 U.S. 579, 589, 125 L. Ed. 2d 469, 113 S. Ct. 2786 (1993)). This requirement will sometimes ask judges to make subtle and sophisticated determinations about scientific methodology and its relation to the conclusions an expert witness seeks to offer—particularly when a case arises in an area where the science itself is tentative or uncertain, or where testimony about general risk levels in human beings or animals is offered to prove individual causation. Yet, as *amici* have pointed out, judges are not scientists and do not have the scientific training that can facilitate the making of such decisions. See, *e.g.*, Brief for Trial Lawyers for Public Justice as *Amicus Curiae* 15; Brief for The New England Journal of Medicine et al. as *Amici Curiae* 2 ("Judges ... are generally not trained scientists ").

Of course, neither the difficulty of the task nor any comparative lack of expertise can excuse the judge from exercising the "gatekeeper" duties that the Federal Rules impose—determining, for example, whether particular expert testimony is reliable and "will assist the trier of fact," Fed. Rule Evid. 702, or whether the "probative value" of testimony is substantially outweighed by risks of prejudice, confusion or waste of time. Fed. Rule Evid. 403. To the contrary, when law and science intersect, those duties often must be exercised with special care.... It is, thus, essential in this science-related area that the courts administer the Federal Rules of Evidence in order to achieve the "ends" that the Rules themselves set forth, not only so that proceedings may be "justly determined," but also so "that the truth may be ascertained." Fed. Rule Evid. 102.

I therefore want specially to note that, as cases presenting significant science-related issues have increased in number, see Judicial Conference of the United States, Report of the Federal Courts Study Committee 97 (Apr. 2, 1990) ("Economic, statistical, technological, and natural and social scientific data are becoming increasingly important in both routine and complex litigation"), judges have increasingly found in the Rules of Evidence and Civil Procedure ways to help them overcome the inherent difficulty of making determinations about complicated scientific or otherwise technical evidence. Among these techniques are an increased use of Rule 16's pretrial conference authority to narrow the scientific issues in dispute, pretrial hearings where potential experts are subject to examination by the court, and the appointment of special masters and specially trained law clerks....

In the present case, the New England Journal of Medicine has filed an *amici* brief "in support of neither petitioners nor respondents" in which the Journal writes:

> "[A] judge could better fulfill this gatekeeper function if he or she had help from scientists. Judges should be strongly encouraged to make greater use of their inherent authority ... to appoint experts.... Reputable experts could be recommended to courts by established scientific organizations, such as the National Academy of Sciences or the American Association for the Advancement of Science."

Brief for The New England Journal of Medicine 18–19; cf. Fed. Rule Evid. 706 (court may "on its own motion or on the motion of any party" appoint an expert to serve on behalf of the court, and this expert may be selected as "agreed upon by the parties" or chosen by the court); see also Weinstein, *supra*, at 116 (a court should sometimes "go beyond the experts proffered by the parties" and "utilize its powers to appoint independent experts under Rule 706 of the Federal Rules of Evidence"). Given this kind of offer of cooperative effort, from the scientific to the legal community, and given the various Rules-authorized methods for facilitating the courts' task, it seems to me that *Daubert's* gatekeeping requirement will not prove inordinately difficult to implement; and that it will help secure the basic objectives of the Federal Rules of Evidence; which are, to repeat, the ascertainment of truth and the just determination of proceedings. Fed. Rule Evid. 102.

Dissent by Justice Stevens, concurring in part and dissenting in part:

The question that we granted certiorari to decide is whether the Court of Appeals applied the correct standard of review. That question is fully answered in Parts I and II of the Court's opinion. Part III answers the quite different question whether the District Court properly held that the testimony of plaintiff 's expert witnesses was inadmissible. Because I am not sure that the parties have adequately briefed that question, or that the Court has adequately explained why the Court of Appeals' disposition was erroneous, I do not join Part III. Moreover, because a proper answer to that question requires a study of the record that can be performed more efficiently by the Court of Appeals than by the nine members of this Court, I would remand the case to that court for application of the proper standard of review.

One aspect of the record will illustrate my concern. As the Court of Appeals pointed out, Joiner's experts relied on "the studies of at least thirteen different researchers, and referred to several reports of the World Health Organization that address the question of whether PCBs cause cancer." 78 F.3d 524, 533 (CA11 1996). Only one of those studies is in the record, and only six of them were discussed in the District Court opinion. Whether a fair appraisal of either the methodology or the conclusions of Joiner's experts can be made on the basis of such an incomplete record is a question that I do not feel prepared to answer.

It does seem clear, however, that the Court has not adequately explained why its holding is consistent with Federal Rule of Evidence 702, ... as interpreted in *Daubert* v. *Merrell Dow Pharmaceuticals, Inc.*, 509 U.S. 579, 125 L. Ed. 2d 469, 113 S. Ct. 2786 (1993).... In general, scientific testimony that is both relevant and reliable must be admitted and testimony that is irrelevant or unreliable must be excluded. *Id.*, at 597. In this case, the District Court relied on both grounds for exclusion.

The relevance ruling was straightforward. The District Court correctly reasoned that an expert opinion that exposure to PCBs, "furans" and "dioxins" together may cause lung cancer would be irrelevant unless the plaintiff had been exposed to those substances. Having already found that there was no evidence of exposure to furans and dioxins, 864 F. Supp. 1310, 1318–1319 (ND Ga. 1994), it necessarily followed that this expert opinion testimony was inadmissible. Correctly applying *Daubert,* the District Court explained that the experts' testimony "manifestly does not fit the facts of this case, and is therefore inadmissible." 864 F. Supp. at 1322. Of course, if the evidence raised a genuine issue of fact on the question of Joiner's exposure to furans and dioxins — as the Court of Appeals held that it did — then this basis for the ruling on admissibility was erroneous, but not because the district judge either abused her discretion or misapplied the law.

The reliability ruling was more complex and arguably is not faithful to the statement in *Daubert* that "the focus, of course, must be solely on principles and methodology, not on the conclusions that they generate." 509 U.S. at 595. Joiner's experts used a "weight of the evidence" methodology to assess whether Joiner's exposure to transformer fluids promoted his lung cancer.... They did not suggest that any one study provided adequate support for their conclusions, but instead relied on all the studies taken together (along with their interviews of Joiner and their review of his medical records). The District Court, however, examined the studies one by one and concluded that none was sufficient to show a link between PCBs and lung cancer. 864 F. Supp. at 1324–1326. The focus of the opinion was on the separate studies and the conclusions of the experts, not on the experts' methodology. ("Defendants ... persuade the court that Plaintiffs' expert testimony would not be admissible ... by attacking the conclusions that Plaintiffs' experts draw from the studies they cite").

The Court of Appeals' discussion of admissibility is faithful to the dictum in *Daubert* that the reliability inquiry must focus on methodology, not conclusions. Thus, even though I fully agree with both the District Court's and this Court's explanation of why each of the studies on which the experts relied was by itself unpersuasive, a critical question remains unanswered: When qualified experts have reached relevant conclusions on the basis of an acceptable methodology, why are their opinions inadmissible? ...

Kumho Tire Company v. Carmichael
526 U.S. 137 (1999)

JUSTICE BREYER delivered the opinion of the Court.

In *Daubert v. Merrell Dow Pharmaceuticals, Inc.*, 509 U.S. 579, 125 L. Ed. 2d 469, 113 S. Ct. 2786 (1993), this Court focused upon the admissibility of scientific expert testimony. It pointed out that such testimony is admissible only if it is both relevant and reliable. And it held that the Federal Rules of Evidence "assign to the trial judge the task of ensuring that an expert's testimony both rests on a reliable foundation and is relevant to the task at hand." Id. at 597. The Court also discussed certain more specific factors, such as testing, peer review, error rates, and "acceptability" in the relevant scientific community, some or all of which might prove helpful in determining the reliability of a particular scientific "theory or technique." Id. at 593–594.

This case requires us to decide how *Daubert* applies to the testimony of engineers and other experts who are not scientists. We conclude that *Daubert*'s general holding—setting forth the trial judge's general "gatekeeping" obligation—applies not only to testimony based on "scientific" knowledge, but also to testimony based on "technical" and "other specialized" knowledge. See Fed. Rule Evid. 702. We also conclude that a trial court *may* consider one or more of the more specific factors that *Daubert* mentioned when doing so will help determine that testimony's reliability. But, as the Court stated in *Daubert*, the test of reliability is "flexible," and *Daubert*'s list of specific factors neither necessarily nor exclusively applies to all experts or in every case. Rather, the law grants a district court the same broad latitude when it decides *how* to determine reliability as it enjoys in respect to its ultimate reliability determination.

See *General Electric Co. v. Joiner*, 522 U.S. 136, 143, 139 L. Ed. 2d 508, 118 S. Ct. 512 (1997) (courts of appeals are to apply "abuse of discretion" standard when reviewing district court's reliability determination). Applying these standards, we determine that the District Court's decision in this case—not to admit certain expert testimony—was within its discretion and therefore lawful.

On July 6, 1993, the right rear tire of a minivan driven by Patrick Carmichael blew out. In the accident that followed, one of the passengers died, and others were severely injured. In October 1993, the Carmichaels brought this diversity suit against the tire's maker and its distributor, whom we refer to collectively as Kumho Tire, claiming that the tire was defective. The plaintiffs rested their case in significant part upon deposition testimony provided by an expert in tire failure analysis, Dennis Carlson, Jr., who intended to testify in support of their conclusion.

Carlson's depositions relied upon certain features of tire technology that are not in dispute. A steel-belted radial tire like the Carmichaels' is made up of a "carcass" containing many layers of flexible cords, called "plies," along which (between the cords and the outer tread) are laid steel strips called "belts." Steel wire loops, called "beads," hold the cords together at the plies' bottom edges. An outer layer, called the "tread," encases the carcass, and the entire tire is bound together in rubber, through the application of heat and various chemicals. See generally, *e.g.*, J. Dixon, Tires, Suspension and Handling 68–72 (2d ed. 1996). The bead of the tire sits upon a "bead seat," which is part of the wheel assembly. That assembly contains a "rim flange," which extends over the bead and rests against the side of the tire. See M. Mavrigian, Performance Wheels & Tires 81, 83 (1998) (illustrations). A. Markovich, How To Buy and Care For Tires 4 (1994).

Carlson's testimony also accepted certain background facts about the tire in question. He assumed that before the blowout the tire had traveled far. (The tire was made in 1988 and had been installed some time before the Carmichaels bought the used mini-van in March 1993; the Carmichaels had driven the van approximately 7,000 additional miles in the two months they had owned it.) Carlson noted that the tire's tread depth, which was 11/32 of an inch when new, App. 242, had been worn down to depths that ranged from 3/32 of an inch along some parts of the tire, to nothing at all along others. Id. at 287. He conceded that the tire tread had at least two punctures which had been inadequately repaired. Id. at 258–261, 322.

Radial-Ply Tire Construction

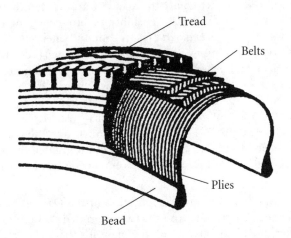

Despite the tire's age and history, Carlson concluded that a defect in its manufacture or design caused the blow-out. He rested this conclusion in part upon three premises which, for present purposes, we must assume are not in dispute: First, a tire's carcass should stay bound to the inner side of the tread for a significant period of time after its tread depth has worn away.... Second, the tread of the tire at issue had separated from its inner steel-belted carcass prior to the accident.... Third, this "separation" caused the blowout....

Carlson's conclusion that a defect caused the separation, however, rested upon certain other propositions, several of which the defendants strongly dispute. First, Carlson said that if a separation is *not* caused by a certain kind of tire misuse called "overdeflection" (which consists of underinflating the tire or causing it to carry too much weight, thereby generating heat that can undo the chemical tread/carcass bond), then, ordinarily, its cause is a tire defect.... Second, he said that if a tire has been subject to sufficient overdeflection to cause a separation, it should reveal certain physical symptoms. These symptoms include (a) tread wear on the tire's shoulder that is greater than the tread wear along the tire's center, id. at 211; (b) signs of a "bead groove," where the beads have been pushed too hard against the bead seat on the inside of the tire's rim, id. at 196–197; (c) sidewalls of the tire with physical signs of deterioration, such as discoloration, id. at 212; and/or (d) marks on the tire's rim flange, id. at 219–220. Third, Carlson said that where he does not find *at least two* of the four physical signs just mentioned (and pre-sumably where there is no reason to suspect a less common cause of separation), he concludes that a manufacturing or design defect caused the separation....

Carlson added that he had inspected the tire in question. He conceded that the tire to a limited degree showed greater wear on the shoulder than in the center, some signs of "bead groove," some discoloration, a few marks on the rim flange, and inadequately filled puncture holes (which can also cause heat that might lead to separation).... in each instance, he testified that the symptoms were not significant, and he explained why he believed that they did not reveal overdeflection. For example, the extra shoulder wear, he said, appeared primarily on one shoulder, whereas an overdeflected tire would reveal equally abnormal wear on both shoulders.... Carlson concluded that the tire did not bear at least two of the four overdeflection symptoms, nor was there any less obvious cause of separation; and since neither overdeflection nor the punctures caused the blowout, a defect must have done so.

Kumho Tire moved the District Court to exclude Carlson's testimony on the ground that his methodology failed Rule 702's reliability requirement. The court agreed with Kumho that it should act as a *Daubert*-type reliability "gatekeeper," even though one might consider Carlson's testimony as "technical," rather than "scientific." ... The court then examined Carlson's methodology in light of the reliability-related factors that *Daubert* mentioned, such as a theory's testability, whether it "has been a subject of peer review or publication," the "known or potential rate of error," and the "degree of acceptance ... within the relevant scientific community." 923 F. Supp. at 1520 (citing *Daubert*, 509 U.S. 579 at 592–594). The District Court found that all those factors argued against the reliability of Carlson's methods, and it granted the motion to exclude the testimony (as well as the defendants' accompanying motion for summary judgment).

The plaintiffs, arguing that the court's application of the *Daubert* factors was too "inflexible," asked for reconsideration. And the Court granted that motion.... After reconsidering the matter, the court agreed with the plaintiffs that *Daubert* should be applied flexibly, that its four factors were simply illustrative, and that other factors could argue in favor of admissibility. It conceded that there may be widespread acceptance of a "visual-inspection method" for some relevant purposes. But the court found insufficient indications of the reliability of

> "the component of Carlson's tire failure analysis which most concerned the Court, namely, the methodology employed by the expert in analyzing the data obtained in the visual inspection, and the scientific basis, if any, for such an analysis." Id. at 6c.

It consequently affirmed its earlier order declaring Carlson's testimony inadmissable and granting the defendants' motion for summary judgment.

The Eleventh Circuit reversed.... It "reviewed ... *de novo*" the "district court's legal decision to apply *Daubert*." ... It noted that "the Supreme Court in *Daubert* explicitly limited its holding to cover only the 'scientific context,'" adding that "a *Daubert* analysis" applies only where an expert relies "on the application of scientific principles," rather than "on skill- or experience-based observation." ... It concluded that Carlson's testimony, which it viewed as relying on experience, "falls outside the scope of *Daubert*," that "the district court erred as a matter of law by applying *Daubert* in this case," and that the case must be remanded for further (non-*Daubert*-type) consideration under Rule 702....

Kumho Tire petitioned for certiorari, asking us to determine whether a trial court "may" consider *Daubert*'s specific "factors" when determining the "admissibility of an engineering expert's testimony." Pet. for Cert. We granted certiorari in light of uncertainty among the lower courts about whether, or how, *Daubert* applies to expert testimony that might be characterized as based not upon "scientific" knowledge, but rather upon "technical" or "other specialized" knowledge. Fed. Rule Evid. 702....

II A

In *Daubert*, this Court held that Federal Rule of Evidence 702 imposes a special obligation upon a trial judge to "ensure that any and all scientific testimony ... is not only relevant, but reliable." 509 U.S. at 589. The initial question before us is whether this basic gatekeeping obligation applies only to "scientific" testimony or to all expert testimony. We, like the parties, believe that it applies to all expert ...

For one thing, Rule 702 itself says:

"If scientific, technical, or other specialized knowledge will assist the trier of fact to understand the evidence or to determine a fact in issue, a witness qualified as an expert by knowledge, skill, experience, training, or education, may testify thereto in the form of an opinion or otherwise."

This language makes no relevant distinction between "scientific" knowledge and "technical" or "other specialized" knowledge. It makes clear that any such knowledge might become the subject of expert testimony. In *Daubert*, the Court specified that it is the Rule's word "knowledge," not the words (like "scientific") that modify that word, that "establishes a standard of evidentiary reliability." ... Hence, as a matter of language, the Rule applies its reliability standard to all "scientific," "technical," or "other specialized" matters within its scope. We concede that the Court in *Daubert* referred only to "scientific" knowledge. But as the Court there said, it referred to "scientific" testimony "because that was the nature of the expertise" at issue....

Neither is the evidentiary rationale that underlay the Court's basic *Daubert* "gatekeeping" determination limited to "scientific" knowledge. *Daubert* pointed out that Federal Rules 702 and 703 grant expert witnesses testimonial latitude unavailable to other witnesses on the "assumption that the expert's opinion will have a reliable basis in the knowledge and experience of his discipline." (pointing out that experts may testify to opinions, including those that are not based on firsthand knowledge or observation). The Rules grant that latitude to all experts, not just to "scientific" ones.

Finally, it would prove difficult, if not impossible, for judges to administer evidentiary rules under which a gatekeeping obligation depended upon a distinction between "scientific" knowledge and "technical" or "other specialized" knowledge. There is no clear line that divides the one from the others. Disciplines such as engineering rest upon scientific knowledge. Pure scientific theory itself may depend for its development upon observation and properly engineered machinery. And conceptual efforts to distinguish the two are unlikely to produce clear legal lines capable of application in particular cases.

Neither is there a convincing need to make such distinctions. Experts of all kinds tie observations to conclusions through the use of what Judge Learned Hand called "general truths derived from ... specialized experience." Hand, Historical and Practical Considerations Regarding Expert Testimony, 15 Harv. L. Rev. 40, 54 (1901). And whether the specific expert testimony focuses upon specialized observations, the specialized translation of those observations into theory, a specialized theory itself, or the application of such a theory in a particular case, the expert's testimony often will rest "upon an experience confessedly foreign in kind to [the jury's] own." *Ibid.* The trial judge's effort to assure that the specialized testimony is reliable and relevant can help the jury evaluate that foreign experience, whether the testimony reflects scientific, technical, or other specialized knowledge.

We conclude that *Daubert's* general principles apply to the expert matters described in Rule 702. The Rule, in respect to all such matters, "establishes a standard of evidentiary reliability." 509 U.S. at 590. It "requires a valid ... connection to the pertinent inquiry as a precondition to admissibility." Id. at 592. And where such testimony's factual basis, data, principles, methods, or their application are called sufficiently into question, see Part III, *infra*, the trial judge must determine whether the testimony has "a reliable basis in the knowledge and experience of [the relevant] discipline." 509 U.S. at 592.

B

The petitioners ask more specifically whether a trial judge determining the "admissibility of an engineering expert's testimony" *may* consider several more specific factors that *Daubert* said might "bear on" a judge's gate-keeping determination. These factors include:

— Whether a "theory or technique ... can be (and has been) tested";

— Whether it "has been subjected to peer review and publication";

— Whether, in respect to a particular technique, there is a high "known or potential rate of error" and whether there are "standards controlling the technique's operation"; and

— Whether the theory or technique enjoys "general acceptance" within a "relevant scientific community." 509 U.S. at 592–594.

Emphasizing the word "may" in the question, we answer that question yes.

Engineering testimony rests upon scientific foundations, the reliability of which will be at issue in some cases. See, *e.g.*, Brief for Stephen Bobo et al. as *Amici Curiae* 23 (stressing the scientific bases of engineering disciplines). In other cases, the relevant reliability concerns may focus upon personal knowledge or experience. As the Solicitor General points out, there are many different kinds of experts, and many different kinds of expertise. See Brief for United States as *Amicus Curiae* 18–19, and n. 5 (citing cases involving experts in drug terms, handwriting analysis, criminal *modus operandi*, land valuation, agricultural practices, railroad procedures, attorney's fee valuation, and others). Our emphasis on the word "may" thus reflects *Daubert's* description of the Rule 702 inquiry as "a flexible one." 509 U.S. at 594. *Daubert* makes clear that the factors it mentions do *not* constitute a "definitive checklist or test." Id. at 593. And *Daubert* adds that the gatekeeping inquiry must be "'tied to the facts'" of a particular "case." Id. at 591 (quoting *United States* v. *Downing*, 753 F.2d 1224, 1242 (CA3 1985)). We agree with the Solicitor General that "the factors identified in *Daubert* may or may not be pertinent in assessing reliability, depending on the nature of the issue, the expert's particular expertise, and the subject of his testimony." Brief for United States as *Amicus Curiae* 19. The conclusion, in our view, is that we can neither rule out, nor rule in, for all cases and for all time the applicability of the factors mentioned in *Daubert*, nor can we now do so for subsets of cases categorized by category of expert or by kind of evidence. Too much depends upon the particular circumstances of the particular case at issue.

Daubert itself is not to the contrary. It made clear that its list of factors was meant to be helpful, not definitive. Indeed, those factors do not all necessarily apply even in every instance in which the reliability of scientific testimony is challenged. It might not be surprising in a particular case, for example, that a claim made by a scientific witness has never been the subject of peer review, for the particular application at issue may never previously have interested any scientist. Nor, on the other hand, does the presence of *Daubert's* general acceptance factor help show that an expert's testimony is reliable where the discipline itself lacks reliability, as, for example, do theories grounded in any so-called generally accepted principles of astrology or necromancy.

At the same time, and contrary to the Court of Appeals' view, some of *Daubert's* questions can help to evaluate the reliability even of experience-based testimony. In certain cases, it will be appropriate for the trial judge to ask, for example, how often an engineering expert's experience-based methodology has produced erroneous results, or whether such a method is generally accepted in the relevant engineering community. Likewise, it will at times be useful to ask even of a witness whose expertise is based purely on experience, say, a perfume tester able to distinguish among 140 odors at a sniff, whether his preparation is of a kind that others in the field would recognize as acceptable.

We must therefore disagree with the Eleventh Circuit's holding that a trial judge may ask questions of the sort *Daubert* mentioned only where an expert "relies on the application of scientific principles," but not where an expert relies "on skill- or experience-based observation." ... We do not believe that Rule 702 creates a schematism that segregates expertise by type while mapping certain kinds of questions to certain kinds of experts. Life and the legal cases that it generates are too complex to warrant so definitive a match.

To say this is not to deny the importance of *Daubert's* gatekeeping requirement. The objective of that requirement is to ensure the reliability and relevancy of expert testimony. It is to make certain that an expert, whether basing testimony upon professional studies or personal experience, employs in the courtroom the same level of intellectual rigor that characterizes the practice of an expert in the relevant field. Nor do we deny that, as stated in *Daubert*, the particular questions that it mentioned will often be appropriate for use in determining the reliability of challenged expert testimony. Rather, we conclude that the trial judge must have considerable leeway in deciding in a particular case how to go about determining whether particular expert testimony is reliable. That is to say, a trial court should consider the specific factors identified in *Daubert* where they are reasonable measures of the reliability of expert testimony.

C

The trial court must have the same kind of latitude in deciding *how* to test an expert's reliability, and to decide whether or when special briefing or other proceedings are needed to investigate reliability, as it enjoys when it decides *whether* that expert's relevant testimony is reliable. Our opinion in *Joiner* makes clear that a court of appeals is to apply an abuse-of-discretion standard when it "reviews a trial court's decision to admit or exclude expert testimony." 522 U.S. at 138–139. That standard applies as much to the trial court's decisions about how to determine reliability as to its ultimate conclusion. Otherwise, the trial judge would lack the discretionary authority needed both to avoid unnecessary "reliability" proceedings in ordinary cases where the reliability of an expert's methods is properly taken for granted, and to require appropriate proceedings in the less usual or more complex cases where cause for questioning the expert's reliability arises. Indeed, the Rules seek to avoid "unjustifiable expense and delay" as part of their search for "truth" and the "just determination" of proceedings. Fed. Rule Evid. 102. Thus, whether *Daubert's* specific factors are, or are not, reasonable measures of reliability in a particular case is a matter that the law grants the trial judge broad latitude to determine.... And the Eleventh Circuit erred insofar as it held to the contrary.

III

We further explain the way in which a trial judge "may" consider *Daubert's* factors by applying these considerations to the case at hand, a matter that has been briefed exhaustively by the parties and their 19 *amici*. The District Court did not doubt Carlson's qualifications, which included a masters degree in mechanical engineering, 10 years' work at Michelin America, Inc., and testimony as a tire failure consultant in other tort cases. Rather, it excluded the testimony because, despite those qualifications, it initially doubted, and then found unreliable, "the methodology employed by the expert in analyzing the data obtained in the visual inspection, and the scientific basis, if any, for such an analysis." Civ. Action No. 93-0860-CB-S (SD Ala., June 5, 1996), App. to Pet. for Cert. 6c. After examining the transcript in "some detail," 923 F. Supp. at 1518–519, n. 4, and after considering respondents' defense of Carlson's methodology, the District Court determined that Carlson's testimony was not reliable. It fell outside the range where experts might reasonably differ, and where the jury must decide among the conflicting views of different experts, even though the evidence is "shaky." *Daubert*, 509 U.S. at 596. In our view, the doubts that triggered the District Court's initial inquiry here were reasonable, as was the court's ultimate conclusion.

For one thing, and contrary to respondents' suggestion, the specific issue before the court was not the reasonableness *in general* of a tire expert's use of a visual and tactile inspection to determine whether overdeflection had caused the tire's tread to separate from its steel-belted carcass. Rather, it was the reasonableness of using such an approach, along with Carlson's particular method of analyzing the data thereby obtained, to draw a conclusion regarding *the particular matter to which the expert testimony was directly relevant*. That matter concerned the likelihood that a defect in the tire at issue caused its tread to separate from its carcass. The tire in question, the expert conceded, had traveled far enough so that some of the tread had been worn bald; it should have been taken out of service; it had been repaired (inadequately) for punctures; and it bore some of the very marks that the expert said indicated, not a defect, but abuse through overdeflection. The relevant issue was whether the expert could reliably determine the cause of *this* tire's separation. Nor was the basis for Carlson's conclusion simply the general theory that, in the absence of evidence of abuse, a defect will normally have caused a tire's separation. Rather, the expert employed a more specific theory to establish the existence (or absence) of such abuse. Carlson testified precisely that in the absence of *at least two* of four signs of abuse (proportionately greater tread wear on the shoulder; signs of grooves caused by the beads; discolored sidewalls; marks on the rim flange) he concludes that a defect caused the separation. And his analysis depended upon acceptance of a further implicit proposition, namely, that his visual and tactile inspection could determine that the tire before him had not been abused despite some evidence of the presence of the very signs for which he looked (and two punctures).

For another thing, the transcripts of Carlson's depositions support both the trial court's initial uncertainty and its final conclusion. Those transcripts cast considerable doubt upon the reliability of both the explicit theory (about the need for two signs of abuse) and the implicit proposition (about the significance of visual inspection in this case). Among other things, the expert could not say whether the tire had traveled more than 10, or 20, or 30, or 40, or 50 thousand miles, adding that 6,000 miles was "about how far" he could "say with any certainty." Id. at 265. The court could reasonably have wondered about the reliability of a method of visual and tactile inspection sufficiently precise to ascertain with some certainty the abuse-related significance of minute shoulder/center relative tread wear differences, but insufficiently precise to tell "with any certainty" from the tread wear whether a tire had traveled less than 10,000 or more than 50,000 miles. And these concerns might have been augmented by Carlson's repeated reliance on the "subjectiveness" of his mode of analysis in response to questions seeking specific information regarding how he could differentiate between a tire that actually had been overdeflected and a tire that merely looked as though it had been. Id. at 222, 224–225, 285–286. They would have been further augmented by the fact that Carlson said he had inspected the tire itself for the first time the morning of his first deposition, and then only for a few hours. (His initial conclusions were based on photographs.)

Moreover, prior to his first deposition, Carlson had issued a signed report in which he concluded that the tire had "not been ... overloaded or underinflated," not because of the absence of "two of four" signs of abuse, but simply because "the rim flange impressions ... were normal." Id. at 335–336. That report also said that the "tread depth remaining was 3/32 inch," id. at 336, though the opposing expert's (apparently undisputed) measurements indicate that the tread depth taken at various positions around the tire actually ranged from .5/32 of an inch to 4/32 of an inch, with the tire apparently showing greater wear along *both* shoulders than along the center.

Further, in respect to one sign of abuse, bead grooving, the expert seemed to deny the sufficiency of his own simple visual-inspection methodology. He testified that most tires have some bead groove pattern, that where there is reason to suspect an abnormal bead groove he would ideally "look at a lot of [similar] tires" to know the grooving's significance, and that he had not looked at many tires similar to the one at issue....

Finally, the court, after looking for a defense of Carlson's methodology as applied in these circumstances, found no convincing defense. Rather, it found (1) that "none" of the *Daubert* factors, including that of "general acceptance" in the relevant expert community, indicated that Carlson's testimony was reliable, 923 F. Supp. at 1521; (2) that its own analysis "revealed no countervailing factors operating in favor of admissibility which could outweigh those identified in *Daubert*," App. to Pet. for Cert. 4c; and (3) that the "parties identified no such factors in their briefs," *ibid.* For these three reasons *taken together,* it concluded that Carlson's testimony was unreliable.

Respondents now argue to us, as they did to the District Court, that a method of tire failure analysis that employs a visual/tactile inspection is a reliable method, and they point both to its use by other experts and to Carlson's long experience working for Michelin as sufficient indication that that is so. But no one denies that an expert might draw a conclusion from a set of observations based on extensive and specialized experience. Nor does anyone deny that, as a general matter, tire abuse may often be identified by qualified experts through visual or tactile inspection of the tire. See Affidavit of H. R. Baumgardner 1–2, cited in Brief for National Academy of Forensic Engineers as *Amici Curiae* 16 (Tire engineers rely on visual examination and process of elimination to analyze experimental test tires). As we said before, *supra,* at 14, the question before the trial court was specific, not general. The trial court had to decide whether this particular expert had sufficient specialized knowledge to assist the jurors "in deciding the particular issues in the case." 4 J. McLaughlin, Weinstein's Federal Evidence P702.05[1], p. 702–33 (2d ed. 1998); see also Advisory Committee's Note on Proposed Fed. Rule Evid. 702, Preliminary Draft of Proposed Amendments to the Federal Rules of Civil Procedure and Evidence: Request for Comment 126 (1998) (stressing that district courts must "scrutinize" whether the "principles and methods" employed by an expert "have been properly applied to the facts of the case").

The particular issue in this case concerned the use of Carlson's two-factor test and his related use of visual/tactile inspection to draw conclusions on the basis of what seemed small observational differences. We have found no indication in the record that other experts in the industry use Carlson's two-factor test or that tire experts such as Carlson normally make the very fine distinctions about, say, the symmetry of comparatively greater shoulder tread wear that were necessary, on Carlson's own theory, to support his conclusions. Nor, despite the prevalence of tire testing, does anyone refer to any articles or papers that validate Carlson's approach. Indeed, no one has argued that Carlson himself, were he still working for Michelin, would have concluded in a report to his employer that a similar tire was similarly defective on grounds identical to those upon which he rested his conclusion here. Of course, Carlson himself claimed that his method was accurate, but, as we pointed out in *Joiner*, "nothing in either *Daubert* or the Federal Rules of Evidence requires a district court to admit opinion evidence that is connected to existing data only by the *ipse dixit* of the expert." 522 U.S. at 146.

Respondents additionally argue that the District Court too rigidly applied *Daubert*'s criteria. They read its opinion to hold that a failure to satisfy any one of those criteria automatically renders expert testimony inadmissible. The District Court's initial opinion might have been vulnerable to a form of this argument. There, the court, after rejecting respondents' claim that Carlson's testimony was "exempted from *Daubert*-style scrutiny" because it was "technical analysis" rather than "scientific evidence," simply added that "none of the four admissibility criteria outlined by the *Daubert* court are satisfied." 923 F. Supp. at 1522. Subsequently, however, the court granted respondents' motion for reconsideration. It then explicitly recognized that the relevant reliability inquiry "should be 'flexible,'" that its "'overarching subject [should be] ... validity' and reliability," and that "*Daubert* was intended neither to be exhaustive nor to apply in every case." App. to Pet. for Cert. 4c (quoting *Daubert*, 509 U.S. at 594–595). And the court ultimately based its decision upon Carlson's failure to satisfy either *Daubert*'s factors *or any other* set of reasonable reliability criteria. In light of the record as developed by the parties, that conclusion was within the District Court's lawful discretion.

In sum, Rule 702 grants the district judge the discretionary authority, reviewable for its abuse, to determine reliability in light of the particular facts and circumstances of the particular case. The District Court did not abuse its discretionary authority in this case. Hence, the judgment of the Court of Appeals is

Reversed.

Concur by Justice Scalia, with whom JUSTICE O'CONNOR and JUSTICE THOMAS join, concurring.

I join the opinion of the Court, which makes clear that the discretion it endorses—trial-court discretion in choosing the manner of testing expert reliability—is not discretion to abandon the gatekeeping function. I think it worth adding that it is not discretion to perform the function inadequately. Rather, it is discretion to choose among *reasonable* means of excluding expertise that is *fausse* and science that is junky. Though, as the Court makes clear today, the *Daubert* factors are not holy writ, in a particular case the failure to apply one or another of them may be unreasonable, and hence an abuse of discretion.

8.3 Mitochondrial DNA

The use of mitochondrial DNA, has been admitted as scientific evidence in several state courts: North Carolina, (*State v. Underwood*, 134 N.C. App. 533, 518 S.E.2d 231

(N.C. Ct. App. 1999)); Tennesse, (*State v. Scott*, 33 S.W.3d 746 (Tenn. 2000)); South Carolina, (*State v. Council*, 335 S.C. 1, 515 S.E.2d 508 (S.C. 1999)); New York, *People v. Klinger*, 185 Misc. 2d 574, 713 N.Y.S. 2d 823 (N.Y. Crim. Ct. 2000)); and Maryland (*Williams v. State*, 342 Md. 724, 679 A.2d 1106 (Md. 1996)). The following case upholds the use of mitochondrial DNA in Ohio.

United States v. Beverly
369 F.3d 516 (6th Cir. 2004)

BOGGS, Chief Judge.

Noah Beverly, Douglas A. Turns, and Johnny P. Crockett were indicted for multiple crimes by a federal grand jury, charging them with conspiracy to commit armed bank robbery, in violation of 18 U.S.C. §371, committing various armed bank robberies, in violation of 18 U.S.C. §2113(a) and (d), and possessing firearms during and in relation to these crimes of violence, in violation of 18 U.S.C. §924(c). After two evidentiary hearings, a jury trial commenced in which all three defendants were tried together. On February 8, 2000, the jury returned a verdict of guilty on all counts against Beverly and Turns. Crockett was found guilty of conspiracy to commit armed bank robbery, of robbing Security National Bank, and the Park National Bank in Hebron, Ohio, and of using a firearm in commission of those crimes, but was found not guilty of robbing two other banks with another defendant not involved in this appeal.

All three defendants have appealed this verdict. Beverly appeals the introduction of mitochondrial DNA (mtDNA) evidence against him at trial, arguing that the evidence was not scientifically reliable and, even if reliable, its probative value was outweighed by its prejudicial effect.... For the reasons set forth below, we affirm the defendants' convictions.

I

This case is about a series of bank robberies that occurred in Ohio between September 1994 and November 1995. Much of what happened was described by two men who testified at trial: Anthony Lavelle Rogers and his half-brother Melvin Warren, Jr..In each of the seven robberies, either Rogers, Warren, or both, participated in the event and so testified to what occurred. Neither Rogers nor Warren are defendants in this case because they both entered into a plea agreement as part of a guilty plea to armed bank robbery.

....

Security National Bank

On May 18, 1995, Warren, Rogers, Beverly, and Crockett robbed the Security National Bank in Springfield, Ohio. The four met before the robbery at Beverly's apartment, where they prepared disguises, including masks and bandannas. They then drove together to Springfield in Warren's tan Lincoln Town Car. Once in Springfield, the four drove to a hospital, where Rogers stole a car to use as a getaway vehicle in the robbery. They found an alley behind some buildings across the street from the bank, where they parked the Lincoln. Rogers, Warren, Beverly, and Crockett entered the bank and Crockett, wearing a pair of pantyhose over his head, jumped over the teller's counter and ordered people to the floor. After robbing the bank, the four used the stolen car to get to the alley where the tan Lincoln was parked. They all left their disguises in the stolen car, which was later recovered by the police. The four escaped with $10,538.47.

During the robbery, bank surveillance cameras were working and took several photographs. Both Warren and Rogers were able to identify each other, as well as Beverly and Crockett, in the photos. The government contends that Beverly's pose, disguise, choice of weapon, and use of his left hand is almost identical in the May 18 and the May 12 robbery photos, and that Beverly's revolver, which appears in the pictures, had the same characteristics as the gun recovered after the November 22, 1995 robbery of the Park National Bank in Hebron, Ohio. (See page 9, infra). The photographs also show a man, identified as Beverly, wearing a "Columbia" hat with holes cut in it as a mask. This hat was later recovered from the abandoned stolen car. It was a hair from this hat that was sent to the lab for the mitochondrial DNA test that was ultimately admitted into evidence at trial.

....

II

The three defendants raise many issues, which we will consider in the following order. All three defendants join in the Batson challenge, so we will deal with it first in Part III. We then turn to the novel issue of Beverly's challenge to the admissibility of mitochondrial DNA evidence in Part IV. Turns and Crockett each appeal the denial of their separate motions for acquittal, and these issues are dealt with in Part V. Turns raises three issues peculiar to his trial and sentence, which we deal with in Part VI. Finally, Crockett raises a number of evidentiary issues and a claim of prosecutorial misconduct, which we address in Part VII.

....

IV

Admissibility of Mitochondrial DNA Testing

Beverly, against whom mitochondrial deoxyribonucleic acid (mtDNA) testing was used in this trial, argues that the district court erred in admitting expert testimony concerning mtDNA evidence. Specifically, Beverly argues that mtDNA testing is not scientifically reliable because the laboratory that did the testing in this case was not certified by an external agency, the procedures used by the laboratory "sometimes yielded results that were contaminated," and the particular tests done in this case were contaminated. In addition, Beverly argues that even if the mtDNA evidence is determined to be sufficiently reliable, its probative value is substantially outweighed by its prejudicial effect. In this part of his argument, Beverly focuses on the statistical analysis presented, which he claims to have artificially enhanced the probative value of the mtDNA evidence. According to Beverly, Dr. Melton, the government's expert, should only have been allowed to testify that Beverly could not be excluded as the source of the sample in question.

We review the district court's decision to admit expert testimony for an abuse of discretion. Kumho Tire Co. v. Carmichael, 526 U.S. 137, 152, 119 S.Ct. 1167, 143 L.Ed.2d 238 (1999); First Tenn. Bank Nat. Ass'n v. Barreto, 268 F.3d 319, 331 (6th Cir.2001).

Federal Rule of Evidence 702 sets forth the requirements for the admissibility of expert testimony as follows:

If scientific, technical, or other specialized knowledge will assist the trier of fact to understand the evidence or to determine a fact in issue, a witness qualified as an expert by knowledge, skill, experience, training, or education, may testify thereto in the form of an opinion or otherwise, if (1) the testimony is based upon sufficient facts or data, (2) the testimony is the product of reliable principles and methods, and (3) the witness has applied the principles and methods reliably to the facts of the case.

The wording of the rule reflects the now-standard inquiry set out in Daubert v. Merrell DOow Pharmaceuticals, Inc., 509 U.S. 579, 113 S.Ct. 2786, 125 L.Ed.2d 469 (1993), which is the basis on which the district court analyzed the expert testimony given in this case. See Nelson v. Tenn. Gas Pipeline Co., 243 F.3d 244, 250 n. 4 (6th Cir.), cert. denied,534 U.S. 822, 122 S.Ct. 56, 151 L.Ed.2d 25 (2001). Therefore, we review this case under Daubert, which set forth a non-exclusive checklist of factors for trial courts to use in assessing the reliability of scientific expert testimony. These include 1) whether the expert's scientific technique or theory can be, or has been, tested; 2) whether the technique or theory has been subject to peer review and publication; 3) the known or potential rate of error of the technique or theory when applied; 4) the existence and maintenance of standards and controls; and 5) whether the technique or theory has been generally accepted in the scientific community. Daubert, 509 U.S. at 592–95, 113 S.Ct. 2786; Hardyman v. Norfolk & W. Ry., 243 F.3d 255, 260 (6th Cir.2001). If the evidence is deemed to be reliable and relevant, the judge must then determine if the probative value of the evidence is outweighed by its prejudicial effect. Daubert, 509 U.S. at 595, 113 S.Ct. 2786.

1. Mitochondrial DNA Testing in General

Before discussing the particular circumstances of this case, it may be helpful to provide some general background concerning mtDNA analysis. Generally speaking, every cell contains two types of DNA: nuclear DNA, which is found in the nucleus of the cell, and mitochondrial DNA, which is found outside of the nucleus in the mitochondrion. The use of nuclear DNA analysis as a forensic tool has been found to be scientifically reliable by the scientific community for more than a decade. The use of mtDNA analysis is also on the rise, and it has been used extensively for some time in FBI labs, as well as state and private crime labs. See, e.g., Micah A. Luftig & Stephen Richey, Symposium: Serenity Now or Insanity Later?: The Impact of Post-Conviction DNA Testing on the Criminal Justice System: Panel One: The Power of DNA, 35 New Eng. L.Rev. 609, 611 (2001). This technique, which generally looks at the differences between people's mitochondrial DNA, has some advantages over nuclear DNA analysis in certain situations. For example, while any given cell contains only one nucleus, there are a vast number of mitochondria. As a result, there is a significantly greater amount of mtDNA in a cell from which a sample can be extracted by a lab technician, as compared to nuclear DNA. Thus, this technique is very useful for minute samples or ancient and degraded samples. Ibid. In addition, mitochondrial DNA can be obtained from some sources that nuclear DNA cannot. For example, mtDNA can be found in shafts of hair, which do not have a nucleus, but do have plenty of mitochondria. Nuclear DNA can only be retrieved from the living root of the hair where the nucleus resides. United States v. Coleman, 202 F.Supp.2d 962, 965 (E.D.Mo.2002) (accepting expert testimony by Dr. Melton, the expert in this case, and admitting evidence based on mtDNA testing).

On the other hand, mtDNA is not as precise an identifier as nuclear DNA. In the case of nuclear DNA, half is inherited from the mother and half from the father, and each individual, with the exception of identical twins, almost certainly has a unique profile. MtDNA, by contrast, is inherited only from the mother and thus all maternal relatives will share the same mtDNA profile, unless a mutation has occurred. Ibid. Because it is not possible to achieve the extremely high level of certainty of identity provided by nuclear DNA, mtDNA typing has been said to be a test of exclusion, rather than one of identification. Id. at 966.

The entire mtDNA sequence, about sixteen thousand base pairs, is considerably shorter than nuclear DNA, which has approximately three billion pairs. Within the mtDNA, two noncoding regions are targeted-Hypervariable-1 (HV1) and Hypervariable-2 (HV2). Each of these regions is about 300 letters in code length and is a region that has a mutation rate five to ten times greater than that of nuclear DNA. Usually there is a one to two percent variance of mtDNA sequence between unrelated individuals. Luftig & Richey, supra, at 612. It has been estimated that mutation within the mtDNA control region is one nucleotide difference every 300 generations. National Commission on the Future of DNA Evidence, The Future of Forensic DNA Testing: Predictions of the Research and Development Working Group 7, Nat'l Inst. of Justice (2000). But see Ann Gibbons, Calibrating the Mitochondrial Clock, 279 Science 28 (1998) (discussing research estimating that mutations occur as frequently as every 40 generations). This academic dispute does not affect this case directly. In general, the slower the mutation rate, the more people who will have the same mtDNA pattern, and vice-versa. However the figures presented to the jury were from a database of actual DNA patterns collected by forensic scientists. The mechanics of the analysis involves a process similar to that used with nuclear DNA. Coleman, 202 F.Supp.2d at 969.

This court has not until now had the opportunity to rule on the admissibility of mtDNA testing. However, mtDNA testing has been admitted into evidence by several state courts and has been upheld on review. See, e.g., State v. Underwood, 134 N.C.App. 533, 518 S.E.2d 231 (1999); State v. Scott, 33 S.W.3d 746 (Tenn.2000); State v. Council, 335 S.C. 1, 515 S.E.2d 508 (1999); People v. Klinger, 185 Misc.2d 574, 713 N.Y.S.2d 823 (Crim.Ct.2000); Williams v. Maryland, 342 Md. 724, 679 A.2d 1106 (1996).

. . . .

2. Mitochondrial DNA in this Case

The district court in this case held a very extensive hearing in order to determine the admissibility of mtDNA evidence at trial. The court determined that the techniques had been established and accepted by the scientific community, accepted by the courts, and had been subject to peer review. Beverly now argues that the district court abused its discretion on the basis of three objections.

Beverly argues that Dr. Melton's laboratory, which had analyzed the sample in this case, has never been certified by an external agency. This point was raised in the pretrial hearing, and, although there is no legal requirement that Dr. Melton's lab be so certified, the district court did question Dr. Melton on this point. Laboratories doing DNA forensic work are accredited through the American Society of Crime Laboratory Directors. However, Dr. Melton's lab, having only been actively engaged in case work for about 11 months at the time of the trial, was not yet able to apply for the accreditation, but was expected to go through the process the following spring. Furthermore, Dr. Melton's own credentials are considerable. Not only has she been working with mtDNA since 1991, she has a Ph.D from Pennsylvania State University in genetics; her thesis investigated mitochondrial DNA as it would apply to forensic applications. In addition, Dr. Melton has published a significant amount of work in this field.

Next, Beverly argues that Dr. Melton's procedures would sometimes yield results that were contaminated, and that furthermore, the sample analyzed in this particular case was contaminated. Testimony given by Dr. Melton and Dr. Kessis, who was Beverly's expert at trial, supported Beverly's general contention, but no evidence demonstrated that any contamination in this case affected the results of the analysis. Dr. Melton testified that "[we] occasionally have what we call sporadic contamination," probably as a result of residue on a piece of equipment brought into the lab. However, Dr. Melton was confident that no contamination of the sample itself had occurred. The reagent blank in the test of the sample itself did not show any indication of contamination, in contrast to a separate reagent blank, used in a different test tube, which was a control in the experiment. Therefore, the actual data relied upon in this case, obtained from the sequencing machine, did not indicate any presence of a contaminant.

Finally, the district court carefully considered during the pretrial hearing the question of whether the relevance of this evidence outweighed its probative value. In particular, Beverly argued that the jury would associate mitochondrial DNA analysis with nuclear DNA analysis and give it the same value, in terms of its ability to "fingerprint" a suspect. The district court, however, decided that this issue was more appropriately dealt with through a vigorous cross-examination, and in fact that was exactly what occurred at trial. Moreover, the court noted the important probative value that this evidence added to the trial. Finally, the court separately considered the scientific reliability of the statistical analysis offered by the government, concluding that:

The predictive effect of the statistical analysis is based upon a formula which is apparently recognized in the scientific community and used in a variety of scientific contexts, and it has been used specifically here in the analysis of mitochondrial DNA results. The Court concludes that it's an accepted and reliable estimate of probability, and in this case, it led to results, interpreted results, which substantially increase the probability that the hair sample is the hair of the defendant in this case.

Based on the record compiled in the district court's careful and extensive hearing on this issue, there was no abuse of discretion in admitting the mtDNA testing results. The scientific basis for the use of such DNA is well established. Any issues going to the conduct of the specific tests in question were fully developed and subject to cross examination. There was no error in finding that the testing methods, and Dr. Melton's testing in particular, were sufficiently reliable to be admissible. Finally, the mathematical basis for the evidentiary power of the mtDNA evidence was carefully explained, and was not more prejudicial than probative.

It was made clear to the jury that this type of evidence could not identify individuals with the precision of conventional DNA analysis. Nevertheless, any particular mtDNA pattern is sufficiently rare, especially when there is no contention that the real culprit might have been a matrilineal relative of the defendant, that it certainly meets the standard for probative evidence: "any tendency to make the existence of any fact that is of consequence to the determination of the action more probable or less probable than it would be without the evidence." Fed.R.Evid. 401. The statistical evidence at trial showed that, at most, less than 1% of the population would be expected to have this mtDNA pattern. Even an article critical of mtDNA stated the most frequent pattern applies in no more than 3% of the population. Erica Beecher-Monas, The Heuristics of Intellectual Due Process: A Primer for Triers of Science, 75 N.Y.U.L.Rev. 1563, 1655 n. 535 (2000). It would be unlikely to find a match between Beverly's hair and the hair of a random individual. The testimony was that, with a high degree of confidence, less than one percent of the population could be expected to have the same pattern as that of the hair recovered from the bank robbery site, and that Beverly did have the same pattern, and thus could not be excluded as the source of the hair. Finding Beverly's mtDNA at the crime scene is essentially equivalent to finding that the last two digits of a license plate of a car owned by defendant matched the last two numbers of a license plate of a getaway car. It would be some evidence—not conclusive, but certainly admissible. We find the same here.

. . . .

VI

A. Severance of Turns's Trial

Turns contends that the district court should not have joined his trial with Beverly's and Crockett's. Turns argues that the alleged conspiracy between Rogers, Warren, and Turns was entirely separate from the alleged conspiracy that existed between Rogers, Warren, and Crockett that, according to Turns, dominated in this case. We do not find this argument persuasive....

Turns also argues that the district court erred in denying his motion to sever the trial, brought under Rule 14 of the Federal Rules of Criminal Procedure. Severance of a joint trial is permitted, if joinder is prejudicial. Fed.R.Crim.P. 14; see also United States v. Critton, 43 F.3d 1089, 1097–98 (6th Cir.1995) ("Rule 14 allows for severance if it appears that a defendant or the government is prejudiced by a joinder of offenses or of defendants.") (internal quotation marks omitted). We review a denial of severance by the district court for a clear abuse of discretion. United States v. Causey, 834 F.2d 1277, 1287 (6th Cir.1987). Furthermore, a strong policy presumption exists in favor of joint trials when charges will be proved by the same evidence and result from the same acts. See United States v. Hamilton, 689 F.2d 1262, 1275 (6th Cir.1982).

Turns argues that his trial was prejudiced by being joined with the other defendants since the credibility of the testimony of Rogers and Warren, the government witnesses who placed Turns at the scene of the crime, was bolstered by additional pieces of incriminating and corroborating evidence in the case against Beverly and Crockett. For example, in Crockett's case, the government presented a photograph taken during one of the bank robberies, which was purported to be of Crockett while he was in the process of robbing the bank. In Beverly's case, there was mtDNA evidence presented that linked Beverly to one of the robberies. These pieces of evidence corroborated the testimony given by Rogers and Crockett, although the evidence would have been inadmissible in a trial focused solely on Turns.

Turns's contention that Rogers's and Warren's testimony was bolstered during the trial by corroborating evidence presented in the case against Beverly and Crockett is unpersuasive. We have stated in Causey, 834 F.2d at 1288, that "a defendant is not entitled to severance simply because the evidence against a co-defendant is far more damaging than the evidence against him." Moreover, a defendant does not have a right to a separate trial, merely because his likelihood of acquittal would be greater if severance were granted. See United States v. Gallo, 763 F.2d 1504, 1526 (6th Cir.1985) (citing United States v. Stirling, 571 F.2d 708, 733 (2d Cir.1978); United States v. Larson, 526 F.2d 256, 260 (5th Cir.1976)). "Absent a showing of substantial prejudice, spillover of evidence from one case to another does not require severance." Ibid. (citing United States v. Ricco, 549 F.2d 264, 270–71 (2d Cir.1977)). Turns has not made a showing of substantial prejudice in this case, and thus the district court did not abuse its discretion by denying Turns's motion for severance.

....

VIII

For the reasons given above, we AFFIRM the convictions of Crockett, Beverly, and Turns.

8.4 Historical Forensics and the Use of DNA Evidence

Use of DNA analysis to answer questions about famous historical persons raises other legal and ethical issues, which should be carefully considered at each step of the planning process and implementation of any experimental work and publication.

Legal and ethical issues must be addressed in contacting family members, obtaining permission for exhumation of remains, permission to be on the property to obtain the remains, permission from communities and tribal leaders, and following the guidelines of the relevant professional societies which may be utilized on the research team.

Care should be taken to accurately describe the scope of the design of the experiment. For example, experiments have been designed to determine whether Abraham Lincoln had Marfan Syndrome and whether Thomas Jefferson fathered children with his slave, Sally Hemings. Design of the experiments in both cases are not scientifically conclusive. In analyzing whether Abraham Lincoln had the gene for Marfan Syndrome, the analysis can only show that he did not have the disease gene. In determining from male descendants of Sally Hemings whether they are also descendants of Thomas Jefferson, it is only possible to determine that they share the same male ancestor with known descendants of Thomas Jefferson. The lack of conclusivity of these research designs does not preclude the use of such methods, but it does indicate that other factors should be considered in making conclusions and that published results must be clear about the limitations.

8.4.1 Thomas Jefferson and Sally Hemings

The allegation was first publicly made September 1, 1802 by James T. Callender, newspaper reporter for the Richmond Recorder, during the elections of 1802. His story read: "it is well known that the man whom it delighteth the people to honor, keeps and for many years has kept as his concubine, one of his own slaves. Her name is SALLY. The name of her eldest son is TOM. His features are said to bear a striking although sable resemblance to those of the President himself. The boy is ten or twelve years of age. His mother went to France in the same vessel with Mr. Jefferson and his two daughters." Callender wrote in November 17, 1802 that his story had ended Thomas Jefferson's political career and that he could not be re-elected in 1804, and he was not. The Thomas Jefferson Heritage Society, *The Jefferson-Hemings Myth: An American Travesty* 16–17 (Jefferson Editions, Charlottesville, VA: 2001).

Meriwether Jones answered the charges made by Callender, denying the story. In fact, in spite of DNA evidence to arguably, the contrary, the Thomas Jefferson Heritage Society vehemently denies that Jefferson had such a relationship. *See,* The Thomas Jefferson Heritage Society, *supra.*

8.4.2 Abraham Lincoln and Marfan Syndrome?

Historians have speculated, at least since a Los Angeles doctor in 1962 made the observation, as to whether the symptoms and physical characteristics of Abraham Lincoln may have indicated that he had Marfan's Syndrome. A reporter during the Civil War wrote that Lincoln was a "tall, lank, lean man considerably over 6 feet in height with stooping shoulders, long pendulous arms terminating in hands of extraordinary dimensions which, however were far exceeded in proportion by his feet."

After DNA testing, experts concluded that Lincoln probably did not have Marfan's syndrome. However, the considerations in the decision to test Lincoln's DNA is discussed in the following excerpt from Philip R. Reilly, Abraham Lincoln's DNA and Other Adventures in Genetics 6–13 (Cold Spring Harbor Laboratory Press, 2000):

> I became involved in the decision over whether or not to test Lincoln's DNA for evidence of Marfan syndrome because of Dr. Victor McKusick, the 1997 winner of the prestigious Lasker Award.... Given that McKusick is the world's authority on Marfan syndrom and works in nearby Baltimore, it was inevitable that Dr. Marc Micozzi, the forensic pathologist who was at the time director of the National Museum of Health and Medicine, would seek his advice on how to handle [the] ... request.... Lynne Wilson, our expert on the preservation of museum collections, reassured by the fact that DNA studies would consume only a tiny fraction of the holdings, concluded that the sacrifice of a tiny bit of bone would not harm the collection or compromise future scholarship.
>
> The really challenging question was to try to determine what Abraham Lincoln would want us to do. Although Lincoln's is among the most studied lives in history, we had no firm historical information to guide us. The Lincoln experts on the panel knew of no action Lincoln had taken or letters he had written from which we could infer that he would either favor or oppose the proposed testing. The scholarly consensus was that Lincoln was not a particularly private person. Neither ethical nor legal analysis posed obvious roadblocks to testing. The law has long recognized that public officials and celebrities may not have the same expectation of privacy as do the rest of us.

Notes

1. Is there an expectation of privacy of the *deceased*? Should the test be for expectation of privacy for the family if the family does not agree to the exhumation and test?

2. What advantages does mitochondrial DNA have over nuclear DNA? Do you agree that mitochondrial DNA meets the criteria for admissibility?

Chapter Nine

Biotechnology and Property Law

9.1 Introduction

Property ownership of the products of biotechnology raise novel questions for which we draw upon our foundations of personal property and intellectual property concepts of ownership. In the landmark case, *Moore v. Regents of University of California*, the California Supreme Court ruled that a person cannot have an ownership interest in his own bodily tissues or organs, under any theory of property ownership.

9.2 Ownership Problems

Moore v. Regents of University of California
793 P.2d 479 (1990)

OPINION by: Judge J. Panelli

I. Introduction

We granted review in this case to determine whether plaintiff has stated a cause of action against his physician and other defendants for using his cells in potentially lucrative medical research without his permission. Plaintiff alleges that his physician failed to disclose preexisting research and economic interests in the cells before obtaining consent to the medical procedures by which they were extracted. The superior court sustained all defendants' demurrers to the third amended complaint, and the Court of Appeal reversed. We hold that the complaint states a cause of action for breach of the physician's disclosure obligations, but not for conversion.

II. Facts

Our only task in reviewing a ruling on a demurrer is to determine whether the complaint states a cause of action. Accordingly, we assume that the complaint's properly pleaded material allegations are true and give the complaint a reasonable interpretation by reading it as a whole and all its parts in their context.... The plaintiff is John Moore (Moore), who underwent treatment for hairy-cell leukemia at the Medical Center of the

University of California at Los Angeles (UCLA Medical Center). The five defendants are: (1) Dr. David W. Golde (Golde), a physician who attended Moore at UCLA Medical Center; (2) the Regents of the University of California (Regents), who own and operate the university; (3) Shirley G. Quan, a researcher employed by the Regents; (4) Genetics Institute, Inc. (Genetics Institute); and (5) Sandoz Pharmaceuticals Corporation and related entities (collectively Sandoz).

Moore first visited UCLA Medical Center on October 5, 1976, shortly after he learned that he had hairy-cell leukemia. After hospitalizing Moore and "withdr[awing] extensive amounts of blood, bone marrow aspirate, and other bodily substances," Golde n1 confirmed that diagnosis. At this time all defendants, including Golde, were aware that "certain blood products and blood components were of great value in a number of commercial and scientific efforts" and that access to a patient whose blood contained these substances would provide "competitive, commercial, and scientific advantages." ...

On October 8, 1976, Golde recommended that Moore's spleen be removed. Golde informed Moore "that he had reason to fear for his life, and that the proposed splenectomy operation ... was necessary to slow down the progress of his disease." Based upon Golde's representations, Moore signed a written consent form authorizing the splenectomy.

Before the operation, Golde and Quan "formed the intent and made arrangements to obtain portions of [Moore's] spleen following its removal" and to take them to a separate research unit. Golde gave written instructions to this effect on October 18 and 19, 1976. These research activities "were not intended to have ... any relation to [Moore's] medical ... care." However, neither Golde nor Quan informed Moore of their plans to conduct this research or requested his permission. Surgeons at UCLA Medical Center, whom the complaint does not name as defendants, removed Moore's spleen on October 20, 1976.

Moore returned to the UCLA Medical Center several times between November 1976 and September 1983. He did so at Golde's direction and based upon representations "that such visits were necessary and required for his health and well-being, and based upon the trust inherent in and by virtue of the physician-patient relationship...." On each of these visits Golde withdrew additional samples of "blood, blood serum, skin, bone marrow aspirate, and sperm." On each occasion Moore travelled to the UCLA Medical Center from his home in Seattle because he had been told that the procedures were to be performed only there and only under Golde's direction.

"In fact, [however,] throughout the period of time that [Moore] was under [Golde's] care and treatment, ... the defendants were actively involved in a number of activities which they concealed from [Moore]...." Specifically, defendants were conducting research on Moore's cells and planned to "benefit financially and competitively ... [by exploiting the cells] and [their] exclusive access to [the cells] by virtue of [Golde's] ongoing physician-patient relationship...."

Sometime before August 1979, Golde established a cell line from Moore's T-lymphocytes. FN2 On January 30, 1981, the Regents applied for a patent on the cell line, listing Golde and Quan as inventors. "[B]y virtue of an established policy..., [the] Regents, Golde, and Quan would share in any royalties or profits ... arising out of [the] patent." The patent issued on March 20, 1984, naming Golde and Quan as the inventors of the cell line and the Regents as the assignee of the patent. (U.S. Patent No. 4,438,032 (Mar. 20, 1984).)

SELECTED NOTES

FN2 A T-lymphocyte is a type of white blood cell. T-lymphocytes produce lymphokines, or proteins that regulate the immune system. Some lymphokines have potential therapeutic value. If the genetic material responsible for producing a particular lymphokine can be identified, it can sometimes be used to manufacture large quantities of the lymphokine through the techniques of recombinant DNA. (See generally U.S. Congress, Office of Technology Assessment, New Developments in Biotechnology: Ownership of Human Tissues and Cells (1987) at pp. 31–46 (hereafter OTA Report); see also fn. 29, *post.*)

While the genetic code for lymphokines does not vary from individual to individual, it can nevertheless be quite difficult to locate the gene responsible for a particular lymphokine. Because T-lymphocytes produce many different lymphokines, the relevant gene is often like a needle in a haystack. (OTA Rep., *supra*, at p. 42.) Moore's T-lymphocytes were interesting to the defendants because they overproduced certain lymphokines, thus making the corresponding genetic material easier to identify. (In published research papers, defendants and other researchers have shown that the overproduction was caused by a virus, and that normal T-lymphocytes infected by the virus will also overproduce. See fn. 30, *post.*)

Cells taken directly from the body (primary cells) are not very useful for these purposes. Primary cells typically reproduce a few times and then die. One can, however, sometimes continue to use cells for an extended period of time by developing them into a "cell line," a culture capable of reproducing indefinitely. This is not, however, always an easy task. "Longterm growth of human cells and tissues is difficult, often an art," and the probability of succeeding with any given cell sample is low, except for a few types of cells not involved in this case. (OTA Rep., *supra*, at p. 5.)

... The Regent's patent also covers various methods for using the cell line to produce lymphokines. Moore admits in his complaint that "the true clinical potential of each of the lymphokines ... [is] difficult to predict, [but] ... competing commercial firms in these relevant fields have published reports in biotechnology industry periodicals predicting a potential market of approximately $ 3.01 Billion Dollars by the year 1990 for a whole range of [such lymphokines]...."

With the Regents' assistance, Golde negotiated agreements for commercial development of the cell line and products to be derived from it. Under an agreement with Genetics Institute, Golde "became a paid consultant" and "acquired the rights to 75,000 shares of common stock." Genetics Institute also agreed to pay Golde and the Regents "at least $ 330,000 over three years, including a pro-rata share of [Golde's] salary and fringe benefits, in exchange for ... exclusive access to the materials and research performed" on the cell line and products derived from it. On June 4, 1982, Sandoz "was added to the agreement," and compensation payable to Golde and the Regents was increased by $ 110,000. "[T]hroughout this period, ... Quan spent as much as 70 [percent] of her time working for [the] Regents on research" related to the cell line ...

III. Discussion

A. *Breach of Fiduciary Duty and Lack of Informed Consent*

Moore repeatedly alleges that Golde failed to disclose the extent of his research and economic interests in Moore's cells n6 before obtaining consent to the medical procedures by which the cells were extracted. These allegations, in our view, state a cause of action against Golde for invading a legally protected interest of his patient. This cause of action can properly be characterized either as the breach of a fiduciary duty to disclose facts material to the patient's consent or, alternatively, as the performance of medical procedures without first having obtained the patient's informed consent.

Our analysis begins with three well-established principles. First, "a person of adult years and in sound mind has the right, in the exercise of control over his own body, to determine whether or not to submit to lawful medical treatment." (*Cobbs* v. *Grant* (1972) 8 Cal.3d 229, 242 [104 Cal.Rptr. 505, 502 P.2d 1]; cf. *Schloendorff* v *New York Hospital* (1914) 211 N.Y. 125 [105 N.E. 92, 93].) Second, "the patient's consent to treatment, to be effective, must be an informed consent." (*Cobbs* v. *Grant, supra*, 8 Cal.3d at p. 242.) Third, in soliciting the patient's consent, a physician has a fiduciary duty to disclose all information material to the patient's decision....

These principles lead to the following conclusions: (1) a physician must disclose personal interests unrelated to the patient's health, whether research or economic, that may affect the physician's professional judgment; and (2) a physician's failure to disclose such interests may give rise to a cause of action for performing medical procedures without informed consent or breach of fiduciary duty.

To be sure, questions about the validity of a patient's consent to a procedure typically arise when the patient alleges that the physician failed to disclose medical risks, as in malpractice cases, and not when the patient alleges that the physician had a personal interest, as in this case. The concept of informed consent, however, is broad enough to encompass the latter. "The scope of the physician's communication to the patient ... must be measured by the patient's need, and that need is whatever information is material to the decision." (*Cobbs* v. *Grant, supra*, 8 Cal.3d at p. 245.)

Indeed, the law already recognizes that a reasonable patient would want to know whether a physician has an economic interest that might affect the physician's professional judgment. As the Court of Appeal has said, "[c]ertainly a sick patient deserves to be free of any reasonable suspicion that his doctor's judgment is influenced by a profit motive." (*Magan Medical Clinic* v. *Cal. State Bd. of Medical Examiners* (1967) 249 Cal.App.2d 124, 132 [57 Cal.Rptr. 256].) The desire to protect patients from possible conflicts of interest has also motivated legislative enactments. Among these is Business and Professions Code section 654.2. Under that section, a physician may not charge a patient on behalf of, or refer a patient to, any organization in which the physician has a "significant beneficial interest, unless [the physician] first discloses in writing to the patient, that there is such an interest and advises the patient that the patient may choose any organization for the purposes of obtaining the services ordered or requested by [the physician]." (Bus. & Prof. Code, §654.2, subd. (a) ...

It is important to note that no law prohibits a physician from conducting research in the same area in which he practices. Progress in medicine often depends upon physicians, such as those practicing at the university hospital where Moore received treatment, who conduct research while caring for their patients.

Yet a physician who treats a patient in whom he also has a research interest has potentially conflicting loyalties. This is because medical treatment decisions are made on the basis of proportionality—weighing the benefits *to the patient* against the risks *to the patient*. As another court has said, "the determination as to whether the burdens of treatment are worth enduring for any individual patient depends upon the facts unique in each case," and "the patient's interests and desires are the key ingredients of the decision-making process." (*Barber* v. *Superior Court* (1983) 147 Cal.App.3d 1006, 1018–1019 [195 Cal.Rptr. 484, 47 A.L.R.4th 1].) A physician who adds his own research interests to this balance may be tempted to order a scientifically useful procedure or test that offers marginal, or no, benefits to the patient. The possibility that an interest extraneous to the patient's health has affected the physician's judgment is something that a reasonable patient would want to know in deciding whether to consent to a proposed course of treatment. It is material to the patient's decision and, thus, a prerequisite to informed consent. (See *Cobbs* v. *Grant, supra*, 8 Cal.3d at p. 245.)

Golde argues that the scientific use of cells that have already been removed cannot possibly affect the patient's medical interests. The argument is correct in one instance but not in another. If a physician has no plans to conduct research on a patient's cells at the time he recommends the medical procedure by which they are taken, then the patient's medical interests have not been impaired. In that instance the argument is correct. On the other hand, a physician who does have a preexisting research interest might, consciously or unconsciously, take that into consideration in recommending the procedure. In that instance the argument is incorrect: the physician's extraneous motivation may affect his judgment and is, thus, material to the patient's consent.

We acknowledge that there is a competing consideration. To require disclosure of research and economic interests may corrupt the patient's own judgment by distracting him from the requirements of his health. But California law does not grant physicians unlimited discretion to decide what to disclose. Instead, "it is the prerogative of the patient, not the physician, to determine for himself the direction in which he believes his interests lie." (*Cobbs* v. *Grant, supra*, 8 Cal.3d at p. 242.) ... However, we made that statement in the context of a physician-patient relationship unaffected by possible conflicts of interest

1. *Dr. Golde*

We turn now to the allegations of Moore's third amended complaint to determine whether he has stated such a cause of action. We first discuss the adequacy of Moore's allegations against Golde, based upon the physician's disclosures prior to the splenectomy.

Moore alleges that, prior to the surgical removal of his spleen, Golde "formed the intent and made arrangements to obtain portions of his spleen following its removal from [Moore] in connection with [his] desire to have regular and continuous access to, and possession of, [Moore's] unique and rare Blood and Bodily Substances." Moore was never informed prior to the splenectomy of Golde's "prior formed intent" to obtain a portion of his spleen. In our view, these allegations adequately show that Golde had an undisclosed research interest in Moore's cells at the time he sought Moore's consent to the splenectomy. Accordingly, Moore has stated a cause of action for breach of fiduciary duty, or lack of informed consent, based upon the disclosures accompanying that medical procedure.

We next discuss the adequacy of Golde's alleged disclosures regarding the postoperative takings of blood and other samples. In this context, Moore alleges that Golde "expressly, affirmatively and impliedly represented ... that these withdrawals of his Blood and Bodily Substances were necessary and required for his health and well-being." However, Moore also alleges that Golde actively concealed his economic interest in Moore's cells during this time period. "[D]uring each of these visits..., and even when [Moore] inquired as to whether there was any possible or potential commercial or financial value or significance of his Blood and Bodily Substances, or whether the defendants had discovered anything ... which was or might be ... related to any scientific activity resulting in commercial or financial benefits..., the defendants repeatedly and affirmatively represented to [Moore] that there was no commercial or financial value to his Blood and Bodily Substances ... and in fact actively discouraged such inquiries."

Moore admits in his complaint that defendants disclosed they "were engaged in strictly academic and purely scientific medical research...." However, Golde's representation that he had no financial interest in this research became false, based upon the allegations, at least by May 1979, when he "began to investigate and initiate the procedures ... for [obtaining] a patent" on the cell line developed from Moore's cells.

In these allegations, Moore plainly asserts that Golde concealed an economic interest in the postoperative procedures. Therefore, applying the principles already discussed, the allegations state a cause of action for breach of fiduciary duty or lack of informed consent.

We thus disagree with the superior court's ruling that Moore had not stated a cause of action because essential allegations were lacking. We discuss each such allegation. First, in the superior court's view, Moore needed but failed to allege that defendants knew his cells had potential commercial value *on October 5, 1976* (the time blood tests were first performed at UCLA Medical Center) and had *at that time* already formed the intent to exploit the cells. We agree with the superior court that the absence of such allegations precludes Moore from stating a cause of action based upon the procedures undertaken on October 5, 1976. But, as already discussed, Moore clearly alleges that Golde had developed a research interest in his cells by October 20, 1976, when the splenectomy was performed. Thus, Moore can state a cause of action based upon Golde's alleged failure to disclose that interest before the splenectomy.

The superior court also held that the lack of essential allegations prevented Moore from stating a cause of action based on the splenectomy. According to the superior court, Moore failed to allege that the operation lacked a therapeutic purpose or that the procedure was totally unrelated to therapeutic purposes. In our view, however, neither allegation is essential. Even if the splenectomy had a therapeutic purpose, FN11 it does not follow that Golde had no duty to disclose his additional research and economic interests. As we have already discussed, the existence of a motivation for a medical procedure unrelated to the patient's health is a potential conflict of interest and a fact material to the patient's decision.

SELECTED FOOTNOTES

FN11 The record shows that the splenectomy did have a therapeutic purpose. The Regents' patent application, which the superior court and the Court of Appeal both accepted as part of the record, shows that Moore had a grossly enlarged spleen and that its excision improved his condition.

... Neither the Court of Appeal's opinion, the parties' briefs, nor our research discloses a case holding that a person retains a sufficient interest in excised cells to support a cause of action for conversion. We do not find this surprising, since the laws governing such things as human tissues, n21 transplantable organs, n22 blood, n23 fetuses, n24 pituitary glands, n25 corneal tissue, n26 and dead bodies n27 deal with human biological materials as objects sui generis, regulating their disposition to achieve policy goals rather than abandoning them to the general law of personal property. It is these specialized statutes, not the law of conversion, to which courts ordinarily should and do look for guidance on the disposition of human biological materials.

SELECTED FOOTNOTES

.... Finally, the subject matter of the Regents' patent—the patented cell line and the products derived from it—cannot be Moore's property. This is because the patented cell line is both factually and legally distinct from the cells taken from Moore's body. FN35 Federal law permits the patenting of organisms that represent the product of "human ingenuity," but not naturally occurring organisms. (*Diamond* v. *Chakrabarty* (1980) 447 U.S. 303, 309–310 [65 L.Ed.2d 144, 150, 100 S.Ct. 2204].) Human cell lines are patentable because "[l]ong-term adaptation and growth of human tissues and cells in culture is difficult—often considered an art...," and the probability of success is low. (OTA Rep., *supra*, at p. 33; see fn. 2, *ante*.) It is this *inventive effort* that patent law rewards, not the discovery of naturally occurring raw materials. Thus, Moore's allegations that he owns the cell line and the products derived from it are inconsistent with the patent, which constitutes an authoritative determination that the cell line is the product of invention. Since such allegations are nothing more than arguments or conclusions of law, they of course do not bind us ...

SELECTED FOOTNOTES

FN35 The distinction between primary cells (cells taken directly from the body) and patented cell lines is not purely a legal one. Cells change while being developed into a cell line and continue to change over time. (OTA Rep., *supra*, at p. 34.) "[I]t is clear that most established cell lines ... are not completely normal. Besides [an] enhanced growth potential relative to primary cells, they frequently have highly abnormal chromosome numbers...." (2 Watson et al., Molecular Biology of the Gene (4th ed. 1987) p. 967; see also OTA Rep., *supra*, at p. 36.)

The cell line in this case, for example, after many replications began to generate defective and rearranged forms of the HTLV-II virus. A published research paper to which defendants contributed suggests that "the defective forms of virus were probably generated during the passage [or replication] of the cells rather than being present in the original tumour cells of the patient." Possibly because of these changes in the virus, the cell line has developed new abilities to grow in different media. (Chen, McLaughlin, Gasson, Clark & Golde, *Molecular Characterization of Genome of a Novel Human T-cell Leukaemia Virus*, Nature (Oct. 6, 1983) vol. 305, p. 505.)

We find it interesting that Justice Mosk, in his dissent, would object to our "summar[y] of the salient conclusions" (*People* v. *Guerra* (1984) 37 Cal.3d 385, 412 [208 Cal.Rptr. 162, 690 P.2d 635] [opn. by Mosk, J.]) of relevant scientific literature in setting forth the technological background of this case. (Dis. opn. of Mosk, J., *post*, at p. 182.) This court has previously cited scientific literature to show, for example, that reports of hypnotic recall "form[ed] a scientifically inadequate basis for drawing conclusions about the memory processes of the large majority of the population" (*People* v. *Shirley* (1982) 31 Cal.3d 18, 59 [181 Cal.Rptr. 243, 723 P.2d 1354] [opn. by Mosk, J.]), and that eyewitness testimony can be unreliable (*People* v. *McDonald* (1984) 37 Cal.3d 351, 365–367 [208 Cal.Rptr. 236, 690 P.2d 709, 46 A.L.R.4th 1011] [opn. by Mosk, J.]).

.... To expand liability by extending conversion law into this area would have a broad impact. The House Committee on Science and Technology of the United States Congress found that "49 percent of the researchers at medical institutions surveyed used human tissues or cells in their research." Many receive grants from the National Institute of Health for this work. (OTA Rep., *supra*, at p. 52.) In addition, "there are nearly 350 commercial biotechnology firms in the United States actively engaged in biotechnology research and commercial product development and approximately 25 to 30 percent appear to be engaged in research to develop a human therapeutic or diagnostic reagent.... Most, but not all, of the human therapeutic products are derived from human tissues and cells, or human cell lines or cloned genes." (*Id.*, at p. 56.)....

IV.

The decision of the Court of Appeal is affirmed in part and reversed in part. The case is remanded to the Court of Appeal, which shall direct the superior court to: (1) overrule Golde's demurrers to the causes of action for breach of fiduciary duty and lack of informed consent; (2) sustain, with leave to amend, the demurrers of the Regents, Quan, Sandoz, and Genetics Institute to the purported causes of action for breach of fiduciary duty and lack of informed consent; (3) sustain, without leave to amend, all defendants' demurrers to the purported cause of action for conversion; and (4) hear and determine all defendants' remaining demurrers.

Miles, Inc. v. Scripps Clinic and Research Foundation
810 F. Supp. 1091 (S.D.Cal. 1993)

Judge John S. Rhoades, Sr.

I. STATEMENT OF FACTS

A. The Parties

Scripps-Miles, Inc. ("Scripps-Miles") was a corporation jointly owned by Plaintiff Miles, Inc. ("Miles"), a pharmaceutical company, and Defendant Scripps Clinic and Research Foundation ("Scripps"), a nonprofit research foundation. One purpose of forming the corporation was to prepare and sell immuno-chemical materials. Defendant Nakamura was hired by Scripps-Miles as Vice President, Technical Operations. Defendant Zimmerman is the executor and personal representative of the Estate of Dr. Theodore Zimmerman. Dr. Zimmerman was retained by Scripps-Miles in 1980 to serve as a consultant in the area of diagnostic immunology. Defendants Armour Pharmaceutical Co. ("Armour") and Revlon, Inc. ("Revlon"), were licensees of Dr. Zimmerman's patent rights. Defendant Rorer Group, Inc. ("Rorer") acquired the license for Dr. Zimmerman's patent when Revlon sold Armour to Rorer....

C. The Technology

This case concerns monoclonal antibodies. The antibodies at issue in this case were used by Dr. Zimmerman to create a purified Factor VIII:C. Factor VIII:C is a substance that permits a hemophiliac's blood to clot. Without Factor VIII:C, hemophiliacs run great risks of blood loss. Purified Factor VIII:C serves its vital function without risk of transmitting AIDS or hepatitis through treatment.

Dr. Zimmerman provided the Scripps-Miles Monoclonal Laboratory with the antigen that eventually led to the production of cell line 2.2.9—the cell line at issue in this suit. A cell line is "a clone or a population of identical cells, derived from a single cell." Created through genetic engineering, cell lines produce cells capable of continuous culture, immortalizing the rare and valuable qualities of a particular cell." ...

D. Other Facts and Allegations

In 1982, Scripps-Miles, Inc. adopted a plan of dissolution and Miles received ownership of the Monoclonal Lab. Dr. Zimmerman and Scripps continued to use cell line 2.2.9, polished articles on the purification of Factor VIII:C through monoclonal antibodies, and obtained a patent for the process of producing Factor VIII:C. Dr. Zimmerman assigned the patent to Scripps, who licensed the patent exclusively to Armour and Revlon. Revlon later sold Armour to Rorer.

Plaintiff alleges that prior to the Scripps-Miles dissolution, Scripps conspired with Dr. Zimmerman and Nakamura to transfer the right to commercialize the cell line to Scripps. Plaintiff further contends that the transfers of the cell line itself from Dr. Zimmerman to Armour and Revlon, and later to Rorer, were inconsistent with Miles's ownership interest in the right to commercialization of the cell line. n3 Plaintiffs further contend that Defendants Scripps, Dr. Zimmerman, and Nakamura breached a fiduciary duty, committed acts of deceit and fraudulent concealment, and committed actual fraud....

II. DISCUSSION

A. Conversion

All Defendants allege that California does not recognize an action for conversion of the "right to commercialize" a cell line. I agree. In its remand to this Court, the Ninth Circuit had the following to say in declining to decide the issue:

While the issues are purely legal, we note that the questions raised by Miles's causes of action are ones of first impression. Miles's conversion claim requires determination of whether a "right to commercialize" a cell line is a property right whose dispossession can give rise to a conversion claim, an issue not yet squarely addressed by California courts....

1. Is There a Conversion Claim?

Under California law, the elements of a conversion claim are (1) plaintiff's ownership or right to possession of the property at the time of the conversion; (2) defendants' conversion by a wrongful act or dispossession of plaintiff's property rights; and (3) damages. The first of these elements is at issue in this case.

Plaintiff agrees that the conversion claim is not as to the cell line itself. Rather, it is the "right to commercialize" that was allegedly converted by Defendants. Therefore, Defendants' extensive arguments that Defendants had a lawful, possessory interest in the cell line do not address Defendants' right to gain financially from the commercialization of an innovation. That Dr. Zimmerman physically was given cell line 2.2.9 is not relevant here; the "property" at issue is the intangible right to commercialize the cell line, not the cell line itself.

2. Ownership or Right to Possession of "Commercialization"

The claim of conversion here relates to an intangible right—a kind of property not traditionally considered capable of being converted. Generally, California law only recognizes "conversion of intangibles represented by documents, such as bonds, notes, bills of exchange, stock certificates, and warehouse receipts." 5 B.E. Witkin Summary of California Law, Torts §§613 (9th ed. 1988). Ordinarily, there can be no conversion of the goodwill of a business, trade secrets, a newspaper route, or a laundry list of customers. Id.…

a. Interest Capable of Precise Definition.

The commercialization of a cell line is an interest capable of precise definition. First, it is undisputed that a cell line is patentable subject matter under 35 U.S.C. §§101. Second, under 35 U.S.C. §§271, the holder of a patent may enforce the exclusive rights flowing from the sale or use of the patentable invention. Thus, using patents as an analogy, the interest at stake here—making money from the commercialization of a cell line—is capable of precise definition.…

Continuing with the analogy, since a patent holder may use a contract—often a licensing agreement—to regulate the "commercialization" of the patentable invention, the interest in the commercialization is similarly protected by contract. Since a commercialization interest may be defined by contract, the interest at stake here is "capable of precise definition" for purposes of this case as well. The first prong of the Rasmussen test is thus met.

b. Capable of Exclusive Possession or Control

Since cell lines may be patented, and since a patent provides the patent holder with exclusive possession or control of the right to exploit the patent for financial gain, the right to commercialize a cell line is, by analogy, also capable of exclusive possession or control. The contract analogy also demonstrates that the interest in commercialization is capable of exclusive possession or control, since contracts are often used to protect similar interests in reaping commercial rewards from biomedical technology. See Moore v. Regents of University of California, 51 Cal. 3d 120, 144–45, 271 Cal. Rptr. 146, 793 P.2d 479 (1990), cert. denied, 113 L. Ed. 2d 444, 111 S. Ct. 1388 (1991). The second prong of Rasmussen is also met.

c. Has Putative Owner Established Claim of Exclusivity?

Plaintiff here has not established an exclusive right to commercialize based on the record before me. It is possible that such a claim could be found within the agreements of incorporation of Scripps-Miles, the hiring contracts for the employee Defendants, or the dissolution agreement. These documents are not before the court at this time. For purposes of this motion, this Court assumes that Plaintiff has established a claim of exclusivity for the right to commercialization of a cell line, so the third and final prong of Rasmussen is also met.

d. Conclusion

Under this analysis, it is possible to own a right to "commercialization." As explained below, however, no cause of action for conversion has been recognized under California law for the alleged conversion of a right to commercialize cell lines. Instead, the intangible property right is one not protected by a conversion cause of action.…

3. California Approach to Conversion of Cell Lines

The California Supreme Court recently analyzed the issue of conversion of cell lines in Moore v. Regents of University of California, 51 Cal. 3d 144 at 144–45:

Thousands of human cell lines already exist in tissue repositories, such as the American Type Culture Collection and those operated by the National Institutes of Health and the American Cancer society.... Since the patent office requires the holders of patents on cell lines to make samples available to anyone, many patent holders place their cell lines in repositories to avoid the administrative burden of responding to requests. At present, human cell lines are routinely copied and distributed to other researchers for experimental purposes, usually free of charge.

The Moore court also noted that exchange of cell lines is "increasingly limited by contract" as "a result of concerns over patent and ownership rights." Id. at 145 n.40. See also In re Lundak, 773 F.2d 1216 (Fed. Cir. 1985) (discussing Patent and Trademark Office requirement that inventors deposit relevant biological materials with an independent depository before a patent application is filed). In refusing to extend California law of conversion to cell lines, the Moore court denied that Moore had a property interest in the cells from his removed spleen.

The instant case is distinguishable because plaintiff does have a property interest in the right to commercialization of the cell line. However, it is not uncommon for a person to have an intangible property right without a cause of action in conversion to protect that right. See generally 5 B. E. Witkin, Summary of California Law, Torts §§ 613 (9th ed. 1988), Rest.2d Torts §§ 242, Pearson v. Dodd, 133 U.S. App. D.C. 279, 410 F.2d 701, 708 (D.C.Cir. 1949) (information in noncommercial documents is a form of property for whose appropriation an action in conversion will not lie). But see A & M Records, Inc. v. Heilman, 75 Cal. App. 3d 554, 142 Cal. Rptr. 390 (1977), cert. denied, 436 U.S. 952, 57 L. Ed. 2d 1118, 98 S. Ct. 3063 (1978) (permitting action for conversion of intangible property right).

California has not recognized a cause of action for conversion of the intangible right to commercialization of a cell line and this Court refuses to extend California conversion law. Instead, this Court follows California's trend of rejecting new theories of tort liability based on contracts, especially when such decisions are more appropriately the subject of legislative deliberation and resolution. See Foley v. Interactive Data Corp., 47 Cal. 3d 654, 694, 254 Cal. Rptr. 211, 765 P.2d 373 n.31 (1988) (declining to apply tort remedies for breach of the covenant of good faith in the employment context); see also 2 B. E. Witkin, Summary of California Law, Agency and Employment §§ 184A (1992 Supp.). Here, Plaintiff is essentially asserting a breach of contract claim. Had the contract claim been brought in a timely manner, the conversion claim would have been unnecessary. Now, Plaintiff seeks to attach a tort action to an expired contract claim. This court refuses to create a new cause of action under California law.

Plaintiff may not argue that the right in question in this case deserves a conversion action on the ground that no other cause of action currently exists. A cause of action for conversion is unnecessary since contract or patent law would cover the alleged violation.[6] Here, Plaintiffs have brought suit based on conversion because they did not protect themselves through other available processes. Plaintiffs' lack of self-protection and the tolling of the statute of limitations on other remedies do not provide a valid reason to extend California's law of conversion, especially given the public policy considerations outlined in Moore.

---

6. This decision does not rest on the fact that other remedies exist for a party in Plaintiff's position. Just as the Moore Court noted the availability of other remedies when it rejected the possibility of a suit for conversion of a cell line, so, too, does this court acknowledge that prudent parties may obviate the need for a conversion cause of action through advance planning.

4. Policy Implications After Moore

In Moore, supra, the California Supreme Court addressed the issue of the rights of a human donor whose cells, through research and experimentation, were eventually engineered to create a profitable drug.

Moore involved the creation of a cell line using cells from plaintiff's diseased spleen, which was removed by defendant out of medical necessity. Although defendant knew of the possible commercial value of the cells before they were removed, plaintiff was never notified of defendant's use of the cells from his spleen. The Moore defendants developed a cell line from plaintiff's cells and received a patent covering the cell line and various methods for using the cell line for commercially valuable medical procedures.

The California Supreme Court rejected Moore's conversion claim and stated that causes of action only existed for breach of fiduciary duty and lack of informed consent against the treating physician. In addition to the important policy consideration of a patient's right to make autonomous medical decisions, the Court addressed the policy of permitting biological sources to assert conversion rights.

According to the Moore court, extending conversion law into this area would threaten the economic incentive to conduct important medical research. "If the use of cells in research is a conversion, then with every cell sample a researcher purchases a ticket in a litigation lottery."

Furthermore, the Moore court explained that a cause of action for conversion of cell lines would not fit within the historical approach to conversion:

No court, however, has ever in a reported decision imposed conversion liability for the use of human cells in medical research. While that fact does not end our inquiry, it raises a flag of caution. In effect, what Moore is asking us to do is to impose a tort duty on scientists to investigate the consensual pedigree of each human cell sample used in research. To impose such a duty, which would affect medical research of importance to all of society, implicates policy concerns far removed from the traditional, two-party ownership disputes in which the law of conversion arose.

Id. at 135 (citing Prosser & Keeton, Torts (5th ed. 1984) §§ 15, p. 89).

The Moore court's concerns that permitting conversion actions for cell line use are only partially related to the instant case. Whereas the Moore plaintiff supplied the raw cells that eventually led to the development of a cell line, here the cell line is the starting point. Thus, Justice Arabian's policy concern that courts may overstep the limits of their competency in fashioning a remedy is not implicated here.[7] No human donor is involved in the analysis at this level of medical research. For this reason, the Moore court's discussion of California's Health and Safety Code is likewise inapplicable here. Furthermore, the chilling effect on medical research that the Moore court feared is not identical here since the parties developing the cell lines are sophisticated researchers capable of protecting themselves legally, not patients who may be unaware of the economic uses for discarded body parts.

The expansion of conversion law into this realm could, however, implicate the policy concerns raised in Moore in other, non-medical contexts. Currently, a regime exists under which readily available cell lines are protected by contract or patent law and par-

---

7. The courts "cannot and should not seek to fashion a remedy for every 'heartache and the thousand natural shocks that flesh is heir to'" Moore, 51 Cal. 3d at 150 (Arabian, J. concurring) (quoting William Shakespeare, Hamlet, act III, scene I).

ties are on notice of possible claims on ownership and control. If these "protections" were expanded to include the strict-liability tort of conversion, then the threat of conversion actions would take away a measure of reliability of source materials and could create a chilling effect on research. The threat of a conversion action would thereby impose a duty of investigation on all subsequent users of cells and cell lines. Researchers would need to determine the "consensual pedigree" n8 of cell lines before beneficial research could be conducted. "Title insurance companies" for cell lines could become the norm. This costly result would add an entirely new procedural dimension to important medical research; time and money would necessarily be diverted to fund the search efforts for ownership rights. This result is unwarranted. Furthermore, it is beyond the competence of this Court to extend California's conversion law, to create a new cell-registry regime. Such a result is better left to the California Legislature.

Plaintiff raises a counter policy consideration, one that was raised in Rasmussen: Since the starting point in this action is with a human-engineered product (and not simply a naturally occurring cell), the opposite chilling effect could result. If entrepreneurs are not permitted the exclusive right to profit from their developments, then inventors will be less likely to invest the necessary time, money and energy into innovation. Rasmussen, 958 F.2d at 900. See also Timothy J. McCoy, Biomedical Process Patents: Should They be Restricted by Ethical Limitations?, 13 Journal of Legal Medicine 501, 518 (1992) ("Without economic incentives, given the high costs and high risks inherent in technological development in health care, it is unlikely that the amazing pace of health care improvements would continue.").

While this economic consideration of profit motive is a valid concern, even devotees of Ayn Rand could not dispute that the available protections provide adequate profit incentives for inventors. Patent and contract law already protect the financial incentives for development of new technologies. n9 No disincentive to ingenuity is created by the absence of a conversion cause of action. For this reason, the absence of a conversion law remedy to the interests at stake here does not implicate the Rasmussen policy concerns....

5. Conclusion

Under the foregoing analysis, Plaintiff does state a property right which is deserving of protection. The protections for that right, however, are not found in an action for conversion. Under existing California law, there is no cause of action for conversion for commercialization of a cell line and strong policy considerations weigh against expanding the conversion cause of action. This Court refuses to extend California law to impose liability—especially a strict-liability tort—for conversion of this type of property.

Defendants' motions to dismiss the conversion claim is therefore GRANTED. The conversion claim is dismissed as to all defendants.

B. Breach of Fiduciary Duty

In Count II of the Fourth Amended Complaint, Plaintiff alleges a breach of fiduciary duty as to Defendants Scripps, Nakamura, and Zimmerman.

For purposes of deciding this motion, it is unnecessary to address the substance of Defendants' arguments. Since the breach of fiduciary duty is dependent upon the cause of action for conversion, no possible action for breach of duty lies here.

In its Fourth Amended Complaint, Plaintiff incorporates the conversion cause of action into its claim for breach of a fiduciary duty. Complaint. P 54. In each and every paragraph alleging a breach of fiduciary duty, Plaintiff mentions conversion. Complaint, PP 54–57. Plaintiff has thus provided the seed for dismissal of the breach of fiduciary duty claim by linking it to the conversion claim, which this Court has found does not exist.

At the hearing on this motion, Plaintiff argued that an attempted conversion would provide an act that justifies a claim for breach of fiduciary duty. Transcript of 11/23/92 Hearing at 29–30. I disagree. This case is one in tort, not an attempt crime. An attempted conversion may not create a breach of fiduciary duty.

Scripps Defendants also argue that there can be no claim for breach of fiduciary duty since these Defendants did not owe Miles a fiduciary duty. I agree.

As explained below, the fact that the entity created by Miles and Scripps was a corporation, not a joint venture, precludes liability for breach of fiduciary duty. By selecting the corporate form as a manner of achieving their goals, Miles and Scripps, both sophisticated parties, elected the benefits granted under that form and rejected the option and the benefits of continuing with a joint venture....

No causes of action remaining, this case is DISMISSED with prejudice in its entirety.

IT IS SO ORDERED:

ORDER GRANTING DEFENDANTS' MOTIONS TO DISMISS

9.3 Special Property Protection Problems of Biotechnology: Patent Ownership Problems

The application of the nonobviousness criteria to gene patents has called for consideration of a higher standard in order to prevent the very effect that patents are intended to prevent—the encouragement of improvement on previous inventions. The following excerpt examines this question.

From, Sara Dastgheib-Vinarov, Comment: *A Higher Nonobviousness Standard for Gene Patents: Protecting Biomedical Research from the Big Chill*, MARQ. INTELL. PROP. L. REV. 143 (2000).

NONOBVIOUS CRITERIA FOR PATENTING PROTEIN AMINO ACID SEQUENCES

SUMMARY:

… The issue was whether knowledge of a partial amino acid sequence from a protein, in conjunction with a general method of cloning, renders the sequence of a gene prima facie obvious.... Both reasoned that the combination of (1) a previously published partial amino acid sequence for heparin-binding growth factor, and (2) the routine method of finding the gene and complete protein sequence rendered the invention obvious. Therefore, on appeal the issue facing the Federal Circuit was "whether the combination of a prior art reference teaching a method of gene cloning, together with a reference disclosing a partial amino acid sequence of a protein, … rendered DNA … molecules encoding the protein prima facie obvious under 103." … The dynamic nature of biotechnology requires that patent law keep pace with advances in technology in order for public policies and constitutional objectives to be upheld.... The Federal Circuit should elevate the nonobviousness standard for many reasons, including: (1) the simplification of obtaining DNA and its corresponding functional protein due to a wealth of new biotechnology information; (2) bombardment of the PTO with "huge sequence" applications; (3) lack of uniformity in gene patenting requirements; (4) exploitation of taxpayer-funded research and private genetic information for corporate profit; (5) the recent wave of state genetic privacy laws; and (6) a general world movement to eliminate patents on life....

I. Introduction

In 1995 the United States Court of Appeals for the Federal Circuit ruled on a controversial issue in the case of In re Deuel. The issue was whether knowledge of a partial amino acid sequence from a protein, in conjunction with a general method of cloning, renders the sequence of a gene prima facie obvious. The court ruled in favor of the patent applicant, holding that the DNA molecules encoding the protein were nonobvious under section 103 of the Patent Act. The court's decision was not surprising considering that the biotechnology industry is highly patent-sensitive. Because enormous expense and risk are involved in the making of every product, it is vital that research institutions and investors be financially rewarded. Since the Federal Circuit's decision in Deuel, companies specializing in genomic research have filed many DNA sequence applications. This new trend of patent filings within the biotechnology field is problematic because genomic research companies are stockpiling DNA sequence patents directed merely to partial DNA sequences that have no known function. Furthermore, these companies are using genetic samples from the American public as the raw materials to obtain these unworthy patents, and the public is being disserved by potentially monopolistic prices.

As a result, there has recently been a public outcry for the government to control and monitor the gene patent activity of the biotechnology industry. This public concern has been exacerbated because of: (1) the explosion of genetic research in the past few years; (2) bombardment of the United States Patent and Trademark Office (PTO) with "huge sequence" applications; (3) new strategies that simplify obtaining DNA and its corresponding functional protein; and (4) lack of genetic privacy, which threatens the future of biomedical research. Furthermore, the recent surge in gene patenting activity has caused politicians, religious leaders, and the media to fuel the public's fear by passing genetic privacy laws, publishing anti-life patenting books, distributing global petitions, and making movies that protest the intrusive applications of genetic testing.

In Re Thomas Deuel
51 F.3d 1552 (1995)

OVERVIEW: Applicants sought a patent for their process of isolating and manufacturing specific DNA molecules. The examiner rejected their application, and the Board of Patent Appeals (Board) affirmed. Applicants appealed, and the court reversed. The court held the Board erred by rejecting the application under the obviousness standard at 35 U.S.C.S. §§ 103. The court agreed with applicants that the Board mistakenly found that the prior art suggested isolating and making the molecules specified in the application and thus were obvious. Rather, the prior art did not disclose the specified molecules; it would have been highly unlikely for one of ordinary skill and art in the field to achieve, based on common teaching, what was achieved by applicants. The fact that there was some similarity in the structure of applicant's molecules and those disclosed by prior art did not render applicants' molecules obvious.

OPINION by LOURIE, Circuit Judge.

Thomas F. Deuel, Yue-Sheng Li, Ned R. Siegel, and Peter G. Milner (collectively "Deuel") appeal from the November 30, 1993 decision of the U.S. Patent and Trademark Office Board of Patent Appeals and Interferences affirming the examiner's final rejection of claims 4–7 of application Serial No. 07/542,232, entitled "Heparin-Binding Growth Factor," as unpatentable on the ground of obviousness under 35 U.S.C. §§ 103 (1988). Ex parte Deuel, 33 USPQ2d 1445 (Bd. Pat. App. Int. 1993). Because the Board erred in concluding that Deuel's claims 5 and 7 directed to specific cDNA molecules would have been obvious in light of the applied references, and no other basis exists in the record to support the rejection with respect to claims 4 and 6 generically covering all possible DNA molecules coding for the disclosed proteins, we reverse.

BACKGROUND

The claimed invention relates to isolated and purified DNA and cDNA molecules encoding heparin-binding growth factors ("HBGFs"). n1 HBGFs are proteins that stimulate mitogenic activity (cell division) and thus facilitate the repair or replacement of damaged or diseased tissue. DNA (deoxyribonucleic acid) is a generic term which encompasses an enormous number of complex macromolecules made up of nucleotide units. DNAs consist of four different nucleotides containing the nitrogenous bases adenine, guanine, cytosine, and thymine. A sequential grouping of three such nucleotides (a "codon") codes for one amino acid. A DNA's sequence of codons thus determines the sequence of amino acids assembled during protein synthesis. Since there are 64 possible codons, but only 20 natural amino acids, most amino acids are coded for by more than one codon. This is referred to as the "redundancy" or "degeneracy" of the genetic code.

DNA functions as a blueprint of an organism's genetic information. It is the major component of genes, which are located on chromosomes in the cell nucleus. Only a small part of chromosomal DNA encodes functional proteins.

Messenger ribonucleic acid ("mRNA") is a similar molecule that is made or transcribed from DNA as part of the process of protein synthesis. Complementary DNA ("cDNA") is a complementary copy ("clone") of mRNA, made in the laboratory by reverse transcription of mRNA. Like mRNA, cDNA contains only the protein-encoding regions of DNA. Thus, once a cDNA's nucleotide sequence is known, the amino acid sequence of the protein for which it codes may be predicted using the genetic code relationship between codons and amino acids. The reverse is not true, however, due to the degeneracy of the code. Many other DNAs may code for a particular protein. The functional relationships between DNA, mRNA, cDNA, and a protein may conveniently be expressed as follows:

genomic
DNA   mRNA   protein
                   cDNA   other DNAs

Collections ("libraries") of DNA and cDNA molecules derived from various species may be constructed in the laboratory or obtained from commercial sources. Complementary DNA libraries contain a mixture of cDNA clones reverse-transcribed from the mRNAs found in a specific tissue source. Complementary DNA libraries are tissue-specific because proteins and their corresponding mRNAs are only made ("expressed") in specific tissues, depending upon the protein. Genomic DNA ("gDNA") libraries, by contrast, theoretically contain all of a species' chromosomal DNA. The molecules present in cDNA and DNA libraries may be of unknown function and chemical structure, and the proteins which they encode may be unknown. However, one may attempt to retrieve molecules of interest from cDNA or gDNA libraries by screening such libraries with a gene probe, which is a synthetic radiolabelled nucleic acid sequence designed to bond ("hybridize") with a target complementary base sequence. Such "gene cloning" techniques thus exploit the fact that the bases in DNA always hybridize in complementary pairs: adenine bonds with thymine and guanine bonds with cytosine. A gene probe for potentially isolating DNA or cDNA encoding a protein may be designed once the protein's amino acid sequence, or a portion thereof, is known.

As disclosed in Deuel's patent application, Deuel isolated and purified HBGF from bovine uterine tissue, found that it exhibited mitogenic activity, and determined the first 25 amino acids of the protein's N-terminal sequence. Deuel then isolated a cDNA molecule encoding bovine uterine HBGF by screening a bovine uterine cDNA library with an oligonucleotide probe designed using the experimentally determined N-terminal sequence of the HBGF. Deuel purified and sequenced the cDNA molecule, which was found to consist of a sequence of 1196 nucleotide base pairs. From the cDNA's nucleotide sequence, Deuel then predicted the complete amino acid sequence of bovine uterine HBGF disclosed in Deuel's application....

During prosecution, the examiner rejected claims 4–7 under 35 U.S.C. §§103 as unpatentable over the combined teachings of Bohlen and Maniatis. The Bohlen reference discloses a group of protein growth factors designated as heparin-binding brain mitogens ("HBBMs") useful in treating burns and promoting the formation, maintenance, and repair of tissue, particularly neural tissue. Bohlen isolated three such HBBMs from human and bovine brain tissue. These proteins have respective molecular weights of 15 kD, 16 kD, and 18 kD. Bohlen determined the first 19 amino acids of the proteins' N-terminal sequences, which were found to be identical for human and bovine HBBMs. Bohlen teaches that HBBMs are brain-specific, and suggests that the proteins may be homologous between species. The reference provides no teachings concerning DNA or cDNA coding for HBBMs....

The examiner asserted that, given Bohlen's disclosure of a heparin-binding protein and its N-terminal sequence and Maniatis's gene cloning method, it would have been prima facie obvious to one of ordinary skill in the art at the time of the invention to clone a gene for HBGF. According to the examiner, Bohlen's published N-terminal sequence would have motivated a person of ordinary skill in the art to clone such a gene because cloning the gene would allow recombinant production of HBGF, a useful protein. The examiner reasoned that a person of ordinary skill in the art could have designed a gene probe based on Bohlen's disclosed N-terminal sequence, then screened a DNA library in accordance with Maniatis's gene cloning method to isolate a gene encoding an HBGF. The examiner did not distinguish between claims 4 and 6 generically directed to all DNA sequences encoding human and bovine HBGFs and claims 5 and 7 reciting particular cDNAs.

In reply, Deuel argued, inter alia, that Bohlen teaches away from the claimed cDNA molecules because Bohlen suggests that HBBMs are brain-specific and, thus, a person of ordinary skill in the art would not have tried to isolate corresponding cDNA clones from human placental and bovine uterine cDNA libraries. The examiner made the rejection final, however, asserting that

> the starting materials are not relevant in this case, because it was well known in
> the art at the time the invention was made that proteins, especially the general

class of heparin binding proteins, are highly homologous between species and tissue type. It would have been entirely obvious to attempt to isolate a known protein from different tissue types and even different species.

No prior art was cited to support the proposition that it would have been obvious to screen human placental and bovine uterine cDNA libraries for the claimed cDNA clones. Presumably, the examiner was relying on Bohlen's suggestion that HBBMs may be homologous between species, although the examiner did not explain how homology between species suggests homology between tissue types....

The Board affirmed the examiner's final rejection. In its opening remarks, the Board noted that it is "constantly advised by the patent examiners, who are highly skilled in this art, that cloning procedures are routine in the art." According to the Board, "the examiners urge that when the sequence of a protein is placed into the public domain, the gene is also placed into the public domain because of the routine nature of cloning techniques." Addressing the rejection at issue, the Board determined that Bohlen's disclosure of the existence and isolation of HBBM, a functional protein, would also advise a person of ordinary skill in the art that a gene exists encoding HBBM. The Board found that a person of ordinary skill in the art would have been motivated to isolate such a gene because the protein has useful mitogenic properties, and isolating the gene for HBBM would permit large quantities of the protein to be produced for study and possible commercial use. Like the examiner, the Board asserted, without explanation, that HBBMs are the same as HBGFs and that the genes encoding these proteins are identical. The Board concluded that "the Bohlen reference would have suggested to those of ordinary skill in this art that they should make the gene, and the Maniatis reference would have taught a technique for 'making' the gene with a reasonable expectation of success." Responding to Deuel's argument that the claimed cDNA clones were isolated from human placental and bovine uterine cDNA libraries, whereas the combined teachings of Bohlen and Maniatis would only have suggested screening a brain tissue cDNA library, the Board stated that "the claims before us are directed to the product and not the method of isolation. Appellants have not shown that the claimed DNA was not present in and could not have been readily isolated from the brain tissue utilized by Bohlen." Deuel now appeals.

On appeal, Deuel challenges the Board's determination that the applied references establish a prima facie case of obviousness. In response, the PTO maintains that the claimed invention would have been prima facie obvious over the combined teachings of Bohlen and Maniatis. Thus, the appeal raises the important question whether the combination of a prior art reference teaching a method of gene cloning, together with a reference disclosing a partial amino acid sequence of a protein, may render DNA and cDNA molecules encoding the protein prima facie obvious under §§ 103....

Deuel argues that the PTO failed to follow the proper legal standard in determining that the claimed cDNA molecules would have been prima facie obvious despite the lack of structurally similar compounds in the prior art. Deuel argues that the PTO has not cited a reference teaching cDNA molecules, but instead has improperly rejected the claims based on the alleged obviousness of a method of making the molecules. We agree

Because Deuel claims new chemical entities in structural terms, a prima facie case of unpatentability requires that the teachings of the prior art suggest the claimed compounds to a person of ordinary skill in the art. Normally a prima facie case of obviousness is based upon structural similarity, i.e., an established structural relationship between a prior art compound and the claimed compound. Structural relationships may provide the requisite motivation or suggestion to modify known compounds to obtain new compounds. For example, a prior art compound may suggest its homologs because homologs often have similar properties and therefore chemists of ordinary skill would ordinarily contemplate making them to try to obtain compounds with improved properties. Similarly, a known compound may suggest its analogs or isomers, either geometric isomers (cis v. trans) or position isomers (e.g., ortho v. para).

In all of these cases, however, the prior art teaches a specific, structurally-definable compound and the question becomes whether the prior art would have suggested making the specific molecular modifications necessary to achieve the claimed invention....

Thus, one could not have conceived the subject matter of claims 5 and 7 based on the teachings in the cited prior art because, until the claimed molecules were actually isolated and purified, it would have been highly unlikely for one of ordinary skill in the art to contemplate what was ultimately obtained. What cannot be contemplated or conceived cannot be obvious....

We today reaffirm the principle, stated in Bell, that the existence of a general method of isolating cDNA or DNA molecules is essentially irrelevant to the question whether the specific molecules themselves would have been obvious, in the absence of other prior art that suggests the claimed DNAs. A prior art disclosure of a process reciting a particular compound or obvious variant thereof as a product of the process is, of course, another matter, raising issues of anticipation under 35 U.S.C. §§ 102 as well as obviousness under §§ 103. Moreover, where there is prior art that suggests a claimed compound, the existence, or lack thereof, of an enabling process for making that compound is surely a factor in any patentability determination....

ANIMAL PATENTS

The following excerpt, Michael E. Sellers, *Patenting Nonnaturally Occurring, Man-Made Life: A Practical Look at the Economic, Environmental, and Ethical Challenges Facing Animal Patents*, 47 ARK. L. REV. 269 (1994) examines animal patents.

> On April 30, 1991, in Animal Legal Defense Fund v. Quigg the United States Court of Appeals for the Federal Circuit held that various animal rights groups and animal husbanders lacked standing to seek both a declaration that animals are not patentable subject matter and an injunction against the issuance of animal patents.... The Animal Legal Defense Fund decision was a defeat for those seeking to curb genetic engineering via the prohibition of animal patenting, but the challenges are far from dead.... The suit was filed in response to a 1987 PTO rule which stated, inter alia, that the PTO considered non-naturally occurring, non-human multicellular organisms, including animals, to be patentable subject matter within the scope of 35 U.S.C. 101. The rule expressly relied upon the decisions of Ex parte Allen, Ex parte Hibberd, and Diamond v. Chakrabarty.... The PTO has noted a significant increase in the number of animal patent applications since the Harvard Mouse patent.... Deliberate release may be necessitated by field testing requirements because the organism's utility cannot be realized absent environmental release.... Based on this observation, one may fairly ask why biotechnology opponents have attacked the patent system with such vigor.... A decision must now be made prescribing how biotechnology and animal patenting will be reconciled with the concerns of all interested groups.... Patenting opponents have attacked the patent system as a means of voicing their concerns over biotechnology....

On April 30, 1991, in Animal Legal Defense Fund v. Quigg . The United States Court of Appeals for the Federal Circuit held that various animal rights groups and animal husbanders lacked standing to seek both a declaration that animals are not patentable subject matter and an injunction against the issuance of animal patents. The action was brought challenging a Public Notice issued by the United States Patent and Trademark Office (PTO) on April 7, 1987, stating in part that the PTO now considers nonnaturally occurring non-human multicellular living organisms, including animals, to be patentable subject matter within the scope of 35 U.S.C. 101. The plaintiffs were concerned with the potential economic, environmental, and ethical problems resulting from this new rule. Unfortunately, because the case was dismissed for lack of standing, the court never reached the issue of whether the PTO's issuance of animal patents exceeded its authority under 35 U.S.C. 101....

Traditionally, animal breeding practices have included selective breeding within species and cross-breeding between closely related species. A breeder seeks to produce animals exhibiting desired characteristics, by selecting animals exhibiting specified or dominant characteristics. The results of selective breeding are unpredictable as there is no guarantee that the desired characteristics will surface in the offspring. Additionally, the breeder cannot select one trait without carrying other, perhaps undesirable, traits with it.

The effectiveness of traditional animal breeding practices has been surpassed by biotechnology. Biotechnology is defined as any technique that uses living organisms or substances from those organisms to make or modify a product, to improve plants or animals, or to develop micro-organisms for specific uses. New species of animals actually are created through various artificial techniques, whereas the results of traditional selective breeding techniques, at least theoretically, are limited to what could have been accomplished without man's intervention. Some of the techniques used today include microinjection, cell fusion, electroporation, and retroviral transformation.

The application of these new technologies to animals is expected to produce many new results, including increased growth performance, higher disease resistance, and certain reproductive traits which will collectively lower costs to farmers and produce a more healthful product for the consumer. Additionally, new breeds of sheep, goats, and cows that secrete valuable human pharmaceutical proteins into their milk are being developed.

Another promising benefit of biotechnology is the development of laboratory animal models for the study of human diseases. On December 29, 1992, the PTO issued patents for three genetically engineered mice strains, the first such animal patents granted since the so-called Harvard Mouse patent was issued in April 1988. One strain of mice, whose males develop enlarged prostrate glands, will be used to test potential drug treatments for prostrate enlargement as well as suspected carcinogens. Another strain, mice that fail to develop a completely functional immune system, will be used in research of immune-system diseases such as AIDS. The other mice, a virus-resistant strain, will be used to study the immune system's response to cancer.

Although many potentially patentable animals are likely to be produced via recombinant DNA (deoxyribonucleic acid) techniques, microinjection is the most commonly used method of transgenic research and the one most likely to lead to practical applications in mammals. This technique involves injecting highly purified copies of certain genes of interest directly into a fertilized animal egg. The egg is then surgically implanted in the reproductive tract of a receptive female which gestates the egg and brings it to term. The injection process is tedious and laborious as it involves delicate and sensitive micromanipulations of the egg. One drawback to this technique is that only a small fraction of injected eggs actually develop into transgenic animals. Approximately 85 percent of every 100 eggs collected are suitable for injection; of the 85 injected eggs, about 60 will survive the delicate microinjection procedure; six of the injected eggs placed in the host female will result in live births; and of these six, only one or two will actually result in a transgenic animal.

Many of these bioengineering techniques also can be used with comparable effectiveness in humans. Scientists already are considering the use of these techniques not only in eliminating harmful genetic traits in humans, but also as a way of genetically designing humans with a wide range of beneficial traits such as enhanced manual dexterity skills and improved memory retention. Such gene therapy also has been hailed as the means for the total eradication of many diseases and disorders in humans, including sickle-cell anemia, Tay-Sachs disease, cystic fibrosis, hemophilia, and other genetic disorders.

In the following case, after the Patent and Trademark Office issued a notice announcing that non-human living organisms, including animals, were patentable. The Animal Legal Defense Fund filed suit to enjoin the PTO Commissioner from issuing such patents, alleging that he had failed to comply with the public notice requirement for rulemaking under the Administrative Procedure Act.

The court held that the PTO Commissioner was not required to comply with the public notice requirements of the APA because he was merely interpreting existing law, not promulgating regulations. Further, the court held that the PTO Commissioner had not exceeded his authority in issuing the notice.

Animal Legal Defense Fund v. Quigg
932 F.2d 920 (Fed. Cir. 1991)

JUDGES: Nies, Chief Judge, and Markey, Archer, Mayer and Lourie, Circuit Judges.

Opinion by Chief Judge NIES:

This is an appeal from the order of the District Court for the Northern District of California (Smith, J.) granting defendants' motion to dismiss the complaint in *Animal Legal Defense Fund v. Quigg*. Various plaintiffs, individual farmers and groups of animal husbanders or nonprofit organizations whose goal is the protection of animals, filed suit in district court under the APA challenging, on procedural and substantive grounds, a Notice issued by the Department of Commerce Patent and Trademark Office (PTO) which stated, *inter alia*, that the PTO "now considers non-naturally occurring, non-human multicellular organisms, including animals, to be patentable subject matter within the scope of 35 U.S.C. §§ 101 [the patent statute]." Plaintiffs seek to impede, indeed, stop issuance of patents for animals. The defendants, Donald Quigg, then Commissioner of Patent & Trademarks, and C. William Verity, then Secretary of Commerce, countered with a motion to dismiss the complaint under Fed. R. Civ. P. 12(b)(6) for failure to state a claim. The district court granted defendants' motion on the grounds that the challenged Notice fell within an exception to the public notice and comment requirements of the APA and that the Commissioner did not exceed his statutory authority in issuing the Notice. The court further held that whether any "animal" patents which might be issued by the PTO would exceed its authority under section 101 was not raised by the suit. We affirm but on the alternative ground that the plaintiffs lack standing. Because of the nature of the injury alleged by some of the parties, however, our ruling on standing subsumes the ground relied on by the district court.

I

Section 101 of Title 35, United States Code, provides the statutory definition of the subject matter upon which a patent may be granted:

§§ 101 Inventions patentable

Whoever invents or discovers any new and useful process, machine, manufacture, or composition of matter, or any new and useful improvement thereof, may obtain a patent therefor, subject to the conditions and requirements of this title.

In 1980, the Supreme Court decided *Diamond v. Chakrabarty*, 447 U.S. 303, 65 L. Ed. 2d 144, 100 S. Ct. 2204 (1980), wherein the Court held that non-naturally occurring man-made living microorganisms fall within the definition of patentable subject matter in section 101. Following that decision, the PTO's Board of Patent Appeals and Interferences applied the *Chakrabarty* decision to conclude that non-naturally occurring man-made multicellular plants were patentable under section 101 in *Ex Parte Hibberd*, 227 U.S.P.Q. (BNA) 443 (Bd. Pat. App. & Int. 1985). Also following that decision, the Board applied *Chakrabarty* to hold that section 101 was not a bar to patentability for a specific non-naturally occurring genetically altered strain of polyploid oysters in *Ex Parte Allen*, 2 U.S.P.Q.2d (BNA) 1425 (Bd. Pat. App. & Int. 1987), *aff'd*, 846 F.2d 77 (Fed. Cir. 1988) (Table). On April 7, 1987, within days of the Board's decision in *Allen*, the PTO issued the following notice:

A decision by the Board of Patent Appeals and Interferences in *Ex parte Allen*, [2 U.S.P.Q.2d (BNA) 1425] (Bd. App. & Int. April 3, 1987), held that claimed polyploid oysters are nonnaturally occurring manufactures or compositions of matter within the meaning of 35 U.S.C. 101. The Board relied upon the opinion of the Supreme Court in *Diamond v. Chakrabarty*, (1980) as it had done in *Ex parte Hibberd*,(1985), as controlling authority that Congress intended statutory subject matter to "include anything under the sun that is made by man." The Patent and Trademark Office now considers nonnaturally occurring non-human multicellular living organisms, including animals, to be patentable subject matter within the scope of 35 U.S.C. 101.

The Board's decision does not affect the principle and practice that products found in nature will not be considered to be patentable subject matter under 35 U.S.C. 101 and/or 102. An article of manufacture or composition of matter occurring in nature will not be considered patentable unless given a new form, quality, properties or combination not present in the original article existing in nature in accordance with existing law. [Citations omitted].

A claim directed to or including within its scope a human being will not be considered to be patentable subject matter under 35 U.S.C. 101. The grant of a limited, but exclusive property right in a human being is prohibited by the Constitution. Accordingly, it is suggested that any claim directed to a non-plant multicellular organism which would include a human being within its scope include the limitation "non-human" to avoid this ground of rejection. The use of a negative limitation to define the metes and bounds of the claimed subject matter is a permissible form of expression.

Accordingly, the Patent and Trademark Office is now examining claims directed to multicellular living organisms, including animals. To the extent that the claimed subject matter is directed to a non-human "nonnaturally occurring manufacture or composition of matter—a product of human ingenuity" (*Diamond v. Chakrabarty*), such claims will not be rejected under 35 U.S.C. 101 as being directed to nonstatutory subject matter.

Every organizational plaintiff in this case alleges that it was injured as a result of its having been denied participation in the PTO's rulemaking process. *See, e.g., Trustees for Alaska v. Hodel*, 806 F.2d 1378, 1380 (9th Cir. 1986) (standing exists based on alleged injury to procedural rights under the National Environmental Policy Act where public comment provision in 40 C.F.R. §§ 1506.8(b)(2)(ii) not properly followed). The allegations of ALDF typify the nature of this alleged "procedural harm":

Plaintiff, ANIMAL LEGAL DEFENSE FUND, (hereinafter "ALDF") is a national non-profit corporation, organized and existing under California law, with its principal place of business in San Rafael, California. ALDF's purposes and activities include: the initiation of and participation in federal and state legal actions and administrative rulemaking proceedings, the provision of information and legal opinions to its members, the general public and governmental agencies, and the advocacy of the interests of its members in connection with: the furtherance of the care and welfare of animals, including farm, research and wild animals, and any rule, policy, act, omission, or neglect which causes or permits physical pain, behavioral distress, suffering, debilitation and/or death to animals. ALDF works to ensure that important governmental decisions affecting the lives and interests of animals are based on a rational analysis and made according to the law. Those of PETA offer little variation:

Plaintiff, People for the Ethical Treatment of Animals (hereinafter "PETA") is a national nonprofit corporation with over 250,000 members and supporters. The purposes and activities of PETA include: to protect and enhance the status of animals, and to educate the general public about the issues of animal rights and systematized animal abuse, to participate in federal and state legislative and administrative rulemaking proceedings, to provide information to its members and the general public and to influence governmental decision-making on behalf of its members. PETA has an interest in providing information to Defendants which may have an impact on Defendants' formulation of any rule regarding the patenting of animals. PETA has an interest in ascertaining the underlying rationale for Defendants' new rule before it becomes finalized and providing its members and the public with such information, along with information about the consequences of such a rule, in order that PETA and its members may participate meaningfully in the decision making process. PETA's purposes, activities and interests have been and will continue to be frustrated and adversely affected by Defendants' refusal to provide the public with notice and the opportunity to comment prior to adopting the new rule. PETA will have to devote significant financial resources to counteract Defendants' unlawful actions.

Whether there is any viability in such allegation of injury by reason of the alleged procedural defect, namely, the Commissioner's failure to provide public notice and comment procedures in adopting the rule, depends on the resolution of an issue of law: Was the Commissioner required to comply with section 553 before issuing the Rule? For reasons which follow, we conclude he was not. Thus, appellants' allegations of injury also fail as a matter of law....

The genesis and effect of the Notice demonstrates that it represents no change in the law effected by the Commissioner and that, in reality, it is merely "interpretative" of prior decisional precedent. As acknowledged by appellants, in 1981 the Supreme Court decided, in *Diamond v. Chakrabarty*, (1980), that live, non-naturally occurring microorganisms fell within the patentable subject matter covered by section 101. Following the Supreme Court's ruling on the scope of section 101, the Board of Patent Appeals decided *Ex Parte Hibberd*, (1985), wherein the Board, relying on the Supreme Court's decision in *Chakrabarty*, held that non-naturally occurring, multicellular living plants were patentable subject matter under section 101. Thereafter, the Board decided *Ex Parte Allen*, (1987), where it reversed an examiner's rejection that claims drawn to a particular non-naturally occurring polyploid oyster were directed to nonpatentable subject matter, although ultimately upholding the examiner's rejection that the oysters would have been obvious in view of prior art under section 103. In this decision, the Board stated that "the Supreme Court made it clear in its decision in *Diamond v. Chakrabarty*, ... that Section 101 includes man-made life forms. The issue, in our view, in determining whether the claimed subject matter is patentable under Section 101 is simply whether that subject matter is made by man."

9.4 Ownership of Human Organs

The following excerpt provides a historical background for the regulation of human tissues.

Marc O. Williams, *The Regulation of Human Tissue in the United States: A Regulatory and Legislative Analysis*, 52 FOOD DRUG L.J. 409 (1997).

FDA'S EARLY REACTIONS TO THE AMERICAN HUMAN TISSUE INDUSTRY

Within a regulatory context, the term "human tissue" is used in connection with "transplants of human bone, heart valves, veins, skin, tendons and cartilage." Human tissue transplants are used both to save lives, as when skin grafts are used on burn victims, and to enhance lives, such as using bone grafts to rebuild the bones of crippled athletes. Human tissue can, depending on the type of tissue, be taken from both living and dead donors. In addition, tissues intended for transplant can ... be processed and stored for long periods of time.

Thus, for regulatory purposes, the definition of "human tissue" does not include whole organs, such as hearts, livers, and kidneys.

Tissue banking, the term that describes the process of removing and then storing human tissue for future use, originated in the United States in the 1940s. The first tissue banks were eye banks, which stored corneas, and bone banks, which stored bone removed during surgery for use in future patients. In 1950, the U.S. Navy established the U.S. Navy Tissue Bank, which pioneered techniques for recovering, processing, and preserving cadaver tissue.

It was not until the late 1960s that the federal government confronted the issue of human tissue regulation. At that time, a group of American ophthalmologists who were concerned about the means used in foreign countries to store corneas donated for transplantation approached the Division of Biologic Standards at the National Institutes of Health to explore the possibility of establishing federal guidelines for corneal storage media. According to FDA's Associate Commissioner for Health Affairs, the Division of Biologic Standards (which later would become part of FDA) had a stance *vis a vis* transplantation that was similar to the one taken by FDA at that time. "Transplantation was regarded as part of the practice of medicine or surgery, and no effort was made to regulate the procedure or the human organs and tissues being transplanted."

In 1976 FDA considered the possibility of regulating tissue banks, but came to the conclusion "that FDA jurisdiction over tissues would be asserted only in response to an immediate need." FDA's human tissue policy remained noninterventionist throughout the 1970s; the goal was to monitor what was taking place in the field of transplantation and be particularly alert to instances of disease transmission by allografts, but to refrain from formal regulation unless it was clearly necessary. As a corollary to this, FDA encouraged the development of voluntary guidelines by those who retrieved, processed, and stored human tissue intended for transplantation.

As the tissue banking industry sought to compensate for the absence of federal regulation, voluntary standards did develop. In 1976 the American Association of Tissue Banks (AATB) "was established to develop standards and procedures and to assist new programs in complying with standards." AATB's accreditation system "evaluates tissue banks for compliance with a comprehensive set of standards through document review and site visits.... The AATB standards cover acquisition, processing, preservation, storage, labeling, and distribution of tissue." As of 1993, AATB estimated that approximately fifty of the 150 to 200 tissue banks in the United States were operating under AATB accreditation. The Eye Bank Association of America (EBAA) serves a similar function for human eye banks. In 1993 over ninety-five percent of its membership was accredited as meeting voluntary medical standards and submitting to site visits.

In 1983 FDA submitted a statement to a U.S. House of Representatives subcommittee that was holding hearings on the National Organ Transplant Act, explaining why the agency had not sought to regulate human organs. In spite of the fact that the statement by its literal terms encompassed only FDA's position on human organs, and did not reference human tissue, the statement was an important one for the human tissue industry. For each of the arguments FDA put forth regarding the regulation of human organs an analogous one could be made regarding the regulation of human tissue. In its statement, FDA maintained that although an organ arguably could be classified as a drug within the meaning of the Federal Food, Drug, and Cosmetic Act (FDCA), such a classification would not be in accord with either "the traditional medical concept of the term 'drug'" or FDA's own current administrative definition of "drug." Likewise, although a transplanted organ might be susceptible to regulation under the Medical Device Amendments of 1976 as an implant, FDA concluded that, because organs are in no respect man-made products, deeming organs to be "devices" would violate legislative intent. Finally, FDA noted that it arguably could regulate organs under the Public Health Service (PHS) Act by labeling organs as "biological products;" the Act allows regulation of material which is "analogous" to, *inter alia*, blood and because blood is essentially a liquid organ, solid organs such as hearts and livers could be considered "analogous products." Nonetheless, FDA rejected this rationale, citing its belief that such an interpretation would be contrary to the legislative history of the PHS Act. Thus, FDA concluded, "Under an expansive legal interpretation, human organ transplants could possibly be regulated as drugs, devices, or biological products. It is, however, by no means clear that such an interpretation would be consistent with the legislative intent underlying the definitions or that it would withstand judicial challenge." This conclusion, that human organs could not be classified easily as drugs, devices, or biological products, was a harbinger of the interpretive difficulties that FDA would encounter in the future as it attempted to regulate human tissue under its statutory authority.

In spite of these doubts regarding its statutory authority to impose regulation, throughout the 1980s FDA continued its 1970s policy of encouraging the development of voluntary industry standards. In 1985, amid growing concern regarding the human immunodeficiency virus (HIV), FDA worked with the Human Milk Banking Association of North America to develop practices that would minimize the possibility of the transmission of HIV through donor breast milk. Then, in 1988, FDA and the Centers for Disease Control and Prevention (CDC) published a joint statement outlining their views on what constituted safe sperm banking practices. This statement received endorsements from several medical organizations.

Despite its progress in encouraging self-imposed voluntary standards, FDA's position by 1990 on the regulation of human tissue was somewhat different from what it had been in 1976. Although it was still FDA's policy "to promote the development of voluntary standards; to remain constantly alert to any hazards to public health," the agency also vowed "to promulgate regulations when needed and to publicize any regulatory intentions on the part of FDA." No longer would FDA confine itself to acting only in the face of "immediate need." FDA, in accordance with the growing concerns over the safety of the human tissue supply, would take a more proactive attitude toward human tissue regulation. The next six years witnessed several FDA regulatory attempts in the human tissue area, as well as a number of congressional attempts to regulate the field.

III. THE IMPETUS TO REGULATION

According to Margaret Porter, FDA's Chief Counsel, two trends were primarily responsible for FDA's move away from its "hands-off" approach to tissue regulation. "First, technological scientific advances in tissue processing have allowed the successful storage, transporting, and preservation of whole organs and parts of organs." As the technology involved in human tissue transplantation advanced, so too did FDA's view that the line between the agency's jurisdiction and the practice of medicine was no longer a sharply-drawn one. The second trend that awakened a regulatory interest in FDA was "the AIDS crisis and the increasing concern with the transmission of communicable diseases. That crisis has led FDA to look much more closely at areas where it has traditionally not asserted jurisdiction."

Concern over the transmission of HIV, hepatitis, and other communicable diseases through human tissue transplants expanded rapidly from the mid-1980s. The evidence suggests, however, that tissue transplants have only rarely resulted in the transmission of these diseases. Indeed, CDC estimates that in the more than 1,000,000 tissue transplants performed since 1985, "only two tissue donors are known to have transmitted AIDS to recipients. (Other diseases, such as hepatitis and rabies, have been transmitted through transplants, though the incidence is extremely low.)" Furthermore, "both AIDS transmission cases occurred in the mid-1980s, during the early days of the AIDS epidemic, when tests for the virus were less sophisticated." Even Senator Paul Simon (D-IL), a chief sponsor of legislation in the human tissue area, has stated, "We shouldn't frighten people. The vast majority of tissue transplants are safe." Perhaps reflecting the move to make the human tissue supply even safer, the Senator did go on to say, "[Tissue transplants] are not as safe as they should be. The whole area of human tissue is unregulated."

One incident in particular fueled the concern over the transmission of HIV through human tissue transplants. In 1991 it came to light that LifeNet, a tissue bank, had in 1985 unwittingly harvested five organs, fifty-four tissue grants, and several vials of bone marrow from an HIV-positive donor. The infected tissue, which apparently tested negative for HIV twice before being delivered, subsequently was transplanted into fifty-six separate recipients. The three recipients who received organs from the donor eventually died, and at least three of the patients who received tissue grafts contracted HIV. LifeNet, an AATB-accredited 0tissue bank, produced records indicating to what hospitals the tissue had been sent, and the bulk of the tissue recipients were notified of the potential problem. Several hospitals, however, that were able to confirm that they had received the tissue could not determine who, if anyone, ultimately had received the donated tissue. Even more disturbing, one hospital had no record of ever having received the tissue. The thought that unknowing patients might contract HIV through a tissue transplant was bad enough, but the notion that ignorance would not only prevent these unfortunate individuals from seeking treatment but also would likely cause them to transmit the virus to other unsuspecting people was horrific. For this reason, the LifeNet incident increased the support for action by FDA and/or Congress, even though statistics indicated that the chance of contracting AIDS as a result of a tissue transplant was minute. By 1991 over 30,000 tissue transplants were occurring in the United States each year, yet the LifeNet incident was the first report of a patient contracting AIDS following a tissue transplant.

Concern over the spread of communicable diseases through human tissue transplants was apparent in the comments made by Senator Simon and Representative (later Senator) Ron Wyden (D-OR) in committee hearings on the human tissue legislation that each of them introduced. For instance, speaking to the Senate Labor and Human Resources Committee on some of the risks present in human tissue transplants, Senator Simon declared, "Even worse, there is the risk that transplanted tissue may bring harm, that it may transmit new, perhaps even fatal, diseases. This risk was tragically demonstrated when three persons became HIV-positive recently as a result of transplantation of tissues from a Virginia donor [the LifeNet incident]." Similarly, Congressman Wyden warned the House Subcommittee on Regulation, Business Opportunities, and Technology of the dangers present in the absence of human tissue regulation.

The window for possible transmission of infectious disease is simply too wide. In just one case [the LifeNet incident], involving just one donor, tissues distributed by one major bank in Virginia resulted in HIV transmission to a number of recipients across the country. At least three of those persons have died from AIDS complications. Importantly, some of that infected tissue is still unaccounted for.

Concerns over the danger of disease transmission were not confined to Congress; the **tissue** banking industry was deeply concerned, leading to many calls for the replacement of voluntary industry guidelines by mandatory federal regulations. In 1991, the year the LifeNet incident surfaced, *Business Insurance* reported that

some of the nation's 700 to 800 tissue banks and organ procurement agencies believe that internal risk management and voluntary quality controls may not be enough to guarantee the safety of the human tissue and organs those facilities process. As a result, some tissue banks and a consultant on federal regulation of medical devices are calling for the Food and Drug Administration to implement regulations that would require tissue banks and other centers that handle skin, bone or ligaments to follow a standardized set of operational procedures during processing.

This type of industry support for federal regulation would be an important theme in later congressional attempts to formulate legislation.

An additional issue that motivated both FDA and Congress to take steps to regulate the human tissue industry was concern over the importation of tissue. This concern, as expressed by Representative Wyden, was that "the so-called 'products' have not always been collected under sanitary conditions. Nevertheless, these products ... are now being marketed directly to U.S. physicians without the provision of any health records on the donor, or data on the methods by which the tissues have been treated and preserved." To highlight his concern, Wyden introduced into the record a copy of a telefax that the Subcommittee had received from the Baltic Tissue Bank in St. Petersburg, which "advertised the availability for sale of a butcher's list of donated tissues, prices attached." By 1993 FDA also had become aware of the potential threat posed by the importation of foreign tissue from unknown sources. The director for FDA's Center for Biologics Evaluation and Research (CBER) noted that

several tissue bank directors have been solicited by individuals offering to sell tissue that originates from other countries. Generally, these contacts have been unwilling to declare the actual source of the tissue, to provide documentation as to the cause of death, the medical records of the donor, the results of donor screening and testing, or to furnish samples of donor serum for testing.

IV. FDA's EARLY ATTEMPTS AT REGULATION: THE PIECEMEAL APPROACH

FDA's initial attempts at regulation were not efforts designed to impose safeguards on the entire human tissue banking industry; rather, FDA sought to regulate the industry with regulations targeted for specific tissues. One approach FDA took when promulgating these regulations was to define the tissue in question as a "medical device," in spite of its 1983 statement to Congress. Gordon Johnson, Director of the Office of Health Affairs at FDA's Center for Devices Radiological Health, defined human tissue devices as "tissues of human origin—usually cadaveric—that have been processed, that have been changed or altered in some way, shape, structure, or character. They may be cut and sculptured, disinfected, sterilized, or freeze-dried. Any number of things may occur. These are tissues that have some structure or structural characters."

Although this broad definition would seem to apply to nearly any banked human tissue, FDA, in accordance with its piecemeal regulatory philosophy regarding human tissue, used it only for specific types of tissue. For example, FDA classified human lenticules, a product derived from human cornea and applied to the cornea to correct vision problems, as post-amendment Class III devices. As such, "manufacturers" of lenticules were required to obtain pre-market approval for those "products." In addition, FDA determined that dura matter (the outer meningeal covering) allografts constituted pre-amendment devices: those distributors who could not document having distributed dura matter allografts prior to May 1976 would have to file premarket notifications, and all distributing facilities were required to register as device manufacturers.

The piecemeal regulation that caused the most controversy was the decision to regulate human heart valves as medical devices. The origins of the controversy lay in a 1987 rule that required "the filing of a premarket approval application or a notice of completion of a product development protocol for the replacement heart valve, a medical device." This regulation attracted little controversy; the notice of proposed rulemaking prompted only one comment, which was not related to FDA's classification of replacement heart valves. FDA embroiled itself in controversy, however, when it published a June 1991 notice of applicability of a final rule (NAFR) stating that the 1987 regulation would apply not only to mechanical replacement heart valves, but to replacement human heart valves as well. Therefore, the premarket approval requirement would apply to replacement human heart valve allografts. FDA reasoned,

Replacement heart valve allografts, by definition, are constructed of biologic materials in that they are human heart valves which are processed to assure shelf life and suitability for implantation in a recipient. There can be little question that the classification regulation for replacement heart valves, when construed to achieve the act's purpose of protecting the public health, must include replacement heart valve allografts.

Unlike FDA, the tissue banking industry strongly questioned whether it was appropriate to regulate a human heart valve as a medical device. Pointing out that it was illogical to test a human heart valve to see if it works safely and effectively in humans (it clearly does), the tissue banking industry argued that forcing companies to go through the lengthy and expensive process of obtaining premarket approval would 1) waste resources, and 2) serve merely to reconfirm what already generally was known, namely that human heart valves are the most effective replacement heart valves available. As the National Head of Tissue Services for the American Red Cross put it, "tissue is not an investigational device or material, but is standard equipment in human beings." Michael Strong, Scientific Director of the Northwest Tissue Center, wrote,

Requiring valve processors to conduct clinical trials to demonstrate the safety and efficacy of a product that was not designed by man makes little sense. Furthermore, current medical device law does not address many of the issues dealing with AIDS transmission, which is the primary impetus for initiating this process.

The cost and rigors of the premarket approval process might force many of the nonprofit tissue banks out of business. Moreover, if human heart valves were to be classified as investigational devices, then many third-party payers might refuse to reimburse the cost of a heart valve allograft, a decision that could have dire consequences for those patients for whom a human heart valve transplant is the most effective, and in some cases the only, treatment. "In such a case, if the patient desperately needing a heart valve to save his or her life is neither covered by Medicare nor wealthy enough to pay the $ 40,000 to $ 60,000 required, then they will be denied the opportunity to obtain a heart valve and they will die."

The tissue banking industry launched a three-pronged attack against FDA's notice of applicability. First, the industry mounted an effort, ultimately successful, to push back the date by which FDA had mandated that investigational device exemptions (IDEs) or premarket approval applications (PMAs) must be in effect to continue marketing. Second, six tissue banks filed suit against FDA, alleging that human heart valves were neither devices nor replacement heart valves within the meaning of FDA's prior regulations. The Seventh Circuit rejected both of these claims, ruling that 1) human heart valves are "implants" within the meaning of section 321(h) of title 21 of the United States Code, and 2) the final rule notice was a reasonable interpretation of prior regulations and "accordingly, the [rule was] an interpretive rule not subject to appellate review." Finally, at an October 16, 1991 FDA-sponsored public hearing on federal regulation of human tissue, the National Tissue Bank Council (NTBC), an organization comprised of nonprofit tissue banks, presented an alternative regulatory plan to FDA. Under NTBC's plan, public standards for dealing with different types or classes of tissues would be promulgated by FDA, following consultation with the public and experts. Such a system, NTBC maintained, would obviate the need for premarket approval.

The tissue banking industry's protestations about the notice of a final FDA rule fell on sympathetic congressional ears. Senator Simon, generally a supporter of federal regulation of human tissue, deemed the rule to be "regulatory overkill" and expressed concerns that were nearly identical to those espoused by the tissue banks.

Treating a wholly human product as if it were a manufactured device requiring investigational device exemption and premarket approval application is not just illogical; it also jeopardizes that availability of human heart valves— which are often the only type of heart valve transplant that will work for infants, children and pregnant women—and it threatens reimbursement for the cost of surgical procedures and the tissue itself by public programs and private medical insurance.

Given the strength of his feelings, it is not surprising that the human tissue legislation that Senator Simon introduced in 1992 and 1993 prevented enforcement of the final rule.

Whether it was the result of congressional pressure, industry pressure, or the sheer force of logic, FDA announced in October 1994 that it would no longer enforce the extension of the regulation to human as well as mechanical heart valves. In explaining its action, FDA cited its belief that "special controls may be more appropriate than premarket approval to ensure the safety and effectiveness of heart valve allografts." The decision to abandon this interpretation NAFR marked not only the end of the human heart valve controversy, but also indicated the end of FDA's attempts to regulate human tissue using a piecemeal approach. Concluding that the piecemeal approach left too many questions unanswered, FDA decided to take a broader approach to the regulation of human tissue, a decision that played a part in the agency's rescission of its rule on human heart valves as well.

V. THE INTERIM RULE: FDA'S DECISION TO ABANDON THE PIECE-MEAL APPROACH

On December 14, 1993, FDA issued an interim rule "to require certain infectious disease testing, donor screening, and recordkeeping to help prevent the transmission of AIDS and hepatitis through human tissue used in transplantation." Unlike FDA's previous regulatory efforts in the area of human tissue, this rule applied not just to one type of tissue, such as heart valves or dura matter, but rather applied to all types of human tissue; the rule was a sweeping regulatory effort that encompassed the entire human tissue industry.

In explaining its reasons for adopting this approach, FDA noted that its prior piecemeal efforts had resulted in incomplete coverage of the human tissue field in that they did not cover "bone, ligaments, tendons, fascia, cartilage, corneas, and skin that are used in the treatment of bone disease, orthopedic injuries, ligamentous and joint complaints, degenerative skeletal disease, blindness due to corneal opacification, and burn wounds." In addition, FDA referenced the fact that AATB, EBAA, and American Red Cross all had expressed support for the notion of federal human tissue regulation. Finally, the agency expressed its concern over the importation of human tissue into the United States from unknown sources and of unknown quality, and discussed its investigation into that issue; "in a relatively brief period of time, the agency was able to ascertain, in a few isolated instances, the availability for importation and distribution of tissue materials that do not meet minimal screening standards for transmission of infectious diseases." FDA concluded,

Donation has occurred and continues to occur, when generally-accepted donor screening through medical history review is largely absent. The agency currently believes that these instances do not represent the predominant practice within the industry. Nonetheless, the traffic in tissue for transplantation without adequate testing or donor screening, whether domestic or imported, cannot be permitted to occur.

FDA promulgated the interim rule not under the FDCA, but instead under the PHS Act, which authorizes the Secretary of the Department of Health and Human Services (DHHS) "to make and enforce such regulations as in his judgement are necessary to prevent the introduction, transmission, or spread of communicable diseases." Interestingly, FDA Chief Counsel, Margaret Porter, had anticipated as early as 1990 that, in the event that FDA should decide to regulate human tissue, it would do so under the PHS Act rather than under the FDCA. If FDA were to classify human tissue as a drug or device under the FDCA, then a sponsor would have to demonstrate that the product was both safe and effective to obtain FDA approval. Noting that "it has been suggested by some that an effectiveness test is inappropriate for human products, and that FDA should only be concerned with such products' safety" (certainly a theme that emerged in the heart valve allografts controversy discussed above), Porter pointed out that if a human tissue regulation were promulgated under the PHS Act, such a problem would be avoided. Porter added that such a use of the PHS Act might leave FDA exposed to judicial challenge.

[The PHS Act's] statutory authority is broad, but its outer limits are untested. FDA has not tried to use it to impose a comprehensive system of good manufacturing practice and licensing requirements. If it tried to do so, some might argue we were circumventing the statutory drug and device approval requirement, although we would, of course, not be prepared to concede that such was occurring.

After explaining its legal basis for issuing the interim rule, FDA explained further that "FDA is issuing this interim rule because of an immediate need to protect the public health from transmission of HIV infection and hepatitis infection through transplantation of tissue from donors infected with or at risk of these diseases." Thus, FDA did not intend that the interim rule serve as a long-term regulatory program, rather, the agency intended that more extensive and specific regulations would be proposed in the near future.

As noted above, the interim rule was a broad rule that applied to all "banked human tissue and to establishments or persons engaged in the recovery, processing, storage, or distribution of banked human tissue," but not to organs or any product currently regulated as a human drug, biological product, or medical device. Responding to the concern over the transmission of communicable diseases through human tissue transplants, the rule mandated that all tissue donors be tested for HIV-1, HIV-2, hepatitis B, and hepatitis C. Furthermore, the rule specified that the process for determining whether banked human tissue was suitable for transplantation must include ascertainment of the donor's identity, as well as a determination that the donor's relevant, accurate medical history "assures freedom from risk factors for or clinical evidence of hepatitis B, hepatitis C, or HIV infection." To minimize the possibility of LifeNet-like confusion, the rule declared that records must be maintained as to the results and interpretations of tests, the destruction of unsuitable banked human tissue, and information on the identity and medical history of the donor. Apparently having learned from the replacement human heart valve debacle, FDA chose not to require premarket approval of banked human tissue. This decision, as noted above, more than likely influenced FDA's decision to promulgate the rule under the PHS Act rather than the FDCA. As for enforcement provisions, the interim rule granted FDA the power to inspect all establishments covered by the rule, and it also provided that, should agency find tissue to be in violation of the rule, FDA had the power either to order its destruction or seize and/or destroy it.

FDA soon began to use the enforcement powers it had granted itself under the interim rule. For example, in February 1993, it ordered AlloTech, a tissue-processing firm that was engaged in the business of importing tissue from Eastern Europe, "to retain or destroy seized tissue and recall previously distributed tissue from about 180 donors." This action was taken despite the fact that there was no evidence that any of the tissue was infected; the action was based on FDA's determination that the firm "lacked adequate documentation of medical history screening and disease testing for the tissue."

The initial reaction of many in the tissue banking industry was that the interim rule was a positive development and that enforcement actions such as that taken against AlloTech could serve a useful purpose. Thus, for instance, Osteotech, a large processor of human bone and connective tissue for transplantation, announced shortly after the rule was issued that it supported FDA's action.

Nonetheless, it did not take long for industry's reaction to cool considerably. As it became clear what procedures FDA planned to follow in implementing the interim rule, the tissue banking industry became concerned. For instance, AATB, traditionally a supporter of the notion of federal regulation, was unhappy with FDA's "development of [inspection] guidelines without the input of tissue banking professionals who are directly affected by those guidelines." In addition, AATB, as well as many independent tissue bank operators, strongly opposed efforts by FDA to apply the interim rule retroactively (i.e., to apply it to tissue processed and distributed prior to the promulgation of the interim rule).

One particular collision between FDA and the tissue banking industry involved Biodynamics International, Inc., a Tampa-based company. After FDA ordered that two of the company's shipments of processed bone allografts be detained, the company successfully sought an injunction against FDA on the theory that "the safety of the processed allografts was not in question, that the tissue recovered was in full compliance with industry standards, including the [interim rule], and that all [Biodynamics'] testing and screening protocols meet or exceed such standards." According to Biodynamics, the problem had arisen because FDA had "sought to require … additional donor screening based upon arbitrary retroactive application of certain unpublished criteria set forth in an internal guidance document for their field inspectors." Biodynamics' complaints regarding the "aggressiveness of FDA field agents" were representative of widespread discontent within the tissue banking industry. Prompted by these sentiments, AATB president Ted Eastlund complained to FDA that tissue banks were left "entirely in the dark" as to what donor screening criteria to use, and that FDA's attempts to force retroactive application were unreasonable, saying "some banks visited by FDA inspectors have been 'encouraged'"—possibly, according to some accounts, instructed—to reassess the adequacy of screening completed months or years before."

These conflicts between FDA and industry were temporary. Executive Director of AATB, Jeanne Mowe, reported that AATB had been "very surprised and gratified at how willing FDA officials have been to work with us to resolve these issues."

Confirming that the initial enforcement problems have subsided, a leading lawyer in the human tissue area remarked that FDA seemingly has "become less agressive" since the Biodynamics incident, and that the interim rule is no longer a controversial rule within the industry. To the contrary, most legitimate tissue bank operators appreciate the rule as a means of eliminating marginal or potentially unsafe operators.

Originally, the interim rule was intended to be just that—a "temporary measure" to last only until FDA could "complete its evaluation of whether additional regulations are necessary," according to Steven Falter, Director of FDA's Division of Bioresearch Monitoring and Regulation. Toward this end, in September 1995 the manager of FDA's Human Tissue Program discussed some issues that might be addressed in a final regulation, such as the possible inclusion of reproductive tissue within the regulatory framework, as well as the establishment of requirements for tissue tracking and for registration of tissue banking establishments. Nonetheless, when FDA promulgated the final rule on July 29, 1997—more than three years subsequent to the issuance of the interim rule—it chose not to expand the coverage of the interim rule.

While the final rule did adopt some new definitions and impose some procedural changes, it left the substance of the regulatory regime established by the interim rule essentially unchanged....

Human organs and tissues are regulated by a number of statutes according to their uses. The excerpt below, from *Moore v. Regents of University of California*, sets out the law on human tissues and organs.

... Neither the Court of Appeal's opinion, the parties' briefs, nor our research discloses a case holding that a person retains a sufficient interest in excised cells to support a cause of action for conversion. We do not find this surprising, since the laws governing such things as human tissues, n21 transplantable organs, n22 blood, n23 fetuses, n24 pituitary glands, n25 corneal tissue, n26 and dead bodies n27 deal with human biological materials as objects sui generis, regulating their disposition to achieve policy goals rather than abandoning them to the general law of personal property. It is these specialized statutes, not the law of conversion, to which courts ordinarily should and do look for guidance on the disposition of human biological materials.

FN21 See Health and Safety Code section 7054.4 (fn. 20, *ante*).

FN22 See the Uniform Anatomical Gift Act, Health and Safety Code section 7150 et seq. The act permits a competent adult to "give all or part of [his] body" for certain designated purposes, including "transplantation, therapy, medical or dental education, research, or advancement of medical or dental science." (Health & Saf. Code, §§ 7151, 7153.) The act does not, however, permit the donor to receive "valuable consideration" for the transfer. (Health & Saf. Code, § 7155.)

FN23 See Health and Safety Code section 1601 et seq., which regulates the procurement, processing, and distribution of human blood. Health and Safety Code section 1606 declares that "[t]he procurement, processing, distribution, or use of whole blood, plasma, blood products, and blood derivatives for the purpose of injecting or transfusing the same ... is declared to be, for all purposes whatsoever, the rendition of a service ... and shall not be construed to be, and is declared not to be, a sale ... for any purpose or purposes whatsoever."

FN24 See Health and Safety Code section 7054.3: "Notwithstanding any other provision of law, a recognizable dead human fetus of less than 20 weeks uterogestation not disposed of by interment shall be disposed of by incineration."

FN25 See Government Code section 27491.46: "The coroner [following an autopsy] shall have the right to retain pituitary glands solely for transmission to a university, for use in research or the advancement of medical science" (*id.*, subd. (a)) or "for use in manufacturing a hormone necessary for the physical growth of persons who are, or may become, hypopituitary dwarfs ..." (*id.*, subd. (b)).

FN26 See Government Code section 27491.47: "The coroner may, in the course of an autopsy [and subject to specified conditions], remove ... corneal eye tissue from a body ..." (*id.*, subd. (a)) for "transplant, therapeutic, or scientific purposes" (*id.*, subd. (a)(5)).

FN27 See Health and Safety Code section 7000 et seq. While the code does not purport to grant property rights in dead bodies, it does give the surviving spouse, or other relatives, "[t]he right to control the disposition of the remains of a deceased person, unless other directions have been given by the decedent...." (Health & Saf. Code, §7100.)

9.5 Ownership of Human Fertilized Eggs

The increase in the use of reproductive technologies and the widespread storage of fertilized human ova have given rise to a number of disputes involving ownership in this material. The potential life of the fertilized eggs, as well as the custody issues that are raised, have given rise to an area of reproductive technology cases.

Kass v. Kass
235 A.D.2d 150 (NY, 1997)

OPINION by Sullivan, J.

The instant case presents this Court with issues of first impression in New York regarding the status and ultimate disposition of fertilized human ova that are the product of an in vitro fertilization (hereinafter IVF) procedure in which one of the prospective parents no longer wishes to participate. Although the parties have raised, *inter alia,* various fundamental legal and policy arguments in support of their respective positions, we conclude that this controversy is governed by the intent of the parties as clearly expressed in the provisions of an informed consent document which they voluntarily executed as participants in the IVF program and in a subsequent "uncontested divorce" instrument which they executed shortly thereafter, both of which manifest their mutual election that the IVF program should retain the cryopreserved pre-zygotes for approved research purposes under the circumstances of this case. Furthermore, by stipulating to the decision of this matter on submissions, the parties have charted their own course and the plaintiff, not having submitted sufficient evidence to support her contentions, cannot prevail.

I

The plaintiff Maureen Kass and the defendant Steven Kass were married on July 4, 1988. Apparently as a result of her in utero exposure to Diethylstilbistrol (DES), the plaintiff experienced difficulty in conceiving a child through coital relations. Accordingly, the parties enrolled in the Long Island IVF program at John T. Mather Memorial Hospital and at that time executed a "General IVF Consent Form No. 1". It is undisputed that the parties underwent 10 unsuccessful attempts to have a child through IVF between March 1990 and June 1993, at a total cost in excess of $ 75,000. The last of these procedures commenced in May 1993. On May 12, 1993, prior to the procedure, the parties executed a single, seven-page informed consent document dealing with cryopreservation and consisting of two sections, to wit: "informed consent form no. 2: cryopreservation of human pre-zygotes", comprising pages one to five of the document, and "INFORMED CONSENT FORM NO. 2—ADDENDUM NO. 2-1: CRYOPRESERVATION—STATEMENT OF DISPOSITION", consisting of pages six and seven. Insofar as relevant, the first section of the document contained the following general language regarding cryopreservation:

"III Disposition of Pre-Zygotes

"We understand that our frozen pre-zygotes will be stored for a maximum of 5 years. We have the principal responsibility to decide the disposition of our frozen pre-zygotes. *Our frozen pre-zygotes will not be released from storage for any purpose without the written consent of both of us,* consistent with the policies of the IVF Program and applicable law. *In the event of divorce, we understand that legal ownership of any stored pre-zygotes must be determined in a property settlement and will be released as directed by order of a court of competent jurisdiction. Should we for any reason no longer wish to attempt to initiate a pregnancy, we understand that we may determine the disposition of our frozen pre-zygotes remaining in storage....*

Subsequently, on May 20, 1993, numerous ova were removed from the plaintiff. Two days later, four fertilized ova were implanted in the plaintiff's sister, who had agreed to act as a surrogate. The five remaining pre-zygotes were cryopreserved by the IVF program pursuant to the parties' express wishes as set forth in "ADDENDUM NO. 2-1" of the informed consent document, set forth above.

II

On June 4, 1993, the parties were advised that a surrogate pregnancy had not resulted from the May 20th procedure, and the plaintiff's sister changed her mind and refused to continue her participation. Their hopes dashed, the parties agreed almost immediately thereafter to dissolve their marriage. Hence, on June 7, 1993, the parties executed a document typed by the plaintiff which provided for an uncontested divorce. Significantly, that instrument set forth their understanding of what they previously had agreed to in the informed consent document with regard to the disposition of the remaining cryopreserved pre-zygotes, as follows: "The disposition of the frozen 5 pre-zygotes at Mather Hospital is that they should be *disposed of [in] the manner outlined in our consent form and that neither Maureen Kass [,] Steve Kass or anyone else will lay claim to custody of these pre-zygotes*" (emphasis supplied).

Notwithstanding the foregoing, the plaintiff changed her mind and, on June 28, 1993, wrote letters to both the hospital and to her IVF physician advising them of the parties' marital difficulties and statingher adamant opposition to the destruction or release of the five pre-zygotes. The plaintiff then commenced this matrimonial action by summons and verified complaint filed July 21, 1993. Among the various items of relief sought therein was the plaintiff's request that she be awarded "sole custody of the frozen fertilized eggs now being held at Mather Memorial Hospital". The plaintiff indicated that she wanted possession of the pre-zygotes so that, rather than having them implanted in her sister as on the previous occasion, the plaintiff herself could undergo yet another IVF implantation procedure. In his verified answer, the defendant opposed both the removal of the pre-zygotes from cryopreservation and any further attempt to achieve a pregnancy, and counterclaimed for specific performance of the parties' election to permit the IVF program to retain the pre-zygotes for study and research, as provided in "ADDENDUM NO. 2-1" of the informed consent document.

In conclusion, we find that the decision to attempt to have children through IVF procedures and the determination of the fate of cryopreserved pre-zygotes resulting therefrom are intensely personal and essentially private matters which are appropriately resolved by the prospective parents rather than the courts. Accordingly, where the parties have indicated their mutual intent regarding the disposition of the pre-zygotes in the event of the occurrence of a contingency, that decision must be scrupulously honored, and the courts must refrain from any interference with the parties' expressed wishes. The documentary evidence overwhelmingly demonstrates that the parties in this case made such a clear and unequivocal choice, and the plaintiff's subsequent change of heart cannot be permitted to unilaterally alter their mutual decision. Accordingly, the judgment is reversed, on the law, with costs, and the matter is remitted to the Supreme Court, Nassau County, for entry of a judgment directing that the disposition of the five pre-zygotes shall be in accordance with paragraph 2 (b) of Addendum No. 2-1 of the parties' informed consent agreement.

9.6 Umbilical Cord Blood Banks

The New York Blood Center is one of the first to make umbilical cord blood accessible for the treatment of many diseases, including leukemia. Private companies have established contractual arrangements with expectant families to store the umbilical cord blood of their child, upon birth, in the event that they develop any of a list of more than 300 disease that may be treated with these blood stem cells.

The following bill was introduced in the U.S. House of Representatives after the success of a number of private umbilical cord blood banks

108TH CONGRESS

1ST SESSION H. R. 2852

To amend the Public Health Service Act to establish a National Cord Blood Stem Cell Bank Network to prepare, store, and distribute human umbilical cord blood stem cells for the treatment of patients and to support peer-reviewed research using such cells.

IN THE HOUSE OF REPRESENTATIVES

JULY 24, 2003

A Bill To amend the Public Health Service Act to establish a National

Cord Blood Stem Cell Bank Network to prepare,

store, and distribute human umbilical cord blood stem

cells for the treatment of patients and to support peer reviewed

research using such cells.

Be it enacted by the Senate and House of Representatives of the United States of America in Congress assembled,

SECTION 1. SHORT TITLE. This Act may be cited as the ''Cord Blood Stem Cell Act of 2003

SEC. 2. FINDINGS. The Congress makes the following findings: (1) Research sponsored by the National Institutes of Health and conducted in full compliance with applicable Food and Drug Administration regulations has demonstrated the feasibility of using cord blood for clinical applications. Stem cells, obtained from the blood contained in the delivered placenta and umbilical cord and donated by the mother, can be used for bone marrow reconstitution by trans-plantation to recipients with certain malignancies (such as leukemia and lymphoma), genetic disorders (such as sickle cell anemia), and acquired diseases. (2) The placenta, umbilical cord, and the neo-natal blood they contain are normally discarded after childbirth. This residual neonatal blood, termed cord blood, is a source of stem cells that can be collected as donor tissue without risk to the donor and can be preserved through freezing for many years and be made immediately available for transplantation in routine or emergency clinical situations. It can also be used for scientific research involving its stem cells. (3) Advantages of cord blood stem cell transplants relative to bone marrow transplants include the reduction of risks to the donor, availability of donor cell units in days rather than months, and lower risk of transplant complications, including graft versus host disease and latent virus infections (such as Epstein-Barr virus or Cytomegalovirus). (4) In conventional bone marrow transplantation, matched siblings are the preferred donors, but only 30 percent of patients have a matched sibling. When no sibling match is found, a search is initiated for an unrelated donor. (5) Finding a fully matched unrelated donor optimizes the chances of successful bone marrow transplantation. In conventional bone marrow transplantation, patients of ethnic minorities generally have difficulty finding fully matched donors, leaving partially matched transplants as their only transplant option. Partially matched bone marrow transplantation leads to a disproportionately high rate of complications, including graft versus host disease and mortality. (6) Cord blood stem cell banks would provide increased genetic diversity in the supply of donors and increase the opportunity to identify fully matched and partially matched transplant units for qualified candidates. Cord blood stem cell transplants using partially matched units reduce the risk of graft versus host disease with its attending morbidity and mortality as compared to conventional bone marrow transplantation.(7) Identifying and delivering an unrelated bone marrow donor from among the several millions in the National registry typically requires many months, sometimes more than 1 year. An inventory of 150,000 cord blood stem cell units, that takes into account the ethnic diversity of the country, would help provide appropriate matches for at least 90 percent of those seeking matched cord blood stem cell transplants, within days of a formal request. (8) Matched donors are more likely within the same ethnic group as the patient's. Some genetic conditions are also more prevalent in members of particular ethnic groups, such as Sickle Cell Anemia, a disease that occurs in one out of 500 African-American newborns. From early infancy, patients with Sickle Cell Anemia have a high risk of severe or fatal bacterial blood infections. Many patients develop painful crises beginning in infancy and occurring up to 20 times per year. Children with recurrent crises, chest syndrome or strokes, are at great risk of dying before the age of 20 years. The median lifepan of a patient with Sickle Cell Disease is 42 years, but patients with severe disease in childhood rarely live beyond 20 years. Cord blood stem cell transplantation has cured patients with Sickle Cell Anemia: 80 percent of children transplanted with related cord blood to correct Sickle Cell Anemia or thalassemia were cured in a recently published study. The earlier in the course of severe disease, the transplant is performed, the better the outcomes. Unrelated cord blood transplants are especially beneficial for African American and other ethnic minority patients because cord blood does not have to match as closely as bone marrow. For this reason, an African American patient is much more likely to find a suitable unrelated cord blood donor as compared to a matched bone marrow donor. With an ethnically balanced national cord blood bank of at least 150,000 units, some 90 percent of African American patients who suffer from Sickle Cell Anemia or other conditions requiring bone marrow replacement would be able to find appropriately matched cord blood stem cells for successful treatment. (9) Since its inception in 1987, the National Marrow Donor Program has facilitated 17,000 bone marrow transplants. Cord blood transplantation complements conventional bone marrow transplantation by providing appropriately matched units to patients, especially those of non-caucasoid ethnicity, who have a much lower probability of finding an adequate match through the National Marrow Donor Program. Cord blood is one of the sources of stem cells used in transplantation, however, its collection, preparation, storage and dissemination require specific systems and expertise. (10) Radiation exposure, from accidents or hostile actions could cause bone marrow failure in a portion of those exposed, requiring treatment including bone marrow reconstitution. In these cases the rapid availability of cryopreserved cord blood stem cell units may be important. Years later, those exposed would incur an increased risk of leukemia or lymphoma, which might also require stem cell transplantation. (11) Recent scientific developments suggest that further research on cord blood stem cells may lead to a greater understanding of certain chronic diseases. This research might improve therapies for, and possibly cure, debilitating diseases such as Parkinson's disease, insulin-dependent diabetes, heart disease, and certain types of cancer. These diseases cause a disproportionately large share of chronic disabilities and account for a large portion of health care expenditures in the United States.

Notes

1. The Cord Blood Stem Cell Center described in the bill and the House Report 108-401 was funded in the appropriations bills in 2004 (HR 2673) and 2005 (HR 4818). Should legislation also be considered to protect the Centers from tort liability, in a manner similar to the Childhood Vaccine Injury Act?

2. For a trial practice exercise in examining the range of legal issues which may arise for the new industry of cord blood stem cell centers, *see*, Sutton, *Madden v. Lifecord, Inc.*, a biotechnology case in product liability, conversion, medical malpractice, negligence, wrongful death, breach of contract, breach of duty of good faith, and misrepresentation, published by the National Institute of Trial Advocacy (2004).

Chapter Ten

Biotechnology and Tort Law

10.1 Intentional Torts

Intentional torts with potential applicability to biotechnology issues include trespass, trespass to land, conversion, private nuisance and public nuisance. Torts have sought as remedies for damages in both human tissues as well as damages from genetically engineered crops. The first is a landmark case in establishing that human tissues are not property. It analyzes the theories of trespass and conversion for profiting on unique tissue taken from a patient without his consent, or remuneration for their commercialization. The second case raises the issues of conversion, private nuisance and public nuisance, in that unique damages can be done by genetically engineered crops in contaminating other crops which become economic losses.

The intentional torts have not proven to be successful legal tools for recovery from damages from the products and practices of biotechnology. The following article suggests that among the intentional torts, trespass to land and conversion may be the most promising.

Excerpt from, Symposium: *Biotechnology and the Law: Biotechnology's Challenge to the Law of Torts*, 32 MᴄGᴇᴏʀɢᴇ L. Rᴇᴠ. 221 (Fall 2000).

There may be liability for intentional torts in the biotechnology context. The two intentional torts most likely to arise are trespass to land and conversion.

A. Trespass to Land

Use of genetically engineered crops creates a significant risk of trespass to land. Trespass to land arises where a defendant intentionally enters the land of another or intentionally causes something to enter the land of another. Although intent is required, it is the intent to enter the land, not the intent to trespass, that is key. Thus, if a defendant enters the plaintiff's land reasonably believing that she has permission to do so, or even under a reasonable belief that the property is hers, she will be liable for trespass to land.

In the biotechnology context, if the defendant knows that it is substantially certain that seeds from her pesticide-resistant plants will find their way on to the plaintiff's property, she can be liable for trespass to land. Further, she is liable for all harm that ensues as a result of the trespass. Genetically engineered crops pose a real risk of trespass to land liability if they cross-pollinate with neighboring plants or otherwise contaminate the land of adjoining land owners.

B. Conversion The intentional tort that thus far has received the most attention in the biotechnology context is the tort of conversion. Conversion arises when a defendant intentionally exercises "dominion and control over a chattel which so seriously interferes with the right of another to control it that the actor may justly be required to pay the other the full value of the chattel." Although an intentional tort, as with trespass to land, it is simply the intent to do the act—here the exercise of dominion and control—that gives rise to liability.

The propriety of a conversion action in the biotechnology context was first considered in the now-famous case of Moore v. Regents of the University of California. Moore had been undergoing medical care for hairy-cell leukemia, a rare and potentially fatal form of cancer. As part of the medical treatment for the disease, Moore's spleen was removed, a standard treatment for the disease. The defendants used Moore's spleen to develop a cell-line that was patented and highly valuable. Moore had no knowledge of the defendants' commercial use of his cells. In fact, Moore was induced to make about a dozen trips to the defendants under the guise of continuing medical treatment when, in fact, the trips were solely to assist the defendants with their ongoing commercial use of Moore's cells. Moore sued, alleging several torts including conversion. A divided California Supreme Court reversed an appellate court that had permitted Moore to pursue a conversion claim.

The Moore decision was a tremendous victory for the biotechnology industry. The decision foreclosed a conversion action against those who exercised dominion and control over the patient's tissue samples without the patient's consent. The majority determined that Moore's cells were not property and, thus, could not be converted. The court admitted that its conclusion was reached in an effort to protect medical research, which, the majority believed, could have been harmed by permitting conversion liability.

The impact of Moore remains substantial and its application to biotechnological harms is yet to be seen. For example, one author argues that the tort of conversion should apply in the context of the misappropriation of human eggs and embryos, notwithstanding the restrictive holding of Moore. Such an action, however, may well be foreclosed if a court elects to adopt the California Supreme Court's reasoning in Moore.

Moore v. Regents of University of California
793 P.2d 479 (1990)

OPINION by: Judge J. Panelli

I. Introduction

We granted review in this case to determine whether plaintiff has stated a cause of action against his physician and other defendants for using his cells in potentially lucrative medical research without his permission. Plaintiff alleges that his physician failed to disclose preexisting research and economic interests in the cells before obtaining consent to the medical procedures by which they were extracted. The superior court sustained all defendants' demurrers to the third amended complaint, and the Court of Appeal reversed. We hold that the complaint states a cause of action for breach of the physician's disclosure obligations, but not for conversion.

II. Facts

Our only task in reviewing a ruling on a demurrer is to determine whether the complaint states a cause of action. Accordingly, we assume that the complaint's properly pleaded material allegations are true and give the complaint a reasonable interpretation by reading it as a whole and all its parts in their context.... The plaintiff is John Moore (Moore), who underwent treatment for hairy-cell leukemia at the Medical Center of the University of California at Los Angeles (UCLA Medical Center). The five defendants are: (1) Dr. David W. Golde (Golde), a physician who attended Moore at UCLA Medical Center; (2) the Regents of the University of California (Regents), who own and operate the university; (3) Shirley G. Quan, a researcher employed by the Regents; (4) Genetics Institute, Inc. (Genetics Institute); and (5) Sandoz Pharmaceuticals Corporation and related entities (collectively Sandoz).

Moore first visited UCLA Medical Center on October 5, 1976, shortly after he learned that he had hairy-cell leukemia. After hospitalizing Moore and "withdr[awing] extensive amounts of blood, bone marrow aspirate, and other bodily substances," Golde n1 confirmed that diagnosis. At this time all defendants, including Golde, were aware that "certain blood products and blood components were of great value in a number of commercial and scientific efforts" and that access to a patient whose blood contained these substances would provide "competitive, commercial, and scientific advantages." ...

On October 8, 1976, Golde recommended that Moore's spleen be removed. Golde informed Moore "that he had reason to fear for his life, and that the proposed splenectomy operation ... was necessary to slow down the progress of his disease." Based upon Golde's representations, Moore signed a written consent form authorizing the splenectomy.

Before the operation, Golde and Quan "formed the intent and made arrangements to obtain portions of [Moore's] spleen following its removal" and to take them to a separate research unit. Golde gave written instructions to this effect on October 18 and 19, 1976. These research activities "were not intended to have ... any relation to [Moore's] medical ... care." However, neither Golde nor Quan informed Moore of their plans to conduct this research or requested his permission. Surgeons at UCLA Medical Center, whom the complaint does not name as defendants, removed Moore's spleen on October 20, 1976.

Moore returned to the UCLA Medical Center several times between November 1976 and September 1983. He did so at Golde's direction and based upon representations "that such visits were necessary and required for his health and well-being, and based upon the trust inherent in and by virtue of the physician-patient relationship...." On each of these visits Golde withdrew additional samples of "blood, blood serum, skin, bone marrow aspirate, and sperm." On each occasion Moore traveled to the UCLA Medical Center from his home in Seattle because he had been told that the procedures were to be performed only there and only under Golde's direction.

"In fact, [however,] throughout the period of time that [Moore] was under [Golde's] care and treatment, ... the defendants were actively involved in a number of activities which they concealed from [Moore]...." Specifically, defendants were conducting research on Moore's cells and planned to "benefit financially and competitively ... [by exploiting the cells] and [their] exclusive access to [the cells] by virtue of [Golde's] ongoing physician-patient relationship...."

Sometime before August 1979, Golde established a cell line from Moore's T-lymphocytes. FN2 On January 30, 1981, the Regents applied for a patent on the cell line, listing Golde and Quan as inventors. "[B]y virtue of an established policy..., [the] Regents,

Golde, and Quan would share in any royalties or profits ... arising out of [the] patent." The patent issued on March 20, 1984, naming Golde and Quan as the inventors of the cell line and the Regents as the assignee of the patent. (U.S. Patent No. 4,438,032 (Mar. 20, 1984).)

SELECTED NOTES

FN2 A T-lymphocyte is a type of white blood cell. T-lymphocytes produce lymphokines, or proteins that regulate the immune system. Some lymphokines have potential therapeutic value. If the genetic material responsible for producing a particular lymphokine can be identified, it can sometimes be used to manufacture large quantities of the lymphokine through the techniques of recombinant DNA. (See generally U.S. Congress, Office of Technology Assessment, New Developments in Biotechnology: Ownership of Human Tissues and Cells (1987) at pp. 31–46 (hereafter OTA Report); see also fn. 29, *post*.)

While the genetic code for lymphokines does not vary from individual to individual, it can nevertheless be quite difficult to locate the gene responsible for a particular lymphokine. Because T-lymphocytes produce many different lymphokines, the relevant gene is often like a needle in a haystack. (OTA Rep., *supra*, at p. 42.) Moore's T-lymphocytes were interesting to the defendants because they overproduced certain lymphokines, thus making the corresponding genetic material easier to identify. (In published research papers, defendants and other researchers have shown that the overproduction was caused by a virus, and that normal T-lymphocytes infected by the virus will also overproduce. See fn. 30, *post*.)

Cells taken directly from the body (primary cells) are not very useful for these purposes. Primary cells typically reproduce a few times and then die. One can, however, sometimes continue to use cells for an extended period of time by developing them into a "cell line," a culture capable of reproducing indefinitely. This is not, however, always an easy task. "Longterm growth of human cells and tissues is difficult, often an art," and the probability of succeeding with any given cell sample is low, except for a few types of cells not involved in this case. (OTA Rep., *supra*, at p. 5.)

... The Regent's patent also covers various methods for using the cell line to produce lymphokines. Moore admits in his complaint that "the true clinical potential of each of the lymphokines ... [is] difficult to predict, [but] ... competing commercial firms in these relevant fields have published reports in biotechnology industry periodicals predicting a potential market of approximately $ 3.01 Billion Dollars by the year 1990 for a whole range of [such lymphokines]...."

With the Regents' assistance, Golde negotiated agreements for commercial development of the cell line and products to be derived from it. Under an agreement with Genetics Institute, Golde "became a paid consultant" and "acquired the rights to 75,000 shares of common stock." Genetics Institute also agreed to pay Golde and the Regents "at least $ 330,000 over three years, including a pro-rata share of [Golde's] salary and fringe benefits, in exchange for ... exclusive access to the materials and research performed" on the cell line and products derived from it. On June 4, 1982, Sandoz "was added to the agreement," and compensation payable to Golde and the Regents was increased by $ 110,000. "[T]hroughout this period, ... Quan spent as much as 70 [percent] of her time working for [the] Regents on research" related to the cell line ...

B. *Conversion*

Moore also attempts to characterize the invasion of his rights as a conversion — a tort that protects against interference with possessory and ownership interests in personal property. He theorizes that he continued to own his cells following their removal from his body, at least for the purpose of directing their use, and that he never consented to their use in potentially lucrative medical research. Thus, to complete Moore's argument, defendants' unauthorized use of his cells constitutes a conversion. As a result of the alleged conversion, Moore claims a proprietary interest in each of the products that any of the defendants might ever create from his cells or the patented cell line.

No court, however, has ever in a reported decision imposed conversion liability for the use of human cells in medical research. n15 While that fact does not end our inquiry, it raises a flag of caution. (**See fn. 16.**) In effect, what Moore is asking us to do is to impose a tort duty on scientists to investigate the consensual pedigree of each human cell sample used in research.[16] To impose such a duty, which would affect medical research of importance to all of society, implicates policy concerns far removed from the traditional, two-party ownership disputes in which the law of conversion arose.[17] Invoking a tort theory originally used to determine whether the loser or the finder of a horse had the better title, Moore claims ownership of the results of socially important medical research, including the genetic code for chemicals that regulate the functions of every human being's immune system.[18]

We have recognized that, when the proposed application of a very general theory of liability in a new context raises important policy concerns, it is especially important to face those concerns and address them openly. [declining to expand negligence law to encompass theory of "clergyman malpractice"];[declining to apply tort remedies for breach of the covenant of good faith in the employment context]; [declining to apply strict products liability to pharmaceutical manufacturers].) Moreover, we should be hesitant to "impose [new tort duties] when to do so would involve complex policy decisions", especially when such decisions are more appropriately the subject of legislative deliberation and resolution. This certainly is not to say that the applicability of common law torts is limited to the historical or factual contexts of existing cases. But on occasions when we have opened or sanctioned new areas of tort liability, we "have noted that the 'wrongs and injuries involved were both comprehensible and assessable within the existing judicial framework.'"

---

16. Imposing liability for conversion is equivalent to the imposition of such a duty, since only through investigation would users of cells be able to avoid liability. "'A tort, whether intentional or negligent, involves a violation of a *legal duty* imposed by statute, contract or otherwise, owed by the defendant to the person injured. Without such a duty, any injury is "damnum absque injuria" — injury without wrong.

17. Conversion arose out of the common law action of trover. "We probably do not have the earliest examples of its use, but they were almost certainly cases in which the finder of lost goods did not return them, but used them himself, or disposed of them to someone else.... By 1554 the allegations of the complaint had become more or less standardized: that the plaintiff was possessed of certain goods, that he casually lost them, that the defendant found them, and that the defendant did not return them, but instead 'converted them to his own use.' From that phrase in the pleading came the name of the tort." (Prosser & Keeton, Torts (5th ed. 1984) §§ 15, p. 89.)

18. Moore alleges, for example, that "genetic sequences ... are his tangible personal property...." We are not, however, bound by that conclusion of law. (*Daar v. Yellow Cab Co., supra*, 67 Cal.2d at p. 713.) Moreover, as already mentioned, the genetic code for lymphokines does not vary from individual to individual. (See fns. 2, *ante*, and 30, *post*.)

Accordingly, we first consider whether the tort of conversion clearly gives Moore a cause of action under existing law. We do not believe it does. Because of the novelty of Moore's claim to own the biological materials at issue, to apply the theory of conversion in this context would frankly have to be recognized as an extension of the theory. Therefore, we consider next whether it is advisable to extend the tort to this context.

1. Moore's Claim Under Existing Law

"To establish a conversion, plaintiff must establish an actual interference with his *ownership* or *right of possession....* Where plaintiff neither has title to the property alleged to have been converted, nor possession thereof, he cannot maintain an action for conversion."[19]

Since Moore clearly did not expect to retain possession of his cells following their removal,[20] to sue for their conversion he must have retained an ownership interest in them. But there are several reasons to doubt that he did retain any such interest. First, no reported judicial decision supports Moore's claim, either directly or by close analogy. Second, California statutory law drastically limits any continuing interest of a patient in excised cells. Third, the subject matters of the Regents' patent—the patented cell line and the products derived from it—cannot be Moore's property.

Neither the Court of Appeal's opinion, the parties' briefs, nor our research discloses a case holding that a person retains a sufficient interest in excised cells to support a cause of action for conversion. We do not find this surprising, since the laws governing such things as human tissues, transplantable organs, blood, fetuses, pituitary glands, corneal tissue, n26 and dead bodies deal with human biological materials as objects sui generis, regulating their disposition to achieve policy goals rather than abandoning them to the general law of personal property. It is these specialized statutes, not the law of conversion, to which courts ordinarily should and do look for guidance on the disposition of human biological materials.

Not only are the wrongful-publicity cases irrelevant to the issue of conversion, but the analogy to them seriously misconceives the nature of the genetic materials and research involved in this case. Moore, adopting the analogy originally advanced by the Court of Appeal, argues that "[i]f the courts have found a sufficient proprietary interest in one's persona, how could one not have a right in one's own genetic material, something far more profoundly the essence of one's human uniqueness than a name or a face?" However, as the defendants' patent makes clear—and the complaint, too, if read with an understanding of the scientific terms which it has borrowed from the patent—the goal and result of defendants' efforts has been to manufacture lymphokines. n29 Lymphokines, unlike a name or a face, have the same molecular structure in every human being and the same, important functions in every human being's immune system.

---

19. While it ordinarily suffices to allege ownership generally (5 Witkin, Cal. Procedure (3d ed. 1985) Pleading, §§ 654, p. 103), it is well established that a complaint's contentions or conclusions of law do not bind us. (*Daar v. Yellow Cab Co., supra,* 67 Cal.2d at p. 713.) Moore's novel allegation that he "owns" the biological materials involved in this case is both a contention and a conclusion of law.

20. In his complaint, Moore does not seek possession of his cells or claim the right to possess them. This is consistent with Health and Safety Code section 7054.4, which provides that "human tissues ... following conclusion of scientific use shall be disposed of by interment, incineration, or any other method determined by the state department [of health services] to protect the public health and safety."

Moreover, the particular genetic material which is responsible for the natural production of lymphokines, and which defendants use to manufacture lymphokines in the laboratory, is also the same in every person; it is no more unique to Moore than the number of vertebrae in the spine or the chemical formula of hemoglobin.

The next consideration that makes Moore's claim of ownership problematic is California statutory law, which drastically limits a patient's control over excised cells. Pursuant to Health and Safety Code section 7054.4, "[n]otwithstanding any other provision of law, recognizable anatomical parts, human tissues, anatomical human remains, or infectious waste following conclusion of scientific use shall be disposed of by interment, incineration, or any other method determined by the state department [of health services] to protect the public health and safety." Clearly the Legislature did not specifically intend this statute to resolve the question of whether a patient is entitled to compensation for the nonconsensual use of excised cells. A primary object of the statute is to ensure the safe handling of potentially hazardous biological waste materials. Yet one cannot escape the conclusion that the statute's practical effect is to limit, drastically, a patient's control over excised cells. By restricting how excised cells may be used and requiring their eventual destruction, the statute eliminates so many of the rights ordinarily attached to property that one cannot simply assume that what is left amounts to "property" or "ownership" for purposes of conversion law.

2. Should Conversion Liability Be Extended?

As we have discussed, Moore's novel claim to own the biological materials at issue in this case is problematic, at best. Accordingly, his attempt to apply the theory of conversion within this context must frankly be recognized as a request to extend that theory. While we do not purport to hold that excised cells can never be property for any purpose whatsoever, the novelty of Moore's claim demands express consideration of the policies to be served by extending liability rather than blind deference to a complaint alleging as a legal conclusion the existence of a cause of action.

There are three reasons why it is inappropriate to impose liability for conversion based upon the allegations of Moore's complaint. First, a fair balancing of the relevant policy considerations counsels against extending the tort. Second, problems in this area are better suited to legislative resolution. Third, the tort of conversion is not necessary to protect patients' rights. For these reasons, we conclude that the use of excised human cells in medical research does not amount to a conversion.

Of the relevant policy considerations, two are of overriding importance. The first is protection of a competent patient's right to make autonomous medical decisions. That right, as already discussed, is grounded in well-recognized and long-standing principles of fiduciary duty and informed consent. This policy weighs in favor of providing a remedy to patients when physicians act with undisclosed motives that may affect their professional judgment. The second important policy consideration is that we not threaten with disabling civil liability innocent parties who are engaged in socially useful activities, such as researchers who have no reason to believe that their use of a particular cell sample is, or may be, against a donor's wishes.

To reach an appropriate balance of these policy considerations is extremely important. In its report to Congress (see fn. 2, ante), the Office of Technology Assessment emphasized that "[u]ncertainty about how courts will resolve disputes between specimen sources and specimen users could be detrimental to both academic researchers and the infant biotechnology industry, particularly when the rights are asserted long after the specimen was obtained. The assertion of rights by sources would affect not only the researcher who obtained the original specimen, but perhaps other researchers as well.

"Biological materials are routinely distributed to other researchers for experimental purposes, and scientists who obtain cell lines or other specimen-derived products, such as gene clones, from the original researcher could also be sued under certain legal theories [such as conversion]. Furthermore, the uncertainty could affect product developments as well as research. Since inventions containing human tissues and cells may be patented and licensed for commercial use, companies are unlikely to invest heavily in developing, manufacturing, or marketing a product when uncertainty about clear title exists." (OTA Rep., *supra*, at p. 27.)

Indeed, so significant is the potential obstacle to research stemming from uncertainty about legal title to biological materials that the Office of Technology Assessment reached this striking conclusion: "[R]egardless of the merit of claims by the different interested parties, resolving the current uncertainty may be more important to the future of biotechnology than resolving it in any particular way." (OTA Rep., *supra*, at p. 27.)

We need not, however, make an arbitrary choice between liability and nonliability. Instead, an examination of the relevant policy considerations suggests an appropriate balance: Liability based upon existing disclosure obligations, rather than an unprecedented extension of the conversion theory, protects patients' rights of privacy and autonomy without unnecessarily hindering research.

To be sure, the threat of liability for conversion might help to enforce patients' rights indirectly. This is because physicians might be able to avoid liability by obtaining patients' consent, in the broadest possible terms, to any conceivable subsequent research use of excised cells. Unfortunately, to extend the conversion theory would utterly sacrifice the other goal of protecting innocent parties. Since conversion is a strict liability tort, it would impose liability on all those into whose hands the cells come, whether or not the particular defendant participated in, or knew of, the inadequate disclosures that violated the patient's right to make an informed decision. In contrast to the conversion theory, the fiduciary-duty and informed-consent theories protect the patient directly, without punishing innocent parties or creating disincentives to the conduct of socially beneficial research.

In Re Starlink Corn Products Liability Litigation
212 F. Supp. 2d 828 (N.D. Ill. 2002)

Memorandum Opinion and Order by Judge James B. Moran

This controversy arises from the discovery of genetically modified corn in various food products. Plaintiffs disseminated a product that contaminated the entire United States' corn supply, increasing their costs and depressing corn prices. Plaintiffs have filed a 57-count master second amended consolidated class action complaint, alleging common law claims for negligence, strict liability, private nuisance, public nuisance and conversion on behalf of a nationwide class of corn farmers.... Defendants filed a motion to dismiss, arguing that the Federal Insecticide, Fungicide and Rodenticide Act (FIFRA), 7 U.S.C. §§ 136 *et seq.*, preempts plaintiffs' state law claims, that the economic loss doctrine bars any recovery, and that the complaint fails to state a claim under any of plaintiffs' purported legal theories. For the following reasons, defendants' motion to dismiss is granted in part and denied in part.

BACKGROUND

Aventis genetically engineered a corn seed to produce a protein known as Cry9C that is toxic to certain insects. The seeds are marketed under the brand name StarLink. Garst is a licensee who produced and distributed Starlink seeds. Aventis applied to register Star-link with the EPA, which is responsible for regulating insecticides under FIFRA, 7 U.S.C. §§ 136 *et seq.* The EPA noted that Cry9C had several attributes similar to known human allergens, and issued only a limited registration, permitting Starlink use for such purposes as animal feed, ethanol production and seed increase, but prohibiting its use for human consumption. Consequently, segregating it from non-StarLink corn, which was fit for human consumption, became of utmost importance. A little background about normal practices for cultivating, harvesting and distributing corn demonstrates the extensive steps necessary to prevent StarLink corn from entering the food supply.

Corn replicates by the transfer of pollen from one corn plant to another, including cross-pollination from one breed to another. Once airborne, corn pollen can drift over considerable distances, meaning that different corn varieties within a farm, and from neighboring farms, regularly cross-breed. With few exceptions, there are not procedures in place to segregate types of corn. Different corn breeds within an individual farm are commingled at the harvesting stage. Corn from hundreds of thousands of farms is then further commingled as it is gathered, stored and shipped through a system of local, re-gional and terminal grain elevators. Elevators, storage and transportation facilities are generally not equipped to test and segregate corn varieties. The commingled corn is then marketed and traded as a fungible commodity.

In light of these general practices in the corn industry, the EPA required special procedures with respect to StarLink. These included mandatory segregation methods to prevent Star-Link from commingling with other corn in cultivation, harvesting, handling, storage and transport, and a 660-foot "buffer zone" around StarLink corn crops to prevent cross-polli-nation with non-StarLink corn plants. The limited registration also made Aventis respon-sible for ensuring these restrictions were implemented, obligating it (a) to inform farmers of the EPA's requirements for the planting, cultivation and use of StarLink; (b) to instruct farmers growing StarLink how to store and dispose of the StarLink seeds, seed bags, and plant detritus; and (c)) to ensure that all farmers purchasing StarLink seeds signed a con-tract binding them to these terms before permitting them to grow StarLink corn.

StarLink was distributed throughout the United States from approximately May 1998 through October 2000. The limited registration initially limited StarLink cultivation to 120,000 acres. In January 1999, Aventis petitioned the EPA to raise this limit to 2.5 mil-lion acres. The EPA agreed, subject to an amended registration that required Aventis to

(a) inform purchasers (i.e. "Growers") at the time of StarLink seed corn sales, of the need to direct StarLink harvest to domestic feed and industrial non-food uses only;

(b) require all Growers to sign a "Grower Agreement" outlining field manage-ment requirements and stating the limits on StarLink corn use;

(c) deliver a Grower Guide, restating the provisions stated in the Grower Agreement, with all seed;

(d) provide all Growers with access to a confidential list of feed outlets and ele-vators that direct grain to domestic feed and industrial uses;

(e) write to Growers prior to planting, reminding them of the domestic and in-dustrial use requirements for StarLink corn;

(f) write to Growers prior to harvest, reminding them of the domestic and industrial use requirements for StarLink corn;

(g) conduct a statistically sound follow-up survey of Growers following harvest, to monitor compliance with the Grower Agreement.

Over this 29-month period, StarLink cultivation expanded from 10,000 acres to 350,000 acres.

In October 2000, after numerous reports that human food products had tested positive for Cry9C, a wave of manufacturers issued recalls for their corn products. On October 12, 2000, Aventis, at EPA's urging, applied to cancel the limited registration, effective February 20, 2001. Fear of StarLink contamination nonetheless continues to affect corn markets. Many U.S. food producers have stopped using U.S. corn, replacing it with imported corn or corn substitutes. South Korea, Japan and other foreign countries have terminated or substantially limited imports of U.S. corn. Grain elevators and transport providers are now mandating expensive testing on all corn shipments.

Plaintiffs allege that the widespread StarLink contamination of the U.S. corn supply is a result of defendants' failure to comply with the EPA's requirements. Aventis did not include the EPA-mandated label on some StarLink packages, did not notify, instruct and remind StarLink farmers of the restrictions on StarLink use, proper segregation methods and buffer zone requirements, and did not require StarLink farmers to sign the obligatory contracts. Prior to the 2000 growing season Aventis allegedly instructed its seed representatives that it was unnecessary for them to advise StarLink farmers to segregate their StarLink crop or create buffer zones because Aventis believed the EPA would amend the registration to permit StarLink use for human consumption. In July 2001, however, an EPA Scientific Advisory Panel reaffirmed its previous position on StarLink's allergenic qualities. Further, the FDA has declared StarLink to be an adulterant under the Food, Drug and Cosmetic Act....

II. Economic Loss Doctrine

This rule limits the types of damages plaintiffs may recover in tort. Physical injuries to persons or property are compensable; solely economic injuries are not. The difficult question is defining what constitutes an "economic" injury....

Non-StarLink corn crops are damaged when they are pollinated by StarLink corn. The pollen causes these corn plants to develop the Cry9C protein and renders what would otherwise be a valuable food crop unfit for human consumption. Non-StarLink corn is also damaged when it is commingled with StarLink corn. Once mixed, there is no way to re-segregate the **corn** into its edible and inedible parts. The entire batch is considered tainted and can only be used for the domestic and industrial purposes for which StarLink is approved. None of that supply can ever be used for human food.

There are at least four different points along the supply chain at which StarLink could have entered the food corn supply, all of which are consistent with the complaint: (1) plaintiffs unknowingly purchased seed containing the Cry9C protein, *i.e.* their suppliers' inventory had been contaminated; (2) plaintiffs' crops were contaminated by pollen from StarLink corn on a neighboring farm; (3) plaintiffs' harvest was contaminated by commingling with StarLink corn in a transport or storage facility; and (4) food manufacturers commingled the corn within their raw material storage or processing activities. The first situation would fall within the economic loss doctrine. Plaintiffs could have negotiated contractual protection from their suppliers and simply did not get what they had bargained for. In the fourth, plaintiffs would have suffered no harm to their property because the corn was commingled after they had relinquished their ownership interest in it. Scenarios 2 and 3, however, present viable claims for harm to their crops. [Resolving the complaint's ambiguous phraseology in plaintiffs' favor, we find that they have sufficiently alleged that their crops were contaminated at some point within that chain.]

The StarLink situation does not fit neatly into traditional economic loss doctrine analysis. Plaintiffs here had no commercial dealings with defendants or defendants' customers. This is more than a lack of direct privity, and not a situation where a party could have negotiated warranty or indemnity protection and chose not to. Plaintiffs had no opportunity to negotiate contractual protection with anyone. Still, as the access cases aptly demonstrate, the economic loss doctrine has grown beyond its original freedom-of-contract based policy justifications. Farmers' expectations of what they will receive for their crops are just that, expectations. Absent a physical injury, plaintiffs cannot recover for drops in market prices. Nor can they recover for any additional costs, such as testing procedures, imposed by the marketplace. But if there was some physical harm to plaintiffs' corn crop, the lack of a transaction with defendants affects what will be considered "other property." [This includes corn commingled at grain elevators because plaintiffs retain ownership rights to corn stored there. Each contributing farmer owns a pro rata share of the entire, now tainted, supply.] Assuming plaintiffs did not buy corn seeds with the Cry9C protein, it cannot be said that a defective part of their crop injured the whole, that a defective product was integrated into a system or that the harm to their crop was a foreseeable consequence of the seeds' failure to perform. These facts are distinguishable from Hapka, 458 N.W.2d at 688 (holding farmer who purchased diseased seeds could not recover for harm to rest of crop). Plaintiffs' seeds, as purchased, were adequate. The StarLink contaminant was wholly external.

Nor does the StarLink controversy present the unlimited or speculative damage concerns common in access cases. There are a finite number of potential plaintiffs—only non-StarLink corn farmers—who can claim injury. This may be a sizeable group, and the damages may be tremendous, but the fact that defendants are alleged to have directly harmed a large number of plaintiffs is not a defense. StarLink's effects on commercial corn farmers are distinct and qualitatively different from society at large. And damages are easily measured through price changes because corn is a regularly traded commodity with a readily measurable market. Further, as discussed above, the contamination of plaintiffs' corn supply is a physical injury.

To the extent plaintiffs allege that their crops were themselves contaminated, either by cross-pollination in the fields or by commingling later in the distribution chain, they have adequately stated a claim for harm to property. Once plaintiffs have established this harm they may be entitled to compensation for certain economic losses....

IV. Conversion

Conversion is defined as "an intentional exercise of dominion or control over a chattel which so seriously interferes with the right of another to control it that the actor may justly be required to pay the other the full value of the chattel." Restatement (Second) of Torts § 222A. Plaintiffs argue that defendants' role in contaminating the corn supply amounts to a conversion of their property. We disagree.

The defining element of conversion, the one that distinguishes it from a trespass to chattels, is the extent of interference with the owner's property rights. If the damage is minor, in duration or severity, plaintiff may only recover for the diminished value. But if the damage is sufficiently severe, plaintiff may recover full value. Conversion is akin to a forced judicial sale. The defendant pays full value for the chattel, and receives title to it. Restatement §222A comment c. Here, plaintiffs have not alleged that defendants destroyed their crops or deprived them of possession. Plaintiffs retained possession and still had total control over the **corn.** Most, if not all of it, was ultimately sold to third parties. The only damages were a lower price, for which plaintiffs could be compensated without forcing a sale.

It is possible to convert a chattel by altering it, without completely destroying it. In particular, commingling fungible goods so that their identity is lost can constitute a conversion. Restatement §226 comment e. To do so, however, the perpetrator must alter the chattel in a way that is "so material as to change the identity of the chattel or its essential character." Restatement §226 comment d. At worst, StarLink contamination changed plaintiffs' yield from being corn fit for human consumption to corn fit only for domestic or industrial use. Plaintiffs do not claim they were growing the corn to eat themselves, but for sale on the commodity markets. The crops were still viable for the purpose for which plaintiffs would normally use them, for sale on the open market. That the market had become less hospitable does not change the product's essential character. As above, the severity of the alteration is indicated by the decrease in market price. This could arguably constitute a trespass to chattels, but does not rise to the level of conversion.

Lastly, negligence cannot support a conversion claim. It requires intent. Restatement §224. The complaint alleges that defendants did not take adequate precautions to ensure that StarLink corn was adequately segregated. Nowhere do plaintiffs claim that defendants intentionally commingled StarLink and non-StarLink corn, or deliberately contaminated the food supply. Even if defendants negligently failed to prevent cross-pollination and commingling, they would not be liable for conversion.

V. Nuisance

A. Private [Nuisance]

The complaint alleges that defendants created a private nuisance by distributing corn seeds with the Cry9C protein, knowing that they would cross-pollinate with neighboring corn crops. [The private nuisance claims appear to be premised exclusively on cross-pollination in the fields, not commingling later in the distribution chain.]

A private nuisance is a nontrespassory invasion of another's interest in the private use and enjoyment of land." Restatement (Second) of Torts §821D. We agree that drifting pollen can constitute an invasion, and that contaminating neighbors' crops interferes with their enjoyment of the land. The issue is whether defendants are responsible for contamination caused by their product beyond the point of sale.

Commingling could not constitute a private nuisance because it does not involve an invasion of any private interests in land. By contrast, the public nuisance claims, discussed below, may be premised on commingling because "unlike a private nuisance, a public nuisance does not necessarily involve interference with use or enjoyment of land." Restatement §821B comment h.

Defendants argue that they cannot be liable for any nuisance caused by StarLink because they were no longer in control of the seeds once they were sold to farmers. But one can be liable for nuisance "not only when he carries on the activity but also when he participates to a substantial extent in carrying it on." Restatement §834. Plaintiffs maintain that defendants' design of the StarLink technology, distribution of the seeds and, most importantly, their failure to fulfill their EPA-mandated duties, constitutes substantial participation.

The paradigm private nuisance case involves a suit between two neighboring landowners, one of whom alleges that the other's activities are somehow interfering with the first's enjoyment of the land. Suing the manufacturer of the product that the neighbor was using appears to be an extension of nuisance law into an area normally regulated by product liability. But there is precedent for such an application under certain circumstances, and it does fit within the definition of a nuisance....

Suppose, however, that [the manufacturer] had not taken steps to alert customers of the risks of the product, or intentionally marketed the product to customers who it knew or should have known would dispose of [it] in a manner that would harm the environment. Nothing in the opinion in City of Bloomington would preclude the imposition of liability on the manufacturer under those facts....

This brings us to the case at bar, which is much closer to mainstream nuisance doctrine than either the asbestos or gun cases. In the asbestos cases, the plaintiffs had themselves purchased the product, consented to having it installed on their property and then sued the manufacturer when it turned out to be harmful. There was no invasion of a neighboring property and plaintiffs had exclusive access to the nuisance-causing agent. Here, plaintiffs did not purchase StarLink seeds, and have alleged that pollen from neighboring farms did enter their premises. Aside from the presence of an invasion, the fact that the alleged nuisance occurred on another's property means that, unlike asbestos purchasers, plaintiffs had no ability to access or control the nuisance themselves. In the gun cases, manufacturers successfully argued that they should not be held responsible for third parties' intentional misuse of their products. Here, however, plaintiffs have not alleged that StarLink farmers defied the manufacturers' instructions, but rather that the instructions themselves violated the EPA's mandates. Moreover, the gun cases alleged a public nuisance and did not implicate plaintiffs' ability to enjoy land or anyone's unreasonable use of land. Private nuisance jurisprudence has always focused on the use and enjoyment of land. Plaintiffs here have alleged that they are unable to enjoy the profits of their land (selling food corn), because of an unreasonable activity on neighboring land (growing StarLink corn).

Another critical factor here is the impact of the limited registration, which negates many of the concerns courts have expressed about holding manufacturers liable for post-sale nuisances. For example, they emphasized that the manufacturers did not have any control over how the purchasers had used their products, or any access to abate the nuisance. Aventis, on the other hand, had an affirmative duty to enforce StarLink farmers' compliance with the Grower Agreements. This arguably gave Aventis some measure of control over StarLink's use, as well as a means to abate any nuisance caused by its misuse. This mirrors Page County Appliance Center, *supra,* where the court found the manufacturer's ongoing service contract with the purchaser gave defendant enough access and control to create a question of fact as to its contribution to the nuisance. Aventis' duties under the limited registration were, by comparison, even more extensive. Similarly, defendants' failure to give StarLink farmers the warnings mandated by the limited registration, and (ultimately incorrect) representations that StarLink need not be segregated because the EPA was going to approve it for human consumption, are also arguably the type of culpable conduct relied upon ...

In summary, of the states involved here Iowa, Wisconsin and Illinois have all held a manufacturer liable for a nuisance related to its product beyond the point of sale....

The lack of state precedent matching these precise facts does not preclude us from applying widely accepted Restatement law to new factual situations. Residue from a product drifting across property lines presents a typical nuisance claim. All parties who substantially contribute to the nuisance are liable. The unique obligations imposed by the limited registration arguably put Aventis in a position to control the nuisance. On a motion to dismiss we may not speculate whether the as yet undeveloped facts will constitute substantial contribution. To the extent the allegations comport with our preemption analysis above, they do state a valid claim for private nuisance.

B. Public [Nuisance]

Plaintiffs also assert that StarLink's contamination of the general food corn supply constitutes a public nuisance. Beyond defendants' argument that they lacked control over the alleged nuisance, discussed above, they assert that plaintiffs cannot establish special harm. At the outset, we note the limited depth of review courts typically undertake on a motion to dismiss a public nuisance claim.

The pleading requirements are not strenuous because the 'concept of common law public nuisance elude[s] precise definition.'... The unreasonableness of the defendant's actions and the substantialness of the right invasion, which lead to the determination of nuisance, are questions of fact for the jury.'

To state a claim, plaintiffs must allege "an unreasonable interference with a right common to the general public." Restatement §821B(1). The Restatement sweeps broadly in defining a "public right," including "the public health, the public safety, the public peace, the public comfort or the public convenience." Restatement §821B(2)(a). Contamination of the food supply implicates health, safety, comfort and convenience, and certainly satisfies this permissive standard.

To state a private action for public nuisance, plaintiffs must also demonstrate that they have been harmed differently than the general public. Restatement §821C. The harm must be of a different type, not merely a difference in severity or imposing a disproportionate share of the burden on plaintiffs. Among the Restatement's specific examples are physical harm to chattels, §821C comment d, and pecuniary loss to businesses, §821C comment h. Both are present here.

The closest analogy and most pertinent discussion is in Burgess v. M/V Tamano, 370 F. Supp. 247, 250 (D. Me. 1973). There, commercial fisherman alleged that an oil spill harmed local waters and marine life. The court found that although fishing the waters was a right of the general public, it affected commercial fishermen differently because they depended on it for their livelihood. This was consistent with the general principle that pecuniary loss to the plaintiff will be regarded as different in kind 'where the plaintiff has an established business making commercial use of the public right with which the defendant interferes....'" Id., quoting Prosser, Law of Torts, §88 at 590 (4th ed. 1971). Here, plaintiffs are commercial corn farmers. While the general public has a right to safe food, plaintiffs depend on the integrity of the corn supply for their livelihood.

Defendants maintain that because plaintiffs purport to represent a group so numerous as a nationwide class of corn farmers, their damages cannot be considered special or unique. But *the special damages requirement does not limit the absolute number of parties affected so much as it restricts the types of harm that are compensable. Class actions and special damages are not mutually exclusive. Commercial corn farmers, as a group, are affected differently than the general public.*

CONCLUSION

For the foregoing reasons, defendants' motion to dismiss is granted with respect to the claims for conversion.... The motion is denied with respect to the claims for negligence *per se*, public nuisance, private nuisance.... The negligence and strict liability claims are dismissed to the extent they rely on a failure to warn, but may proceed under the theories outlined above.

10.2 Unintentional Torts

The unintentional torts include negligence, strict liability, products liability, and abnormally dangerous activities

Strict Liability

Strict liability, though quite rare and controversial in modern American tort law, may apply to biotechnologically created harms. In general, strict liability applies in very limited contexts, such as injuries caused by wild animals, abnormally dangerous activities, and defective products. The latter two may be relevant in the biotechnology context and are examined in turn.

Abnormally Dangerous Activities

Excerpt from, Symposium: *Biotechnology and the Law: Biotechnology's Challenge to the Law of Torts,"* 32 McGeorge L. Rev. 221 (Fall 2000).

Where a defendant is engaged in a so-called abnormally dangerous activity, she is strictly liable for harm she causes even absent proof of fault on her part. While there are many proffered explanations for this rule, an underlying justification is that there are certain undertakings that are so inherently dangerous that fairness dictates that those engaging in them should bear the costs of harms that ensue. Biotechnology-related harms arising from a defendant's activity may prove to be exactly the sort of undertaking that will be deemed abnormally dangerous, thereby leading to strict liability.

For strict liability to apply in the abnormally dangerous context, two factors are key: first, the activity must present a high level of unavoidable danger, and, second, the activity must not be a common one. Ironically, those who advocate most strongly for the exemption of biotechnologically created injuries from the tort system may ultimately be making the strongest case for strict liability in the abnormally dangerous activity context. For example, in their thoughtful article, Burk and Boczar repeatedly point out that no matter how well tested and despite the degree of care used, biotechnology may create harm. They note, for example, that "biotechnology products arise in the highly complex milieu of living organisms, where the interaction of hundreds of biochemical pathways lends an atmosphere of inherent unpredictability to the technology." Further, while the use of biotechnologically created products is increasing, it still is unlikely to be viewed as commonplace.

In fact, the modern development of strict liability arose in the context of competing land uses, situations where a plaintiff's land was injured due to activity by the defendant on the defendant's neighboring property. This is exactly the context in which biotechnological-based strict liability will most likely arise. For example, if a farmer planted a crop genetically designed to resist application of certain pesticides, and the crop spread to neighboring property, it could pass the pesticide resistance on to other plants, such as weeds, which could harm the neighbor's crops. The use of genetically engineered plants is one that involves an unavoidable risk of serious harm and it is not a common-place activity. Strict liability appears to be an appropriate theory in such a situation.

10.2.1 Wrongful Birth/Wrongful Life: Medical Malpractice

Shroeder v. Perkel
432 A.2d 834(1981)

Opinion by Pollock:

The sole issue on this appeal is the propriety of a grant of partial summary judgment to defendant physicians in a "wrongful conception" or "wrongful birth" action brought by the parents of a child with cystic fibrosis.

The parents allege that the negligent failure of defendants to diagnose cystic fibrosis, a hereditary disease, in their first child deprived the parents of an informed choice whether to have a second child. Consequently, the parents seek to recover the incremental medical costs associated with raising the second child who also suffers from cystic fibrosis. They claim that these costs are attributable directly to the negligence of the defendants.

The trial court denied defendants' motion for summary judgment, but the Appellate Division reversed. We granted certification, 84 *N.J.* 438 (1980). We reverse the judgment of the Appellate Division and remand the matter for trial.

Defendants, Dr. Perkel and his associate Dr. Venin, are pediatricians certified by the American Board of Pediatrics and licensed to practice medicine in this state. They treated infant plaintiff, Ann Schroeder, from May 1970 until September 1974. During that time, they failed to diagnose Ann's illness as cystic fibrosis, a genetically transferred disease. Because Mr. and Mrs. Schroeder, Ann's parents, were not told that they were carriers of cystic fibrosis, they claim that they were deprived of an informed choice of whether to assume the risk of a second child. Before they learned that Ann suffered from cystic fibrosis, Mrs.Schroeder became pregnant. One month after learning of Ann's affliction, Mrs. Schroeder gave birth to a second child, Thomas, who also suffers from cystic fibrosis.

Cystic fibrosis is one of the most common fatal genetic diseases in the United States and affects approximately one out of every 1,800 babies. An insidious and incurable disease, cystic fibrosis is carried by some parents as a recessive gene. There is no reasonably certain method of detecting whether a parent is a "carrier" of the disease, and parents may be carriers without knowing it. When both parents are carriers, they may anticipate that cystic fibrosis will affect their children according to the Mendelian ratio. The statistical probability that cystic fibrosis will affect the children is: 25% probability of a normal child, 50% probability of a carrier child, and 25% probability of an afflicted child.

In general, cystic fibrosis causes certain glands to malfunction and produce abnormally thick mucous. The most commonly affected body systems are the digestive tract and the respiratory system. In the digestive tract, mucous blocks ducts in the pancreas, preventing enzymes from reaching the intestines. One result is an inability to digest fats. Respiratory problems, however, are the most serious symptoms of cystic fibrosis. In the respiratory system, mucous clogs passages and causes air to become trapped in the lungs. Respiratory problems cause chronic pulmonary infection, emphysema and over 90% of all deaths of patients with cystic fibrosis. *Metabolic Basis of Inherited Disease* 1684 (4 ed. 1978).

Standard treatment of cystic fibrosis consists of antibiotics to control pulmonary infection and a restricted diet. Mucous is drained from the lungs by elevating the victim's feet above the head and clapping or gently pounding the back and chest. Hospital or institutional care frequently is not required except in emergencies or until the terminal stages of the illness.

In many respects, people afflicted with cystic fibrosis may lead normal lives. The prospects for one suffering from cystic fibrosis, however, are grim. Life expectancy is foreshortened, and death usually occurs in the late teen years.

Cystic fibrosis cannot be detected in a fetus. A safe, simple and highly reliable test, however, can be performed shortly after birth. Known as the "sweat test," it involves an analysis of perspiration, which contains an abnormally high concentration of salt in someone suffering from cystic fibrosis. A positive test indicates not only that both parents are carriers, but also the probabilities that future children of those parents will be afflicted with cystic fibrosis.

As an infant, Ann suffered from a digestive disorder diagnosed by Dr. Swiney, a general practitioner, as colic. When the symptoms persisted through her second year, Dr. Swiney referred Ann to the defendant physicians.

Dr. Venin diagnosed Ann's condition as a malabsorption syndrome resulting from an intolerance for fats. He prescribed a special diet low in starch and high in protein. The diet, which relieved her symptoms, is the same diet prescribed for persons suffering from cystic fibrosis. Dr. Venin did not deem the diagnosis final, however, and indicated that alternative diagnoses should be considered and eliminated. His notes from his initial interview with Ann show the entry "R.O. [meaning "rule out"] cystic fibrosis."

Dr. Venin did not perform a sweat test. Instead, he relied on a stool test performed by Dr. Swiney, and he assured Mr. and Mrs. Schroeder that the stool test ruled out cystic fibrosis. Nonetheless, Dr. Venin admits that the stool test is not the correct or preferred test to use in diagnosing cystic fibrosis. Between May 1970 and September 1974, Dr. Venin also treated Ann for respiratory complaints that he diagnosed as an allergic problem.

In June 1974, Mr. and Mrs. Schroeder read a newspaper article describing the symptoms of cystic fibrosis. Feeling that the article described Ann's condition, they asked Dr. Venin about the possibility of cystic fibrosis. According to Mrs. Schroeder, Dr. Venin told her in July 1974 that Ann "couldn't possibly have cystic fibrosis," an assertion disputed by Dr. Venin. Mrs. Schroeder stated that Dr. Venin informed her that the stool test performed by Dr. Swiney had eliminated the possibility of cystic fibrosis and that Ann definitely was not suffering from this disease.

When Ann's condition worsened in September 1974, Dr. Venin referred her to Dr. Grotsky, a specialist in digestive disorders. Dr. Grotsky performed the sweat test. The test established that Ann suffered from cystic fibrosis. Unfortunately, by that date Mrs. Schroeder was in the eighth month of her pregnancy with Thomas. The delay in the diagnosis had precluded Mr. and Mrs. Schroeder from making an informed choice as to whether or not to assume the risk of conceiving a second child with cystic fibrosis. The delay also had prevented them from making an informed choice whether Mrs. Schroeder should have an abortion.

On depositions, Mrs. Schroeder testified:

Q. If you had been made aware at an earlier time that Ann had cystic fibrosis, would you have become pregnant with Thomas? ...

A. No. I would not have....

Q. If you had been told that Ann had cystic fibrosis in late January or early February of 1974 would you have aborted the pregnancy?

A. Yes.

A consideration of the risk of cystic fibrosis for subsequent children led Mr. Schroeder to submit to a vasectomy even before the birth of Thomas. A sweat test performed on Thomas two weeks after his birth revealed that he, like his sister, was afflicted with cystic fibrosis.

Mr. and Mrs. Schroeder instituted this action on behalf of themselves and Ann and Thomas. In an amended complaint, they asserted four causes of action. In Count One, Mrs. Schroeder, as guardian ad litem of Ann, sought damages for pain and suffering caused by the allegedly negligent failure of defendants to diagnose that Ann suffered from cystic fibrosis. In Count Two, Mr. and Mrs. Schroeder asserted their own claim for the costs of past medical care for Ann. In Count Three, Mr. and Mrs. Schroeder sought damages in a "wrongful birth" action for the failure of defendants to advise them that Ann suffered from cystic fibrosis, thereby depriving Mr. and Mrs. Schroeder of the alternative of preventing the conception of Thomas. They sought damages not only for the incremental medical costs, but also for the mental anguish involved in caring for Thomas. In Count Four, Mrs. Schroeder, as guardian ad litem of Thomas, asserted a claim for his wrongful life. In that claim she sought damages for his pain and suffering resulting from his birth and life as a child afflicted with cystic fibrosis.

In determining the rights and duties of the parties, we must consider initially whether the defendant physicians owed a duty to Mr. and Mrs. Schroeder to diagnose Ann's affliction and to inform them that she suffered from cystic fibrosis. If that duty exists, we must then consider whether Mr. and Mrs. Schroeder have asserted facts establishing a breach of the duty. Finally, we shall consider whether Mr. and Mrs. Schroeder have asserted sufficient facts to establish that the breach of duty proximately caused the extraordinary medical expenses that they claim they will sustain in caring for Thomas.

Defendants contend that Ann was their patient and that their duty was to her, not her parents. In effect, they contend that they had no duty to Mr. and Mrs. Schroeder to advise them that their infant child was suffering from cystic fibrosis. The implication is that, if defendants had no duty to Mr. and Mrs. Schroeder, then defendants cannot be liable for depriving them of the decision not to have another child. Consequently, the defendants argue they cannot be liable for the expenses Mr. and Mrs. Schroeder will sustain in caring for Thomas. We disagree. The contention of the defendant physicians takes too myopic a view of the responsibilities of a physician treating a child with a genetically transferable disease such as cystic fibrosis. *See* Note, "Father and Mother Know Best: Defining the Liability of Physicians for Genetic Counseling," 87 *Yale L.J.* 1488, 1494 (1978).

The scope of duty in negligence, except as limited by policy considerations, is coextensive with the reasonable foreseeability of the consequences of a negligent act. *Portee v. Jaffee, supra*, 84 *N.J.* at 94–96 (emotional distress of mother from viewing suffering and death of child sufficiently foreseeable to impose liability on tortfeasor causing injury to child); *Trentacost* v. Brussel, 82 *N.J.* 214, 223 (1980) (mugging of tenant was foreseeable result of landlord's negligent failure to provide locks on apartment house entrance door); *Hill v. Yaskin*, 75 *N.J.* 139, 144–146 (1977) (foreseeability of theft of car left unlocked in high crime area and subsequent attempt by police to intercept thieves sufficient to impose liability on car owner for injuries sustained by police officer while apprehending thieves in stolen car).

The foreseeability of injury to members of a family other than one immediately injured by the wrongdoing of another must be viewed in light of the legal relationships among family members. A family is woven of the fibers of life; if one strand is damaged, the whole structure may suffer. The filaments of family life, although individually spun, create a web of interconnected legal interests. This Court has recognized that a wrongdoer who causes a direct injury to one member of the family may indirectly damage another. Consequently, husbands and wives have causes of action for loss of consortium when the other spouse is injured. *Ekalo v. Constructive Serv. Corp.*, 46 *N.J.* 82, 95 (1965) (recognition of claim by wife for loss of husband's consortium); *Nuzzi v. United States Cas. Co.*, 121 *N.J.L.* 249, 254 (E. & A. 1938) (husband has an action for loss of consortium of wife). Parents can recover for loss of companionship and advice in an action for the wrongful death of a minor child, *Green v. Bittner*, 85 *N.J.* 1, 4 (1980); an infant can recover against a tortfeasor for prenatal injuries suffered as a result of injuries to the mother in an automobile accident, *Smith v. Brennan*, 31 *N.J.* 353, 361 (1960). A parent has a cause of action for mental anguish resulting from viewing the suffering and death of a child caused by the negligence of a tortfeasor. *Portee v. Jaffee, supra*, 84 *N.J.* at 101. As a corollary to their duty to provide medical care for their children, parents can maintain an independent action to recover from a tortfeasor for medical expenses incurred for a child. *Friedrichsen v. Niemotka*, 71 *N.J. Super.* 398, 402 (Law Div.1962); *cf. Greenspan v. Slate*, 12 *N.J.* 426, 443 (1953) (parents under legal obligation to pay for necessary medical care provided to child in an emergency).

Foreseeability of harm to parents from an injury to a child flows not only from the bonds between parent and child, but also from the responsibility of parents to provide medical care for their children. In a theoretical sense, the primary obligation to pay for the medical expense incurred by a child may be that of the estate of the child. *Gleitman, supra*, 49 *N.J.* at 64 (Weintraub, C.J., dissenting in part). Generally, however, parents pay for the medical expenses of their children. Indeed, the willful failure of parents to provide "proper and sufficient" medical care for their child is a crime. In this case, we were informed at oral argument that Mr. and Mrs. Schroeder have borne and will continue to bear the expense of the medical treatment of Thomas. It would be unreasonable to compel parents to bear the expense of medical treatment required by a child and to allow the wrongdoer to go scot-free. In this context, a wrong should not go unrequited and an entire family left to suffer because of the dry technicality that Thomas has the primary obligation to pay for his own medical expenses. In addition, exoneration of the defendants would provide no deterrent to professional irresponsibility and would be contrary to the direction of our decisions in family torts.

A physician's duty thus may extend beyond the interests of a patient to members of the immediate family of the patient who may be adversely affected by a breach of that duty. Here, the physicians had not only a duty to Ann, but an independent duty to Mr. and Mrs. Schroeder to disclose to them that Ann suffered from cystic fibrosis. The wrong allegedly committed by defendants was the failure to disclose material information. The defendants should have foreseen that parents of childbearing years, such as Mr. and Mrs. Schroeder, would, in the absence of knowledge that Ann suffered from cystic fibrosis, conceive another child. They should have foreseen also that a second child could suffer from cystic fibrosis and that, if so afflicted, would sustain certain medical expenses. *See generally* Note, 87 *Yale L.J., supra,* at 1506–1508.

In his separate opinion, our colleague Justice Handler would extend the duty of the physicians to Thomas. (*Post* at 74–75). That is, Justice Handler would recognize in Thomas a cause of action for the diminution in the capacity of his parents to love and care for him. This Court, however, has declined to recognize claims for diminished parenthood and wrongful life. *Berman, supra,* 80 *N.J.* at 429; *id.* at 434 (Handler, J., concurring in part and dissenting in part). Furthermore, Mr. and Mrs. Schroeder do not assert any such claims on this appeal. Policy considerations suggest that we proceed judiciously in recognizing causes of action in one member of a family for direct injury to another member. Given the "sensitive and subtle judgments" involved (*post* at 76), we believe the more judicious course of action is not to pass upon a claim for diminished parenthood on this appeal.... Inherent in all the cases are sensitive issues concerning procreation and the right to prevent it by contraception or abortion. Those issues may affect judicial nerves differently with correspondingly different reactions. Another consideration that may affect courts in different ways is that the cause of action involves injury arising out of the conception and birth of a person not yet born. Also, courts may vary in their perception of the relationships and responsibilities of one family member to another. In brief, the problems of wrongful conception and wrongful birth involve an evaluation not only of law, but also of morals, medicine and society. Thus, it is not surprising that the same issue may elicit divergent judicial responses.... By limiting damages to those expenses that are actually attributable to the affliction, we are not conferring a windfall on Mr. and Mrs. Schroeder. Although they may derive pleasure from Thomas, that pleasure will be derived in spite of, rather than because of, his affliction. Mr. and Mrs. Schroeder will receive no compensating pleasure from incurring extraordinary medical expenses on behalf of Thomas. There is no joy in watching a child suffer and die from cystic fibrosis.... The medical expenses attributable to the cystic fibrosis of their son are part of Mr. and Mrs. Schroeder's loss caused by the deprivation of their right to choose whether to conceive a second child. If it is proved at trial that the defendant physicians deprived Mr. and Mrs. Schroeder of their right to choose whether or not to give birth to a child afflicted with cystic fibrosis, defendants should be liable for the incremental medical costs of a child born with that affliction. In the changing landscape of family torts our decision in this case merely advances the frontier a little farther....

SCHREIBER, J., dissenting.

The majority implicitly clings to the rule that there is no cause of action for "wrongful life," but its reasoning completely undercuts the rule's *raison d'etre*. It accepts the thesis that the infant has no cause of action based on whether he or she should not have been born. It accepts the public policy that the child's existence outweighs any discomfort the parents might endure in rearing and caring for the child. The consequence of adopting these propositions is that the parents can have no claim for medical expenses unless they are injured in their own right. Conversely, once the parents are held to have such a claim, it follows logically and conceptually that the child should be entitled to recover for its incapacity and the parents for the added costs in rearing the child....

HANDLER, J., concurring in part, dissenting in part.

The wrongful conduct of a physician, in contexts such as are present here, is a tort to the entire family. A doctor's wrongdoing, which directly leads to the otherwise avoidable conception and birth of a gravely congenitally handicapped infant, can be considered no less than a wrong to all who comprise the family unit. The Court itself recognizes that concept in this case, *viz*:

> A family is woven of the fibers of life; if one strand is damaged, the whole structure may suffer. The filaments of family life, although individually spun, create a web of interconnected legal interests. This Court has recognized that a wrongdoer who causes a direct injury to one member of the family may indirectly damage another....

A physician's duty thus may extend beyond the interests of a patient to members of the immediate family of the patient who may be adversely affected by a breach of that duty.... I believe that what I am urging as a cognizable cause of action on behalf of the hapless child in this situation is not inconsistent with the philosophy of the Court expressed in the case it decides today. The familial nature of the tort is acknowledged. We have given voice to the common understanding that the physician's professional duty and responsibility, in treating a patient in matters involving procreation, pregnancy and childbirth, extend to that person not simply as an individual but as a member of a family whose entire welfare is bound up in the patient's health and well-being.

Reed v. Campagnolo
630 A.2d 1145 (Md 1993)

The certified questions are:

"I. Whether the State of Maryland recognizes a tort cause of action for wrongful birth when the doctor does not inform the patient about an available diagnostic test which might reveal the possibility of neural tube defects of the fetus, when these defects are genetically caused, when further diagnostic testing would be required to determine the nature and extent of any fetal defects, and when the plaintiff asserts she would have aborted the child had she been made aware of the fetus's deformities.

"ii. Whether the continuation of a pregnancy is a decision requiring the informed consent of the patient which can give rise to a Maryland tort cause of action for lack of informed consent when the allegedly negligent course of treatment is the defendant physician's failure to inform a pregnant patient about the availability, risks and benefits of diagnostic testing which might reveal birth defects, and failure to inform the patient about the benefits and risks associated with aborting a severely deformed fetus."

Reed v. Campagnolo, 810 F.Supp. 167, 172–73 (D. Md.1993)....

Plaintiffs, Tina Smedley Reed and Frederick E. Reed, seek damages against defendants, Mary Campagnolo, M.D. and Bruce Grund, M.D. Defendants rendered prenatal care to Mrs. Reed and her unborn child at a Caroline County Health Department maternity clinic beginning in January 1986, the third month of Mrs. Reed's pregnancy ...

The essence of the Reeds' allegations are

> "that defendants failed in the course of pre-natal care to 'inform plaintiffs of the existence or need for routine [a-fetoprotein] ("AFP") testing of maternal

serum to detect serious birth defects such as spina bifida and imperforate anus.'
Had they been informed about AFP testing they would have requested it. Had
such testing been done, it would have revealed elevated protein levels, indicative of an abnormal fetus, which would have led plaintiffs to request amniocentesis. Amniocentesis, claim plaintiffs, would have revealed the extent of the
fetus's defects and plaintiffs ultimately would have chosen to terminate the
pregnancy."

Reed, 810 F.Supp. at 169 (references to complaint omitted).

"The parties agree Mrs. Reed was never informed about AFP testing, a procedure which reveals abnormal levels of [*230] proteins produced by the fetus.
Abnormal protein levels may indicate genetically caused neural tube defects,
including spina bifida. This test must be performed between weeks 16 and 18
of the pregnancy to obtain reliable results."

Id. (footnotes omitted).

"The [Reeds'] child, Ashley Nicole, suffers from a variety of genetically caused
abnormalities, including meningomyelocele (spina bifida), hydrocephaly, imperforate anus, and ambiguous genitalia. The infant also has only one kidney, a
fistula connecting her bladder and intestines, and increased head circumfer-
ence, which required the insertion of a cerebral-abdominal shunt after
birth." ...

The issue presented by the first certified question is whether the claim is simply a traditional negligence claim, as the Reeds contend, or whether the claim fails to withstand
traditional tort analysis, as the defendants contend. If the latter, then the defendants
submit that this Court should not recognize it as a new tort, but rather should defer to
the General Assembly.... Simply put, have we here a duty, a breach of that duty, and an
injury proximately caused by the breach?

There is no dispute that the defendant physicians owed a duty of care to Mrs. Reed....
Subsidiary to the concept of duty is whether, under the particular circumstances of the
instant matter, the standard of care was violated. The defendant physicians contend that
it was not, but that is a matter of proof that is not before us on these certified questions.
If the applicable standard of care required that the AFP and amniocentesis tests be offered or performed, that standard was violated, because it is undisputed that the tests
were not offered or performed.

If the standard of care contended for by the Reeds had been fulfilled by the defendant
physicians, and if Mrs. Reed had determined to terminate the pregnancy by abortion
because of genetic defects revealed by the tests, then the defendants', or any successor or
consulting physicians', common law duty of care to the unborn child would have been
overridden by the former Maryland abortion statute. n2 At the time of the negligence
alleged here, that statute provided in relevant part:

"A physician licensed by the State of Maryland may terminate a human pregnancy or aid or assist or attempt a termination of a human pregnancy if said
termination takes place in a hospital accredited by the Joint Commission for
Accreditation of Hospitals and licensed by the State Board of Health and Mental Hygiene and if one or more of the following conditions exist:

....“(3) There is substantial risk of the birth of the child with grave and permanent physical deformity or mental retardation...."

Md.Code (1982, 1990 Repl.Vol.), §§ 20–208(a) of the Health-General Article (HG). n3....

The links in the chain of causation alleged by the Reeds, if supported by the evidence and believed by the trier of fact, constitute proximate cause. The first link in that chain, the alleged failure of the defendants to advise concerning the availability in the medical community of AFP testing and its purpose, connected to the next link, requiring a fact-finding that the testing would have been done, and so forth, through to abortion, present a form of proximate cause reasoning that is analogous to that applied in informed consent cases. *See Sard v. Hardy*, 281 Md. 432, 450–51, 379 A.2d 1014, 1024–25 (1977). Plaintiffs in these cases must prove causation in the sense that they must convince the fact finder that they would in fact have acted as alleged, had the information concerning testing been made available. n4 In the instant matter the Reeds have alleged this causal nexus....

We now consider legal injury. The clear majority of courts that has considered the type of medical malpractice case alleged by the Reeds has concluded that there is legally cognizable injury, proximately caused by a breach of duty.... The defendants' basic argument is that the Reeds have not suffered any legally cognizable injury. The argument adopts the analysis of the majority of the Supreme Court of North Carolina in its four-three decision in *Azzolino v. Dingfelder*, 377 S.E.2d 528. That court said:

"Courts which purport to analyze wrongful birth claims in terms of 'traditional' tort analysis are able to proceed to this point [*i.e.*, injury] but no further before their 'traditional' analysis leaves all tradition behind or begins to break down. In order to allow recovery such courts must then take a step into *entirely untraditional analysis* by holding that the existence of a human life can constitute an injury cognizable at law. Far from being 'traditional' tort analysis, such a step requires a view of human life previously unknown to the law of this jurisdiction. We are unwilling to take any such step because we are unwilling to say that life, even life with severe defects, may ever amount to a legal injury.".... Thus, those courts that recognize the cause of action alleged by the Reeds permit, at a minimum, damages measured by the extraordinary cost, at least through minority, of supporting the child with severe birth defects as compared to supporting a child who is not so afflicted.... The defendant physicians also suggest that they cannot be liable because they have not caused the impairments suffered by Ashley Nicole. This argument espouses the view advanced by the dissenting judge of the New York Court of Appeals in *Becker v. Schwartz*, 413 N.Y.S.2d at 904, 386 N.E.2d at 816:

> "The heart of the problem in these cases is that the physician cannot be said to have caused the defect. The disorder is genetic and not the result of any injury negligently inflicted by the doctor. In addition it is incurable and was incurable from the moment of conception. Thus the doctor's alleged negligent failure to detect it during prenatal examination cannot be considered a cause of the condition by analogy to those cases in which the doctor has failed to make a timely diagnosis of a curable disease. The child's handicap is an inexorable result of conception and birth.".... We do not agree, because this argument takes too narrow a view of proximate or legal cause. Under Restatement (Second) of Torts §§431 (1965), an actor's negligent conduct is a legal cause if it is "a substantial factor" and if no rule of law relieves the actor from liability because of the manner in which the negligence resulted in harm. Even though the physical forces producing Ashley Nicole's birth defects were already in operation at the time of the alleged negligence of the physicians, under the chain of causation alleged by the Reeds the physicians could have prevented the harm to the parents. Those allegations, if proved, would present sufficient evidence from which the trier of fact could find that the alleged negligence of the physicians

was a substantial factor in the legal harm to the parents. *See* Restatement (Second) of Torts §§ 302, comment c.

In argument before this Court, counsel for the defendants also presented an "over utilization" argument. The submission is that, faced with the possibility of liability in these cases, physicians will order tests for which there is no medical justification, and that this form of defensive medicine will become so widespread that it would create the appearance of the standard of care. Obviously, whether the defendants should have offered or recommended certain tests to Mrs. Reed is a matter for proof at trial. Further, although we acknowledge a general public interest in medical cost containment, that public interest, as currently manifested in cost containment legislation, is not a prohibition against legally recognized medical malpractice actions.

For the foregoing reasons, the answer to the first certified question is that Maryland does recognize the tort cause of action therein described....

The second certified question is directed to that count of the Reeds' complaint which casts their allegations in the mold of a lack of informed consent action. The Reeds, emphasizing that they were not told by the defendants about AFP and amniocentesis tests, say that they lacked informed consent. But one's informed consent must be to some treatment. Here, the defendants never proposed that the tests be done. Whether the defendants had a duty to offer or recommend the tests is analyzed in relation to the professional standard of care. Application of that standard may or may not produce a result identical with the informed consent criterion of what reasonable persons, in the same circumstances as the Reeds, would want to know ... facts in *Pratt v. University of Minn. Affiliated Hosps. & Clinics*, 414 N.W.2d 399 (Minn. 1987). There parents sought genetic testing because the third of their three children suffered from multiple, congenital abnormalities. The defendants non-negligently advised the parents "that their chance[s] of conceiving another child with birth defects were about the same as parents in general." 414 N.W.2d at 400. Thereafter the plaintiffs had their fourth child who also suffered from birth defects. It was held that there was no liability on a theory of negligent nondisclosure for failure to advise of alternate possible causes of the third child's anomalies so that the parents "could make an informed decision on whether to conceive another child."

To support their informed consent argument, the Reeds submit:

"Defendants fail to recognize that there was indeed something for the Reeds to consent to, *i.e.*, forgoing maternal serum AFP testing, amniocentesis, and an elective abortion in the face of knowledge (which would have been acquired through those tests) that the fetus was severely impaired and would be born, if at all, with serious birth defects."…. One commentator well stated the overview:

"Counseling about genetic risks in reproduction has traditionally occurred after the birth of a family's first child with a genetic disorder. Increasingly, however, reproductive counseling involves predictive 'diagnosis' based upon risk factors, rather than upon the appearance of a genetically impaired child in the family. The development of more sophisticated biochemical and cytogenetic tests for assaying amniotic fluid and maternal and fetal blood has also significantly enhanced the importance of the reproductive counseling aspect of medical genetics. As is true for other kinds of diagnosis, the process of reproductive counseling is strewn with opportunities for missteps. First, there is the need to possess and employ expert knowledge, a matter that would be determined according to professional standards. The physician must understand enough about the patient's apparent condition to obtain proper clinical and laboratory tests and to gather relevant facts through a medical, and perhaps a family, history. It is as necessary to discern the correct tests as to perform them properly. Moreover, small differences in diagnostic results may be crucial in determining the medical condition involved and in recognizing whether it is classified as a 'genetic disorder.'"

A.M. Capron, *Tort Liability in Genetic Counseling*, 79 Colum.L.Rev. 618, 626 (1979) (footnotes omitted).

For the foregoing reasons, our answer to the second question is in the negative.

————————

From Jeri E. Reutenaue, Note: *Medical Malpractice Liability in the Era of Genetic Susceptiblity Testing*, 19 Quinnipiac L. Rev. 539 (2000).

III. The Development of Genetic Malpractice Through Wrongful Birth and Wrongful Life Litigation

A cause of action for medical malpractice derives from tort law. The law of torts creates a new cause of action "whenever it becomes clear that the plaintiff's interests are entitled to legal protection against the conduct of the defendant." This Note adopts the term "genetic malpractice," which has been proposed previously as the nomenclature for a medical malpractice suit in which the claim is based on a genetic condition. In general, the traditional medical malpractice principles for negligence analysis have been applied in suits alleging genetic malpractice, such as wrongful birth and wrongful life.

In a suit alleging genetic malpractice, a plaintiff must satisfy the four elements of negligence in order to prevail. First, the plaintiff must show that the physician owed a duty to him or her. Whether a duty is owed in a particular situation "is a question of whether the defendant is under any obligation for the benefit of the particular plaintiff." In order to prove that the defendant owes the plaintiff a legal duty, the plaintiff must demonstrate that, as a matter of public policy, a duty should exist. "The problem of duty is ... [that] ... no universal test for it has ever been formulated.... As our ideas of human relations change the law as to duties changes with them.... Changing social conditions lead constantly to the recognition of new duties." The universal rule is that a physician has a duty to use reasonable skill and care in the diagnosis and treatment of his or her patients.

Next, the plaintiff must demonstrate that the physician failed to conform to the standard required and, therefore, breached his or her duty. Today the typical standard applied in measuring the reasonableness of the physician's skill and care is the average standard within the profession. The standard of care in malpractice actions is generally measured by a national standard. Under this standard of care, "[a] physician who undertakes a mode or form of treatment which a reasonable and prudent member of the medical profession would undertake under the same or similar circumstances shall not be subject to liability for harm caused thereby to the patient."

It is important to note that the standard of care in the medical profession, including the field of genetic diagnostics, is continually evolving. As the technology advances, the medical community becomes aware of these new developments, and as the new methods are employed in practice, the standard of care changes. Once a large number of physicians adopt a test, its use becomes the standard of care, and then failure to test may give rise to liability. Under this developing standard, "advances in the profession, availability of facilities, specialization or general practice, proximity of specialists and special facilities, together with all other relevant considerations, are to be taken into account." Therefore, it is possible that a court may hold a physician liable for genetic malpractice based on his or her failure to inform a patient of the availability of genetic counseling services if that failure did not conform to the established standard of care.

In order to satisfy the third element of negligence, the plaintiff must show that the physician's acts or omissions proximately caused the injury. There must be a "reasonably close causal connection between the conduct and the resulting injury." In most genetic malpractice actions, the plaintiff asserts that the physician negligently failed to detect or disclose the genetic risks preceding the eventual manifestation of the genetic disorder. For example, in a typical wrongful birth suit, the plaintiff must show that the physician's acts or omissions proximately caused the "defective" child to be born. In general, the parents are required to show that they would not have had the child if they had known of the foreseeable genetic risks. The parents must prove this by clear and convincing evidence, thus providing a potential safeguard against false claims.

Establishing proximate cause in a genetic malpractice case in which genetic susceptibility testing was not discussed or offered might be more problematic. Although individuals who have a genetic susceptibility to a particular disorder face an increased risk of developing that specific disorder, a positive test result does not guarantee that they will develop that disorder. This uncertainty could hinder the plaintiff in meeting the burden of proof because it would be difficult to show that the physician proximately caused an injury.

According to section 431 of the Restatement (Second) of Torts, however, an actor's negligent conduct is a legal cause if it is a "substantial factor" in causing the injury and if no rule of law relieves the actor from liability because of the manner in which the negligence resulted in harm. Applying this type of reasoning, courts have upheld liability for a missed diagnosis in other areas of medicine, even though the healthcare provider did not cause the ailment. For example, in Ferrell v. Rosenbaum, the mother of a young child brought a suit for medical malpractice against both her child's geneticist and the medical center. In the complaint, the plaintiff alleged that the geneticist failed to diagnose her child with Fanconi's anemia while the plaintiff and her husband were still together and could have conceived another child, who may have been a compatible bone marrow donor. Therefore, the plaintiff argued that the geneticist proximately caused the loss of her child's best opportunity for transplant from the potential sibling donor.

In this case, the court applied a two-prong test to determine whether there was proximate causation, specifically addressing whether the defendants' negligence caused the loss of opportunity for the best treatment. The first prong of the court's analysis was to determine the plaintiff's chance of survival if properly diagnosed and treated, and the second prong was to ascertain the extent to which the defendants' negligence reduced this chance. Based on this inquiry, the court held that the plaintiff had sufficiently demonstrated that the alleged negligence was a substantial factor in the loss of her child's best chance of survival. Thus, whether the plaintiff can prove, by a preponderance of the evidence, that the asserted negligence was a "substantial factor" in causing the injury may be a test for proximate causation.

Similarly, some courts have viewed causation in medical malpractice cases in terms of "lost chance" or "loss of chance." "Loss of chance" refers to "injury sustained by the plaintiff whose medical providers are alleged to have negligently deprived the plaintiff of a chance to survive or recover from a health problem, or where the malpractice has lessened the effectiveness of treatment or increased the risk of an unfavorable outcome to the plaintiff." The court in Holton v. Memorial Hospital applied the lost chance doctrine. In that case, the court explained that the plaintiff may present evidence that the defendant's act or omission, to a reasonable degree of certainty, proximately caused the risk of harm or lost chance of recovery, if that negligent act or omission lessened a plaintiff's chance of survival.

Finally, the fourth element the plaintiff must demonstrate in order to bring a medical malpractice claim is that he or she was in fact injured. "The threat of future harm, not yet realized, is not enough." Despite this requirement, plaintiffs have pled a broad range of compensable injuries in genetic malpractice suits. For instance, courts have awarded damages for the pain and suffering of the child affected with a genetic disorder, as well as damages for the emotional stress and mental anguish suffered by the parents of that child.

The courts first addressed the legal issues involved in the dissemination of genetic information in cases of wrongful birth and wrongful life. Various courts have held that physicians have a duty to disclose information to prospective parents regarding the genetic risks to their potential offspring and a duty to disclose diagnostic procedures that are available to ascertain those risks. This information would provide the parents with the option to decide to refrain from conceiving or to abort a fetus with a serious disorder.

A. Wrongful Birth

"Wrongful birth" refers to a claim brought by parents who allege that they would have avoided conception or terminated the pregnancy by abortion but for the negligence of those charged with prenatal testing or counseling the parents regarding the likelihood of giving birth to a physically or mentally impaired child. These claims often arise when physicians fail to warn prospective parents that they are at risk of giving birth to a child with a genetic disorder. The first cases of wrongful birth found the courts reluctant to recognize it as a cause of action. In contrast to the situation in traditional malpractice cases, this reluctance resulted from the fact that nothing that the physician could have done would have prevented the harm to the child. Early case law that dealt with wrongful birth actions held that the failure to warn parents of the risk of a serious defect to their offspring was not actionable because the physician was not the proximate cause of the defect.

In addition, courts were hesitant to recognize a cause of action for wrongful birth because, at that time, abortion was illegal. However, under Roe v. Wade, which legalized abortions performed during the first two-trimesters of a pregnancy, this reasoning is no longer valid. Referring to the decision in Roe v. Wade, one court explained that failure to recognize a cause of action for wrongful birth "could impermissibly burden the constitutional rights involved in conception, procreation, and other familial decisions."

Today a majority of jurisdictions recognize wrongful birth suits. Only a handful of states has refused to recognize this cause of action. A claim for wrongful birth may be brought when a physician fails to warn prospective parents that they are at risk of conceiving or giving birth to a child with a serious genetic disorder. Potential liability includes instances when a reasonable physician should have known of the risk because the couple's previous child was born with a genetic disorder or because of the woman's advanced maternal age. Liability can also arise when the physician fails to advise prospective parents of known risks because one or both parents are of a particular ethnic or racial descent. Moreover, liability may exist when a physician fails to discuss the availability of genetic services. Finally, it is possible for courts to hold a physician liable for failing to inform a couple about the availability of carrier testing or prenatal diagnosis or failing to offer such testing.

Some courts have explained that public policy supports wrongful birth suits by upholding the proposition that parents should not be denied the opportunity to terminate a pregnancy. One court even stated that refusal to recognize wrongful birth actions would insulate from liability those persons who fail to provide proper care to persons who would otherwise choose to exercise their constitutional right to abort a fetus that, if born, would suffer from serious genetic (or other) problems. Another court explained that recognizing a cause of action for wrongful birth might even encourage the proper performance and interpretation of genetic testing.

B. Wrongful Life

In contrast to a wrongful birth claim, a wrongful life claim is one "brought on behalf of a severely defective infant, against a physician, … contending that the physician negligently failed to inform the child's parents of the possibility of their bearing a severely defective child, thereby preventing parental choice to avoid the child's birth." In an action for wrongful life, the child does not allege that the defendant's negligence caused his impaired condition, but instead that the defendant's negligence resulted in birth in an impaired condition.

Wrongful life suits are not recognized in most jurisdictions. The debate surrounding this action is based on the nature of the claim, namely, the allegation that one would be better off not existing than existing in an impaired state. Courts have found it contrary to public policy to hold that, as a matter of law, nonexistence is preferable to an "impaired life" when both our society and our legal system seem to place the highest value on human life. In Gleitman v. Cosgrove, the court rejected the wrongful life claim, protesting that it could not "weigh the value of life with impairments against the nonexistence of life itself." The cause of action requires a calculation of damages dependent upon the relative benefits of an impaired life as opposed to no life at all, "[a] comparison the law is not equipped to make."

There are a few states, however, that have recognized a cause of action for wrongful life. In Turpin v. Sortini, the plaintiffs had consulted a speech and hearing specialist regarding a suspected hearing deficiency in their two-year-old daughter. After being assured that their child's hearing was within normal range, when in fact she was totally deaf, the plaintiffs conceived a second child, who was born with the same hereditary total deafness. The plaintiffs then brought suit against the physician and the hospital on behalf of their child seeking damages for the defendants' failure to advise them of the possibility of hereditary deafness, thereby depriving them of the opportunity to choose not to conceive the child.

In Turpin, the Supreme Court of California upheld the claim for wrongful life. The court qualified its decision, however, by explaining that although the child could not recover general damages for being born impaired as opposed to not being born at all, she could recover special damages for the extraordinary expenses necessary to treat her hereditary ailment. The Turpin court held that an award of general damages would be unjustified, stating that it is "inconsistent with basic tort principles to view the injury for which defendants are legally responsible solely by reference to plaintiff's present condition without taking into consideration the fact that if defendants had not been negligent she would not have been born at all."

The Supreme Court of Washington, in Harbeson v. Parke-Davis, Inc., also upheld a claim for wrongful life, finding liability for the failure of a physician to inform an epileptic mother of the potential effects that medication could have on her fetus. The court found that although general damages are impossible to calculate with reasonable certainty, special damages for the extraordinary expenses of medical care could be proved. Similarly, in Procanik v. Cillo, the Supreme Court of New Jersey also upheld a wrongful life claim. In that case, the court found that the infant plaintiff could seek to recover special damages for extraordinary medical expenses attributable to congenital rubella syndrome with which he was born, but could not seek to recover general damages for an impaired childhood.

In all of these cases, the supreme courts of California, New Jersey, and Washington permitted children to pursue wrongful life actions limited to the recovery of special damages attributable to the extraordinary medical expenses expected to be incurred during the child's lifetime.

IV. Liability for Failure to Advise of Genetic Risks and Failure to Offer Genetic Susceptibility or Presymptomatic Testing for Adult Diseases

Until recently, most genetic risk assessments have occurred in the setting of genetic testing for carrier status and prenatal diagnosis. Typically, physicians have been presented with two healthy individuals who are at risk of having a child with a single-gene disorder or a chromosomal abnormality. Newly developing genetic technologies do not specifically offer information about future risks to one's offspring, but instead reveal information about one's own future health risks. These tests allow individuals to discover if they are susceptible to developing a specific disorder.

At the present time, genetic susceptibility testing can determine if someone is at an increased risk for breast or colon cancer, and presymptomatic testing is available for Huntington's Disease. Eventually, it may be possible for every individual to learn of the illnesses he or she may develop in the future. The benefits these individuals can derive from this knowledge includes early utilization of screening and treatment programs in order to reduce the chance of mortality of such illnesses and enhanced preparation, both emotionally and financially, for these potential health problems.

As the capability of genetic testing expands, the duty to inform individuals of the existence of the genetic risks and the availability of services will affect physicians and healthcare providers in all fields of medicine. Questions regarding when the duty to inform individuals of possible genetic risks should be imposed on physicians and other healthcare providers will arise from genetic susceptibility testing. To date, most of the legal precedent has established physician liability for failure to inform patients about the risk of serious genetic disorders that may affect a child. However, with continuing advances in genetic testing, particularly in the area of presymptomatic testing for adult-onset disorders and genetic susceptibility testing, courts will confront issues regarding whether healthcare providers are liable for failure to advise of genetic risks and failure to offer testing. The advances in genetic testing technology thus present a number of questions that must be addressed to determine whether or not the healthcare provider should be held liable.

A. When Is the Risk Sufficient to Discuss and Offer Testing?

The first consideration in resolving whether the risk is sufficient for physicians to discuss and offer testing is to determine and define the appropriate persons. In accomplishing this, a standard of care consisting of the requisite criteria for testing should be established. The appropriate standard, as seen by the court in Munro v. Regents of the University of California, acknowledged the requirement that a patient must be in a sufficiently high risk group in order for a physician to have a duty to offer a particular genetic test.

In that case, the plaintiffs consulted a physician for genetic counseling when the wife became pregnant with the couple's second child. The physician took the plaintiffs' family history and asked about their ethnic background. Mrs. Munro had stated that her father's background was "primarily German" and that her mother's background was English and Canadian. She also informed the physician that her husband's heritage was Scottish, Norwegian, and "some peculiar kind of French." Based on the family history information that Mrs. Munro provided, the physician did not recommend genetic testing for Tay-Sachs disease because the incidence is extremely low, except among people of Ashkenazi (Eastern European) Jewish ancestry.

Several months after Mrs. Munro gave birth, the baby was diagnosed with Tay-Sachs disease. Subsequently, the plaintiffs brought an action against both the physician and the university hospital for medical malpractice based on the physician's failure to test the parents for Tay-Sachs disease. The plaintiffs claimed that they sought the services of the defendants for the purpose of diagnosing and treating any genetic fetal abnormality. The plaintiffs argued that the physician should have informed them that they were excluded from Tay-Sachs testing because they were not Jewish, asserting that they would have undergone the testing if the physician had offered it. The plaintiffs' contention was that the "defendants had a duty to disclose material information to enable [them] to make an informed decision whether to take the Tay-Sachs test."

The defense presented expert evidence to support its assertion that "since it is medically impossible to screen all patients for all genetic abnormalities, the standard of care requires that specific screening tests be performed only on those patients who meet specific profile characteristics that warrant such tests." The court of appeals affirmed the superior court's decision, holding that summary judgment was properly awarded to the defendants on the issue of medical malpractice because the plaintiffs failed to present expert evidence that genetic testing for Tay-Sachs disease was indicated.

Taking a narrow view regarding the disclosure duties of physicians, the court expressed that there is "no duty to disclose where no diagnostic testing or treatment is recommended." This decision seems to establish a bright-line rule when there is a question regarding whether a physician has a duty to disclose. The standard of care, however, continues to determine the requisite criteria for recommending testing or treatment. Furthermore, this decision seems to contradict the decisions of prior courts, which have held, in cases of wrongful birth, that physicians have a duty to advise patients of the availability of genetic tests.

A less drastic standard, which may resolve the contradictory decisions in wrongful birth cases, can be found in the concurring opinion in the Munro case. This standard provides a more subjective rule stating that the "scope of the physician's duty to disclose is measured by the amount of knowledge a patient needs in order to make an informed choice." Based on this type of facts-and-circumstances test, the court would need to determine the necessary amount of information a particular patient required in order to make an informed decision. Therefore, a physician's duty would vary with the amount of knowledge required by each patient.

B. How Accurate and Predictive Must the Genetic Testing Be?

The quality of data which can be gleaned from the currently available genetic testing is another factor taken into account in determining whether it is appropriate to hold a physician or other healthcare professional liable for failing to provide information about the genetic risks. In the initial wrongful birth and wrongful life cases, the available genetic testing could assess, with a high degree of certainty, whether a particular disorder affected the fetus. Some of the latest genetic tests, however, do not have the same accuracy and predictive ability as many of the definitive tests used in carrier testing or prenatal diagnosis. Optimally, genetic testing should be both precise and accurate. However, with the current level of genetic understanding and capability, absolute precision and accuracy in testing is not possible with genetic susceptibility testing.

For example, the accuracy of the genetic susceptibility testing may vary depending on the testing process or the technique used. As researchers have learned more about the human genome, they have found that a variety of mutations, in one gene or several genes, can each cause the same disorder or predisposition for a disorder. As an example to illustrate this point, in testing for breast cancer susceptibility there are hundreds of different possible mutations on at least two different genes. Therefore, based on the present level of knowledge, full gene sequencing is likely to be much more accurate than only testing for the presence of a specific mutation or mutations when testing for genetic susceptibility to developing breast cancer.

Further considerations include whether the testing is sufficiently predictive of the disease, and, in the case of a positive test result, whether there are options for screening or prevention. With susceptibility testing, patients will want to know what their individual chances are of developing the specific disease and by what age it may develop. Although researchers are frantically trying to ascertain precise risk figures for some of the presently identified susceptibility genes, the exact predictive value of a positive test result may not be known. Therefore, it is important that information ascertained by genetic susceptibility testing "be interpreted with caution if it is to serve as a basis for [medical] action."

Researchers assert that interpreting the results of genetic susceptibility testing for breast cancer can be very difficult, because the specific risk associated with each mutation is unknown. Also, because there are no proven preventive or management strategies, physicians may not know what follow-up testing to recommend. Although increased surveillance, including frequent mammograms, is possible, studies have not proven its effectiveness in women less than fifty years of age. In addition, some women may decide to have their healthy breasts or ovaries surgically removed as a preventive measure. Despite these preventive actions, there can be no assurance that all tissue has been removed, and thus the residual risk of developing cancer remains uncertain. Further complicating this matter is the fact that individuals tend to have unrealistic expectations about the accuracy and certainty of genetic information.

E. Does the Physician Have a Duty to Warn Third Parties?

A somewhat controversial issue that courts may encounter is whether a physician has a duty to warn a third party that he or she may be at risk for a genetic disease because a relative had a positive test result. In this scenario, a woman who develops breast cancer may attempt to sue her sister's physician for failing to warn her that she might have a significantly increased risk for breast cancer due to a genetic susceptibility gene that had been previously identified in her sister. Should the doctor be held liable for this woman who was never his or her patient? Since the inception of genetic susceptibility testing, cases, such as the one presented by this hypothetical, are likely to arise in courtrooms throughout the country.

The duty of a physician to warn the relatives of one of his or her patients of the presence of genetic risk has not been extensively addressed in the law. Only a few cases have dealt with this issue directly. Most cases confronting third party liability address the general duty to disclose information, including medical information.

The leading case regarding a duty to disclose information to third parties is Tarasoff v. Regents of the University of California. This California case has had a significant impact on many other jurisdictions regarding the duty of disclosure. The facts of this case are as follows. In October 1969, Prosenjit Poddar killed his girlfriend, Tatiana Tarasoff. Although Poddar had confided in Dr. Moore, his psychologist employed by a University of California hospital, of his intent to kill Tarasoff two months prior to her death, Dr. Moore did not warn Tarasoff of the potential risk to her life. As a result, Tarasoff's parents brought a malpractice suit against the physician, the hospital and the university, claiming that the defendants were liable because of their failure to warn Tarasoff of the impending danger and failure to confine Poddar.

Discussing the defendants' duty, the California Supreme Court explained that although one person has no duty to control the conduct of another or to warn those endangered by such conduct, an exception exists if the defendant stands in some special relationship either with the person whose conduct needs to be controlled or with the foreseeable victim of that conduct. Applying the exception, the court held that Moore did have a duty to warn Tarasoff of the potential impending danger. The court noted that a relationship of the defendant-therapist to either Tarasoff or Poddar sufficed to establish a duty of care. In its decision, the court relied on section 315 of the Restatement (Second) of Torts, which provides that a duty of care may arise from either "(a) a special relation ... between the actor and the third person which imposes a duty upon the actor to control the third person's conduct, or (b) a special relation ... between the actor and the other which gives to the other a right of protection."

Subsequent to the Tarasoff case, the legal duty to disclose genetic information to third parties began to evolve. As genetic research has increased our knowledge in the detection of future medical risks, the legal system has encountered the next generation of failure to warn cases. Three recent cases, specifically dealing with genetic information, have each recognized a duty of disclosure to relatives.

Schroeder v. Perkel appears to be the first genetic disclosure case. In that case, the parents of two children born with cystic fibrosis brought an action on behalf of themselves and their children against the pediatricians who treated their first-born child and allegedly failed to diagnose the condition in time for the parents to prevent or abort the second pregnancy. Although the trial court denied the defendants' motion for summary judgment, the appellate court reversed the decision of the trial court and the Supreme Court of New Jersey then granted review. In its decision, the Supreme Court of New Jersey held that the physicians not only had a duty to the first born child, but also had an independent duty to the parents to disclose that the child suffered from cystic fibrosis. The court further explained that the physician's failure to diagnosis cystic fibrosis and to advise the parents that their child suffered from such a disease was a breach of the physician's duty to disclose material information to the parents.

The pediatricians argued that they owed no duty to the plaintiffs because there was no doctor-patient relationship between themselves and the plaintiffs, but the court rejected the argument as a "myopic" view of the pediatricians' responsibilities. It observed that "the scope of duty in negligence, except as limited by policy considerations, is coextensive with the reasonable foreseeability of the consequences of a negligent act." The case was then remanded for trial.

VII. Conclusion

Holding healthcare professionals liable for not advising their patients about genetic risks may ensure that some genetic information is conveyed. However, physicians and other healthcare professionals should not be bound by fears of frivolous lawsuits. Courts will provide relief to a plaintiff only when the physician failed to utilize the appropriate medical practices, in cases in which the physician was negligent.

Clearly the courts should not shape what is proper or improper medical care; physicians have established, and should continue to establish, the standard of care in medicine. But the courts retain the responsibility for determining what level of care is applied in each case, determining whether it is a national standard or local community standard, and determining whether it is based on a medical specialty or that of a general practitioner.

The manner in which a court determines what standard of care to apply in each case should involve a thorough analysis of the various issues presented in this Note. It is imperative for courts to take careful consideration of all of these issues before setting the standard of care and establishing whether the healthcare provider has a duty. Despite the rapid advances in genetic technology, courts must be cautious when they hold physicians liable for negligence based on a failure to warn of genetic risks. Legislation regarding medical practice guidelines will foster the courts' ability to set the standard of care and assist in determining whether a physician was negligent.

Most importantly, the medical community must strive to maintain reasonable standards of care regarding new genetic technologies. Physicians and other healthcare providers must keep abreast of current developments in genetics so they can provide their patients with all relevant information. Despite the fact that genetic malpractice suits may inevitably result from these newly developing genetic technologies, it is the medical community that must continue to establish and abide by the standards of care. Then, it is in the hands of the courts to decide whether a physician is liable for genetic malpractice based upon the specific circumstances of the case.

10.2.2 Products Liability

Strict products liability, manufacturing defects, and failure to warn claims are all potential actions for recovery of damages from biotechnologies. The following excerpt describes the potential for these theories of recovery.

Symposium: *Biotechnology and the Law: Biotechnology's Challenge to the Law of Torts*, 32 McGeorge L. Rev. 221 (Fall 2000):

Strict Products Liability

As products created by biotechnological methods make their way into the marketplace, it seems likely that if and when personal injury or property damage result, the victims will invoke the theory of strict liability for defective products. Despite the fact that the biotech industry has been developing products for the last twenty-five years, biotechnology products have not been the subject of strict products liability actions until very recently. Despite the virtual absence of litigation, enough genetically engineered products now exist on the market that the potential for liability is real.

As noted at the beginning of this Article, the overriding policy issue in this area is whether biotechnology products, or the biotechnology industry, are so different from other products and manufacturers that departure from traditional tort law is warranted. A number of commentators strongly believe that the biotechnology industry is so important to human health and to national self-interest, that strict products liability should not apply. These arguments merit serious consideration. Commentators believe that product liability law will erode innovation and commercial growth within the biotechnolog industry. Some believe that medical products produced through biotechnological techniques offer unique benefits, above and beyond those that can be provided by traditional drugs, and that current case law is a disincentive to the development of those products. In addition, because American law has not yet addressed issues involving biotechnology and the application of strict products liability, potential defendants such as biotechnology firms lack the ability to predict how courts will address liability when the issues arise. Other countries, such as Germany, have enacted legislation that will govern liability for some injuries that arise from use of biotechnology.

As we noted above, neither courts nor legislatures have yet accepted arguments for completely exempting biotech products from strict products liability. It may well be that the protection existing law gives to producers of other products of high social utility, such as prescription drugs, will be deemed sufficient.

Assuming then that injuries occurring as result of products created through biotechnology receive the same treatment by the legal system as other products, we can begin to think through the major issues that will arise. It appears likely that firms that design and implement bio-engineered products can properly be included within the reach of strict products liability law. Under the Restatement and the law of most jurisdictions, strict products liability applies to manufacturers and others in the chain of supply. Further, the law in many jurisdictions is quite broad as to the range of potential plaintiffs who may bring suit, encompassing persons injured by products who are not the purchaser or even the user. Thus, it seems fair to say there may be a large group of potential plaintiffs. For example, if Farmer A purchases genetically engineered cotton seed that produces blue cotton, and that blue cotton cross-pollinates with white cotton grown by Farmer B a mile away, damaging B's crop, under current law B should be permitted to bring suit against the blue cotton manufacturer even though B did not purchase or use the genetically engineered cotton.

The largest hurdle in strict liability cases is proving that the product is defective in design or manufacture. Manufacturing defects are typically the easiest types of defect to prove; under the Restatement (Second) of Torts, the question is whether the product performed as safely as the ordinary consumer would expect. While this test is easy to apply in cases of exploding coke bottles or faulty hasps on a truck, it may be harder to apply when products are created through bio-engineering. The average consumer may have no expectation regarding the product he or she buys, or, may have a general expectation of safety without any true understanding of certain risks or side effects, even if these are explained. The ambiguity of the consumer expectation test, however, is common also to non-biotechnology cases.

It is difficult to predict whether the ambiguity of the test for a production defect will in fact be problematic in cases involving bio-engineered products. Courts have simply not yet confronted the dilemma of whether and how alleged defects in bio-engineered products fit within the traditional analytical niches. To anticipate how these questions will be answered, one must predict whether defects that occur will pervade every bio-engineered product of a certain type that is produced and therefore be deemed design flaws, or whether the defects will be sporadic and easily identifiable as a departure from the intended output and therefore deemed manufacturing flaws. Also, defects could arise that hybridize the two existing concepts. For example, a defect in an inspection or quality control process could result in failure to detect an impurity in a bio-engineered product. A defect of this character would share attributes of both manufacturing and design defects. For purposes of this Article, however, one can reasonably assume that some types of design defect will be alleged. The question then, will become how the vast case law regarding design defect liability will apply.

Under both the Second and Third Restatements of Torts, certain products are exempt from liability for design defects. This protection is commonly afforded to prescription drugs, and is likely to be sought for many products that are developed through biotechnology methods. In many jurisdictions, courts decide which products are to be exempt from design defect analysis on a case by case basis. Thus, they could evaluate a new vaccine and determine if its usefulness is high enough, and its risks unavoidable enough, to merit protection from design defect analysis. Some products viewed as central to health would qualify without question; others, such as hair-growth drugs, or weight loss panaceas, might well not qualify. In some jurisdictions, such as California, all prescription drugs are exempt from liability on the basis of design defects. The California court was convinced that unless manufacturers knew from the outset that they would not be strictly liable for design defects, they would not invest the money necessary to develop drugs. Given the enormous costs associated with production of new products using biotechnology, the same arguments could no doubt be made forcefully. However, it remains to be seen whether courts are willing to grant the biotech industries such broad protection. The Restatement (Third) of Torts, if adopted by courts, will expand the protection that comment k affords in the Restatement (Second), because it specifically encompasses prescription drugs and medical devices. However, even this expanded protection from design defect liability could leave unprotected significant areas such as agriculture.

Assuming then, that at least some injury-producing products created through biotechnological methods are subjected to strict liability for defective design, the question is whether the analysis will differ in any significant way from ordinary design defect cases. In jurisdictions that use a risk/utility balancing test, and in jurisdictions that require proof of a reasonable alternate design, plaintiffs may have to be creative in applying the law. As an example, consider a genetically engineered fungus which is under development by Ag/Bio Con. The purpose of this fungus is to attack marijuana plants, and thereby serve as a tool in crime prevention. One fear, of course, is that the fungus might possibly mutate once released, injuring crops and the environment. If that fear were realized, the plaintiff alleging a design defect would, of course, be required to present evidence, from which the jury would evaluate the risks of the design, the probability it would produce injury, and design alternatives. To meet this burden of proof, the plaintiff would most likely need an expert to testify as to scientifically feasible design alternatives. The need for such evidence is even clearer under the Restatement (Third), because proof of a reasonable alternative design is mandatory. Regardless of the standard used, one wonders whether the plaintiff could actually present the required evidence. What is the alternative to a genetically-engineered fungus? Would the plaintiff need to prove that another bio-engineered fungus would not be subject to the defect? Given the secrecy with which biotechnology companies surround their products and patents, obtaining evidence of the design of other bio-engineered fungi, if they even exist, could be difficult. In short, application of the law relating to design defects appears possible, but would seem to require some unique adjustments and potentially difficult proof on the part of the plaintiff. It is not as easy to compare designs of genetically-engineered products as it is to compare, for example, different designs of a motor or lawn chair.

Failure to warn claims appear to be a much more fertile area for tort litigation regarding products that are made using biotechnology. Such claims are generally evaluated using a negligence standard. These claims may occur more frequently with bio-engineered products because, due to the extremely high cost of developing the products, extensive testing is sometimes not financially feasible. For example, Monsanto apparently rushed a Roundup Ready cotton to the market avoiding the customary three years of testing, with the result that Monsanto apparently did not know that the yield of cotton would be decreased. Of course, regulatory processes, such as FDA approval, ensure that there is agency oversight of testing of many products, but still, the Monsanto example shows that sometimes under-tested products can make their way to the marketplace. Liability for failure to warn of harm-causing properties may follow.

There are many other issues that may arise with respect to products that are manufactured using biotechnology. For example, biotechnology companies may argue that FDA approval should constitute a complete defense to tort liability; if this proposition were accepted, it would be a radical departure from the way tort law treats other products. It might possibly be justified by the enormous amount of money that must be spent to gain FDA approval for bio-engineered products. However, if this defense were to be recognized, there would soon be a clamor from drug and chemical companies to afford them the same protection, and to do so would require major change in the law.

New issues will continue to emerge as the industry develops. For example, it is now possible to grow human body parts in petri dishes in a laboratory. In a sense, a laboratory grown ear might be considered a product, but will it be subjected to the traditional rules regarding strict products liability, or will it be covered by the Restatement Third's exemption of human blood and tissue products? It depends how broadly the Restatement's exemption is construed, and as yet we have no guidance. As more genetically engineered food, such as bio-engineered grain, makes its way into the marketplace, we may find litigants arguing over whether defective food should be analyzed under section 7 (which covers food products) or under Section 2 (design defects) of the Third Restatement. Section 7 is intended to cover easy cases like glass shards in tuna salad, using the reasonable consumer expectations test, while Section 2 addresses the complex issues design cases raise. The better choice appears to be Section 2, since any alleged defects probably pervade all products the defendant has brought to market. However, litigants and judges will find the issue to be a difficult one.

While it is true that litigation about products manufactured using biotechnology has not yet flooded the courts, there is reason to believe that when it does, litigators will encounter juries with strong preconceptions and biases about biotechnology. Burk and Boczar fear that anti-biotechnology bias, coupled with the inability to understand the basic science, bodes poorly for the ability of the industry to defend itself. Certainly, near hysterical public reaction to products such as bST, a hormone treatment for cows, bears out their apprehension. No scientific evidence produced to date indicates the hormone is dangerous to humans, yet there has been regulatory litigation to challenge its use, as well as a threatened boycott of milk produced by cows treated with the hormone. In addition, public opposition to genetically engineered food seems to be growing, in the United States as well as in Europe and Asia..

In the Starlink case *supra*, the plaintiffs also sought recovery based on a failure to warn theory. The court discusses the preemption claim for labeling under FIFRA, finding that for theories of recovery, FIFRA did not preempt state law.

In Re Starlink Corn Products Liability Litigation
212 F. Supp. 2d 828 (N.D. Ill. 2002)

Memorandum Opinion and Order by Judge James B. Moran

[facts are the same as Starlink, *supra*.]

This controversy arises from the discovery of genetically modified corn in various food products.

I. Preemption

FIFRA regulates the use, sale and labeling of pesticides such as the Cry9C protein found in StarLink corn. The EPA approved StarLink's label and issued a limited registration for it to be distributed. Defendants argue that FIFRA preempts plaintiffs' state law claims.

FIFRA does not preempt all state laws respecting pesticides. The statute expressly authorizes states to regulate pesticide use. But it also prohibits states from imposing any labeling requirements beyond those imposed by the EPA.

The Supreme Court has made clear that "requirements" includes both positive law, in the form of statutory and regulatory obligations, and any common law standards which could give rise to civil damages. FIFRA uses nearly identical language to the Cigarette

Act, and its preemptive effect is equivalent. FIFRA therefore preempts any claims based on the inadequacy of StarLink's label or defendants' failure to warn StarLink farmers.

First, plaintiffs allege that defendants sold StarLink seeds without the EPA-required label, and otherwise failed to comply with the limited registration's terms.

There is no federal private right of action to redress FIFRA violations. Only the EPA has standing to enforce it. FIFRA does not, however, prevent states from creating civil remedies for violating the federal standard. The statute only prohibits additional requirements, not identical ones. Although potential civil liability obviously increases the manufacturer's incentive to comply, if the state is merely adopting as its standard of care that which is already required under federal law, no additional obligation is imposed. FIFRA, therefore, does not preempt plaintiffs' negligence *per se* claims.

Next, plaintiffs assert that defendants made voluntary statements regarding StarLink beyond those on the EPA-approved label that contributed to the contamination.

Claims based on off-label representations are preempted if they merely reiterate information contained in the label. They are not preempted, however, to the extent the representations substantially differ from the label. The complaint alleges that Aventis instructed seed representatives to tell farmers that StarLink was safe for human consumption and that the EPA was going to issue a tolerance for Cry9C in food products. Such statements directly contradict the approved label ...

Plaintiffs also advance the theory that defendants failed to adequately inform those who handled corn further down the distribution chain, *e.g.*, grain elevator operators and transport providers, of the required warnings.

Courts have noted the distinction between failure to warn the initial purchaser and failure to warn third parties.

> FIFRA "labeling" is designed to be read and followed by the end user. Generally it is conceived as being attached to the immediate container of the product in such a way that it can be expected to remain affixed during the period of use ... By contrast, the target audience of the [state] notification program is those innocent members of the general public who may unwittingly happen upon an area where strong poisons are present, as well as those who contract to have pesticides applied.

New York State Pesticide Coalition,(upholding regulation requiring placards be posted to notify third parties of pesticide use). Parties who handle StarLink corn down the supply chain will not see the label on the original seed bag and, consequently, will not know that a particular batch of corn is unfit for human consumption and must be segregated and handled differently.

States can reasonably require that pesticide manufacturers share the same EPA-approved warnings with parties beyond the immediate purchaser. Similar to permitting state causes of action for directly violating FIFRA, because the state standard here would mirror the federal one in substance, it does not interfere with the EPA's prerogative with respect to labeling and does not constitute an additional requirement.

Finally, plaintiffs allege that StarLink corn is a defective product. They assert that, as currently designed, StarLink cannot be safely used for its intended non-food purposes because it will inevitably commingle and cross-pollinate with the food supply.

The EPA's approval of a product's FIFRA label does not constitute a finding or an endorsement that its design is safe. Here we must be careful to determine whether their allegations are really challenging the product design, which is permissible, or effectively challenging the accompanying warnings, which would be preempted. The test most frequently articulated is, when confronted with a type of harm, would the manufacturer change the design or the label to prevent its recurrence?

Defendants' failure to prevent commingling has nothing to do with StarLink's design. Plaintiffs acknowledge that, although it is not the general practice, there are means to segregate types of corn such that they maintain their identity. It is a matter of ensuring that everyone who handles the corn adheres to certain procedures. Confronted with commingling, a manufacturer would more likely change the warnings than the design. This constitutes a failure to warn, not a design defect, and therefore FIFRA preempts it.

The allegations regarding StarLink's tendency to cross-pollinate with non-StarLink corn can be read two ways. One is that defendants should have known that the 660-foot buffer zone was insufficient to prevent cross-pollination. The 660-foot requirement was incorporated in the limited registration and would have been communicated to farmers by the EPA-approved label. A state standard of care demanding more than a 660-foot buffer would be an additional requirement in the form of a different warning. FIFRA preempts such a claim.

It is also possible to view plaintiffs' cross-pollination charge as asserting that no buffer zone could prevent it. The theory posits that, given the way corn reproduces, cross-pollination between corn targeted for non-food uses and corn intended for the human food supply is inevitable. Defendants, therefore, had a duty to design insect-resistant corn such that it is fit for human consumption — use a protein that is safer than Cry9C. This still attacks the label because it is premised on the idea that the buffer zone warning was not sufficient to prevent cross-pollination. The EPA approved the label with the knowledge that StarLink was unfit for human consumption. It deemed the 660-foot buffer zone an adequate warning to preserve the integrity of the food supply. Plaintiffs' defect claims implicitly challenge this warning and are therefore preempted.

In summary, plaintiffs may proceed on the theory that defendants (1) violated duties imposed by the limited registration; (2) made representations to StarLink growers that contradicted the EPA-approved label; and (3) failed to inform parties handling StarLink corn downstream of the EPA-approved warnings.

II. Economic Loss Doctrine

This rule limits the types of damages plaintiffs may recover in tort. Physical injuries to persons or property are compensable; solely economic injuries are not. The difficult question is defining what constitutes an "economic" injury....

Non-StarLink corn crops are damaged when they are pollinated by StarLink corn. The pollen causes these corn plants to develop the Cry9C protein and renders what would otherwise be a valuable food crop unfit for human consumption. Non-StarLink corn is also damaged when it is commingled with StarLink corn. Once mixed, there is no way to re-segregate the **corn** into its edible and inedible parts. The entire batch is considered tainted and can only be used for the domestic and industrial purposes for which StarLink is approved. None of that supply can ever be used for human food.

There are at least four different points along the supply chain at which StarLink could have entered the food corn supply, all of which are consistent with the complaint: (1) plaintiffs unknowingly purchased seed containing the Cry9C protein, *i.e.* their suppliers' inventory had been contaminated; (2) plaintiffs' crops were contaminated by pollen from StarLink corn on a neighboring farm; (3) plaintiffs' harvest was contaminated by commingling with StarLink corn in a transport or storage facility; and (4) food manu-facturers commingled the corn within their raw material storage or processing activi-ties. The first situation would fall within the economic loss doctrine. Plaintiffs could have negotiated contractual protection from their suppliers and simply did not get what they had bargained for. In the fourth, plaintiffs would have suffered no harm to their property because the corn was commingled after they had relinquished their ownership interest in it. Scenarios 2 and 3, however, present viable claims for harm to their crops. [Resolving the complaint's ambiguous phraseology in plaintiffs' favor, we find that they have sufficiently alleged that their crops were contaminated at some point within that chain.]

The StarLink situation does not fit neatly into traditional economic loss doctrine analy-sis. Plaintiffs here had no commercial dealings with defendants or defendants' cus-tomers. This is more than a lack of direct privity, and not a situation where a party could have negotiated warranty or indemnity protection and chose not to. Plaintiffs had no opportunity to negotiate contractual protection with anyone. Still, as the access cases aptly demonstrate, the economic loss doctrine has grown beyond its original freedom-of-contract based policy justifications. Farmers' expectations of what they will receive for their crops are just that, expectations. Absent a physical injury, plaintiffs cannot re-cover for drops in market prices. Nor can they recover for any additional costs, such as testing procedures, imposed by the marketplace. But if there was some physical harm to plaintiffs' corn crop, the lack of a transaction with defendants affects what will be con-sidered "other property." [This includes corn commingled at grain elevators because plaintiffs retain ownership rights to corn stored there. Each contributing farmer owns a pro rata share of the entire, now tainted, supply.] Assuming plaintiffs did not buy corn seeds with the Cry9C protein, it cannot be said that a defective part of their crop in-jured the whole, that a defective product was integrated into a system or that the harm to their crop was a foreseeable consequence of the seeds' failure to perform. These facts are distinguishable from Hapka, 458 N.W.2d at 688 (holding farmer who purchased diseased seeds could not recover for harm to rest of crop). Plaintiffs' seeds, as pur-chased, were adequate. The StarLink contaminant was wholly external.

Nor does the StarLink controversy present the unlimited or speculative damage con-cerns common in access cases. There are a finite number of potential plaintiffs—only non-StarLink corn farmers—who can claim injury. This may be a sizeable group, and the damages may be tremendous, but the fact that defendants are alleged to have di-rectly harmed a large number of plaintiffs is not a defense. StarLink's effects on com-mercial corn farmers are distinct and qualitatively different from society at large. And damages are easily measured through price changes because corn is a regularly traded commodity with a readily measurable market. Further, as discussed above, the contam-ination of plaintiffs' corn supply is a physical injury.

To the extent plaintiffs allege that their crops were themselves contaminated, either by cross-pollination in the fields or by commingling later in the distribution chain, they have adequately stated a claim for harm to property. Once plaintiffs have established this harm they may be entitled to compensation for certain economic losses.

III. Negligence

Defendants challenge three separate elements: duty, proximate cause and damages. Al-though cast in terms of a balance between foreseeability, reasonableness and public pol-icy, the essence of their argument is remoteness—any effect StarLink may have had on corn markets is too far removed from defendants' conduct. Defendants contend that the causal relationship involved six distinct steps: (1) the EPA approved the registration for Cry9C; (2) seed companies incorporated the StarLink technology into seed corn; (3) growers purchased StarLink seeds; (4) the StarLink seeds/corn was handled in such a way as to allow cross-pollination and commingling; (5) the tainted corn was introduced into the mainstream corn supply, leading to food product recalls; and (6) the discovery of StarLink in the main food supply hurt corn prices.

In presenting their version of the causal chain, however, defendants have imposed their own construction on the complaint.

On a motion to dismiss we must not only accept plaintiffs' version, but also any set of facts consistent with it. First, defendants' argument used their own characterization of Aventis' role, or lack thereof, in bringing StarLink to market. Aventis denies any involvement in numerous steps leading to the widespread StarLink contamination. This is a simple factual dispute. The complaint plainly alleges that Aventis (or its predecessors) were involved in developing and licensing StarLink. Moreover, it alleges that pursuant to the limited registration Aventis was responsible for monitoring and enforcing compliance by StarLink farmers. For now we must accept plaintiffs' version of Aventis' involvement in introducing StarLink into the food supply.

We must also collapse defendants' purported chain from the other end. Although they attempt to characterize the complaint as asserting some remote duty to preserve the market price of **corn,** the duty alleged is to prevent contamination. The effects on corn markets are merely a way to measure the damages. As we discussed above, we read the complaint to allege direct harm to plaintiffs' corn. Defendants are correct that the complaint does not make this charge specifically, but it is a set of facts that is consistent with plaintiffs' allegations about the impact on the **corn** system as a whole. At this stage of litigation we must construe this ambiguity in plaintiffs' favor.

Presuming Aventis' more active involvement with StarLink, and presuming further that the latter physically harmed plaintiffs' corn, the chain becomes substantially shorter. Aventis had a duty to ensure that StarLink did not enter the human food supply, and their failure to do so caused plaintiffs' corn to be contaminated.

Lastly, Aventis argues that even if plaintiffs suffered direct harm to their corn, its SES program would fully compensate them. Plaintiffs have alleged otherwise, and for now, that is sufficient.

10.2.3 Strict Liability Legislation

One solution to the StarLink problem, may be to create a standard of strict liability for companies which produce genetically modified organisms. Legislation was proposed in the 108th Congress to create such a standard, but failed to go further than Committee assignment.

H. R. 2919, 108th Cong., 1st Sess. (July 25, 2003)

To assign liability for injury caused by genetically engineered organisms.

Sponsored by Mr. Kucinich and others

A BILL To assign liability for injury caused by genetically engineered organisms. Be it enacted by the Senate and House of Representatives of the United States of America in Congress assembled,

SECTION 1. SHORT TITLE.

This Act may be cited as the 'Genetically Engineered Organism Liability Act of 2003'.

SEC. 2. FINDINGS.

The Congress finds the following:

(1) The negative consequences of genetically engineered crops may impact farmers who grow these crops, neighbor farmers who do not grow these crops, and consumers.

(2) Biotech companies are selling a technology that is being commercialized ahead of the new and unknown science of genetic engineering.

(3) Farmers may suffer from crop failures, neighbor and nearby farmers may suffer from cross pollination, increased insect resistance, and unwanted volunteer genetically engineered plants, and consumers may suffer from health and environmental impacts.

(4) Therefore, biotech companies should be found liable for the failures of genetically engineered crops when they arise.

SEC. 3. LIABILITY.

(a) CAUSE OF ACTION—A biotech company is liable to any party injured by the release of a genetically engineered organism into the environment if that injury results from that genetic engineering. The prevailing plaintiff in an action under this subsection may recover reasonable attorney's fees and other litigation expenses as a part of the costs.

(b) INDEMNITY—For the purposes of subsection (a), the term 'injury' includes any liability of a person who uses that organism in accordance with applicable Federal and other law, if that liability arises from that use.

(c) NOT WAIVABLE—The liability created by subsection (a) may not be waived or otherwise avoided by contract.

(d) DEFINITION—As used in this section, the term 'biotech company' means a person—

(1) engaged in the business of genetically engineering an organism; or

(2) obtaining the patent rights to such an organism for the purposes of commercial exploitation of that organism.

[The bill was assigned to the Committee on Health, and died there.]

———————

Chapter Eleven

The Future of Biotechnology and Law

Predictions are difficult, particularly when they are about the future

—old Chinese proverb

The future of biotechnology and law is certain to continue to move together as society embraces or rejects the scientific developments of biotechnology. While the thought that biotechnology is ahead of the law, and the courts available resources to deal with it, it is almost certain that this will change to meet the demands of an ever-increasing technological world.

The nine types of biotechnologies which were described at the beginning of this book, grew to this number only in the last twenty years. It is likely that new biotechnologies not yet contemplated will be added to this list in the coming decade. Biotechnologies not only for human health, but for agriculture and manufacturing. For example, University of California at Santa Barbara researchers are using the biochemical processes of a marine sponge, which are capable of assembling silicon structures, in hopes of constructing semi-conductors with the same process. The Massachusetts Institute for Technology has evolved viruses that can organize and make nano-size wires and magnetic components which could be used in a manufacturing process. Andrew Pollack, *Army Center to Study New Uses of Biotechnology*, NEW YORK TIMES, Aug. 27, 2003.

The following article by Prof. Henry Greely, a leading professor in the field of law and biotechnology, describes some of the potential legal issues that will arise as we address these new questions in biotechnolog

Speech: *The Revolution in Human Genetics: Implications for Human Societies*, 52 S.C. L. REV. 377 (Winter 2001).

Specifically, I want to cover the possible social consequences of six major areas touched by the new genetics: (1) social effects of medical advances, (2) issues of identity, (3) predicting the **future,** (4) manipulating genomes, (5) ownership and control, and (6) changed understandings. Before that, I must stress two overriding themes. First, the issues about human genetics in human society are not really new. They have arisen in the past with respect to other technologies and other changes—genetics, for the most part, just puts the same issues in a slightly different context. Second, human genetics is both extremely powerful and sometimes relatively weak. We all must avoid assuming, as I think the public too often does, that genetic effects are always powerful. Sometimes they are—sometimes they are not.

II. Medical Advances

Let us start with the social and legal consequences of some of the medical implications of genetics research. The potentially wonderful medical benefits coming from increased research in human genetics affect not only what we think of as genetic diseases, but also other diseases that have mild genetic components, and still other diseases that are not "caused" at all by genetic variations but for which genes play a role in either the disease progress or the disease treatment. The last two classes of disease have really been driving this revolution. Scientists are interested in genetics largely for its own sake, but the legislatures, pharmaceutical companies, venture capitalists, and individual investors who have been paying for this research are interested in products that will improve human life (while improving bottom lines) through the treatment and prevention of disease. I do not think we are going to live to be two hundred years old or even that our children are going to live to be two hundred years old, but genetics research will contribute significantly to an increase in life span and a decrease in misery during life. That is great news, which is usually overlooked by people like me who look at the ethical, legal, and social implications of genetics — we tend to be a gloomy lot.

But every silver lining has a gray cloud wrapped around it. Law students in the audience, ask yourselves this: If my generation lives to be ninety-five, who is going to be paying for our Social Security? Not just you, but your children, and our Medicare and our nursing homes. What if we can cure the physical diseases of old age before we cure some of the mental deterioration and we end up with a country with tens of millions of demented nonagenarians and centenarians? Even before we get to that stage, when we have exciting new — and usually expensive — drugs, who is going to get these drugs in a country where approximately forty-four million Americans have no health insurance? This is not so much a problem in the rest of the rich world, which is civilized enough to make sure that all of its citizens get health insurance, but we have not become that civilized yet. Even if we do adopt universal coverage and decide that people with low cost health insurance or people without health insurance will have access to these drugs, what about the ninety-five percent of the human species that lives outside of the United States? Consider the people in sub-Saharan Africa who are dying of HIV right now and who are causing great tension in international intellectual property law by seeking (and sometimes getting) deep discounts for life saving therapies? Effective new therapies can be wonderful things, but they will bring a set of problems that we are going to have to deal with, as a result of the genetic revolution.

III. Identity

The basic issues with respect to the forensic use of DNA in court are now resolved. Judges and juries throughout the country understand that DNA evidence is very powerful — except in the O.J. Simpson case. But even the O.J. Simpson case is a nice example that no matter how powerful the technology, the police still have to prove the traditional issues of physical evidence: the origin of the DNA sample, that the sample was not contaminated, that it was not tampered with, and so on. In the area of forensic identification, we have now moved to a second type of DNA identification that does not look at known suspects and known crime scenes, but actually involves checking the DNA from a crime scene against a database of criminals, people who have been accused of crimes, and people who have been arrested. Every state now has a DNA database and repository for forensic purposes. But there is not a lot of agreement on whose DNA should be in it. In some states the database includes only convicted sex offenders, in other states it includes all convicted felons, and in the United Kingdom, for example, it includes anybody who has been arrested. Where are we going with this? We are all potential subjects of this database. Is that a good thing or a bad thing? I have been fingerprinted a number of times for various purposes, including for admission to the bar. My fingerprints are on file in many places. Is DNA different?

Two important issues here will have to be resolved, probably within the next ten years. First, how broad should the collections be? Should they include just convicted people, or all arrested people? Should they include the entire population? These collections are not only useful for solving crimes but also for identification of remains, and, if samples are taken early enough, for identification of stolen or kidnaped children. Second, what kind of information should be kept? Information about the thirteen markers considered the "DNA fingerprint" does not tell us much about an individual. It does not tell us anything about a person's medical risks, height, sex, or anything else. But if we keep the actual physical samples, and not just the analysis of a few meaningless markers, then potentially we can know a lot about those people. Watch this issue of DNA collections. They can be a powerful tool in criminal justice, especially for solving cold cases—cases where you have some physical evidence but no suspect—but they also raise powerful issues about privacy.

IV. Predicting the Future

The power of DNA to predict the future is the area that concerns people the most. There are five subparts to this issue.

A. Prenatal or Early Postnatal Situations

The use of genetic testing in prenatal or early postnatal situations is one way DNA predicts the future. Postnatal tests, some of which are required by law in every state in the union, identify genetic disease like phenylketonuria (PKU) or galactosemia. We require these tests because babies identified with the genetic defects can receive medical interventions to limit, or eliminate, the diseases' ill effects.

Prenatal genetic tests can predict many diseases, most untreatable. Should we require that testing? When should we require hospitals and doctors to offer that testing to individuals? My state, California, requires that all pregnant women be offered a test called Maternal Serum Alpha-Fetoprotein testing. That test shows whether a fetus is at heightened risk for Downs Syndrome, Spina Bifida, Anencephaly, and a number of other severe conditions. By requiring that it be offered, we encourage people to take the test. By encouraging people to take the test, we encourage people, probably, to abort fetuses who test positive. Is that something we as a society want to do?

B. Testing for Adult Onset Diseases

The second subpart of using genetic testing is predicting the future health of people who are already alive and old enough to make their own decisions through genetic tests for adult onset diseases. Adult onset testing exists for diseases like Huntington's disease, for the heightened susceptibility to breast and ovarian cancers that come from mutations in BRCA1 and BRCA2 genes, and for a number of other genetic conditions. We can say something about your future health by doing a test of your genes.

On the other hand, we usually cannot say much. There are not very many diseases where DNA can predict your future perfectly. There are a few, such as Huntington's disease, a very nasty, untreatable, lingering—and rare—neurological disorder. As far as we know, if you have one copy of the disease-linked version of the gene that leads to Huntington's disease, the only way to avoid getting the disease is to die first from something else. It is what geneticists call one hundred percent penetrant—one hundred percent of the people with the genotype get the disease.

Most genetic diseases are not like that. Many can be treated. My nearsightedness, which is quite extreme, is partially genetic. My glasses work fine; many people now get surgery for several thousand dollars that they think works even better than my glasses. There are also many diseases which we know have a genetic component to them, but the genetic variations do not lead to disease one hundred percent—or zero percent—of the time. Such strong associations are (relatively) easy to find. The effects of genetic variations on disease usually are going to be more subtle. They may raise your risk of a disease from eight percent to eleven percent. Or maybe they reduce your risk from eight percent to five percent. What do we make of that information? Why do we want those predictions? These are questions we are all going to face as patients. When do you want to be tested and why? The answer will be a balance that will vary with each individual and each kind of test. If there is good medical intervention for the disease, the test is a lot more attractive. With colon cancer, good medical interventions, particularly increased monitoring, now exist. There are interventions for breast cancer, but their value is more questionable. Huntington's disease has no interventions. That makes a difference.

There are also the risks. People might worry about insurance or employment discrimination. Those are the risks most talked about. Most states have taken steps in a haphazard, patchwork way to try to combat the risks of health insurance discrimination, but they have not done so with life insurance. And some states have taken steps with respect to employment discrimination. I believe most people exaggerate the risks of health insurance discrimination because most of us who are fortunate enough to have health insurance get it in ways that do not allow medical underwriting. Our insurers do not get to pick and choose whom to cover because most of us get insurance through our employers, medicare, or medicaid, none of whom do medical underwriting. Only ten to fifteen percent of the insurance market is medically underwritten. If I left my tenured position with a solvent university and became a freelance writer, I would be in that position as well. For one—and for most of us—this kind of discrimination is a potential threat. It is not a very real threat yet, but it is good that people are trying to take action with respect to it. But there are other costs to adult onset testing which are much less frequently talked about that I think are often more important than the insurance issue.

People in families with a history of genetic disease tell me that genetic testing often causes discord within the family. One sister wants to get tested for BRCA1 or BRCA2, the other sister doesn't. They fight, they are unhappy. The mother feels guilty when she learns that she has passed on a gene for increased Alzheimer's risk to her children. And I think in some ways, issues surrounding genetic testing are toughest in marriages. If you take a genetic test and discover you are at high risk for Huntington's disease or early onset Alzheimer's disease or breast cancer, do you tell your spouse? If you do tell your spouse, what is going to happen? Is he or she going to leave you? Well, that would be a little dramatic. Is he or she going to become emotionally distant from you? Perhaps. The familial consequences of genetic testing are a real cost for a lot of people and an issue that is not talked about very much.

The other serious cost that is often over-looked involves the personal, psychological consequences for some people. Most genetic research has been done with Huntington's disease, which is one hundred percent penetrant, has a one hundred percent death rate, and no treatment. And the good news is, on average, most people who take the test are about as happy or unhappy a year later as they were before, whether they test positive or negative. But that is an average and the average conceals extremes. Some people go to pieces and some people feel better. As you might expect, often times people who do not have the Huntington's disease gene feel better. People who test positive feel worse, but not always. Sometimes people who test positive feel better. Why? Maybe because they are no longer uncertain. Sometimes people who test negative—they won't get the disease—feel much worse. Why? A sense of guilt, perhaps, that all of their relatives have had this and they are spared somehow? Nancy Wexler, the psychologist who was largely responsible for the effort that led to the finding of the gene, tells about a thirty-four year old man who had always assumed he was going to get Huntington's disease (his father had it) but finally decided to get tested at the age of thirty-four. The test was negative, but he suffered an emotional breakdown anyway. Why? He had dropped out of three colleges, declared bankruptcy twice, had never had a long term relationship, and had been arrested on white collar criminal charges. He had always assumed he only had thirty-five years to live. At thirty-four he found that he had another forty years to live—and that he had ruined them.

The deeper point here is that the psychological reactions can be strong, and they can be unpredictable. With respect to any of these genetic tests for adult onset diseases, whether it is a good test or it is a bad test is a question that can only be answered in the context of the specific test, the specific disease, and the specific individual—his or her life situation, job, family, and personality.

C. Behavioral Genetics

For some reason, the covers of news magazines seem to be particularly susceptible to news stories about behavioral genetics. It is almost as if things like cancer and diabetes are not as exciting as math ability or sexual preference or violence or other behavioral characteristics. It is clear that there are some genetic links to behavior. Our genes are different from those of chimpanzees. Not very different, but different. And we behave differently. People with "Fragile X" Syndrome are mentally retarded because of genetic differences. Mental retardation is behavior. There is a nasty genetic disease called Lesch-Nyhan Syndrome where children end up engaging in very self-destructive behaviors. It is clearly a genetic disease—and a prime example that genes and behavior can be related. But these behavioral genetic relationships, at least thus far, are really hard to tease out. When you read things saying a "gay gene" has been found, do not believe it. In general it is wise not to believe any gene discovery until it has been replicated at least four or five times; this is particularly true of behavioral genetics. I believe there ultimately will be some associations between genetic variations and behavior, but those associations are not going to be very powerful. There will not be a "math ability gene," but there might be a genetic variant where twenty percent of the people with the variant have significantly better math ability. But, at the same time, perhaps ten percent will have below-average math ability. The effects of genes on behavior will likely be small.

D. Eugenics

Eugenics is a bad word in the West, thanks to the Nazis, who took eugenic principles so far as to wipe out whole groups of people they thought should not be allowed to breed. But eugenics was not another Nazi outrage. By 1932, at least twenty-six states in the United States passed, on eugenic principles, laws providing for compulsory sterilization of people with bad genes. By 1950, as many as sixty-thousand Americans had been sterilized for their genetic diseases, such as feeblemindedness, shiftlessness, and criminal tendencies, so they would not pass them on to their progeny. I believe we have now been immunized against eugenics. The Nazi exaggeration of the United States experience is sufficiently fresh that the West will probably not go down this path again—at least not in my lifetime, and I hope not in the lifetime of anyone here.

But eugenics, of course, can play more subtle roles. If we pay for prenatal genetic tests as part of health insurance and pay for abortions but do not pay for treatment, is that eugenics? If we pay for phenylketonuria (PKU) tests—and in fact require them—but do not pay for the special and expensive medical diet that people with PKU need, the PKU test requirement potentially encourages abortions. Is that eugenics?

More directly, the West is not all of the world. About three years ago, China, the home of one-fifth of our species, passed a maternal and infant health law that required couples getting married to get a certificate from a doctor. And if the doctor finds either person has a serious genetic condition, the couple can only get the certificate if they promise to be sterilized or use long term contraception. I am also told that in China that if you are not married, you do not have children. Further, if the couple gets pregnant and the doctor believes the fetus is at risk for a serious genetic disease, the woman must get prenatal testing and—in some very controversially translated Chinese characters—the law says that she "should" follow the doctor's advice. No one is quite clear what that "should" means. But the statue can be read as saying that if your doctor says your fetus has this condition and you should have an abortion, you must have the abortion.

E. Free Market Eugenics

Washington, or even Sacramento or Columbia, is not likely any time soon to tell us we can or cannot reproduce. But parents always want the best for their kids, so why not the best genes? Until recently that has been hard to do. Not very many couples are going to get pregnant over and over again and keep aborting fetuses because they do not have the right genes for height or hair color or what they think might be an athletic ability. But if a couple is undergoing in vitro fertilization, they can have a procedure called pre-implantation genetic diagnosis.

This procedure is performed when the embryo grows to about sixteen cells. Technicians can take one cell out without hurting the embryo and can then test its DNA. Typically, a round of in vitro fertilization produces ten, twelve, or twenty embryos. They are not all implanted at one time because no one wants the risk of a woman trying to carry twelve fetuses to term. Instead, the clinic will implant three or four; in some places as many as five or six. The clinic must pick which embryos to implant. Right now they look at them under a microscope and they pick out the healthiest looking ones. But they could also do pre-implantation genetic diagnosis and say to the parents, "You are at risk for passing on cystic fibrosis. These eight embryos would be carriers but not have the disease, these four embryos would not be carriers, and these four embryos would have cystic fibrosis. Parents, which ones do you want to implant?"

And if they are testing one gene, they could test many more, someday thousands. So, the clinic could say to the parents, "By the way, of the four that won't be carriers for cystic fibrosis, these two are male, these two are female. This one will be particularly tall, this one will be short—or at least has a better chance of being tall or short." Designer babies will be a reality for at least the next generation, if not my generation. What should we do about it? Should we care about it? I am a parent. Part of my job is to shape my child, to make sure that my son and daughter know right from wrong, are loving and good people, study hard, and root for Stanford. That is my responsibility. I do it through enormous post-birth intervention in their environment. Is it different if I try to shape them, in part, before birth by genetic selection? I do not know the answer to that.

V. Manipulation

The fourth major area is manipulation. Is there something wrong or odd about taking genes from one species and putting them in another? This has been a major issue recently with respect to food. Many people do not realize that many of the new drugs, and even many old drugs like insulin, are currently being produced by organisms that are part human and part non-human. Genetically, these cells are 99.99% E. coli or yeast or Chinese hamster; and .01% human. You take the human gene, you put it in some other kind of cell, and have the cell churn things out. Is that troublesome? Probably not.

But what if we start making things that are half human and non-human? What if, like the firm Advanced Cell Technologies, we put the nucleus from a human cell into a cow's egg cell? Does that trouble us? The more direct area of this kind of manipulation is human gene therapy, which ultimately will stand and fall on its medical merits and which does not raise particularly difficult ethical issues. But some of these broader issues of creation of chimeras are going to be troubling.

VI. Ownership and Control

Ownership and control issues span a wide range of controversies. One set concerns "gene patents." There are two kinds of objections to the current patent process for genes. One objection questions what we should and should not allow to be patented, and what rights should follow from patenting. It does not claim that these patents are bad or good in the abstract, but that we must balance the incentive patents give to firms like Celera to accelerate the Human Genome Project versus the cost, the resulting monopoly. There is another, much more fundamentalist kind of objection coming from religious groups, deep environmentalists and a variety of anti-globalization forces. These groups are strongly against "patents on life" as a fundamental issue. The first set of issues are alive in the policy arena; the second in the political. We cannot know yet how these patent questions are going to be resolved, but they are important issues to follow.

Genetic privacy is another hot issue in the ownership and control of genetic information. Many states have passed legislation protecting genetic privacy. In other states, genetic information is protected, just as medical information is protected. This means that in law, genetic information is protected everywhere, and, in fact, it is hardly protected at all. I believe genetic information really is just another form of medical information. It cannot and should not be separated from the medical information category. Rather than trying to protect specifically genetic information, we should improve our protection for all medical information.

One argument for that regulation is that it is impossible to determine what medical information is "genetic," and what is not. My blood type is "A positive." I have just given you genetic information about myself—about two different gene systems, the ABO system and the Rhesus factor system. My physical audience can make a pretty good guess that I am carrying a Y chromosome (my readers will make the same guess from my first name). Genetic information is everywhere. When a doctor takes a family history, she gets probabilistic genetic information. Genetic privacy laws will be extremely difficult to administer. How does the law limit information that can be inferred broadly and found anywhere? We leave biological information about ourselves everywhere. We shed hair, skin cells, and other small, DNA-bearing biological matter, all accessible to someone who really wanted it. How does the law control that?

It might be impossible to regulate effectively the collection of tissues that have DNA, but perhaps we could control the analysis of the information. A lab, for example, might only be allowed to test a sample if it had signed permission from the person who left it. But even that has problems—for example, what happens if someone gives a blood sample, with full permission, to a doctor for a simple medical test? Could that doctor then test the sample for any disease, or is the doctor limited to the test the patient consented to? While these issues may seem clear, in practice they are not—it is going to be increasingly difficult to protect people from unlimited testing of DNA samples.

VII. Changed Understandings

The deepest effects of the revolution in human genetics on our societies may be the ways in which it could change our understandings of ourselves and our place in the living world. Three areas stand out.

First, comparison of the genes and genomes of different species shows, very concretely, that all life on earth is related. DNA sequences from vastly different organisms show strong similarities. About ninety-nine percent of human genes seem to be closely related to genes in mice; over a third of human genes are found in single-celled yeast. Darwin's claim that all life is related by descent from a common ancestor can be seen in these similarities in DNA. It is unclear what cultural significance this will have. It should not, for example, lead to vegetarianism because the evidence shows that carrots and corn, like sheep and cattle, are our relatives. It might, however, promote greater respect for other forms of life, as reflected in stronger environmental sentiment.

Second, the evidence from human genetics shows that all humans are very closely related. We are all cousins. Our DNA differs, on average, at one spot in one thousand. In the regions of the genome that make proteins, the differences are one in ten thousand. Humans from opposite ends of the earth are far more similar to each other genetically than are chimpanzees from the same band. Genetic theories provided support for a "scientific" racism in the first part of the twentieth century. The new genetic evidence should provide conclusive evidence against such racism.

Third, genetics may shift the balance in the debate between nature and nurture. DNA may appear to prove that individuals are powerfully shaped by forces beyond their control, but, in reality, science paints a much more complex picture. Genes play a role in the development of many traits or diseases, but environment or luck are also often essential. Most of the time, the correct answer to "nature or nurture?" is "yes." The general population, however, seems to hold a much stronger belief in the power of genes. For that reason, the new genetics could end up promoting a more closed and fatalistic view of human life and abilities than either current society holds or than science would support. That reaction may prove to be the most significant ethical challenge—and, in the long run, the most important harm—of the revolution in human genetics.

VIII. Conclusion

Our new knowledge of human genetics will change human societies forever. It will do that partially through providing new and powerful tools. Like all powerful tools, these can be used well or poorly: they will give us a greater ability to cure or prevent human suffering; they also give us a greater ability to inflict such suffering. The revolution in human genetics, however, provides not just knowledge for creating tools, but knowledge—about ourselves and all other life—that, in itself, can have powerful effects. The consequences of the knowledge gained from genetics may be greater than the consequences of the tools it provides.

At this point, so close to the beginning of the revolution, we are really only guessing about the consequences. Some of the effects seem quite clear; undoubtedly, we are completely overlooking others. It will be the task of those living through this revolution, from our generation and from future generations, to work to ensure that we realize as many of the benefits—and as few of the harms—as possible. For that reason, all of us—as professionals in law, medicine, and science and as citizens—need to follow, and to influence, the implications of the human genetics revolution for human society.

———————

Appendix 1

Primer on Cell Biology

From the 1950s we understood that cells were either "eucaryotes" or "procaryotes". Eucaryotes were cells having a true nucleus in complex animals; and procaryotes were cells with no defined nucleus such as bacteria, but both were understood to have evolved from the same ancestral cell. From the ancestral procaryote, blue-green algae (cyanobacteria), purple bacteria and gram positive bacteria developed on one branch, and on the other branch, the archaebacteria (*halobacteria*).

Bacteria are the simplest organisms found in most environments. They duplicate the population of the earth in 11 hours. Through mutations, the bacteria can adapt rapidly to its environment. Fats, hydrocarbons, jet fuel, nitrogen gas are all potential sources of nutrient for bacteria.

The **structure of the cell** of the bacteria includes a cell wall, which provides rigidity; an inner plasma membrane, which provides permeability for the cell; cytoplasm; and floating within the cytoplasm, is the DNA, which is loosely contained in one area of the cell.

The **plasma membrane** includes a phospholipid bilayer, permeable gases, water (H_2O), impermeable large molecules, and channels through which materials pass in and out of the cell. The **internal membranes** are connected to the plasma membrane.

The *phospholipid bilayer* is made up of hydrocarbon chains and lipids which create a layer impervious to water, or hydrophobic. The utility in this mechanism is to keep the cell in tact, and to prevent water from rushing into the cell body and destroying it. The phospholipid bilayer can become porous with the opening and closing of the channels.

Bacteria can be **gram negative** or **gram positive**, and this becomes very important in the selection of antibiotics, for example, where the type of bacteria requires certain antibiotics, while others will be ineffective against the bacteria.

Gram negative bacteria has an *inner membrane*, or the **plasma membrane**, and an **outer membrane**. Between these two membranes is a **cell wall**, plus a **periplastic space**. Within this space are the peptidoglycans (proteins + oligosaccharides).

Gram positive bacteria has only a **plasma membrane** and a **cell wall**, but it is thicker. There is no **outer membrane**.

Eucaryotes' cells have, in addition to the bacteria structures, organelles; and membrane binding these structures, involving an extensive internal network of membranes. The typical animal cell, or eucaryote, includes:

mitochondria which performs oxygenation, and provides storage for small molecules;

nucleolus, where synthesis of RNA takes place;

447

smooth and rough endoplasmic reticulum, where proteins and lipids are synthesized;

golgi vesicles, which direct activities in the cell;

cytoskeleton, which provides rigidity and is involved in motion; and

centrioles, which are involved in cell division.

Procaryotes' cells, or plant cells, in contrast include a **cell wall** which contains cellulose.

There are many common organelles in both plant and animal cells; however there are a few unique organelles in plant cells:

chloroplast where photosynthesis occurs;

large vacuoles which stores waste; and

plasmodesmata which connects cells and allows communication.

Other than these structural differences between the eucaryotes and procaryotes, other important comparisons can be useful:

	Eucaryote	*Procaryote*
1. Volume	200x that of bacteria	
2. Similarities	70 % H2O	
	23% macromolecules	
	7% small molecules	
3. Different amounts of DNA	Humans—> 2 sets of 23 chromosomes, 30,000 genes. The fruit Fly has 13,000 genes; the round-worm, *c. elegans* has 19,000 genes. *E. coli* Reptiles have more. Humans have And about 500,000 proteins.	
4. DNA package	DNA is divided between 2 or More chromosomes. Chromosomes are contained in the nucleus. The number and size of chromosomes vary widely. Yeast—> 12–18 chromosomes (Each has 20% of the DNA that would occur in *e. coli*. Of that in an *e. coli* chromosome. Each contains a single, linear double-stranded DNA molecule. Each chromosome contains histones, Which are charged proteins in DNA interaction.	One single circular DNA molecule (since there is no nucleus, the DNA is folded on itself and has several attachments to the cell wall Some contain plasmids.
Similarities	1. Biochemical pathways 2. Translation of mRNA—> protein. These mechanisms Have been preserved throughout the evolutionary process.	

The eucaryotes and procaryotes on a cellular basis have been described in terms of their structure and function. Single cell organisms gave rise to multicellular organisms, and those differences are important to address at this point.

Single cell organisms make up a large part of the earth's biomass, or total biological, living material. What is the advantage then, from going from a single to a multicellular organism?

Multicellular organisms can exploit resources whereas a single cell organism cannot. Evolutionary innovations, such as movement, sensory capability and the ability to communicate assist in exploiting resources in the organism's changing environment.

There are two essential features to the move to multicellular organization: (1) cells become specialized; and (2) cells cooperate with each other. When the food supply is exhausted, plants grow fruiting bodies and aggregate; produce spores, which survives the dirth. Green algae, cells connected by cytoplasmic bridges is its highest multicellular form. There are specialized cells for reproduction.

Animals. An extracellular matrix is required for a multicellular animal, e.g., sponges which have epithelium, contain five types of cells, which form channels and pores. These channels and pores serve as filters for H2O and food. There is no nervous system. This simple organization means that there are no size limits for the sponge. Sponges pushed through a sieve would break into cells and simply reassemble themselves. The sheet of cells is useful in closing the organism's spaces. Once you have a closed internal space, you can contain it and create the kind of environment desireable for the organism.

Hydra, a simple multicellular animal, has a primitive nervous system. The outer layer is the **ectoderm**; the inner layer is the **endoderm**. Specialized cells in the ectoderm include some with muscle properties, some with sting cells and some sensory cells. In the **endoderm**, there are gland cells and digestive cells. The hydra, as you know from Greek myths, can regenerate; so signals must pass through cell to cell.

In all higher organisms, epithelial cells line all internal and external surfaces.

Embryonic development is very similar in the beginning for fish, chickens and humans. Complexity increases with the vertebrates, which have more than 200 specialized cells.

THE FOCUSES OF BIOTECHNOLOGY IN CELL BIOLOGY

Cell processes which are areas of focus in manipulating cell function, include the replication, which is the process of replicating genetic material during the reproduction of cells; the **regulation** of gene expression; gene regulation involving **interactions between proteins** and other molecules; **maintenance chemicals**, each characteristic to cell membranes that differs depending upon the external environment that must be maintained; **metabolic enzymes**, which are utilized by the cell for making their component parts and carrying out their specific tasks; and **receptors**, or cells functions which respond to stimuli and communicate with other cells.

Appendix 2

Primer on Molecular Biology

A. Biological Molecules

Biological molecules are the large macromolecules unique to living organisms, carbohdrates, lipids, proteins and nucleic acids. DNA and proteins are biological molecules. Molecules or monomers are the smallest unit in which that specific protein exits; as compared to an element whose smallest unit is an atom.

Class of biological molecule	Example	Monomer, or smallest unit	Example
Carbohydrate	starch, cellulose, chitin, glycogen, hyaluronic acid	simple sugars (monosaccharides)	Monosaccharides: glucose, fructose, glycerol Disaccharides: sucrose, lactose, maltose
Protein (polypeptide)	enzymes, antibodies, collagen, hemoglobin, insulin, interferon, actin	nucleotides (nitrogenous bases)	lysine, methionine, serine, glutamic acid, cysteine, tryptophan
Nucleic Acd	DNA, RNA	nucleotides (nitrogenous bases)	adensosine monphosphate, guanosine monphosphate, ATP, cyclic AMP
Lipid	triglycerides, fatty acids, estrogen, testosterone, vitamins A&E, cortisone	There is no simple building block molecule common to all lipids. The class is defined by water-insolubility	

B. Chemistry of Cells

The kinds of chemical bonds in the molecules of cells define the work of the cell in much of its activities. The work of a cell involves in part, making and breaking covalent bonds.

Covalent bonds. These bonds have a requirement of energy for their formation of 50–200 kcalories per mole to form a covalent bond.

Non-covalent bonds. These bonds are weaker bonds, with a requirement of energy for their formation of only 1–5 kcal per mole. However, many concurrent bonds create a very strong bond.

Covalent bonds share two atoms, or electrons, in their outer shell.

Diagram 2.

Some of the basic elements and their number of possible bonds compare as follows:

A.	.	..	..	..	..
H	•C•	•N•	•P•	•O•	•S•
	.	.	.	..	..

No. of bonds   1   4   3 or 5   2 to 6

H3C - C3H—> • CH3 + • CH3

This illustrates the covalent bond between the carbons which is very stable, and the result of the breaking of the covalent bond—two less stable molecules of _____. Only 1 in 10–12 occur at room temperature, where any of these exist as radicals, as shown in the second step of the equation.

Orientation. Orientation of different molecules results in bonds occurring in different planes, or in other words, something other than two-dimensional form. **Rotation** around various bonds may occur because of the effects of the space being taken by the outer shell electrons. Simply, the molecule positions itself with the least stress on the bonds, and the least crowding.

For example, if carbon is forming a double bond, the carbons will be on the same plane, and there will be no rotation around the double bond.

H2 C = C H2

The bond formation of water, in H2O, results in a 104.5% angle, because of the effect of the oxygen's outer electrons:

O
/ \
H H
104.5 %

Dipoles. Dipoles describe another type of bonding which involves certain atoms with an unequal sharing of electrons in the bond. A dipolar bond includes two atoms differing in electronegativity, compared to nonpolar bonds, which share electrons equally.

Electronegativity. Nitrogen (N) and Oxygen (O) have very high electronegativity, and the hierarchy of elements is as follows:

O > N > S y C > P > H H, being NOT very electronegative

Electron's spend more time around O than around Hs; making O slightly negative, in water, for example.

Noncovalent bonds. There are four types of noncovalent bonds: (1) hydrogen bonds; (2) ionic bonds; (3) Van der Waals interactions; and (4) hydrophobic bonds.

1. Hydrogen bonds. These bonds involve a donor atom with a hydrogen attached. In a reversible action, the donor, donates the H+. H is always closer to the donor. For example:

D-H	+	A	⇔	D-H ••••• A
dipolar		non-bonding		Hydrogen bond

2. Ionic bonds. These bonds are created by the lack of one electron in the shell of one molecule, sharing the extra electron in the shell of another molecule. For example, NaCl, common table salt, is the combination of the cation Na+ and the anion Cl-.

The important molecules for cellular chemistry are Na+, Cl-, K+, Mg+2 in forming ionic bonds.

3. Van der Waals interactions. When two atoms approach each other, they create a weak, but attractive force. A momentary shift in molecules creates a transient dipole bond.

4. Hydrophobic interactions. These involve non-polar molecules. Hydrocarbons bond through Van der Waal forces and hydrophobic interactions outside the hydrocarbons. There is no hydrogen bonding. These hydrophobic set of interactions makes the bond insoluble in H_2O, which is a useful mechanism for the integrity of the cell.

Amino acids, which are the combination of molecules, which always include a nitrogen molecule, that are the building blocks of proteins. Amino acids can be attached by all four types of non-covalent bonds. Amino acids include guanine (G), alanine (A), cytosine (C), and tyrosine (T), which are the amino acids which combine to create the sequence of code in the DNA molecule. In the formation and replication process of DNA, these non-covalent bonds are broken and reformed in the repeating process.

C. DNA and Proteins: Structure

DNA is made up of a chain of nucleotides. The sequence of these nucleotides in DNA determines the sequence of amino acids in a protein.

A protein is made up of a group of amino acids in a three dimensional structure.

D. DNA and Proteins: Function

DNA contains the code for making living organisms, which are made up of biological molecules and minerals.

A protein functions by binding to another molecule. Changing a protein's structure changes its ability to function, and may completely disable the protein.

E. Genetic Variation: Creation and Analysis

Recombination of DNA occurs in nature to produce mutations and changes in gene combinations. Genetic variation is a tool for identifying diseases, disease genes, compare DNA samples to crime scene DNA evidence.

Techniques for examining genetic variation include RFLPs, PCR/STRPs/VNTR and SNPs.

Appendix 3

Primer on DNA

A. History of DNA

The discovery of DNA originated with a group of meticulous experiments performed on pea plants by an Augustinian monk in the year 1865. For centuries humans had breed plants and animals to select for desirable traits, yet it remained unclear how traits were inherited from one generation to the next. Mendel made careful observations of the appearance or disappearance of a number of traits, including the texture and color of the seeds and pods of these pea plants over several generations. From these observations, Mendel was eventually able to postulate a set of rules governing inheritance of traits. He proposed that certain hereditary particles, now referred to as genes, are transmitted from generation to generation.

Then, in the year 1928, Frederick Griffith made a puzzling observation in the course of experiments involving the bacterium *Streptococcus pneumoniae*. A mixture of live, avirulent, rough *S. pneumoniae* cells and heat-killed, virulent, smooth *S. pneumoniae* cells lead to the death of mice when injected, and live, virulent, smooth *S. pneumoniae* cells were recovered from these dead mice. This suggested that somehow debris from the heat-killed smooth cells had converted the live rough cells into live smooth cells. Griffith called this process "transformation", and referred to the debris as the "transforming agent."

The question remained which chemical component of the heat-killed cells constituted this "transforming agent." Building upon the work of Griffith, experiments performed by Oswald Avery, C. M. MacLeod, and M. McCarty confirmed that DNA was the "transforming agent" responsible for heredity.

The next piece of the puzzle was provided by James Watson and Francis Crick in a paper published in the scientific journal *Nature* in 1953. Years earlier, Erwin Chargaff established empirical rules about the amounts of each type of nucleotide found in DNA: that the amount of pyrimidines (T + C) always equals the amount of purines (A + G). Watson and Crick observed X-ray diffraction data on the DNA structure performed by Rosalind Franklin in the laboratory of Maurice Wilkins. Franklin's data suggested that DNA had a helical structure. They combined this X-ray data with their knowledge of Chargaff's empirical rules and were able to suggest an accurate structure for DNA in which two side by side nucleotide chains are twisted into a double helix. A sugar-phosphate backbone holds together the strands of bases, which are bound to each other by chemical bonds formed between the bases A and T and between the bases C and G.

Another important discovery involving DNA, the importance of which will be explained later in this paper, was the introduction of Polymerase Chain Reaction (PCR) by Kary Mullis in 1985. PCR uses a heat stable DNA polymerase from a heat-loving bacteria strain to amplify large amounts of a specific DNA fragment starting with a very small amount of DNA. This process involves allowing specific oligonucleotide primers to bind to either side of the target DNA molecule that is to be amplified. DNA polymerase and a mixture of free DNA bases are then added and the polymerase is allowed to amplify the DNA through several cycles of temperature change.

The human genome project formally began and announced its mission to determine the sequence of every gene of every chromosome of the human body in the year 1990. By the year 2000, a rough draft of the complete nucleotide sequence of the human genome had been assimilated. Complete genome sequences of other organisms have been and continue to be determined as well. These will become increasingly important as organisms are used more frequently as model systems for the human organism.

B. Description of DNA

The human body consists of trillions of cells, each containing a material that allows the cells to replicate and determines the genetic characteristics of that human body. This material is deoxyribonucleic acid, more commonly known as DNA.

All cells of the human body except red blood cells contain DNA. Within each cell, the DNA is confined to the nucleus and to mitochondria, an organelle that provides the cell with its energy. DNA occurs as forty-six separate units, known as chromosomes, which control DNA so that only the right genes are utilized at any given time. DNA consists of several sub-unit bases, Adenine ("A"), Cytosine ("C"), Guanine ("G"), and Thymine ("T"). These bases are strung throughout DNA, attached to a sugar-phosphate backbone. DNA is organized as two strands, with a simple pairing rule in which A pairs opposite T, and G pairs opposite C. Today, it is common knowledge that DNA, the hereditary material, is responsible for giving humans our human characteristics. But, until the very recent past, this was not the case.

DNA tests were originally used by molecular biologists searching for the chromosomal locations of certain disease causing genes. These tests allow for the diagnosis of a genetic predisposition for a particular disease and also might lead to eventual development of treatments for the particular disease. Today, DNA tests also serve as a useful source of evidence in the courts. This type of evidence serves several purposes in courts, including linking a criminal to a crime scene from which evidence has been taken, resolving paternity, and identifying human remains.

C. DNA Testing Techniques

1. Restriction Fragment Length Polymorphism Technique

The Restriction Fragment Length Polymorphism ("RFLP") Technique is the most common of the DNA testing techniques currently available. This technique enables the testing of small amounts of DNA, such as a dime sized sample of blood, or an eraser sized sample of semen. RFLP consists of seven basic testing steps. In the first step, DNA is extracted from a sample such as blood or semen, and purified. Second, the DNA is treated enzymatically with specific enzymes called restriction endonucleases. These enzymes act like chemical scissors and cut DNA at very specific short recognition sequences. In some individuals some recognition sequences may be missing, or there may be an additional recognition sequence present. Thus, the length of the DNA fragments cut by the restriction endonucleases, and the number of repeat base pair sequences, called Variable Number of Tandem Repeats ("VNTRs"), will vary with each individual.

Third, the fragments are separated by size on an electrophoresis gel. The DNA is loaded on one side of the gel and an electric current is passed through the gel, driving the DNA through the gel. Smaller fragments have a lower molecular weight, and thus are driven further down the gel in a given time period. The electrophoresis results cannot be seen, therefore, further steps are required to visualize the results. So, in the fourth step, a nylon membrane is placed on the electrophoresis gel and allowed to draw up the DNA from the gel. Once on the membrane, the DNA is immobilized by heating. This step is referred to as Southern Blotting. In the fifth step, called hybridization, probes which recognize specific DNA sequences are placed on the membrane. These probes are either radioactive, or more commonly today, luminescent. The sixth step involves either visualizing the radioactive probes using an X-ray film or observing the luminescence depending on which type of probe is used. This step produces a visual DNA profile.

Finally, the seventh step involves interpretation of the results. Two samples at issue, for example a suspect's DNA and DNA taken from the scene of a crime, are compared for similarities in VNTRs. If they seem to visually match, then a computer analysis is performed. A standard number of allowable differences in base pairs of DNA is used in the computer analysis and if the difference exceeds this standard number, then the tests are declared inconclusive.

After the seventh step, any matches determined to be conclusive must be analyzed for statistical significance. This is because a match has no evidentiary significance in court unless it is determined to be statistically significant. In other words, if a large percentage of the population would also have tested positive for a match, then the match is not very incriminating to the particular person. Statistical significance is determined by measuring the likelihood that a random person would match the same bands as those matched in the particular test performed.

In a typical statistical significance analysis, the frequency of each allele, or alternative form of DNA, is determined for a particular population, which is usually the race of the person being tested. The matches for the person tested are compared to the population database, and the product rule, or the Hardy Weinburg equation, is used to determine the probability of the result obtained. The product rule states that in order to determine the probability of an overall occurrence, one must multiply the probability of each individual occurrence. For example, if allele 1 is present in one of every ten people, allele 2 is present in one of every twenty people, and allele 3 is present in every one of thirty people, the product rule says that the probability that a person will have all three alleles is (1/10 x 1/20 x 1/30=1/6000), one in every six thousand persons. Probabilities used in DNA analysis often approach numbers such as one out of millions or even billions of persons, giving DNA analysis its strong evidentiary power.

2. Polymerase Chain Reaction Technique

Mullis' discovery of PCR provided a DNA testing technique with unprecedented sensitivity. PCR testing targets and amplifies sections of DNA where polymorphisms are likely to occur, and thus is able to test very small and disintegrated samples that could not otherwise be used for DNA testing. Polymorphic sections of DNA are targeted, and the replication system inherent in DNA is utilized to produce millions of copies of that section in an extremely fast and efficient manner.

One way in which the PCR technique can be applied is through dot blot analysis. To perform a dot blot analysis, it is necessary that the PCR be known to produce a definite number of different products that do not differ in length, but do differ in their DNA sequence. An example of a dot blot analysis system is the DQa system. This system uses a variable region on a chromosome for which four alleles are known and easily tested. Four spots of the PCR products are immobilized on a nylon membrane and denatured with heat. A different probe, one for each type of allele, is then added to each spot. The probes are designed such that only those that bind to their exact counterpart in the PCR product will remain and give a colored product. Matches are then analyzed in the same manner as described above with RFLP.

3. Short Tandem Repeat Technique

Areas of DNA that do not code for any protein product are spread throughout the genome of most organisms. Within these areas are short sections of DNA that are repeated, the number of which varies from person to person. These areas are called Short Tandem Repeats ("STRs"). A common STR Technique utilizes PCR and is based upon a repeat of four bases. A frequency database for a particular STR can be consulted, and a frequency for a number of repeats appearing in that STR in the population determined. Several STR results can be combined, and a progressively decreasing value for the probability of a combination determined. The use of the STR Technique of DNA testing has greatly increased, and as of the year 2000, STR analysis was the method of choice used by all major forensic science services in the world.

4. Single Nucleotide Polymorphism Technique

The Single Nucleotide Polymorphism ("SNP") Technique targets a single base in the genome and looks at how it varies between individuals. In order to measure the presence of a SNP, the nature of the expected change and the sequence of DNA on either side of the SNP must be known. A modified form of PCR in which the growing DNA chain is terminated when it reaches the SNP is used in this type of analysis. A single SNP analysis is relatively uninformative, but many SNPs combined generate very high probabilities with relative ease.

5. Direct Sequencing Technique (Mitochondrial DNA)

Direct DNA sequencing was originally a very slow process that required high technical expertise. The process, however, is faster and cheaper each day because of increasing automation of DNA sequencing techniques. Sequencing an entire genome seems unnecessary since DNA testing techniques look for variation between individuals, and large portions of the genome do not vary between individuals. Sequencing of short sections of Mitochondrial DNA, however, could be of great use in forensic testing. Mitochondrial DNA is maternally inherited, so all descendants originating from the female line will have the same Mitochondrial DNA. Thus, this type of analysis has little use in paternity determinations. Mitochondrial DNA analysis could prove extremely useful, however, in the case of identifying the remains of a badly decayed corpse. Nuclear DNA, which quickly degrades, may be of little or no use, whereas Mitochondrial DNA, which is found in hair shafts and bone itself, degrades at a much slower rate.

6. Simple Sequence Length Polymorphism Technique

The Simple Sequence Length Polymorphism ("SSLP") Technique is a recently developed technique, not yet commonly used for forensic analysis. Two types of SSLPs, minisatellite markers and microsatellite markers, are routinely used in genomic analysis. While a RFLP usually has only one or two different gene forms in a population, a SSLP can have up to fifteen different forms. As a consequence, multiple alleles can be tracked with SSLP, making it a potentially much more reliable forensic analysis technique. Because of its potential for accurate analysis, the SSLP Technique will likely be used more and more in forensic DNA testing.

SOURCES CONSULTED:

WILSON WALL, GENETICS AND DNA TECHNOLOGY: LEGAL ASPECTS 24 (2002).

ANTHONY J.F. GRIFFITHS ET AL., INTRODUCTION TO GENETIC ANALYSIS 29–30 (8th ed. 2005)

William Thompson and Simon Ford, *DNA Typing: Acceptance and Weight of the New Genetic Identification Techniques*, 75 VA. L. REV. 45, 65 (1989).

Margann Bennett, *Admissibility Issues of Forensic DNA Evidence*, 44 U. KAN. L. REV. 141, 147 (1995).

Ryan McDonald, Juries and Crime Labs: Correcting the Weak Links in the DNA Chain, 24 AM. J.L. & MED. 345, 351 (1998).

Appendix 4

Glossary

A

Amino acids
Basic chemical building blocks of proteins. There are 20 common amino acids: alanine, arginine, aspargine, aspartic acid, cysteine, glutamic acid, glutamine, glycine, histidine, isoleucine, leucine, lysine, methionine, phenylalanine, proline, serine, threonine, tryptophan, tyrosine, and valine. In addition, two other amino acids have been discovered in microbes: selenocysteine and pyrolysine.

Antibody
A protein produced by humans and higher animals through an immune response to the presence of a specific antigen.

Antigen
A substance that, when introduced into the body, induces an immune response.

Antisense
One of an emerging set of "RNA interference" approaches in biotechnology, intended to modify a cell's normal processes of gene expression, for therapeutic purposes (e.g., to suppress the effect of genes involved in induction of human cancers) or to fine-tune the particular characteristics of commercially significant agricultural commodities (such as fruits with improved shelf life characteristics).

Aquaculture
Growth of aquatic organisms in controlled environment, particularly for marine food products. Application of biotechnology can help increase production, productivity, and quality, including improved genetic traits in fish and shellfish, growth factors, and defense mechanisms to fight microbial infections.

Assay (bioassay)
Analytical techniques to measure a biological response. For example, determination of the biochemical response of an animal cell system when exposed to a possible therapeutic compound.

B

Base pair
Two complementary nucleotide bases on opposite strands of the DNA molecule that weakly bond. Nature is strict in the pairings of bases allowed: adenine pairs only with thymine (DNA) or uracil (RNA), and guanine pairs only with cytosine.

Bioassay
Determination of the effectiveness of a compound by measuring its effect on animals, tissues, or organisms in comparison with a standard preparation.

Bioaugmentation
Increasing the activity of bacteria that break down pollutants by adding more of their kind. A technique used in bioremediation.

Biocatalyst
In bioprocessing, an enzyme that activates or speeds up a biochemical reaction.

Biodegradable
Capable of being reduced to water and carbon dioxide by the action of microorganisms.

Bioenrichment
A bioremediation strategy that involves adding nutrients or oxygen, thereby bolstering the activity of microbes as they break down pollutants.

Bioinformatics
The science of information as applied to biological research. Informatics is the management and analysis of data using advanced computing techniques. Bioinformatics is particularly important as an adjunct to genomics research, because of the large amount of data and complex relationships among bioactive molecules that this research generates.

Bioleaching
Use of natural or laboratory-altered microorganisms to extract and concentrate metals and other minerals from their location of deposit.

Biomass
The totality of biological matter in a given area. As commonly used in biotechnology, refers to the use of cellulose, a renewable resource, for the production of chemicals that can be used to generate energy or as alternative feedstocks for the chemical industry to reduce dependence on nonrenewable fossil fuels.

Biomaterials
Biological molecules (such as proteins, complex sugars) used to make devices such as structural elements for reconstructive surgery.

Biopharmaceuticals
Pharmaceutical drugs such as proteins, antibodies, and enzymes derived from biotechnology methods.

Bioprocess engineering
Process that uses complete living cells or their components (e.g., enzymes, chloroplasts) to effect desired physical or chemical changes.

Bioremediation
Use of natural or laboratory-altered microorganisms to degrade, detoxify, or accumulate contaminants for cleanup. Provides a control technology approach to render hazardous wastes nonhazardous.

Biosensors
Combination of molecular biology, advanced materials, and microelectronics to produce sophisticated monitoring devices capable of being activated by or measuring minute levels of bioactive molecules.

Biotransformation
The use of enzymes in chemical synthesis to produce chemical compounds of a desired stereochemistry.

C

Catalyst (biocatalyst)
An agent—such as an enzyme or a metal complex—that facilitates the kinetics of a chemical reaction.

Cell culture
Growth and maintenance of cells isolated from multicellular organisms in artificial (in vitro) conditions.

Chemical genomics
Use of structural and functional genomic information about biological molecules, especially proteins, to identify useful small molecules and alter their structure to improve their efficacy (e.g., as therapeutic drugs).

Clinical studies (clinical trials)
Generally, studies in human populations that are designed to measure the safety and efficacy of a new drug or other biologic treatment. Clinical trials come in various forms (Phases I, II, III) and are mandatory for new drugs and biologics under Food and Drug Administration (FDA) regulations. Complex experimental designs and control groups are typically involved in such trials.

Cloning
In recombinant DNA technology: the process of using a variety of DNA manipulation procedures to produce multiple copies of a single gene or segment of DNA.

Combinatorial chemistry
An approach to drug discovery that has evolved in recent years. The process enables rapid synthesis and screening of as many as several million molecules with similar structure in order to find molecules with desired properties. (See also *drug design*.)

Computational biology
A subdiscipline of bioinformatics, which involves chiefly computation-based research directed at understanding basic biological processes.

Confined release assessment (field trial)
Component of a government regulatory process in which an advance determination is made of the risk to the environment, including to health, of the release of an agricultural organism with novel features (e.g., seeds from a transgenic plant). Confined release is generally a research step, involving strict terms and conditions, such as reproductive isolation and restrictions in the use of the harvested material and field plot in subsequent growing seasons. (Compare with *unconfined release assessment*.)

Cost of goods sold (COGS)
The costs of producing goods and services sold. These may include production costs such as raw materials, supplies, and labor.

Cross-licensing
A legal, contractual procedure in which two or more firms with established intellectual property (IP) rights (e.g., a patent) to technologies mutually needed for continuing R&D and execution of company business plans strike a business deal (e.g., through mutual patent licensing) such that all parties can get access to the needed technologies. Cross-licensing helps to avoid both conflicts over IP rights and subsequent legal actions such as infringement suits.

D

Deoxyribonucleic acid (DNA)
Molecule that carries the genetic information for most organisms living on earth. The DNA molecule is comprised by a varied sequence of four nucleotide bases (adenine, cytosine, guanine, and thymine) along with a sugar-phosphate backbone. Structurally, these components are arrayed in paired strands that wind together in the form of a double helix.

Diagnostic tests
Laboratory and health care tools/products that can reliably measure biochemical and other biological parameters which are helpful in diagnosing disease or other medical conditions. Both monoclonal antibodies and DNA probes are useful diagnostic products.

DNA amplification
Process by which a very large number of copies of a target DNA sequence is synthesized (usually in a laboratory test tube). This kind of multiplication is normally needed for adequate DNA analysis in contemporary molecular biology. The widely known polymerase chain reaction (PCR) is frequently used to perform this amplification, which can quickly produce a million or more extremely accurate copies of a target sequence.

DNA hybridization
Procedure in which single-stranded nucleic acid segments are allowed to bind with complementary segments (following nature's nucleotide base pairing rules) to form a doublestranded helix.

DNA library
A large, systematic collection of DNA fragments. Such libraries help scientists to catalog and distinguish the millions, or even billions, of nucleotides in the genomes of organisms. There are many types of libraries. A "genomic library" contains all the different types of DNA sequences found in a genome (coding, noncoding, and repetitive DNA sequences). A "complementary DNA (cDNA) library" includes only genes that are expressed, i.e., genes that get transcribed in messenger-RNA, which is then translated into proteins. A "chromosome-specific library" focuses on the DNA associated with a single chromosome.

DNA microarray (Gene chip, Genome chip)
A recent new technology in the field of molecular biology and genetics. The microarray is a laboratory microscale sampling and analysis membrane which systematically incorporates many different DNA probes. An experiment with a single DNA microarray can provide research information on the involvement of thousands of genes in cellular functions.

DNA polymerase
An enzyme that replicates DNA. DNA polymerase is the basis of the polymerase chain reaction.

DNA probes
Various analytical techniques have been developed, based on the hybridization process and its selective base pairing logic, to locate a specific sequence along a DNA strand. A short piece of DNA (a "probe"), which is complementary to a nucleotide sequence of interest (and often explicitly synthesized for this purpose), is mixed with the target DNA strand. As a result of hybridization, the probe will bind and form a region of double-stranded DNA wherever the probe sequence encounters a complementary sequence along the target DNA strand. Such areas of hybridization are typically identified and analyzed through standard laboratory blotting and radiographic methods.

DNA sequencing
Identification of the specific sequence of nucleotide bases (adenine, cytosine, guanine, thymine) that comprise a segment of DNA. Cutting-edge laboratory technology and computers have greatly automated the chemical and analytical steps needed for these determinations. The recently completed international project to sequence the human genome involved identifying some 3 billion nucleotide base pairs.

DNA synthesis (oligonucleotides)
Current biotechnology methods enable a wide range of artificial DNAs, with known base sequences in one or more regions, to be synthesized for use as tools and reagents for laboratory research and diagnostic test applications. In fact, the principal purpose of a significant segment of the present biotechnology industry is preparing such oligonucleotides to commercial order, at high accuracy and purity.

Drug delivery
Process by which a formulated drug is administered to a patient. The traditional routes have been oral or intravenous perfusion. New methods provide for delivery through the skin with a transdermal patch or across the nasal membrane with an aerosol spray.

Drug design (rational drug design)
The now rapidly advancing scientific knowledge of cell functions in molecular terms, in both healthy and disease states, and improved ability to model the chemical and biological pathways involved provide an improved basis to infer the chemical identity and threedimensional structure of molecules with likelihood of providing positive therapeutic effects. This "rational approach" to drug design stands in some contrast to the longstanding prior approach in which the identification of new therapeutic drugs depended chiefly on doseresponse screening (often serendipitous) of many molecules for biological activity.

E

Enzyme
A protein catalyst that promotes specific chemical or metabolic reactions necessary for cell functioning and development.

Expression
In genetics, manifestation of a characteristic that is specified by a gene. With hereditary disease, for example, a person can carry the gene for the disease but not actually have the disease. In this case, the gene is present but not expressed. In industrial biotechnology the term is often used to mean the production of a protein by a gene that has been inserted into a new host organism.

Extraction, separation, purification
Process of isolating a compound of interest in a mixture of many compounds and refining the purity. Is a standard problem in most all chemistry, irrespective of the state of matter (solid, liquid, gas) at hand. In biotechnology, this problem often arises as a need to identify, isolate, concentrate, and/or purify specific proteins, gene fragments, or other bioactive molecules from the integrated, functioning cells in which they naturally exist.

Extremophiles
Microorganisms that live at extreme levels of pH, temperature, pressure, and salinity. An example is the Taq polymerase, which facilities the widely used polymerase chain reaction (PCR) technique for quickly amplifying nucleotide chains. This enzyme was iso-

lated from the thermophilic bacterium *Thermus Aquaticus,* which exists in hot spring-like conditions.

F

Fermentation
An (anaerobic) process for growing microorganisms for the production of various chemical or pharmaceutical compounds. Microbes are normally incubated under specific conditions in the presence of nutrients in large tanks called fermentors.

Functional foods (nutraceuticals)
Foods containing compounds with beneficial health effects beyond those provided by the basic nutrients, minerals, and vitamins.

Functional genomics
A field of research that aims to understand what each gene does, how it is regulated and how it interacts with other genes. (See also *genomics.*)

G

Gene
The fundamental physical and functional unit of heredity. A segment of a chromosome. An ordered sequence of nucleotide base pairs that produce a specific product or have an assigned function. Some genes direct the syntheses of proteins, while others have regulatory functions.

Gene mapping
Determination of the relative locations of genes on a chromosome. Genetic maps use landmarks called genetic markers—any observable variation that results from a known **alteration** or mutation at a specific genetic locus—to guide scientists in the hunt for the specific physical location of a gene on a chromosome.

Gene therapy
Replacement of a defective gene in an organism suffering from a genetic disease. Recombinant DNA techniques are becoming increasingly more able to successfully insert a functional form of the gene into relevant cells, thereby relieving the disease. More than 300 single-gene genetic disorders have been identified to date in humans. A significant percentage of these may be amenable to gene therapy.

Genetic engineering (Genetic modification)
Various techniques now available—such as selective breeding, mutagenesis, transposon insertions, and recombinant DNA technology—that can be used to alter the genetic material of cells in order to make them capable of producing new substances, performing new functions, or blocking the production of substances.

Genetic screening
Use of genetic analysis procedures to screen for inherited diseases or medical conditions. Testing can be conducted prenatally to check for metabolic defects and congenital disorders in the developing fetus, as well as postnatally to screen for carriers of heritable diseases.

Genetics
The scientific study of heredity and how particular qualities or traits are transmitted from parents to offspring.

Genome
All the genetic material in the chromosomes of a particular organism. Its size is generally measured as its total number of nucleotide base pairs.

Genomics

The scientific study of genes and their functions. Recent advances in genomics are bringing about a revolution in our understanding of the molecular mechanisms of disease, including the complex interplay of genetic and environmental factors. Genomics is also stimulating the discovery of breakthrough health care products by revealing thousands of new biological targets for the development of drugs and by giving scientists innovative ways to design new drugs, vaccines, and DNA diagnostics. Genomic-based therapeutics may include "traditional" small chemical drugs, protein drugs, and gene therapy.

Genotype

The genetic constitution of an organism. (Compare with *phenotype*.)

H

Hormone

A protein or other biochemical that acts as a messenger or stimulatory signal, relaying instructions to stop or start certain physiological activities. Hormones are synthesized in one type of cell and then released to direct the function of other cell types.

I

Immunodiagnostics

The use of specific antibodies to measure a substance of interest. This kind of analytical tool is useful in diagnosing infectious diseases and the presence of foreign substances in a variety of human and animal fluids.

Immunology

The study of the biology and biochemistry of the body's immune response to pathogens and other foreign substances.

Inducer

A molecule or substance that increases the rate of enzyme synthesis, usually by blocking the action of the corresponding repressor.

M

Microbial ecology

General reference to the biological nature and interrelationships of the system of microorganisms in an ecosystem.

Microbial herbicides and pesticides

Microorganisms that are selectively toxic to specific plants or insects. Because of their narrow host range and limited toxicity, these microorganisms can be preferable to conventional synthetic chemical herbicides and pesticides for certain pest control applications.

Molecular genetics

Study of how genes function to control cellular activities.

Monoclonal antibody (MAb)

A highly specific, purified antibody derived from a single clone of specialized cells that recognizes only one antigen.

N

Net revenues

Total of all receipts of an enterprise. This may include receipts from sales of products, services, or merchandise; and earnings from interest, dividends, rents, wages, and technology licensing.

Net sales
Gross receipts from sales of goods or services minus returns, discounts, or allowances.

Nucleotide (nucleotide base)
The building blocks of nucleic acids such as DNA and RNA. Each nucleotide is composed of sugar, phosphate, and one of four nitrogen bases. The sugar in DNA is deoxyribose and RNA's sugar is ribose. The sequence of the bases along the nucleic acid's molecular chain directs the synthesis of the sequence of amino acids in a protein.

O

Operating income
A measure of a company's earning power from ongoing operations. In the present survey, operating income is defined as net sales minus the cost of goods sold and selling, general, and administrative expenses.

P

Pharmacogenetics
Study of hereditary influences on drug response.

Phenotype
Observable characteristics of an organism produced by the organism's genotype interacting with the environment. (Compare with *genotype*.)

Phytoremediation
The use of plants to clean up pollution.

Pre-clinical studies
Studies that test a potential new drug, diagnostic, or other medical treatment on animals and in other nonhuman test systems. For example, safety information derived from such studies is often used to support an Investigational New Drug application (IND) filed with the Food and Drug Administration (FDA).

Protein (polypeptide)
A molecule composed of a chemically linked sequence of amino acids. There are many types of proteins, and each cell produces thousands of proteins. These proteins carry out different functions essential for cell functioning and development.

Protein sequencing
The process of ascertaining the identity and order of the amino acids that comprise a protein molecule of interest.

Proteomics
The set of proteins in a cell is termed the proteome. Unlike the genome, which is constant irrespective of cell type, the proteome varies from one type of cell to another. The science of proteomics strives to characterize the protein profile of each cell type, assess protein differences between healthy and diseased cells, and analyze each protein's specific function and how it interacts with the other proteins in the cell.

R

Radioimmunoassay (RIA)
A test combining radioisotopes and immunology to detect trace substances. Such tests are useful for studying antibody interaction with cell receptors and can be developed into clinical diagnostics.

Recombinant DNA
General reference to the broad range of techniques involved in manipulating genetic material in organisms. The term is often used synonymously with "genetic engineering."

Recombination
The process of breaking and rejoining DNA strands, which occurs naturally in the course of cellular functioning. This produces new combinations of genes and, thus, generates genetic variation.

Research tools
In the realm of contemporary biotechnology R&D, this term is frequently used to refer to genes, gene fragments, DNA mutations, and related proteins, whose biochemical identity and availability as isolated molecules are regarded as essential foundations for productive further research in molecular biology.

Restriction fragment length polymorphism (RFLP)
The variation in the length of DNA fragments produced by a restriction endonuclease that cuts at a polymorphic locus. This is a key tool in DNA fingerprinting and is based on the presence of different alleles in an individual. RFLP mapping is also used in plant breeding to see if a key trait such as disease resistance is inherited.

Ribonucleic acid (RNA)
Also a nucleic acid, composed of a chemically linked sequence of nucleotide bases. RNA exists in three forms (messenger RNA, transfer RNA, and ribosomal RNA) responsible for translating the genetic information encoded in an organism's DNA into the proteins essential for cell functioning and development. RNA is also the hereditary material for some viruses.

RNA interference
An emerging approach to genetic engineering—whether in developing new therapeutic drugs or organisms with altered traits—that seeks to selectively influence the cellular processes of RNA translation and transcription that yield the proteins essential for cellular functioning.

S

Selling, general, and administrative expenses (SGAE)
Expenses and costs not linked to the production of specific goods, but including all selling, general company expense, and administrative expenses. These expenses may include salespersons' salaries, advertising, salaries for executives, and other administrative expenses.

Somatic cell gene therapy
Gene therapy approach that involves inserting genes into cells for therapeutic purposes—for example, to induce such treated cells to produce a protein that the body is missing. This does not affect the genetic makeup of a patient's offspring and generally does not change all, or even most, cells in the recipient. Somatic cell gene therapy is one of several possible ways use genomics to improve health care.

Structural biology
Biological science that focuses on systematic understanding of the biological structures that both distinguish different organisms and allow them to function.

Structural gene
A gene that codes for a protein, such as an enzyme.

Systems biology
A hypothesis-driven field of research that creates predictive mathematical models of complex biological processes or organ systems.

T

Three-dimensional molecular modeling

Typically, this is directed at identifying a protein's shape (structure). The three-dimensional structure of these molecules—beyond simple chemical composition and amino acid sequence—is increasingly recognized as key in determining biological function. Identifying this structure is, however, no easy analytical feat. Present methods involve such tools as X-ray crystallography, nuclear magnetic resonance spectroscopy, and extensive computer modeling.

Transcription, Translation

Critical cellular processes, involving DNA and RNA, involved in transforming genetic information in synthesized proteins essential for cell functioning and development. Transcription is synthesis of messenger RNA (mRNA) from the genetic (DNA) template. Translation is the process of turning the mRNA instructions (nucleotide sequence) into polypeptide chains of amino acids, which then fold into proteins.

Transgenic organism

Animals, plants, microbes, and other organisms whose hereditary DNA has been augmented by the addition of DNA from a source other than parental germplasm. Such organisms are made possible by the availability of recombinant DNA techniques.

U

Unconfined release assessment

Component of a government regulatory process whereby an advance determination is made of the risk to the environment, including to health, of the release of an agricultural organism with novel features (e.g., seeds from a transgenic plant). Unconfined release generally means release into the environment with limited or no restrictions (i.e., near to release associated with full product commercialization). (Compare with *confined release assessment*.)

V

Vaccine

A preparation of attenuated or killed microorganisms (e.g., viruses or bacteria) that when inoculated is capable of conferring immunity or otherwise counteracting the pathological effects of the original microorganisms. Until recently, vaccines have been prepared through natural or synthetic processes. However, the recombinant DNA techniques now provide a way to modify the genetic content of these microorganisms in ways that yield much more effective vaccines with fewer side effects.

Value added

An industry's net addition to gross domestic product. The term "net" signifies that purchases from other industries have been subtracted out of the gross sales of the industry to eliminate double-counting.

Virology

The scientific study of viruses and viral diseases.

Virus

Any of a large group of organisms containing genetic material, but which are unable to reproduce outside a host cell. To replicate, a virus must invade another cell and use parts of that cell's reproductive machinery

X

Xenobiotics
Synthetic chemicals believed to be resistant to environmental degradation. A branch of biotechnology called bioremediation is seeking to develop biological methods to degrade such compounds.

Additional sources for definitions and background information on science and technology include http://bio.org, http://www.ncbi.nlm.nih.gov/About/primer/index.html, and http://agnic.umd.ed/. For additional information on financial analysis terms and concepts see InvestorWords.com at http://www.investorwords.com, Universal Accounting at http://www. accounting-andbookkeeping-tips.com/learning-accounting/, and Solution Matrix, Ltd.'s business case analysis web site at http://www.solutionmatrix.com/.

SOURCE:
This entire appendix is from "A Survey of the Use of Biotechnology in Industry," (Dept. of Commerce, 2003) at: http://www.technology.gov/reports/Biotechnology/CD120a_ 0310.pdf

Index